Java Fundamental Classes Reference

THE JAVA SERIES™

Exploring Java

Java Threads

Java Network Programming

Java Virtual Machine

Java AWT Reference

Java Language Reference

Java Fundamental Classes Reference

Also from O'Reilly

Java in a Nutshell, Second Edition

Java Fundamental Classes Reference

Mark Grand and Jonathan Knudsen

O'REILLY

Cambridge · Köln · Paris · Sebastopol · Tokyo

Java Fundamental Classes Reference
by Mark Grand and Jonathan Knudsen

Copyright © 1997 O'Reilly & Associates, Inc. All rights reserved.
Printed in the United States of America.

Published by O'Reilly & Associates, Inc., 101 Morris Street, Sebastopol, CA 95472.

Editor: Paula Ferguson

Production Editor: Mary Anne Weeks Mayo

Printing History:

> May 1997:   First Edition

This book is printed on acid-free paper with 85% recycled content, 15% post-consumer waste. O'Reilly & Associates is committed to using paper with the highest recycled content available consistent with high quality.

ISBN: 1-56592-241-7

Table of Contents

Preface

This book is a reference manual for the *fundamental classes* in the Java programming environment; it covers version 1.1 of the Java API. We've defined fundamental classes to mean those classes in the Java Development Kit (JDK) that every Java programmer is likely to need, minus the classes that comprise the Abstract Window Toolkit (AWT). (The classes in the AWT are covered by a companion volume, the *Java AWT Reference*, from O'Reilly & Associates.) Thus, this book covers the classes in the java.lang and java.io packages, among others, and is essential for the practicing Java programmer.

This is an exciting time in the development of Java. Version 1.1 introduces a massive amount of infrastructure that more than doubles the size of the core Java APIs. This new infrastructure provides many new facilities, such as:

- Java is now more dynamic. An expanded Class class, in conjunction with the new java.lang.reflect package, allows objects to access methods and variables of objects that they were not compiled with.

- There are classes in java.io that build on the new dynamic capabilities to provide the ability to read and write objects as streams of bytes.

- There is increased support for internationalization. The support includes a Locale class and classes to format and parse data in locale-specific ways. There is also support for loading external locale-specific resources, such as textual strings.

- The java.util.zip package provides the ability to read and write compressed files.

- The `java.math` package provides the ability to perform arithmetic operations to any degree of precision that is necessary.

There are also more ways to package and distribute Java programs. In addition to being able to build command-line based applications and applets that are hosted by browsers, we now have the Java Servelet API that allows Java programs to function as part of a web server. Furthermore, the nature of applets may be changing. Instead of waiting for large applet to be downloaded by a browser, we now have push technologies such as Marimba's Castanet that ensure that the most current version of an applet is already on our machine when we want to run it.

Many new uses for Java have appeared or are on the horizon. For example, NASA is using Java applets to monitor telemetry data, instead of building more large, dedicated hardware consoles. Cellular phone manufacturers have committed to making cellular phone models that support Java, so in the future we may see Java programs that run on cellular phones and allow us to check e-mail or view location maps. Many additional APIs are also on the way, from Sun and other companies. These APIs not only supply infrastructure, but also provide frameworks for building domain-specific applications, in such areas as electronic commerce and manufacturing.

This book is about the classes that provide the most fundamental infrastructure for Java. As you use this book, we hope that you will share our enthusiasm for the richness of what is provided and the anticipation of what is yet to come.

What This Book Covers

The *Java Fundamental Classes Reference* is the definitive resource for programmers working with the core, non-AWT classes in Java. It covers all aspects of these fundamental classes as of version 1.1.1 of Java. If there are any changes to these classes after 1.1.1 (at least one more patch release is expected), we will integrate them as soon as possible. Watch the book's web site, *http://www.ora.com/catalog/javafund/*, for details on changes.

Specifically, this book completely covers the following packages:

- `java.io` (1.0 and 1.1)
- `java.lang` (1.0 and 1.1)
- `java.lang.reflect` (new in 1.1)
- `java.math` (new in 1.1)

- java.net (1.0 and 1.1)
- java.text (new in 1.1)
- java.util (1.0 and 1.1)
- java.util.zip (new in 1.1)

As you can see from the list above, this book covers four packages that are completely new in Java 1.1. In addition, it includes material on all of the new features in the four original 1.0 packages. Here are the highlights of what is new in Java 1.1:

java.lang

This package contains the new Byte, Short, and Void classes that are needed for the new Reflection API. The Class class also defines a number of new methods for the Reflection API. Chapter 12, *The java.lang Package*, contains reference material on all of the classes in the java.lang package.

java.io

This package contains a number of new classes, mostly for object serialization and character streams. Chapter 11, *The java.io Package*, contains reference material on all of the classes in the java.io package.

java.net

This package contains a new MulticastSocket class that supports multicast sockets and several new exception types for more detailed networking exceptions. Chapter 15, *The java.net Package*, contains reference material on all of the classes in the java.net package.

java.util

This package includes a handful of new classes for internationalization, such as Locale and ResourceBundle. The package also defines the base classes that support the new AWT event model. The new Calendar and TimeZone classes provide increased support for working with dates and times. Chapter 17, *The java.util Package*, contains reference material on all of the classes in the java.util package.

java.lang.reflect

This new package defines classes that implement the bulk of the new Reflection API. The classes in the package represent the fields, methods, and constructors of a class. Chapter 13, *The java.lang.reflect Package*, contains reference material on all of the classes in the java.lang.reflect package.

java.math

> This new package includes two classes that support arithmetic: one with arbitrarily large integers and another with arbitrary-precision floating-point numbers. Chapter 14, *The java.math Package*, contains reference material on all of the classes in the java.math package.

java.text

> This new package contains the majority of the classes that implement the internationalization capabilities of Java 1.1. It includes classes for formatting dates, times, numbers, and textual messages for any specified locale. Chapter 16, *The java.text Package*, contains reference material on all of the classes in the java.text package.

java.util.zip

> This new package defines classes that support general-purpose data compression and decompression using the ZLIB compression algorithms, as well as classes that work with the popular GZIP and ZIP formats. Chapter 18, *The java.util.zip Package*, contains reference material on all of the classes in the java.util.zip package.

Organization

The *Java Fundamental Classes Reference* is divided into two parts. The first part is a brief guide to using many of the features provided by the fundamental classes in Java. This book is not meant to be read from cover to cover, but these chapters can be read in order to learn about some of the basic functionality of the Java API. These tutorial-style chapters provide short examples where appropriate, to illustrate the use of various features. However, this section is by no means a comprehensive tutorial on the fundamental classes.

The second part is the meat of the book. It contains a set of documentation pages typical of what you find in most reference sets. It is organized alphabetically by package, and within each package, alphabetically by class. The reference page for a class tells you everything you need to know about using that class. It provides a detailed description of the class as a whole, followed by a complete description of every variable, constructor, and method defined by the class.

The beginning of each reference page also gives you a synopsis of the class, including information about its availability (i.e., whether the class is available in Java 1.0 or is new in Java 1.1). All new variables, constructors, and methods in Java 1.1 are also clearly marked, so that you can use the reference pages for programming with either Java 1.0.2 or Java 1.1.

Related Books

O'Reilly & Associates is developing an entire series of books on Java. This series consists of introductory books, reference manuals, and advanced programming guides.

The following books on Java are currently available or due to be released soon from O'Reilly & Associates:

Exploring Java, by Patrick Niemeyer and Joshua Peck
> A comprehensive tutorial that provides a practical, hands-on approach to learning Java.

Java Language Reference, by Mark Grand
> A complete reference for the Java programming language itself.

Java AWT Reference, by John Zukowski
> A comprehensive reference manual for the AWT-related packages in the core Java API.

Java Virtual Machine, by Jon Meyer and Troy Downing
> A programming guide and reference manual for the Java virtual machine.

Java in a Nutshell, by David Flanagan
> A quick-reference guide to Java which lists all of the classes, methods, and variables in the core Java API.

Java Threads, by Scott Oaks and Henry Wong
> An advanced programming guide to working with threads in Java.

Java Network Programming, by Elliotte Rusty Harold
> A complete guide to writing sophisticated network applications.

Database Programming with JDBC and Java, by George Reese
> An advanced tutorial on JDBC that presents a robust model for developing Java database programs.

Developing Java Beans, by Robert Englander
> A complete guide to writing components that work with the JavaBeans API.

Look for additional advanced programming guides on such topics as distributed computing and electronic commerce from O'Reilly in the near future.

Online Resources

There are many sources for information about Java. Sun Microsystems' official web site for Java topics is *http://www.javasoft.com/*. You should look here for the latest news, updates, and Java releases. This site is where you'll find the Java Development Kit (JDK), which includes the compiler, the interpreter, and all of the classes in the Java API.

The various *comp.lang.java.** newsgroups can be a good source of information about Java. The *comp.lang.java.announce* newsgroup is for announcements that may be of interest to Java developers. The *comp.lang.java.api* newsgroup is for discussion of the Java application programming interface; it's also a good place to ask intelligent questions. There are a number of other Java newsgroups for various kinds of specialized discussions. You should read the FAQ to find out more. The FAQ is maintained on the Web at *http://sunsite.unc.edu/javafaq/javafaq.html.*

Another large source of Java-related resources and Java code is *http://www.gamelan.com/*, also known as *http://java.developer.com/.*

You should also visit O'Reilly & Associates' Java site at *http://www.ora.com/ publishing/java.* There you'll find information about other books in O'Reilly's Java series.

Conventions Used in This Book

Italic is used for:

- New terms where they are defined.
- Pathnames, filenames, and program names.
- Internet addresses, such as domain names and URLs.

Typewriter Font is used for:

- Anything that might appear in a Java program, including keywords, operators, data types, constants, method names, variable names, class names, and interface names.
- Command lines and options that should be typed verbatim on the screen.
- Tags that might appear in an HTML document.

Request for Comments

We invite you to help us improve our books. If you have an idea that could make this a more useful language reference, or if you find a bug in an example or an error in the text, let us know by sending mail to *bookquestions@ora.com.*

As Java continues to evolve, we may find it necessary to issue errata for this book or to release updated examples or reference information. This information will be found on the book's web site, *http://www.ora.com/catalog/javafund/*.

Acknowledgments

Mark would like to acknowledge the patience, love, and support that his wonderful wife Ginni provided during the long months he spent writing this book. I also want to thank my daughters Rachel and Shana for their understanding when they had to compete with this book for my attention. I also want to thank Mike Loukides and Andy Cohen for their valuable suggestions on the content of this book. I particularly want to thank Paula Ferguson, who spent many long hours above and beyond the call of duty poring over the details of this book to edit it into its final form.

Jonathan sends many thanks to Kristen, who helps him reach for his dreams and does a lot of proofreading, too. To Daphne, thanks for reminding me every day exactly how great it is to work at home. To my cats, Asher and Basteet, thanks for attending my meetings and helping me type. Thanks also to Paula Ferguson for her unflagging attention to detail.

The class hierarchy diagrams in this book were borrowed from David Flanagan's book, *Java in a Nutshell.* These diagrams were based on similar diagrams for Java 1.1 by Charles L. Perkins.

Finally, a big round of applause to the design and production staff at O'Reilly & Associates for putting out this tome on a very tight schedule. Mary Anne Weeks Mayo was the production manager. Quality was assured through the services of Ellie Fountain Maden and Sheryl Avruch. Seth Maislin wrote the index. Erik Ray, Ellen Siever, and Lenny Muellner contributed their tool-tweaking prowess. Chris Reilley was responsible for illustrations, Nancy Priest for the interior design, Hanna Dyer created the back cover, and Edie Freedman designed the front cover.

1

Introduction

The phenomenon that is Java continues to capture new supporters every day. What began as a programming environment for writing fancy animation applets that could be embedded in web browsers is growing up to be a sophisticated platform for delivering all kinds of portable, distributed applications. If you are already an experienced Java programmer, you know just how powerful the portability of Java is. If you are just now discovering Java, you'll be happy to know that the days of porting applications are over. Once you write a Java application, it can run on UNIX workstations, PCs, and Macintosh computers, as well as on many other supported platforms.

This book is a complete programmer's reference to the "fundamental classes" in the Java programming environment. The fundamental classes in the Java Development Kit (JDK) provide a powerful set of tools for creating portable applications; they are an important component of the toolbox used by every Java programmer. This reference covers the classes in the java.lang, java.io, java.net, java.util, java.lang.reflect, java.math, java.text, and java.util.zip packages. This chapter offers an overview of the fundamental classes in each of these packages.

This reference assumes you are already familiar with the Java language and class libraries. If you aren't, *Exploring Java*, by Pat Niemeyer and Josh Peck, provides a general introduction, and other books in the O'Reilly Java series provide detailed references and tutorials on specific topics. Note that the material herein does not cover the classes that comprise the Abstract Window Toolkit (AWT): the AWT is covered by a companion volume, the *Java AWT Reference*, by John Zukowski. In addition, this book does not cover any of the new "enterprise" APIs in the core 1.1 JDK, such as the classes in the java.rmi, java.sql, and java.security packages. These packages will be covered by forthcoming books on distributed computing and database programming. See the Preface for a complete list of titles in the O'Reilly Java series.

You should be aware that this book covers two versions of Java: 1.0.2 and 1.1. Version 1.1 of the Java Development Kit (JDK) was released in February 1997. This release includes many improvements and additions to the fundamental Java classes; it represents a major step forward in the evolution of Java. Although Java 1.1 has a number of great new features, you may not want to switch to the new version right away, especially if you are writing mostly Java applets. You'll need to keep an eye on the state of Java support in browsers to help you decide when to switch to Java 1.1. Of course, if you are writing Java applications, you can take the plunge today.

This chapter points out new features of Java 1.1 as they come up. However, there is one "feature" that deserves mention that doesn't fit naturally into an overview. As of Java 1.1, classes, methods, and constructors available in Java 1.0.2 can be deprecated in favor of new classes, methods, and constructors in Java 1.1. The Java 1.1 compiler issues a warning whenever you use a deprecated entity.

1.1 The java.lang Package

The java.lang package contains classes and interfaces essential to the Java language. For example, the Object class is the ultimate superclass of all other classes in Java. Object defines some basic methods for thread synchronization that are inherited by all Java classes. In addition, Object defines basic methods for equality testing, hashcode generation, and string conversion that can be overridden by subclasses when appropriate.

The java.lang package also contains the Thread class, which controls the operation of each thread in a multithreaded application. A Thread object can be used to start, stop, and suspend a thread. A Thread must be associated with an object that implements the Runnable interface; the run() method of this interface specifies what the thread actually does. See Chapter 3, *Threads*, for a more detailed explanation of how threads work in Java.

The Throwable class is the superclass of all error and exception classes in Java, so it defines the basic functionality of all such classes. The java.lang package also defines the standard error and exception classes in Java. The error and exception hierarchies are rooted at the Error and Exception subclasses of Throwable. See Chapter 4, *Exception Handling*, for more information about the exception-handling mechanism.

The Boolean, Character, Byte, Double, Float, Integer, Long, and Short classes encapsulate the Java primitive data types. Byte and Short are new in Java 1.1, as is the Void class. All of these classes are necessary to support the new Reflection API and class literals in Java 1.1 The Class class also has a number of new methods in Java 1.1 to support reflection.

All strings in Java are represented by String objects. These objects are immutable. The StringBuffer class in java.lang can be used to work with mutable text strings. Chapter 2, *Strings and Related Classes*, offers a more detailed description of working with strings in Java.

See Chapter 12, *The java.lang Package*, for complete reference material on all of the classes in the java.lang package.

1.2   The java.lang.reflect Package

The java.lang.reflect package is new in Java 1.1. It contains classes and interfaces that support the new Reflection API. *Reflection* refers to the ability of a class to reflect upon itself, or look inside of itself, to see what it can do. The new JavaBeans API depends upon the Reflection API, as does the object-serialization functionality in Java 1.1.

The Reflection API makes it possible to discover the variables, methods, and constructors of any class and manipulate those members as appropriate. For example, you can use a Method object to call a particular method in an object, even if your code was not compiled with any information about the class that contains that method. The java.lang.reflect package also defines an Array class that can be used to manipulate arbitrary arrays.

All of the classes in java.lang.reflect work in conjunction with the Class class in the java.lang package.

See Chapter 13, *The java.lang.reflect Package*, for complete reference material on all of the classes in the java.lang.reflect package.

1.3   The java.io Package

The java.io package contains the classes that handle fundamental input and output operations in Java. Almost all fundamental I/O in Java is based on streams. A stream represents a flow of data, or a channel of communication, with a reading process at one end of the stream and a writing process at the other end, at least conceptually. As of Java 1.1, the java.io package is the largest of the fundamental packages. See Chapter 6, *I/O*, for a more in-depth description of the basic I/O capabilities provided by this package.

Java 1.0 supports only byte streams. The InputStream class is the superclass of all of the Java 1.0 byte input streams, while OutputStream is the superclass of all the byte output streams. A number of other byte stream classes extend the functionality of these basic streams. For example, the FileInputStream and FileOutputStream classes read from and write to files, respectively, while DataInputStream and DataOutputStream read and write binary representations of the primitive Java data types. The main problem with these byte streams is that they do not handle the conversion between the Unicode character set used internally by Java and other character sets used when reading or writing data.

As of Java 1.1, java.io contains classes that represent character streams. These character stream classes convert other character encodings that appear in I/O streams to and from Unicode characters. The Reader class is the superclass of all the Java 1.1 character input streams, while Writer is the superclass of all character output streams. Many of the reader and writer classes have analogous behavior to corresponding byte stream classes. For instance, FileReader and FileWriter are character streams that read from and write to files, respectively.

The InputStreamReader and OutputStreamWriter classes provide a bridge between byte streams and character streams. If you wrap an InputStreamReader around an InputStream object, the bytes in the byte stream are read and converted to characters using the character encoding scheme specified by the InputStream-Reader. Likewise, you can wrap an OutputStreamWriter around any OutputStream object, which allows you to write characters and have them converted to bytes.

As of Java 1.1, java.io also contains classes to support *object serialization*. Object serialization is the ability to write the complete state of an object to an output stream, and then later recreate that object by reading in the serialized state from an input stream. The ObjectOutputStream and ObjectInputStream classes handle serializing and deserializing objects, respectively. These classes provide basic serialization capabilities for all objects that implement the Serializable interface. Chapter 7, *Object Serialization,* provides a more detailed explanation of the new object serialization functionality in Java 1.1.

The RandomAccessFile class is the only class in java.io that does not use a stream for reading or writing data. As its name implies, RandomAccessFile provides nonsequential access to a file, so you can use it to read from or write to specific locations in a file.

The File class represents a file on the local filesystem. The class provides methods to identify a file, both in terms of its path and its filename. There are also methods that retrieve information about a file, such as its status as a directory or a file, its length, and its last modification time.

See Chapter 11, *The java.io Package*, for complete reference material on all of the classes in the `java.io` package.

1.4   *The java.net Package*

The `java.net` package contains classes and interfaces that provide a powerful infrastructure for networking in Java. Many of the classes in this package provide support for working with sockets in Java. For example, the `Socket` and `Server-Socket` classes make it possible to implement client and server programs that communicate using a reliable, connection-oriented protocol. The `DatagramSocket`, `DatagramPacket`, and `MulticastSocket` classes, on the other hand, all provide support for communication over a connectionless protocol. The `MulticastSocket` class is new in Java 1.1.

The `URL` and `URLConnection` classes define methods for working with uniform resource locators (URLs). The `URL` class supports basic access to data stored at a URL, while `URLConnection` offers complete control over all aspects of working with a URL.

The `InetAddress` class represents network addresses, so `InetAddress` objects are used by a number of the methods in other classes in `java.net`.

Chapter 8, *Networking*, offers a short tutorial on using the networking classes provided by the `java.net` package. See Chapter 15, *The java.net Package*, for complete reference material on all of the classes in this package.

1.5   *The java.util Package*

The `java.util` package contains a number of useful classes and interfaces that support fundamental data structures and notification-related design patterns. Java depends directly on several of the classes in this package, and you may find many of these indispensable.

A number of classes in `java.util` are designed to help you manage a collection of objects. For example, the `Vector` class supports variable-length arrays of objects, while the `Hashtable` class can be used to create hashtables, or associative arrays, that contain key/value pairs of objects. In addition, the `Enumeration` interface defines methods for iterating through a collection of elements. Chapter 5, *Collections*, provides more detailed information on using these classes effectively in your Java programs.

The `StringTokenizer` class parses strings into distinct tokens separated by delimiter characters. This class is described in more detail in Chapter 2.

The java.util package contains a number of new classes in Java 1.1 to support internationalization. Many of these classes work in conjuction with the classes defined in the new java.text package. The most important new class is the Locale class, which represents a particular locale, or country and language, for internationalization purposes. The new Calendar and TimeZone classes interpret the value of a Date object in the context of a particular calendar system; the Date class existed in Java 1.0.2, but many of its methods are deprecated in Java 1.1. Finally, the ResourceBundle class and its subclasses, ListResourceBundle and PropertyResourceBundle, represent sets of localized data in Java 1.1.

Two other new entities in java.util are the EventObject class and the EventListener interface. These items form the basis of the new event model in Java 1.1.

See Chapter 17, *The java.util Package*, for complete reference material on all of the classes in the java.util package.

1.6 *The java.text Package*

The java.text package is new in Java 1.1. It contains classes that support the parsing and formatting of data. These classes also support the internationalization of Java programs. Internationalization refers to the process of making a program flexible enough to run correctly in any locale. An internationalized program must, however, be localized to enable it to run in a particular locale. The internationalization capabilities in Java are quite significant, especially in this age of the global Internet.

Many of the classes in java.text are meant to handle formatting string representations of dates, times, numbers, and messages based on the conventions of a locale. The Format class is the superclass of all of the classes that generate and parse string representations of various types of data.

The DateFormat class formats and parses dates and times according to the customs and language of a particular locale. By the same token, the NumberFormat class formats and parses numbers, including currency values, in a locale-dependent manner. The MessageFormat class creates a textual message from a pattern string, while ChoiceFormat maps numerical ranges to strings. By themselves, these classes do not provide different results for different locales. However, they can be used in conjunction with ResourceBundle objects from java.util that generate locale-specific pattern strings.

The Collator class handles collating strings according to the rules of a particular locale. Different languages have different characters and different rules for sorting those characters; Collator and its subclass, RuleBasedCollator, are designed to take those differences into account when collating strings. In addition, the CollationKey class optimizes the sorting of a large collection of strings.

The BreakIterator class finds various boundaries, such as word boundaries and line boundaries, in textual data. As you might expect, BreakIterator locates these boundaries according to the rules of a particular locale.

See Chapter 16, *The java.text Package*, for complete reference material on all of the classes in the java.text package.

1.7 The java.math Package

The java.math package is new in Java 1.1. It contains two classes that support arithmetic on arbitrarily large integers and floating-point numbers: BigInteger and BigDecimal. The BigInteger class also defines some methods for handling modular arithmetic and determining primality that are needed for cryptographic purposes. See Chapter 14, *The java.math Package*, for complete reference material on the two classes in this package.

1.8 The java.util.zip Package

The java.util.zip package is new in Java 1.1. It contains classes that provide support for general-purpose data compression and decompression using the ZLIB compression algorithms. The important classes in java.util.zip are those that provide the means to read and write data that is compatible with the popular GZIP and ZIP formats: GZIPInputStream, GZIPOutputStream, ZipInputStream, and ZipOutputStream.

The GZIP and ZIP classes are easy to use because they subclass java.io.FilterInputStream and java.io.FilterOutputStream. While a GZIP file is simply a stream of compressed data, a ZIP file, or archive, can contain multiple compressed files. A ZipEntry object represents each compressed file in the archive. The ZipFile class is provided as a convenience for reading an archive; it allows nonsequential access to the entries in a ZIP file while the ZipInputStream class provides only sequential access.

The remainder of the classes in java.util.zip support the GZIP and ZIP classes. The generic Deflater and Inflater classes implement the ZLIB algorithms; they are used by DeflaterOutputStream and InflaterInputStream to decompress and compress data. The Checksum interface and the classes that implement it, Adler32 and CRC32, define algorithms that generate checksums from stream data. These checksums are used by the CheckedInputStream and CheckedOutputStream classes.

See Chapter 18, *The java.util.zip Package*, for complete reference material on all of the classes in the java.util.zip package.

I

USING THE FUNDAMENTAL CLASSES

- Chapter 2, *Strings and Related Classes*
- Chapter 3, *Threads*
- Chapter 4, *Exception Handling*
- Chapter 5, *Collections*
- Chapter 6, *I/O*
- Chapter 7, *Object Serialization*
- Chapter 8, *Networking*
- Chapter 9, *Security*
- Chapter 10, *Accessing the Environment*

This part of the book, Chapters 2 through 10, provides a brief guide to many of the features of the fundamental classes in Java. These tutorial-style chapters are meant to help you learn about some of the basic functionality of the Java API. They provide short examples where appropriate that illustrate the use of various features.

Strings and Related Classes

As with most programming languages, strings are used extensively throughout Java, so the Java API has quite a bit of functionality to help you manipulate strings. This chapter describes the following classes:

- The `java.lang.String` class represents all textual strings in Java. A `String` object is immutable; once you create a `String` object, there is no way to change the sequence of characters it represents or the length of the string.

- The `java.lang.StringBuffer` class represents a variable-length, mutable sequence of characters. With a `StringBuffer` object, you can insert characters anywhere in the sequence and add characters to the end of the sequence.

- The `java.util.StringTokenizer` class provides support for parsing a string into a sequence of words, or tokens.

2.1 String

You can create a `String` object in Java simply by assigning a string literal to a `String` variable:

```
String quote = "To be or not to be";
```

All string literals are compiled into `String` objects. Although the Java compiler does not generally treat expressions involving object references as compile-time constants, references to `String` objects created from string literals are treated as compile-time constants.

Of course, there are many other ways to create a `String` object. The `String` class has a number of constructors that let you create a `String` from an array of bytes, an array of characters, another `String` object, or a `StringBuffer` object.

If you are a C or C++ programmer, you may be wondering if String objects are null-terminated. The answer is no, and, in fact, the question is irrelevant. The String class actually uses a character array internally. Since arrays in Java are actual objects that know their own length, a String object also knows its length and does not require a special terminator. Use the length() method to get the length of a String object.

Although String objects are immutable, the String class does provide a number of useful methods for working with strings. Any operation that would otherwise change the characters or the length of the string returns a new String object that copies the necessary portions of the original String.

The following methods access the contents of a String object:

- substring() creates a new String object that contains a sub-sequence of the sequence of characters represented by a String object.

- charAt() returns the character at a given position in a String object.

- getChars() and getBytes() return a range of characters in a char array or a byte array.

- toCharArray() returns the entire contents of a String object as a char array.

You can compare the contents of String objects with the following methods:

- equals() returns true if two String objects have the exact same contents, while equalsIgnoreCase() returns true if two objects have the same contents ignoring differences between upper- and lowercase versions of the same character.

- regionMatches() determines if two sub-strings contain the same sequence of characters.

- startsWith() and endsWith() determine if a String object begins or ends with a particular sequence of characters.

- compareTo() determines if the contents of one String object are less than, equal to, or greater than the contents of another String object.

Use the following methods to search for characters in a string:

- indexOf() searches forward through a string for a given character or string.

- lastIndexOf() searches backwards through a string for a given character or string.

The following methods manipulate the contents of a string and return a new, related string:

- concat() returns a new String object that is the concatenation of two String objects.

- replace() returns a new String object that contains the same sequence of characters as the original string, but with a given character replaced by another given character.

- toLowerCase() and toUpperCase() return new String objects that contain the same sequence of characters as the original string, but converted to lower- or uppercase.

- trim() returns a new String object that contains the same character sequence as the original string, but with leading and trailing white space and control characters removed.

The String class also defines a number of static methods named valueOf() that return string representations of primitive Java data types and objects. The Object class defines a toString() method, and, since Object is the ultimate superclass of every other class, every class inherits a basic toString() method. Any class that has a string representation should override the toString() method to produce the appropriate string.

2.2 StringBuffer

StringBuffer objects are similar to String objects in that they both represent sequences of characters. The main difference is that a StringBuffer is mutable, while a String is not. The StringBuffer class defines a number of append() methods for adding characters to the end of the sequence, as well as a number of insert() methods for inserting characters anywhere in the sequence.

Many computations that produce a String object use a StringBuffer internally to build the string. For example, to write a method that takes a String object and returns a new String that contains the sequence of characters in reverse, you use a StringBuffer as follows:

```
public static String reverse(String s) {
    StringBuffer buf = new StringBuffer(s.length());
    for (int i = s.length()-1; i >= 0; i--) {
        buf.append(s.charAt(i));
    }
    return buf.toString();
}
```

After creating a new StringBuffer object, the method loops over the given string from the last character to the first character and appends each character to the end of the StringBuffer object. When the loop finishes, the StringBuffer object contains a sequence of characters that is the reverse of the sequence of characters in the given String object. The method finishes by calling the toString() method of the StringBuffer; this method returns a String object that contains the same sequence of characters as the StringBuffer object.

2.3 String Concatenation

Java's string concatenation operator (+) provides special support for the String and StringBuffer classes. If either operand of the binary + operator is a reference to a String or StringBuffer object, the operator is the string concatenation operator instead of the arithmetic addition operator. The string concatenation operator produces a new String object that contains the concatenation of its operands; the characters of the left operand precede the characters of the right operand in the newly created string.

If one of the operands of the + operator is a reference to a string object and the other is not, the operator converts the nonstring operand to a string object using the following rules:

- A null operand is converted to the string literal "null".

- If the operand is a non-null reference to an object that is not a string, the object's toString() method is called. The result of the conversion is the value returned by the object's toString() method, unless the return value is null, in which case the result of the conversion is the string literal "null".

- A char operand is converted to a reference to a string object that has a length of one and contains that character.

- An integer operand (other than char) is converted to a string object that contains the base 10 string representation of its value. If the value is negative, the string starts with a minus sign; if it is positive there is no sign character. If the value is zero, the result of the conversion is "0". Otherwise, the string representation of the integer does not have any leading zeros.

- If the operand is a floating-point value, the exact string representation depends on the value being converted. If its absolute value is greater than or equal to 10^{-3} or less than or equal to 10^7, it is converted to a string with an optional minus sign (if the value is negative) followed by up to eight digits before the decimal point, a decimal point, and the necessary number of digits after the decimal point (but no trailing zero if there is more than one significant digit). There is always a minimum of one digit after the decimal point.

- Otherwise, the value is converted to a string with an optional minus sign (if the value is negative), followed by a single digit, a decimal point, the necessary number of digits after the decimal point (but no trailing zero if there is more than one significant digit), and the letter E followed by a plus or a minus sign and a base 10 exponent of at least one digit. Again, there is always a minimum of one digit after the decimal point.

- The values NaN, NEGATIVE_INFINITY, POSITIVE_INFINITY, -0.0, and +0.0 are represented by the strings "NaN", "-Infinity", "Infinity", "-0.0", and "0.0", respectively.

- A boolean operand is converted to either the string literal "true" or the string literal "false".

The following is a code example that uses the string concatenation operator:

```
// format seconds into hours, minutes, and seconds
String formatTime(int t) {
    int minutes, seconds;
    seconds = t%60;
    t /= 60;
    minutes = t%60;
    return t/60 + ":" + minutes + ":" + seconds;
}
```

Java uses StringBuffer objects to implement string concatenation. Consider the following code:

```
String s, s1, s2;
s = s1 + s2
```

To compute the string concatenation, Java's compiler generates this code:

```
s = new StringBuffer().append(s1).append(s2).toString()
```

2.4 *StringTokenizer*

The java.util.StringTokenizer class provides support for parsing a string into a sequence of words, or *tokens*, that are separated by some set of delimiter characters. Here is an example of how to use the StringTokenizer class:

```
StringTokenizer s = new StringTokenizer("This is it");
while (s.hasMoreTokens())
    System.out.println(s.nextToken());
```

This example begins by creating a StringTokenizer object to pick tokens out of the specified string. The example uses a StringTokenizer constructor that does not specify what delimiters to use, so the new StringTokenizer object uses the default delimiters: space, tab ('\t'), carriage return ('\r'), and newline ('\n').

The while loop does the actual work of getting the tokens from the StringTokenizer object. The hasMoreTokens() method returns true while there are still
more tokens to be fetched from the StringTokenizer object, while nextToken()
returns the next token. Here is the output from the example:

```
This
is
it
```

You can also use a StringTokenizer to extract tokens from a string that uses delimiters other than whitespace. For example, suppose that you need to extract tokens
that are separated by commas, such as from a string that looks like this:

```
abc,def,123,789
```

In this case, you use a StringTokenizer constructor that takes a parameter that
specifies the characters to be treated as delimiters. For example:

```
StringTokenizer s = new StringTokenizer(commaString, ",");
```

The second argument to this constructor specifies the delimiter characters, so in
this case, the only delimiter character is the comma character.

3

Threads

Threads provide a way for a Java program to do multiple tasks concurrently. A thread is essentially a flow of control in a program and is similar to the more familiar concept of a process. An operating system that can run more than one program at the same time uses processes to keep track of the various programs that it is running. However, processes generally do not share any state, while multiple threads within the same application share much of the same state. In particular, all of the threads in an application run in the same address space, sharing all resources except the stack. In concrete terms, this means that threads share field variables, but not local variables.

When multiple processes share a single processor, there are times when the operating system must stop the processor from running one process and start it running another process. The operating system must execute a sequence of events called a *context switch* to transfer control from one process to another. When a context switch occurs, the operating system has to save a lot of information for the process that is being paused and load the comparable information for the process being resumed. A context switch between two processes can require the execution of thousands of machine instructions. The Java virtual machine is responsible for handling context switches between threads in a Java program. Because threads share much of the same state, a context switch between two threads typically requires the execution of less than 100 machine instructions.

There are a number of situations where it makes sense to use threads in a Java program. Some programs must be able to engage in multiple activities and still be able to respond to additional input from the user. For example, a web browser should be able to respond to user input while fetching an image or playing a sound. Because threads can be suspended and resumed, they can make it easier to control multiple activities, even if the activities do not need to be concurrent. If a program models real world objects that display independent, autonomous behavior, it makes sense to use a separate thread for each object. Threads can also implement asynchronous methods, so that a calling method does not have to wait for the method it calls to complete before continuing with its own activity.

Java applets make considerable use of threads. For example, an animation is generally implemented with a separate thread. If an applet has to download extensive information, such as an image or a sound, to initialize itself, the initialization can take a long time. This initialization can be done in a separate thread to prevent the initialization from interfering with the display of the applet. If an applet needs to process messages from the network, that work generally is done in a separate thread so that the applet can continue painting itself on the screen and responding to mouse and keyboard events. In addition, if each message is processed separately, the applet uses a separate thread for each message.

For all of the reasons there are to use threads, there are also some compelling reasons not to use them. If a program uses inherently sequential logic, where one operation starts another operation and then must wait for the other operation to complete before continuing, one thread can implement the entire sequence. Using multiple threads in such a case results in a more complex program with no accompanying benefits. There is considerable overhead in creating and starting a thread, so if an operation involves only a few primitive statements, it is faster to handle it with a single thread. This can even be true when the operation is conceptually asynchronous. When multiple threads share objects, the objects must use synchronization mechanisms to coordinate thread access and maintain consistent state. Synchronization mechanisms add complexity to a program, can be difficult to tune for optimal performance, and can be a source of bugs.

3.1 Using Thread Objects

The Thread class in the java.lang package creates and controls threads in Java programs. The execution of Java code is always under the control of a Thread object. The Thread class provides a static method called currentThread() that provides a reference to the Thread object that controls the current thread of execution.

3.1.1 Associating a Method with a Thread

The first thing you need to do to make a Thread object useful is to associate it with a method you want it to run. Java provides two ways of associating a method with a Thread:

- Declare a subclass of Thread that defines a run() method.

- Pass a reference to an object that implements the Runnable interface to a Thread constructor.

For example, if you need to load the contents of a URL as part of an applet's initialization, but the applet can provide other functionality before the content is loaded, you might want to load the content in a separate thread. Here is a class that does just that:

```
import java.net.URL;

class UrlData extends Thread   {
    private Object data;
    private URL url

    public UrlData(String urlName) throws MalformedURLException {
        url = new URL(urlName);
        start();
    }

    public void run(){
        try {
            data = url.getContent();
        } catch (java.io.IOException  e) {
        }
    }

    public Object getUrlData(){
        return data;
    }
}
```

The UrlData class is declared as a subclass of Thread so that it can get the contents of the URL in a separate thread. The constructor creates a java.net.URL object to fetch the contents of the URL, and then calls the start() method to start the thread. Once the thread is started, the constructor returns; it does not wait for the contents of the URL to be fetched. The run() method is executed after the thread is started; it does the real work of fetching the data. The getUrlData() method is an access method that returns the value of the data variable. The value of this variable is null until the contents of the URL have been fetched, at which time it contains a reference to the actual data.

Subclassing the Thread class is convenient when the method you want to run in a separate thread does not need to belong to a particular class. Sometimes, however, you need the method to be part of a particular class that is a subclass of a class other than Thread. Say, for example, you want a graphical object that is displayed in a window to alternate its background color between red and blue once a

second. The object that implements this behavior needs to be a subclass of the
java.awt.Canvas class. However, at the same time, you need a separate thread to
alternate the color of the object once a second.

In this situation, you want to tell a Thread object to run code in another object that
is not a subclass of the Thread class. You can accomplish this by passing a reference
to an object that implements the Runnable interface to the constructor of the
Thread class. The Runnable interface requires that an object has a public method
called run() that takes no arguments. When a Runnable object is passed to the
constructor of the Thread class, it creates a Thread object that calls the Runnable
object's run() method when the thread is started. The following example shows
part of the code that implements an object that alternates its background color
between red and blue once a second:

```
class AutoColorChange extends java.awt.Canvas implements Runnable {
    private Thread myThread;

    AutoColorChange () {
        myThread = new Thread(this);
        myThread.start();
        ...
    }

    public void run() {
        while (true) {
            setBackground(java.awt.Color.red);
            repaint();
            try {
                myThread.sleep(1000);
            } catch (InterruptedException e) {}
            setBackground(java.awt.Color.blue);
            repaint();
            try {
                myThread.sleep(1000);
            } catch (InterruptedException e) {}
        }
    }
}
```

The AutoChangeColor class extends java.awt.Canvas, alternating the background
color between red and blue once a second. The constructor creates a new Thread
by passing the current object to the Thread constructor, which tells the Thread to
call the run() method in the AutoChangeColor class. The constructor then starts
the new thread by calling its start() method, so that the color change happens
asynchronously of whatever else is going on. The class has an instance variable
called myThread that contains a reference to the Thread object, so that can control
the thread. The run() method takes care of changing the background color, using
the sleep() method of the Thread class to temporarily suspend the thread and
calling repaint() to redisplay the object after each color change.

3.1.2 Controlling a Thread

As shown in the previous section, you start a Thread by calling its start() method. Before the start() method is called, the isAlive() method of the Thread object always returns false. When the start() method is called, the Thread object becomes associated with a scheduled thread in the underlying environment. After the start() method has returned, the isAlive() method always returns true. The Thread is now scheduled to run until it dies, unless it is suspended or in another unrunnable state.

It is actually possible for isAlive() to return true before start() returns, but not before start() is called. This can happen because the start() method can return either before the started Thread begins to run or after it begins to run. In other words, the method that called start() and the new thread are now running concurrently. On a multiprocessor system, the start() method can even return at the same time the started Thread begins to run.

Thread objects have a parent-child relationship. The first thread created in a Java environment does not have a parent Thread. However, after the first Thread object is created, the Thread object that controls the thread used to create another Thread object is considered to be the parent of the newly created Thread. This parent-child relationship is used to supply some default values when a Thread object is created, but it has no further significance after a Thread has been created.

3.1.2.1 Stopping a thread

A thread dies when one of the following things happens:

*   The run() method called by the Thread returns.
*   An exception is thrown that causes the run() method to be exited.
*   The stop() method of the Thread is called.

The stop() method of the Thread class works by throwing a ThreadDeath object in the run() method of the thread. Normally, you should not catch ThreadDeath objects in a try statement. If you need to catch ThreadDeath objects to detect that a Thread is about to die, the try statement that catches ThreadDeath objects should rethrow them.

When an object (ThreadDeath or otherwise) is thrown out of the run() method for the Thread, the uncaughtException() method of the ThreadGroup for that Thread is called. If the thrown object is an instance of the ThreadDeath class, the thread dies, and the thrown object is ignored. Otherwise, if the thrown object is of any other class, uncaughtException() calls the thrown object's printStackTrace()

method, the thread dies, and the thrown object is ignored. In either case, if there are other nondaemon threads running in the system, the current program continues to run.

3.1.2.2 Interrupting a thread

There are a number of methods in the Java API, such as wait() and join(), that are declared as throwing an InterruptedException. What these methods have in common is that they temporarily suspend the execution of a thread. In Java 1.1, if a thread is waiting for one of these methods to return and another thread calls interrupt() on the waiting thread, the method that is waiting throws an InterruptedException.

The interrupt() method sets an internal flag in a Thread object. Before the interrupt() method is called, the isInterrupted() method of the Thread object always returns false. After the interrupt() method is called, isInterrupted() returns true.

Prior to version 1.1, the methods in the Java API that are declared as throwing an InterruptedException do not actually do so. However, the isInterrupted() method does function as described above. Thus, if the code in the run() method for a thread periodically calls isInterrupted(), the thread can respond to a call to interrupt() by shutting down in an orderly fashion.

3.1.2.3 Thread priority

One of the attributes that controls the behavior of a thread is its priority. Although Java does not guarantee much about how threads are scheduled, it does guarantee that a thread with a priority that is higher than that of another thread will be scheduled to run at least as often, and possibly more often, than the thread with the lower priority. The priority of a thread is set when the Thread object is created, by passing an argument to the constructor that creates the Thread object. If an explicit priority is not specified, the Thread inherits the priority of its parent Thread object.

You can query the priority of a Thread object by calling its getPriority() method. Similarly, you can set the priority of a Thread using its setPriority() method. The priority you specify must be greater than or equal to Thread.MIN_PRIORITY and less than or equal to Thread.MAX_PRIORITY.

Before actually setting the priority of a Thread object, the setPriority() method checks the maximum allowable priority for the ThreadGroup that contains the Thread by calling getMaxPriority() on the ThreadGroup. If the call to setPriority() tries to set the priority to a value that is higher than the maximum allowable priority for the ThreadGroup, the priority is instead set to the maximum priority. It is possible for the current priority of a Thread to be greater than the maximum allowable priority for the ThreadGroup. In this case, an attempt to raise the priority of the Thread results in its priority being lowered to the maximum priority.

3.1.2.4 Daemon threads

A daemon thread is a thread that runs continuously to perform a service, without having any connection with the overall state of the program. For example, the thread that runs the garbage collector in Java is a daemon thread. The thread that processes mouse events for a Java program is also a daemon thread. In general, threads that run application code are not daemon threads, and threads that run system code are daemon threads. If a thread dies and there are no other threads except daemon threads alive, the Java virtual machine stops.

A Thread object has a boolean attribute that specifies whether or not a thread is a daemon thread. The daemon attribute of a thread is set when the Thread object is created, by passing an argument to the constructor that creates the Thread object. If the daemon attribute is not explicitly specified, the Thread inherits the daemon attribute of its parent Thread object.

The daemon attribute is queried using the isDaemon() method; it is set using the setDaemon() method.

3.1.2.5 Yielding

When a thread has nothing to do, it can call the yield() method of its Thread object. This method tells the scheduler to run a different thread. The value of calling yield() depends largely on whether the scheduling mechanism for the platform on which the program is running is preemptive or nonpreemptive.

By choosing a maximum length of time a thread can continuously, a *preemptive* scheduling mechanism guarantees that no single thread uses more than its fair share of the processor. If a thread runs for that amount of time without yielding control to another thread, the scheduler preempts the thread and causes it to stop running so that another thread can run.

A *nonpreemptive* scheduling mechanism cannot preempt threads. A nonpreemptive scheduler relies on the individual threads to yield control of the processor frequently, so that it can provide reasonable performance. A thread explicitly yields control by calling the Thread object's yield() method. More often, however, a thread implicitly yields control when it is forced to wait for something to happen elsewhere.

Calling a Thread object's yield() method during a lengthy computation can be quite valuable on a platform that uses a nonpreemptive scheduling mechanism, as it allows other threads to run. Otherwise, the lengthy computation can prevent other threads from running. On a platform that uses a preemptive scheduling mechanism, calling yield() does not usually make any noticeable difference in the responsiveness of threads.

Regardless of the scheduling algorithm that is being used, you should not make any assumptions about when a thread will be scheduled to run again after it has called yield(). If you want to prevent a thread from being scheduled to run until a specified amount of time has elapsed, you should call the sleep() method of the Thread object. The sleep() method takes an argument that specifies a minimum number of milliseconds that must elapse before the thread can be scheduled to run again.

3.1.2.6 Controlling groups of threads

Sometimes is it necessary to control multiple threads at the same time. Java provides the ThreadGroup class for this purpose. Every Thread object belongs to a ThreadGroup object. By passing an argument to the constructor that creates the Thread object, the ThreadGroup of a thread can be set when the Thread object is created. If an explicit ThreadGroup is not specified, the Thread belongs to the same ThreadGroup as its parent Thread object.

3.2 Synchronizing Multiple Threads

The correct behavior of a multithreaded program generally depends on multiple threads cooperating with each other. This often involves threads not doing certain things at the same time or waiting for each other to perform certain tasks. This type of cooperation is called *synchronization*. This section discusses some common strategies for synchronization and how they can be implemented in Java.

The simplest strategy for ensuring that threads are correctly synchronized is to write code that works correctly when executed concurrently by any number of threads. However, this is more easily said than done. Most useful computations involve doing some activity, such as updating an instance variable or updating a display, that must be synchronized in order to happen correctly.

If a method only updates its local variables and calls other methods that only modify their local variables, the method can be invoked by multiple threads without any need for synchronization. Math.sqrt() and the length() method of the String class are examples of such methods.

A method that creates objects and meets the above criterion may not require synchronization. If the constructors invoked by the method do not modify anything but their own local variables and instance variables of the object they are constructing, and they only call methods that do not need to be synchronized, the method itself does not need to be synchronized. An example of such a method is the substring() in the String class.

Beyond these two simple cases, it is impossible to give an exhaustive list of rules that can tell you whether or not a method needs to be synchronized. You need to consider what the method is doing and think about any ill effects of concurrent execution in order to decide if synchronization is necessary.

3.2.1 Single-Threaded Execution

When more than one thread is trying to update the same data at the same time, the result may be wrong or inconsistent. Consider the following example:

```
class CountIt {
    int i = 0;

    void count() {
        i = i + 1;
    }
}
```

The method count() is supposed to increment the variable i by one. However, suppose that there are two threads, A and B, that call count() at the same time. In this case, it is possible that i could be incremented only once, instead of twice. Say the value of i is 7. Thread A calls the count() method and computes i+1 as 8. Then thread B calls the count() method and computes i+1 as 8 because thread A has not yet assigned the new value to i. Next, thread A assigns the value 8 to the variable i. Finally, thread B assigns the value 8 to the variable i. Thus, even though the count() method is called twice, the variable has only been incremented once when the sequence is finished.

Clearly, this code can fail to produce its intended result when it is executed concurrently by more than one thread. A piece of code that can fail to produce its intended result when executed concurrently is called a *critical section*. However, a critical section does behave correctly when it is executed by only one thread at a time. The strategy of single-threaded execution is to allow only one thread to execute a critical section of code at a time. If a thread wants to execute a critical section that another thread is already executing, the thread has to wait until the first thread is done and no other thread is executing that code before it can proceed.

Java provides the synchronized statement and the synchronized method modifier for implementing single-threaded execution. Before executing the block in a synchronized statement, the current thread must obtain a lock for the object referenced by the expression. If a method is declared with the synchronized modifer, the current thread must obtain a lock before it can invoke the method. If the method is not declared static, the thread must obtain a lock associated with the object used to access the method. If the method is declared static, the thread must obtain a lock associated with the class in which the method is declared. Because a thread must obtain a lock before executing a synchronized method, Java guarantees that synchronized methods are executed one thread at a time.

Modifying the count() method to make it a synchronized method ensures that it works as intended.

```
class CountIt {
    int i = 0;

    synchronized void count() {
        i = i + 1;
    }
}
```

The strategy of single-threaded execution can also be used when multiple methods update the same data. Consider the following example:

```
class CountIt2 {
    int i = 0;

    void count() {
        i = i + 1;
    }
    void count2() {
        i = i + 2;
    }
}
```

By the same logic used above, if the count() and count2() methods are executed concurrently, the result could be to increment i by 1, 2, or 3. Both the count() and count2() methods can be declared as synchronized to ensure that they are not executed concurrently with themselves or each other:

```
class CountIt2 {
    int i = 0;

    synchronized void count() {
        i = i + 1;
    }
    synchronized void count2() {
        i = i + 2;
    }
}
```

Sometimes it's necessary for a thread to make multiple method calls to manipulate an object without another thread calling that object's methods at the same time.

Consider the following example:

```
System.out.print(new Date());
System.out.print(" : ");
System.out.println(foo());
```

If the code in the example is executed concurrently by multiple threads, the output from the two threads will be interleaved. The synchronized keyword provides a way to ensure that only one thread at a time can execute a block of code. Before executing the block in a synchronized statement, the current thread must obtain a lock for the object referenced by the expression. The above code can be modified to give a thread exclusive access to the OutputStream object referenced by System.out:

```
synchronized (System.out) {
    System.out.print(new Date());
    System.out.print(" : ");
    System.out.println(foo());
}
```

Note that this approach only works if other code that wants to call methods in the same object also uses similar synchronized statements, or if the methods in question are all synchronized methods. In this case, the print() and println() methods are synchronized, so other pieces of code that need to use these methods do not need to use a synchronized statement.

Another situation in which simply making a method synchronized does not provide the needed single-threaded execution occurs when an inner class is updating fields in its enclosing instance. Consider the following code:

```
public class Z extends Frame {
    int pressCount = 0;
    ...
    private class CountButton extends Button
                             implements ActionListener {
        public void actionPerformed(ActionEvent evt) {
            pressCount ++;
        }
    }
    ...
}
```

If a Z object instantiates more than one instance of CountButton, you need to use single-threaded execution to ensure that updates to pressCount are done correctly. Unfortunately, declaring the actionPerformed() method of CountButton to be synchronized does not accomplish that goal because it only forces the method to acquire a lock on the instance of CountButton it is associated with before it executes. The object you need to acquire a lock for is the enclosing instance of Z.

One way to have a CountButton object capture a lock on its enclosing instance of Z is to update pressCount inside of a synchronized statement:

```
synchronized (Z.this) {
    pressCount ++;
}
```

The drawback to this approach is that every piece of code that accesses pressCount in any inner class of Z must be in a similar synchronized statement. Otherwise, it is possible for pressCount to be updated incorrectly. The more pieces of code that need to be inside of synchronized statements, the more places there are to introduce bugs in your program.

A more robust approach is to have the inner class update a field in its enclosing instance by calling a synchronized method in the enclosing instance:

```
public class Z extends Frame {
    int pressCount = 0;
    synchronized incrementPressCount() {
        pressCount++;
    }
    ...
    private class CountButton extends Button
                             implements ActionListener {
        public void actionPerformed(ActionEvent evt) {
            incrementPressCount();
        }
    }
    ...
}
```

3.2.2 Optimistic Single-Threaded Execution

When multiple threads are updating a data structure, single-threaded execution is the obvious strategy to use to ensure correctness of the operations on the data structure. However, single-threaded execution can cause some problems of its own. Consider the following example:

```
public class Queue extends java.util.Vector {
    synchronized public void put(Object obj) {
        addElement(obj);
    }

    synchronized public Object get() throws EmptyQueueException {
        if (size() == 0)
            throw new EmptyQueueException();
        Object obj = elementAt(0);
```

```
            removeElementAt(0);
            return obj;
        }
    }
```

This example implements a first-in, first-out (FIFO) queue. If the get() method of a Queue object is called when the queue is empty, the method throws an exception. Now suppose that you want to write the get() method so that when the queue is empty, the method waits for an item to be put in the queue, rather than throwing an exception. In order for an item to be put in the queue, the put() method of the queue must be invoked. But using the single-threaded execution strategy, the put() method will never be able to run while the get() method is waiting for the queue to receive an item. A good way to solve this dilemma is to use a strategy called *optimistic single-threaded execution*.

The optimistic single-threaded execution strategy is similar to the single-threaded execution strategy. They both begin by getting a lock on an object to ensure that the currently executing thread is the only thread that can execute a piece of code, and they both end by releasing that lock. The difference is what happens in between. Using the optimistic single-threaded execution strategy, if a piece of code discovers that conditions are not right to proceed, the code releases the lock it has on the object that enforces single-threaded execution and waits. When another piece of code changes things in such a way that might allow the first piece of code to proceed, it notifies the first piece of code that it should try to regain the lock and proceed.

To implement this strategy, the Object class provides methods called wait(), notify(), and notifyAll(). These methods are inherited by every other class in Java. The following example shows how to implement a queue that uses the optimistic single-threaded execution strategy, so that when the queue is empty, its get() method waits for the queue to have an item put in it:

```
public class Queue extends java.util.Vector {
    synchronized public void put(Object obj) {
        addElement(obj);
        notify();
    }

    synchronized public Object get() throws EmptyQueueException {
        while (size() == 0)
            wait();
        Object obj = elementAt(0);
        removeElementAt(0);
        return obj;
    }
}
```

In the above implementation of the Queue class, the get() method calls wait() when the queue is empty. The wait() method releases the lock that excludes other threads from executing methods in the Queue object, and then waits until another thread calls the put() method. When put() is called, it adds an item to the queue and calls notify(). The notify() method tells a thread that is waiting to return from a wait() method that it should attempt to regain its lock and proceed. If there is more than one thread waiting to regain the lock on the object, notify() chooses one of the threads arbitrarily. The notifyAll() method is similar to notify(), but instead of choosing one thread to notify, it notifies all of the threads that are waiting to regain the lock on the object.

Notice that the get() method calls wait() inside a while loop. Between the time that wait() is notified that it should try to regain its lock and the time it actually does regain the lock, another thread may have called the get() method and emptied the queue. The while loop guards against this situation.

3.2.3 Rendezvous

Sometimes it is necessary to have a thread wait to continue until another thread has completed its work and died. This type of synchronization uses the rendezvous strategy. The Thread class provides the join() method for implementing this strategy. When the join() method is called on a Thread object, the method returns immediately if the thread is dead. Otherwise, the method waits until the thread dies and then returns.

3.2.4 Balking

Some methods should not be executed concurrently and have a time-sensitive nature that makes postponing calls to them a bad idea. This is a common situation when software is controlling real-world devices. Suppose you have a Java program that is embedded in an electronic control for a toilet. There is a method called flush() that is responsible for flushing a toilet, and flush() can be called from more than one thread. If a thread calls flush() while another thread is already executing flush(), the second call should do nothing. A toilet is capable of only one flush at a time, and having a concurrent call to the flush() method result in a second flush would only waste water.

This scenario suggests the use of the balking strategy. The balking strategy allows no more than one thread to execute a method at a time. If another thread attempts to execute the method, the method simply returns without doing anything. Here is an example that shows what such a flush() method might look like:

```
boolean busy;
void flush() {
    synchronized (this) {
```

```
            if (busy)
                return;
            busy = true;
        }
        // code to make flush happen goes here
        busy = false;
    }
```

3.2.5 *Explicit Synchronization*

When the synchronization needs of a thread are not known in advance, you can use a strategy called explicit synchronization. The explicit synchronization strategy allows you to explicitly tell a thread when it can and cannot run. For example, you may want an animation to start and stop in response to external events that happen at unpredictable times, so you need to be able to tell the animation when it can run.

To implement this strategy, the Thread class provides methods called suspend() and resume(). You can suspend the execution of a thread by calling the suspend() method of the Thread object that controls the thread. You can later resume execution of the thread by calling the resume() method on the Thread object.

4

In this chapter:
• *Handling Exceptions*
• *Declaring Exceptions*
• *Generating Exceptions*

Exception Handling

Exception handling is a mechanism that allows Java programs to handle various exceptional conditions, such as semantic violations of the language and program-defined errors, in a robust way. When an exceptional condition occurs, an *exception* is thrown. If the Java virtual machine or run-time environment detects a semantic violation, the virtual machine or run-time environment implicitly throws an exception. Alternately, a program can throw an exception explicitly using the throw statement. After an exception is thrown, control is transferred from the current point of execution to an appropriate catch clause of an enclosing try statement. The catch clause is called an exception handler because it handles the exception by taking whatever actions are necessary to recover from it.

4.1 Handling Exceptions

The try statement provides Java's exception-handling mechanism. A try statement contains a block of code to be executed. Putting a block in a try statement indicates that any exceptions or other abnormal exits in the block are going to be handled appropriately. A try statement can have any number of optional catch clauses that act as exception handlers for the try block. A try statement can also have a finally clause. The finally block is always executed before control leaves the try statement; it cleans up after the try block. Note that a try statement must have either a catch clause or a finally clause.

Here is an example of a try statement that includes a catch clause and a finally clause:

```
try {
    out.write(b);
} catch (IOException e) {
    System.out.println("Output Error");
```

```
  } finally {
      out.close();
  }
```

If out.write() throws an IOException, the exception is caught by the catch clause. Regardless of whether out.write() returns normally or throws an exception, the finally block is executed, which ensures that out.close() is always called.

A try statement executes the block that follows the keyword try. If an exception is thrown from within the try block and the try statement has any catch clauses, those clauses are searched, in order, for one that can handle the exception. If a catch clause handles an exception, that catch block is executed.

However, if the try statement does not have any catch clauses that can handle the exception (or does not have any catch clauses at all), the exception propagates up through enclosing statements in the current method. If the current method does not contain a try statement that can handle the exception, the exception propagates up to the invoking method. If this method does not contain an appropriate try statement, the exception propagates up again, and so on. Finally, if no try statement is found to handle the exception, the currently running thread terminates.

A catch clause is declared with a parameter that specifies the type of exception it can handle. The parameter in a catch clause must be of type Throwable or one of its subclasses. When an exception occurs, the catch clauses are searched for the first one with a parameter that matches the type of the exception thrown or is a superclass of the thrown exception. When the appropriate catch block is executed, the actual exception object is passed as an argument to the catch block. The code within a catch block should do whatever is necessary to handle the exceptional condition.

The finally clause of a try statement is always executed, no matter how control leaves the try statement. Thus it is a good place to handle clean-up operations, such as closing files, freeing resources, and closing network connections.

4.2 Declaring Exceptions

If a method is expected to throw any exceptions, the method declaration must declare that fact in a throws clause. If a method implementation contains a throw statement, it is possible that an exception will be thrown from within the method. In addition, if a method calls another method declared with a throws clause, there is the possibility that an exception will be thrown from within the method. If the

exception is not caught inside the method with a `try` statement, it will be thrown
out of the method to its caller. Any exception that can be thrown out of a method
in this way must be listed in a `throws` clause in the method declaration. The classes
listed in a `throws` clause must be `Throwable` or any of its subclasses; the `Throwable`
class is the superclass of all objects that can be thrown in Java.

However, there are certain types of exceptions that do not have to be listed in a
`throws` clause. Specifically, if the exception is an instance of `Error`, `RunTimeExcep-`
`tion`, or a subclass of one of those classes, it does not have to be listed in a `throws`
clause. Subclasses of the `Error` class correspond to situations that are not easily
predicted, such as the system running out of memory. Subclasses of `RunTimeExcep-`
`tion` correspond to many common run-time problems, such as illegal casts and
array index problems. The reason that these types of exceptions are treated spe-
cially is that they can be thrown from such a large number of places that essentially
every method would have to declare them.

Consider the following example:

```
import java.io.IOException;

class throwsExample {
    char[] a;
    int position;
    ...
    // Method explicitly throws an exception
    int read() throws IOException {
        if (position >= a.length)
            throw new IOException();
        return a[position++];
    }

    // Method implicitly throws an exception
    String readUpTo(char terminator) throws IOException {
        StringBuffer s = new StringBuffer();
        while (true) {
            int c = read(); // Can throw IOException
            if (c == -1 || c == terminator) {
                return s.toString();
            }
            s.append((char)c);
        }
        return s.toString();
    }

    // Method catches an exception internally
    int getLength() {
        String s;
        try {
            s = readUpTo(':');
        } catch (IOException e) {
            return 0;
```

```
        }
        return s.length();
    }

    // Method can throw a RunTimeException
    int getAvgLength() {
        int count = 0;
        int total = 0;
        int len;
        while (true){
            len = getLength();
            if (len == 0)
                break;
            count++;
            total += len;
        }
        return total/count; // Can throw ArithmeticException
    }
}
```

The method read() can throw an IOException, so it declares that fact in its throws clause. Without that throws clause, the compiler would complain that the method must either declare IOException in its throws clause or catch it. Although the readUpTo() method does not explicitly throw any exceptions, it calls the read() method that does throw an IOException, so it declares that fact in its throws clause. Whether explicitly or implicitly thrown, the requirement to catch or declare an exception is the same. The getLength() method catches the IOException thrown by readUpTo(), so it does not have to declare the exception. The final method, getAvgLength(), can throw an ArithmeticException if count is zero. Because ArithmeticException is a subclass of RuntimeException, the fact that it can be thrown out of getAvgLength() does not need to be declared in a throws clause.

4.3 Generating Exceptions

A Java program can use the exception-handling mechanism to deal with program-specific errors in a clean manner. A program simply uses the throw statement to signal an exception. The throw statement must be followed by an object that is of type Throwable or one of its subclasses. For program-defined exceptions, you typically want an exception object to be an instance of a subclass of the Exception class. In most cases, it makes sense to define a new subclass of Exception that is specific to your program.

Consider the following example:

```
class WrongDayException extends Exception {
    public WrongDayException () {}
    public WrongDayException(String msg) {
```

```
            super(msg);
        }
    }


public class ThrowExample {
    void doIt() throws WrongDayException{
        int dayOfWeek =(new java.util.Date()).getDay();
        if (dayOfWeek != 2  && dayOfWeek != 4)
            throw new WrongDayException("Tue. or Thur.");
        // The rest of doIt's logic goes here
        System.out.println("Did it");
    }
    public static void main (String [] argv) {
        try {
            (new ThrowExample()).doIt();
        } catch (WrongDayException e) {
            System.out.println("Sorry, can do it only on "
                               + e.getMessage());
        }
    }
}
```

The code in this example defines a class called WrongDayException to represent the specific type of exception thrown by the example. The Throwable class, and most subclasses of Throwable, have at least two constructors. One constructor takes a string argument that is used as a textual message that explains the exception, while the other constructor takes no arguments. Thus, the WrongDayException class defines two constructors.

In the class ThrowExample, if the current day of the week is neither Tuesday nor Thursday, the doIt() method throws a WrongDayException. Note that the Wrong-DayException object is created at the same time it is thrown. It is common practice to provide some information about an exception when it is thrown, so a string argument is used in the allocation statement for the WrongDayException. The method declaration for the doIt() method contains a throws clause, to indicate the fact that it can throw a WrongDayException.

The main() method in ThrowExample encloses its call to the doIt() method in a try statement, so that it can catch any WrongDayException thrown by doIt(). The catch block prints an error message, using the getMessage() method of the exception object. This method retrieves the string that was passed to the constructor when the exception object was created.

4.3.1 Printing Stack Traces

When an exception is caught, it can be useful to print a stack trace to figure out where the exception came from. A stack trace looks like the following:

```
java.lang.ArithmeticException: / by zero
        at t.cap(t.java:16)
        at t.doit(t.java:8)
        at t.main(t.java:3)
```

You can print a stack trace by calling the `printStackTrace()` method that all `Throwable` objects inherit from the `Throwable` class. For example:

```
int cap (x) {return 100/x}

try {
    cap(0);
} catch(ArithmeticException e) {
    e.printStackTrace();
}
```

You can also print a stack trace anywhere in an application, without actually throwing an exception. For example:

```
new Throwable().printStackTrace();
```

4.3.2 Rethrowing Exceptions

After an exception is caught, it can be rethrown if is appropriate. The one choice that you have to make when rethrowing an exception concerns the location from where the stack trace says the object was thrown. You can make the rethrown exception appear to have been thrown from the location of the original exception throw, or from the location of the current rethrow.

To rethrow an exception and have the stack trace indicate the original location, all you have to do is rethrow the exception:

```
try {
    cap(0);
} catch(ArithmeticException e) {
    throw e;
}
```

To arrange for the stack trace to show the actual location from which the exception is being rethrown, you have to call the exception's `fillInStackTrace()` method. This method sets the stack trace information in the exception based on the current execution context. Here's an example using the `fillInStackTrace()` method:

```
try {
    cap(0);
} catch(ArithmeticException e) {
    throw (ArithmeticException)e.fillInStackTrace();
}
```

It is important to call `fillInStackTrace()` on the same line as the `throw` statement, so that the line number specified in the stack trace matches the line on which the `throw` statement appears. The `fillInStackTrace()` method returns a reference to the `Throwable` class, so you need to cast the reference to the actual type of the exception.

In this chapter:
- *Enumerations*
- *Vectors*
- *Stacks*
- *Hashtables*

Collections

Java provides a number of utility classes that help you to manage a collection of objects. These collection classes allow you to work with objects without regard to their types, so they can be extremely useful for managing objects at a high level of abstraction. This chapter describes the following collection classes:

- The java.util.Vector class, which represents a dynamic array of objects.

- The java.util.Stack class, which represents a dynamic stack of objects.

- The java.util.Dictionary class, which is an abstract class that manages a collection of objects by associating a key with each object.

- The java.util.Hashtable class, which is a subclass of java.util.Dictionary that implements a specific algorithm to associate keys with objects. Given a key, a Hashtable can retrieve the associated object with little or no searching.

- The java.util.Enumeration interface, which supports sequential access to a set of elements.

5.1 Enumerations

The Enumeration interface is implemented by classes that provide serial access to a set of elements, or objects, in a collection. An object that implements the Enumeration interface provides two methods for dealing with the set: nextElement() and hasMoreElements(). The nextElement() method returns a value of type Object, so it can be used with any kind of collection. When you remove an object from an Enumeration, you may need to cast the object to the appropriate type before using it. You can iterate through the elements in an Enumeration only once; there is no way to reset it to the beginning or move backwards through the elements.

Here is an example that prints the contents of an object the implements the Enumeration interface:

```
static void printEnumeration(Enumeration e) {
    while (e.hasMoreElements()) {
        System.out.println(e.nextElement());
    }
```

Note that the above method is able to print all of the objects in the Enumeration without knowing their class types because the println() method handles objects of any type.

A number of classes in the Java API provide a method that returns a reference to an Enumeration object, rather than implementing the Enumeration interface directly. For example, as you'll see shortly, the Vector class provides an elements() method that returns an Enumeration of the objects in a Vector object.

5.2 Vectors

The Vector class implements a variable-length array that can hold any kind of object. Like an array, the elements in a Vector are accessed with an integer index. However, unlike an array, the size of a Vector can grow and shrink as needed to accommodate a changing number of objects. Vector provides methods to add and remove elements, as well as ways to search for objects in a Vector and iterate through all of the objects.

You can create a Vector object using the constructor that takes no arguments.

```
Vector v = new Vector()
```

This constructor creates an empty Vector with an initial capacity of 10. The capacity of a Vector specifies how many objects it can contain before more space must be allocated. You can improve the performance of a Vector by setting its initial capacity to a more appropriate value when you create it. For example, if you know that you are going to be storing close to 100 objects in a Vector, you could set the initial capacity as follows:

```
Vector v = new Vector(100)
```

It can be time-consuming for a Vector to increase its capacity, so it is better to set the initial capacity based on a rough estimate of the number of objects a Vector will contain than to simply use the default capacity.

The capacity increment of a Vector specifies how much more space is allocated each time the Vector needs to increase its capacity. If you do not specify a capacity increment when you create a Vector, it uses the default value of 0, which causes the Vector to double in size every time it needs to increase its capacity. Doubling in size is a good way for a Vector to become large enough quickly when you have no idea what size it needs to be. However, if you do have a rough idea of the final size of a Vector, specifying a positive capacity increment is less wasteful of memory. For example, if you know that you will be putting 100 or so objects in a Vector, you could create it as follows:

```
Vector v = new Vector(110, 20)
```

Once you have created an empty Vector object, you can put object references in it using the addElement() and insertElementAt() methods. The addElement() method adds an element to the end of a Vector. The following code fragment shows the use of the addElement() method:

```
Vector v = new Vector();
v.addElement("abc");
v.addElement("jkl");
v.addElement("xyz");
```

The insertElementAt() method inserts a new element into a Vector before a given position, so it can be used to insert an element at any position in a Vector except the last. Like arrays, Vector objects are indexed starting at 0. Here's how to insert an object at the beginning of the Vector object created above:

```
v.insertElementAt("123", 0);
```

The size() method returns the number of elements in a Vector object.

After you have added some elements to a Vector object, you can retrieve elements with a number of different methods. For example, the elementAt() method fetches the object at the specified position in the Vector, while the firstElement() and lastElement() methods return the first and last objects in the Vector, respectively. Finally, the elements() method returns an Enumeration object that accesses the elements in the Vector object.

The setElementAt() method allows you to change the object stored at a specified position in the Vector, while the removeElementAt() method removes the object at a specified position from the Vector. The removeElement() method takes an object reference as an argument and removes the first element in the Vector that refers to the given object, if there is such an element. You can also remove all of the elements from the Vector using the removeAllElements() method.

The Vector class also provides some methods for searching the contents of a Vector object. For example, the contains() method returns true if a Vector contains a reference to a specified object. The `indexOf()` and `lastIndexOf()` methods return the positions of the first and last elements, respectively, in a `Vector` that match a specified object.

5.3 Stacks

The `Stack` class is a subclass of `Vector` that implements a last-in-first-out (LIFO) object stack. The `Stack` class uses the following methods to provide stack behavior:

- The `push()` method pushes an object onto the top of the stack.

- The `pop()` method removes and returns the top element from the stack. If the stack is empty, `pop()` throws an `EmptyStackException`.

- The `peek()` method returns, but does not remove, the top element from the stack. If the stack is empty, `peek()` throws an `EmptyStackException`.

- The `empty()` method returns `true` if and only if the stack is empty.

5.4 Hashtables

The `Dictionary` class is an `abstract` class that defines methods for associating key objects with value objects. Given a key, an instance of `Dictionary` is able to return its associated value. The `Hashtable` class is a concrete subclass of `Dictionary` that uses a data structure called a *hashtable* and a technique called *chained hashing* to allow values associated with keys to be fetched with minimal searching. You might use a `Hashtable` object to associate weather reports with the names of cities and towns, for example.

Before explaining hashtables or chained hashing, consider the problem of finding a key/value pair in an array that contains references to key/value pairs in no particular order. The array might look something like what is shown in Figure 5-1.

Since we cannot make any assumptions about where in the array a key is to be found, the most reasonable search strategy is a linear search that starts at one end of the array and looks at each array element until it finds what it is looking for or reaches the other end of the array. For an array with just a few elements, a linear search is a reasonable strategy, but for an array with hundreds of elements it is not. If we know where in the array to look for a key, however, we can eliminate most of the searching effort. Knowing where to look for a key is the idea behind a hashtable.

With a hashtable, each key object has a relatively unique integer value that is called a *hashcode*. The `Object` class defines a `hashCode()` method, so every object in Java has such a method. The hashcode returned by this method computes an array index for a key object as follows:

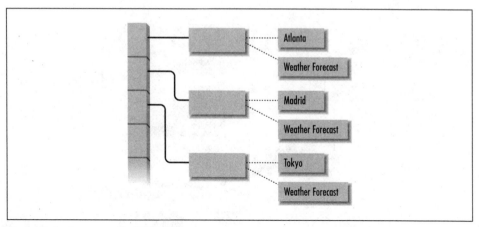

Figure 5–1: An array of key/value pairs

```
array.length % hashCode()
```

This array index, or hash index, stores the key/value pair in a hashtable array. If there is nothing stored at that index, the key/value pair is placed at that position in the array. However, if there is already a key/value pair at that hash index, the Hashtable stores the key/value pair in a linked list at that position in the array. This strategy for managing multiple keys with the same hash index is called *chained hashing*. The array for hashtable that uses this strategy might look like Figure 5-2.

Now, when we want to fetch a key/value pair, all we have to do is recalculate the hash index for the key object and look at that position in the hashtable array. If the key stored at that hash index is the right key, then we have found what we are looking for by examining only one array element instead of searching. However, if the key is not the right key, all we have to do is search the items in the linked list at that position to find our key/value pair.

You can create a Hashtable object using the constructor that takes no arguments:

```
Hashtable h = new Hashtable()
```

This constructor creates an empty Hashtable. There are other constructors that take parameters to allow you to tune the performance of a Hashtable object. The first parameter you can specify is the capacity of the hash table, which is the length of the array used to implement it. The longer the array, the less likely it is that multiple keys will share the same hash index. The default array length is 101. To create a Hashtable object with an array length of 1009, use the following constructor:

```
Hashtable h = new Hashtable(1009);
```

The number that you choose for the array length should be a prime number. If it is not, the key/value pairs stored in the array will tend to be less evenly distributed.

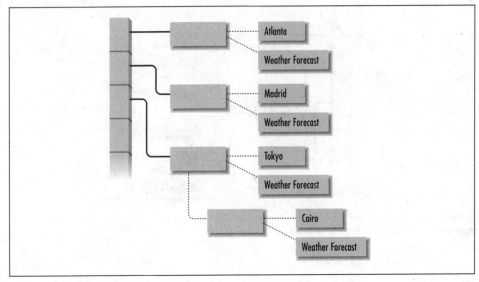

Figure 5–2: An array of key/value pairs that uses chained hashing

The load factor of a hashtable is the ratio of the number of key/value pairs in the hashtable to the array length. A load factor of 0 means that the Hashtable is empty. As the load factor increases, so does the likelihood that multiple key/value pairs will share the same hash index. When the load factor becomes greater than 1, it means that the number of key/value pairs in a hashtable is greater than the array length, so that at least one hash index is being shared by multiple key/value pairs. Clearly, a low load factor is better than a high load factor in terms of performance. You can specify the maximum permissible load factor for a Hashtable object when you create it. For example:

```
Hashtable h = new Hashtable(1009, .62);
```

If not specified, the maximum load factor for a Hashtable object is .75. When a key/value pair is added to a Hashtable that would otherwise cause the load factor to exceed the maximum value, the Hashtable performs a rehash. This means that the Hashtable creates a new array with a length one greater than double the length of the old array. It then recomputes the hash index for each key/value pair in the old array and stores each key/value pair in the new array at the new hash index. Obviously, this is an undesirable performance hit, so if you know approximately how many items you will add to a Hashtable, you should create one with an appropriate initial capacity.

After you have created a `Hashtable` object, you can add new key/value pairs to it, or modify the value in an existing key/value pair, by calling the `put()` method. The `put()` method takes two arguments: a reference to a key object and a reference to a value object. It first looks for a key/value pair in the hashtable with the key equal to the specified key. If there is such a key/value pair, the `put()` method replaces the previous value with the specified value and returns a reference to the previous value object. If, however, there is no such key/value pair, the `put()` method creates a new key/value pair, adds it to the hashtable and returns `null`. Here is a fragment of a class that uses a `Hashtable` to store weather forecasts.

```
import java.util.Hashtable;

class WeatherForecastDictionary {
    private Hashtable ht = new Hashtable(13291);

    public void putForecast(String locale, WeatherForecast forecast) {
        ht.put(locale, forecast);
    }
...
```

The `get()` method returns the value associated with a given key in a `Hashtable` object. It takes one argument that is a reference to the key it should search for. If the `get()` method does not find a key/value pair with a key equal to the specified key, it returns `null`. Here is a method that uses the `get()` method to retrieve a weather forecast:

```
public WeatherForecast getForecast(String locale) {
    return (WeatherForecast)ht.get(locale);
}
```

The various equality tests done by a `Hashtable` use a given key object's `equals()` method. Because of the way that an object's `hashCode()` and `equals()` methods are used by the `Hashtable` class, it is important that if you override the definition of either of these methods, you do so in a consistent way. In other words, if two objects are considered equal by the `equals()` method for the class, then the `hashCode()` method for each object must return the same hashcode value. If that is not the case, when those objects are used as keys in a `Hashtable` object, the `Hashtable` will produce inconsistent results.

Once you have added key/value pairs to a `Hashtable`, you can use the `keys()` and `elements()` methods to get `Enumeration` objects that iterate through the key and value objects, respectively. The `containsKey()` method allows you to search the `Hashtable` for a particular key object, while `contains()` searches for a particular value object. The `Hashtable` class also defines a `remove()` method for removing key/value pairs from a `Hashtable`.

6

In this chapter:
- *Input Streams and Readers*
- *Output Streams and Writers*
- *File Manipulation*

I/O

The `java.io` package contains the fundamental classes for performing input and output operations in Java. These I/O classes can be divided into four basic groups:

- Classes for reading input from a stream.
- Classes for writing output to a stream.
- Classes for manipulating files.
- Classes for serializing objects.

All fundamental I/O in Java is based on *streams.* A stream represents a flow of data, or a channel of communication. Conceptually, there is a reading process at one end of the stream and a writing process at the other end. Java 1.0 supported only byte streams, which meant that Unicode characters were not always handled correctly. As of Java 1.1, there are classes in `java.io` for both byte streams and character streams. The character stream classes, which are called *readers* and *writers*, handle Unicode characters appropriately.

The rest of this chapter describes the classes in `java.io` that read from and write to streams, as well as the classes that manipulate files. The classes for serializing objects are described in Chapter 7, *Object Serialization*.

6.1 Input Streams and Readers

The `InputStream` class is an `abstract` class that defines methods to read sequentially from a stream of bytes. Java provides subclasses of the `InputStream` class for reading from files, `StringBuffer` objects, and byte arrays, among other things. Other subclasses of `InputStream` can be chained together to provide additional logic, such as keeping track of the current line number or combining multiple input sources into one logical input stream. It is also easy to define a subclass of InputStream that reads from any other kind of data source.

In Java 1.1, the Reader class is an abstract class that defines methods to read sequentially from a stream of characters. Many of the byte-oriented InputStream subclasses have character-based Reader counterparts. Thus, there are subclasses of Reader for reading from files, character arrays, and String objects.

6.1.1 InputStream

The InputStream class is the abstract superclass of all other byte input stream classes. It defines three read() methods for reading from a raw stream of bytes:

```
read()
read(byte[] b)
read(byte[] b, int off, int len)
```

If there is no data available to read, these methods block until input is available. The class also defines an available() method that returns the number of bytes that can be read without blocking and a skip() method that skips ahead a specified number of bytes. The InputStream class defines a mechanism for marking a position in the stream and returning to it later, via the mark() and reset() methods. The markSupported() method returns true in subclasses that support these methods.

Because the InputStream class is abstract, you cannot create a "pure" Input-Stream. However, the various subclasses of InputStream can be used interchangeably. For example, methods often take an InputStream as a parameter. Such a method accepts any subclass of InputStream as an argument.

InputStream is designed so that read(byte[]) and read(byte[], int, int) both call read(). Thus, when you subclass InputStream, you only need to define the read() method. However, for efficiency's sake, you should also override read(byte[], int, int) with a method that can read a block of data more efficiently than reading each byte separately.

6.1.2 Reader

The Reader class is the abstract superclass of all other character input stream classes. It defines nearly the same methods as InputStream, except that the read() methods deal with characters instead of bytes:

```
read()
read(char[] cbuf)
read(char[] cbuf, int off, int len)
```

The `available()` method of `InputStream` has been replaced by the `ready()` method of `Reader`, which simply returns a flag that indicates whether or not the stream must block to read the next character.

`Reader` is designed so that `read()` and `read(char[])` both call `read(char[], int, int)`. Thus, when you subclass `Reader`, you only need to define the `read(char[], int, int)` method. Note that this design is different from, and more efficient than, that of `InputStream`.

6.1.3 InputStreamReader

The `InputStreamReader` class serves as a bridge between `InputStream` objects and `Reader` objects. Although an `InputStreamReader` acts like a character stream, it gets its input from an underlying byte stream and uses a character encoding scheme to translate bytes into characters. When you create an `InputStreamReader`, specify the underlying `InputStream` and, optionally, the name of an encoding scheme. For example, the following code fragment creates an `InputStreamReader` that reads characters from a file that is encoded using the ISO 8859-5 encoding:

```
String fileName = "encodedfile.txt"; String encodingName = "8859_5";
InputStreamReader in;

try {
  x FileInputStream fileIn = new FileInputStream(fileName);
    in = new InputStreamReader(fileIn, encodingName);
} catch (UnsupportedEncodingException e1) {
    System.out.println(encodingName + " is not a supported encoding scheme.");
} catch (IOException e2) {
    System.out.println("The file " + fileName + " could not be opened.");
}
```

6.1.4 FileInputStream and FileReader

The `FileInputStream` class is a subclass of `InputStream` that allows a stream of bytes to be read from a file. The `FileInputStream` class has no explicit open method. Instead, the file is implicitly opened, if appropriate, when the `FileInput-Stream` is created. There are three ways to create a `FileInputStream`:

- You can create a `FileInputStream` by passing the name of a file to be read:

    ```
    FileInputStream f1 = new FileInputStream("foo.txt");
    ```

- You can create a `FileInputStream` with a `File` object:

    ```
    File f = new File("foo.txt");
    FileInputStream f2 = new FileInputStream(f);
    ```

- You can create a `FileInputStream` with a `FileDescriptor` object. A `FileDescriptor` object encapsulates the native operating system's representation of an open file. You can get a `FileDescriptor` from a `RandomAccessFile` by calling its `getFD()` method. You create a `FileInputStream` that reads from the open file associated with a `RandomAccessFile` as follows:

```
RandomAccessFile raf;
raf = new RandomAccessFile("z.txt","r");
FileInputStream f3 = new FileInputStream(raf.getFD());
```

The `FileReader` class is a subclass of `Reader` that reads a stream of characters from a file. The bytes in the file are converted to characters using the default character encoding scheme. If you do not want to use the default encoding scheme, you need to wrap an `InputStreamReader` around a `FileInputStream`, as shown above. You can create a `FileReader` from a filename, a `File` object, or a `FileDescriptor` object, as described above for `FileInputStream`.

6.1.5 StringReader and StringBufferInputStream

The `StringReader` class is a subclass of `Reader` that gets its input from a `String` object. The `StringReader` class supports mark-and-reset functionality via the `mark()` and `reset()` methods. The following example shows the use of `StringReader`:

```
StringReader sr = new StringReader("abcdefg");
try {
    char[] buffer = new char[3];
    sr.read(buffer);
    System.out.println(buffer);
} catch (IOException e) {
    System.out.println("There was an error while reading.");
}
```

This code fragment produces the following output:

```
abc
```

The `StringBufferInputStream` class is the byte-based relative of `StringReader`. The entire class is deprecated as of Java 1.1 because it does not properly convert the characters of the string to a byte stream; it simply chops off the high eight bits of each character. Although the `markSupported()` method of `StringBufferInput-Stream` returns `false`, the `reset()` method causes the next read operation to read from the beginning of the `String`.

6.1.6 CharArrayReader and ByteArrayInputStream

The CharArrayReader class is a subclass of Reader that reads a stream of characters from an array of characters. The CharArrayReader class supports mark-and-reset functionality via the mark() and reset() methods. You can create a CharArrayReader by passing a reference to a char array to a constructor like this:

```
char[] c;
...
CharArrayReader r;
r = new CharArrayReader(c);
```

You can also create a CharArrayReader that only reads from part of an array of characters by passing an offset and a length to the constructor. For example, to create a CharArrayReader that reads elements 5 through 24 of a char array you would write:

```
r = new CharArrayReader(c, 5, 20);
```

The ByteArrayInputStream class is just like CharArrayReader, except that it deals with bytes instead of characters. In Java 1.0, ByteArrayInputStream did not fully support mark() and reset(); in Java 1.1 these methods are completely supported.

6.1.7 PipedInputStream and PipedReader

The PipedInputStream class is a subclass of InputStream that facilitates communication between threads. Because it reads bytes written by a connected PipedOutputStream, a PipedInputStream must be connected to a PipedOutputStream to be useful. There are a few ways to connect a PipedInputStream to a PipedOutputStream. You can first create the PipedOutputStream and pass it to the PipedInputStream constructor like this:

```
PipedOutputStream po = new PipedOutputStream();
PipedInputStream pi = new PipedInputStream(po);
```

You can also create the PipedInputStream first and pass it to the PipedOutputStream constructor like this:

```
PipedInputStream pi = new PipedInputStream();
PipedOutputStream po = new PipedOutputStream(pi);
```

The PipedInputStream and PipedOutputStream classes each have a connect() method you can use to explicitly connect a PipedInputStream and a PipedOutputStream as follows:

```
PipedInputStream pi = new PipedInputStream();
PipedOutputStream po = new PipedOutputStream();
pi.connect(po);
```

Or you can use connect() as follows:

```
PipedInputStream pi = new PipedInputStream();
PipedOutputStream po = new PipedOutputStream();
po.connect(pi);
```

Multiple PipedOutputStream objects can be connected to a single PipedInput-Stream at one time, but the results are unpredictable. If you connect a PipedOut-putStream to an already connected PipedInputStream, any unread bytes from the previously connected PipedOutputStream are lost. Once the two PipedOutput-Stream objects are connected, the PipedInputStream reads bytes written by either PipedOutputStream in the order that it receives them. The scheduling of different threads may vary from one execution of the program to the next, so the order in which the PipedInputStream receives bytes from multiple PipedOutputStream objects can be inconsistent.

The PipedReader class is the character-based equivalent of PipedInputStream. It works in the same way, except that a PipedReader is connected to a PipedWriter to complete the pipe, using either the appropriate constructor or the connect() method.

6.1.8 FilterInputStream and FilterReader

The FilterInputStream class is a wrapper class for InputStream objects. Conceptually, an object that belongs to a subclass of FilterInputStream is wrapped around another InputStream object. The constructor for this class requires an InputStream. The constructor sets the object's in instance variable to reference the specified InputStream, so from that point on, the FilterInputStream is associated with the given InputStream. All of the methods in FilterInputStream work by calling the corresponding methods in the underlying InputStream. Because the close() method of a FilterInputStream calls the close() method of the Input-Stream that it wraps, you do not need to explicitly close the underlying Input-Stream.

A FilterInputStream does not add any functionality to the object that it wraps, so by itself it is not very useful. However, subclasses of the FilterInputStream class do add functionality to the objects that they wrap in two ways:

- Some subclasses add logic to the InputStream methods. For example, the InflaterInputStream class in the java.util.zip package decompresses data automatically in the read() methods.

- Some subclasses add new methods. An example is `DataInputStream`, which provides methods for reading primitive Java data types from the stream.

The `FilterReader` class is the character-based equivalent of `FilterInputStream`. A `FilterReader` is wrapped around an underlying `Reader` object; the methods of `FilterReader` call the corresponding methods of the underlying `Reader`. However, unlike `FilterInputStream`, `FilterReader` is an abstract class, so you cannot instantiate it directly.

6.1.9 DataInputStream

The `DataInputStream` class is a subclass of `FilterInputStream` that provides methods for reading a variety of data types. The `DataInputStream` class implements the `DataInput` interface, so it defines methods for reading all of the primitive Java data types.

You create a `DataInputStream` by passing a reference to an underlying `InputStream` to the constructor. Here is an example that creates a `DataInputStream` and uses it to read an `int` that represents the length of an array and then to read the array of `long` values:

```
long[] readLongArray(InputStream in) throws IOException {
    DataInputStream din = new DataInputStream(in);
    int count = din.readInt();
    long[] a = new long[count];
    for (int i = 0; i < count; i++) {
        a[i] = din.readLong();
    }
    return a;
}
```

6.1.10 BufferedReader and BufferedInputStream

The `BufferedReader` class is a subclass of `Reader` that buffers input from an underlying `Reader`. A `BufferedReader` object reads enough characters from its underlying `Reader` to fill a relatively large buffer, and then it satisfies read operations by supplying characters that are already in the buffer. If most read operations read just a few characters, using a `BufferedReader` can improve performance because it reduces the number of read operations that the program asks the operating system to perform. There is generally a measurable overhead associated with each call to the operating system, so reducing the number of calls into the operating system improves performance. The `BufferedReader` class supports mark-and-reset functionality via the `mark()` and `reset()` methods.

Here is an example that shows how to create a `BufferedReader` to improve the efficiency of reading from a file:

```
try {
    FileReader fileIn = new FileReader("data.dat");
    BufferedReader in = new BufferedReader(fileIn);
    // read from the file
} catch (IOException e) {
    System.out.println(e);
}
```

The `BufferedInputStream` class is the byte-based counterpart of `BufferedReader`. It works in the same way as `BufferedReader`, except that it buffers input from an underlying `InputStream`.

6.1.11 LineNumberReader and LineNumberInputStream

The `LineNumberReader` class is a subclass of `BufferedReader`. Its `read()` methods contain additional logic to count end-of-line characters and thereby maintain a line number. Since different platforms use different characters to represent the end of a line, `LineNumberReader` takes a flexible approach and recognizes "\n", "\r", or "\r\n" as the end of a line. Regardless of the end-of-line character it reads, `LineNumberReader` returns only "\n" from its `read()` methods.

You can create a `LineNumberReader` by passing its constructor a `Reader`. The following example prints out the first five lines of a file, with each line prefixed by its number. If you try this example, you'll see that the line numbers begin at 0 by default:

```
try {
    FileReader fileIn = new FileReader("text.txt");
    LineNumberReader in = new LineNumberReader(fileIn);
    for (int i = 0; i < 5; i++)
        System.out.println(in.getLineNumber() + " " + in.readLine());
}catch (IOException e) {
    System.out.println(e);
}
```

The `LineNumberReader` class has two methods pertaining to line numbers. The `getLineNumber()` method returns the current line number. If you want to change the current line number of a `LineNumberReader`, use `setLineNumber()`. This method does not affect the stream position; it merely sets the value of the line number.

The `LineNumberInputStream` is the byte-based equivalent of `LineNumberReader`. The entire class is deprecated in Java 1.1 because it does not convert bytes to characters properly. Apart from the conversion problem, `LineNumberInputStream` works the same as `LineNumberReader`, except that it takes its input from an `Input-Stream` instead of a `Reader`.

6.1.12 SequenceInputStream

The `SequenceInputStream` class is used to sequence together multiple `Input-Stream` objects. Consider this example:

```
FileInputStream f1 = new FileInputStream("data1.dat");
FileInputStream f2 = new FileInputStream("data2.dat");
SequenceInputStream s = new SequenceInputStream(f1, f2);
```

This example creates a `SequenceInputStream` that reads all of the bytes from f1 and then reads all of the bytes from f2 before reporting that it has encountered the end of the stream. You can also cascade `SequenceInputStream` object themselves, to allow more than two input streams to be read as if they were one. You would write it like this:

```
FileInputStream f3 = new FileInputStream("data3.dat");
SequenceInputStream s2 = new SequenceInputStream(s, f3);
```

The `SequenceInputStream` class has one other constructor that may be more appropriate for wrapping more than two `InputStream` objects together. It takes an `Enumeration` of `InputStream` objects as its argument. The following example shows how to create a `SequenceInputStream` in this manner:

```
Vector v = new Vector();
v.add(new FileInputStream("data1.dat"));
v.add(new FileInputStream("data2.dat"));
v.add(new FileInputStream("data3.dat"));
Enumeration e = v.elements();
SequenceInputStream s = new SequenceInputStream(e);
```

6.1.13 PushbackInputStream and PushbackReader

The `PushbackInputStream` class is a `FilterInputStream` that allows data to be pushed back into the input stream and reread by the next read operation. This functionality is useful for implementing things like parsers that need to read data and then return it to the input stream. The Java 1.0 version of `PushbackInput-Stream` supported only a one-byte pushback buffer; in Java 1.1 this class has been enhanced to support a larger pushback buffer.

To create a `PushbackInputStream`, pass an `InputStream` to its constructor like this:

```
FileInputStream ef = new FileInputStream("expr.txt");
PushbackInputStream pb = new PushbackInputStream(ef);
```

This constructor creates a `PushbackInputStream` that uses a default one-byte push-back buffer. When you have data that you want to push back into the input stream to be read by the next read operation, you pass the data to one of the `unread()` methods.

The `PushbackReader` class is the character-based equivalent of `PushbackInput-Stream`. In the following example, we create a `PushbackReader` with a pushback buffer of 48 characters:

```
FileReader fileIn = new FileReader("expr.txt");
PushbackReader in = new PushbackReader(fileIn, 48);
```

Here is an example that shows the use of a `PushbackReader`:

```
public String readDigits(PushbackReader pb) {
    char c;
    StringBuffer buffer = new StringBuffer();

    try {
        while (true) {
            c = (char)pb.read();
            if (!Character.isDigit(c))
                break;
            buffer.append(c);
        }
        if (c != -1)
            pb.unread(c);
    }catch (IOException e) {}
    return buffer.toString();
}
```

The above example shows a method that reads characters corresponding to digits from a `PushbackReader`. When it reads a character that is not a digit, it calls the `unread()` method so that the nondigit can be read by the next read operation. It then returns a string that contains the digits that were read.

6.2 Output Streams and Writers

The `OutputStream` class is an abstract class that defines methods to write a stream of bytes sequentially. Java provides subclasses of the `OutputStream` class for writing to files and byte arrays, among other things. Other subclasses of `OutputStream` can be chained together to provide additional logic, such as writing multibyte data types or converting data to a string representation. It is also easy to define a subclass of `OutputStream` that writes to another kind of destination.

In Java 1.1, the Writer class is an abstract class that defines methods to write to a stream of characters sequentially. Many of the byte-oriented subclasses of Output-Stream have counterparts in the character-oriented world of Writer objects. Thus, there are subclasses of Writer for writing to files and character arrays.

6.2.1 OutputStream

The OutputStream class is the abstract superclass of all other byte output stream classes. It defines three write() methods for writing to a raw stream of bytes:

```
write(int b)
write(byte[] b)
write(byte[] b, int off, int len)
```

Some OutputStream subclasses may implement buffering to increase efficiency. OutputStream provides a method, flush(), that tells the OutputStream to write any buffered output to the underlying device, which may be a disk drive or a network.

Because the OutputStream class is abstract, you cannot create a "pure" Output-Stream. However, the various subclasses of OutputStream can be used interchange-ably. For example, methods often take OutputStream parameters. This means that such a method accepts any subclass of OutputStream as an argument.

OutputStream is designed so that write(byte[]) and write(byte[], int, int) call write(int). Thus, when you subclass OutputStream, you only need to define the write() method. However, for efficiency's sake, you should also override write(byte[], int, int) with a method that can write a block of data more effi-ciently than writing each byte separately.

6.2.2 Writer

The Writer class is the abstract parent class of all other character output stream classes. It defines nearly the same methods as OutputStream, except that the write() methods deal with characters instead of bytes:

```
write(int c)
write(char[] cbuf)
write(char[] cbuf, int off, int len)
write(String str)
write(String str, int off, int len)
```

Writer also includes a flush() method that forces any buffered data to be written to the stream.

Writer is designed so that write(int) and write(char[]) both call write(char[], int, int). Thus, when you subclass Writer, you only need to define the write(char[], int, int) method. Note that this design is different from, and more efficient than, that of OutputStream.

6.2.3 OutputStreamWriter

The OutputStreamWriter class serves as a bridge between Writer objects and OutputStream objects. Although an OutputStreamWriter acts like a character stream, it converts its characters to bytes using a character encoding scheme and writes them to an underlying OutputStream. This class is the output counterpart of InputStreamReader. When you create an OutputStreamWriter, specify the underlying OutputStream and, optionally, the name of an encoding scheme. The following example shows how to construct an OutputStreamWriter that writes characters to a file, encoded using the ISO 8859-5 encoding:

```
String fileName = "encodedfile.txt";
String encodingName = "8859_5";
OutputStreamWriter out;

try {
    FileOutputStream fileOut = new FileOutputStream (fileName);
    out = new OutputStreamWriter (fileOut, encodingName);
} catch (UnsupportedEncodingException e1) {
    System.out.println(encodingName + " is not a supported encoding scheme.");
} catch (IOException e2) {
    System.out.println("The file " + fileName + " could not be opened.");
}
```

6.2.4 FileWriter and FileOutputStream

The FileOutputStream class is a subclass of OutputStream that writes a stream of bytes to a file. The FileOutputStream class has no explicit open method. Instead, the file is implicitly opened, if appropriate, when you create the FileOutputStream object. There are several ways to create a FileOutputStream:

- You can create a FileOutputStream by passing the name of a file to be written:

  ```
  FileOutputStream f1 = new FileOutputStream("foo.txt");
  ```

- Another constructor is available in Java 1.1 that allows you to specify whether you want to append to the file or overwrite it. The following example constructs a FileOutputStream that appends the given file:

  ```
  FileOutputStream f1 = new FileOutputStream("foo.txt", true);
  ```

- You can create a FileOutputStream with a File object:

  ```
  File f = new File("foo.txt");
  FileOutputStream f2 = new FileOutputStream(f);
  ```

- You can create a FileOutputStream with a FileDescriptor object. A FileDescriptor encapsulates the native operating system's representation of

an open file. You can get a `FileDescriptor` from a `RandomAccessFile` by calling its `getFD()` method. You create a `FileOutputStream` that writes to the open
file associated with a `RandomAccessFile` as follows:

```
RandomAccessFile raf;
raf = new RandomAccessFile("z.txt","rw");
FileInputStream f3 = new FileOutputStream(raf.getFD());
```

The `FileWriter` class is a subclass of `Writer` that writes a stream of characters
to a file. The characters to be written are converted to bytes using the default
character encoding scheme. If you do not want to use the default encoding
scheme, you need to wrap an `OutputStreamWriter` around a `FileOutput-
Stream` as shown above. You can create a `FileWriter` from a filename, a `File`
object, or a `FileDescriptor` object, as described above for `FileOutputStream`.

6.2.5 StringWriter

The `StringWriter` class is a subclass of `Writer` that stores its data in a `String`
object. Internally, it uses a `StringBuffer`, which can be examined using `get-
Buffer()`. A `String` containing the data that has been written can be obtained with
`toString()`. The following example creates a `StringWriter` and writes data into it:

```
StringWriter out = new StringWriter();
char[] buffer = {'b', 'o', 'o', '!', 'h', 'a'};

out.write('B');
out.write("uga");
out.write(buffer, 0, 4);

System.out.println(out.toString());
```

This example produces the following output:

```
Bugaboo!
```

6.2.6 CharArrayWriter and ByteArrayOutputStream

The `CharArrayWriter` class is a subclass of `Writer` that writes characters to an internal array. There are three ways to retrieve the data that has been written to the
`CharArrayWriter`:

- The `toCharArray()` method returns a reference to a copy of the internal array.

- The `toString()` method returns a `String` constructed from the internal array.

- The `writeTo()` method writes the internal array to another `Writer`.

This example demonstrates how to create a `CharArrayWriter`, write data into it,
and retrieve the data:

```
CharArrayWriter out = new CharArrayWriter();

try {
    out.write("Daphne");
}catch (IOException e) {}

char[] buffer = out.toCharArray();
System.out.println(buffer);

String result = out.toString();
System.out.println(result);
```

This example produces the following output:

```
Daphne
Daphne
```

The internal buffer of the CharArrayWriter is expanded as needed when data is written. If you know how many characters you will be writing, you can make your CharArrayWriter a little more efficient by passing an initial size to its constructor.

ByteArrayOutputStream is the byte-oriented equivalent of CharArrayWriter. It works in much the same way, with the following exceptions:

- The write() methods deal with bytes, not characters. Additionally, ByteArray-OutputStream does not have the write(String) methods that CharArray-Writer defines.

- Instead of toCharArray(), ByteArrayOutputStream has a toByteArray() method.

- Three toString() methods are provided. The one with no arguments converts the bytes in the internal array to characters using the default encoding scheme.[*] In Java 1.1, the toString(int) method is deprecated, since it does not convert bytes to characters appropriately. Instead, pass an encoding name to toString(String); this method correctly converts the internal byte array to a character string.

6.2.7 PipedOutputStream and PipedWriter

The PipedOuputStream class is a subclass of OutputStream that facilitates communication between threads. A PipedOutputStream must be connected to a PipedInputStream to be useful, as it writes bytes that can be read by a connected PipedInputStream. There are a few ways to connect a PipedOutputStream to a PipedInputStream. You can first create the PipedInputStream and pass it to the PipedOutputStream constructor like this:

---

[*] In Java 1.1, the default encoding scheme is used for the conversion. In earlier versions, characters are simply created using the eight bits of each byte as the low eight bits of the character.

```
PipedInputStream pi = new PipedInputStream();
PipedOutputStream po = new PipedOutputStream(pi);
```

You can also create the `PipedOutputStream` first and pass it to the `PipedInput-Stream` constructor like this:

```
PipedOutputStream po = new PipedOutputStream();
PipedInputStream pi = new PipedInputStream(po);
```

The `PipedOutputStream` and `PipedInputStream` classes each have a `connect()` method you can use to explicitly connect a `PipedOutputStream` and a `PipedInput-Stream` as follows:

```
PipedOutputStream po = new PipedOutputStream();
PipedInputStream pi = new PipedInputStream();
po.connect(pi);
```

Or you can use `connect()` as follows:

```
PipedOutputStream po = new PipedOutputStream();
PipedInputStream pi = new PipedInputStream();
pi.connect(po);
```

Only one `PipedInputStream` can be connected to a `PipedOutputStream` at a time. If you use a `connect()` method to connect a `PipedOutputStream` to an already connected `PipedInputStream`, any unread bytes from the previously connected `Piped-OutputStream` are lost.

`PipedWriter` is the character-based equivalent of `PipedOutputStream`. It works in the same way, except that a `PipedWriter` is connected to a `PipedReader` to complete the pipe, using either the appropriate constructor or the `connect()` method.

6.2.8 FilterOutputStream and FilterWriter

The `FilterOutputStream` class is a wrapper class for `OutputStream` objects. Conceptually, objects that belong to a subclass of `FilterOutputStream` are wrapped around another `OutputStream` object. The constructor for this class requires an `OutputStream`. The constructor sets the object's out instance variable to reference the specified `OutputStream`, so from that point on, the `FilterOutputStream` is associated with the given `OutputStream`. All of the methods of `FilterOutputStream` work by calling the corresponding methods in the underlying `OutputStream`. Because the `close()` method of a `FilterOutputStream` calls the `close()` method of the `OutputStream` that it wraps, you do not need to explicitly close the underlying `OutputStream`.

A `FilterOutputStream` does not add any functionality to the object that it wraps, so by itself it is not very useful. However, subclasses of the `FilterOutputStream` class do add functionality to the objects that they wrap in two ways:

- Some subclasses add logic to the methods of OutputStream. For example, the BufferedOutputStream class adds logic that buffers write operations.

- Other subclasses add new methods. An example of this is DataOutputStream, which provides methods for writing primitive Java data types to the stream.

The FilterWriter class is the character-based equivalent of FilterOutputStream. A FilterWriter is wrapped around an underlying Writer object; the methods of FilterWriter call the corresponding methods of the underlying Writer. However, unlike FilterOutputStream, FilterWriter is an abstract class, so you cannot instantiate it directly.

6.2.9 DataOutputStream

The DataOutputStream class is a subclass of the FilterOutputStream class that provides methods for writing a variety of data types to an OutputStream. The DataOutputStream class implements the DataOutput interface, so it defines methods for writing all of the primitive Java data types.

You create a DataOutputStream by passing a reference to an underlying OutputStream to the constructor. Here is an example that creates a DataOutputStream and uses it to write the length of an array as an int and then to write the values in array as long values:

```
void writeLongArray(OutputStream out, long[] a) throws IOException {
    DataOutputStream dout = new DataOutputStream(out);
    dout.writeInt(a.length);
    for (int i = 0; i < a.length; i++) {
        dout.writeLong(a[i]);
    }
}
```

6.2.10 BufferedWriter and BufferedOutputStream

The BufferedWriter class is a subclass of Writer that stores output destined for an underlying Writer in an internal buffer. When the buffer fills up, the entire buffer is written, or flushed, to the underlying Writer. Using a BufferedWriter is usually faster than using a regular Writer because it reduces the number of calls that must be made to the underlying device, be it a disk or a network. You can use the flush() method to force a BufferedWriter to write the contents of the buffer to the underlying Writer.

The following example shows how to create a BufferedWriter around a network socket's output stream:

```
public Writer getBufferedWriter(Socket s) throws IOException {
    OutputStreamWriter converter = new OutputStreamWriter(s.getOutputStream());
    return new BufferedWriter(converter);
}
```

First, create an OutputStreamWriter that converts characters to bytes using the default encoding scheme. After they are converted, the bytes are written to the socket. Then simply wrap a BufferedWriter around the OutputStreamWriter to buffer the output.

The BufferedOutputStream class is the byte-based equivalent of BufferedWriter. It works in the same way as BufferedWriter, except that it buffers output for an underlying OutputStream. Here's how you would rewrite the previous example to create a BufferedOutputStream around a socket:

```
public OutputStream getBufferedOutputStream(Socket s) throws IOException {
    return new BufferedOutputStream(s.getOutputStream());
}
```

6.2.11 PrintWriter and PrintStream

The PrintWriter class is a subclass of Writer that provides a set of methods for printing string representations of every Java data type. A PrintWriter can be wrapped around an underlying Writer object or an underlying OutputStream object. In the case of wrapping an OutputStream, any characters written to the PrintWriter are converted to bytes using the default encoding scheme.[*] Additional constructors allow you to specify if the underlying stream should be flushed after every line-separator character is written.

The PrintWriter class provides a print() and a println() method for every primitive Java data type. As their names imply, the println() methods do the same thing as their print() counterparts, but also append a line separator character.

The following example demonstrates how to wrap a PrintWriter around an OutputStream:

```
boolean b = true;
char c = '%'
double d = 8.31451
int i = 42;
String s = "R = ";
```

---

[*] You can achieve the same effect using an OutputStreamWriter, but it is easier to use the PrintWriter(OutputStream) constructor. However, if you want to use an encoding scheme other than the default one, you need to create your own OutputStreamWriter.

```
PrintWriter out = new PrintWriter(System.out, true);

out.print(s);
out.print(d);
out.println();
out.println(b);
out.println(c);
out.println(i);
```

This example produces the following output:

```
R = 8.31451
true
%
42
```

PrintWriter objects are often used to report errors. For this reason, the methods of this class do not throw exceptions. Instead, the methods catch any exceptions thrown by any downstream OutputStream or Writer objects and set an internal flag, so that the object can remember that a problem occurred. You can query the internal flag by calling the checkError() method.

Although you can create a PrintWriter that flushes the underlying stream every time a line-separator character is written, this may not always be exactly what you want. Suppose that you are writing a program that has a character-based user interface, and that you want the program to output a prompt and then allow the user to input a response on the same line. In order to make this work with a PrintWriter, you need to get the PrintWriter to write the characters in its buffer without writing a line separator. You can do this by calling the flush() method.

PrintWriter is new as of Java 1.1; it is more capable than the PrintStream class. You should use PrintWriter instead of PrintStream because it uses the default encoding scheme to convert characters to bytes for an underlying OutputStream. The constructors for PrintStream are deprecated in Java 1.1. In fact, the whole class probably would have been deprecated, except that it would have generated a lot of compilation warnings for code that uses System.out and System.err.

6.3 File Manipulation

While streams are used to handle most types of I/O in Java, there are some non-stream-oriented classes in java.io that are provided for file manipulation. Namely, the File class represents a file on the local filesystem, while the RandomAccessFile class provides nonsequential access to data in a file. In addition, the Filename-Filter interface can be used to filter a list of filenames.

6.3.1 File

The `File` class represents a file on the local filesystem. You can use an instance of the `File` class to identify a file, obtain information about the file, and even change information about the file. The easiest way to create a `File` is to pass a filename to the `File` constructor, like this:

```
new File("readme.txt")
```

Although the methods that the `File` class provides for manipulating file information are relatively platform independent, filenames must follow the rules of the local filesystem. The `File` class does provide some information that can be helpful in interpreting filenames and path specifications. The variable `separatorChar` specifies the system-specific character used to separate the name of a directory from what follows.[*] In a Windows environment, this is a backslash (\), while in a UNIX or Macintosh environment it is a forward slash (/). You can create a `File` object that refers to a file called `readme.txt` in a directory called `myDir` as follows:

```
new File("myDir" + File.separatorChar + "readme.txt")
```

The `File` class also provides some constructors that make this task easier. For example, there is a `File` constructor that takes two strings as arguments: the first string is the name of a directory and the second string is the name of a file. The following example does the exact same thing as the previous example:

```
new File("myDir", "readme.txt")
```

The `File` class has another constructor that allows you to specify the directory of a file using a `File` object instead of a `String`:

```
File dir = new File("myDir");
File f = new File(dir, "readme.txt");
```

Sometimes a program needs to process a list of files that have been passed to it in a string. For example, such a list of files is passed to the Java environment by the `CLASSPATH` environment variable and can be accessed by the expression:

```
System.getProperty("java.class.path")
```

This list contains one or more filenames separated by separator characters. In a Windows or Macintosh environment, the separator character is a semicolon (;), while in a UNIX environment, the separator character is a colon (:). The system-specific separator character is specified by the `pathSeparatorChar` variable. Thus, to turn the value of `CLASSPATH` into a collection of `File` objects, we can write:

---

[*] This information is also available as `System.getProperty("file.separator")`, which is how the `File` class gets it.

```
StringTokenizer s;
Vector v = new Vector();
s = new StringTokenizer(System.getProperty("java.class.path"),
                        File.pathSeparator);
while (s.hasMoreTokens())
    v.addElement(new File(s.nextToken()));
```

You can retrieve the pathname of the file represented by a `File` object with `get-Path()`, the filename without any path information with `getName()`, and the directory name with `getParent()`.

The `File` class also defines methods that return information about the actual file represented by a `File` object. Use `exists()` to check whether or not the file exists. `isDirectory()` and `isFile()` tell whether the file is a file or a directory. If the file is a directory, you can use `list()` to get an array of filenames for the files in that directory. The `canRead()` and `canWrite()` methods indicate whether or not a program is allowed to read from or write to a file. You can also retrieve the length of a file with `length()` and its last modified date with `lastModified()`.

A few `File` methods allow you to change the information about a file. For example, you can rename a file with `rename()` and delete it with `delete()`. The `mkdir()` and `mkdirs()` methods provide a way to create directories within the filesystem.

Many of these methods can throw a `SecurityException` if a program does not have permission to access the filesystem, or particular files within it. If a `Security-Manager` has been installed, the `checkRead()` and `checkWrite()` methods of the `SecurityManager` verify whether or not the program has permission to access the filesystem.

6.3.2   FilenameFilter

The purpose of the `FilenameFilter` interface is to provide a way for an object to decide which filenames should be included in a list of filenames. A class that implements the `FilenameFilter` interface must define a method called `accept()`. This method is passed a `File` object that identifies a directory and a `String` that names a file. The `accept()` method is expected to return `true` if the specified file should be included in the list, or `false` if the file should not be included. Here is an example of a simple `FilenameFilter` class that only allows files with a specified suffix to be in a list:

```
import java.io.File;
import java.io.FilenameFilter;

public class SuffixFilter implements FilenameFilter {
    private String suffix;

    public SuffixFilter(String suffix) {
        this.suffix = "." + suffix;
```

```
        }

        public boolean accept(File dir, String name) {
            return name.endsWith(suffix);
        }
    }
```

A `FilenameFilter` object can be passed as a parameter to the `list()` method of `File` to filter the list that it creates. You can also use a `FilenameFilter` to limit the choices shown in a `FileDialog`.

6.3.3 RandomAccessFile

The `RandomAccessFile` class provides a way to read from and write to a file in a nonsequential manner. The `RandomAccessFile` class has two constructors that both take two arguments. The first argument specifies the file to open, either as a `String` or a `File` object. The second argument is a `String` that must be either `"r"` or `"rw"`. If the second argument is `"r"`, the file is opened for reading only. If the argument is `"rw"`, however, the file is opened for both reading and writing. The `close()` method closes the file. Both constructors and all the methods of the `RandomAccessFile` class can throw an `IOException` if they encounter an error.

The `RandomAccessFile` class defines three different `read()` methods for reading bytes from a file. The `RandomAccessFile` class also implements the `DataInput` interface, so it provides additional methods for reading from a file. Most of these additional methods are related to reading Java primitive types in a machine-independent way. Multibyte quantities are read assuming the most significant byte is first and the least significant byte is last. All of these methods handle an attempt to read past the end of file by throwing an `EOFException`.

The `RandomAccessFile` class also defines three different `write()` methods for writing bytes of output. The `RandomAccessFile` class also implements the `DataOutput` interface, so it provides additional methods for writing to a file. Most of these additional methods are related to writing Java primitive types in a machine-independent way. Again, multibyte quantities are written with the most significant byte first and the least significant byte last.

The `RandomAccessFile` class would not live up to its name if it did not provide a way to access a file in a nonsequential manner. The `getFilePointer()` method returns the current position in the file, while the `seek()` method provides a way to set the position. Finally, the `length()` method returns the length of the file in bytes.

7

Object Serialization

The object serialization mechanism in Java 1.1 provides a way for objects to be written as a stream of bytes and then later recreated from that stream of bytes. This facility supports a variety of interesting applications. For example, object serialization provides persistent storage for objects, whereby objects are stored in a file for later use. Also, a copy of an object can be sent through a socket to another Java program. Object serialization forms the basis for the remote method invocation mechanism in Java that facilitates distributed programs. Object serialization is supported by a number of new classes in the `java.io` package in Java 1.1.

7.1 Object Serialization Basics

If a class is designed to work with object serialization, reading and writing instances of that class is quite simple. The process of writing an object to a byte stream is called *serialization.* For example, here is how you can write a `Color` object to a file:

```
FileOutputStream out = new FileOutputStream("tmp");
ObjectOutput objOut = new ObjectOutputStream(out);
objOut.writeObject(Color.red);
```

All you need to do is create an `ObjectOutputStream` around another output stream and then pass the object to be written to the `writeObject()` method. If you are writing objects to a socket or any other destination that is time-sensitive, you should call the `flush()` method after you are finished passing objects to the `ObjectOutputStream`.

The process of reading an object from byte stream is called *deserialization.* Here is how you can read that `Color` object from its file:

```
FileInputStream in = new FileInputStream("tmp");
ObjectInputStream objIn = new ObjectInputStream(in);
Color c = (Color)objIn.readObject();
```

Here all you need to do is create an ObjectInputStream object around another
input stream and call its readObject() method.

7.2 *Writing Classes to Work with Serialization*

Writing a class that works with serialization is a bit more complicated than simply
using that class for serialization. Essentially, an ObjectOutputStream must write
enough of an object's state information so that the object can be reconstructed. If
an object refers to other objects, those objects must be written, and so on, until all
of the objects the original object refers to, directly or indirectly, are written. An
ObjectOutputStream does not actually write a Class object that describes an object
it is serializing. Instead, an ObjectOutputStream writes an ObjectStreamClass
object that identifies the class of the object. Thus, a program that reads a serialized
object must have access to a Class object that describes the object being deserialized.

When you are writing a new class, you need to decide whether or not it should be
serializable. Serialization does not make sense for every class. For example, a
Thread object encapsulates information that is meaningful only within the process
that created it, so serialization is not appropriate. In order for instances of a class
to be serializable, the class must implement the Serializable interface. The Serializable interface does not declare any methods or variables, so it simply acts as
an indicator of serializability. The writeObject() method of an ObjectOutput-
Stream throws a NotSerializableException if it is asked to serialize an object that
does not implement the Serializable interface.

The default serialization mechanism is implemented by the writeObject()
method in ObjectOutputStream. When an object is serialized, the class of the
object is encoded, along with the class name, the signature of the class, the values
of the non-static and non-transient fields of the object, including any other
objects referenced by the object (except those that do not implement the Serializable interface themselves). Multiple references to the same object are encoded
using a reference-sharing mechanism, so that a graph of objects can be restored
appropriately. Strings and arrays are objects in Java, so they are treated as objects
during serialization (and deserialization).

The default deserialization mechanism mirrors the serialization mechanism. The default deserialization mechanism is implemented by the readObject() method in ObjectInputStream. When an object is deserialized, the non-static and non-transient fields of the object are restored to the values they had when the object was serialized, including any other objects referenced by the object (except for those objects that do not implement the Serializable interface themselves). New object instances are always allocated during the deserialization process, to prevent existing objects from being overwritten. Deserialized objects are returned as instances of type Object, so they should be cast to the appropriate type.

Some classes can simply implement the Serializable interface and make use of the default serialization and deserialization mechanisms. However, a class may need to handle two other issues in order to work with serialization:

- If any of the superclasses of the class do not implement the Serializable interface, the class must take care of writing any necessary state information for those superclasses during serialization and reading the information back during deserialization.

  When an object is serialized, all of the serializable state information defined by its class and any superclasses that implement the Serializable interface is written to the byte stream. However, any state information defined by superclasses that do not implement the Serializable interface is not written to the byte stream.

  When an object is deserialized, the state information defined by its Serializable superclasses is restored from the byte stream. By default, the state information for a superclass that does not implement the Serializable interface is initialized by called the no-argument constructor for the superclass. If that superclass does not have a no-argument constructor, deserialization fails and the readObject() method throws a NoSuchMethodError.

  If the objects of a class refer to other objects that are not Serializable, the class must take care of writing any necessary state information for the referenced objects during serialization and reading the information back during deserialization.

A class can override the default serialization logic by defining the following method:

```
private void writeObject(ObjectOutputStream stream) throws IOException
```

Now, when an object of the class is serialized, this method is called instead of the default mechanism. Note that writeObject() is private, so it is not inherited by subclasses. The implementation of a writeObject() method normally begins by

calling the defaultWriteObject() method of ObjectOutputStream, which implements the default serialization logic. After that, a writeObject() method normally
goes on to write whatever information is appropriate to reconstruct values that are
not directly serialized.

By the same token, a class can override the default deserialization logic by defining
the following method:

```
private void readObject(ObjectInputStream stream)
            throws IOException, ClassNotFoundException
```

Now, when an object of the class is deserialized, this method is called instead of the
default mechanism. readObject() is also private and thus not inherited by subclasses. The implementation of a readObject() method normally begins by calling
the defaultReadObject() method of ObjectInputStream, which implements the
default deserialization logic. After that, a readObject() method normally goes on
to read whatever information is appropriate to reconstruct the values that are not
directly serialized.

Let's take a look at a Serializable class that has writeObject() and readObject()
methods. The example below is a partial listing of a class that accesses data using a
RandomAccessFile object. RandomAccessFile objects are not Serializable
because they encapsulate information that is meaningful only on the local system
and only for a limited amount of time.

```
public class TextFileReader implements Serializable {
    private transient RandomAccessFile file;
    private String browseFileName;
    ...
    private void writeObject(ObjectOutputStream stream) throws IOException{
        stream.defaultWriteObject();
        stream.writeLong(file.getFilePointer());
    }
    private void readObject(ObjectInputStream stream) throws IOException {
        try {
            stream.defaultReadObject();
        }catch (ClassNotFoundException e) {
            String msg = "Unable to find class";
            if (e.getMessage() != null)
                msg += ": " + e.getMessage();
            throw new IOException(msg);
        }
        file = new RandomAccessFile(browseFileName, "r");
        file.seek(stream.readLong());
    }
}
```

The above example gets around being unable to serialize RandomAccessFile objects by having enough information during deserialization to construct a RandomAccessFile object that is similar to the original. The name of the file accessed by the RandomAccessFile object is specified by the browseFileName variable; this state information is handled by the default serialization mechanism. In addition, the writeObject() method writes out the current value returned by the original RandomAccessFile object's getFilePointer() method, so that readObject() can pass that value to the seek() method of a new RandomAccessFile object.

Some sets of objects are more complicated to reconstruct than an instance of the above class and its RandomAccessFile object. In such cases, the information to reconstruct the objects may be spread out over multiple objects in the set. The ObjectInputValidation interface provides a way to handle this situation. As the readObject() method of ObjectInputStream reads a set of objects, it notices which of those objects implement the ObjectInputValidation interface. After readObject() is done reading a set of objects, but before it returns, it calls the validateObject() method for each object in the set that implements the Object-InputValidation interface. If one of those methods is unable to properly reconstruct something or detects an inconsistency of some sort, it should throw an ObjectInvalidException. Note that the order in which the validateObject() methods are called is not documented.

It is also possible for a class to take complete control over its serialized representation, using the Externalizable interface. The Externalizable interface extends the Serializable interface and defines two methods: writeExternal() and readExternal(). During serialization, if an object implements Externalizable, its writeExternal() method is called. The writeExternal() method is responsible for writing all of the information in the object. Similarly, during deserialization, if an object implements Externalizable, its readExternal() method is called. The readExternal() method is responsible for reading all of the information in the object. Note that the Externalizable mechanism is used instead of, not in addition to, the mechanism for handling Serializable objects.

7.3 Versioning of Classes

One you have written a class that works with serialization, the next concern is that serialized instances of that class can be deserialized by programs that use a different version of the same class.

After a class is written, it is often necessary to modify its definition as requirements change or new features are needed. Deserialization may fail if the definition of a class in use when an instance was serialized is different than the definition in use when the instance is deserialized. If you do not take any measures to assure the serialization mechanism that the two classes are different versions of the same class, deserialization fails by throwing an `InvalidClassException`. And even if the serialization mechanism is satisfied that the two class definitions represent different versions of the same class, it may find incompatible differences between the definitions.

The following changes to the definition of a class are noticed by the serialization mechanism:

- Adding or deleting instance variables.

- Moving a class up or down the inheritance hierarchy.

- Making a non-static, non-transient variable either `static` or `transient` has the same effect as deleting the variable. Similarly, changing a variable that is `static` or `transient` to be non-static or non-transient has the same effect as adding the variable.

- Changing the data type of a `transient` variable from a primitive data type to an object reference type or from an object reference type to a primitive data type.

- Changing the `readObject()` or `writeObject()` method of a class so that it calls `defaultReadObject()` or `defaultWriteObject()` when it did not previously, or so that it does not call one of these methods when it did previously. The removal or addition of a `readObject()` or `writeObject()` method that does not call `defaultReadObject()` or `defaultWriteObject()` has a similar effect.

- Changing a class from `Serializable` to `Externalizable` or from `Externalizable` to `Serializable`.

It's possible to code around some of these problems if you can first convince the serialization mechanism that the two class definitions are different versions of the same class. In order to convince the serialization mechanism of such a thing, the class definition used for deserialization of an object must define a `static final long` variable named `serialVersionUID`. If the class used for serialization also defined that variable with the same value, the two class definitions are assumed to define different versions of the same class.

If the class used for serialization does not define `serialVersionUID`, the serialization mechanism performs the comparison using a value that is computed by calling the `ObjectStreamClass.getSerialVersionUID()` method. That computation is based on the fields defined by the class. To take advantage of this automatic computation when you define serialVersionUID, you should use the *serialver* program that comes with the JDK to determine the appropriate value for serialVersionUID. The *serialver* program computes a value for serialVersionUID by calling the ObjectStreamClass.getSerialVersionUID() method.

Assuming you've convinced the serialization mechanism that the two class definitions represent different versions of the same class, here is some advice on how to deal with the differences that can be worked around:

Missing variables

If the class used to deserialize an object defines variables the class used to serialize the object did not define, the serialized object does not contain any values for those variables. This situation can also arise if the class used to serialize the object defined a variable as static or transient, while the class used to deserialize the object defines it as non-static or non-transient.

When an object is deserialized and there are variables missing in its serialized form, the variables in the deserialized object are set to default values. In other words, the value of such a variable is true if it has an arithmetic data type, false if it has a boolean data type, or null if it has an object reference type. Deserialization ignores intializers in variable declarations.

When you add variables to a Serializable class, consider the possibility that the new version of the class will deserialize an object serialized with an older version of the class. If that happens and it is unacceptable for the new variables to have default values after deserialization, you can define a validateObject() method for the class to check for the default values and provide acceptable values or throw an InvalidObjectException.

Extra variables

If the serialized form of an object contains values for variables that are not defined by the class used to deserialize that object, the values are read and then ignored. If the value of such a variable is an object, the object is created and immediately becomes a candidate for garbage collection.

Missing classes

If the class used to deserialize an object inherits from an ancestor class that the class used to serialize the object did not inherit from, the serialized object does not contain any values for the variables of the additional ancestor class. Just as with missing variables, those variables are deserialized with their default values.

When you add an ancestor class to a Serializable class, consider the possibility that the new version of the class will deserialize an object serialized with an older version of the class. If that happens and it is unacceptable for instance variables in the new ancestor class to have default values after deserialization, you can define a `validateObject()` method for the class to check for the default values and provide acceptable values or throw an `InvalidObjectException`.

Extra classes

If the class used to serialize an object inherits from an ancestor class that the class used to deserialize the object does not inherit from, the values for the variables defined by that extra ancestor class are read but not used.

Adding writeObject() and readObject() methods

You can add `writeObject()` and `readObject()` methods to a class that did not have them. In order to deserialize objects that were serialized using the older class definition, the new methods must begin by calling `defaultWriteObject()` and `defaultReadObject()`. That ensures that information written out using default logic is still processed using default logic.

If the `writeObject()` and `readObject()` methods write and read additional information to and from the byte stream, you should also add an additional variable to the class to serve as a version indicator. For example, you might declare an `int` variable and initialize it to one. If, after `defaultReadObject()` returns, the value of that variable is `0`, you know the object was serialized using the old class definition and that any additional information that would have been written by the `writeObject()` method will not be there.

Removing writeObject() and readObject() methods

If you remove `writeObject()` and `readObject()` methods from a class and deserialize an object using the new class definition, the information written by a call to `writeObject()` is simply read by the default logic and any additional information is ignored.

Changing a class so that it implements Serializable

If a superclass of an object did not implement `Serializable` when the object was serialized, and that superclass does implement `Serializable` when the object is deserialized, the result is similar to the missing class situation. There is no information about the variables of the newly `Serializable` superclass in the byte stream, so its instance variables are initialized to default values.

Changing a class so that it does not implement Serializable

If a superclass of an object implemented `Serializable` when the object was serialized, and that superclass does not implement `Serializable` when the object is deserialized, the result is similar to the extra class situation. The information in the byte stream for that class is read and discarded.

8

Networking

The java.net package provides two basic mechanisms for accessing data and other resources over a network. The fundamental mechanism is called a socket. A socket allows programs to exchange groups of bytes called packets. There are a number of classes in java.net that support sockets, including Socket, Server-Socket, DatagramSocket, DatagramPacket, and MulticastSocket. The java.net package also includes a URL class that provides a higher-level mechanism for accessing and processing data over a network.

8.1 Sockets

A socket is a mechanism that allows programs to send packets of bytes to each other. The programs do not need to be running on the same machine, but if they are running on different machines, they do need to be connected to a network that allows the machines to exchange data. Java's socket implementation is based on the socket library that was originally part of BSD UNIX. Programmers who are familiar with UNIX sockets or the Microsoft WinSock library should be able to see the similarities in the Java implementation.

When a program creates a socket, an identifying number called a port number is associated with the socket. Depending on how the socket is used, the port number is either specified by the program or assigned by the operating system. When a socket sends a packet, the packet is accompanied by two pieces of information that specify the destination of the packet:

- A network address that specifies the system that should receive the packet.

- A port number that tells the receiving system to which socket to deliver the data.

Sockets typically work in pairs, where one socket acts as a client and the other functions as a server. A server socket specifies the port number for the network communication and then listens for data that is sent to it by client sockets. The port numbers for server sockets are well-known numbers that are known to client programs. For example, an FTP server uses a socket that listens at port 21. If a client program wants to communicate with an FTP server, it knows to contact a socket that listens at port 21.

The operating system normally specifies port numbers for client sockets because the choice of a port number is not usually important. When a client socket sends a packet to a server socket, the packet is accompanied by the port number of the client socket and the client's network address. The server is then able to use that information to respond to the client.

When using sockets, you have to decide which type of protocol that you want it to use to transport packets over the network: a connection-oriented protocol or a connectionless protocol. With a connection-oriented protocol, a client socket establishes a connection to a server socket when it is created. Once the connection has been established, a connection-oriented protocol ensures that data is delivered reliably, which means:

- For every packet that is sent, the packet is delivered. Every time a socket sends a packet, it expects to receive an acknowledgement that the packet has been received successfully. If the socket does not receive that acknowledgement within the time it expects to receive it, the socket sends the packet again. The socket keeps trying until transmission is successful, or it decides that delivery has become impossible.

- Packets are read from the receiving socket in the same order that they were sent. Because of the way that networks work, packets may arrive at the receiving socket in a different order than they were sent. A reliable, connection-oriented protocol allows the receiving socket to reorder the packets it receives, so that they can be read by the receiving program in the same order that they were sent.

A connectionless protocol allows a best-effort delivery of packets. It does not guarantee that packets are delivered or that packets are read by the receiving program in the same order they were sent. A connectionless protocol trades these deficiencies for performance advantages over connection-oriented protocols. Here are two types of situations in which connectionless protocols are frequently preferred over connection-oriented protocols:

- When only a single packet needs to be sent and guaranteed delivery is not crucial, a connectionless protocol eliminates the overhead involved in creating and destroying a connection. For comparison purposes, the connection-oriented TCP/IP protocol uses seven packets to send a single packet, while the connectionless UDP/IP protocol uses only one. A protocol for getting the current time typically uses a connectionless protocol to request the current time from the server and to return the time to the requester.

- For extremely time-sensitive applications, such as sending audio in real time, the guarantee of reliable transmission is not an advantage and may be a disadvantage. Pausing until a missing piece of data is received can cause noticeable clicks or pauses in the audio. Techniques for sending audio over a network that use a connectionless protocol have been developed and they work noticeably better. For example, RealAudio uses a protocol that runs on top of a connectionless protocol to transmit sound over a network.

Table 8-1 shows the roles of the various socket classes in the java.net package.

Table 8–1: Socket Classes in java.net

	Client	Server
Connection-oriented Protocol	Socket	ServerSocket
Connectionless Protocol	DatagramSocket	DatagramSocket

As of Java 1.1, the java.net package also contains a MulticastSocket class that supports connectionless, multicast data communication.

8.1.1 Sockets for Connection-Oriented Protocols

When you are writing code that implements the server side of a connection-oriented protocol, your code typically follows this pattern:

- Create a ServerSocket object to accept connections.

- When the ServerSocket accepts a connection, it creates a Socket object that encapsulates the connection.

- The Socket is asked to create InputStream and OutputStream objects that read and write bytes to and from the connection.

- The ServerSocket can optionally create a new thread for each connection, so that the server can listen for new connections while it is communicating with clients.

The code that implements the client side of a connection-oriented protocol is quite simple. It creates a Socket object that opens a connection with a server, and then it uses that Socket object to communicate with the server.

Now let's look at an example. The example consists of a pair of programs that allows a client to get the contents of a file from a server. The client requests the contents of a file by opening a connection to the server and sending it the name of a file followed by a newline character. If the server is able to read the named file, it responds by sending the string "Good:\n" followed by the contents of the file. If the server is not able to read the named file, it responds by sending the string "Bad:" followed by the name of the file and a newline character. After the server has sent its response, it closes the connection.

Here's the program that implements the server side of this file transfer:

```
public class FileServer extends Thread {

    public static void main(String[] argv) {
        ServerSocket s;
        try {
            s = new ServerSocket(1234, 10);
        }catch (IOException e) {
            System.err.println("Unable to create socket");
            e.printStackTrace();
            return;
        }
        try {
            while (true) {
                new FileServer(s.accept());
            }
        }catch (IOException e) {
        }
    }

    private Socket socket;

    FileServer(Socket s) {
        socket = s;
        start();
    }

    public void run() {
        InputStream in;
        String fileName = "";
        PrintStream out = null;
        FileInputStream f;
        try {
            in = socket.getInputStream();
            out = new PrintStream(socket.getOutputStream());
            fileName = new DataInputStream(in).readLine();
            f = new FileInputStream(fileName);
        }catch (IOException e) {
            if (out != null)
                out.print("Bad:"+fileName+"\n");
            out.close();
            try {
```

```
                    socket.close();
                }catch (IOException ie) {
                }
                return;
            }
            out.print("Good:\n");
            // send contents of file to client.
            byte[] buffer = new byte[4096];
            try {
                int len;
                while ((len = f.read(buffer)) > 0) {
                    out.write(buffer, 0, len);
                }// while
            }catch (IOException e) {
            }finally {
                try {
                    in.close();
                    out.close();
                    socket.close();
                }catch (IOException e) {
                }
            }
        }
    }
}
```

The `FileServer` class implements the server side of the file transfer; it is a subclass of `Thread` to make it easier to write code that can handle multiple connections at the same time. The `main()` method provides the top-level logic for the program. The first thing that `main()` does is to create a `ServerSocket` object to listen for connections. The constructor for `ServerSocket` takes two parameters: the port number for the socket and a value that specifies the maximum length of the pending connections queue. The operating system can accept connections on behalf of the socket when the server program is busy doing something other than accepting connections. If the second parameter is greater than zero, the operating system can accept up to that many connections on behalf of the socket and store them in a queue. If the second parameter is zero, however, the operating system does not accept any connections on behalf of the server program. The remainder of the `main()` method accepts a connection, creates a new instance of the `FileServer` class to process the connection, and then waits for the next connection.

Each `FileServer` object is responsible for handling a connection accepted by its `main()` method. A `FileServer` object uses a private variable, `socket`, to refer to the `Socket` object that allows it to communicate with the client program on the other end of the connection. The constructor for `FileServer` sets its socket variable to refer to the `Socket` object that is passed to it by the `main()` method and then calls its `start()` method. The `FileServer` class inherits the `start()` method from the Thread class; the start() method starts a new thread that calls the run() method. Because the rest of the connection processing is done asynchronously in a separate thread, the constructor can return immediately. This allows the main() method to accept another connection right away, instead of having to wait for this connection to be fully processed before accepting another.

The run() method uses the in and out variables to refer to InputStream and PrintStream objects that read from and write to the connection associated with the Socket object, respectively. These streams are created by calling the getInput-Stream() and getOutputStream() methods of the Socket object. The run() method then reads the name of the file that the client program wants to receive and creates a FileInputStream to read that file. If any of the methods called up to this point have detected a problem, they throw some kind of IOException. In this case, the server sends a response to the client that consists of the string "Bad: " followed by the filename and then closes the socket and returns, which kills the thread.

If everything up to this point has been fine, the server sends the string "Good: " and then copies the contents of the file to the socket. The copying is done by repeatedly filling a buffer with bytes from the file and writing the buffer to the socket. When the contents of the file are exhausted, the streams and the socket are closed, the run() method returns, and the thread dies.

Now let's take a look at the client part of this program:

```
public class FileClient {

    private static boolean usageOk(String[] argv) {
        if (argv.length != 2) {
            String msg = "usage is: " + "FileClient server-name file-name";
            System.out.println(msg);
            return false;
        }
        return true;
    }

    public static void main(String[] argv) {
        int exitCode = 0;
        if (!usageOk(argv))
            return;
        Socket s = null;
        try {
            s = new Socket(argv[0], 1234);
        }catch (IOException e) {
            String msg = "Unable to connect to server";
            System.err.println(msg);
            e.printStackTrace();
            System.exit(1);
        }
```

```
            InputStream in = null;
            try {
                OutputStream out = s.getOutputStream();
                new PrintStream(out).print(argv[1]+"\n");
                in = s.getInputStream();
                DataInputStream din = new DataInputStream(in);
                String serverStatus = din.readLine();
                if (serverStatus.startsWith("Bad")) {
                    exitCode = 1;
                int ch;
                while((ch = in.read()) >= 0) {
                    System.out.write((char)ch);
                }// while
            }catch (IOException e) {
            }finally {
                try {
                    s.close();
                }catch (IOException e) {
                }
            }
        }
    }
}
```

The usageOk() method is simply a utility method that verifies that the correct number of arguments have been passed to the client application. It outputs a help message if the number of arguments is not what is expected. It is generally a good idea to include a method like this in a Java application that uses command-line parameters.

The main() method does the real work of FileClient. After it verifies that it has the correct number of parameters, it attempts to create a socket connected to the server program running on the specified host and listening for connections on port number 1234. The socket that it creates is encapsulated by a Socket object. The constructor for the Socket object takes two arguments: the name of the machine the server program is running on and the port number. After the socket is successfully opened, the client sends the specified filename, followed by a new line character, to the server. The client then gets an InputStream from the socket to read what the server is sending and reads the success/failure code that the server sends back. If the request is a success, the client reads the contents of the requested file.

Note that the finally clause at the end closes the socket. If the program did not explicitly close the socket, it would be closed automatically when the program terminates. However, it is a good programming practice to explicitly close a socket when you are done with it.

8.1.2 Sockets for Connectionless Protocols

Communicating with a connectionless protocol is simpler than using a connection-oriented protocol, as both the client and the server use `DatagramSocket` objects. The code for the server-side program has the following pattern:

- Create a `DatagramSocket` object associated with a specified port number.

- Create a `DatagramPacket` object and ask the `DatagramSocket` to put the next piece of data it receives in the `DatagramPacket`.

On the client-side, the order is simply reversed:

- Create a `DatagramPacket` object associated with a piece of data, a destination network address, and a port number.

- Ask a `DatagramSocket` object to send the data associated with the `Datagram-Packet` to the destination associated with the `DatagramSocket`.

Let's look at an example that shows how this pattern can be coded into a server that provides the current time and a client that requests the current time. Here's the code for the server class:

```
public class TimeServer {
    static DatagramSocket socket;

    public static void main(String[] argv) {
        try {
            socket = new DatagramSocket(7654);
        }catch (SocketException e) {
            System.err.println("Unable to create socket");
            e.printStackTrace();
            System.exit(1);
        }
        DatagramPacket datagram;
        datagram = new DatagramPacket(new byte[1], 1);
        while (true) {
            try {
                socket.receive(datagram);
                respond(datagram);
            }catch (IOException e) {
                e.printStackTrace();
            }
        }
    }

    static void respond(DatagramPacket request) {
        ByteArrayOutputStream bs;
        bs = new ByteArrayOutputStream();
        DataOutputStream ds = new DataOutputStream(bs);
        try {
            ds.writeLong(System.currentTimeMillis());
        }catch (IOException e) {
```

```
        }
        DatagramPacket response;
        byte[] data = bs.toByteArray();
        response = new DatagramPacket(data, data.length,
                    request.getAddress(), request.getPort());
        try {
            socket.send(response);
        }catch (IOException e) {
            // Give up, we've done our best.
        }
    }
}
```

The `main()` method of the `TimeServer` class begins by creating a `DatagramSocket` object that uses port number 7654. The socket variable refers to this `Datagram-Socket`, which is used to communicate with clients. Then the `main()` method creates a `DatagramPacket` object to contain data received by the `DatagramSocket`. The two-argument constructor for `DatagramPacket` creates objects that receive data. The first argument is an array of bytes to contain the data, while the second argument specifies the number of bytes to read. When a `DatagramSocket` is asked to receive a packet into a `DatagramPacket`, only the specified number of bytes are read. Even though the client is not really sending any information to the server, we still create a `DatagramPacket` with a 1-byte buffer. In theory, all that the server needs is an empty packet that specifies the client's network address and port number, but attempting to receive a zero-byte packet does not work. When the `receive()` method of a `DatagramSocket` is called to receive a zero-byte packet, it returns immediately, rather than waiting for a packet to arrive. Finally, the server enters an infinite loop that receives requests from clients using the `receive()` method of the `DatagramSocket`, and sends responses.

The `respond()` method handles sending responses. It starts by writing the current time as a `long` value to an array of bytes. Next, the `respond()` method prepares to send the array of bytes by creating a `DatagramPacket` object that encapsulates the array and the address and port number of the client that requested the time. Notice that the constructor used to create a `DatagramPacket` object for sending a packet takes four arguments: an array of bytes, the number of bytes to send, the client's network address, and the client's port number. The address and port are retrieved from the request `DatagramPacket` with the `getAddress()` and `getPort()` methods. The `respond()` method finishes its work by actually sending the `Data-gramPacket` using the `send()` method of the `DatagramSocket`.

Now here's the code for the corresponding client program:

```
public class TimeClient {
    private static boolean usageOk(String[] argv) {
        if (argv.length != 1) {
            String msg = "usage is: " + "TimeClient server-name";
```

```
            System.out.println(msg);
            return false;
        }
        return true;
    }

    public static void main(String[] argv) {
        if (!usageOk(argv))
            System.exit(1);
        DatagramSocket socket;
        try {
            socket = new DatagramSocket();
        }catch (SocketException e) {
            System.err.println("Unable to create socket");
            e.printStackTrace();
            System.exit(1);
            return;
        }
        long time;
        try {
            byte[] buf = new byte[1];
            socket.send(new DatagramPacket(buf, 1,
                            InetAddress.getByName(argv[0]), 7654));
            DatagramPacket response = new DatagramPacket(new byte[8],8);
            socket.receive(response);
            ByteArrayInputStream bs;
            bs = new ByteArrayInputStream(response.getData());
            DataInputStream ds = new DataInputStream(bs);
            time = ds.readLong();
        }catch (IOException e) {
            e.printStackTrace();
            System.exit(1);
            return;
        }
        System.out.println(new Date(time));
        socket.close();
    }
}
```

The main() method does the real work of TimeClient. After it verifies that it has
the correct number of parameters with usageOk(), it creates a DatagramSocket
object for communicating with the server. Note that the constructor for this DatagramSocket does not specify any parameters; a client DatagramSocket is not explicitly connected to a specific port. Then the main() method creates a
DatagramPacket object to contain the request to be sent to the server. Since this
DatagramPacket is being used to send a packet, the code uses the four-argument
constructor that specifies an array of bytes, the number of bytes to send, the specified network address for a time server, and the server's port number. The DatagramPacket is then sent to the server with the send() method of the
DatagramSocket.

Now the `main()` method creates another `DatagramPacket` to receive the response from the server. The two-argument constructor is used this time because the object is being created to receive data. After calling the `receive()` method of the `Data-gramSocket` to get the response from the server, the `main()` method gets the data from the response `DatagramPacket` by calling `getData()`. The data is wrapped in a `DataInputStream` so that the data can be read as a `long` value. If everything has gone smoothly, the client finishes by printing the current time and closing the socket.

8.2 URL Objects

The `URL` class provides higher-level access to data than sockets do. A `URL` object encapsulates a Uniform Resource Locator (URL) specification. Once you have created a `URL` object, you can use it to access the data in the location specified by the `URL`. A `URL` allows you to access the data without needing to be aware of the details of the protocol being used, such as HTTP or FTP. For some types of data, a `URL` object provides a way to get the data already encapsulated in an appropriate kind of object. For example, a `URL` can provide JPEG data encapsulated in an `ImagePro-ducer` object or text data encapsulated in a `String` object.

You can create a `URL` object as follows:

```
try {
    URL js = new URL("http://www.javasoft.com/index.html");
}catch (MalformedURLException e) {
    return;
}
```

This type of URL specification is called an absolute URL specification because it completely specifies where to find the data. It is also possible to create a `URL` object with a relative URL specification that is combined with an absolute specification:

```
try {
    URL jdk = new URL(js,"java.sun.com/products/JDK/index.html");
}catch (MalformedURLException e) {
    return;
}
```

In this example, the `URL` created in the previous example is combined with a relative URL specification that doesn't specify a network address or a root directory. The constructor can only combine the specifications if the protocol for both specifications is the same. If no protocol is specified, HTTP is assumed. The rules for combining the specifications depend on the protocol. In fact, the syntax rules for the portion of the URL after the protocol and up to an optional # depend on the protocol. If there's a # in the URL specification, the portion of the spec after the # is considered reference information that specifies a location within a file.

Once you have created a URL object, you can use the following access methods to get the information that the URL object encapsulates:

- getProtocol()
- getHost()
- getFile()
- getPort()
- getRef()

If you want to determine if two URL objects refer to the same file, you can use the sameFile(URL) method, which compares all the information in two URL objects except the reference information.

The highest level of functionality available from a URL object is provided by the getContent() method. The getContent() method tries to determine the type of data in the file specified by the URL, and then it returns the contents of the file encapsulated in an appropriate object for that type of data. For example, if the file contains GIF data, getContent() returns an ImageProducer object. If the type of data is not explicitly specified, getContent() tries to guess the type from the file-name extension and possibly also from the contents of the file. The data type names that Java uses conform to the naming scheme for MIME data types, as do the filename extensions that are recognized. The data types that correspond to various file extensions are shown in Table 8-2.

Table 8–2: File Extensions and Data Types

Suffix	Data Type	Suffix	Data Type
.a[a]	application/octet-stream	.ms	application/x-troff-ms
.ai	application/postscript	.mv	video/x-sgi-movie
.aif	audio/x-aiff	.nc	application/x-netcdf
.aifc	audio/x-aiff	.o[a]	application/octet-stream
.aiff	audio/x-aiff	.obj[b]	application/octet-stream
.arc	application/octet-stream	.oda	application/oda
.au	audio/basic	.pbm	image/x-portable-bitmap
.avi	application/x-troff-msvideo	.pdf	application/pdf
.bcpio	application/x-bcpio	.pgm	image/x-portable-graymap
.bin	application/octet-stream	.pl	text/plain
.c	text/plain	.pnm	image/x-portable-anymap
.c++	text/plain	.ppm	image/x-portable-pixmap
.cc	text/plain	.ps	application/postscript
.cdf	application/x-netcdf	.qt	video/quicktime
.cpio	application/x-cpio	.ras	image/x-cmu-rast

Table 8–2: File Extensions and Data Types (continued)

Suffix	Data Type	Suffix	Data Type
.dump	application/octet-stream	*.rgb*	image/x-rgb
.dvi	application/x-dvi	*.roff*	application/x-troff
.el	text/plain	*.rtf* [b]	application/rtf
.eps	application/postscript	*.rtx*	application/rtf
.etx	text/x-setext	*.saveme*	application/octet-stream
.exe	application/octet-stream	*.sh*	application/x-shar
.gif	image/gif	*.shar*	application/x-shar
.gtar	application/x-gtar	*.snd*	audio/basic
.gz	application/octet-stream	*.src*	application/x-wais-source
.h	text/plain	*.sv4cpio*	application/x-sv4cpio
.hdf	application/x-hdf	*.sv4crc*	application/x-sv4crc
.hqx	application/octet-stream	*.t*	application/x-troff
.htm	text/html	*.tar*	application/x-tar
.html	text/html	*.tex*	application/x-tex
.ief	image/ief	*.texi*	application/x-texinfo
.java	text/plain	*.texinfo*	application/x-texinfo
.jfif	image/jpeg	*.text*	text/plain
.jfif-tbnl	image/jpeg	*.tif*	image/tiff
.jpe	image/jpeg	*.tiff*	image/tiff
.jpeg	image/jpeg	*.tr*	application/x-troff
.jpg	image/jpeg	*.tsv*	text/tab-separated-values
.latex	application/x-latex	*.txt*	text/plain
.lib [b]	application/octet-stream	*.ustar*	application/x-ustar
.man	application/x-troff-man	*.uu*	application/octet-stream
.me	application/x-troff-me	*.wav*	audio/x-wav
.mime	message/rfc822	*.wsrc*	application/x-wais-source
.mov	video/quicktime	*.xbm*	image/x-xbitmap
.movie	video/x-sgi-movie	*.xpm*	image/x-xpixmap
.mpe	video/mpeg	*.xwd*	image/x-xwindowdump
.mpeg	video/mpeg	*.z* [b]	application/octet-stream
.mpg	video/mpeg	*.zip* [b]	application/zip

[a] UNIX only.
[b] Windows only.

If the filename does not end with a recognized extension, the first few bytes of the file are examined. If the first few bytes match the signature of a known type, the file is assumed to be of that type. Table 8-3 shows the byte combinations that are recognized.

Table 8–3: File Contents and Corresponding File Type

File Begins with	Inferred Data Type
"GIF8"	image/gif
"#def"	image/x-bitmap
"! XPM2"	image/x-pixmap
"<html>"	text/html
"<head>"	text/html
"<body>"	text/html

If you want to access the raw contents of a file instead of getting it encapsulated in an object, you can call the openStream() method of a URL. The openStream() method returns a reference to an InputStream object that you can use to read the file.

8.2.1 URLConnection Objects

After a URL object has parsed its specification, it actually creates a URLConnection object that is responsible for the protocol that it uses. The URLConnection is also responsible for determining the type of data in the file. The object is an instance of a subclass of URLConnection that is specific to the protocol specified by the URL object. As of Java 1.1, the java.net package includes the HttpURLConnection class for the HTTP protocol.

The URLConnection object for a URL provides complete control over the downloading of data from that URL. Unfortunately, the functionality of URLConnection is quite complex and goes beyond the scope of this book. For a detailed explanation of URLConnection, see *Java Network Programming* by Eliotte Rusty Harold, published by O'Reilly & Associates.

9

Security

Java uses a "sandbox" security model to ensure that applets cannot cause security problems. The idea is that an applet can do whatever it wants within the constraints of its sandbox, but that nothing done inside the sandbox has any consequences outside of the sandbox.

9.1 SecurityManager

Java implements the sandbox model using the `java.lang.SecurityManager` class. An instance of `SecurityManager` is passed to the method `System.setSecurityManager()` to establish the security policy for an application. Before `setSecurityManager()` is called, a Java program can access any resources available on the system. After `setSecurityManager()` is called, however, the `SecurityManager` object is responsible for providing a security policy. Once a security policy has been set by calling `setSecurityManager`, the method cannot be called again. Subsequent calls simply throw a `SecurityException`.

All methods in the Java API that can access resources outside of the Java environment call a `SecurityManager` method to ask permission before doing anything. If the `SecurityManager` method throws a `SecurityException`, the exception is thrown out of the calling method, and access to the resource is denied. The `SecurityManager` class defines a number of methods for asking for permission to access specific resources. Each of these methods has a name that begins with the word "check." Table 9-1 shows the names of the `check` methods provided by the `SecurityManager` class.

Table 9–1: The Check Methods of SecurityManager

Method Name	Permission
checkAccept()	To accept a network connection
checkAccess()	To modify a Thread or ThreadGroup
checkAwtEventQueueAccess()	To access the AWT event queue
checkConnect()	To establish a network connection or send a datagram
checkCreateClassLoader()	To create a ClassLoader object
checkDelete()	To delete a file
checkExec()	To call an external program
checkExit()	To stop the Java virtual machine and exit the Java environment
checkLink()	To dynamically link an external library into the Java environment
checkListen()	To listen for a network connection
checkMemberAccess()	To access the members of a class
checkMulticast()	To use a multicast connection
checkPackageAccess()	To access the classes in a package
checkPackageDefinition()	To define classes in a package
checkPrintJobAccess()	To initiate a print job request
checkPropertiesAccess()	To get or set the Properties object that defines all of the system properties
checkPropertyAccess()	To get or set a system property
checkRead()	To read from a file or input stream
checkSecurityAccess()	To perform a security action
checkSetFactory()	To set a factory class that determines classes to be used for managing network connections and their content
checkSystemClipboardAccess()	To access the system clipboard
checkTopLevelWindow()	To create a top-level window on the screen
checkWrite()	To write to a file or output stream

The SecurityManager class provides implementations of these methods that always refuse the requested permission. To implement a more permissive security policy, you need to create a subclass of SecurityManager that implements that policy.

In Java 1.0, most browsers consider an applet to be trusted or untrusted. An untrusted applet is one that does not come from the local filesystem. An untrusted applet is treated as follows by most popular browsers:

- It can establish network connections to the network address from which it came.

- It can create new windows on the screen. However, a notice is displayed on the bottom of the window that the window was created by an untrusted applet.

- It cannot access any other external resources. In particular, untrusted applets cannot access local files.

As of Java 1.1, an applet can have a digital signature attached to it. When an applet has been signed by a trusted entity, a browser may consider the applet to be trusted and relax its security policy.

9.2   ClassLoader

Java supports dynamically loaded classes, so the class loading mechanism plays an important role in the Java security model. The default class loading mechanism in Java loads classes from local files found relative to directories specified by the CLASSPATH environment variable. The CLASSPATH environment variable should have a value made up of one or more directory paths separated by a colon. The path implied by the package of a class is relative to the directories specified in the CLASSPATH environment variable.

In contrast, an instance of the java.lang.ClassLoader class defines how classes are loaded over the network. You can specify a security policy for loading classes by defining a subclass of ClassLoader that implements the policy. The loadClass() method of a ClassLoader loads a top-level class, such as a subclass of Applet. That ClassLoader object then becomes associated with the loaded class. You can retrieve the ClassLoader object that loads the class by calling the getClass-Loader() of an instance of the loaded class; every class in Java inherits this method from the Object class.

An object of a class loaded using a ClassLoader can attempt to load additional classes without explicitly using a ClassLoader object. The object does this by calling the forName() method of the Class class. However, if a ClassLoader object is associated with any pending method invocation in the current thread, the for-Name() method uses that ClassLoader to load the additional classes. In essence, this means that the object can only load classes through its associated Class-Loader.

If Java security is implemented correctly, an untrusted applet cannot escape the security policy implemented by the ClassLoader object used to load it because it cannot access any other ClassLoader objects. An applet should not be able to create its own ClassLoader objects. It is the responsibility of the checkCreateClass-Loader() method of SecurityManager to enforce this restriction.

Because a SecurityManager can determine the ClassLoader, if any, used to load a class, it can use the ClassLoader to help determine the trustworthiness of the class. Classes loaded by different ClassLoader objects cannot accidentally be mixed up because a class is identified by the combination of its fully qualified name and its ClassLoader.

In this chapter:
- *I/O*
- *System Properties*
- *Environment Variables*
- *External Program Execution*
- *Garbage Collection*
- *Self Termination*

10

Accessing the Environment

The `java.lang.System` and `java.lang.Runtime` classes provide a variety of methods that allow a Java program to access information and resources for the environment in which it is running. This environment includes the Java virtual machine and the native operating system.

10.1 I/O

The `System` class defines three `static` variables for the three default I/O stream objects that are used by Java programs:

`in` This variable refers to an `InputStream` that is associated with the process's standard input.

`out`
This variable refers to a `PrintStream` object that is associated with the process's standard output. In an applet environment, the `PrintStream` is likely to be associated with a separate window or a file, although this is not guaranteed.

This stream is the most commonly used of the three I/O streams provided by the `System` class. Even in GUI-based applications, sending output to this stream can be useful for debugging purposes. The usual idiom for sending output to this stream is:

```
System.out.println("some string");
```

`err`
This variable refers to a `PrintStream` object that is associated with the process's standard error output. In an applet environment, the `PrintStream` is likely to be associated with a separate window or a file, although this is not guaranteed.

10.2 System Properties

System properties provide a mechanism for getting information about the environment. You can get the value of a system property by passing its name to the `System.getProperty(String)` method. This method returns the value of the named property as a `String`, or it returns `null` if the property is not defined. Since it is common to assume a default value if a property is not specified, there is also a `System.getProperty(String, String)` method that takes the name of a property and a default `String` value to return if the property is not defined.

Table 10-1 lists the standard system properties for a Java environment. Many of these properties are guaranteed to be defined in any Java environment. Note, however, that untrusted applets aren't allowed to access many of these properties.

Table 10–1: Standard System Properties

Property Name	Description
file.encoding	The character encoding for the default locale (Java 1.1 only)
file.encoding.pkg	The package that contains the converters that handle converting between local encodings and Unicode (Java 1.1 only)
file.separator	The platform-dependent file separator (e.g., "/" on UNIX, "\" for Windows)
java.class.path	The value of the CLASSPATH environment variable
java.class.version	The version of the Java API
java.compiler	The just-in-time compiler to use, if any. The *java* interpreter provided with the JDK initializes this property from the environment variable JAVA_COMPILER
java.home	The directory in which Java is installed
java.version	The version of the Java interpreter
java.vendor	A vendor-specific string
java.vendor.url	A vendor URL
line.separator	The platform-dependent line separator (e.g., "\n" on UNIX, "\r\n" for Windows)
os.name	The name of the operating system
os.arch	The system architecture
os.version	The operating system version
path.separator	The platform-dependent path separator (e.g., ":" on UNIX, "," for Windows)
user.dir	The current working directory when the properties were initialized
user.home	The home directory of the current user

Table 10–1: Standard System Properties (continued)

Property Name	Description
user.language	The two-letter language code of the default locale (Java 1.1 only)
user.name	The username of the current user
user.region	The two-letter country code of the default locale (Java 1.1 only)
user.timezone	The default time zone (Java 1.1 only)

The Java API also provides some convenience methods for getting the value of a system property that should be interpreted as a data type other than `String`:

- `Boolean.getBoolean()` returns the value of a named system property as a `boolean`.

- `Color.getColor()` returns a `Color` object that represents the color specified by the value of a named system property interpreted as an RGB value. For example, the value `0xFFFFFF` is white, `0xFF000` is red, `0x00FF00` is green, and `0x0000FF` is blue.

- `Font.getFont()` returns a `Font` object that is mapped to a font in the native windowing system. If the string passed to `getFont()` is `"poster"`, the method uses the value of the system property `awt.font.poster` as the name of the native font.

  By default, the font style is plain and the font size is 12 points. If the font name is prefixed with `bold-`, `italic-` or `bolditalic-`, that style is used instead. If the font name is prefixed with a size and a `-`, that size is used instead. If both style and size are specified, style must come first. For example, passing `"italic-14-timesRoman"` to `getFont()` causes it to return a `Font` object that uses the native font identified by the system property `awt.font.timesRoman`. That font should be an italic, 14-point, TimesRoman font.

- `Integer.getInteger()` returns the value of a named system property as an `int`.

- `Long.getLong()` returns the value of a named system property as a `long`.

  There are two built-in mechanisms for setting system properties. Note that you can use these mechanisms to set the standard system properties or to define specific system properties for your own application.

- You can define properties from the command line of the Java virtual machine using the `-D` command line option. For example, to define a property named `time.server` with the value `tm02`, you can invoke the interpreter like this:

```
C:\> java -Dtime.server=tm02
```

- You can define any number of system properties using -D, as long as each property is specified with its own -D option.

You can programmatically define properties by calling the System.setProperties() method. The Properties object that you pass to System.setProperties() becomes the new source for all system property values.

If a program is running in a browser or other environment that has a SecurityManager installed, it may be denied any access to system properties.

10.3 Environment Variables

Java does not provide any way to directly access environment variables defined on a system. There is a System.getEnv() method that served that purpose before Java 1.0 was released. However, in released versions of Java, the System.getEnv() method just throws an exception with a message explaining that it is not supported.

However, an environment variable can be made available as a system property if it is defined as a system property on the command line that invokes the Java virtual machine. For example, to make the environment variable PRINTER available as a system property in a Windows environment, you can write:

```
C:\> java -Dprinter=%PRINTER%
```

In a UNIX environment, you can use:

```
% java -Dprinter=$PRINTER
```

10.4 External Program Execution

The Runtime.exec() method allows a Java program to run an external program. There are four forms of the exec() method, but they all expect to receive command-line-style information about the program to be run. The simplest exec() method takes a single String argument that contains the name of the program and its arguments. For example, to print a file named *foo.ps* in a Windows environment, you can use the following:

```
getRuntime().exec("copy foo.ps lpt1:");
```

Another form of exec() takes an array of String objects as its argument. The first element of the array is the name of the program to run; the remaining array elements are arguments to the program. The other two forms of exec() take a second argument that specifies the environment variables that are available to the program. The second argument should be an array of strings that are all of the form *name=value*.

The external program started by exec() is run asynchronously from the Java program that started it. All forms of the exec() method return immediately; they return a reference to a Process object that you can use to communicate with the external program. The three standard I/O streams for the external program can be accessed by calling the getInputStream(), getOutputStream(), and getErrorStream() methods of the Process object. If you want to wait for the external program to complete, you can call the waitFor() method. This method returns the program's exit code. The exitValue() method returns the program's exit code if it is called after the program has completed. If it is called before the program completes, it throws an IllegalThreadStateException. You can kill the external program by calling the destroy() method.

If a program is running in a browser or other environment that has a SecurityManager installed, it may be denied the ability to execute external programs.

10.5 Garbage Collection

The garbage-collection process in Java normally runs continuously in the background in a low-priority thread. In an environment that has nonpreemptive thread scheduling, you may want to run the Java virtual machine with the −noasyncgc option to ensure the best possible response from your application. The −noasyncgc option prevents garbage collection from running in the background. In this case, the only time that garbage collection occurs automatically is when the Java virtual machine runs out of memory. Since this can cause unexpected pauses in a program, you should try to avoid the problem by running the garbage collector at convenient or appropriate times by calling System.gc().

10.6 Self Termination

The very last communication a program has with its environment occurs when it terminates itself. A Java application can terminate itself by calling the System.exit() method. This method terminates an application by exiting the Java virtual machine; its argument is the exit code that is returned to the environment that invoked the Java virtual machine.

If a program is running in a browser or other environment that has a SecurityManager installed, it may be denied the ability to call System.exit().

II

REFERENCE

This part of the book is a complete reference to all of the fundamental classes in the core Java API. The material is organized alphabetically by package, and within each package, alphabetically by class. The reference page for a class tells you everything you need to know about using that class. It provides a detailed description of the class as a whole, followed by a complete description of every variable, constructor, and method defined by the class.

11

The java.io Package

The package java.io contains the classes that handle fundamental input and output operations in Java. The I/O classes can be grouped as follows:

- Classes for reading input from a stream of data.
- Classes for writing output to a stream of data.
- Classes that manipulate files on the local filesystem.
- Classes that handle object serialization.

I/O in Java is based on streams. A stream represents a flow of data or a channel of communication. Java 1.0 supports only byte streams. The InputStream class is the superclass of all of the Java 1.0 byte input streams, while OutputStream is the superclass of all the byte output streams. The drawback to these byte streams is that they do not always handle Unicode characters correctly.

As of Java 1.1, java.io contains classes that represent character streams. These character stream classes handle Unicode characters appropriately by using a character encoding to convert bytes to characters and vice versa. The Reader class is the superclass of all the Java 1.1 character input streams, while Writer is the superclass of all character output streams.

The InputStreamReader and OutputStreamWriter classes provide a bridge between byte streams and character streams. If you wrap an InputStreamReader around an InputStream object, the bytes in the byte stream are read and converted to characters using the character encoding scheme specified by the InputStream-Reader. Likewise, you can wrap an OutputStreamWriter around any OutputStream object so that you can write characters and have them converted to bytes.

As of Java 1.1, java.io also contains classes to support object serialization. Object serialization is the ability to write the complete state of an object to an output stream, and then later recreate that object by reading in the serialized state from an input stream. The ObjectOutputStream and ObjectInputStream classes handle serializing and deserializing objects, respectively.

The RandomAccessFile class is the only class that does not use a stream for reading or writing data. As its name implies, RandomAccessFile provides nonsequential access to a file for both reading and writing purposes.

The File class represents a file on the local file system. The class provides methods to identify and retrieve information about a file.

Figure 11-1 shows the class hierarchy for the java.io package. The java.io package defines a number of standard I/O exception classes. These exception classes are all subclasses of IOException, as shown in Figure 11-2.

11.1   BufferedInputStream

Synopsis

Class Name: java.io.BufferedInputStream
Superclass: java.io.FilterInputStream
Immediate Subclasses: None
Interfaces Implemented: None
Availability: JDK 1.0 or later

Description

A BufferedInputStream object provides a more efficient way to read just a few bytes at a time from an InputStream. BufferedInputStream object use a buffer to store input from an associated InputStream. In other words, a large number of bytes are read from the underlying stream and stored in an internal buffer. A BufferedInputStream is more efficient than a regular InputStream because reading data from memory is faster than reading it from a disk or a network. All reading is done directly from the internal buffer; the disk or network needs to be accessed only occasionally to fill up the buffer.

You should wrap a BufferedInputStream around any InputStream whose read() operations may be time consuming or costly, such as a FileInputStream.

BufferedInputStream provides a way to mark a position in the stream and subsequently reset the stream to that position, using mark() and reset().

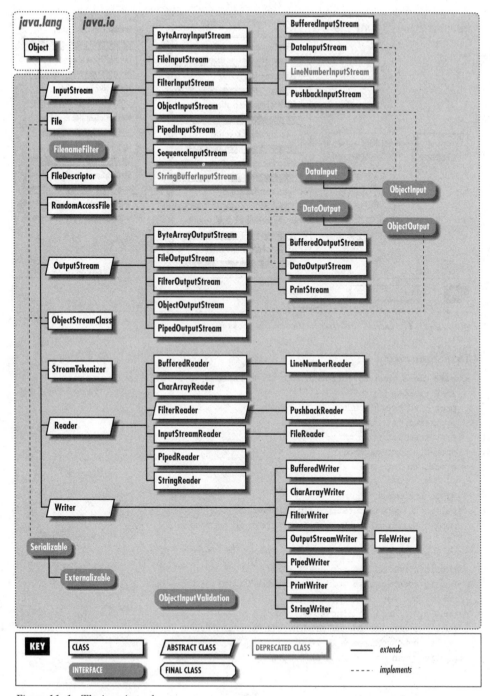

Figure 11–1: The java.io package

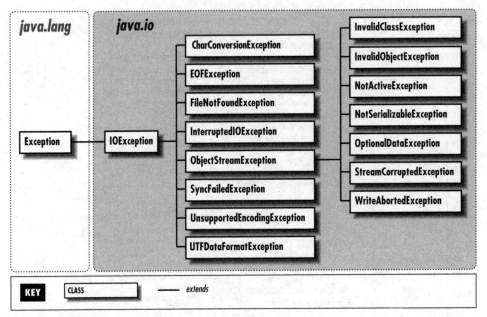

Figure 11–2: The exception classes in the java.io package

Class Summary

```
public class java.io.BufferedInputStream extends java.io.FilterInputStream {
    // Variables
    protected byte[] buf;
    protected int count;
    protected int marklimit;
    protected int markpos;
    protected int pos;

    // Constructors
    public BufferedInputStream(InputStream in);
    public BufferedInputStream(InputStream in, int size);

    // Instance Methods
    public synchronized int available();
    public synchronized void mark(int readlimit);
    public boolean markSupported();
    public synchronized int read();
    public synchronized int read(byte[] b, int off, int len);
    public synchronized void reset();
    public synchronized long skip(long n);
}
```

Variables

buf

protected byte[] buf

    Description   The buffer that stores the data from the input stream.

count

protected int count

    Description   A placeholder that marks the end of valid data in the buffer.

marklimit

protected int marklimit

    Description   The maximum number of bytes that can be read after a call to mark() before a call to reset() fails.

markpos

protected int markpos

    Description   The position of the stream when mark() was called. If mark() has not been called, this variable is -1.

pos

protected int pos

    Description   The current position in the buffer, or in other words, the index of the next character to be read.

Constructors

BufferedInputStream

public BufferedInputStream(InputStream in)

    Parameters   in   The input stream to buffer.

    Description   This constructor creates a BufferedInputStream that buffers input from the given InputStream, using a buffer with the default size of 2048 bytes.

public BufferedInputStream(InputStream in, int size)

    Parameters   in   The input stream to buffer.

                     size   The size of buffer to use.

    Description   This constructor creates a BufferedInputStream that buffers input from the given InputStream, using a buffer of the given size.

Instance Methods

available

public synchronized int available() throws IOException

Returns	The number of bytes that can be read without blocking.
Throws	IOException If any kind of I/O error occurs.
Overrides	FilterInputStream.available()
Description	This method returns the number of bytes that can be read without having to wait for more data to become available. The returned value is the sum of the number of bytes remaining in the object's buffer and the number returned as the result of calling the available() method of the underlying InputStream object.

mark

public synchronized void mark(int readlimit)

Parameters	readlimit The maximum number of bytes that can be read before the saved position becomes invalid.
Overrides	FilterInputStream.mark()
Description	This method causes the BufferedInputStream to remember its current position. A subsequent call to reset() causes the object to return to that saved position, and thus reread a portion of the buffer.

markSupported

public synchronized boolean markSupported()

Returns	The boolean value true.
Overrides	FilterInputStream.markSupported()
Description	This method returns true to indicate that this class supports mark() and reset().

read

public synchronized int read() throws IOException

Returns	The next byte of data or –1 if the end of the stream is encountered.
Throws	IOException If any kind of I/O error occurs.
Overrides	FilterInputStream.read()
Description	This method returns the next byte from the buffer. If all the bytes in the buffer have been read, the buffer is filled from the underlying InputStream and the next byte is returned. If the buffer does not need to be filled, this method returns immedi-

ately. If the buffer needs to be filled, this method blocks until data is available from the underlying InputStream, the end of the stream is reached, or an exception is thrown.

public synchronized int read(byte b[], int off, int len)
                 throws IOException

Parameters	b	An array of bytes to be filled from the stream.
	off	An offset into the byte array.
	len	The number of bytes to read.
Returns	The actual number of bytes read or –1 if the end of the stream is encountered immediately.	
Throws	IOException If any kind of I/O error occurs.	
Overrides	FilterInputStream.read(byte[], int, int)	
Description	This method copies bytes from the internal buffer into the given array b, starting at index off and continuing for up to len bytes. If there are any bytes in the buffer, this method returns immediately. Otherwise the buffer needs to be filled; this method blocks until the data is available from the underlying InputStream, the end of the stream is reached, or an exception is thrown.	

reset

public synchronized void reset() throws IOException

Throws	IOException If there was no previous call to this BufferedInputStream's mark method, or the saved position has been invalidated.	
Overrides	FilterInputStream.reset()	
Description	This method sets the position of the BufferedInputStream to a position that was saved by a previous call to mark(). Subsequent bytes read from this BufferedInputStream will begin from the saved position and continue normally.	

skip

public synchronized long skip(long n) throws IOException

Parameters	n	The number of bytes to skip.
Returns	The actual number of bytes skipped.	
Throws	IOException If any kind of I/O error occurs.	
Overrides	FilterInputStream.skip()	
Description	This method skips n bytes of input. If the new position of the stream is still within the data contained in the buffer, the method returns immediately. Otherwise the skip() method of the underlying stream is called. A subsequent call to read() forces the buffer to be filled.	

Inherited Methods

Method	Inherited From	Method	Inherited From
clone()	Object	close()	FilterInput-Stream
equals(Object)	Object	finalize()	Object
getClass()	Object	hashCode()	Object
notify()	Object	notifyAll()	Object
read(byte[])	FilterInput-Stream	toString()	Object
void wait()	Object	void wait(long)	Object
void wait(long, int)	Object		

See Also

FilterInputStream, InputStream, IOException

11.2   BufferedOutputStream

Synopsis

Class Name:	java.io.BufferedOutputStream
Superclass:	java.io.FilterOutputStream
Immediate Subclasses:	None
Interfaces Implemented:	None
Availability:	JDK 1.0 or later

Description

A BufferedOutputStream object provides a more efficient way to write just a few bytes at a time to an OutputStream. BufferedOutputStream objects use a buffer to store output for an associated OutputStream. In other words, a large number of bytes are stored in an internal buffer and only written when the buffer fills up or is explicitly flushed. A BufferedOutputStream is more efficient than a regular OutputStream because the data is written to memory, rather than a disk or a network. Minimizing the number of write operations to a disk or the network minimizes the cumulative overhead for these operations.

You should wrap a BufferedOutputStream around any OutputStream whose write() operations may be time consuming or costly, such as a FileOutputStream.

Class Summary

```
public class java.io.BufferedOutputStream
            extends java.io.FilterOutputStream {
  // Variables
  protected byte[] buf;
  protected int count;

  // Constructors
  public BufferedOutputStream(OutputStream out);
  public BufferedOutputStream(OutputStream out, int size);

  // Instance Methods
  public synchronized void flush();
  public synchronized void write(int b);
  public synchronized void write(byte[] b, int off, int len);
}
```

Variables

buf

protected byte[] buf

    Description   The buffer that stores the data for the output stream.

count

protected int count

    Description   The current position in the buffer.

Constructors

BufferedOutputStream

public BufferedOutputStream(OutputStream out)

    Parameters   out   The output stream to buffer.

    Description   This constructor creates a BufferedOutputStream that acts on the specified OutputStream, using a buffer with the default size of 512 bytes.

public BufferedOutputStream(OutputStream out, int size)

    Parameters   out   The output stream to buffer.

                  size   The size of buffer to use.

    Description   This constructor creates a BufferedOutputStream that acts on the specified OutputStream, using a buffer that is size bytes long.

Instance Methods

flush

`public synchronized void flush() throws IOException`

Throws	IOException If any kind of I/O error occurs.
Overrides	FilterOutputStream.flush()
Description	This method writes the contents of the buffer to the underlying output stream. It is called automatically when the buffer fills up. You can also call it before the buffer is full. This is known as "flushing" the buffer. This method blocks until the underlying write() is complete.

write

`public synchronized void write(int b) throws IOException`

Parameters	b	The value to write.
Throws	IOException	If any kind of I/O error occurs.
Overrides	FilterOutputStream.write(int)	
Description	This method places a byte containing the low-order eight bits of the given integer into the buffer. If the buffer is full, it is flushed, and the value b is placed in the newly empty buffer. If the buffer is flushed, this method blocks until flush() returns; otherwise this method returns immediately.	

`public synchronized void write(byte b[], int off, int len)`
                              `throws IOException`

Parameters	b	An array of bytes to write to the stream.
	off	An offset into the byte array.
	len	The number of bytes to write.
Throws	IOException	If any kind of I/O error occurs.
Overrides	FilterOutputStream.write(byte[], int, int)	
Description	This method copies len bytes from b, starting at off, into the buffer. If there is enough space left in the buffer for the new data, it is copied into the buffer and the method returns immediately. Otherwise, the buffer is flushed, and the new data is written directly to the underlying stream. This is subtly different from the behavior of write(int), which places new data in the buffer after a flush().	

Inherited Methods

Method	Inherited From	Method	Inherited From
clone()	Object	close()	FilterOutputStream
equals(Object)	Object	finalize()	Object
getClass()	Object	hashCode()	Object
notify()	Object	notifyAll()	Object
toString()	Object	wait()	Object
wait(long)	Object	wait(long, int)	Object
write(byte[])	FilterOutputStream		

See Also

FilterOutputStream, IOException, OutputStream

11.3 BufferedReader

Synopsis

Class Name:	java.io.BufferedReader
Superclass:	java.io.Reader
Immediate Subclasses:	None
Interfaces Implemented:	None
Availability:	New as of JDK 1.1

Description

A BufferedReader object provides a more efficient way to read just a few characters at a time from a Reader. BufferedReader objects use a buffer to store input from an associated Reader. In other words, a large number of characters are read from the underlying reader and stored in an internal buffer. A BufferedReader is more efficient than a regular Reader because reading data from memory is faster than reading it from a disk or a network. All reading is done directly from the buffer; the disk or network needs to be accessed only occasionally to fill up the buffer.

You should wrap a BufferedReader around any Reader whose read() operations may be time consuming or costly, such as a FileReader or InputStreamReader.

BufferedReader provides a way to mark a position in the stream and subsequently reset the stream to that position, using mark() and reset().

A BufferedReader is similar to a BufferedInputStream, but it operates on a stream of Java characters instead of a byte stream, which makes it easier to support internationalization.

Class Summary

```
public class java.io.BufferedReader extends java.io.Reader {
    // Constructors
    public BufferedReader(Reader in);
    public BufferedReader(Reader in, int sz);

    // Instance Methods
    public void close();
    public void mark(int readAheadLimit);
    public boolean markSupported();
    public int read();
    public int read(char[] cbuf, int off, int len);
    public String readLine();
    public boolean ready();
    public void reset();
    public long skip(long n);
}
```

Constructors

BufferedReader

public BufferedReader(Reader in)

Parameters	in	The reader to buffer.
Description		This constructor creates a BufferedReader that buffers input from the given Reader using a buffer with the default size of 8192 characters.

public BufferedReader(Reader in, int sz)

Parameters	in	The reader to buffer.
	sz	The size of buffer to use.
Throws	IllegalArgumentException	
		If the specified size is less than 0.
Description		This constructor creates a BufferedReader that buffers input from the given Reader, using a buffer of the given size.

Instance Methods

close

public void close() throws IOException

Throws	IOException	If any kind of I/O error occurs.

Overrides   `Reader.close()`

Description   This method closes this `BufferedReader` and its underlying `Reader`.

mark

`public void mark(int readAheadLimit) throws IOException`

Parameters   `readlimit`   The maximum number of bytes that can be read before the saved position becomes invalid.

Throws   `IOException`   If the stream is closed.

Overrides   `Reader.mark(int)`

Description   This method causes the `BufferedReader` to remember its current position. A subsequent call to `reset()` causes the object to return to that saved position, and thus reread a portion of the buffer.

markSupported

`public boolean markSupported()`

Returns   The `boolean` value `true`.

Overrides   `Reader.markSupported()`

Description   This method returns `true` to indicate that this class supports `mark()` and `reset()`.

read

`public int read() throws IOException`

Returns   The next character of data, or `-1` if the end of the stream is encountered.

Throws   `IOException`   If any kind of I/O error occurs.

Overrides   `Reader.read()`

Description   This method returns the next character from the buffer. If all the characters in the buffer have been read, the buffer is filled from the underlying `Reader`, and the next character is returned. If the buffer does not need to be filled, this method returns immediately. If the buffer needs to be filled, this method blocks until data is available from the underlying `Reader`, the end of the stream is reached, or an exception is thrown.

`public int read(char[] cbuf, int off, int len) throws IOException`

Parameters   `cbuf`   An array of characters to be filled from the stream.

	off	Offset into the character array.
	len	Number of characters to read.
Returns		The actual number of characters read or -1 if the end of the stream is encountered immediately.
Throws		IOException If any kind of I/O error occurs.
Overrides		Reader.read(char[], int, int)
Description		This method reads characters from the internal buffer into the given array cbuf, starting at index off and continuing for up to len bytes. If there are any characters in the buffer, this method returns immediately. Otherwise the buffer needs to be filled; this method blocks until the data is available from the underlying InputStream, the end of the stream is reached, or an exception is thrown.

readLine

public String readLine() throws IOException

Returns	A String containing the line just read, or null if the end of the stream has been reached.
Throws	IOException If any kind of I/O error occurs.
Description	This method reads a line of text. Lines are terminated by "\n", "\r", or "\r\n". The line terminators are not returned with the line string.

ready

public boolean ready() throws IOException

Returns	A boolean value that indicates whether the stream is ready to be read.
Throws	IOException If the stream is closed.
Overrides	Reader.ready()
Description	If there is data in the buffer, or if the underlying stream is ready, this method returns true. The underlying stream is ready if the next read() is guaranteed to not block. Note that a return value of false does not guarantee that the next read operation will block.

reset

public void reset() throws IOException

Throws	IOException If the reader is closed, mark() has not been called, or the saved position has been invalidated.

Overrides   `Reader.reset()`

Description   This method sets the position of the `BufferedReader` to a position that was saved by a previous call to `mark()`. Subsequent characters read from this `BufferedReader` will begin from the saved position and continue normally.

skip

`public long skip(long n) throws IOException`

Parameters   n   The number of characters to skip.

Returns   The actual number of characters skipped.

Throws   `IOException`   If any kind of I/O error occurs.

Overrides   `Reader.skip()`

Description   This method skips n characters of input. If the new position of the stream is still within the data contained in the buffer, the method returns immediately. Otherwise the buffer is repeatedly filled until the requested position is available.

Inherited Methods

Method	Inherited From	Method	Inherited From
clone()	Object	equals(Object)	Object
finalize()	Object	getClass()	Object
hashCode()	Object	notify()	Object
notifyAll()	Object	read(char[])	Reader
toString()	Object	void wait()	Object
void wait(long)	Object	void wait(long, int)	Object

See Also

`IllegalArgumentException, IOException, Reader, String`

11.4 BufferedWriter

Synopsis

Class Name: `java.io.BufferedWriter`

Superclass: `java.io.Writer`

Immediate Subclasses: None

Interfaces Implemented: None
Availability: New as of JDK 1.1

Description

A BufferedWriter object provides a more efficient way to write just a few characters at a time to a Writer. BufferedWriter objects use a buffer to store output for an associated Writer. In other words, a large number of characters are stored in an internal buffer and only written when the buffer fills up or is explicitly flushed. A BufferedWriter is more efficient than a regular Writer because the data is written to memory, rather than a disk or a network. Minimizing the number of write operations to a disk or the network minimizes the cumulative overhead for these operations.

You should wrap a BufferedWriter around any Writer whose write() operations may be time consuming or costly, such as a FileWriter or a OutputStreamWriter.

This class is very similar to BufferedOutputStream, but it operates on a stream of Java characters instead of a byte stream; this makes it easier to support internationalization.

Class Summary

```
public class java.io.BufferedWriter extends java.io.Writer {
    // Constructors
    public BufferedWriter(Writer out);
    public BufferedWriter(Writer out, int size);

    // Instance Methods
    public void close();
    public void flush();
    public void newLine();
    public void write(int c);
    public void write(char[] cbuf, int off, int len);
    public void write(String s, int off, int len);
}
```

Constructors

BufferedWriter

public BufferedWriter (Writer out)

Parameters   out   The output stream to buffer.
Description   This constructor creates a BufferedWriter that acts on the specified Writer, using a buffer with the default size of 8192 characters.

```
public BufferedWriter (Writer out, int size)
```
Parameters	out	The output stream to buffer.
	size	The size of buffer to use.
Throws	IllegalArgumentException	
		If the specified size is less than 0.
Description		This constructor creates a BufferedWriter that acts on the specified Writer, using a buffer that is size bytes long.

Instance Methods

close

```
public void close() throws IOException
```
Throws	IOException	If any kind of I/O error occurs.
Overrides	Writer.close()	
Description		This method closes this BufferedWriter and its underlying Writer.

flush

```
public void flush() throws IOException
```
Throws	IOException	If any kind of I/O error occurs.
Overrides	Writer.flush()	
Description		This method writes the contents of the buffer to the underlying Writer and calls flush() on the underlying Writer. It is called automatically when the buffer fills up. You can also call it before the buffer is full. This is known as "flushing" the buffer. This method blocks until the underlying write() is complete.

newLine

```
public void newLine() throws IOException
```
Throws	IOException	If any kind of I/O error occurs.
Description		This method writes the newline character or characters to the stream. It uses System.getProperty("line.separator") to choose the newline appropriate for the run-time system. Calling this method is preferable to explicitly writing a newline character.

write

```
public void write(int c) throws IOException
```
Parameters	c	The value to write.
Throws	IOException	If any kind of I/O error occurs.

Overrides `Writer.write(int)`

Description This method places the low-order 16 bits of the specified value into the buffer. If the buffer is full, it is flushed, and the value c is placed in the newly empty buffer. If the buffer is flushed, this method blocks while the data is written; otherwise this method returns immediately.

```
public void write(char[] cbuf, int off, int len)
        throws IOException
```

Parameters `cbuf` An array of characters to write.

  `off` An offset into the character array.

  `len` The number of characters to write.

Throws `IOException` If any kind of I/O error occurs.

Overrides `Writer.write(char[], int, int)`

Description This method copies `len` characters from `cbuf`, starting at `off`, into the buffer. If there is enough space left in the buffer for the new data, it is copied into the buffer, and the method returns immediately. Otherwise, the buffer is filled and flushed repeatedly until all the new data has been copied into the buffer.

```
public void write(String s, int off, int len) throws IOException
```

Parameters `s` The string to be written.

  `off` An offset into the string.

  `len` The number of characters to write.

Throws `IOException` If an I/O error occurs.

Overrides `Writer.write(String, int, int)`

Description This method copies `len` characters from `s`, starting at `off`, into the buffer. If there is enough space left in the buffer for the new data, it is copied into the buffer and the method returns immediately. Otherwise, the buffer is filled and flushed repeatedly until all the new data has been copied into the buffer.

Inherited Methods

Method	Inherited From	Method	Inherited From
clone()	Object	equals(Object)	Object
finalize()	Object	getClass()	Object
hashCode()	Object	notify()	Object
notifyAll()	Object	toString()	Object
wait()	Object	wait(long)	Object
wait(long, int)	Object	write(char[])	Writer

Method	Inherited From	Method	Inherited From
write(String)	Writer		

See Also

IllegalArgumentException, IOException, String, Writer

11.5   ByteArrayInputStream

Synopsis

Class Name:	java.io.ByteArrayInputStream
Superclass:	java.io.InputStream
Immediate Subclasses:	None
Interfaces Implemented:	None
Availability:	JDK 1.0 or later

Description

A ByteArrayInputStream is a stream whose data comes from a byte array. None of the methods of this class throw an IOException because the data comes from an array instead of an actual I/O device. This class does not support the ability to mark a position in the stream. A call to reset(), however, does position the stream at the beginning of the byte array.

The position of the end of the stream depends on the constructor used. If the ByteArrayInputStream(byte[] buf) constructor is used, the end of the stream is the end of the byte array. If the ByteArrayInputStream(byte[] buf, int offset, int length) constructor is used, the end of the stream is reached at the index given by offset+length.

Class Summary

```
public class java.io.ByteArrayInputStream extends java.io.InputStream {
    // Variables
    protected byte[] buf;
    protected int count;
    protected int pos;

    // Constructors
    public ByteArrayInputStream(byte[] buf);
    public ByteArrayInputStream(byte[] buf, int offset, int length);

    // Instance Methods
    public synchronized int available();
```

```
    public synchronized int read();
    public synchronized int read(byte[] b, int off, int len);
    public synchronized void reset();
    public synchronized long skip(long n);
}
```

Variables

buf

protected byte[] buf

Description   The buffer represented by this stream.

count

protected int count

Description   A placeholder that marks the end of the data this ByteArrayInputStream represents.

pos

protected int pos

Description   The current position in the buffer.

Constructors

ByteArrayInputStream

public ByteArrayInputStream(byte[] buf)

Parameters   buf   The stream source.
Description   This constructor creates a ByteArrayInputStream object that
uses the given array of bytes as its data source. The data is not
copied, so changes made to the array affect the data the
ByteArrayInputStream returns.

public ByteArrayInputStream(byte[] buf, int offset, int length)

Parameters   buf   The stream source.
              offset   An index into the buffer where the stream
                             should begin.
              length   The number of bytes to read.
Description   This constructor creates a ByteArrayInputStream that uses, as
its data source, length bytes in a given array of bytes, starting at
offset bytes from the beginning of the array. The data is not
copied, so changes made to the array affect the data the
ByteArrayInputStream returns.

Instance Methods

available

public synchronized int available()

Returns	The number of bytes remaining to be read in the array.
Overrides	InputStream.available()
Description	This method returns the number of bytes remaining to be read in the byte array.

read

public synchronized int read()

Returns	The next byte or –1 if the end of the stream is encountered.
Overrides	InputStream.read()
Description	This method returns the next byte in the array.

public synchronized int read(byte[] b, int off, int len)

Parameters	b	An array to read bytes into.
	off	An offset into b.
	len	The number of bytes to read.
Returns	The number of bytes read or –1 if the end of the stream is encountered.	
Overrides	InputStream.read(byte[], int, int)	
Description	This method copies up to len bytes from its internal byte array into the given array b, starting at index off.	

reset

public synchronized void reset()

Overrides	InputStream.reset()
Description	This method resets the position of the input stream to the beginning of the byte array. If you specified an offset into the array, you might expect this method to reset the position to where you first started reading from the stream, but that is not the case.

skip

public synchronized long skip(long n)

Parameters	n	The number of bytes to skip.
Returns	The number of bytes skipped.	
Overrides	InputStream.skip()	
Description	This method skips n bytes of input. If you try to skip past the end of the array, the stream is positioned at the end of the array.	

Inherited Methods

Method	Inherited From	Method	Inherited From
clone()	Object	close()	InputStream
equals (Object)	Object	finalize()	Object
getClass()	Object	hashCode()	Object
mark(int)	InputStream	markSupported ()	InputStream
notify()	Object	notifyAll()	Object
read(byte[])	InputStream	toString()	Object
wait()	Object	wait(long)	Object
wait(long, int)	Object		

See Also

InputStream, String

11.6   ByteArrayOutputStream

Synopsis

Class Name:	java.io.ByteArrayOutputStream
Superclass:	java.io.FilterOutputStream
Immediate Subclasses:	None
Interfaces Implemented:	None
Availability:	JDK 1.0 or later

Description

A ByteArrayOutputStream is a stream whose data is written to an internal byte array. None of the methods of this class throws an IOException because the data is written to an array instead of an actual I/O device.

The data for a ByteArrayOutputStream can be sent to another OutputStream using the writeTo() method. A copy of the array can be obtained using the toCharArray() method.

Class Summary

```
public class java.io.ByteArrayOutputStream extends java.io.OutputStream {
    // Variables
    protected byte[] buf;
    protected int count;
```

```
// Constructors
public ByteArrayOutputStream();
public ByteArrayOutputStream(int size);

// Instance Methods
public synchronized void reset();
public int size( );
public synchronized byte[] toByteArray();
public String toString();
public String toString(int hibyte);          // Deprecated in 1.1
public String toString(String enc);          // New in 1.1
public synchronized void write(int b);
public synchronized void write(byte[] b, int off, int len);
public synchronized void writeTo(OutputStream out);
}
```

Variables

buf

protected byte[] buf

Description   The buffer that holds data for this stream.

count

protected int count

Description   A placeholder that marks the end of the data in the buffer.

Constructors

ByteArrayOutputStream

public ByteArrayOutputStream()

Description   This constructor creates a ByteArrayOutputStream with an internal buffer that has a default size of 32 bytes. The buffer grows automatically as data is written to the stream.

public ByteArrayOutputStream(int size)

Parameters   size   The initial buffer size.

Description   This constructor creates a ByteArrayOutputStream with an internal buffer that has a size of size bytes. The buffer grows automatically as data is written to the stream.

Instance Methods

reset

`public synchronized void reset()`

Description   This method discards the current contents of the buffer and resets the position of the stream to zero. Subsequent data is written starting at the beginning of the array.

size

`public int size()`

Description   This method returns the number of bytes currently stored in this object's internal buffer. It is a count of the number of bytes that have been written to the stream.

toByteArray

`public synchronized byte[] toByteArray()`

Returns   A copy of the data that has been written to this ByteArrayOutputStream.

Description   This method copies the data in the internal array and returns a reference to the copy. The returned array is as long as the data that has been written to the stream, i.e., the same as `size()`.

toString

`public String toString()`

Returns   A copy of the data that has been written to this ByteArrayOutputStream.

Overrides   `Object.toString()`

Description   This method returns a reference to a `String` object that contains a copy of the bytes currently stored in this object's internal buffer. The bytes are assumed to represent characters in the encoding that is customary for the native platform, so the bytes are converted to Unicode characters based on that assumption.

`public String toString(int hibyte)`

Availability   Deprecated as of JDK 1.1

Parameters   hibyte   A value to use as the high byte of each character.

Returns   A copy of the data that has been written to this ByteArrayOutputStream, where each character in the string has a high byte of hibyte and a low byte taken from the corresponding byte in the array.

Description   This method provides a way to convert from bytes to characters. As of 1.1, it is deprecated and replaced with `toString(String)`.

`public String toString(String enc) throws UnsupportedEncodingException`

Availability   New as of JDK 1.1

Parameters   enc   The encoding scheme to use.

Returns   A copy of the data that has been written to this `ByteArrayOut-putStream`, converted from bytes to characters via the named encoding scheme `enc`.

Throws   `UnsupportedEncodingException`
                  The specified encoding is not supported.

Description   This method returns a Java `String` created from the byte array of this stream. The conversion is performed according to the encoding scheme `enc`.

write

`public synchronized void write(int b)`

Parameters   b   The value to write.

Overrides   `OutputStream.write(int)`

Description   This method writes the low-order 8 bits of the given value into the internal array. If the array is full, a larger array is allocated.

`public synchronized void write(byte b[], int off, int len)`

Parameters   b   The array to copy from.

                off   Offset into the byte array.

                len   Number of bytes to write.

Overrides   `OutputStream.write(byte[], int, int)`

Description   This method copies `len` bytes to this object's internal array from `b`, starting `oset` elements from the beginning of the supplied array `b`. If the internal array is full, a larger array is allocated.

writeTo

`public synchronized void writeTo(OutputStream out)`
`                          throws IOException`

Parameters   out   The destination stream.

Throws   `IOException`   If any kind of I/O error occurs.

Description   This method writes the contents of this object's internal buffer to the given `OutputStream`. All the data that has been written to this `ByteArrayOutputStream` is written to out.

Inherited Methods

Method	Inherited From	Method	Inherited From
clone()	Object	close()	OutputStream
equals(Object)	Object	finalize()	Object
flush()	OutputStream	getClass()	Object
hashCode()	Object	notify()	Object
notifyAll()	Object	wait()	Object
wait(long)	Object	wait(long, int)	Object
write(byte[])	OutputStream		

See Also

IOException, OutputStream, String, UnsupportedEncodingException

11.7   CharArrayReader

Synopsis

Class Name:	java.io.CharArrayReader
Superclass:	java.io.Reader
Immediate Subclasses:	None
Interfaces Implemented:	None
Availability:	New as of JDK 1.1

Description

The CharArrayReader class represents a stream whose data comes from a character array. This class is similar to ByteArrayInputStream, but it deals with a Java character stream rather than a byte stream. Furthermore, this class supports marking a position in the stream, which ByteArrayInputStream does not.

The position of the end of the stream depends on the constructor used. If the CharArrayReader(char[] buf) constructor is used, the end of the stream is the end of the character array. If the CharArrayReader(char[] buf, int offset, int length) constructor is used, the end of the stream is reached at the index given by offset+length.

Class Summary

```
public class java.io.CharArrayReader extends java.io.Reader {
    // Variables
    protected char[] buf;
    protected int count;
    protected int markedPos;
    protected int pos;

    // Constructors
    public CharArrayReader(char[] buf);
    public CharArrayReader(char[] buf, int offset, int length);

    // Instance Methods
    public void close();
    public void mark(int readAheadLimit);
    public boolean markSupported();
    public int read();
    public int read(char[] b, int off, int len);
    public boolean ready();
    public void reset();
    public long skip(long n);
}
```

Variables

buf

```
protected char[] buf
```

    Description   The buffer represented by this reader.

count

```
protected int count
```

    Description   The size of the buffer, or in other words, the length of the array.

markedPos

```
protected int markedPos
```

    Description   The buffer position when mark() was called. If mark() has not been called, this variable is 0.

pos

```
protected int pos
```

    Description   The current position in the buffer.

Constructors

CharArrayReader

```
public CharArrayReader(char[] buf)
```
Parameters	buf	The reader source.
Description		This constructor creates a CharArrayReader object that uses the given array of characters as its data source. The data is not copied, so changes made to the array affect the data that the CharArrayReader returns.

```
public CharArrayReader(char[] buf, int offset, int length)
```
Parameters	buf	The reader source.
	offset	An offset into the array.
	length	The number of bytes to read.
Description		This constructor creates a CharArrayReader that uses, as its data source, length characters in a given array of bytes, starting at offset characters from the beginning of the array. The data is not copied, so changes made to the array affect the data that the CharArrayReader returns.

Instance Methods

close

```
public void close()
```
Overrides	Reader.close()
Description	This method closes the reader by removing the link between this CharArrayReader and the array it was created with.

mark

```
public void mark(int readAheadLimit) throws IOException
```
Parameters	readAheadLimit	
		The maximum number of characters that can be read before the saved position becomes invalid.
Throws	IOException	If the stream is closed or any other kind of I/O error occurs.
Overrides	Reader.mark(int)	
Description		This method causes the CharArrayReader to remember its current position. A subsequent call to reset() causes the object to return to that saved position, and thus reread a portion of the buffer. Because the data for this stream comes from a char array, there is no limit on reading ahead, so readAheadLimit is ignored.

markSupported

`public boolean markSupported()`

Returns	The boolean value true.
Overrides	Reader.markSupported()
Description	This method returns true to indicate that this class supports mark() and reset().

read

`public int read() throws IOException`

Returns	The next character or -1 if the end of the stream is encountered.
Throws	IOException If the stream is closed or any other kind of I/O error occurs.
Overrides	Reader.read()
Description	This method returns the next character in the array.

`public int read(char[] b, int off, int len) throws IOException`

Parameters	b	An array of characters to be filled from the stream.
	off	An offset into the character array.
	len	The number of characters to read.
Returns		The actual number of characters read or -1 if the end of the stream is encountered immediately.
Throws		IOException If the stream is closed or any other kind of I/O error occurs.
Overrides		Reader.read(char[], int, int)
Description		This method copies up to len characters from its internal array into the given array b, starting at index off.

ready

`public boolean ready() throws IOException`

Returns	A boolean value that indicates whether the stream is ready to be read.
Throws	IOException If the stream is closed or any other kind of I/O error occurs.
Overrides	Reader.ready()
Description	If there is any data left to be read from the character array, this method returns true.

reset

```
public void reset() throws IOException
```

Throws	IOException If the stream is closed or any other kind of I/O error occurs.
Overrides	Reader.reset()
Description	This method resets the position of the CharArrayReader to the position that was saved by calling the mark() method. If mark() has not been called, the CharArrayReader is reset to read from the beginning of the array.

skip

```
public long skip(long n) throws IOException
```

Parameters	n	The number of characters to skip.
Returns	The actual number of characters skipped.	
Throws	IOException If the stream is closed or any other kind of I/O error occurs.	
Overrides	Reader.skip()	
Description	This method skips n characters of input. If you try to skip past the end of the array, the stream is positioned at the end of the array.	

Inherited Methods

Method	Inherited From	Method	Inherited From
clone()	Object	equals (Object)	Object
finalize()	Object	getClass()	Object
hashCode()	Object	notify()	Object
notifyAll()	Object	read(char[])	Reader
toString()	Object	wait()	Object
wait(long)	Object	wait(long, int)	Object

See Also

IOException, Reader, String

11.8   CharArrayWriter

Synopsis

Class Name: java.io.CharArrayWriter
Superclass: java.io.Writer
Immediate Subclasses: None
Interfaces Implemented: None
Availability: New as of JDK 1.1

Description

The CharArrayWriter class represents a stream whose data is written to an internal character array. This class is similar to ByteArrayOutputStream, but it operates on an array of Java characters instead of a byte array.

The data from a CharArrayWriter can be sent to another Writer using the writeTo() method. A copy of the array can be obtained using the toCharArray() method.

Class Summary

```
public class java.io.CharArrayWriter extends java.io.Writer {
    // Variables
    protected char[] buf;
    protected int count;

    // Constructors
    public CharArrayWriter();
    public CharArrayWriter(int initialSize);

    // Instance Methods
    public void close();
    public void flush();
    public void reset();
    public int size();
    public char[] toCharArray();
    public String toString();
    public void write(int c);
    public void write(char[] c, int off, int len);
    public void write(String str, int off, int len);
    public void writeTo(Writer out);
}
```

Variables

buf

> `protected char[] buf`
> > Description   The buffer that holds data for this stream.

count

> `protected int count`
> > Description   A placeholder that marks the end of the data in the buffer.

Constructors

CharArrayWriter

> `public CharArrayWriter()`
> > Description   This constructor creates a `CharArrayWriter` with an internal buffer that has a default size of 32 characters. The buffer grows automatically as data is written to the stream.

> `public CharArrayWriter(int initialSize)`
> > Parameters   `initialSize`   The initial buffer size.
> > Description   This constructor creates a `CharArrayWriter` with an internal buffer that has a size of `initialSize` characters. The buffer grows automatically as data is written to the stream.

Instance Methods

close

> `public void close()`
> > Overrides   `Writer.close()`
> > Description   This method does nothing. For most subclasses of `Writer`, this method releases any system resources that are associated with the `Writer` object. However, the `CharArrayWriter`'s internal array may be needed for subsequent calls to `toCharArray()` or `writeTo()`. For this reason, `close()` does nothing, and the internal array is not released until the `CharArrayWriter` is garbage collected.

flush

> `public void flush()`
> > Overrides   `Writer.flush()`
> > Description   This method does nothing. The `CharArrayWriter` writes data directly into its internal array; thus it is never necessary to flush the stream.

reset

    public void reset()

   Description   This method discards the current contents of the buffer and
                  resets the position of the stream to zero. Subsequent data is
                  written starting at the beginning of the array.

size

    public int size()

   Description   This method returns the number of characters currently stored
                  in this object's internal buffer. It is a count of the number of
                  characters that have been written to the stream.

toCharArray

    public char[] toCharArray()

   Returns   A copy of the data that has been written to this CharArray-
                  Writer in the form of a char array.

   Description   This method copies the data in the internal array and returns a
                  reference to the copy. The returned array is as long as the data
                  that has been written to the stream, i.e., the same as size().

toString

    public String toString()

   Returns   A copy of the data that has been written to this CharArray-
                  Writer in the form of a String.

   Overrides   Object.toString()

   Description   This method returns a reference to a String object created
                  from the characters stored in this object's internal buffer.

write

    public void write(int c)

   Parameters   c   The value to write.

   Overrides   Writer.write(int)

   Description   This method writes the low-order 16 bits of the given value into
                  the internal array. If the array is full, a larger array is allocated.

    public void write(char[] c, int off, int len)

   Parameters   c   An array of characters to write to the stream.
                  off   An offset into the character array.
                  len   The number of characters to write.

   Overrides   Writer.write(char[], int, int)

Description   This method copies len characters to this object's internal array from c, starting off elements from the beginning of the array. If the internal array is full, a larger array is allocated.

public void write(String str, int off, int len)
Parameters   str   A String to write to the stream.
              off   An offset into the string.
              len   The number of characters to write.
Overrides   Writer.write(String, int, int)
Description   This method copies len characters to this object's internal array from str, starting off characters from the beginning of the given string. If the internal array is full, a larger array is allocated.

writeTo

public void writeTo(Writer out) throws IOException
Parameters   out   The destination stream.
Throws   IOException If any kind of I/O error occurs.
Description   This method writes the contents of this object's internal buffer to the given Writer. All the data that has been written to this CharArrayWriter is written to out.

Inherited Methods

Method	Inherited From	Method	Inherited From
clone()	Object	equals(Object)	Object
finalize()	Object	getClass()	Object
hashCode()	Object	notify()	Object
notifyAll()	Object	wait()	Object
wait(long)	Object	wait(long, int)	Object
write(char[])	Writer	write(String)	Writer

See Also

IOException, String, Writer

11.9   CharConversionException

Synopsis

Class Name: java.io.CharConversionException
Superclass: java.io.IOException
Immediate Subclasses: None
Interfaces Implemented: None
Availability: New as of JDK 1.1

Description

A CharConversionException object is thrown when a problem occurs in converting a character to a byte.

Class Summary

```
public class java.io.CharConversionException extends java.io.IOException {
  // Constructors
  public CharConversionException();
  public CharConversionException(String s);
}
```

Constructors

CharConverionException

```
public CharConversionException()
```

Description   This constructor creates a CharConversionException with no detail message.

```
public CharConversionException(String s)
```

Parameters   s   The detail message.

Description   This constructor creates a CharConversionException with the specified detail message.

Inherited Methods

Method	Inherited From	Method	Inherited From
clone()	Object	equals(Object)	Object
fillInStackTrace()	Throwable	finalize()	Object
getClass()	Object	getLocalizedMessage()	Throwable
getMessage()	Throwable	hashCode()	Object
notify()	Object	notifyAll()	Object
printStackTrace()	Throwable	printStack-Trace(PrintStream)	Throwable

Method	Inherited From	Method	Inherited From
printStack-Trace(PrintWriter)	Throwable	toString()	Object
wait()	Object	wait(long)	Object
wait(long, int)	Object		

See Also

Exception, IOException, Throwable

11.10   DataInput

Synopsis

Interface Name:	java.io.DataInput
Super-interface:	None
Immediate Sub-interfaces:	
	java.io.ObjectInput
Implemented By:	java.io.DataInputStream, java.io.RandomAccessFile
Availability:	JDK 1.0 or later

Description

The DataInput interface defines methods for reading primitive data types and lines of text from an input stream in a machine-independent manner. All multi-byte quantities are assumed to be in a format that stores the most significant byte as the first byte and the least significant byte as the last byte.

Interface Declaration

```
public abstract interface java.io.DataInput {
    // Methods
    public abstract boolean readBoolean();
    public abstract byte readByte();
    public abstract char readChar();
    public abstract double readDouble();
    public abstract float readFloat();
    public abstract void readFully(byte[] b);
    public abstract void readFully(byte[] b, int off, int len);
    public abstract int readInt();
    public abstract String readLine();
    public abstract long readLong();
    public abstract short readShort();
    public abstract int readUnsignedByte();
    public abstract int readUnsignedShort();
```

```
      public abstract String readUTF();
      public abstract int skipBytes(int n);
}
```

Methods

readBoolean

public abstract boolean readBoolean() throws IOException

Returns	The boolean value read from the stream.
Throws	EOFException
	If the end of the file is encountered.
	IOException If any other kind of I/O error occurs.
Description	This method reads a byte as a boolean value. A byte that contains a zero is read as false; that which contains a nonzero is read as true.

readByte

public abstract byte readByte() throws IOException

Returns	The byte value read from the stream.
Throws	EOFException
	If the end of the file is encountered.
	IOException If any other kind of I/O error occurs.
Description	This method reads a signed 8-bit byte.

readChar

public abstract char readChar() throws IOException

Returns	The char value read from the stream.
Throws	EOFException
	If the end of the file is encountered.
	IOException If any other kind of I/O error occurs.
Description	This method reads a 16-bit char.

readDouble

public abstract double readDouble() throws IOException

Returns	The double value read from the stream.
Throws	EOFException
	If the end of the file is encountered.
	IOException If any other kind of I/O error occurs.
Description	This method reads a 64-bit double quantity.

readFloat

`public abstract float readFloat() throws IOException`

Returns	The float value read from the stream.
Throws	EOFException
	If the end of the file is encountered.
	IOException If any other kind of I/O error occurs.
Description	This method reads a 32-bit float quantity.

readFully

`public abstract void readFully(byte[] b) throws IOException`

Parameters	b	The array to fill.
Throws	EOFException	
	If the end of the file is encountered.	
	IOException If any other kind of I/O error occurs.	
Description	This method reads bytes into the given array b until the array is full.	

`public abstract void readFully(byte[] b, int off, int len)`
                        `throws IOException`

Parameters	b	The array to fill.
	off	An offset into the array.
	len	The number of bytes to read.
Throws	EOFException	
	If the end of the file is encountered.	
	IOException If any other kind of I/O error occurs.	
Description	This method reads len bytes into the given array, starting at offset off.	

readInt

`public abstract int readInt() throws IOException`

Returns	The int value read from the stream.
Throws	EOFException
	If the end of the file is encountered.
	IOException If any other kind of I/O error occurs.
Description	This method reads a 32-bit int quantity.

readLine

`public abstract String readLine() throws IOException`

Returns	A String that contains the line read from the stream.

Throws EOFException

If the end of the file is encountered.

IOException If any other kind of I/O error occurs.

Description This method reads a String from the current position through the next line terminator. Implementations of this method should take care to look for any line terminator: "\n", "\r", or "\r\n".

readLong

```
public abstract long readLong() throws IOException
```
Returns The long value read from the stream.

Throws EOFException

If the end of the file is encountered.

IOException If any other kind of I/O error occurs.

Description This method reads a 64-bit long quantity.

readShort

```
public abstract short readShort() throws IOException
```
Returns The short value read from the stream.

Throws EOFException

If the end of the file is encountered.

IOException If any other kind of I/O error occurs.

Description This method reads a 16-bit short quantity.

readUnsignedByte

```
public abstract int readUnsignedByte() throws IOException
```
Returns The unsigned byte value read from the stream.

Throws EOFException

If the end of the file is encountered.

IOException If any other kind of I/O error occurs.

Description This method reads an 8-bit byte as an unsigned quantity.

readUnsignedShort

```
public abstract int readUnsignedShort() throws IOException
```
Returns The unsigned short value read from the stream.

Throws EOFException

If the end of the file is encountered.

IOException If any other kind of I/O error occurs.

Description This method reads a 16-bit short as an unsigned quantity.

readUTF

public abstract String readUTF() throws IOException

Returns   The String read from the stream.

Throws   EOFException

                       If the end of the file is encountered.

               IOException   If any other kind of I/O error occurs.

               UTFDataFormatException

                       If the bytes do not represent a valid UTF-8
                       encoding.

Description   This method reads a UTF-8 format String. See Appendix B,
               The UTF-8 Encoding, for information on the UTF-8 encoding.

skipBytes

public abstract int skipBytes(int n) throws IOException

Parameters   n   The number of bytes to skip.

Returns   The actual number of skipped bytes.

Throws   EOFException

                       If the end of the file is encountered.

               IOException   If any other kind of I/O error occurs.

Description   This method skips over n bytes.

See Also

DataInputStream, EOFException, IOException, ObjectInput, RandomAccessFile,
UTFDataFormatException

11.11   DataInputStream

Synopsis

Class Name: java.io.DataInputStream
Superclass: java.io.FilterInputStream
Immediate Subclasses: None
Interfaces Implemented: java.io.DataInput
Availability: JDK 1.0 or later

Description

The DataInputStream class provides methods for reading primitive data types and lines of text from an underlying input stream in a machine-independent manner. Many of the methods of DataInputStream read a single primitive data type, in binary format, from an underlying input stream. All multibyte quantities are assumed to be in a format that stores the most significant byte as the first byte and the least significant byte as the last byte.

Class Summary

```
public class java.io.DataInputStream extends java.io.FilterInputStream
                                implements java.io.DataInput {
// Constructors
public DataInputStream(InputStream in);

// Class Methods
public final static String readUTF(DataInput in);

// Instance Methods
public final int read(byte[] b);
public final int read(byte[] b, int off, int len);
public final boolean readBoolean();
public final byte readByte();
public final char readChar();
public final double readDouble();
public final float readFloat();
public final void readFully(byte[] b);
public final void readFully(byte[] b, int off, int len);
public final int readInt();
public final String readLine();                 // Deprecated in 1.1
public final long readLong();
public final short readShort();
public final int readUnsignedByte();
public final int readUnsignedShort();
public final String readUTF() throws IOException;
public final int skipBytes(int n) throws IOException;
}
```

Constructors

DataInputStream

public DataInputStream(InputStream in)

Parameters   in   The input stream to use.

Description   This constructor creates a DataInputStream object that reads from, or wraps, the given input stream.

Class Methods

readUTF

```
public final static String readUTF(DataInput in)
                              throws IOException
```

Parameters   in   The data input stream to use.

Returns   The String read from the stream.

Throws   EOFException
                                If the end of the file is encountered.

              IOException   If any other kind of I/O error occurs.

              UTFDataFormatException
                                If the bytes do not represent a valid UTF-8
                                encoding.

Description   This method reads a UTF-8 encoded string from the given
              DataInput object. To get the number of bytes in the encoded
              string, the first two bytes are read as an unsigned short value.
              Then the following bytes are read and interpreted as UTF-8
              encoded bytes; these bytes are converted into characters for the
              resulting String. This method blocks until all of the bytes in
              the encoded string have been read, the end of the stream is
              encountered, or an exception is thrown.

              For details on the UTF-8 encoding, see Appendix B.

Instance Methods

read

```
public final int read(byte b[]) throws IOException
```

Parameters   b   An array of bytes to be filled from the stream.

Returns   The number of bytes read, or –1 if the end of file is encoun-
              tered immediately.

Throws   IOException   If any kind of I/O error occurs.

Overrides   FilterInputStream.read(byte[])

Description   This method reads bytes of input into the given array by calling
              the read() method of the underlying stream. The method
              reads up to b.length bytes of data from the stream. The
              method blocks until there is some input available.

```
public final int read(byte b[], int off, int len)
                  throws IOException
```

Parameters   b   An array of bytes to be filled from the stream.

off   An offset into the byte array.

len   The number of bytes to read.

Returns   The number of bytes read, or -1 if the end of file is encountered immediately.

Throws   IOException If any kind of I/O error occurs.

Overrides   FilterInputStream.read(byte[], int, int)

Description This method reads up to len bytes of input into the given array starting at index off. The method reads the bytes by calling the read() method of the underlying stream and blocks until there is some input available.

readBoolean

```
public final boolean readBoolean() throws IOException
```

Returns   The boolean value read from the stream.

Throws   EOFException

             If the end of the file is encountered.

             IOException If any other kind of I/O error occurs.

Implements   DataInput.readBoolean()

Description This method reads a byte as a boolean value from the underlying input stream. A byte that contains a zero is read as false; that which contains any other value is read as true. The method blocks until the byte is read, the end of the stream is encountered, or an exception is thrown.

readByte

```
public final byte readByte() throws IOException
```

Returns   The byte value read from the stream.

Throws   EOFException

             If the end of the file is encountered.

             IOException If any other kind of I/O error occurs.

Implements   DataInput.readByte()

Description This method reads a signed 8-bit value—a byte—from the underlying input stream. The method blocks until the byte is read, the end of the stream is encountered, or an exception is thrown.

readChar

```
public final char readChar() throws IOException
```

Returns   The char value read from the stream.

Throws	EOFException
	If the end of the file is encountered.
	IOException If any other kind of I/O error occurs.
Implements	DataInput.readChar()
Description	This method reads a 16-bit Unicode character from the stream. The method reads two bytes from the underlying input stream and then creates a char value, using the first byte read as the most significant byte. The method blocks until the two bytes are read, the end of the stream is encountered, or an exception is thrown.

readDouble

public final double readDouble() throws IOException

Returns	The double value read from the stream.
Throws	EOFException
	If the end of the file is encountered.
	IOException If any other kind of I/O error occurs.
Implements	DataInput.readDouble()
Description	This method reads a 64-bit double quantity from the stream. The method reads a long value from the underlying input stream as if using the readLong() method. The long value is then converted to a double using the longBitsToDouble() method in Double. The method blocks until the necessary eight bytes are read, the end of the stream is encountered, or an exception is thrown.

readFloat

public final float readFloat() throws IOException

Returns	The float value read from the stream.
Throws	EOFException
	If the end of the file is encountered.
	IOException If any other kind of I/O error occurs.
Implements	DataInput.readFloat()
Description	This method reads a 32-bit float quantity from the stream. The method reads an int value from the underlying input stream as if using the readInt() method. The int value is then converted to a float using the intBitsToFloat() method in Float. The method blocks until the necessary four bytes are read, the end of the stream is encountered, or an exception is thrown.

readFully

public final void readFully(byte b[]) throws IOException

Parameters	b	The array to fill.
Throws	EOFException	
		If the end of the file is encountered.
	IOException	If any other kind of I/O error occurs.
Implements	DataInput.readFully(byte[])	
Description	This method reads bytes into the given array b until the array is full. The method reads repeatedly from the underlying stream to fill the array. The method blocks until all of the bytes are read, the end of the stream is encountered, or an exception is thrown.	

public final void readFully(byte b[], int off, int len)
                    throws IOException

Parameters	b	The array to fill.
	off	An offset into the array.
	len	The number of bytes to read.
Throws	EOFException	
		If the end of the file is encountered.
	IOException	If any other kind of I/O error occurs.
Implements	DataInput.readFully(byte[], int, int)	
Description	This method reads len bytes into the given array, starting at offset off. The method reads repeatedly from the underlying stream to fill the array. The method blocks until all the bytes are read, the end of the stream is encountered, or an exception is thrown.	

readInt

public final int readInt() throws IOException

Returns	The int value read from the stream.	
Throws	EOFException	
		If the end of the file is encountered.
	IOException	If any other kind of I/O error occurs.
Implements	DataInput.readInt()	
Description	This method reads a signed 32-bit int quantity from the stream. The method reads four bytes from the underlying input stream and then creates an int quantity, using the first byte read as the most significant byte. The method blocks until the four bytes are read, the end of the stream is encountered, or an exception is thrown.	

readLine

public final String readLine() throws IOException

Availability	Deprecated as of JDK 1.1
Returns	A String that contains the line read from the stream.
Throws	EOFException
	If the end of the file is encountered.
	IOException If any other I/O error occurs.
Implements	DataInput.readLine()
Description	This method reads the next line of text from the stream. The method reads bytes of data from the underlying input stream until it encounters a line terminator. A line terminator is a carriage return ("\r"), a newline character ("\n"), a carriage return immediately followed by a newline character, or the end of the stream. The method blocks until a line terminator is read, the end of the stream is encountered, or an exception is thrown.

This method is deprecated as of JDK 1.1 because it does not convert bytes to characters correctly. It's replaced by BufferedReader.readLine().

readLong

public final long readLong() throws IOException

Returns	The long value read from the stream.
Throws	EOFException
	If the end of the file is encountered.
	IOException If any other kind of I/O error occurs.
Implements	DataInput.readLong()
Description	This method reads a signed 64-bit long quantity from the stream. The method reads eight bytes from the underlying input stream and then creates a long quantity, using the first byte read as the most significant byte. The method blocks until the eight bytes are read, the end of the stream is encountered, or an exception is thrown.

readShort

public final short readShort() throws IOException

Returns	The short value read from the stream.

Throws   `EOFException`

If the end of the file is encountered.

`IOException`   If any other kind of I/O error occurs.

Implements   `DataInput.readShort()`

Description   This method reads a signed 16-bit short quantity from the stream. The method reads two bytes from the underlying input stream and then creates a short quantity, using the first byte read as the most significant byte. The method blocks until the two bytes are read, the end of the stream is encountered, or an exception is thrown.

readUnsignedByte

`public final int readUnsignedByte() throws IOException`

Returns   The unsigned byte value read from the stream.

Throws   `EOFException`

If the end of the file is encountered.

`IOException`   If any other kind of I/O error occurs.

Implements   `DataInput.readUnsignedByte()`

Description   This method reads an unsigned 8-bit quantity from the stream. The method reads a byte from the underlying input stream and returns that byte, and blocks until the byte is read, the end of the stream is encountered, or an exception is thrown.

readUnsignedShort

`public final int readUnsignedShort() throws IOException`

Returns   The unsigned short value read from the stream.

Throws   `EOFException`

If the end of the file is encountered.

`IOException`   If any other kind of I/O error occurs.

Implements   `DataInput.readUnsignedShort()`

Description   This method reads an unsigned 16-bit quantity from the stream. The method reads two bytes from the underlying input stream and creates an unsigned short quantity, using the first byte read as the most significant byte. The method blocks until the two bytes are read, the end of the stream is encountered, or an exception is thrown.

readUTF

public final String readUTF() throws IOException

Returns | The String read from the stream.
Throws | EOFException
|| If the end of the file is encountered.
| IOException | If any other kind of I/O error occurs.
| UTFDataFormatException
|| If the bytes do not represent a valid UTF-8 encoding.
Implements | DataInput.readUTF()
Description | This method reads a UTF-8 encoded string from the stream. See the description of the readUTF(DataInput) class method for more information.

skipBytes

public final int skipBytes(int n) throws IOException

Parameters | n | The number of bytes to skip.
Returns | The actual number of skipped bytes.
Throws | EOFException
|| If the end of the file is encountered.
| IOException | If any other kind I/O error occurs.
Implements | DataInput.skipBytes()
Description | This method skips over n bytes in the underlying input stream. The method blocks until all of the bytes are skipped, the end of the stream is encountered, or an exception is thrown.

Inherited Methods

Method	Inherited From	Method	Inherited From
available ()	FilterInputStream	clone()	Object
close()	FilterInputStream	equals(Object)	Object
finalize()	Object	getClass()	Object
hashCode()	Object	mark(int)	FilterInputStream
markSupported()	FilterInputStream	notify()	Object
notifyAll()	Object	read()	FilterInputStream
reset()	FilterInputStream	skip(long)	FilterInputStream
toString()	Object	wait()	Object
wait(long)	Object	wait(long, int)	Object

See Also

DataOutputStream, Double, EOFException, FilterInputStream, Float, Input-Stream, IOException, String, UTFDataFormatException

11.12   DataOutput

Synopsis

Interface Name:	java.io.DataOutput
Super-interface:	None
Immediate Sub-interfaces:	
	java.io.ObjectOutput
Implemented By:	java.io.DataOutputStream,
	java.io.RandomAccessFile
Availability:	JDK 1.0 or later

Description

The DataOutput interface defines methods for writing primitive data types to an output stream in a machine-independent manner. All multibyte quantities are written in a format that stores the most significant byte as the first byte and the least significant byte as the last byte.

Interface Declaration

```
public abstract interface java.io.DataOutput {
  // Methods
  public abstract void write(byte[] b);
  public abstract void write(byte[] b, int off, int len);
  public abstract void write(int b);
  public abstract void writeBoolean(boolean v);
  public abstract void writeByte(int v);
  public abstract void writeBytes(String s);
  public abstract void writeChar(int v);
  public abstract void writeChars(String s);
  public abstract void writeDouble(double v);
  public abstract void writeFloat(float v);
  public abstract void writeInt(int v);
  public abstract void writeLong(long v);
  public abstract void writeShort(int v);
  public abstract void writeUTF(String str);
}
```

Methods

write

```
public abstract void write(int b) throws IOException
```
Parameters   b   The value to write.

Throws   IOException   If any kind of I/O error occurs.

Description   This method writes the low-order 8 bits of the given integer b.

```
public abstract void write(byte[] b) throws IOException
```
Parameters   b   An array of values to write.

Throws   IOException   If any kind of I/O error occurs.

Description   This method writes all of the 8-bit bytes in the given array.

```
public abstract void write(byte[] b, int off, int len)
                  throws IOException
```
Parameters   b   An array of values to write.

                off   An offset into the array.

                len   The number of bytes to write.

Throws   IOException   If any kind of I/O error occurs.

Description   This method writes len bytes from the given array, starting off elements from the beginning of the array.

writeBoolean

```
public abstract void writeBoolean(boolean v) throws IOException
```
Parameters   v   The boolean value to write.

Throws   IOException   If any kind of I/O error occurs.

Description   If v is true, this method writes a byte that contains the value 1. If v is false, the method writes a byte that contains the value 0.

writeByte

```
public abstract void writeByte(int v) throws IOException
```
Parameters   v   The value to write.

Throws   IOException   If any kind of I/O error occurs.

Description   This method writes an 8-bit byte using the low-order eight bits of the integer v.

writeBytes

```
public abstract void writeBytes(String s) throws IOException
```
Parameters   s   The String to write.

Throws   IOException   If any kind of I/O error occurs.

Description   This method writes the characters in the given String as a sequence of 8-bit bytes. The high-order bytes of the characters in the string are ignored.

writeChar

```
public abstract void writeChar(int v) throws IOException
```

Parameters   v   The value to write.

Throws   IOException If any kind of I/O error occurs.

Description   This method writes a 16-bit char using the low-order 16 bits of the given integer v.

writeChars

```
public abstract void writeChars(String s) throws IOException
```

Parameters   s   The String to write.

Throws   IOException If any kind of I/O error occurs.

Description   This method writes the characters in the given String object as a sequence of 16-bit characters.

writeDouble

```
public abstract void writeDouble(double v) throws IOException
```

Parameters   v   The double value to write.

Throws   IOException If any kind of I/O error occurs.

Description   This method writes a 64-bit double.

writeFloat

```
public abstract void writeFloat(float v) throws IOException
```

Parameters   v   The value to write.

Throws   IOException If any kind of I/O error occurs.

Description   This method writes a 32-bit float.

writeInt

```
public abstract void writeInt(int v) throws IOException
```

Parameters   v   The int value to write.

Throws   IOException If any kind of I/O error occurs.

Description   This method writes a 32-bit int.

writeLong

```
public abstract void writeLong(long v) throws IOException
```

Parameters   v   The long value to write.

Throws   IOException If any kind of I/O error occurs.

Description   This method writes a 64-bit long.

writeShort

public abstract void writeShort(int v) throws IOException

Parameters	v	The short value to write.
Throws	IOException	If any kind of I/O error occurs.
Description	This method writes a 16-bit short.	

writeUTF

public abstract void writeUTF(String str) throws IOException

Parameters	str	The String to write.
Throws	IOException	If any kind of I/O error occurs.
Description	This method writes the given String using UTF-8 encoding. See Appendix B for information on the UTF-8 encoding.	

See Also

DataOutputStream, IOException, ObjectOutput, RandomAccessFile

11.13 DataOutputStream

Synopsis

Class Name:	java.io.DataOutputStream
Superclass:	java.io.FilterOutputStream
Immediate Subclasses:	None
Interfaces Implemented:	java.io.DataOutput
Availability:	JDK 1.0 or later

Description

The DataOutputStream class defines methods for writing primitive data types to an output stream in a machine-independent manner. Many of the methods of DataOutputStream write a single primitive data type, in binary format, to an underlying output stream. All multibyte quantities are written in a format that stores the most significant byte as the first byte and the least significant byte as the last byte.

Class Summary

```
public class java.io.DataOutputStream extends java.io.FilterOutputStream
                                implements java.io.DataOutput {
    // Variables
    protected int written;

    // Constructors
    public DataOutputStream(OutputStream out);
```

```
// Instance Methods
public void flush();
public final int size();
public synchronized void write(int b);
public synchronized void write(byte[] b, int off, int len);
public final void writeBoolean(boolean v);
public final void writeByte(int v);
public final void writeBytes(String s);
public final void writeChar(int v);
public final void writeChars(String s);
public final void writeDouble(double v);
public final void writeFloat(float v);
public final void writeInt(int v);
public final void writeLong(long v);
public final void writeShort(int v);
public final void writeUTF(String str);
}
```

Variables

written

protected int written

> Description   The number of bytes that have been written to this output stream.

Constructors

DataOutputStream

public DataOutputStream(OutputStream out)

> Parameters   out   The output stream to use.
> Description   This constructor creates a DataOutputStream that uses out as its underlying stream.

Instance Methods

flush

public void flush() throws IOException

> Throws   IOException   If any kind of I/O error occurs.
> Overrides   FilterOutputStream.flush()
> Description   This method flushes the stream, forcing any buffered output to be written. The method calls the flush() method of the underlying output stream.

size

`public final int size()`

Returns	The number of bytes written.
Description	This method returns the number of bytes that have been written to the stream (i.e., it returns the value of the variable written).

write

`public synchronized void write(int b) throws IOException`

Parameters	b	The value to write.
Throws	IOException	If any kind of I/O error occurs.
Overrides	FilterOutputStream.write(int)	
Implements	DataOutput.write(int)	
Description	This method writes the low-order eight bits of b to the underlying stream as a byte.	

`public synchronized void write(byte b[], int off, int len)`
                    `throws IOException`

Parameters	b	An array of bytes to write.
	off	An offset into the byte array.
	len	The number of bytes to write.
Throws	IOException	If any kind of I/O error occurs.
Overrides	FilterOutputStream.write(byte[], int, int)	
Implements	DataOutput.write(byte[], int, int)	
Description	This method writes len bytes from the given array, starting off elements from the beginning of the array, to the underlying stream.	

writeBoolean

`public final void writeBoolean(boolean v) throws IOException`

Parameters	v	The boolean value to write.
Throws	IOException	If any kind of I/O error occurs.
Implements	DataOutput.writeBoolean()	
Description	If v is true, this method writes a byte that contains the value 1 to the underlying stream. If v is false, the method writes a byte that contains the value 0.	

writeByte

`public final void writeByte(int v) throws IOException`

Parameters	v	The value to write.

Throws   IOException   If any kind of I/O error occurs.
Implements   DataOutput.writeByte()
Description   This method writes an 8-bit byte to the underlying stream, using the low-order eight bits of the given integer v.

writeBytes

public final void writeBytes(String s) throws IOException
Parameters   s   The String to write.
Throws   IOException   If any kind of I/O error occurs.
Implements   DataOutput.writeBytes()
Description   This method writes the characters in the given String to the underlying stream as a sequence of 8-bit bytes. The high-order bytes of the characters in the string are ignored.

writeChar

public final void writeChar(int v) throws IOException
Parameters   v   The value to write.
Throws   IOException   If any kind of I/O error occurs.
Implements   DataOutput.writeChar()
Description   This method writes a 16-bit char to the underlying stream, using the low-order 16 bits of the given integer v.

writeChars

public final void writeChars(String s) throws IOException
Parameters   s   The String to write.
Throws   IOException   If any kind of I/O error occurs.
Implements   DataOutput.writeChars()
Description   This method writes the characters in the given String object to the underlying stream as a sequence of 16-bit characters.

writeDouble

public final void writeDouble(double v) throws IOException
Parameters   v   The double value to write.
Throws   IOException   If any kind of I/O error occurs.
Implements   DataOutput.writeDouble()
Description   This method writes a 64-bit double to the underlying stream. The double value is converted to a long using doubleToLong-Bits() of Double; the long value is then written to the underlying stream as eight bytes with the high-order byte first.

writeFloat

```
public final void writeFloat(float v) throws IOException
```

Parameters	v	The float value to write.
Throws	IOException	If any kind of I/O error occurs.
Implements	DataOutput.writeFloat()	
Description		This method writes a 32-bit float to the underlying stream. The float value is converted to a int using floatToIntBits() of Float; the int value is then written to the underlying stream as four bytes with the high-order byte first.

writeInt

```
public final void writeInt(int v) throws IOException
```

Parameters	v	The int value to write.
Throws	IOException	If any kind of I/O error occurs.
Implements	DataOutput.writeInt()	
Description		This method writes a 32-bit int to the underlying stream. The value is written as four bytes with the high-order byte first.

writeLong

```
public final void writeLong(long v) throws IOException
```

Parameters	v	The long value to write.
Throws	IOException	If any kind of I/O error occurs.
Implements	DataOutput.writeLong()	
Description		This method writes a 64-bit long to the underlying stream. The value is written as eight bytes with the high-order byte first.

writeShort

```
public final void writeShort(int v) throws IOException
```

Parameters	v	The value to write.
Throws	IOException	If any kind of I/O error occurs.
Implements	DataOutput.writeShort()	
Description		This method writes a 16-bit short to the underlying stream, using the low-order two bytes of the given integer v.

writeUTF

```
public final void writeUTF(String str) throws IOException
```

Parameters	str	The String to write.
Throws	IOException	If any kind of I/O error occurs.
Implements	DataOutput.writeUTF()	

Description   This method writes the given String to the underlying stream using the UTF-8 encoding. First, two bytes are written as an unsigned short value; this value specifies the number of bytes to follow. The value is the actual number of bytes in the UTF-8 encoding, not the length of the string. Then each character of the string is written as UTF-8 encoded bytes.

See Appendix B for more information on the UTF-8 encoding.

Inherited Methods

Method	Inherited From	Method	Inherited From
clone()	Object	close()	FilterOut-putStream
equals(Object)	Object	finalize()	Object
getClass()	Object	hashCode()	Object
notify()	Object	notifyAll()	Object
toString()	Object	wait()	Object
wait(long)	Object	wait(long, int)	Object
write(byte[])	FilterOut-putStream		

See Also

DataInputStream, DataOutput, Double, FilterOutputStream, Float, IOException, OutputStream

11.14   EOFException

Synopsis

Class Name: java.io.EOFException
Superclass: java.io.IOException
Immediate Subclasses: None
Interfaces Implemented: None
Availability: JDK 1.0 or later

Description

An EOFException is thrown in response to an attempt to read past the end of a file.

Many file-handling routines indicate the end of a file with a special return code. For example, many read() methods return -1 to indicate that the end of file has been reached. However, in some cases, the program clearly expects a certain format of data in a file. If it's not all there, throwing an exception is an appropriate way to flag the unusual condition of the file. So, for example, a DataInputStream throws an EOFException if it comes to the end of file in the middle of read-Float(). In the java.io package, EOFException is used in the classes that implement the DataInput and ObjectInput interfaces, namely DataInputStream, ObjectInputStream, and RandomAccessFile.

Class Summary

```
public class java.io.EOFException extends java.io.IOException {
  // Constructors
  public EOFException();
  public EOFException(String s);
}
```

Constructors

EOFException

public EOFException()

    Description   This constructor creates an EOFException with no detail message.

public EOFException(String s)

    Parameters   s   The detail message.

    Description   This constructor creates an EOFException with the specified detail message.

Inherited Methods

Method	Inherited From	Method	Inherited From
clone()	Object	equals(Object)	Object
fillInStackTrace()	Throwable	finalize()	Object
getClass()	Object	getLocalizedMessage()	Throwable
getMessage()	Throwable	hashCode()	Object
notify()	Object	notifyAll()	Object
printStackTrace()	Throwable	printStack-Trace(PrintStream)	Throwable
printStack-Trace(PrintWriter)	Throwable	toString()	Object

Method	Inherited From	Method	Inherited From
wait()	Object	wait(long)	Object
wait(long, int)	Object		

See Also

DataInput, DataInputStream, Exception, IOException, ObjectInput, ObjectInputStream, RandomAccessFile, Throwable

11.15   Externalizable

Synopsis

Interface Name:	java.io.Externalizable
Super-interface:	java.io.Serializable
Immediate Sub-interfaces:	
	None
Implemented By:	None
Availability:	New as of JDK 1.1

Description

The Externalizable interface is an extension of the Serializable interface. Whereas a Serializable object is automatically saved and loaded (in most cases), an Externalizable object has sole responsibility for saving and loading its state via the writeExternal() and readExternal() methods. If a class implements the Externalizable interface, it must handle any versioning issues that occur.

The methods of Externalizable are public, which can pose a security risk. If security is a concern, Externalizable objects should not write or read sensitive information, or the Serializable interface should be used instead.

Interface Declaration

```
public abstract interface java.io.Externalizable
                    extends java.io.Serializable {
    // Methods
    public abstract void readExternal(ObjectInput in);
    public abstract void writeExternal(ObjectOutput out);
}
```

Methods

readExternal

```
public abstract void readExternal(ObjectInput in)
                throws IOException, ClassNotFoundException
```

Parameters   in   The object input stream to use.

Throws   ClassNotFoundException

                If the class of the object being deserialized cannot be found.

             IOException   If any kind of I/O error occurs.

Description   This method reads an object from the given stream. This method has full responsibility for restoring the object's state. The implementation of readExternal() should read data in the format that is written out by writeExternal(). In general, an implementation should call methods of DataInput to read primitive types and methods of ObjectInput to read objects, strings, and arrays.

writeExternal

```
public abstract void writeExternal(ObjectOutput out)
                throws IOException
```

Parameters   out   The object output stream to use.

Throws   IOException   If any kind of I/O error occurs.

Description   This method writes an object to the given stream. This method has full responsibility for saving the object's state. The implementation of writeExternal() should write data in the format that is read by readExternal(). In general, an implementation should call methods of DataOutput to write primitive types and methods of ObjectOutput to write objects, strings, and arrays.

See Also

ClassNotFoundException, DataInput, DataOutput, IOException, ObjectInput, ObjectOutput, Serializable

11.16   File

Synopsis

Class Name:	java.io.File
Superclass:	java.lang.Object
Immediate Subclasses:	None
Interfaces Implemented:	None
Availability:	JDK 1.0 or later

Description

The File class provides methods to obtain information about files and directories. A File object encapsulates the name of a file or a directory. A File object can list the files in a directory, check the existence and type of a file, create new directories, and rename and delete files, among other things. However, the File class does not handle I/O to files. Actual reading and writing is accomplished using RandomAccessFile, FileReader, FileWriter, FileInputStream, and FileOutputStream objects.

The File class also defines some constants for the platform-specific directory and path separator characters. If you want to avoid putting system-dependent path information in your program, you may want to reference all files relative to the directory in which your program is running (i.e., the current directory). Alternatively, you can use java.awt.FileDialog to prompt the user for system-dependent paths.

Many of the methods in File throw a SecurityException if the application does not have sufficient privileges for the requested operation. This happens in two steps. First, System.getSecurityManager() is called. If a SecurityManager has been installed, it is queried for the appropriate permission. For example, File.canRead() calls SecurityManager.canRead(). If the application does not have permission to read the specified file, the SecurityManager throws a SecurityException, which in turn is thrown by File.canRead().

Class Summary

```
public class java.io.File extends java.lang.Object
                    implements java.io.Serializable {
  // Constants
  public final static String pathSeparator;
  public final static char pathSeparatorChar;
  public final static String separator;
  public final static char separatorChar;

  // Constructors
  public File(String path);
```

```
    public File(String path, String name);
    public File(File dir, String name);

    // Instance Methods
    public boolean canRead();
    public boolean canWrite();
    public boolean delete();
    public boolean equals(Object obj);
    public boolean exists();
    public String getAbsolutePath();
    public String getCanonicalPath();              // New in 1.1
    public String getName();
    public String getParent();
    public String getPath();
    public int hashCode();
    public native boolean isAbsolute();
    public boolean isDirectory();
    public boolean isFile();
    public long lastModified();
    public long length();
    public String[] list();
    public String[] list(FilenameFilter filter);
    public boolean mkdir();
    public boolean mkdirs();
    public boolean renameTo(File dest);
    public String toString();
}
```

Constants

pathSeparator

public final static String pathSeparator

    Description   This string holds the value of System.getProperty("path.separator"). It contains the character that separates paths in a path list. Usually it is ":" or ";".

pathSeparatorChar

public final static char pathSeparatorChar

    Description   This variable holds the first (and only) character in pathSeparator.

separator

public final static String separator

    Description   This string holds the value of System.getProperty("file.separator"). It contains the character that separates directory and filenames in a path string. Usually it is "/" or "\".

separatorChar

   public final static char separatorChar

      Description   This variable holds the first (and only) character in separator.

Constructors

File

   public File(String path)

      Parameters   path   A full pathname (i.e., a directory and filename).

      Description   This constructor creates a File object that represents the file specified by path.

   public File(String path, String name)

      Parameters   path   A directory path.

                     name   A filename.

      Description   This constructor creates a File object that represents the file with the specified name in the directory described by path. In other words, the full pathname is the directory, followed by the separator character, followed by the filename.

                     If path is null, the constructor creates a File that represents the file with the specified name in the current directory. The current directory is the directory in which the program is running.

   public File(File dir, String name)

      Parameters   dir   A File object that represents a directory.

                     name   A filename.

      Description   This constructor creates a File object that represents the file with the specified name in the directory described by the File object dir. In other words, the full pathname is the directory represented by dir, followed by the separator character, followed by the filename.

                     If dir is null, the constructor creates a File that represents the file with the specified name in the current directory. The current directory is the directory in which the program is running.

Instance Methods

canRead

   public boolean canRead()

      Returns   A boolean value that indicates if the file is readable.

Throws   SecurityException

                    If the application does not have permission to read the File.

Description   This method returns true if File corresponds to an existing, readable file or directory. Otherwise it returns false.

canWrite

public boolean canWrite()

Returns   A boolean value that indicates if the file is writable.

Throws   SecurityException

                    If the application does not have permission to write to the File.

Description   This method returns true if File corresponds to an existing, writable file or directory. Otherwise it returns false.

delete

public boolean delete()

Returns   true if the file is deleted; otherwise false.

Throws   SecurityException

                    If the application does not have permission to delete the file.

Description   This method attempts to delete the file or directory associated with this File object. A directory is only deleted if it is empty.

equals

public boolean equals(Object obj)

Parameters   obj   The Object to be compared.

Returns   true if the objects are equal; false if they are not.

Overrides   Object.equals()

Description   This method returns true if obj is an instance of File that encapsulates the same pathname as this object.

exists

public boolean exists()

Returns   true if the file or directory exists; false otherwise.

Throws   SecurityException

                    If the application does not have permission to read the File.

Description   This method returns true if this File corresponds to an existing file or directory.

getAbsolutePath

```
public String getAbsolutePath()
```
Returns   A String that contains the absolute pathname.

Description   This method returns the absolute pathname of the file or directory associated with this File.

getCanonicalPath

```
public String getCanonicalPath() throws IOException
```
Availability   New as of JDK 1.1

Returns   A String that contains the canonical, or exact, pathname.

Throws   IOException   If any kind of I/O error occurs.

Description   This method returns the canonical pathname of the file or directory associated with this File.

getName

```
public String getName()
```
Returns   A String that contains the filename.

Description   This method returns the filename associated with this File. The string returned does not include the name of the directory.

getParent

```
public String getParent()
```
Returns   A String that contains the parent directory of the file, or null if it does not exist.

Description   This method returns the name of the parent directory of the file or directory associated with this File. The algorithm used returns everything in the pathname before the last separator character.

getPath

```
public String getPath()
```
Returns   A String that contains the pathname of the file.

Description   This method returns the full pathname associated with this File.

hashCode

```
public int hashCode()
```
Returns   A hashcode value for this file.

Overrides   Object.hashCode()

Description   This method returns a hashcode based on the pathname associated with this File.

isAbsolute

public native boolean isAbsolute()

Returns   true if the File represents an absolute path; false otherwise.

Description   This method indicates if the File represents an absolute path; what constitutes an absolute path is system-dependent.

isDirectory

public boolean isDirectory()

Returns   true if the File represents a directory; false otherwise.

Throws   SecurityException

If the application does not have permission to read the File.

Description   This method returns true if this File corresponds to a directory.

isFile

public boolean isFile()

Returns   true if the File represents a normal file; false otherwise.

Throws   SecurityException

If the application does not have permission to read the File.

Description   This method returns true if this File corresponds to a normal file, as opposed to an alternative, such as a directory, a named pipe, or a device.

lastModified

public long lastModified()

Returns   The time the file was last modified, or 0L if the file does not exist.

Throws   SecurityException

If the application does not have permission to read the File.

Description   This method returns the modification time of the file or directory that corresponds to this File. The format of the time returned is useful for comparing modification times; it's not meant to be used for other purposes.

length

public long length()

Returns	The file length, in bytes, or 0L if the file does not exist.
Throws	SecurityException
	If the application does not have permission to read the File.
Description	This method returns the length of the file or directory that corresponds to this File.

list

public String[] list()

Returns	An array of the names of the files and directories contained by this File, or null if this File is not a directory.
Throws	SecurityException
	If the application does not have permission to read the File.
Description	This method returns the contents of a directory. The current directory and the parent directory are not included in the list.

public String[] list(FilenameFilter filter)

Parameters	filter	A filter to use.
Returns	An array of the names of the files and directories contained by this File and filtered by filter, or null if this File is not a directory.	
Throws	SecurityException	
	If the application does not have permission to read the File.	
Description	This method returns of the contents of a directory as selected by the given FilenameFilter object. Specifically, a name is included if the FilenameFilter object's accept() method returns true for that name.	

If filter is null, this method is equivalent to, but slower than, list().

mkdir

public boolean mkdir()

Returns	true if the directory is created; false otherwise.
Throws	SecurityException
	If the application does not have permission to write to the File.

Description   This method creates a directory with the pathname specified by this `File`.

mkdirs

```
public boolean mkdirs()
```
Returns   true if the directory is created; false otherwise.
Throws   `SecurityException`
                If the application does not have permission to write to the `File`.
Description   This method creates a directory with the pathname specified by this `File`. The method also creates all the parent directories if necessary.

renameTo

```
public boolean renameTo(File dest)
```
Parameters   dest   A `File` that specifies the new name.
Returns   true if the name is changed; false otherwise.
Throws   `SecurityException`
                  If the application does not have permission to write to this `File` or the file represented by dest.
Description   This method changes the pathname of this `File` to the pathname specified by dest.

toString

```
public String toString()
```
Returns   A `String` that contains the pathname of this `File`.
Overrides   `Object.toString()`
Description   This method returns a string representation of this `File` object.

Inherited Methods

Method	Inherited From	Method	Inherited From
clone()	Object	finalize()	Object
getClass()	Object	notify()	Object
notifyAll()	Object	wait()	Object
wait(long)	Object	wait(long, int)	Object

See Also

FileInputStream, FilenameFilter, FileOutputStream, FileReader, FileWriter, IOException, SecurityException

11.17   FileDescriptor

Synopsis

Class Name: java.io.FileDescriptor
Superclass: java.lang.Object
Immediate Subclasses: None
Interfaces Implemented: None
Availability: JDK 1.0 or later

Description

The FileDescriptor class encapsulates system-specific handles for files and sockets. Instances of this class can be properly constructed only by native methods of other classes. In other words, you should not be constructing your own file descriptors. Currently, file descriptors are returned by the following methods:

*   DatagramSocketImpl.getFileDescriptor()
*   FileInputStream.getFD()
*   FileOutputStream.getFD()
*   RandomAccessFile.getFD()
*   SocketImpl.getFileDescriptor()

A file descriptor can be used in the constructors for FileInputStream, FileOutputStream, FileReader, and FileWriter.

Class Summary

```
public final class java.io.FileDescriptor extends java.lang.Object {
    // Constants
    public final static FileDescriptor err;
    public final static FileDescriptor in;
    public final static FileDescriptor out;

    // Instance Methods
    public native void sync();                    // New in 1.1
    public native boolean valid();
}
```

Constants

err

```
public final static FileDescriptor err
```
    Description   The file descriptor for standard error. See System.err, which is constructed from this constant.

in

```
public final static FileDescriptor in
```
    Description   The file descriptor for standard input. See System.in, which is constructed from this constant.

out

```
public final static FileDescriptor out
```
    Description   The file descriptor for standard output. See System.out, which is constructed from this constant.

Instance Methods

sync

```
public native void sync() throws SyncFailedException
```
    Availability   New as of JDK 1.1
    Throws   SyncFailedException
                  If synchronization cannot be accomplished.
    Description   This method causes the underlying device to be updated to a current state, which typically involves asking the operating system to flush its buffer. For example, if this FileDescriptor refers to a file on a physical disk, the disk is physically updated to reflect the current state of the object this descriptor represents. This method allows an application to put a device in a known state, which could be useful for transaction processing.

valid

```
public native boolean valid()
```
    Returns   true if the FileDescriptor represents a valid, open device; false otherwise.
    Description   This method returns a boolean value that indicates the validity of the file descriptor.

Inherited Methods

Method	Inherited From	Method	Inherited From
clone()	Object	equals(Object)	Object
finalize()	Object	getClass()	Object
hashCode()	Object	notify()	Object
notifyAll()	Object	toString()	Object
wait()	Object	wait(long)	Object
wait(long, int)	Object		

See Also

FileInputStream, FileOutputStream, FileReader, FileWriter, SyncFailedException, System

11.18   FileInputStream

Synopsis

Class Name:	java.io.FileInputStream
Superclass:	java.io.InputStream
Immediate Subclasses:	None
Interfaces Implemented:	None
Availability:	JDK 1.0 or later

Description

The FileInputStream class represents a byte stream that reads data from a file. The file can be specified using a FileDescriptor, a File object, or a String that represents a pathname. All of the constructors can throw a SecurityException if the application does not have permission to read from the specified file.

FileInputStream provides a low-level interface for reading data from a file. You should wrap a FileInputStream with a DataInputStream if you need a higher-level interface that can handle reading strings and binary data. You should also think about wrapping a FileInputStream with a BufferedInputStream to increase reading efficiency.

Data must be read sequentially from a FileInputStream; you can skip forward, but you cannot move back. If you need random access to file data, use the RandomAccessFile class instead.

Class Summary

```
public class java.io.FileInputStream extends java.io.InputStream {
    // Constructors
    public FileInputStream(String name);
    public FileInputStream(File file);
    public FileInputStream(FileDescriptor fdObj);

    // Public Instance Methods
    public native int available();
    public native void close();
    public final FileDescriptor getFD();
    public native int read();
    public int read(byte[] b);
    public int read(byte[] b, int off, int len);
    public native long skip(long n);

    // Protected Instance Methods
    protected void finalize();
}
```

Constructors

FileInputStream

public FileInputStream(String name) throws FileNotFoundException

Parameters	name	A String that contains the pathname of the file to be accessed. The path must conform to the requirements of the native operating system.
Throws	FileNotFoundException	
		If the named file cannot be found.
	SecurityException	
		If the application does not have permission to read the named file.
Description		This constructor creates a FileInputStream that gets its input from the file named by the specified String.

public FileInputStream(File file) throws FileNotFoundException

Parameters	file	The File to use as input.
Throws	FileNotFoundException	
		If the named file cannot be found.
	SecurityException	
		If the application does not have permission to read the named file.
Description		This constructor creates a FileInputStream that gets its input from the file represented by the specified File.

```
public FileInputStream(FileDescriptor fdObj)
```
Parameters   fdObj   The FileDescriptor of the file to use as input.

Throws   SecurityException

                               If the application does not have permission to
                               read the specified file.

                 NullPointerException

                               If FileDescriptor is null.

Description   This constructor creates a FileInputStream that gets its input
                 from the file identified by the given FileDescriptor.

Public Instance Methods

available

```
public native int available() throws IOException
```
Returns   The number of bytes that can be read from the file without
                 blocking.

Throws   IOException   If any kind of I/O error occurs.

Overrides   InputStream.available()

Description   This method returns the number of available bytes of data. Ini-
                 tially, this is the length of the file.

close

```
public native void close() throws IOException
```
Throws   IOException   If any kind of I/O error occurs.

Overrides   InputStream.close()

Description   This method closes this file input stream and releases any
                 resources used by it.

getFD

```
public final FileDescriptor getFD() throws IOException
```
Returns   The file descriptor for the file that supplies data for this stream.

Throws   IOException   If there is no FileDescriptor associated with
                               this object.

Description   This method returns the file descriptor associated with the data
                 source of this FileInputStream.

read

```
public native int read() throws IOException
```
Returns   The next byte of data or –1 if the end of the stream is encoun-
                 tered.

Throws   IOException   If any kind of I/O error occurs.

Overrides   InputStream.read()

Description   This method reads the next byte of data from the file. The method blocks if no input is available.

`public int read(byte[] b) throws IOException`

Parameters   b   An array of bytes to be filled from the stream.

Returns   The actual number of bytes read or –1 if the end of the stream is encountered immediately.

Throws   IOException   If any kind of I/O error occurs.

Overrides   InputStream.read(byte[])

Description   This method reads data into the given array. The method fills the array if enough bytes are available. The method blocks until some input is available.

`public int read(byte[] b, int off, int len) throws IOException`

Parameters   b   An array of bytes to be filled from the stream.

                off   An offset into the byte array.

                len   The number of bytes to read.

Returns   The actual number of bytes read or –1 if the end of the stream is encountered immediately.

Throws   IOException   If any kind of I/O error occurs.

Overrides   InputStream.read(byte[], int, int)

Description   This method reads len bytes of data into the given array, starting at element off. The method blocks until some input is available.

skip

`public native long skip(long n) throws IOException`

Parameters   n   The number of bytes to skip.

Returns   The actual number of bytes skipped.

Throws   IOException   If any kind of I/O error occurs.

Overrides   FilterInputStream.skip()

Description   This method skips n bytes of input in the stream.

Protected Instance Methods

finalize

`protected void finalize() throws IOException`

Throws   IOException   If any kind of I/O error occurs.

Overrides   Object.finalize()

Description   This method is called when the FileInputStream is garbage collected to ensure that close() is called. If the stream has a valid file descriptor, the close() method is called to free the system resources used by this stream.

Inherited Methods

Method	Inherited From	Method	Inherited From
clone()	Object	equals(Object)	Object
getClass()	Object	hashCode()	Object
mark(int)	InputStream	markSupported()	InputStream
notify()	Object	notifyAll()	Object
reset()	InputStream	toString()	Object
wait()	Object	wait(long)	Object
wait(long, int)	Object		

See Also

BufferedInputStream, DataInputStream, File, FileDescriptor, FileNotFoundException, InputStream, IOException, NullPointerException, RandomAccessFile, SecurityException

11.19   FilenameFilter

Synopsis

Interface Name: java.io.FilenameFilter
Super-interface: None
Immediate Sub-interfaces:

                None
Implemented by: None
Availability: JDK 1.0 or later

Description

The FilenameFilter interface is implemented by a class that wants to filter the filenames that should be included in a list of filenames. For example, the list() method of the File class can take a FilenameFilter object to filter the filenames that are listed. The java.awt.FileDialog class also uses a FilenameFilter to limit the choices that are presented to the user.

Interface Declaration

```
public abstract interface java.io.FilenameFilter {
    // Methods
    public abstract boolean accept(File dir, String name);
}
```

Methods

accept

`public abstract boolean accept(File dir, String name)`

Parameters	dir	The directory that contains the file.
	name	The name of the file.
Returns		true if the file should be shown; false otherwise.
Description		This method returns a boolean value that indicates whether or not a file should be included in a list of filenames. The method should return true if a file should be included; otherwise it should return false. A simple filter might return true for filenames with a certain extension, like .java. A more complex filter could check the directory name, the file's readability, and last modification time, for example.

See Also

File

11.20   FileNotFoundException

Synopsis

Class Name:	java.io.FileNotFoundException
Superclass:	java.io.IOException
Immediate Subclasses:	None
Interfaces Implemented:	None
Availability:	JDK 1.0 or later

Description

A FileNotFoundException is thrown when a specified file cannot be located.

Class Summary

```
public class java.io.FileNotFoundException extends java.io.IOException {
    // Constructors
    public FileNotFoundException();
    public FileNotFoundException(String s);
}
```

Constructors

FileNotFoundException

public FileNotFoundException()

Description	This constructor creates a FileNotFoundException with no detail message.

public FileNotFoundException(String s)

Parameters	s	The detail message.
Description	This constructor creates a FileNotFoundException with the specified detail message.

Inherited Methods

Method	Inherited From	Method	Inherited From
clone()	Object	equals(Object)	Object
fillInStackTrace()	Throwable	finalize()	Object
getClass()	Object	getLocalizedMessage()	Throwable
getMessage()	Throwable	hashCode()	Object
notify()	Object	notifyAll()	Object
printStackTrace()	Throwable	printStack-Trace(PrintStream)	Throwable
printStack-Trace(PrintWriter)	Throwable	toString()	Object
wait()	Object	wait(long)	Object
wait(long, int)	Object		

See Also

Exception, IOException, Throwable

11.21   FileOutputStream

Synopsis

Class Name: java.io.FileOutputStream
Superclass: java.io.OutputStream
Immediate Subclasses: None
Interfaces Implemented: None
Availability: JDK 1.0 or later

Description

The FileOutputStream class represents a byte stream that writes data to a file. The file can be specified using a FileDescriptor, a File object, or a String that represents a pathname. All of the constructors can throw a SecurityException if the application does not have permission to write to the specified file.

FileOutputStream provides a low-level interface for writing data to a file. Wrap a FileOutputStream with a DataOutputStream or a PrintStream if you need a higher-level interface that can handle writing strings and binary data. You should also think about wrapping a FileOutputStream with a BufferedOutputStream to increase writing efficiency.

Data must be written sequentially to a FileOutputStream; you can either overwrite existing data or append data to the end of the file. If you need random access to file data, use the RandomAccessFile class instead.

Class Summary

```
public class java.io.FileOutputStream extends java.io.OutputStream {
    // Constructors
    public FileOutputStream(String name);
    public FileOutputStream(String name, boolean append);    // New in 1.1
    public FileOutputStream(File file);
    public FileOutputStream(FileDescriptor fdObj);

    // Public Instance Methods
    public native void close();
    public final FileDescriptor getFD();
    public native void write(int b);
    public void write(byte[] b);
    public void write(byte[] b, int off, int len);

    // Protected Instance Methods
    protected void finalize();
}
```

Constructors

FileOutputStream

public FileOutputStream(String name) throws IOException

Parameters	name	A String that contains the pathname of the file to be used for output. The path must conform to the requirements of the native operating system.
Throws	FileNotFoundException	
		If the named file cannot be found.
	SecurityException	
		If the application does not have permission to write to the named file.
Description		This constructor creates a FileOutputStream that sends its output to the file named by the specified String.

public FileOutputStream(String name, boolean append)
    throws IOException

Availability	New as of JDK 1.1	
Parameters	name	A String that contains the pathname of the file to be used for output. The path must conform to the requirements of the native operating system.
	append	Specifies whether or not data is appended to the output stream.
Throws	FileNotFoundException	
		If the named file cannot be found.
	SecurityException	
		If the application does not have permission to write to the named file.
Description		This constructor creates a FileOutputStream that sends its output to the named file. If append is true, the stream is positioned at the end of the file, and data is appended to the end of the file. Otherwise, if append is false, the stream is positioned at the beginning of the file, and any previous data is overwritten.

public FileOutputStream(File file) throws IOException

Parameters	file	The File to use as output.
Throws	FileNotFoundException	
		If the named file cannot be found.
	SecurityException	
		If the application does not have permission to write to the named file.

Description   This constructor creates a `FileOutputStream` that sends its output to the file represented by the specified `File`.

`public FileOutputStream(FileDescriptor fdObj)`

Parameters   fdObj   The `FileDescriptor` of the file to use as output.

Throws   SecurityException
                              If the application does not have permission to write to the specified file.

               NullPointerException
                              If `FileDescriptor` is `null`.

Description   This constructor creates a `FileOutputStream` that sends its output to the file identified by the given `FileDescriptor`.

Public Instance Methods

close

`public native void close() throws IOException`

Throws   IOException   If any kind of I/O error occurs.

Overrides   `OutputStream.close()`

Description   This method closes this file output stream and releases any resources used by it.

getFD

`public final FileDescriptor getFD() throws IOException`

Throws   IOException   If there is no `FileDescriptor` associated with this object.

Description   This method returns the file descriptor associated with the data source of this `FileOutputStream`.

write

`public native void write(int b) throws IOException`

Parameters   b   The value to write to the stream.

Throws   IOException   If any kind of I/O error occurs.

Overrides   `OutputStream.write(int)`

Description   This method writes a byte containing the low-order eight bits of the given value to the output stream.

`public void write(byte[] b) throws IOException`

Parameters   b   An array of bytes to write to the stream.

Throws   IOException   If any kind of I/O error occurs.

Overrides   `OutputStream.write(byte[])`

Description   This method writes the entire contents of the given array to the output stream.

```
public void write(byte[] b, int off, int len) throws IOException
```
    Parameters   b   An array of bytes to write to the stream.

                      off   An offset into the byte array.

                      len   The number of bytes to write.

Throws   IOException   If any kind of I/O error occurs.

Overrides   OutputStream.write(byte[], int, int)

Description   This method writes len bytes from the given array, starting at element off, to the output stream.

Protected Instance Methods

finalize

```
protected void finalize() throws IOException
```
Throws   IOException   If any kind of I/O error occurs.

Description   This method is called when the FileOutputStream is garbage-collected to ensure that close() is called. If the stream has a valid file descriptor, the close() method is called to free the system resources used by this stream.

Inherited Methods

Method	Inherited From	Method	Inherited From
clone()	Object	equals(Object)	Object
flush()	OutputStream	getClass()	Object
hashCode()	Object	notify()	Object
notifyAll()	Object	toString()	Object
wait()	Object	wait(long)	Object
wait(long, int)	Object		

See Also

BufferedOutputStream, DataOutputStream, File, FileDescriptor, FileNot-FoundException, IOException, NullPointerException, OutputStream, PrintStream, RandomAccessFile, SecurityException

11.22   FileReader

Synopsis

Class Name:	java.io.FileReader
Superclass:	java.io.InputStreamReader
Immediate Subclasses:	None
Interfaces Implemented:	None
Availability:	New as of JDK 1.1

Description

The FileReader class represents a character stream that reads data from a file. It is a subclass of InputStreamReader that uses a default buffer size (8192 bytes) to read bytes from a file and the default character encoding scheme to convert the bytes to characters. If you need to specify the character encoding or the buffer size, wrap an InputStreamReader around a FileInputStream.

The file can be specified using a FileDescriptor, a File object, or a String that represents a pathname. All of the constructors can throw a SecurityException if the application does not have permission to read from the specified file.

FileReader provides a low-level interface for reading character data from a file. You should think about wrapping a FileReader with a BufferedReader to increase reading efficiency.

If you need to read binary data from a file, you should use a FileInputStream wrapped by a DataInputStream instead.

Class Summary

```
public class java.io.FileReader extends java.io.InputStreamReader {
    // Constructors
    public FileReader(String fileName);
    public FileReader(File file);
    public FileReader(FileDescriptor fd);
}
```

Constructors

FileInputStream

public FileReader(String fileName) throws FileNotFoundException

Parameters   fileName   A String that contains the pathname of the file to be accessed. The path must conform to the requirements of the native operating system.

Throws   `FileNotFoundException`

>   If the named file cannot be found.

                `SecurityException`

>   If the application does not have permission to read the named file.

Description   This constructor creates a `FileReader` that gets its input from the file named by the specified `String`.

`public FileReader(File file) throws FileNotFoundException`

Parameters   `file`   The `File` to use as input.

Throws   `FileNotFoundException`

>   If the named file cannot be found.

                `SecurityException`

>   If the application does not have permission to read the named file.

Description   This constructor creates a `FileReader` that gets its input from the file represented by the specified `File`.

`public FileReader(FileDescriptor fdObj)`

Parameters   `fdObj`   The `FileDescriptor` of the file to use as input.

Throws   `SecurityException`

>   If the application does not have permission to read the specified file.

                `NullPointerException`

>   If `FileDescriptor` is `null`.

Description   This constructor creates a `FileReader` that gets its input from the file identified by the given `FileDescriptor`.

Inherited Methods

Method	Inherited From	Method	Inherited From
clone()	Object	close()	InputStreamReader
equals(Object)	Object	finalize()	Object
getClass()	Object	getEncoding()	InputStreamReader
hashCode()	Object	mark(int)	Reader
markSupported()	Reader	notify()	Object
notifyAll()	Object	read()	InputStreamReader
read(char[])	Reader	read(char[], int, int)	InputStreamReader
ready()	InputStreamReader	reset()	Reader
skip(long)	Reader	toString()	Object
wait()	Object	wait(long)	Object
wait(long, int)	Object		

See Also

BufferedReader, DataInputStream, File, FileDescriptor, FileInputStream, FileNotFoundException, InputStreamReader, IOException, NullPointerException, Reader, SecurityException

---

11.23   FileWriter

Synopsis

Class Name:	java.io.FileWriter
Superclass:	java.io.OutputStreamWriter
Immediate Subclasses:	None
Interfaces Implemented:	None
Availability:	New as of JDK 1.1

Description

The FileWriter class represents a character stream that writes data to a file. It is a subclass of OutputStreamWriter that uses a default buffer size (8192 bytes) to write bytes to a file and the default character encoding scheme to convert characters to bytes. If you need to specify the character encoding or the buffer size, wrap an OutputStreamWriter around a FileOutputStream.

The file can be specified using a FileDescriptor, a File object, or a String that represents a pathname. All of the constructors can throw a SecurityException if the application does not have permission to write to the specified file.

FileWriter provides a low-level interface for writing character data to a file. You should think about wrapping a FileWriter with a BufferedWriter to increase writing efficiency.

If you need to write binary data to a file, you should use a FileOutputStream wrapped by a DataOutputStream or a PrintStream instead.

Class Summary

```
public class java.io.FileWriter extends java.io.OutputStreamWriter {
  // Constructors
  public FileWriter(String fileName);
  public FileWriter(String fileName, boolean append);
  public FileWriter(File file);
  public FileWriter(FileDescriptor fd);
}
```

Constructors

FileWriter

public FileWriter(String fileName) throws IOException

Parameters	fileName	The pathname of the file to use as output.
Throws	FileNotFoundException	
		If the named file cannot be found.
	SecurityException	
		If the application does not have permission to write to the named file.
Description		This constructor creates a FileWriter that sends its output to the file named by the specified String.

public FileWriter(String fileName, boolean append)
      throws IOException

Parameters	fileName	The pathname of the file to use as output.
	append	Specifies whether or not data is appended to the output stream.
Throws	FileNotFoundException	
		If the named file cannot be found.
	SecurityException	
		If the application does not have permission to write to the named file.
Description		This constructor creates a FileWriter that sends its output to the named file. If append is true, the stream is positioned at the end of the file, and data is appended to the end of the file. Otherwise, if append is false, the stream is positioned at the beginning of the file, and any previous data is overwritten.

public FileWriter(File file) throws IOException

Parameters	file	The File to use as output.
Throws	FileNotFoundException	
		If the named file cannot be found.
	SecurityException	
		If the application does not have permission to write to the named file.
Description		This constructor creates a FileWriter that sends its output to the file represented by the specified File object.

public FileWriter(FileDescriptor fdObj)

Parameters	fdObj	The FileDescriptor of the file to use as output.

Throws   SecurityException

>   If the application does not have permission to write to the specified file.

NullPointerException

>   If FileDescriptor is null.

Description   This constructor creates a FileWriter that sends its output to the file identified by the given FileDescriptor.

Inherited Methods

Method	Inherited From	Method	Inherited From
clone()	Object	close()	Output-StreamWriter
equals(Object)	Object	finalize()	Object
flush()	Output-StreamWriter	getClass()	Object
getEncoding()	Output-StreamWriter	hashCode()	Object
notify()	Object	notifyAll()	Object
toString()	Object	wait()	Object
wait(long)	Object	wait(long, int)	Object
write(int)	Output-StreamWriter	write(char[])	Writer
write(char[], int, int)	Output-StreamWriter	write(String)	Writer
write(String, int, int)	Output-StreamWriter		

See Also

BufferedWriter, DataOutputStream, File, FileDescriptor, FileNotFoundException, FileOutputStream, IOException, NullPointerException, OutputStreamWriter, SecurityException, Writer

11.24   FilterInputStream

Synopsis

Class Name:	java.io.FilterInputStream
Superclass:	java.io.InputStream
Immediate Subclasses:	java.io.BufferedInputStream,
	java.io.DataInputStream,
	java.io.LineNumberInputStream,
	java.io.PushbackInputStream,
	java.util.zip.CheckedInputStream,
	java.util.zip.InflaterInputStream
Interfaces Implemented:	None
Availability:	JDK 1.0 or later

Description

The FilterInputStream class is the superclass of all of the input stream classes that filter input. Each of the subclasses of FilterInputStream works by wrapping an existing input stream, called the *underlying input stream*, and providing additional functionality. The methods of FilterInputStream simply override the methods of InputStream with versions that call the corresponding methods of the underlying stream.

FilterInputStream cannot be instantiated directly; it must be subclassed. An instance of one of the subclasses of FilterInputStream is constructed with another InputStream object. The methods of a subclass of FilterInputStream should override some methods in order to extend their behavior or provide some sort of filtering.

Class Summary

```
public class java.io.FilterInputStream extends java.io.InputStream {
  // Variables
  protected InputStream in;

  // Constructors
  protected FilterInputStream(InputStream in);

  // Instance Methods
  public int available();
  public void close();
  public synchronized void mark(int readlimit);
  public boolean markSupported();
  public int read();
  public int read(byte[] b);
  public int read(byte[] b, int off, int len);
```

```
    public synchronized void reset();
    public long skip(long n);
}
```

Variables

in

protected InputStream in

    Description   The underlying stream that this FilterInputStream wraps or filters.

Constructors

FilterInputStream

protected FilterInputStream(InputStream in)

    Parameters   in   The input stream to filter.

    Description   This constructor creates a FilterInputStream that gets its data from in.

Instance Methods

available

public int available() throws IOException

    Returns   The number of bytes that can be read without blocking.

    Throws   IOException   If any kind of I/O error occurs.

    Overrides   InputStream.available()

    Description   This method calls the available() method of the underlying stream and returns the result.

close

public void close() throws IOException

    Throws   IOException   If any kind of I/O error occurs.

    Overrides   InputStream.close()

    Description   This method calls the close() method of the underlying stream, which releases any system resources associated with this object.

mark

public synchronized void mark(int readlimit)

    Parameters   readlimit   The maximum number of bytes that can be read before the saved position becomes invalid.

    Overrides   InputStream.mark()

Description   This method calls the mark() method of the underlying stream. If the underlying stream supports mark() and reset(), this method causes the FilterInputStream to remember its current position. A subsequent call to reset() causes the object to return to that saved position, and thus re-read a portion of the input.

markSupported

```
public boolean markSupported()
```

Returns   true if this stream supports mark() and reset(); false otherwise.

Overrides   InputStream.markSupported()

Description   This method calls the markSupported() method of the underlying stream and returns the result.

read

```
public int read() throws IOException
```

Returns   The next byte of data or –1 if the end of the stream is encountered.

Throws   IOException   If any kind of I/O error occurs.

Overrides   InputStream.read()

Description   This method calls the read() method of the underlying stream and returns the result. This method blocks until some data is available, the end of the stream is detected, or an exception is thrown.

```
public int read(byte[] b) throws IOException
```

Parameters   b   An array of bytes to be filled from the stream.

Returns   The actual number of bytes read or –1 if the end of the stream is encountered immediately.

Throws   IOException   If any kind of I/O error occurs.

Overrides   InputStream.read(byte[])

Description   This method reads bytes of input to fill the given array. It does this by calling read(b, 0, b.length), which allows subclasses to only override read(byte[], int, int) and have read(byte[]) work automatically. The method blocks until some data is available.

```
public int read(byte[] b, int off, int len) throws IOException
```

Parameters   b   An array of bytes to be filled from the stream.

off	An offset into the byte array.
len	The number of bytes to read.

Returns   The actual number of bytes read or -1 if the end of the stream is encountered immediately.

Throws   IOException   If any kind of I/O error occurs.

Overrides   InputStream.read(byte[], int, int)

Description   This method reads up to len bytes of input into the given array starting at index off. It does this by calling the read(byte[], int, int) method of the underlying stream and returning the result. The method blocks until some data is available.

reset

```
public synchronized void reset() throws IOException
```

Throws   IOException   If there was no previous call to the mark() method or the saved position has been invalidated.

Overrides   InputStream.reset()

Description   This method calls the reset() method of the underlying stream. If the underlying stream supports mark() and reset(), this method sets the position of the FilterInputStream to a position that was saved by a previous call to mark(). Subsequent bytes read from this FilterInputStream will begin from the saved position and continue normally.

skip

```
public long skip(long n) throws IOException
```

Parameters   n   The number of bytes to skip.

Returns   The actual number of bytes skipped.

Throws   IOException   If any kind of I/O error occurs.

Overrides   InputStream.skip()

Description   This method skips n bytes of input. It calls the skip() method of the underlying stream.

Inherited Methods

Method	Inherited From	Method	Inherited From
clone()	Object	equals(Object)	Object
finalize()	Object	getClass()	Object
hashCode()	Object	notify()	Object
notifyAll()	Object	toString()	Object
wait()	Object	wait(long)	Object

Method	Inherited From	Method	Inherited From
wait(long, int)	Object		

See Also

BufferedInputStream, CheckedInputStream, DataInputStream, FilterInput-Stream, InflaterInputStream, InputStream, IOException, LineNumberInput-Stream, PushbackInputStream

11.25   FilterOutputStream

Synopsis

Class Name:	java.io.FilterOutputStream
Superclass:	java.io.ObjectStream
Immediate Subclasses:	java.io.BufferedOutputStream,
	java.io.DataOutputStream,
	java.io.PrintStream,
	java.util.zip.CheckedOutputStream,
	java.util.zip.DeflaterOutputStream
Interfaces Implemented:	None
Availability:	JDK 1.0 or later

Description

The FilterOutputStream class is the superclass of all of the output stream classes that filter output. Each of the subclasses of FilterOutputStream works by wrapping an existing output stream, called the *underlying output stream*, and providing additional functionality. The methods of FilterOutputStream simply override the methods of OutputStream with versions that call the corresponding methods of the underlying stream.

FilterOutputStream cannot be instantiated directly; it must be subclassed. An instance of one of the subclasses of FilterOutputStream is constructed with another OutputStream object. The methods of a subclass of FilterOutputStream should override some methods in order to extend their behavior or provide some sort of filtering.

Class Summary

```
public class java.io.FilterOutputStream extends java.io.OutputStream {
    // Variables
    protected OutputStream out;

    // Constructors
    public FilterOutputStream(OutputStream out);

    // Instance Methods
    public void close();
    public void flush();
    public void write(int b);
    public void write(byte[] b);
    public void write(byte[] b, int off, int len);
}
```

Variables

out

protected OutputStream out

  Description   The underlying stream that this FilterOutputStream wraps or
                 filters.

Constructors

FilterOutputStream

public FilterOutputStream(OutputStream out)

  Parameters   out   The output stream to filter.
  Description   This constructor creates a FilterOutputStream that sends its
                 data to out.

Instance Methods

close

public void close() throws IOException

  Throws   IOException   If any kind of I/O error occurs.
  Overrides   OutputStream.close()
  Description   This method calls the close() method of the underlying
                 stream, which releases any system resources associated with this
                 object.

flush

> public void flush() throws IOException

Throws	IOException If any kind of I/O error occurs.
Overrides	OutputStream.flush()
Description	This method calls the flush() method of the underlying stream, which forces any bytes that may be buffered by this FilterOutputStream to be written to the underlying device.

write

> public void write(int b) throws IOException

Parameters	b The value to write.
Throws	IOException If any kind of I/O error occurs.
Overrides	OutputStream.write(int)
Description	This method writes a byte containing the low-order eight bits of the given integer value. The method calls the write(int) method of the underlying stream.

> public void write(byte[] b) throws IOException

Parameters	b An array of bytes to write to the stream.
Throws	IOException If any kind of I/O error occurs.
Overrides	OutputStream.write(byte[])
Description	This method writes the bytes contained in the given array. To accomplish this, it calls write(b, 0, b.length). Subclasses need override only write(byte[], int, int) for this method to work automatically.

> public void write(byte[] b, int off, int len) throws IOException

Parameters	b An array of bytes to write to the stream.
	off An offset into the byte array.
	len The number of bytes to write.
Throws	IOException If any kind of I/O error occurs.
Overrides	OutputStream.write(byte[], int, int)
Description	This method writes len bytes contained in the given array, starting at offset off. It does this by calling write(int) for each element to be written in the array. This is inefficient, so subclasses should override write(byte[], int, int) with a method that efficiently writes a block of data.

Inherited Methods

Method	Inherited From	Method	Inherited From
clone()	Object	equals(Object)	Object
finalize()	Object	getClass()	Object
hashCode()	Object	notify()	Object
notifyAll()	Object	toString()	Object
wait()	Object	wait(long)	Object
wait(long, int)	Object		

See Also

BufferedOutputStream, CheckedOutputStream, DataOutputStream, DeflaterOutputStream, IOException, OutputStream, PrintStream

11.26   FilterReader

Synopsis

Class Name: java.io.FilterReader
Superclass: java.io.Reader
Immediate Subclasses: java.io.PushbackReader
Interfaces Implemented: None
Availability: New as of JDK 1.1

Description

The FilterReader class is the superclass of all of the reader classes that filter input. A subclass of FilterReader works by wrapping an existing reader, called the *underlying reader*, and providing additional functionality. The methods of Filter-Reader simply override the methods of Reader with versions that call the corresponding methods of the underlying reader.

FilterReader cannot be instantiated directly; it must be subclassed. An instance of a subclass of FilterReader is constructed with another Reader object. The methods of a subclass of FilterReader should override some methods in order to extend their behavior or provide some sort of filtering.

FilterReader is like FilterInputStream, except that it deals with a character stream instead of a byte stream.

Class Summary

```
public abstract class java.io.FilterReader extends java.io.Reader {
   // Variables
   protected Reader in;

   // Constructors
   protected FilterReader(Reader in);

   // Instance Methods
   public void close();
   public void mark(int readAheadLimit);
   public boolean markSupported();
   public int read();
   public int read(char[] cbuf, int off, int len);
   public boolean ready();
   public void reset();
   public long skip(long n);
}
```

Variables

in

protected Reader in

    Description   The underlying reader that this FilterReader wraps or filters.

Constructors

FilterReader

protected FilterReader(Reader in)

    Parameters   in   The input reader to filter.

    Description   This constructor creates a FilterReader that gets data from in.

Instance Methods

close

public void close() throws IOException

    Throws   IOException   If any kind of I/O error occurs.

    Overrides   Reader.close()

    Description   This method calls the close() method of the underlying reader, which releases any system resources associated with this object.

mark

```
public void mark(int readAheadLimit) throws IOException
```

Parameters   readAheadLimit

The maximum number of characters that can be read before the saved position becomes invalid.

Throws   IOException   If any kind of I/O error occurs.

Overrides   Reader.mark()

Description   This method calls the mark() method of the underlying reader. If the underlying reader supports mark() and reset(), this method causes the FilterReader to remember its current position. A subsequent call to reset() causes the object to return to that saved position, and thus re-read a portion of the input.

markSupported

```
public boolean markSupported()
```

Returns   true if this reader supports mark() and reset(); false otherwise.

Overrides   Reader.markSupported()

Description   This method calls the markSupported() method of the underlying reader and returns the result.

read

```
public int read() throws IOException
```

Returns   The next character of data or −1 if the end of the stream is encountered.

Throws   IOException   If any kind of I/O error occurs.

Overrides   Reader.read()

Description   This method calls the read() method of the underlying reader and returns the result. The method blocks until data is available, the end of the stream is detected, or an exception is thrown.

```
public int read(char[] cbuf, int off, int len) throws IOException
```

Parameters   cbuf   An array of characters to be filled from the stream.

              off   An offset into the array.

              len   The number of characters to read.

Returns   The actual number of characters read or −1 if the end of the stream is encountered immediately.

Throws   IOException   If any kind of I/O error occurs.
Overrides   Reader.read(char[], int, int)
Description   This method reads up to len characters of input into the given
               array starting at index off. It does this by calling the
               read(char[], int, int) method of the underlying reader and
               returning the result. The method blocks until some data is
               available.

ready

public boolean ready() throws IOException
Returns   A boolean value that indicates whether the reader is ready to be
               read.
Throws   IOException   If the stream is closed.
Overrides   Reader.ready()
Description   This method calls the ready() method of the underlying
               reader and returns the result. If the underlying stream is ready,
               this method returns true. The underlying stream is ready if the
               next read() is guaranteed not to block.

reset

public void reset() throws IOException
Throws   IOException   If the stream is closed, mark() has not been
                             called, or the saved position has been invali-
                             dated.
Overrides   Reader.reset()
Description   This method calls the reset() method of the underlying
               reader. If the underlying reader supports mark() and reset(),
               this method sets the position of the FilteredReader to a posi-
               tion that was saved by a previous call to mark(). Subsequent
               characters read from this FilteredReader will begin from the
               saved position and continue normally.

skip

public long skip(long n) throws IOException
Parameters   n   The number of characters to skip.
Returns   The actual number of characters skipped.
Throws   IOException   If any kind of I/O error occurs.
Overrides   Reader.skip()
Description   This method skips n characters of input. It calls the skip()
               method of the underlying reader.

Inherited Methods

Method	Inherited From	Method	Inherited From
clone()	Object	equals(Object)	Object
finalize()	Object	getClass()	Object
hashCode()	Object	notify()	Object
notifyAll()	Object	toString()	Object
wait()	Object	wait(long)	Object
wait(long, int)	Object		

See Also

FilterInputStream, IOException, PushbackReader, Reader

11.27   FilterWriter

Synopsis

Class Name:	java.io.FilterWriter
Superclass:	java.io.Writer
Immediate Subclasses:	None
Interfaces Implemented:	None
Availability:	New as of JDK 1.1

Description

The FilterWriter class is the superclass of all of the writer classes that filter output. A subclass of FilterWriter works by wrapping an existing writer, called the *underlying writer,* and providing additional functionality. The methods of Filter-Writer simply override the methods of Writer with versions that call the corresponding methods of the underlying writer.

FilterWriter cannot be instantiated directly; it must be subclassed. An instance of a subclass of FilterWriter is constructed with another Writer object. The methods of a subclass of FilterWriter should override some methods in order to extend their behavior or provide some sort of filtering.

FilterWriter is like FilterOutputStream, except that it deals with a character stream instead of a byte stream.

Class Summary

```
public abstract class java.io.FilterWriter extends java.io.Writer {
  // Variables
  protected Writer out;

  // Constructors
  protected FilterWriter(Writer out);

  // Instance Methods
  public void close();
  public void flush();
  public void write(int c);
  public void write(char[] cbuf, int off, int len);
  public void write(String str, int off, int len);
}
```

Variables

out

protected Writer out

    Description   The underlying writer that this FilterWriter wraps or filters.

Constructors

FilterWriter

public FilterWriter(Writer out)

    Parameters   out   The output writer to filter.
    Description   This constructor creates a FilterWriter that sends data to out.

Instance Methods

close

public void close() throws IOException

    Throws   IOException   If any kind of I/O error occurs.
    Overrides   Writer.close()
    Description   This method calls the close() method of the underlying writer, which releases any system resources associated with this object.

flush

public void flush() throws IOException

    Throws   IOException   If any kind of I/O error occurs.
    Overrides   Writer.flush()
    Description   This method calls the flush() method of the underlying writer, which forces any characters that may be buffered by this FilterWriter to be written to the underlying device.

write

public void write(int c) throws IOException

Parameters	c	The value to write.
Throws	IOException	If any kind of I/O error occurs.
Overrides	Writer.write(int)	
Description	This method writes a character containing the low-order 16 bits of the given integer value. It calls the write(int) method of the underlying writer.	

public void write(char[] cbuf, int off, int len)
       throws IOException

Parameters	cbuf	An array of characters to write to the stream.
	off	An offset into the array.
	len	The number of characters to write.
Throws	IOException	If any kind of I/O error occurs.
Overrides	Writer.write(char[], int, int)	
Description	This method writes len characters contained in the given array, starting at offset off. It does this by calling the write(char[], int, int) method of the underlying writer.	

public void write(String str, int off, int len) throws IOException

Parameters	str	A string to write to the stream.
	off	An offset into the string.
	len	The number of characters to write.
Throws	IOException	If any kind of I/O error occurs.
Overrides	Writer.write(String, int, int)	
Description	This method writes len characters contained in the given string, starting at offset off. It does this by calling the write(String, int, int) method of the underlying writer.	

Inherited Methods

Method	Inherited From	Method	Inherited From
clone()	Object	equals(Object)	Object
finalize()	Object	getClass()	Object
hashCode()	Object	notify()	Object
notifyAll()	Object	toString()	Object
wait()	Object	wait(long)	Object
wait(long, int)	Object		

See Also

FilterOutputStream, IOException, String, Writer

11.28   InputStream

Synopsis

Class Name: java.io.InputStream
Superclass: java.lang.Object
Immediate Subclasses: java.io.ByteArrayInputStream,
                               java.io.FileInputStream,
                               java.io.FilterInputStream,
                               java.io.ObjectInputStream,
                               java.io.PipedInputStream,
                               java.io.SequenceInputStream,
                               java.io.StringBufferInputStream
Interfaces Implemented: None
Availability: JDK 1.0 or later

Description

The InputStream class is an abstract class that is the superclass of all classes that represent input byte streams. InputStream defines the basic input methods that all input streams provide. A similar hierarchy of classes, based around Reader, deals with character streams instead of byte streams.

InputStream is designed so that read(byte[]) and read(byte[], int, int) both call read(). Thus, a subclass can simply override read(), and all the read methods will work. However, for efficiency sake, read(byte[], int, int) should also be overridden with a method that can read a block of data more efficiently than reading each byte separately.

InputStream also defines a mechanism for marking a position in the stream and returning to it later, via the mark() and reset() methods. Another method, mark-Supported(), indicates whether or not this mark-and-reset functionality is available in a particular subclass.

Class Summary

```
public abstract class java.io.InputStream extends java.lang.Object {
   // Instance Methods
   public abstract int available();
   public void close();
   public synchronized void mark(int readlimit);
   public boolean markSupported();
```

```
    public abstract int read();
    public int read(byte[] b);
    public int read(byte[] b, int off, int len);
    public synchronized void reset();
    public long skip(long n);
}
```

Instance Methods

available

`public abstract int available() throws IOException`

Returns	The number of bytes that can be read without blocking.
Throws	`IOException` If any kind of I/O error occurs.
Description	This method returns the number of bytes that can be read without having to wait for more data to become available, or in other words, blocking.

A subclass of `InputStream` must implement this method.

close

`public void close() throws IOException`

Throws	`IOException` If any kind of I/O error occurs.
Description	This method closes the input stream and releases any resources associated with it.

The implementation of the `close()` method in `InputStream` does nothing; a subclass should override this method to handle cleanup for the stream.

mark

`public synchronized void mark(int readlimit)`

Parameters	`readlimit` The maximum number of bytes that can be read before the saved position can become invalid.
Description	This method tells this `InputStream` object to remember its current position, so that the position can be restored by a call to the `reset()` method. The `InputStream` can read `readlimit` bytes beyond the marked position before the mark becomes invalid.

The implementation of the `mark()` method in `InputStream` does nothing; a subclass must override the method to provide the mark-and-reset functionality.

markSupported

public boolean markSupported()

Returns   true if this input stream supports mark() and reset(); false otherwise.

Description   This method returns a boolean value that indicates whether or not this object supports mark-and-reset functionality.

The markSupported() method in InputStream always returns false. A subclass that implements the mark-and-reset functionality should override the method to return true.

read

public abstract int read() throws IOException

Returns   The next byte of data or –1 if the end of the stream is encountered.

Throws   IOException   If any kind of I/O error occurs.

Description   This method reads the next byte of input. The byte is returned as an integer in the range 0 to 255. The method blocks until the byte is read, the end of stream is encountered, or an exception is thrown.

A subclass of InputStream must implement this method.

public int read(byte[] b) throws IOException

Parameters   b   An array of bytes to be filled from the stream.

Returns   The actual number of bytes read or –1 if the end of the stream is encountered immediately.

Throws   IOException   If any kind of I/O error occurs.

Description   This method reads bytes of input to fill the given array by calling read(b, 0, b.length). The method blocks until some data is available.

A subclass does not usually need to override this method as it can override read(byte[], int, int) and have read(byte[]) work automatically.

public int read(byte[] b, int off, int len) throws IOException

Parameters   b   An array of bytes to be filled from the stream.

off   An offset into the array.

len   The number of bytes to read.

Returns   The actual number of bytes read or –1 if the end of the stream is encountered immediately.

Throws   IOException   If any kind of I/O error occurs.

Description This method reads up to len bytes of input into the given array starting at index off. The method blocks until some data is available.

The implementation of this method in InputStream uses read() repeatedly to fill the array. Although it is not strictly necessary, a subclass should override this method to read a block of data more efficiently.

reset

public synchronized void reset() throws IOException

Throws   IOException   If there was no previous call to the mark() method or the saved position has been invalidated.

Description This method restores the position of the stream to the position that was saved by a previous call to mark().

The implementation of the reset() method in InputStream throws an exception to indicate that mark-and-reset functionality is not supported by default. A subclass must override the method to provide the functionality.

skip

public long skip(long n) throws IOException

Parameters   n   The number of bytes to skip.

Returns   The actual number of bytes skipped.

Throws   IOException   If any kind of I/O error occurs.

Description   This method skips n bytes of input. In other words, it moves the position of the stream forward by n bytes.

The implementation of the skip() method in InputStream simply calls read(b) where b is a byte array n bytes long. A subclass may want to override this method to implement a more efficient skipping algorithm.

Inherited Methods

Method	Inherited From	Method	Inherited From
clone()	Object	equals(Object)	Object
finalize()	Object	getClass()	Object
hashCode()	Object	notify()	Object
notifyAll()	Object	toString()	Object

Method	Inherited From	Method	Inherited From
wait()	Object	wait(long)	Object
wait(long, int)	Object		

See Also

ByteArrayInputStream, FileInputStream, FilterInputStream, IOException, ObjectInputStream, PipedInputStream, SequenceInputStream, StringBufferInputStream

11.29   InputStreamReader

Synopsis

Class Name:	java.io.InputStreamReader
Superclass:	java.io.Reader
Immediate Subclasses:	java.io.FileReader
Interfaces Implemented:	None
Availability:	New as of JDK 1.1

Description

The InputStreamReader class is a bridge between the byte-oriented world of the InputStream class and the character-oriented world of the Reader class. The InputStreamReader represents a character stream, but it gets its input from an underlying byte stream. An encoding scheme is responsible for translating the bytes to Unicode characters. An InputStreamReader can be created using an explicit encoding scheme or a default encoding scheme.

For example, to read an ISO-8859-5 byte stream as a Unicode character stream, you can construct an InputStreamReader with the encoding "8859_5" as follows:

```
InputStreamReader inr = new InputStreamReader(in, "8859_5");
```

Each time you read from an InputStreamReader object, bytes may be read from the underlying byte stream. To improve efficiency, you may want to wrap the InputStreamReader in a BufferedReader.

Class Summary

```
public class java.io.InputStreamReader extends java.io.Reader {
    // Constructors
    public InputStreamReader(InputStream in);
    public InputStreamReader(InputStream in, String enc);
```

```
// Instance Methods
public void close();
public String getEncoding();
public int read();
public int read(char[] cbuf, int off, int len);
public boolean ready();
}
```

Constructors

InputStreamReader

public InputStreamReader(InputStream in)

Parameters	in	The input stream to use.
Description		This constructor creates an InputStreamReader that gets its data from in and translates bytes to characters using the system's default encoding scheme.

public InputStreamReader(InputStream in, String enc)
        throws UnsupportedEncodingException

Parameters	in	The input stream to use.
	enc	The name of an encoding scheme.
Throws	UnsupportedEncodingException	
		If enc is not a supported encoding scheme.
Description		This constructor creates an InputStreamReader that gets its data from in and translates bytes to characters using the given encoding scheme.

Instance Methods

close

public void close() throws IOException

Throws	IOException	If any kind of I/O error occurs.
Overrides	Reader.close()	
Description		This method calls the close() method of the underlying input stream, which releases any system resources associated with this object.

getEncoding

public String getEncoding()

Returns		A String that contains the name of the character encoding scheme of this reader.
Description		This method returns the name of the character encoding scheme this InputStreamReader is currently using.

read

public int read() throws IOException

Returns	The next character of data or -1 if the end of the stream is encountered.
Throws	IOException If any kind of I/O error occurs.
Overrides	Reader.read()
Description	This method reads a character of input. The method returns the next character that has been read and converted from the underlying byte-oriented InputStream. The InputStreamReader class uses buffering internally, so this method returns immediately unless the buffer is empty. If the buffer is empty, a new block of bytes is read from the InputStream and converted to characters. The method blocks until the character is read, the end of stream is encountered, or an exception is thrown.

public int read(char[] cbuf, int off, int len) throws IOException

Parameters	cbuf	An array of characters to be filled from the stream.
	off	An offset into the array.
	len	The number of characters to read.
Returns		The actual number of characters read or -1 if the end of the stream is encountered immediately.
Throws		IOException If any kind of I/O error occurs.
Overrides		Reader.read(char[], int, int)
Description		This method reads up to len characters of input into the given array starting at index off. The InputStreamReader class uses buffering internally, so this method returns immediately if there is enough data in the buffer. If there is not enough data, a new block of bytes is read from the InputStream and converted to characters. The method blocks until some data is available.

ready

public boolean ready() throws IOException

Returns	true if the reader is ready to be read; false otherwise.
Throws	IOException If the reader is closed or any other kind of I/O error occurs.
Overrides	Reader.ready()
Description	This method returns a boolean value that indicates whether or not the reader is ready to be read. If there is data available in the internal buffer or if there are bytes available to be read from the underlying byte stream, the method returns true. Otherwise it returns false.

Inherited Methods

Method	Inherited From	Method	Inherited From
clone()	Object	equals(Object)	Object
finalize()	Object	getClass()	Object
hashCode()	Object	notify()	Object
notifyAll()	Object	mark()	Reader
markSupported()	Reader	read(char[])	Reader
reset()	Reader	skip(long)	Reader
toString()	Object	wait()	Object
wait(long)	Object	wait(long, int)	Object

See Also

BufferedReader, FileReader, InputStream, IOException, , Reader, UnsupportedEncodingException

11.30 InterruptedIOException

Synopsis

Class Name:	java.io.InterruptedIOException
Superclass:	java.io.IOException
Immediate Subclasses:	None
Interfaces Implemented:	None
Availability:	JDK 1.0 or later

Description

An InterruptedIOException is thrown when an I/O operation is interrupted. This can occur when a thread is waiting for data to become available for a PipedInput-Stream or PipedReader to read. It can also occur when a thread is waiting for buffer space to become available for a PipedOutputStream or PipedWriter to write to. If the thread's interrupt() method is called while the thread is waiting, the read() or write() method in question throws an InterruptedIOException.

Class Summary

```
public class java.io.InterruptedIOException extends java.io.IOException {
    // Variables
    public int bytesTransferred;

    // Constructors
    public InterruptedIOException();
```

```
    public InterruptedIOException(String s);
}
```

Variables

bytesTransferred

public int bytesTransferred

Description   The number of bytes that had been transferred before the interruption.

Constructors

InterruptedIOException

public InterruptedIOException()

Description   This constructor creates an InterruptedIOException with no detail message.

public InterruptedIOException(String s)

Parameters   s   The detail message.

Description   This constructor creates an InterruptedIOException with the specified detail message.

Inherited Methods

Method	Inherited From	Method	Inherited From
clone()	Object	equals(Object)	Object
fillInStackTrace()	Throwable	finalize()	Object
getClass()	Object	getLocalizedMessage()	Throwable
getMessage()	Throwable	hashCode()	Object
notify()	Object	notifyAll()	Object
printStackTrace()	Throwable	printStack-Trace(PrintStream)	Throwable
printStack-Trace(PrintWriter)	Throwable	toString()	Object
wait()	Object	wait(long)	Object
wait(long, int)	Object		

See Also

Exception, IOException, Throwable

11.31   InvalidClassException

Synopsis

Class Name: java.io.InvalidClassException
Superclass: java.io.ObjectStreamException
Immediate Subclasses: None
Interfaces Implemented: None
Availability: New as of JDK 1.1

Description

An InvalidClassException is thrown during object serialization. It indicates that the run-time environment does not support a serialized class for one of the following reasons:

- The version of the class does not match the serial version of the class in the stream.
- The class contains unknown data types.

An InvalidClassException can also indicate one of these problems with the class itself:

- The class implements only one of writeObject() and readObject().
- The class is not public.
- The class does not have an accessible constructor that takes no arguments.

Class Summary

```
public class java.io.InvalidClassException
            extends java.io.ObjectStreamException {
    // Variables
    public String classname;

    // Constructors
    public InvalidClassException(String reason);
    public InvalidClassException(String cname, String reason);

    // Instance Methods
    public String getMessage();
}
```

Variables

classname

public String classname

> Description   The name of the class that caused the exception.

Constructors

InvalidClassException

public InvalidClassException(String reason)

> Parameters   reason   The reason the exception was thrown.
>
> Description   This constructor creates an InvalidClassException with the specified reason string.

public InvalidClassException(String cname, String reason)

> Parameters   cname   The name of the class.
>
>   reason   The reason the exception was thrown.
>
> Description   This constructor creates an InvalidClassException with the specified class name and reason string.

Instance Methods

getMessage

public String getMessage()

> Returns   The reason string for this exception.
>
> Overrides   Throwable.getMessage()
>
> Description   This method returns the reason string for this exception. If a class name has also been specified, it is prepended to the reason string with a semicolon.

Inherited Methods

Method	Inherited From	Method	Inherited From
clone()	Object	equals(Object)	Object
fillInStackTrace()	Throwable	finalize()	Object
getClass()	Object	getLocalizedMessage()	Throwable
getMessage()	Throwable	hashCode()	Object
notify()	Object	notifyAll()	Object
printStackTrace()	Throwable	printStack-Trace(PrintStream)	Throwable
printStack-Trace(PrintWriter)	Throwable	toString()	Object
wait()	Object	wait(long)	Object
wait(long, int)	Object		

See Also

Exception, ObjectStreamException, Throwable

11.32   InvalidObjectException

Synopsis

Class Name:	java.io.InvalidObjectException
Superclass:	java.io.ObjectStreamException
Immediate Subclasses:	None
Interfaces Implemented:	None
Availability:	New as of JDK 1.1

Description

An InvalidObjectException is thrown by an object to indicate that it cannot validate itself during object deserialization.

Class Summary

```
public class java.io.InvalidObjectException
          extends java.io.ObjectStreamException {
    // Constructors
    public InvalidObjectException(String reason);
}
```

Constructors

InvalidObjectException

public InvalidObjectException(String reason)

Parameters	reason	The detail message.
Description		This constructor creates an InvalidObjectException with the specified detail message, which should be the name of the class.

Inherited Methods

Method	Inherited From	Method	Inherited From
clone()	Object	equals(Object)	Object
fillInStackTrace()	Throwable	finalize()	Object
getClass()	Object	getLocalizedMessage()	Throwable
getMessage()	Throwable	hashCode()	Object
notify()	Object	notifyAll()	Object

Method	Inherited From	Method	Inherited From
printStackTrace()	Throwable	printStack-Trace(PrintStream)	Throwable
printStack-Trace(PrintWriter)	Throwable	toString()	Object
wait()	Object	wait(long)	Object
wait(long, int)	Object		

See Also

Exception, ObjectStreamException, Throwable

11.33   IOException

Synopsis

Class Name: java.io.IOException
Superclass: java.lang.Exception
Immediate Subclasses: java.io.CharConversionException,
                         java.io.EOFException,
                         java.io.FileNotFoundException,
                         java.io.InterruptedIOException,
                         java.io.ObjectStreamException,
                         java.io.SyncFailedException,
                         java.io.UnsupportedEncodingException,
                         java.io.UTFDataFormatException,
                         java.net.MalformedURLException,
                         java.net.ProtocolException,
                         java.net.SocketException,
                         java.net.UnknownHostException,
                         java.net.UnknownServiceException,
                         java.util.zip.ZipException
Interfaces Implemented: None
Availability: JDK 1.0 or later

Description

The IOException class is the superclass for all of the exceptions that represent anything that can go wrong with input or output.

Class Summary

```
public class java.io.IOException extends java.lang.Exception {
    // Constructors
    public IOException();
    public IOException(String s);
}
```

Constructors

IOException

public IOException()

Description   This constructor creates an IOException with no detail message.

public IOException(String s)

Parameters   s   The detail message.

Description   This constructor creates an IOException with the specified detail message.

Inherited Methods

Method	Inherited From	Method	Inherited From
clone()	Object	equals(Object)	Object
fillInStackTrace()	Throwable	finalize()	Object
getClass()	Object	getLocalizedMessage()	Throwable
getMessage()	Throwable	hashCode()	Object
notify()	Object	notifyAll()	Object
printStackTrace()	Throwable	printStack-Trace(PrintStream)	Throwable
printStack-Trace(PrintWriter)	Throwable	toString()	Object
wait()	Object	wait(long)	Object
wait(long, int)	Object		

See Also

CharConversionException, EOFException, Exception, FileNotFoundException, InterruptedException, MalformedURLException, ObjectStreamException, ProtocolException, SocketException, SyncFailedException, Throwable, UnknownHostException, UnknownServiceException, UnsupportedEncodingException, UTFDataFormatException, ZipException

11.34   LineNumberInputStream

Synopsis

Class Name:	java.io.LineNumberInputStream
Superclass:	java.io.FilterInputStream
Immediate Subclasses:	None
Interfaces Implemented:	None
Availability:	Deprecated as of JDK 1.1

Description

The LineNumberInputStream class is an InputStream that keeps track of line numbers. The line number starts at 0 and is incremented each time an end-of-line character is encountered. LineNumberInputStream recognizes "\n", "\r", or "\r\n" as the end of a line. Regardless of the end-of-line character it reads, LineNumberInputStream returns only "\n". The current line number is returned by getLineNumber(). The mark() and reset() methods are supported, but only work if the underlying stream supports mark() and reset().

The LineNumberInputStream class is deprecated as of JDK 1.1 because it does not perform any byte to character conversions. Incoming bytes are directly compared to end-of-line characters. If you are developing new code, you should use LineNumberReader instead.

Class Summary

```
public class java.io.LineNumberInputStream
            extends java.io.FilterInputStream {
  // Constructors
  public LineNumberInputStream(InputStream in);

  // Instance Methods
  public int available();
  public int getLineNumber();
  public void mark(int readlimit);
  public int read();
  public int read(byte[] b, int off, int len);
  public void reset();
  public void setLineNumber(int lineNumber);
  public long skip(long n);
}
```

Constructors

LineNumberInputStream

   public LineNumberInputStream(InputStream in)

      Parameters   in   The input stream to use.

      Description   This constructor creates a LineNumberInputStream that gets its data from in.

Instance Methods

available

   public int available() throws IOException

      Returns   The number of bytes that can be read without blocking.

      Throws   IOException If any kind of I/O error occurs.

      Overrides   FilterInputStream.available()

      Description   This method returns the number of bytes of input that can be read without having to wait for more input to become available.

getLineNumber

   public int getLineNumber()

      Returns   The current line number.

      Description   This method returns the current line number.

mark

   public void mark(int readlimit)

      Parameters   readlimit   The maximum number of bytes that can be read before the saved position becomes invalid.

      Overrides   FilterInputStream.mark()

      Description   This method tells the LineNumberInputStream to remember its current position. A subsequent call to reset() causes the object to return to that saved position and thus reread a portion of the input. The method calls the mark() method of the underlying stream, so it only works if the underlying stream supports mark() and reset().

read

   public int read() throws IOException

      Returns   The next byte of data or –1 if the end of the stream is encountered.

      Throws   IOException If any kind of I/O error occurs.

Overrides   `FilterInputStream.read()`

Description   This method reads a byte of input from the underlying stream. If `"\n"`, `"\r"`, or `"\r\n"` is read from the stream, `"\n"` is returned. Otherwise, the byte read from the underlying stream is returned verbatim. The method blocks until the byte is read, the end of stream is encountered, or an exception is thrown.

`public int read(byte[] b, int off, int len) throws IOException`

Parameters   b   An array of bytes to be filled from the stream.

                off   An offset into the byte array.

                len   The number of bytes to read.

Returns   The actual number of bytes read or -1 if the end of the stream is encountered immediately.

Throws   `IOException`   If any kind of I/O error occurs.

Overrides   `FilterInputStream.read(byte[], int, int)`

Description   This method reads up to `len` bytes of input into the given array starting at index `off`. If `"\n"`, `"\r"`, or `"\r\n"` is read from the stream, `"\n"` is returned. The method does this by repeatedly calling `read()`, which is not efficient, especially if the underlying stream is not buffered. The method blocks until some data is available.

reset

`public void reset() throws IOException`

Throws   `IOException`   If there was no previous call to this `FilterInputStream`'s `mark()` method or the saved position has been invalidated.

Overrides   `FilterInputStream.reset()`

Description   This method calls the `reset()` method of the underlying stream. If the underlying stream supports `mark()` and `reset()`, this method sets the position of the stream to a position that was saved by a previous call to `mark()`. Subsequent bytes read from this stream will begin from the saved position and continue normally. The method also restores the line number to its correct value for the mark location. The method only works if the underlying stream supports `mark()` and `reset()`.

setLineNumber

`public void setLineNumber(int lineNumber)`

Parameters   lineNumber   The new line number.

Description   This method sets the current line number of the LineNumber-
                  InputStream. The method does not change the position of the
                  stream.

skip

```
public long skip(long n) throws IOException
```
Parameters   n   The number of bytes to skip.
Returns   The actual number of bytes skipped.
Throws   IOException   If any kind of I/O error occurs.
Overrides   FilterInputStream.skip()
Description   This method skips n bytes of input. Note that since LineNumber-
                  InputStream returns "\r\n" as a single character, "\n", this
                  method may skip over more bytes than you expect.

Inherited Methods

Method	Inherited From	Method	Inherited From
clone()	Object	close()	FilterInputStream
equals(Object)	Object	finalize()	Object
getClass()	Object	hashCode()	Object
markSupported()	FilterInputStream	notify()	Object
notifyAll()	Object	read(byte[])	FilterInputStream
toString()	Object	wait()	Object
wait(long)	Object	wait(long, int)	Object

See Also

FilterInputStream, InputStream, IOException, LineNumberReader

11.35   LineNumberReader

Synopsis

Class Name: java.io.LineNumberReader
Superclass: java.io.BufferedReader
Immediate Subclasses: None
Interfaces Implemented: None
Availability: New as of JDK 1.1

Description

The LineNumberReader class is a BufferedReader that keeps track of line numbers. The line number starts at 0 and is incremented each time an end-of-line character is encountered. LineNumberReader recognizes "\n", "\r", or "\r\n" as the end of a line. Regardless of the end-of-line character it reads, ReaderInputStream returns only "\n". The current line number is returned by getLineNumber().

The LineNumberReader class is the JDK 1.1 replacement for LineNumberInput-Stream. Not only does it correctly handle byte to character conversions (via Reader), it implements read(byte[], int, int) and skip() more efficiently than its predecessor.

Class Summary

```
public class java.io.LineNumberReader extends java.io.BufferedReader {
    // Constructors
    public LineNumberReader(Reader in);
    public LineNumberReader(Reader in, int sz);

    // Instance Methods
    public int getLineNumber();
    public void mark(int readAheadLimit);
    public int read();
    public int read(char[] cbuf, int off, int len);
    public String readLine();
    public void reset();
    public void setLineNumber(int lineNumber);
    public long skip(long n);
}
```

Constructors

LineNumberReader

public LineNumberReader(Reader in)

Parameters	in	The reader to use.
Description		This constructor creates a LineNumberReader that gets its data from in and uses a default sized buffer. The default buffer size for BufferedReader is 8192 characters.

public LineNumberReader(Reader in, int sz)

Parameters	in	The reader to use.
	sz	The buffer size.
Description		This constructor creates a LineNumberReader that gets its data from in and uses a buffer of the given size.

Instance Methods

getLineNumber

```
public int getLineNumber()
```

Returns   The current line number.

Description   This method returns the current line number.

mark

```
public void mark(int readAheadLimit) throws IOException
```

Parameters   readAheadLimit

The maximum number of characters that can be
read before the saved position becomes invalid.

Throws   IOException   If any kind of I/O error occurs.

Overrides   BufferedReader.mark()

Description   This method causes the LineNumberReader to remember its current position. A subsequent call to reset() causes the object to
return to that saved position and thus reread a portion of the
input.

read

```
public int read() throws IOException
```

Returns   The next character of data or –1 if the end of the stream is
encountered.

Throws   IOException   If any kind of I/O error occurs.

Overrides   BufferedReader.read()

Description   This method reads a character of input from the underlying
reader. If "\n", "\r", or "\r\n" is read from the stream, "\n" is
returned. Otherwise the character read from the underlying
BufferedReader is returned verbatim. The method blocks until
it reads the character, the end of stream is encountered, or an
exception is thrown.

```
public int read(char[] cbuf, int off, int len) throws IOException
```

Parameters   cbuf   An array of characters to be filled from the
stream.

              off   An offset into the array.

              len   The number of characters to read.

Returns   The actual number of characters read or –1 if the end of the
stream is encountered immediately.

Throws   IOException   If any kind of I/O error occurs.

Overrides   `BufferedReader.read(char[], int, int)`

Description   This method reads up to `len` characters of input into the given array starting at index `off`. This method, unlike `read()`, returns end-of-line characters exactly as they come from the underlying `BufferedReader`. The method blocks until data is available.

readLine

`public String readLine() throws IOException`

Returns   A `String` containing the line just read, or `null` if the end of the stream has been reached.

Throws   `IOException` If any kind of I/O error occurs.

Overrides   `BufferedReader.readLine()`

Description   This method reads a line of text. Lines are terminated by `"\n"`, `"\r"`, or `"\r\n"`. The line terminators are not returned with the line string.

reset

`public void reset() throws IOException`

Throws   `IOException` If the reader is closed, `mark()` has not been called, or the saved position has been invalidated.

Overrides   `BufferedReader.reset()`

Description   This method sets the position of the reader to a position that was saved by a previous call to `mark()`. Subsequent characters read from this reader will begin from the saved position and continue normally. The method also restores the line number to its correct value for the mark location.

setLineNumber

`public void setLineNumber(int lineNumber)`

Parameters   `lineNumber` The new line number.

Description   This method sets the current line number of the `LineNumberReader`. The method does not change the position of the reader.

skip

`public long skip(long n) throws IOException`

Parameters   `n`   The number of characters to skip.

Returns	The actual number of bytes skipped.
Throws	`IOException` If any kind of I/O error occurs.
Overrides	`BufferedReader.skip()`
Description	This method skips n characters of input.

Inherited Methods

Method	Inherited From	Method	Inherited From
clone()	Object	close()	BufferedReader
equals(Object)	Object	finalize()	Object
getClass()	Object	hashCode()	Object
notify()	Object	notifyAll()	Object
markSupported()	BufferedReader	read(char[])	Reader
ready()	BufferedReader	toString()	Object
wait()	Object	wait(long)	Object
wait(long, int)	Object		

See Also

`BufferedReader, Reader, IOException, LineNumberInputStream`

11.36   NotActiveException

Synopsis

Class Name:	`java.io.NotActiveException`
Superclass:	`java.io.ObjectStreamException`
Immediate Subclasses:	None
Interfaces Implemented:	None
Availability:	New as of JDK 1.1

Description

A `NotActiveException` is thrown to indicate that an inappropriate method is being
called when serialization or deserialization is not in progress.

Class Summary

```
public class java.io.NotActiveException
          extends java.io.ObjectStreamException {
  // Constructors
  public NotActiveException();
  public NotActiveException(String reason);
}
```

Constructors

NotActiveException

`public NotActiveException()`

    Description   This constructor creates a `NotActiveException` with no detail message.

`public NotActiveException(String reason)`

    Parameters   reason   The detail message.

    Description   This constructor creates a `NotActiveException` with the specified detail message.

Inherited Methods

Method	Inherited From	Method	Inherited From
clone()	Object	equals(Object)	Object
fillInStackTrace()	Throwable	finalize()	Object
getClass()	Object	getLocalizedMessage()	Throwable
getMessage()	Throwable	hashCode()	Object
notify()	Object	notifyAll()	Object
printStackTrace()	Throwable	printStack-Trace(PrintStream)	Throwable
printStack-Trace(PrintWriter)	Throwable	toString()	Object
wait()	Object	wait(long)	Object
wait(long, int)	Object		

See Also

Exception, ObjectStreamException, Throwable

11.37 NotSerializableException

Synopsis

Class Name: java.io.NotSerializableException

Superclass: java.io.ObjectStreamException

Immediate Subclasses: None

Interfaces Implemented: None

Availability: New as of JDK 1.1

Description

A NotSerializableException is thrown to indicate that a class can't be serialized.

Class Summary

```
public class java.io.NotSerializableException
            extends java.io.ObjectStreamException {
  // Constructors
  public NotSerializableException();
  public NotSerializableException(String classname);
}
```

Constructors

NotSerializableException

public NotSerializableException()

    Description   This constructor creates a NotSerializableException with no class name.

public NotSerializableException(String classname)

    Parameters   classname   The name of the class that can't be serialized.

    Description   This constructor creates a NotSerializableException with the specified class name.

Inherited Methods

Method	Inherited From	Method	Inherited From
clone()	Object	equals(Object)	Object
fillInStackTrace()	Throwable	finalize()	Object
getClass()	Object	getLocalizedMessage()	Throwable
getMessage()	Throwable	hashCode()	Object
notify()	Object	notifyAll()	Object
printStackTrace()	Throwable	printStack-Trace(PrintStream)	Throwable
printStack-Trace(PrintWriter)	Throwable	toString()	Object
wait()	Object	wait(long)	Object
wait(long, int)	Object		

See Also

Exception, ObjectStreamException, Throwable

11.38   ObjectInput

Synopsis

Interface Name:	java.io.ObjectInput
Super-interface:	java.io.DataInput
Immediate Sub-interfaces:	
	None
Implemented By:	java.io.ObjectInputStream
Availability:	New as of JDK 1.1

Description

The ObjectInput interface extends the DataInput interface for object serialization. While DataInput defines methods for reading primitive types from a stream, ObjectInput defines methods for reading objects and arrays of bytes.

Interface Declaration

```
public abstract interface java.io.ObjectInput extends java.io.DataInput {
    // Methods
    public abstract int available();
    public abstract void close();
    public abstract int read();
    public abstract int read(byte[] b);
    public abstract int read(byte[] b, int off, int len);
    public abstract Object readObject();
    public abstract long skip(long n);
}
```

Methods

available

public abstract int available() throws IOException

Returns	The number of bytes that can be read without blocking.
Throws	IOException If any kind of I/O error occurs.
Description	This method returns the number of bytes that can be read from the stream without accessing a physical device, like a disk or a network.

close

public abstract void close() throws IOException

Throws	IOException If any kind of I/O error occurs.
Description	This method closes the stream and releases any system resources associated with it.

read

```
public abstract int read() throws IOException
```

Returns	The next byte of data or –1 if the end of the stream is encountered.
Throws	IOException If any kind of I/O error occurs.
Description	This method returns the next byte of data from the stream. The method blocks until the byte is read, the end of stream is detected, or an exception is thrown.

```
public abstract int read(byte[] b) throws IOException
```

Parameters	b	An array of bytes to be filled from the stream.
Returns		The actual number of bytes read or –1 if the end of the stream is encountered immediately.
Throws		IOException If any kind of I/O error occurs.
Description		This method reads bytes from the stream to fill the given array. The method blocks until some data is available.

```
public abstract int read(byte[] b, int off, int len)
                  throws IOException
```

Parameters	b	An array of bytes to be filled from the stream.
	off	An offset into the array.
	len	The number of bytes to read.
Returns		The actual number of bytes read or –1 if the end of the stream is encountered immediately.
Throws		IOException If any kind of I/O error occurs.
Description		This method reads up to len bytes of input into the given array starting at index off. The method blocks until some data is available.

readObject

```
public abstract Object readObject()
                  throws ClassNotFoundException, IOException
```

Returns	An Object that has been deserialized from the stream.
Throws	ClassNotFoundException
	If the class of the serialized object cannot be found in the run-time environment.
	IOException If any kind of I/O error occurs.
Description	This method reads and returns an object instance from the stream; in other words, it deserializes an object from the stream. The class that implements this interface determines exactly how the object is to be read.

skip

```
public abstract long skip(long n) throws IOException
```

Parameters	n	The number of bytes to skip.
Returns		The actual number of bytes skipped.
Throws	`IOException`	If any kind of I/O error occurs.
Description		This method skips n bytes of input.

Inherited Methods

Method	Inherited From	Method	Inherited From
readBoolean()	DataInput	readByte()	DataInput
readChar()	DataInput	readDouble()	DataInput
readFloat(byte[])	DataInput	readFully(byte[])	DataInput
readFully(byte[], int, int)	DataInput	readInt()	DataInput
readLine()	DataInput	readLong()	DataInput
readShort()	DataInput	readUnsignedByte()	DataInput
readUnsignedChar()	DataInput	readUTF()	DataInput
skipBytes(int)	DataInput		

See Also

`DataInput`, `ObjectInputStream`

11.39   ObjectInputStream

Synopsis

Class Name:	`java.io.ObjectInputStream`
Superclass:	`java.io.InputStream`
Immediate Subclasses:	None
Interfaces Implemented:	`java.io.ObjectInput`
Availability:	New as of JDK 1.1

Description

The `ObjectInputStream` class can read both primitive types and object instances from an underlying `InputStream`. The objects and other data must have been written by an `ObjectOutputStream`. These two classes can provide persistent storage of objects when they are used in conjunction with `FileInputStream` and `FileOutput-Stream`. The classes can also be used with socket streams to pass objects across the network.

Only objects that are instances of classes that implement the Serializable or Externalizable interfaces can be deserialized from an input stream. The default deserialization mechanism is implemented by readObject(). When an object is deserialized, the non-static and non-transient fields of the object are restored to the values they had when the object was serialized, including any other objects referenced by the object (except for those objects that do not implement the Serializable interface themselves). Graphs of objects are restored using a reference sharing mechanism. New object instances are always allocated during the deserialization process, to prevent existing objects from being overwritten. Deserialized objects are returned as instances of type Object, so they should be cast to the appropriate type. Strings and arrays are objects in Java, so they are treated as objects during deserialization.

For example, the following code opens a file called *color.ser* and reads a Color object:

```
FileInputStream fileIn;
ObjectInputStream in;
Color color;
try {
    fileIn = new FileInputStream("color.ser");
    in = new ObjectInputStream(fileIn);
    color = (Color)in.readObject();
    in.close();
}
catch (Exception e) {
    System.out.println("Error reading: " + e);
}
```

Classes that have transient instance variables may require special handling to reconstruct the values of these variables when objects are deserialized. Special handling may also be necessary to correctly deserialize objects that were serialized with a different version of their class than is in use when they are deserialized. Classes that require special handling during serialization and deserialization must implement the following methods (with these exact signatures):

```
private void readObject(ObjectOutputStream stream)
        throws IOException, ClassNotFoundException
private void writeObject(ObjectOutputStream stream) throws IOException
```

The writeObject() method is responsible for writing the state of the object for the particular class so that it can be restored by readObject(). The readObject() method registers an object validation callback by calling registerValidation() as its first action. The readObject() method doesn't need to handle reading the state for the object's superclass or any of its subclasses except in the case where the superclass doesn't itself implement the Serializable interface. In this case, the nonserializable class must have a no-argument constructor that can be called to initialize its fields, and it is the responsibility of the subclass to restore the state of its superclass.

A class that inherits the implementation of Serializable prevents itself from being serialized by defining readObject() and writeObject() methods that throw NotSerializableException objects.

If a class needs complete control over the contents and formatting of the serialized form of its objects, it should implement the Externalizable interface.

Class Summary

```
public class java.io.ObjectInputStream extends java.io.InputStream
            implements java.io.ObjectInput {
   // Constructors
   public ObjectInputStream(InputStream in);

   // Public Instance Methods
   public int available();
   public void close();
   public final void defaultReadObject();
   public int read();
   public int read(byte[] data, int offset, int length);
   public boolean readBoolean();
   public byte readByte();
   public char readChar();
   public double readDouble();
   public float readFloat();
   public void readFully(byte[] data);
   public void readFully(byte[] data, int offset, int size);
   public int readInt();
   public String readLine();
   public long readLong();
   public final Object readObject();
   public short readShort();
   public int readUnsignedByte();
   public int readUnsignedShort();
   public String readUTF();
   public synchronized void
           registerValidation(ObjectInputValidation obj, int prio);
   public int skipBytes(int len);

   // Protected Instance Methods
   protected final boolean enableResolveObject(boolean enable);
   protected void readStreamHeader();
   protected Class resolveClass(ObjectStreamClass v);
   protected Object resolveObject(Object obj);
}
```

Constructors

ObjectInputStream

```
public ObjectInputStream(InputStream in)
        throws IOException, StreamCorruptedException
```

Parameters | in | The underlying input stream.
Throws | IOException | If any kind of I/O error occurs.
| StreamCorruptedException
| | If the stream header is not correct.
Description | This constructor creates an ObjectInputStream that reads from the given input stream. The constructor attempts to read the stream header, which consists of a magic number and a version number, and if something goes wrong, an appropriate exception is thrown. If all of the bytes of the stream header are not available, the constructor does not return until they become available.

Public Instance Methods

available

```
public int available() throws IOException
```

Returns | The number of bytes that can be read without blocking.
Throws | IOException   If any kind of I/O error occurs.
Implements | ObjectInput.available()
Overrides | InputStream.available()
Description | This method returns the number of bytes that can be read without having to wait for more data to become available.

close

```
public void close() throws IOException
```

Throws | IOException   If any kind of I/O error occurs.
Implements | ObjectInput.close()
Overrides | InputStream.close()
Description | This method closes the stream and releases any system resources that are associated with it.

defaultReadObject

```
public final void defaultReadObject()
                throws IOException, ClassNotFoundException,
                    NotActiveException
```

Throws | IOException   If any kind of I/O error occurs.

ClassNotFoundException

    If the class of the object being read cannot be found.

NotActiveException

    If serialization is not active.

Description   This method reads the fields of the current object that are not static and not transient. The method can only be called from the private readObject() method of an object that is being deserialized; it throws a NotActiveException if it is called at any other time. This method implements the default deserialization mechanism.

read

```
public int read() throws IOException
```

Returns   The next byte of data or -1 if the end of the stream is encountered.

Throws   IOException   If any kind of I/O error occurs.

Implements   ObjectInput.read()

Overrides   InputStream.read()

Description   This method reads the next byte from the stream. The method blocks until some data is available, the end of the stream is detected, or an exception is thrown.

```
public int read(byte[] data, int offset, int length)
        throws IOException
```

Parameters   data   Array of bytes to be filled from the stream.

    offset   An offset into the byte array.

    length   The number of bytes to read.

Returns   The number of bytes read or -1 if the end of the stream is encountered immediately.

Throws   IOException   If any kind of I/O error occurs.

Implements   ObjectInput.read(byte[], int, int)

Overrides   InputStream.read(byte[], int, int)

Description   This method reads up to length bytes of input into the given array starting at index offset. The method blocks until there is some input available.

readBoolean

```
public boolean readBoolean() throws IOException
```

Returns   The boolean value read from the stream.

Throws	EOFException
	If the end of the file is encountered.
	IOException If any other kind of I/O error occurs.
Implements	DataInput.readBoolean()
Description	This method reads a byte as a boolean value from the underlying input stream. A byte that contains a zero is read as false. A byte that contains any other value is read as true. The method blocks until the byte is read, the end of the stream is encountered, or an exception is thrown.

readByte

```
public byte readByte() throws IOException
```

Returns	The byte value read from the stream.
Throws	EOFException
	If the end of the file is encountered.
	IOException If any other kind of I/O error occurs.
Implements	DataInput.readByte()
Description	This method reads a signed 8-bit value, a byte, from the underlying input stream. The method blocks until the byte is read, the end of the stream is encountered, or an exception is thrown.

readChar

```
public char readChar() throws IOException
```

Returns	The char value read from the stream.
Throws	EOFException
	If the end of the file is encountered.
	IOException If any other kind of I/O error occurs.
Implements	DataInput.readChar()
Description	This method reads a 16-bit Unicode character from the stream. The method reads two bytes from the underlying input stream and then creates a char value using the first byte read as the most significant byte. The method blocks until the two bytes are read, the end of the stream is encountered, or an exception is thrown.

readDouble

```
public double readDouble() throws IOException
```

Returns	The double value read from the stream.

Throws   EOFException

If the end of the file is encountered.

IOException   If any other kind of I/O error occurs.

Implements   DataInput.readDouble()

Description   This method reads a 64-bit double quantity from the stream. The method reads a long value from the underlying input stream as if using the readLong() method. The long value is then converted to a double using the longBitsToDouble() method in Double. The method blocks until the necessary eight bytes are read, the end of the stream is encountered, or an exception is thrown.

readFloat

```
public float readFloat() throws IOException
```
Returns   The float value read from the stream.

Throws   EOFException

If the end of the file is encountered.

IOException   If any other kind of I/O error occurs.

Implements   DataInput.readFloat()

Description   This method reads a 32-bit float quantity from the stream. The method reads an int value from the underlying input stream as if using the readInt() method. The int value is then converted to a float using the intBitsToFloat() method in Float. The method blocks until the necessary four bytes are read, the end of the stream is encountered, or an exception is thrown.

readFully

```
public void readFully(byte[] b) throws IOException
```
Parameters   b   The array to fill.

Throws   EOFException

If the end of the file is encountered.

IOException   If any other kind of I/O error occurs.

Implements   DataInput.readFully(byte[])

Description   This method reads bytes into the given array b until the array is full. The method reads repeatedly from the underlying stream to fill the array. The method blocks until all of the bytes are read, the end of the stream is encountered, or an exception is thrown.

```
public void readFully(byte[] data, int offset, int size)
        throws IOException
```

Parameters	data	The array to fill.
	offset	An offset into the array.
	length	The number of bytes to read.
Throws	EOFException	
		If the end of the file is encountered.
	IOException	If any other kind of I/O error occurs.
Implements	DataInput.readFully(byte[], int, int)	
Description	This method reads len bytes into the given array, starting at offset off. The method reads repeatedly from the underlying stream to fill the array. The method blocks until all of the bytes are read, the end of the stream is encountered, or an exception is thrown.	

readInt

```
public int readInt() throws IOException
```

Returns	The int value read from the stream.	
Throws	EOFException	
		If the end of the file is encountered.
	IOException	If any other kind of I/O error occurs.
Implements	DataInput.readInt()	
Description	This method reads a signed 32-bit int quantity from the stream. The method reads four bytes from the underlying input stream and then creates an int quantity, using the first byte read as the most significant byte. The method blocks until the four bytes are read, the end of the stream is encountered, or an exception is thrown.	

readLine

```
public String readLine() throws IOException
```

Returns	A String that contains the line read from the stream.	
Throws	EOFException	
		If the end of the file is encountered.
	IOException	If any other I/O error occurs.
Implements	DataInput.readLine()	
Description	This method reads the next line of text from the stream. The method reads bytes of data from the underlying input stream until it encounters a line terminator. A line terminator is a carriage return ("\r"), a newline character ("\n"), a carriage return immediately followed by a newline character, or the end of the stream. The method blocks until a line terminator is	

read, the end of the stream is encountered, or an exception is thrown. Note that this method calls the `readLine()` method of `DataInputStream`, which is deprecated in 1.1.

readLong

`public long readLong() throws IOException`

Returns	The `long` value read from the stream.
Throws	`EOFException`
	If the end of the file is encountered.
	`IOException` If any other kind of I/O error occurs.
Implements	`DataInput.readLong()`
Description	This method reads a signed 64-bit `long` quantity from the stream. The method reads eight bytes from the underlying input stream and then creates a `long` quantity, using the first byte read as the most significant byte. The method blocks until the eight bytes are read, the end of the stream is encountered, or an exception is thrown.

readObject

`public final Object readObject()`
`                throws OptionalDataException,`
`                        ClassNotFoundException, IOException`

Returns	An `Object` that has been deserialized from the stream.
Throws	`ClassNotFoundException`
	If the object being deserialized has an unrecognized class.
	`InvalidClassException`
	If there is a problem with the class of the deserialized object.
	`StreamCorruptedException`
	If the stream serialization information is not correct.
	`OptionalDataException`
	If the stream contains primitive data instead of an object.
	`IOException` If any kind of I/O error occurs.
Implements	`ObjectInput.readObject()`
Description	This method deserializes an object from the stream and returns a reference to the object. The non-static and non-transient fields of the object are restored to the values they had when the object was serialized. If the object contains references to other objects, these objects are also deserialized (as long as they

implement the Serializable interface). Graphs of objects are restored using a reference-sharing mechanism. New object instances are always allocated during the deserialization process, to prevent existing objects from being overwritten. Deserialized objects are returned as instances of type Object, so they should be cast to the appropriate type.

Once an object has been completely restored (i.e., all of its fields and any objects it references have been restored), any object validation callbacks for the object or any of the objects it references are called in an order based on their priority. An object validation callback is registered by the private readObject() method for an object.

readShort

public short readShort() throws IOException

Returns	The short value read from the stream.
Throws	EOFException
	If the end of the file is encountered.
	IOException If any other kind of I/O error occurs.
Implements	DataInput.readShort()
Description	This method reads a signed 16-bit short quantity from the stream. The method reads two bytes from the underlying input stream and then creates a short quantity, using the first byte read as the most significant byte. The method blocks until the two bytes are read, the end of the stream is encountered, or an exception is thrown.

readUnsignedByte

public int readUnsignedByte() throws IOException

Returns	The unsigned byte value read from the stream.
Throws	EOFException
	If the end of the file is encountered.
	IOException If any other kind of I/O error occurs.
Implements	DataInput.readUnsignedByte()
Description	This method reads an unsigned 8-bit quantity from the stream. The method reads a byte from the underlying input stream and returns that byte. The method blocks until the byte is read, the end of the stream is encountered, or an exception is thrown.

readUnsignedShort

public int readUnsignedShort() throws IOException

Returns | The unsigned short value read from the stream.

Throws | EOFException

If the end of the file is encountered.

IOException | If any other kind of I/O error occurs.

Implements | DataInput.readUnsignedShort()

Description | This method reads an unsigned 16-bit quantity from the stream. The method reads two bytes from the underlying input stream and creates an unsigned short quantity using the first byte read as the most significant byte. The method blocks until the two bytes are read, the end of the stream is encountered, or an exception is thrown.

readUTF

public String readUTF() throws IOException

Returns | The String read from the stream.

Throws | EOFException

If the end of the file is encountered.

IOException | If any other kind of I/O error occurs.

UTFDataFormatException

If the bytes do not represent a valid UTF-8 encoding.

Implements | DataInput.readUTF()

Description | This method reads a UTF-8 encoded string from the stream. See the description of DataInputStream.readUTF(DataInput) for more information.

registerValidation

public synchronized void registerValidation(
                    ObjectInputValidation obj, int prio)
    throws NotActiveException, InvalidObjectException

Parameters | obj | The object requesting validation.

prio | The priority of the validation callback; use zero as a default.

Throws | NotActiveException

If serialization is not active.

InvalidObjectException

If obj is null.

Description   This method may be called from an object's `private readOb-ject()` method to register a validation callback. An object performs internal validation by implementing the `ObjectInput-Validation` interface and registering itself with the `ObjectInputStream` via this function. When `ObjectInputStream` has completely deserialized an object (i.e., restored all of its fields and any objects it references), the stream calls `ObjectInputValidation.validateObject()` for every object that has an object validation callback. Objects that register with higher priority values get validated before objects that register with lower priority values. Within a priority value, the callbacks are not processed in any particular order.

skipBytes

```
public int skipBytes(int len) throws IOException
```

Parameters   `len`   The number of bytes to skip.

Returns   The actual number of skipped bytes.

Throws   `EOFException`

        If the end of the file is encountered.

    `IOException`   If any other kind I/O error occurs.

Implements   `DataInput.skipBytes()`

Description   This method skips over n bytes in the underlying input stream. The method blocks until all of the bytes are skipped, the end of the stream is encountered, or an exception is thrown.

Protected Instance Methods

enableResolveObject

```
protected final boolean enableResolveObject(boolean enable)
                    throws SecurityException
```

Parameters   `enable`   A boolean value that specifies whether or not object replacement is enabled.

Returns   `true` if object replacement was previously enabled; `false` otherwise.

Throws   `SecurityException`

        If `enable` is `true` and `getClassLoader()` called on the class of the stream does not return `null`.

Description   This method determines if a trusted subclass of `ObjectInputStream` is allowed to replace deserialized objects. If the method is called with `true`, object replacement is enabled. Each time an object is deserialized, `resolveObject()` is called to give the `ObjectInputStream` a chance to replace the object. A trusted stream is one whose class has no `ClassLoader`.

readStreamHeader

protected void readStreamHeader()
                  throws IOException, StreamCorruptedException

Throws	StreamCorruptedException
	If the stream header is not correct.
	IOException If any kind of I/O error occurs.
Description	This method attempts to read the stream header, which consists of a magic number and a version number. If something goes wrong, an appropriate exception is thrown. This method is called by the constructor for ObjectInputStream and is the source of the exceptions it throws. If you subclass ObjectInput-Stream, you can override this method to provide your own stream header checking.

resolveClass

protected Class resolveClass(ObjectStreamClass v)
                   throws IOException, ClassNotFoundException

Parameters	v The ObjectStreamClass to be resolved.
Returns	The Class that corresponds to the given ObjectStreamClass.
Throws	ClassNotFoundException
	If the class of the given ObjectStreamClass cannot be found.
	IOException If any kind of I/O error occurs.
Description	This method attempts to find the Class object that corresponds to the supplied ObjectStreamClass. When a object is deserialized, its class information is read into an ObjectStreamClass object, which is then resolved to a Class if possible. Subclasses of ObjectInputStream can override this method to allow classes to be fetched from alternate sources. The version of the ObjectStreamClass and the Class must match.

resolveObject

protected Object resolveObject(Object obj) throws IOException

Parameters	obj The object to be replaced.
Returns	A replacement for the given object.
Throws	IOException If any kind of I/O error occurs.
Description	If object replacement is enabled for this ObjectInputStream (see enableResolveObject()), this method is called with each deserialized object to give the stream a chance to replace the object. In ObjectInputStream, this method simply returns the object that was passed to it. Subclasses can override this method to provide more useful functionality.

Inherited Methods

Method	Inherited From	Method	Inherited From
clone()	Object	equals(Object)	Object
finalize()	Object	getClass()	Object
hashCode()	Object	mark()	InputStream
markSupported()	InputStream	notify()	Object
notifyAll()	Object	read(byte[])	InputStream
reset()	InputStream	skip(long n)	InputStream
toString()	Object	wait()	Object
wait(long)	Object	wait(long, int)	Object

See Also

Class, ClassNotFoundException, DataInput, Double, EOFException, Externaliz-able, Float, InputStream, InvalidClassException, IOException, NotActiveException, ObjectInput, ObjectInputValidation, ObjectOuputStream, ObjectStreamClass, OptionalDataException, SecurityException, Serializable, StreamCorruptedException, String, UTFDataFormatException

11.40   ObjectInputValidation

Synopsis

Interface Name: java.io.ObjectInputValidation
Super-interface: None
Immediate Sub-interfaces:
                         None
Implemented By: None
Availability: New as of JDK 1.1

Description

The ObjectInputValidation interface defines a callback for object validation. A class implements this interface if it needs to validate deserialized objects. A class that needs to perform object validation on deserialized instances should pass a validation object to ObjectInputStream.registerValidation() at the beginning of its private readObject() method. When an object of that class is deserialized, the validateObject() method in the validation object is called. If the method is satisfied with the state of the deserialized object, it returns quietly; otherwise it should throw an InvalidObjectException.

The simplest case is to have a class do its own validation by implementing `Object-InputValidation` itself and passing `this` to the `registerValidation()` method. For example, the following code fragment shows how to register for validation in `readObject()`. The `validateObject()` method always throws an exception:

```
public class ValidateMe
    implements Serializable, ObjectInputValidation {

    private void readObject(ObjectInputStream in)
                throws IOException, ClassNotFoundException {
        in.registerValidation(this, 0);
        in.defaultReadObject();
    }

    public void validateObject() throws InvalidObjectException {
        // if (this object is not valid)
            throw new InvalidObjectException("Object not valid!");
    }
...
}
```

Interface Declaration

```
public abstract interface java.io.ObjectInputValidation {
    // Methods
    public abstract void validateObject();
}
```

Methods

validateObject

public void validateObject() throws InvalidObjectException

    Throws   InvalidObjectException

                       If the method is not satisfied with its state.

    Description This method allows an object to check its own validity. An InvalidObjectException should be thrown if anything is invalid.

See Also

ObjectInput, ObjectInputStream

11.41   ObjectOutput

Synopsis

Interface Name: java.io.ObjectOutput
Super-interface: java.io.DataOutput
Immediate Sub-interfaces:
                         None
Implemented By: java.io.ObjectOutputStream
Availability: New as of JDK 1.1

Description

The ObjectOutput interface extends the DataOutput interface for object serialization. While DataOutput defines methods for reading primitive types from a stream, ObjectOutput defines methods for writing objects and arrays of bytes.

Interface Declaration

```
public abstract interface java.io.ObjectOutput extends java.io.DataOutput {
    // Methods
    public abstract void close();
    public abstract void flush();
    public abstract void write(int b);
    public abstract void write(byte[] b);
    public abstract void write(byte[] b, int off, int len);
    public abstract void writeObject(Object obj);
}
```

Methods

close

```
public abstract void close() throws IOException
```

Throws   IOException   If any kind of I/O error occurs.
Description   This method closes the stream and releases any system resources associated with it.

flush

```
public abstract void flush() throws IOException
```

Throws   IOException   If any kind of I/O error occurs.
Description   If the stream uses a buffer, this method forces any bytes that may be buffered by the output stream to be written to the underlying physical device.

write

public abstract void write(int b) throws IOException

Parameters	b	The value to write.
Throws	IOException	If any kind of I/O error occurs.
Overrides	DataOutput.write(int)	
Description	This method writes the lowest eight bits of the given integer b to the stream.	

public abstract void write(byte[] b) throws IOException

Parameters	b	An array of bytes to write to the stream.
Throws	IOException	If any kind of I/O error occurs.
Overrides	DataOutput.write(byte[])	
Description	This method writes all of the 8-bit bytes in the given array to the stream.	

public abstract void write(byte[] b, int off, int len)
            throws IOException

Parameters	b	An array of bytes to write to the stream.
	off	An offset into the byte array.
	len	The number of bytes to write.
Throws	IOException	If any kind of I/O error occurs.
Overrides	DataOutput.write(byte[], int, int)	
Description	This method writes len bytes from the given array, starting off elements from the beginning of the array, to the stream.	

writeObject

public abstract void writeObject(Object obj) throws IOException

Throws	IOException	If any kind of I/O error occurs.
Description	This method writes the given object to the stream, or in other words, it serializes an object to the stream. The class that implements this interface determines how the object is written.	

Inherited Methods

Method	Inherited From	Method	Inherited From
writeBoolean(boolean)	DataOutput	writeByte(int)	DataOutput
writeBytes(String)	DataOutput	writeChar(int)	DataOutput
writeChars(String)	DataOutput	writeDouble(double)	DataOutput
writeFloat(float)	DataOutput	writeInt(int)	DataOutput
writeLong(long)	DataOutput	writeShort(int)	DataOutput
writeUTF(String)	DataOutput		

See Also

DataOutput, ObjectOutputStream

11.42   ObjectOutputStream

Synopsis

Class Name:	java.io.ObjectOutputStream
Superclass:	java.io.OutputStream
Immediate Subclasses:	None
Interfaces Implemented:	java.io.ObjectOutput
Availability:	New as of JDK 1.1

Description

The ObjectOutputStream class can write both primitive types and object instances to an underlying OutputStream. The objects and other data can then be read by an ObjectInputStream. These two classes provide persistent storage of objects when they are used in conjunction with FileInputStream and FileOutputStream. The classes can also be used with socket streams to pass objects across the network.

Only objects that are instances of classes that implement the Serializable or Externalizable interfaces can be serialized to an output stream. The default serialization mechanism is implemented by writeObject(). When an object is serialized, the class of the object is encoded, along with the class name, the signature of the class, the values of the non-static and non-transient fields of the object, including any other objects referenced by the object (except those that do not implement the Serializable interface themselves). Multiple references to the same object are encoded using a reference sharing mechanism, so that a graph of the object can be restored appropriately. Strings and arrays are objects in Java, so they are treated as objects during serialization.

For example, the following code opens a file called *color.ser* and writes out a Color object:

```
FileOutputStream fileOut;
ObjectOutputStream out;
try {
    fileOut = new FileOutputStream("color.ser");
    out = new ObjectOutputStream(fileOut);
    out.writeObject(Color.blue);
    out.close();
}
catch (IOException e) {
    System.out.println("Error writing: " + e);
}
```

Classes that require special handling during serialization and deserialization must implement the following methods (with these exact signatures):

```
private void readObject(ObjectOutputStream stream)
            throws IOException, ClassNotFoundException
private void writeObject(ObjectOutputStream stream) throws IOException
```

The writeObject() method is responsible for writing the state of the object for the particular class so that it can be restored by readObject(). The writeObject() method does not need to handle writing the state for the object's superclass or any of its subclasses except in the case where the superclass does not itself implement the Serializable interface. In this case, the nonserializable class must have a no-argument constructor that can be called to initialize its fields, and it is the responsibility of the subclass to save the state of its superclass.

A class that inherits the implementation of Serializable prevents itself from being serialized by defining readObject() and writeObject() methods that throw NotSerializableException objects.

If a class needs complete control over the contents and formatting of the serialized form of its objects, it should implement the Externalizable interface.

Class Summary

```
public class java.io.ObjectOutputStream extends java.io.OutputStream
            implements java.io.ObjectOutput {
   // Constructors
   public ObjectOutputStream(OutputStream out);

   // Instance Methods
   public void close();
   public final void defaultWriteObject();
   public void flush();
   public void reset();
   public void write(int data);
   public void write(byte[] b);
   public void write(byte[] b, int off, int len);
   public void writeBoolean(boolean data);
   public void writeByte(int data);
   public void writeBytes(String data);
   public void writeChar(int data);
   public void writeChars(String data);
   public void writeDouble(double data);
   public void writeFloat(float data);
   public void writeInt(int data);
   public void writeLong(long data);
   public final void writeObject(Object obj);
   public void writeShort(int data);
   public void writeUTF(String data);
```

```
// Protected Instance Methods
protected void annotateClass(Class cl);
protected void drain();
protected final boolean enableReplaceObject(boolean enable);
protected Object replaceObject(Object obj);
protected void writeStreamHeader();
}
```

Constructors

ObjectOutputStream

public ObjectOutputStream(OutputStream out) throws IOException

Parameters	out	The underlying output stream.
Throws	IOException	If any kind of I/O error occurs.
Description		This constructor creates an ObjectOutputStream that writes to the given output stream. The constructor writes the stream header, which consists of a magic number and version number, in preparation for serialization.

Instance Methods

close

public void close() throws IOException

Throws	IOException	If any kind of I/O error occurs.
Implements	ObjectOutput.close()	
Overrides	OutputStream.close()	
Description		This method closes the stream and releases any system resources that are associated with it.

defaultWriteObject

public final void defaultWriteObject() throws IOException

Throws	IOException	If any kind of I/O error occurs.
	NotActiveException	
		If serialization is not active.
Description		This method writes the fields of the object that are not static or transient. The method can only be called from the private writeObject() method of an object that is being serialized; it throws a NotActiveException if it is called at any other time. This method implements the default serialization mechanism.

flush

```
public void flush() throws IOException
```
Throws	IOException If any kind of I/O error occurs.
Implements	ObjectOutput.flush()
Overrides	OutputStream.flush()
Description	This method takes any buffered output and forces it to be written to the underlying stream.

reset

```
public void reset() throws IOException
```
Throws	IOException If any kind of I/O error occurs.
Description	This method sets the state of the ObjectOutputStream to the same state as when it was created. As objects are serialized to the stream, the ObjectOutputStream remembers which ones are already serialized. If the program requests that already serialized objects be written again, the ObjectOutputStream just writes out a reference to the previous object. Calling reset() causes the ObjectOutputStream to forget what it has done before, so all subsequent objects are fully serialized.

write

```
public void write(int data) throws IOException
```
Parameters	data The value to write.
Throws	IOException If any kind of I/O error occurs.
Implements	ObjectOutput.write(int)
Overrides	OutputStream.write(int)
Description	This method writes the lowest eight bits of b to the underlying stream as a byte.

```
public void write(byte[] b) throws IOException
```
Parameters	b An array of bytes to write.
Throws	IOException If any kind of I/O error occurs.
Implements	ObjectOutput.write(byte[])
Overrides	OutputStream.write(byte[])
Description	This method writes the given array of bytes to the underlying stream.

```
public void write(byte[] b, int off, int len) throws IOException
```
Parameters	b An array of bytes to write to the stream.
	off An offset into the byte array.

len	The number of bytes to write.
Throws	IOException If any kind of I/O error occurs.
Implements	ObjectOutput.write(byte[], int, int)
Overrides	OutputStream.write(byte[], int, int)
Description	This method writes len bytes from the given array, starting off elements from the beginning of the array, to the underlying stream.

writeBoolean

```
public void writeBoolean(boolean data) throws IOException
```

Parameters	data The boolean value to write.
Throws	IOException If any kind of I/O error occurs.
Implements	DataOutput.writeBoolean()
Description	If data is true, this method writes a byte that contains the value 1 to the underlying stream. If data is false, the method writes a byte that contains the value 0.

writeByte

```
public void writeByte(int data) throws IOException
```

Parameters	data The value to write.
Throws	IOException If any kind of I/O error occurs.
Implements	DataOutput.writeByte()
Description	This method writes an 8-bit byte to the underlying stream, using the lowest eight bits of the given integer data.

writeBytes

```
public void writeBytes(String data) throws IOException
```

Parameters	data The String to write.
Throws	IOException If any kind of I/O error occurs.
Implements	DataOutput.writeBytes()
Description	This method writes the characters in the given String to the underlying stream as a sequence of 8-bit bytes. The high-order bytes of the characters in the string are ignored.

writeChar

```
public void writeChar(int data) throws IOException
```

Parameters	data The value to write.
Throws	IOException If any kind of I/O error occurs.
Implements	DataOutput.writeChar()

Description   This method writes a 16-bit char to the underlying stream, using the lowest two bytes of the given integer data.

writeChars

```
public void writeChars(String data) throws IOException
```
Parameters   data   The String to write.
Throws   IOException   If any kind of I/O error occurs.
Implements   DataOutput.writeChars()
Description   This method writes the characters in the given String object to the underlying stream as a sequence of 16-bit characters.

writeDouble

```
public void writeDouble(double data) throws IOException
```
Parameters   data   The double value to write.
Throws   IOException   If any kind of I/O error occurs.
Implements   DataOutput.writeDouble()
Description   This method writes a 64-bit double to the underlying stream. The double value is converted to a long using doubleToLongBits() of Double; the long value is then written to the underlying stream as eight bytes with the highest byte first.

writeFloat

```
public void writeFloat(float data) throws IOException
```
Parameters   data   The float value to write.
Throws   IOException   If any kind of I/O error occurs.
Implements   DataOutput.writeFloat()
Description   This method writes a 32-bit float to the underlying stream. The float value is converted to a int using floatToIntBits() of Float; the int value is then written to the underlying stream as four bytes with the highest byte first.

writeInt

```
public void writeInt(int data) throws IOException
```
Parameters   data   The int value to write.
Throws   IOException   If any kind of I/O error occurs.
Implements   DataOutput.writeInt()
Description   This method writes a 32-bit int to the underlying stream. The value is written as four bytes with the highest byte first.

writeLong

```
public void writeLong(long data) throws IOException
```

Parameters	data	The long value to write.
Throws	IOException	If any kind of I/O error occurs.
Implements	DataOutput.writeLong()	
Description	This method writes a 64-bit long to the underlying stream. The value is written as eight bytes with the highest byte first.	

writeObject

```
public final void writeObject(Object obj)
                throws IOException, InvalidClassException,
                    NotSerializableException
```

Parameters	obj	The object to be serialized.
Throws	InvalidClassException	
		If there is a problem with the class of the object.
	NotSerializableException	
		If the object does not implement Serializable or Externalizable.
	IOException	If any kind of I/O error occurs.
Implements	ObjectOutput.writeObject()	
Description	This method serializes the given object to the stream. The class of the object is encoded, along with the class name, the signature of the class, the values of the non-static and non-transient fields of the object, including any other objects referenced by the object (except those that do not implement the Serializable interface themselves). Multiple references to the same object are encoded using a reference sharing mechanism, so that a graph of object can be restored appropriately.	

writeShort

```
public void writeShort(int data) throws IOException
```

Parameters	data	The value to write.
Throws	IOException	If any kind of I/O error occurs.
Implements	DataOutput.writeShort()	
Description	This method writes a 16-bit short to the underlying stream, using the lowest two bytes of the given integer data.	

writeUTF

> public void writeUTF(String data) throws IOException

Parameters	data	The String to write.
Throws	IOException	If any kind of I/O error occurs.
Implements	DataOutput.writeUTF()	
Description	This method writes the given String to the underlying stream using the UTF-8 encoding. See the description of DataOutput-Stream.writeUTF(String) for more information.	

Protected Instance Methods

annotateClass

> protected void annotateClass(Class cl) throws IOException

Parameters	cl	The class to be serialized.
Throws	IOException	If any kind of I/O error occurs.
Description	This method is called once for each unique class during serialization. The implementation in ObjectOutputStream does nothing; subclasses can override this method to write out more information about a class. A corresponding subclass of Object-InputStream should override the resolveClass() method to read the extra class information.	

drain

> protected void drain() throws IOException

Throws	IOException	If any kind of I/O error occurs.
Description	This method is a helper method for flush(). It forces a write of any buffered data in the ObjectOutputStream, but does not call flush() on the underlying stream.	

enableReplaceObject

> protected final boolean enableReplaceObject(boolean enable)
>   throws SecurityException

Parameters	enable	A boolean value that specifies whether or not object replacement is enabled.
Returns	true if object replacement was previously enabled; false otherwise.	
Throws	SecurityException	
		If enable is true and getClassLoader() called on the class of the stream does not return null.
Description	This method determines if a trusted subclass of ObjectOutput-Stream is allowed to replace serialized objects. If the method is called with true, replacement is enabled. Each time an object is serialized, replaceObject() is called to give the	

ObjectOutputStream a chance to replace the object. A trusted stream is one whose class has no ClassLoader.

replaceObject

protected Object replaceObject(Object obj) throws IOException

Parameters	obj The object to be replaced.
Returns	A replacement for the given object.
Throws	IOException If any kind of I/O error occurs.
Description	If object replacement is enabled for this ObjectOutputStream (see enableReplaceObject()), this method is called with each object to be serialized to give the stream a chance to replace the object. In ObjectOutputStream, this method simply returns the object that was passed to it. Subclasses can override this method to provide more useful functionality.

writeStreamHeader

protected void writeStreamHeader() throws IOException

Throws	IOException If any kind of I/O error occurs.
Description	This method writes the serialization stream header, which consists of a magic number and a version number. This method is called by the constructor for ObjectOutputStream. If you subclass ObjectOutputStream, you can override this method to provide your own stream header.

Inherited Methods

Method	Inherited From	Method	Inherited From
clone()	Object	equals(Object)	Object
finalize()	Object	getClass()	Object
hashCode()	Object	notify()	Object
notifyAll()	Object	toString()	Object
wait()	Object	wait(long)	Object
wait(long, int)	Object		

See Also

Class, DataOutput, Double, Externalizable, Float, InvalidClassException, IOException, NotActiveException, NotSerializableException, ObjectInputStream, ObjectOutput, OutputStream, SecurityException, Serializable, String

11.43   ObjectStreamClass

Synopsis

Class Name: java.io.ObjectStreamClass
Superclass: java.lang.Object
Immediate Subclasses: None
Interfaces Implemented: None
Availability: New as of JDK 1.1

Description

The ObjectStreamClass class represents a Java class during object serialization. When an object is deserialized, its class information is read into an ObjectStream-Class, which is then resolved to a Class if possible. An ObjectStreamClass instance contains the name and version information for a class.

Class Summary

```
public class java.io.ObjectStreamClass extends java.lang.Object
            implements java.io.Serializable {
  // Class Methods
  public static ObjectStreamClass lookup(Class cl);

  // Instance Methods
  public Class forClass();
  public String getName();
  public long getSerialVersionUID();
  public String toString();
}
```

Class Methods

lookup

```
public static ObjectStreamClass lookup(Class cl)
```

Parameters	cl	The Class to find.
Returns		An ObjectStreamClass that corresponds to the given Class.
Description		This method finds an ObjectStreamClass for the given Class. If the appropriate ObjectStreamClass does not already exist, this method creates an ObjectStreamClass for the given Class. The method returns null if cl is not serializable.

Instance Methods

forClass

```
public Class forClass()
```
    Returns   The `Class` that corresponds to this `ObjectStreamClass`.

    Description   This method returns the `Class` in the run-time system that corresponds to this `ObjectStreamClass`. If there is no corresponding class, `null` is returned.

getName

```
public String getName()
```
    Returns   The `class name`.

    Description   This method returns the name of the class this `ObjectStream-Class` represents.

getSerialVersionUID

```
public long getSerialVersionUID()
```
    Returns   The `class version`.

    Description   This method returns the version of the class this `ObjectStream-Class` represents.

toString

```
public String toString()
```
    Returns   A `string representation of this` object.

    Overrides   `Object.toString()`

    Description   This method returns a string that contains the class name and version information for this `ObjectStreamClass`.

Inherited Methods

Method	Inherited From	Method	Inherited From
clone()	Object	equals(Object)	Object
finalize()	Object	getClass()	Object
hashCode()	Object	notify()	Object
notifyAll()	Object	wait()	Object
wait(long)	Object	wait(long, int)	Object

See Also

Class, `ObjectInputStream`, `ObjectOutputStream`, `Serializable`

11.44   ObjectStreamException

Synopsis

Class Name:	`java.io.ObjectStreamException`
Superclass:	`java.io.IOException`
Immediate Subclasses:	`java.io.InvalidClassException,`
	`java.io.InvalidObjectException,`
	`java.io.NotActiveException,`
	`java.io.NotSerializableException,`
	`java.io.OptionalDataException,`
	`java.io.StreamCorruptedException,`
	`java.io.WriteAbortedException`
Interfaces Implemented:	None
Availability:	New as of JDK 1.1

Description

The `ObjectStreamException` class is the superclass for all of the serialization exceptions.

Class Summary

```
public class java.io.ObjectStreamException extends java.io.IOException {
  // Constructors
  protected ObjectStreamException();
  protected ObjectStreamException(String classname);
}
```

Constructors

ObjectStreamException

protected ObjectStreamException()

Description   This constructor creates an `ObjectStreamException` with no detail message.

protected ObjectStreamException(String classname)

Parameters   classname   The name of the class.

Description   This constructor creates an `ObjectStreamException` with the specified detail message, which should be the name of the class that caused the exception.

Inherited Methods

Method	Inherited From	Method	Inherited From
clone()	Object	equals(Object)	Object
fillInStackTrace()	Throwable	finalize()	Object
getClass()	Object	getLocalizedMessage()	Throwable
getMessage()	Throwable	hashCode()	Object
notify()	Object	notifyAll()	Object
printStackTrace()	Throwable	printStack-Trace(PrintStream)	Throwable
printStack-Trace(PrintWriter)	Throwable	toString()	Object
wait()	Object	wait(long)	Object
wait(long, int)	Object		

See Also

Exception, InvalidClassException, InvalidObjectException, IOException, NotActiveException, NotSerializableException, OptionalDataException, StreamCorruptedException, WriteAbortedException

11.45   OptionalDataException

Synopsis

Class Name: java.io.OptionalDataException
Superclass: java.io.ObjectStreamException
Immediate Subclasses: None
Interfaces Implemented: None
Availability: New as of JDK 1.1

Description

An OptionalDataException is thrown during object deserialization to indicate that primitive data has been encountered instead of objects. Either the eof flag is true, or the length variable indicates the number of bytes that are available to be read.

Class Summary

```
public class java.io.OptionalDataException
            extends java.io.ObjectStreamException {
  // Variables
  public boolean eof;
  public int length;
}
```

Variables

eof

public boolean eof

Description   A boolean value that indicates if the stream is at its end.

length

public int length

Description   The number of available bytes of data.

Inherited Methods

Method	Inherited From	Method	Inherited From
clone()	Object	equals(Object)	Object
fillInStackTrace()	Throwable	finalize()	Object
getClass()	Object	getLocalizedMessage()	Throwable
getMessage()	Throwable	hashCode()	Object
notify()	Object	notifyAll()	Object
printStackTrace()	Throwable	printStack-Trace(PrintStream)	Throwable
printStack-Trace(PrintWriter)	Throwable	toString()	Object
wait()	Object	wait(long)	Object
wait(long, int)	Object		

See Also

Exception, ObjectInputStream, ObjectStreamException, Throwable

11.46   OutputStream

Synopsis

Class Name:	java.io.OutputStream
Superclass:	java.lang.Object
Immediate Subclasses:	java.io.ByteArrayOutputStream,
	java.io.FileOutputStream,
	java.io.FilterOutputStream,
	java.io.ObjectOutputStream,
	java.io.PipedOutputStream
Interfaces Implemented:	None
Availability:	JDK 1.0 or later

Description

The OutputStream class is an abstract class that is the superclass of all classes that represent output byte streams. OutputStream defines the basic output methods that all output streams provide. A similar hierarchy of classes, based around Writer, deals with character streams instead of byte streams.

OutputStream is designed so that write(byte[]) and write(byte[], int, int) call write(int b). Thus, a subclass can simply override write(), and all the write methods will work. However, for efficiency's sake, write(byte[], int, int) should also be overridden with a method that can write a block of data more efficiently than writing each byte separately.

Some OutputStream subclasses may implement buffering to increase efficiency. OutputStream provides a method, flush(), that tells the OutputStream to write any buffered output to the underlying device, which may be a disk drive or a network.

Class Summary

```
public abstract class java.io.OutputStream extends java.lang.Object {
    // Instance Methods
    public void close();
    public void flush();
    public abstract void write(int b);
    public void write(byte[] b);
    public void write(byte[] b, int off, int len);
}
```

Instance Methods

close

public void close() throws IOException

Throws	IOException	If any kind of I/O error occurs.
Description	This method closes the output stream and releases any resources associated with it.	

The implementation of the close() method in OutputStream does nothing; a subclass should override this method to handle cleanup for the stream.

flush

public void flush() throws IOException

Throws	IOException	If any kind of I/O error occurs.
Description	This method forces any bytes that may be buffered by the output stream to be written.	

The implementation of flush() in OutputStream does nothing; a subclass should override this method as needed.

write

public abstract void write(int b) throws IOException

Parameters	b	The value to write to the stream.
Throws	IOException	If any kind of I/O error occurs.
Description	This method writes a byte of output. The method blocks until the byte is actually written.	

A subclass of OutputStream must implement this method.

public void write(byte[] b) throws IOException

Parameters	b	An array of bytes to write to the stream.
Throws	IOException	If any kind of I/O error occurs.
Description	This method writes the bytes from the given array by calling write(b, 0, b.length). The method blocks until the bytes are actually written.	

A subclass does not usually need to override this method, as it can override write(byte[], int, int) and have write(byte[]) work automatically.

```
public void write(byte[] b, int off, int len) throws IOException
```
Parameters	b	An array of bytes to write to the stream.
	off	An offset into the byte array.
	len	The number of bytes to write.
Throws	IOException	If any kind of I/O error occurs.
Description		This method writes len bytes of output from the given array, starting at offset off. The method blocks until the bytes are actually written.

The implementation of this method in OutputStream uses write(int) repeatedly to write the bytes. Although it is not strictly necessary, a subclass should override this method to write a block of data more efficiently.

Inherited Methods

Method	Inherited From	Method	Inherited From
clone()	Object	equals(Object)	Object
finalize()	Object	getClass()	Object
hashCode()	Object	notify()	Object
notifyAll()	Object	toString()	Object
wait()	Object	wait(long)	Object
wait(long, int)	Object		

See Also

ByteArrayOutputStream, FileOutputStream, FilterOutputStream, IOException, ObjectOutputStream, PipedOutputStream

11.47   OutputStreamWriter

Synopsis

Class Name:	java.io.OutputStreamWriter
Superclass:	java.io.Writer
Immediate Subclasses:	java.io.FileWriter
Interfaces Implemented:	None
Availability:	New as of JDK 1.1

Description

The OutputStreamWriter class is a bridge between the byte-oriented world of the OutputStream class and the character-oriented world of the Writer class. The OutputStreamWriter represents a character stream, but it sends its output to an underlying byte stream. A character encoding scheme is responsible for translating the Unicode characters to bytes. An OutputStreamWriter can be created using an explicit encoding scheme or a default encoding scheme.

For example, to write a Unicode character stream as an ISO-8859-5 byte stream, you can construct an OutputStreamWriter with the encoding 8859_5 as follows:

```
OutputStreamWriter outr = new OutputStreamWriter(out, "8859_5");
```

Each time you write to an OutputStreamWriter object, bytes may be written to the underlying byte stream. To improve efficiency, you may want to wrap the OutputStreamWriter in a BufferedWriter.

Class Summary

```
public class java.io.OutputStreamWriter extends java.io.Writer {
    // Constructors
    public OutputStreamWriter(OutputStream out);
    public OutputStreamWriter(OutputStream out, String enc);

    // Instance Methods
    public void close();
    public void flush();
    public String getEncoding();
    public void write(int c);
    public void write(char[] cbuf, int off, int len);
    public void write(String str, int off, int len);
}
```

Constructors

OutputStreamWriter

public OutputStreamWriter(OutputStream out)

    Parameters   out   The output stream to use.

    Description   This constructor creates an OutputStreamWriter that writes its data to out and translates characters to bytes using the system's default encoding scheme.

```
public OutputStreamWriter(OutputStream out, String enc)
    throws UnsupportedEncodingException
```

Parameters | out | The output stream to use.
| enc | The name of an encoding scheme.
Throws | UnsupportedEncodingException
| | If enc is not a supported encoding scheme.
Description | This constructor creates an OutputStreamWriter that writes its data to out and translates characters to bytes using the given encoding scheme.

Instance Methods

close

```
public void close() throws IOException
```

Throws | IOException If any kind of I/O error occurs.
Overrides | Writer.close()
Description | This method calls the close() method of the underlying output stream, which releases any system resources associated with this object.

flush

```
public void flush() throws IOException
```

Throws | IOException If any kind of I/O error occurs.
Overrides | Writer.flush()
Description | This method writes out any buffered data in the internal buffer and calls the flush() method of the underlying output stream, which forces any bytes that may be buffered to be written to the underlying device.

getEncoding

```
public String getEncoding()
```

Returns | A String that contains the name of the character encoding scheme of this writer.
Description | This method returns the name of the character encoding scheme this OutputStreamWriter is currently using.

write

```
public void write(int c) throws IOException
```

Parameters | c | The value to write.
Throws | IOException If any kind of I/O error occurs.

Overrides   `Writer.write(int)`

Description   This method converts the given character to bytes using the current encoding scheme and places the converted bytes into an internal buffer. When the buffer fills up, it is written to the underlying byte stream.

```
public void write(char[] cbuf, int off, int len)
          throws IOException
```

Parameters   `cbuf`   An array of characters to write.

                `off`   An offset into the character array.

                `len`   The number of characters to write.

Throws   `IOException`   If any kind of I/O error occurs.

Overrides   `Writer.write(char[], int, int)`

Description   This method converts `len` characters from the array `cbuf` to bytes, starting at offset `off`, using the current encoding scheme. The method places the converted bytes into an internal buffer. When the buffer fills up, it is written to the underlying byte stream.

```
public void write(String str, int off, int len) throws IOException
```

Parameters   `str`   The string to be written.

                `off`   An offset into start in the string.

                `len`   The number of characters to write.

Throws   `IOException`   If any kind of I/O error occurs.

Overrides   `Writer.write(String, int, int)`

Description   This method converts `len` characters from the string `str` to bytes, starting at offset `off`, using the current encoding scheme. The method places the converted bytes into an internal buffer. When the buffer fills up, it is written to the underlying byte stream.

Inherited Methods

Method	Inherited From	Method	Inherited From
clone()	Object	equals(Object)	Object
finalize()	Object	getClass()	Object
hashCode()	Object	notify()	Object
notifyAll()	Object	toString()	Object
wait()	Object	wait(long)	Object
wait(long, int)	Object	write(char[])	Writer
write(String)	Writer		

See Also

BufferedWriter, FileWriter, IOException, OutputStream, UnsupportedEncodingException, Writer

11.48   PipedInputStream

Synopsis

Class Name: java.io.PipedInputStream
Superclass: java.io.InputStream
Immediate Subclasses: None
Interfaces Implemented: None
Availability: JDK 1.0 or later

Description

The PipedInputStream class represents half of a communication pipe; a PipedInputStream must be connected to a PipedOutputStream. When the two halves of a
communication pipe are connected, data written to the PipedOutputStream can be
read from the PipedInputStream. The communication pipe formed by a PipedInputStream and a PipedOutputStream should be used to communicate between
threads. If both ends of a pipe are used by the same thread, the thread can hang.

Class Summary

```
public class java.io.PipedInputStream extends java.io.InputStream {
    // Variables
    protected byte[] buffer;                        // New in 1.1
    protected int in;                               // New in 1.1
    protected int out;                              // New in 1.1
    protected final static int PIPE_SIZE;           // New in 1.1

    // Constructors
    public PipedInputStream();
    public PipedInputStream(PipedOutputStream src);

    // Public Instance Methods
    public synchronized int available();            // New in 1.1
    public void close();
    public void connect(PipedOutputStream src);
    public synchronized int read();
    public synchronized int read(byte[] b, int off, int len);
```

```
    // Protected Instance Methods
    protected synchronized void receive(int b);      // New in 1.1
}
```

Variables

buffer

protected byte[] buffer

Availability   New as of JDK 1.1

Description   The internal data buffer. The buffer receives data from the connected PipedOutputStream and supplies data for the calls to
read().

in

protected int in

Availability   New as of JDK 1.1

Description   An index into the buffer that points to the byte after the last
byte of valid data. A value of -1 indicates that the buffer is
empty.

out

protected int out

Availability   New as of JDK 1.1

Description   An index into the buffer that points to the next byte that will be
returned by read().

PIPE_SIZE

public final static int PIPE_SIZE = 1024

Availability   New as of JDK 1.1

Description   The size of the internal data buffer. The buffer receives data
from the connected PipedOutputStream and supplies data for
the calls to read().

Constructors

PipedInputStream

public PipedInputStream()

Description   This constructor creates a PipedInputStream that is not connected to a PipedOutputStream. The created object must be
connected to a PipedOutputStream before it can be used.

```
public PipedInputStream(PipedOutputStream src) throws IOException
```
    Parameters   src   The `PipedOutputStream` to connect.

    Throws   `IOException`   If any kind of I/O error occurs.

    Description   This constructor creates a `PipedInputStream` that receives data from the given `PipedOutputStream`.

Public Instance Methods

available

```
public synchronized int available() throws IOException
```
    Availability   New as of JDK 1.1

    Returns   The number of bytes that can be read without blocking.

    Throws   `IOException`   If any kind of I/O error occurs.

    Overrides   `InputStream.available()`

    Description   This method returns the number of bytes that can be read without having to wait for more data to become available. More data becomes available in the `PipedInputStream` when data is written to the connected `PipedOutputStream`.

close

```
public void close() throws IOException
```
    Throws   `IOException`   If any kind of I/O error occurs.

    Overrides   `InputStream.close()`

    Description   This method closes the stream and releases the system resources that are associated with it.

connect

```
public void connect(PipedOutputStream src) throws IOException
```
    Parameters   src   The `PipedOutputStream` to connect.

    Throws   `IOException`   If another `PipedOutputStream` is already connected to this `PipedInputStream`.

    Description   This method connects the given `PipedOutputStream` to this `PipedInputStream` object. If there is already a connected `PipedOutputStream`, an exception is thrown.

read

```
public synchronized int read() throws IOException
```
    Returns   The next byte of data or −1 if the end of the stream is encountered.

Throws	IOException	If the pipe is broken. In other words, if this PipedInputStream is closed or if the connected PipedOutputStream is dead.
	InterruptedIOException	
		While this method is waiting for input, if the interrupted() method of the thread that invoked this method is called.
Overrides	InputStream.read()	
Description	This method returns the next byte from the pipe buffer. If the buffer is empty, the method waits until data is written to the connected PipedOutputStream. The method blocks until the byte is read, the end of the stream is encountered, or an exception is thrown.	

```
public synchronized int read(byte b[], int off, int len)
                    throws IOException
```

Parameters	b	An array of bytes to be filled.
	off	An offset into the byte array.
	len	The number of bytes to read.
Returns	The actual number of bytes read or -1 if the end of the stream is encountered immediately.	
Throws	IOException	If the pipe is broken. In other words, if this PipedInputStream is closed or if the connected PipedOutputStream is dead.
	InterruptedIOException	
		While this method is waiting for buffer space to become available, if the interrupted() method of the thread that invoked this method is called.
Overrides	InputStream.read(byte[], int, int)	
Description	This method copies bytes from the pipe buffer into the given array b, starting at index off and continuing for len bytes. If there is at least one byte in the buffer, the method returns as many bytes as are in the buffer (up to len). If the buffer is empty, the method blocks until data is written to the connected PipedOutputStream.	

Protected Instance Methods

receive

```
protected synchronized void receive(int b) throws IOException
```

Availability	New as of JDK 1.1	
Parameters	b	The byte being received.
Throws	IOException	If the pipe is broken. In other words, if this `PipedInputStream` is closed.
Description		This method is called by the connected `PipedOutputStream` object to provide the given value as a byte of input to this `PipedInputStream` object.

Inherited Methods

Method	Inherited From	Method	Inherited From
clone()	Object	equals(Object)	Object
finalize()	Object	getClass()	Object
hashCode()	Object	mark(int)	InputStream
markSupported()	InputStream	notify()	Object
notifyAll()	Object	read(byte[])	InputStream
reset()	InputStream	skip(long)	InputStream
toString()	Object	wait()	Object
wait(long)	Object	wait(long, int)	Object

See Also

InputStream, IOException, PipedOutputStream

11.49   PipedOutputStream

Synopsis

Class Name:	java.io.PipedOutputStream
Superclass:	java.io.OutputStream
Immediate Subclasses:	None
Interfaces Implemented:	None
Availability:	JDK 1.0 or later

Description

The PipedOutputStream class represents half of a communication pipe; a Piped-OutputStream must be connected to a PipedOutputStream. When the two halves of a communication pipe are connected, data written to the PipedOutputStream can be read from the PipedInputStream. The communication pipe formed by a Piped-OutputStream and a PipedInputStream should be used to communicate between threads. If both ends of a pipe are used by the same thread, the thread can hang.

Class Summary

```
public class java.io.PipedOutputStream extends java.io.OutputStream {
    // Constructors
    public PipedOutputStream();
    public PipedOutputStream(PipedInputStream snk);

    // Instance Methods
    public void close();
    public void connect(PipedInputStream snk);
    public synchronized void flush();                    // New in 1.1
    public void write(int b);
    public void write(byte[] b, int off, int len);
}
```

Constructors

PipedOutputStream

public PipedOutputStream()

Description   This constructor creates a PipedOutputStream that is not connected to a PipedInputStream. The created object must be connected to a PipedInputStream before it can be used.

public PipedOutputStream(PipedInputStream snk)

Parameters   snk   The PipedInputStream to connect.

Throws   IOException   If any kind of I/O error occurs.

Description   This constructor creates a PipedOutputStream that sends data to the given PipedInputStream.

Instance Methods

close

public void close() throws IOException

Throws   IOException   If any kind of I/O error occurs.

Overrides   OutputStream.close()

Description   This method closes the stream and releases the system resources that are associated with it.

connect

public void connect(PipedInputStream snk) throws IOException

Parameters	snk	The PipedInputStream to connect.
Throws	IOException	If another PipedInputStream is already connected to this PipedOutputStream or this PipedOutputStream is already connected.
Description		This method connects this PipedOutputStream object to the given PipedInputStream. If this PipedOutputStream or snk is already connected, an exception is thrown.

flush

public synchronized void flush() throws IOException

Availability	New as of JDK 1.1	
Throws	IOException	If any kind of I/O error occurs.
	InterruptedIOException	
		While this method is waiting for buffer space to become available, if the interrupted() method of the thread that invoked this method is called.
Overrides	OutputStream.flush()	
Description		This method flushes the stream, which tells the connected PipedInputStream to notify its readers to read any available data.

write

public void write(int b) throws IOException

Parameters	b	The value to write.
Throws	IOException	If any kind of I/O error occurs.
	InterruptedIOException	
		While this method is waiting for buffer space to become available, if the interrupted() method of the thread that invoked this method is called.
Overrides	OutputStream.write(int)	
Description		This method writes a byte of output. The method passes the given value directly to the connected PipedInputStream.

public void write(byte b[], int off, int len) throws IOException

Parameters	b	An array of bytes to write to the stream.
	off	An offset into the byte array.
	len	The number of bytes to write.

Throws	IOException If any kind of I/O error occurs.
	InterruptedIOException
	While this method is waiting for buffer space to become available, if the interrupted() method of the thread that invoked this method is called.
Overrides	OutputStream.write(byte[], int, int)
Description	This method writes len bytes of output from the given array, starting at offset off. The method passes the given data to the connected PipedInputStream.

Inherited Methods

Method	Inherited From	Method	Inherited From
clone()	Object	equals(Object)	Object
finalize()	Object	getClass()	Object
hashCode()	Object	notify()	Object
notifyAll()	Object	toString()	Object
wait()	Object	wait(long)	Object
wait(long, int)	Object	write(byte[])	OutputStream

See Also

IOException, OutputStream, PipedInputStream

11.50   PipedReader

Synopsis

Class Name:	java.io.PipedReader
Superclass:	java.io.Reader
Immediate Subclasses:	None
Interfaces Implemented:	None
Availability:	New as of JDK 1.1

Description

The PipedReader class represents half of a communication pipe; a PipedReader must be connected to a PipedWriter. When the two halves of a communication pipe are connected, data written to the PipedWriter can be read from the PipedReader. The communication pipe formed by a PipedReader and a PipedWriter should be used to communicate between threads. If both ends of a pipe are used by the same thread, the thread can hang.

The PipedReader class is the character-based equivalent of the byte-based PipedInputStream.

Class Summary

```
public class java.io.PipedReader extends java.io.Reader {
    // Constructors
    public PipedReader();
    public PipedReader(PipedWriter src);

    // Instance Methods
    public void close();
    public void connect(PipedWriter src);
    public int read(char[] cbuf, int off, int len);
}
```

Constructors

PipedReader

public PipedReader ()

Description	This constructor creates a PipedReader that is not connected to a PipedWriter. The created object must be connected to a PipedWriter before it can be used.

public PipedReader(PipedWriter src) throws IOException

Parameters	src	The PipedWriter to connect.
Throws	IOException	If any kind of I/O error occurs.
Description	This constructor creates a PipedReader that receives data from the given PipedWriter.	

Instance Methods

close

public void close() throws IOException

Throws	IOException	If any kind of I/O error occurs.
Overrides	Reader.close()	
Description	This method closes the reader and releases the system resources that are associated with it.	

connect

public void connect(PipedWriter src) throws IOException

Parameters	src	The PipedWriter to connect.
Throws	IOException	If another PipedWriter is already connected to this PipedReader.

Description   This method connects the given PipedWriter to this PipedReader object. If there is already a connected PipedWriter, an exception is thrown.

read

```
public int read(char[] cbuf, int off, int len) throws IOException
```

Parameters   cbuf   An array of characters to be filled.

                  off   An offset into the array.

                  len   The number of characters to read.

Returns   The actual number of characters read or –1 if the end of the stream is encountered immediately.

Throws   IOException   If the pipe is broken. In other words, if this PipedReader is closed or if the connected PipedWriter is dead.

                  InterruptedIOException

                  While this method is waiting for input, if the interrupted() method of the thread that invoked this method is called.

Overrides   Reader.read(char[], int, int)

Description   This method copies characters from the pipe buffer into the given array cbuf, starting at index off and continuing for len characters. If there is at least one character in the buffer, the method returns as many characters as are in the buffer (up to len). If the buffer is empty, the method blocks until data is written to the connected PipedWriter.

Inherited Methods

Method	Inherited From	Method	Inherited From
clone()	Object	equals(Object)	Object
finalize()	Object	getClass()	Object
hashCode()	Object	mark(int)	Reader
markSupported()	Reader	notify()	Object
notifyAll()	Object	read()	Reader
read(char[])	Reader	reset()	Reader
skip(long)	Reader	toString()	Object
wait()	Object	wait(long)	Object
wait(long, int)	Object		

See Also

IOException, PipedInputStream, PipedWriter, Reader

11.51   PipedWriter

Synopsis

Class Name:	java.io.PipedWriter
Superclass:	java.io.Writer
Immediate Subclasses:	None
Interfaces Implemented:	None
Availability:	New as of JDK 1.1

Description

The PipedWriter class represents half of a communication pipe; a PipedReader must be connected to a PipedWriter. When the two halves of a communication pipe are connected, data written to the PipedWriter can be read from the PipedReader. The communication pipe formed by a PipedWriter and a PipedReader should be used to communicate between threads. If both ends of a pipe are used by the same thread, the thread can hang.

The PipedWriter class is the character-based equivalent of the byte-based Piped-OutputStream.

Class Summary

```
public class java.io.PipedWriter extends java.io.Writer {
    // Constructors
    public PipedWriter();
    public PipedWriter(PipedReader sink);

    // Instance Methods
    public void close();
    public void connect(PipedReader sink);
    public void flush();
    public void write(char[] cbuf, int off, int len;
}
```

Constructors

PipedWriter

public PipedWriter()

Description   This constructor creates a PipedWriter that is not connected to a PipedReader. The created object must be connected to a PipedReader before it can be used.

public PipedWriter(PipedReader sink)

Parameters   sink   The PipedReader to connect.

Throws   IOException   If any kind of I/O error occurs.

Description   This constructor creates a PipedWriter that sends data to the given PipedReader.

Instance Methods

close

public void close() throws IOException

Throws   IOException   If any kind of I/O error occurs.

Overrides   Writer.close()

Description   This method closes the writer and releases the system resources that are associated with it.

connect

public void connect(PipedReader sink) throws IOException

Parameters   sink   The PipedReader to connect.

Throws   IOException   If another PipedReader is already connected to this PipedWriter or this PipedWriter is already connected.

Description   This method connects this PipedWriter object to the given PipedReader. If this PipedWriter or sink is already connected, an exception is thrown.

flush

public void flush() throws IOException

Throws   IOException   If any kind of I/O error occurs.

                 InterruptedIOException

                 While this method is waiting for buffer space to become available, if the interrupted() method of the thread that invoked this method is called.

Overrides   Writer.flush()

Description   This method flushes the writer, which tells the connected PipedReader to notify its readers to read any available data.

write

```
public void write(char[] cbuf, int off, int len)
          throws IOException
```

Parameters   cbuf   An array of characters to write to the stream.

off   An offset into the character array.

len   The number of characters to write.

Throws   IOException   If any kind of I/O error occurs.

Overrides   Writer.write(char[], int, int)

Description   This method writes len characters of output from the given array, starting at offset off. The method passes the given data to the connected PipedReader.

Inherited Methods

Method	Inherited From	Method	Inherited From
clone()	Object	equals(Object)	Object
finalize()	Object	getClass()	Object
hashCode()	Object	notify()	Object
notifyAll()	Object	toString()	Object
wait()	Object	wait(long)	Object
wait(long, int)	Object	write(int)	Writer
write(char[])	Writer	write(String)	Writer
write(String, int, int)	Writer		

See Also

IOException, PipedOutputStream, PipedReader, Writer

11.52   PrintStream

Synopsis

Class Name: java.io.PrintStream

Superclass: java.io.FilterOutputStream

Immediate Subclasses: None

Interfaces Implemented: None
Availability: JDK 1.0 or later

Description

The PrintStream class provides support for writing string representations of primitive data types and objects to an underlying output stream. As of JDK 1.1, PrintStream uses the system's default encoding scheme to convert characters to bytes and uses the system's own specific line separator, rather than the newline character, for separating lines of text. Although this class is not officially deprecated, its constructors are, and you should use PrintWriter instead of PrintStream in new code.

Prior to JDK 1.1, PrintStream did not handle Unicode characters. Any PrintStream methods that wrote characters only wrote the low eight bits of each character. In addition, prior to JDK 1.1, PrintStream used the newline character to separate lines of text, regardless of the platform. These problems have been corrected as of JDK 1.1.

All of the methods of PrintStream that write multiple times to the underlying output stream handle synchronization internally, so that PrintStream objects are thread-safe.

A PrintStream object is often used to write to a BufferedOutputStream object. Note that you can specify that the PrintStream be flushed every time it writes the line separator or the newline character by using the constructor that takes a boolean argument.

PrintStream objects are often used to report errors. For this reason, the methods of this class do not throw exceptions. Instead, the methods catch any exceptions thrown by any downstream OutputStream objects and set an internal flag, so that the object can remember that a problem occurred. You can query the internal flag by calling the checkError() method.

Class Summary

```
public class java.io.PrintStream extends java.io.FilterOutputStream {
   // Constructors
   public PrintStream(OutputStream out);                  // Deprecated in 1.1
   public PrintStream(OutputStream out,
                       boolean autoFlush);                 // Deprecated in 1.1

   // Public Instance Methods
   public boolean checkError();
   public void close();
   public void flush();
   public void print(boolean b);
   public void print(char c);
```

```
    public void print(char[] s);
    public void print(double d);
    public void print(float f);
    public void print(int i);
    public void print(long l);
    public void print(String s);
    public void print(Object obj);
    public void println();
    public void println(boolean b);
    public void println(char c);
    public void println(char[] s);
    public void println(double d);
    public void println(float f);
    public void println(int i);
    public void println(long l);
    public void println(Object obj);
    public void println(String s);
    public void write(int b);
    public void write(byte[] buf, int off, int len);

    // Protected Instance Methods
    protected void setError();                          // New in 1.1
  }
```

Constructors

PrintStream

public PrintStream(OutputStream out)

Availability	Deprecated as of JDK 1.1
Parameters	out	The output stream to use.
Description	This constructor creates a PrintStream object that sends output to the given OutputStream.

public PrintStream(OutputStream out, boolean autoflush)

Availability	Deprecated as of JDK 1.1
Parameters	out	The output stream to use.
	autoflush	A boolean value that indicates whether or not the print stream is flushed every time a newline is output.
Description	This constructor creates a PrintStream object that sends output to the given OutputStream. If autoflush is true, every time the PrintStream object writes a newline character or line separator, it calls its flush() method. Note that this is different than with a PrintWriter object, which only calls its flush() method when a println() method is called.

Public Instance Methods

checkError

> public boolean checkError()
>
> | Returns | true if any error has occurred; false otherwise. |
> |---|---|
> | Description | This method flushes any buffered output and returns true if any error has occurred. Once the error flag for a PrintStream object has been set, it is never cleared. |

close

> public void close()
>
> | Overrides | FilterOutputStream.close() |
> |---|---|
> | Description | This method closes this print stream and releases any resources associated with the object. The method does this by calling the close() method of the underlying output stream and catching any exceptions that are thrown. |

flush

> public void flush()
>
> | Overrides | FilterOutputStream.flush() |
> |---|---|
> | Description | This method flushes this print stream, forcing any bytes that may be buffered to be written to the underlying output stream. The method does this by calling the flush() method of the underlying output stream and catching any exceptions that are thrown. |

print

> public void print(boolean b)
>
> | Parameters | b | The boolean value to print. |
> |---|---|---|
> | Description | This method writes "true" to the underlying output stream if b is true; otherwise it writes "false". | |
>
> public void print(char c)
>
> | Parameters | c | The char value to print. |
> |---|---|---|
> | Description | This method writes the given character to the underlying output stream. | |
>
> public void print(char[] s)
>
> | Parameters | s | The char array to print. |
> |---|---|---|
> | Description | This method writes the characters in the given array to the underlying output stream. | |

```
public void print(double d)
```
    Parameters   d   The `double` value to print.

    Description   This method writes a string representation of the given `double` value to the underlying output stream. The string representation is identical to the one returned by calling `Double.toString(d)`.

```
public void print(float f)
```
    Parameters   f   The `float` value to print.

    Description   This method writes a string representation of the given `float` value to the underlying output stream. The string representation is identical to the one returned by calling `Float.toString(f)`.

```
public void print(int i)
```
    Parameters   i   The `int` value to print.

    Description   This method writes a string representation of the given `int` value to the underlying output stream. The string representation is identical to the one returned by calling `Integer.toString(i)`.

```
public void print(long l)
```
    Parameters   l   The `long` value to print.

    Description   This method writes a string representation of the given `long` value to the underlying output stream. The string representation is identical to the one returned by calling `Long.toString(l)`.

```
public void print(Object obj)
```
    Parameters   obj   The `Object` to print.

    Description   This method writes the string representation of the given `Object` to the underlying output stream. The string representation is that returned by calling the `toString()` method of `Object`.

```
public void print(String s)
```
    Parameters   s   The `String` to print.

    Description   This method writes the given `String` to the underlying output stream. If `String` is `null`, the method writes `"null"`.

println

```
public void println()
```
    Description   This method writes a line separator to the underlying output stream.

```
public void println(boolean b)
```
Parameters b   The `boolean` value to print.

Description This method writes `"true"` to the underlying output stream if `b` is true, otherwise it writes `"false"`. In either case, the string is followed by a line separator.

```
public void println(char c)
```
Parameters c   The `char` value to print.

Description This method writes the given character, followed by a line separator, to the underlying output stream.

```
public void println(char[] s)
```
Parameters s   The `char` array to print.

Description This method writes the characters in the given array, followed by a line separator, to the underlying output stream.

```
public void println(double d)
```
Parameters d   The `double` value to print.

Description This method writes a string representation of the given `double` value, followed by a line separator, to the underlying output stream. The string representation is identical to the one returned by calling `Double.toString(d)`.

```
public void println(float f)
```
Parameters f   The `float` value to print.

Description This method writes a string representation of the given `float` value, followed by a line separator, to the underlying output stream. The string representation is identical to the one returned by calling `Float.toString(f)`.

```
public void println(int i)
```
Parameters i   The `int` value to print.

Description This method writes a string representation of the given `int` value, followed by a line separator, to the underlying output stream. The string representation is identical to the one returned by calling `Integer.toString(i)`.

```
public void println(long l)
```
Parameters l   The `long` value to print.

Description This method writes a string representation of the given `long` value, followed by a line separator, to the underlying output stream. The string representation is identical to the one returned by calling `Long.toString(l)`.

```
public void println(Object obj)
```
    Parameters   obj   The Object to print.

    Description   This method writes the string representation of the given Object, followed by a line separator, to the underlying output stream. The string representation is that returned by calling the toString() method of Object.

```
public void println(String s)
```
    Parameters   s   The String to print.

    Description   This method writes the given String, followed by a line separator, to the underlying output stream. If String is null, the method writes "null" followed by a line separator.

write

```
public void write(int b)
```
    Parameters   b   The value to write to the stream.

    Overrides   FilterOutputStream.write(int)

    Description   This method writes the lowest eight bits of b to the underlying stream as a byte. The method does this by calling the write() method of the underlying output stream and catching any exceptions that are thrown. If necessary, the method blocks until the byte is written.

```
public void write(byte b[], int off, int len)
```
    Parameters   b   An array of bytes to write to the stream.

                     off   An offset into the byte array.

                     len   The number of bytes to write.

    Overrides   FilterOutputStream.write(byte[], int, int)

    Description   This method writes the lowest eight bits of each of len bytes from the given array, starting off elements from the beginning of the array, to the underlying output stream. The method does this by calling write(b, off, len) for the underlying output stream and catching any exceptions that are thrown. If necessary, the method blocks until the bytes are written.

Protected Instance Methods

setError

```
protected void setError()
```
    Availability   New as of JDK 1.1

    Description   This method sets the error state of the PrintStream object to true. Any subsequent calls to getError() return true.

Inherited Methods

Method	Inherited From	Method	Inherited From
clone()	Object	equals(Object)	Object
finalize()	Object	getClass()	Object
hashCode()	Object	notify()	Object
notifyAll()	Object	toString()	Object
wait()	Object	wait(long)	Object
wait(long, int)	Object	write(byte[])	FilterOut- putStream

See Also

Double, FilterOutputStream, Float, Integer, Long, OutputStream

11.53   PrintWriter

Synopsis

Class Name:	java.io.PrintWriter
Superclass:	java.io.Writer
Immediate Subclasses:	None
Interfaces Implemented:	None
Availability:	New as of JDK 1.1

Description

The PrintWriter class provides support for writing string representations of primitive data types and objects to an underlying output stream. PrintWriter uses the system's default encoding scheme to convert characters to bytes. PrintWriter also uses the system's own specific line separator, rather than the newline character, for separating lines of text. This line separator is equivalent to the value returned by:

```
System.getProperty("line.separator")
```

A PrintWriter object can be created using a Writer object or an OutputStream object as its underlying stream. When a PrintWriter is created using an Output-Stream, the constructor creates the intermediate OutputStreamWriter that handles the conversion of characters to bytes using the default character encoding.

All of the methods of PrintWriter that write multiple times to the underlying output stream handle synchronization internally, so that PrintWriter objects are thread-safe.

A PrintWriter object is often used to write to a BufferedWriter object. Note that you can specify that the PrintWriter should be flushed every time a println() method is called by using a constructor that takes a boolean argument.

PrintWriter objects are often used to report errors. For this reason, the methods of this class do not throw exceptions. Instead, the methods catch any exceptions thrown by any downstream OutputStream or Writer objects and set an internal flag, so that the object can remember that a problem occurred. You can query the internal flag by calling the checkError() method.

Class Summary

```
public class java.io.PrintWriter extends java.io.Writer {
    // Constructors
    public PrintWriter(OutputStream out);
    public PrintWriter(OutputStream out, boolean autoFlush);
    public PrintWriter(Writer out);
    public PrintWriter(Writer out, boolean autoFlush);

    // Public Instance Methods
    public boolean checkError();
    public void close();
    public void flush();
    public void print(boolean b);
    public void print(char c);
    public void print(char[] s);
    public void print(double d);
    public void print(float f);
    public void print(int i);
    public void print(long l);
    public void print(Object obj);
    public void print(String s);
    public void println();
    public void println(boolean b);
    public void println(char c);
    public void println(char[] s);
    public void println(double d);
    public void println(float f);
    public void println(int i);
    public void println(long l);
    public void println(Object obj);
    public void println(String s);
    public void write(int c);
    public void write(char[] buf);
    public void write(char[] buf, int off, int len);
    public void write(String s);
    public void write(String s, int off, int len);
```

```
// Protected Instance Methods
protected void setError();
}
```

Constructors

PrintWriter

public PrintWriter(OutputStream out)

Parameters	out	The output stream to use.
Description		This constructor creates a PrintWriter object that sends output to the given OutputStream. The constructor creates the intermediate OutputStreamWriter that converts characters to bytes using the default character encoding.

public PrintWriter(OutputStream out, boolean autoFlush)

Parameters	out	The output stream to use.
	autoFlush	A boolean value that indicates whether or not the print stream is flushed every time a println() method is called.
Description		This constructor creates a PrintWriter object that sends output to the given OutputStream. The constructor creates the intermediate OutputStreamWriter that converts characters to bytes using the default character encoding. If autoFlush is true, every time a println() method is called, the PrintWriter object calls its flush() method. This behavior is different from that of a PrintStream object, which calls its flush() method each time a line separator or newline character is written.

public PrintWriter(Writer out)

Parameters	out	The output stream to use.
Description		This constructor creates a PrintWriter object that sends output to the given Writer.

public PrintStream(Writer out, boolean autoFlush)

Parameters	out	The output stream to use.
	autoFlush	A boolean value that indicates whether or not the print stream is flushed every time a println() method is called.
Description		This constructor creates a PrintWriter object that sends output to the given Writer. If autoFlush is true, every time a println() method is called, the PrintWriter object calls its flush() method. Note that this behavior is different from that of a PrintStream object, which calls its flush() method every time a newline character or line separator is written.

Public Instance Methods

checkError

```
public boolean checkError()
```
Returns   true if any error has occurred; false otherwise.

Description   This method flushes any buffered output and returns true if an error occurs. Once the error flag for a PrintWriter object is set, it's never cleared.

close

```
public void close()
```
Overrides   Writer.close()

Description   This method closes this print stream and releases any resources associated with the object. The method does this by calling the close() method of the underlying output stream and catching any exceptions that are thrown.

flush

```
public void flush()
```
Overrides   Writer.flush()

Description   This method flushes this print stream, forcing any bytes that may be buffered to be written to the underlying output stream. The method does this by calling the flush() method of the underlying output stream and catching any exceptions that are thrown.

print

```
public void print(boolean b)
```
Parameters   b   The boolean value to print.

Description   This method writes "true" to the underlying output stream if b is true; otherwise it writes "false".

```
public void print(char c)
```
Parameters   c   The char value to print.

Description   This method writes the given character to the underlying output stream.

```
public void print(char[] s)
```
Parameters   s   The char array to print.

Description   This method writes the characters in the given array to the underlying output stream.

```
public void print(double d)
```
    Parameters   d   The `double` value to print.

    Description   This method writes a string representation of the given `double` value to the underlying output stream. The string representation is identical to the one returned by calling `Double.toString(d)`.

```
public void print(float f)
```
    Parameters   f   The `float` value to print.

    Description   This method writes a string representation of the given `float` value to the underlying output stream. The string representation is identical to the one returned by calling `Float.toString(f)`.

```
public void print(int i)
```
    Parameters   i   The `int` value to print.

    Description   This method writes a string representation of the given `int` value to the underlying output stream. The string representation is identical to the one returned by calling `Integer.toString(i)`.

```
public void print(long l)
```
    Parameters   l   The `long` value to print.

    Description   This method writes a string representation of the given `long` value to the underlying output stream. The string representation is identical to the one returned by calling `Long.toString(l)`.

```
public void print(Object obj)
```
    Parameters   obj   The `Object` to print.

    Description   This method writes the string representation of the given `Object` to the underlying output stream. The string representation is that returned by calling the `toString()` method of `Object`.

```
public void print(String s)
```
    Parameters   s   The `String` to print.

    Description   This method writes the given `String` to the underlying output stream. If `String` is `null`, the method writes `"null"`.

println

```
public void println()
```
    Description   This method writes a line separator to the underlying output stream.

```
public void println(boolean b)
```
Parameters   b   The `boolean` value to print.

Description   This method writes `"true"` to the underlying output stream if `b` is true, otherwise it writes `"false"`. In either case, the string is followed by a line separator.

```
public void println(char c)
```
Parameters   c   The `char` value to print.

Description   This method writes the given character, followed by a line separator, to the underlying output stream.

```
public void println(char[] s)
```
Parameters   s   The `char` array to print.

Description   This method writes the characters in the given array, followed by a line separator, to the underlying output stream.

```
public void println(double d)
```
Parameters   d   The `double` value to print.

Description   This method writes a string representation of the given `double` value, followed by a line separator, to the underlying output stream. The string representation is identical to the one returned by calling `Double.toString(d)`.

```
public void println(float f)
```
Parameters   f   The `float` value to print.

Description   This method writes a string representation of the given `float` value, followed by a line separator, to the underlying output stream. The string representation is identical to the one returned by calling `Float.toString(f)`.

```
public void println(int i)
```
Parameters   i   The `int` value to print.

Description   This method writes a string representation of the given `int` value, followed by a line separator, to the underlying output stream. The string representation is identical to the one returned by calling `Integer.toString(i)`.

```
public void println(long l)
```
Parameters   l   The `long` value to print.

Description   This method writes a string representation of the given `long` value, followed by a line separator, to the underlying output stream. The string representation is identical to the one returned by calling `Long.toString(l)`.

```
public void println(Object obj)
```
  Parameters   obj   The Object to print.
  Description   This method writes the string representation of the given
                 Object, followed by a line separator, to the underlying output
                 stream. The string representation is that returned by calling the
                 toString() method of Object.

```
public void println(String s)
```
  Parameters   s   The String to print.
  Description   This method writes the given String, followed by a line separa-
                 tor, to the underlying output stream. If String is null, the
                 method writes "null" followed by a line separator.

write

```
public void write(int c)
```
  Parameters   c   The value to write to the stream.
  Overrides   Writer.write(int)
  Description   This method writes the character specified by the lowest two
                 bytes of the given integer c to the underlying stream. The
                 method does this by calling the write() method of the underly-
                 ing output stream and catching any exceptions that are thrown.
                 If necessary, the method blocks until the character is written.

```
public void write(char[] buf)
```
  Parameters   buf   An array of characters to write to the stream.
  Overrides   Writer.write(char[])
  Description   This method writes the given array of characters to the underly-
                 ing output stream. The method does this by calling write(buf,
                 0, buf.length) for the underlying output stream and catching
                 any exceptions that are thrown. If necessary, the method
                 blocks until the characters are written.

```
public void write(char[] buf, int off, int len)
```
  Parameters   buf   An array of characters to write to the stream.
                  off   An offset into the array.
                  len   The number of characters to write.
  Overrides   Writer.write(char[], int, int)
  Description   This method writes len characters from the given array, starting
                 off elements from the beginning of the array, to the underlying
                 output stream. The method does this by calling write(buf,
                 off, len) for the underlying output stream and catching any
                 exceptions that are thrown. If necessary, the method blocks
                 until the characters are written.

```
public void write(String s)
```
    Parameters   s   A `String` to write to the stream.

    Overrides   `Writer.write(String)`

    Description   This method writes the given `String` to the underlying output stream. The method does this by calling `write(s, 0, s.length)` for the underlying output stream and catching any exceptions that are thrown. If necessary, the method blocks until the `String` is written.

```
public void write(String s, int off, int len)
```
    Parameters   s   A `String` to write to the stream.

                   off   An offset into the string.

                   len   The number of characters to write.

    Overrides   `Writer.write(String, int, int)`

    Description   This method writes `len` characters from the given `String`, starting `off` elements from the beginning of the string, to the underlying output stream. The method does this by calling `write(s, off, len)` for the underlying output stream and catching any exceptions that are thrown. If necessary, the method blocks until the characters of the `String` are written.

Protected Instance Methods

setError

```
protected void setError()
```
    Description   This method sets the error state of the `PrintWriter` object to true. Any subsequent calls to `getError()` will return true.

Inherited Methods

Method	Inherited From	Method	Inherited From
clone()	Object	equals(Object)	Object
finalize()	Object	getClass()	Object
hashCode()	Object	notify()	Object
notifyAll()	Object	toString()	Object
wait()	Object	wait(long)	Object
wait(long, int)	Object		

See Also

Double, Float, Integer, Long, OutputStream, OutputStreamWriter, Writer

11.54   PushbackInputStream

Synopsis

Class Name:	java.io.PushbackInputStream
Superclass:	java.io.FilterInputStream
Immediate Subclasses:	None
Interfaces Implemented:	None
Availability:	JDK 1.0 or later

Description

The PushbackInputStream class represents a byte stream that allows data to be pushed back into the stream. In other words, after data has been read from a PushbackInputStream, it can be pushed back into the stream so that it can be reread. This functionality is useful for implementing things like parsers that need to read data and then return it to the input stream.

The PushbackInputStream has been enhanced as of JDK 1.1 to support a pushback buffer that is larger than one byte. Prior to JDK 1.1, the class supported only a one-byte buffer using the protected variable pushBack. As of 1.1, that variable has been replaced by the buf and pos variables.

Class Summary

```
public class java.io.PushbackInputStream extends java.io.FilterInputStream {
    // Variables
    protected byte[] buf;                        // New in 1.1
    protected int pos;                           // New in 1.1

    // Constructors
    public PushbackInputStream(InputStream in);
    public PushbackInputStream(InputStream in,
                            int size);           // New in 1.1

    // Instance Methods
    public int available();
    public boolean markSupported();
    public int read();
    public int read(byte[] b, int off, int len);
    public void unread(int b);
```

```
    public void unread(byte[] b);                    // New in 1.1
    public void unread(byte[] b, int off, int len); // New in 1.1
}
```

Variables

buf

protected byte[] buf

Availability	New as of JDK 1.1
Description	The buffer that holds data that has been pushed back.

pos

protected int pos

Availability	New as of JDK 1.1
Description	The position of pushed-back data in the buffer. When there is no pushed-back data, pos is buf.length. As data is pushed back, pos decreases. As pushed-back data is read, pos increases. When the pushback buffer is full, pos is 0.

Constructors

PushbackInputStream

public PushbackInputStream(InputStream in)

Parameters	in	The input stream to wrap.
Description		This constructor creates a PushbackInputStream that reads from the given InputStream, using a pushback buffer with the default size of one byte.

public PushBackInputStream(InputStream in, int size)

Availability	New as of JDK 1.1	
Parameters	in	The input stream to wrap.
	size	The size of the pushback buffer.
Description		This constructor creates a PushbackInputStream that reads from the given InputStream, using a pushback buffer of the given size.

Instance Methods

available

public int available() throws IOException

Returns	The number of bytes that can be read without blocking.
Throws	IOException If any kind of I/O error occurs.
Overrides	FilterInputStream.available()

Description   This method returns the number of bytes that can be read without having to wait for more data to become available. This is b + u, where b is the number of bytes in the pushback buffer and u is the number of available bytes in the underlying stream.

markSupported

public boolean markSupported()

Returns   The boolean value false.

Overrides   FilterInputStream.markSupported()

Description   This method returns false to indicate that this class does not support mark() and reset().

read

public int read() throws IOException

Returns   The next byte of data, or -1 if the end of the stream is encountered.

Throws   IOException   If any kind of I/O error occurs.

Overrides   FilterInputStream.read()

Description   This method reads a byte of data. If there is any data in the pushback buffer, the method returns the next byte in the pushback buffer. Otherwise, it calls the read() method of the underlying stream. The method blocks until the byte is read, the end of the stream is encountered, or an exception is thrown.

public int read(byte b[], int off, int len) throws IOException

Parameters   b   An array of bytes to be filled from the stream.

             off   An offset into the byte array.

             len   The number of bytes to read.

Returns   The actual number of bytes read, or -1 if the end of the stream is encountered immediately.

Throws   IOException   If any kind of I/O error occurs.

Overrides   FilterInputStream.read(byte[], int, int)

Description   This method copies bytes from the stream into the given array b, starting at index off and continuing for len bytes. If the array can be populated solely from the pushback buffer, the method returns immediately. Otherwise, the read(byte[], int, int) method of the underlying stream is called to make up the difference. The method blocks until some data is available.

unread

    public void unread(int b) throws IOException

Parameters	b	The value to push back.
Throws	IOException	If the pushback buffer is full.
Description		This method puts the given byte into the pushback buffer.

    public void unread(byte[] b) throws IOException

Availability	New as of JDK 1.1	
Parameters	b	An array of bytes to push back.
Throws	IOException	If the pushback buffer is full.
Description		This method puts all of the bytes in the given array into the pushback buffer.

    public void unread(byte[] b, int off, int len) throws IOException

Availability	New as of JDK 1.1	
Parameters	b	An array of bytes to push back.
	off	An offset into the array.
	len	The number of bytes to push back.
Throws	IOException	If the pushback buffer is full.
Description		This method puts len bytes from the given array, starting at offset off, into the pushback buffer.

Inherited Methods

Method	Inherited From	Method	Inherited From
clone()	Object	close()	FilterInputStream
equals(Object)	Object	finalize()	Object
getClass()	Object	hashCode()	Object
mark(int)	FilterInputStream	notify()	Object
notifyAll()	Object	read(byte[])	FilterInputStream
reset()	FilterInputStream	skip(long)	FilterInputStream
toString()	Object	wait()	Object
wait(long)	Object	wait(long, int)	Object

See Also

FilterInputStream, InputStream, IOException

11.55   PushbackReader

Synopsis

Class Name:	java.io.PushbackReader
Superclass:	java.io.FilterReader
Immediate Subclasses:	None
Interfaces Implemented:	None
Availability:	New as of JDK 1.1

Description

The PushbackReader class represents a character stream that allows data to be pushed back into the stream. In other words, after data has been read from a PushbackReader, it can be pushed back into the stream so that it can be reread. This functionality is useful for implementing things like parsers that need to read data and then return it to the input stream. PushbackReader is the character-oriented equivalent of PushbackInputStream.

Class Summary

```
public class java.io.PushbackReader extends java.io.FilterReader {
    // Constructors
    public PushbackReader(Reader in);
    public PushbackReader(Reader in, int size);

    // Instance Methods
    public void close();
    public boolean markSupported();
    public int read();
    public int read(char[] cbuf, int off, int len);
    public boolean ready();
    public void unread(int c);
    public void unread(char[] cbuf);
    public void unread(char[] cbuf, int off, int len);
}
```

Constructors

PushbackReader

public PushbackReader(Reader in)

Parameters	in	The reader to wrap.
Description		This constructor creates a PushbackReader that reads from the given Reader, using a pushback buffer with the default size of one byte.

```
public PushbackReader(Reader in, int size)
```
    Parameters   in   The reader to wrap.

                      size   The size of the pushback buffer.

    Description   This constructor creates a PushbackReader that reads from the given Reader, using a pushback buffer of the given size.

Instance Methods

close

```
public void close() throws IOException
```
    Throws   IOException If any kind of I/O error occurs.

    Overrides   FilterReader.close()

    Description   This method closes the reader and releases the system resources that are associated with it.

markSupported

```
public boolean markSupported()
```
    Returns   The boolean value false.

    Overrides   FilterReader.markSupported()

    Description   This method returns false to indicate that this class does not support mark() and reset().

read

```
public int read() throws IOException
```
    Returns   The next character of data or –1 if the end of the stream is encountered.

    Throws   IOException If any kind of I/O error occurs.

    Overrides   FilterReader.read()

    Description   This method reads a character of data. If there is any data in the pushback buffer, the method returns the next character in the pushback buffer. Otherwise, it calls the read() method of the underlying stream. The method blocks until the character is read, the end of the stream is encountered, or an exception is thrown.

```
public int read(char[] cbuf, int off, int len) throws IOException
```
    Parameters   cbuf   An array of characters to be filled from the stream.

                      off   An offset into the array.

                      len   The number of characters to read.

    Returns   The actual number of characters read or –1 if the end of the stream is encountered immediately.

Throws   IOException   If any kind of I/O error occurs.

Overrides   FilterReader.read(char[], int, int)

Description   This method copies characters from the stream into the given array cbuf, starting at index off and continuing for len characters. If the array can be populated solely from the pushback buffer, the method returns immediately. Otherwise, the read(char[], int, int) method of the underlying stream is called to make up the difference. The method blocks until some data is available.

ready

public boolean ready() throws IOException

Returns   A boolean value that indicates whether the stream is ready to be read.

Throws   IOException   If the stream is closed.

Overrides   FilterReader.ready()

Description   If there is data in the pushback buffer, or if the underlying stream is ready, this method returns true. The underlying stream is ready if the next read() is guaranteed not to block.

unread

public void unread(int c) throws IOException

Parameters   c   The value to push back.

Throws   IOException   If the pushback buffer is full.

Description   This method puts the given character into the pushback buffer.

public void unread(char[] cbuf) throws IOException

Parameters   cbuf   An array of characters to push back.

Throws   IOException   If the pushback buffer is full.

Description   This method puts all of the characters in the given array into the pushback buffer.

public void unread(char[] cbuf, int off, int len) throws IOException

Parameters   cbuf   An array of characters to push back.

                off   An offset into the array.

                len   The number of characters to push back.

Throws   IOException   If the pushback buffer is full.

Description   This method puts len characters from the given array, starting at offset off, into the pushback buffer.

Inherited Methods

Method	Inherited From	Method	Inherited From
clone()	Object	equals(Object)	Object
finalize()	Object	getClass()	Object
hashCode()	Object	mark(int)	FilterReader
notify()	Object	notifyAll()	Object
read(char[])	FilterReader	reset()	FilterReader
skip(long)	FilterReader	toString()	Object
wait()	Object	wait(long)	Object
wait(long, int)	Object		

See Also

FilterReader, IOException, Reader

11.56   RandomAccessFile

Synopsis

Class Name: java.io.RandomAccessFile
Superclass: java.lang.Object
Immediate Subclasses: None
Interfaces Implemented: java.io.DataInput, java.io.DataOutput
Availability: JDK 1.0 or later

Description

The RandomAccessFile class reads data from and writes data to a file. The file is specified using a File object or a String that represents a pathname. Both constructors take a mode parameter that specifies whether the file is being opened solely for reading, or for reading and writing. Each of the constructors can throw a SecurityException if the application does not have permission to access the specified file using the given mode.

Unlike FileInputStream and FileOutputStream, RandomAccessFile supports random access to the data in the file; the seek() method allows you to alter the current position of the file pointer to any location in the file. RandomAccessFile implements both the DataInput and DataOutput interfaces, so it supports reading and writing of all the primitive data types.

Class Summary

```
public class java.io.RandomAccessFile extends java.lang.Object
            implements java.io.DataInput, java.io.DataOutput {
    // Constructors
    public RandomAccessFile(File file, String mode);
    public RandomAccessFile(String name, String mode);

    // Instance Methods
    public native void close();
    public final FileDescriptor getFD();
    public native long getFilePointer();
    public native long length();
    public native int read();
    public int read(byte[] b);
    public int read(byte[] b, int off, int len);
    public final boolean readBoolean();
    public final byte readByte();
    public final char readChar();
    public final double readDouble();
    public final float readFloat();
    public final void readFully(byte[] b);
    public final void readFully(byte[] b, int off, int len);
    public final int readInt();
    public final String readLine();
    public final long readLong();
    public final short readShort();
    public final String readUTF();
    public final int readUnsignedByte();
    public final int readUnsignedShort();
    public native void seek(long pos);
    public int skipBytes(int n);
    public native void write(int b);
    public void write(byte[] b);
    public void write(byte[] b, int off, int len);
    public final void writeBoolean(boolean v);
    public final void writeByte(int v);
    public final void writeBytes(String s);
    public final void writeChar(int v);
    public final void writeChars(String s);
    public final void writeDouble(double v);
    public final void writeFloat(float v);
    public final void writeInt(int v);
    public final void writeLong(long v);
    public final void writeShort(int v);
    public final void writeUTF(String str);
}
```

Constructors

RandomAccessFile

`public RandomAccessFile(File file, String mode) throws IOException`

Parameters	file	The file to be accessed.
	mode	The mode of access to the file: either "r" for read access or "rw" for read/write access.
Throws	IOException	If any kind of I/O error occurs.
	IllegalArgumentException	
		If mode is not "r" or "rw".
	SecurityException	
		If the application does not have permission to read the named file, or if mode is "rw" and the application does not have permission to write to the named file.
Description		This constructor creates a RandomAccessFile to access the specified File in the specified mode.

`public RandomAccessFile(String name, String mode) throws IOException`

Parameters	name	A String that contains the pathname of the file to be accessed. The path must conform to the requirements of the native operating system.
	mode	The mode of access to the file: either "r" for read access or "rw" for read/write access.
Throws	IOException	If any kind of I/O error occurs.
	IllegalArgumentException	
		If mode is not "r" or "rw".
	SecurityException	
		If the application does not have permission to read the named file, or if mode is "rw" and the application does not have permission to write to the named file.
Description		This constructor creates a RandomAccessFile to access the file with the specified name in the specified mode.

Instance Methods

close

`public native void close() throws IOException`

Throws	IOException	If any kind of I/O error occurs.
Description		This method closes the file and releases the system resources that are associated with it.

getFD

```
public final FileDescriptor getFD() throws IOException
```

Returns	The file descriptor for the file that supplies data for this object.
Throws	IOException If there is no FileDescriptor associated with this object.
Description	This method returns the file descriptor associated with this RandomAccessFile.

getFilePointer

```
public native long getFilePointer() throws IOException
```

Returns	The current position in the file.
Throws	IOException If any kind of I/O error occurs.
Description	This method returns the current position in the file. The position is the offset, in bytes, from the beginning of the file where the next read or write operation occurs.

length

```
public native long length() throws IOException
```

Returns	The length of the file.
Throws	IOException If any kind of I/O error occurs.
Description	This method returns the length of the file in bytes.

read

```
public native int read() throws IOException
```

Returns	The next byte or –1 if the end of file is encountered.
Throws	IOException If any kind of I/O error occurs.
Description	This method reads the next byte from the file. The method blocks until the byte is read, the end of the file is encountered, or an exception is thrown.

```
public int read(byte b[]) throws IOException
```

Parameters	b An array of bytes to be filled from the stream.
Returns	The number of bytes read or –1 if the end of file is encountered immediately.
Throws	IOException If any kind of I/O error occurs.
Description	This method reads bytes from the file into the given array. The method reads up to b.length bytes of data from the stream. The method blocks until there is some data available.

```
public int read(byte b[], int off, int len) throws IOException
```

Parameters	b	An array of bytes to be filled.
	off	An offset into the array.
	len	The number of bytes to read.
Returns		The number of bytes read or –1 if the end of file is encountered immediately.
Throws	IOException	If any kind of I/O error occurs.
Description		This method reads up to len bytes from the file into the given array, starting at index off. The method blocks until there is some input available.

readBoolean

```
public final boolean readBoolean() throws IOException
```

Returns		The boolean value read from the file.
Throws	EOFException	
		If the end of the file is encountered.
	IOException	If any other kind of I/O error occurs.
Implements	DataInput.readBoolean()	
Description		This method reads a byte as a boolean value from the file. A byte that contains a zero is read as false. A byte that contains any other value is read as true. The method blocks until the byte is read, the end of the file is encountered, or an exception is thrown.

readByte

```
public final byte readByte() throws IOException
```

Returns		The byte value read from the file.
Throws	EOFException	
		If the end of the file is encountered.
	IOException	If any other kind of I/O error occurs.
Implements	DataInput.readByte()	
Description		This method reads a signed 8-bit value, a byte, from the file. The method blocks until the byte is read, the end of the file is encountered, or an exception is thrown.

readChar

```
public final char readChar() throws IOException
```

Returns		The char value read from the file.

Throws   EOFException

                      If the end of the file is encountered.

         IOException   If any other kind of I/O error occurs.

Implements   `DataInput.readChar()`

Description   This method reads a 16-bit Unicode character from the file. The method reads two bytes from the file and then creates a char value using the first byte read as the most significant byte. The method blocks until the two bytes are read, the end of the file is encountered, or an exception is thrown.

readDouble

`public final double readDouble() throws IOException`

Returns   The double value read from the file.

Throws   EOFException

                      If the end of the file is encountered.

         IOException   If any other kind of I/O error occurs.

Implements   `DataInput.readDouble()`

Description   This method reads a 64-bit double quantity from the file. The method reads a long value from the file as if using the readLong() method. The long value is then converted to a double using the longBitsToDouble() method in Double. The method blocks until the necessary eight bytes are read, the end of the file is encountered, or an exception is thrown.

readFloat

`public final float readFloat() throws IOException`

Returns   The float value read from the file.

Throws   EOFException

                      If the end of the file is encountered.

         IOException   If any other kind of I/O error occurs.

Implements   `DataInput.readFloat()`

Description   This method reads a 32-bit float quantity from the file. The method reads an int value from the file as if using the readInt() method. The int value is then converted to a float using the intBitsToFloat() method in Float. The method blocks until the necessary four bytes are read, the end of the file is encountered, or an exception is thrown.

readFully

```
public final void readFully(byte b[]) throws IOException
```

Parameters   b   The array to fill.

Throws   EOFException

If the end of the file is encountered.

IOException   If any other kind of I/O error occurs.

Implements   DataInput.readFully(byte[])

Description   This method reads bytes into the given array b until the array is
full. The method reads repeatedly from the file to fill the array.
The method blocks until all of the bytes are read, the end of
the file is encountered, or an exception is thrown.

```
public final void readFully(byte b[], int off, int len) throws IOException
```

Parameters   b   The array to fill.

off   An offset into the array.

len   The number of bytes to read.

Throws   EOFException

If the end of the file is encountered.

IOException   If any other kind of I/O error occurs.

Implements   DataInput.readFully(byte[], int, int)

Description   This method reads len bytes into the given array, starting at offset off. The method reads repeatedly from the file to fill the
array. The method blocks until all of the bytes are read, the end
of the file is encountered, or an exception is thrown.

readInt

```
public final int readInt() throws IOException
```

Returns   The int value read from the stream.

Throws   EOFException

If the end of the file is encountered.

IOException   If any other kind of I/O error occurs.

Implements   DataInput.readInt()

Description   This method reads a signed 32-bit int quantity from the file.
The method reads four bytes from the file and then creates an
int quantity, using the first byte read as the most significant
byte. The method blocks until the four bytes are read, the end
of the file is encountered, or an exception is thrown.

readLine

`public final String readLine() throws IOException`

Returns   A String that contains the line read from the stream.

Throws   EOFException

If the end of the file is encountered.

IOException   If any other I/O error occurs.

Implements   DataInput.readLine()

Description   This method reads the next line of text from the file. The method reads bytes of data from the file until it encounters a line terminator. A line terminator is a carriage return ("\r"), a newline character ("\n"), a carriage return immediately followed by a newline character, or the end of the file. The method blocks until a line terminator is read, the end of the file is encountered, or an exception is thrown.

The method does not convert bytes to characters correctly.

readLong

`public final long readLong() throws IOException`

Returns   The long value read from the stream.

Throws   EOFException

If the end of the file is encountered.

IOException   If any other kind of I/O error occurs.

Implements   DataInput.readLong()

Description   This method reads a signed 64-bit long quantity from the file. The method reads eight bytes from the file and then creates a long quantity, using the first byte read as the most significant byte. The method blocks until the eight bytes are read, the end of the file is encountered, or an exception is thrown.

readShort

`public final short readShort() throws IOException`

Returns   The short value read from the stream.

Throws   EOFException

If the end of the file is encountered.

IOException   If any other kind of I/O error occurs.

Implements   DataInput.readShort()

Description   This method reads a signed 16-bit short quantity from the file. The method reads two bytes from the file and then creates a short quantity, using the first byte read as the most significant byte. The method blocks until the two bytes are read, the end of the file is encountered, or an exception is thrown.

readUnsignedByte

`public final int readUnsignedByte() throws IOException`

Returns	The unsigned byte value read from the stream.
Throws	EOFException
	If the end of the file is encountered.
	IOException If any other kind of I/O error occurs.
Returns	
Implements	DataInput.readUnsignedByte()
Description	This method reads an unsigned 8-bit quantity from the file. The method reads a byte from the file and returns that byte. The method blocks until the byte is read, the end of the file is encountered, or an exception is thrown.

readUnsignedShort

`public final int readUnsignedShort() throws IOException`

Returns	The unsigned short value read from the stream.
Throws	EOFException
	If the end of the file is encountered.
	IOException If any other kind of I/O error occurs.
Implements	DataInput.readUnsignedShort()
Description	This method reads an unsigned 16-bit quantity from the file. The method reads two bytes from the file and creates an unsigned short quantity using the first byte read as the most significant byte. The method blocks until the two bytes are read, the end of the file is encountered, or an exception is thrown.

readUTF

`public final String readUTF() throws IOException`

Returns	The String read from the stream.
Throws	EOFException
	If the end of the file is encountered.
	IOException If any other kind of I/O error occurs.
	UTFDataFormatException
	If the bytes do not represent a valid UTF-8 encoding.
Implements	DataInput.readUTF()
Description	This method reads a UTF-8 encoded string from the file. The method reads the first two bytes from the file as unsigned short values, to get the number of bytes in the encoded string. Then the following bytes are read and interpreted UTF-8 encoded bytes; these bytes are converted into characters for the resulting

String. This method blocks until all of the bytes in the
encoded string have been read, the end of the file is encountered, or an exception is thrown. See Appendix B for information about the UTF-8 encoding.

seek

public native void seek(long pos) throws IOException

Parameters	pos	The new position in the file.
Throws	IOException	If any kind of I/O error occurs.
Description		This method sets the current file position to the specified posi-tion. The position is the offset, in bytes, from the beginning of the file where the next read or write operation occurs.

skipBytes

public int skipBytes(int n) throws IOException

Parameters	n	The number of bytes to skip.
Returns	The actual number of skipped bytes.	
Throws	EOFException	
		If EOF is encountered.
	IOException	If any I/O error occurs.
Implements	DataInput.skipBytes()	
Description	This method skips over n bytes.	

write

public native void write(int b) throws IOException

Parameters	b	The value to write.
Throws	IOException	If any kind of I/O error occurs.
Implements	DataOutput.write(int)	
Description		This method writes the low-order eight bits of b to the file as a byte.

public void write(byte b[]) throws IOException

Parameters	b	An array of bytes to write.
Throws	IOException	If any kind of I/O error occurs.
Implements	DataOutput.write(byte[])	
Description		This method writes the bytes in the given array to the file.

```
public void write(byte b[], int off, int len) throws IOException
```
    Parameters   `b`   An array of bytes to write.

                      `off`   An offset into the byte array.

                      `len`   The number of bytes to write.

    Throws   `IOException` If any kind of I/O error occurs.

    Implements   `DataOutput.write(byte[], int, int)`

    Description   This method writes `len` bytes from the given array, starting `off` elements from the beginning of the array, to the file.

writeBoolean

```
public final void writeBoolean(boolean v) throws IOException
```
    Parameters   `v`   The `boolean` value to write.

    Throws   `IOException` If any kind of I/O error occurs.

    Implements   `DataOutput.writeBoolean()`

    Description   If `v` is true, this method writes a byte that contains the value 1 to the file. If `v` is false, the method writes a byte that contains the value 0.

writeByte

```
public final void writeByte(int v) throws IOException
```
    Parameters   `v`   The value to write.

    Throws   `IOException` If any kind of I/O error occurs.

    Implements   `DataOutput.writeByte()`

    Description   This method writes an 8-bit byte to the file, using the low-order eight bits of the given integer `v`.

writeBytes

```
public final void writeBytes(String s) throws IOException
```
    Parameters   `s`   The `String` to write.

    Throws   `IOException` If any kind of I/O error occurs.

    Implements   `DataOutput.writeBytes()`

    Description   This method writes the characters in the given `String` to the file as a sequence of 8-bit bytes. The high-order bytes of the characters in the string are ignored.

writeChar

```
public final void writeChar(int v) throws IOException
```
    Parameters   `v`   The value to write.

    Throws   `IOException` If any kind of I/O error occurs.

Implements   `DataOutput.writeChar()`

Description   This method writes a 16-bit `char` to the file, using the low-order 16 bits of the given integer v.

writeChars

`public final void writeChars(String s) throws IOException`

Parameters   `s`   The `String` to write.

Throws   `IOException`   If any kind of I/O error occurs.

Implements   `DataOutput.writeChars()`

Description   This method writes the characters in the given `String` object to the file as a sequence of 16-bit characters.

writeDouble

`public final void writeDouble(double v) throws IOException`

Parameters   `v`   The `double` value to write.

Throws   `IOException`   If any kind of I/O error occurs.

Implements   `DataOutput.writeDouble()`

Description   This method writes a 64-bit `double` to the file. The `double` value is converted to a `long` using `doubleToLongBits()` of Double; the `long` value is then written to the file as eight bytes with the high-order byte first.

writeFloat

`public final void writeFloat(float v) throws IOException`

Parameters   `v`   The `float` value to write.

Throws   `IOException`   If any kind of I/O error occurs.

Implements   `DataOutput.writeFloat()`

Description   This method writes a 32-bit `float` to the file. The `float` value is converted to a int using `floatToIntBits()` of Float; the int value is then written to the file as four bytes with the high-order byte first.

writeInt

`public final void writeInt(int v) throws IOException`

Parameters   `v`   The int value to write.

Throws   `IOException`   If any kind of I/O error occurs.

Implements   `DataOutput.writeInt()`

Description   This method writes a 32-bit int to the file. The value is written as four bytes with the high-order byte first.

writeLong

public final void writeLong(long v) throws IOException

Parameters	v	The long value to write.
Throws	IOException	If any kind of I/O error occurs.
Implements	DataOutput.writeLong()	
Description	This method writes a 64-bit long to the file. The value is written as eight bytes with the high-order byte first.	

writeShort

public final void writeShort(int v) throws IOException

Parameters	v	The value to write.
Throws	IOException	If any kind of I/O error occurs.
Implements	DataOutput.writeShort()	
Description	This method writes a 16-bit short to the file, using the low-order 16 bits of the given integer v.	

writeUTF

public final void writeUTF(String str) throws IOException

Parameters	str	The String to write.
Throws	IOException	If any kind of I/O error occurs.
Implements	DataOutput.writeUTF()	
Description	This method writes the given String to the file using the UTF-8 encoding. See Appendix B for information about the UTF-8 encoding.	

Inherited Methods

Method	Inherited From	Method	Inherited From
clone()	Object	equals(Object)	Object
finalize()	Object	getClass()	Object
hashCode()	Object	notify()	Object
notifyAll()	Object	toString()	Object
wait()	Object	wait(long)	Object
wait(long, int)	Object		

See Also

DataInput, DataOutput, File, FileInputStream, FileOutputStream, Double, Float, Integer, IllegalArgumentException, IOException, Long

11.57   Reader

Synopsis

Class Name: java.io.Reader
Superclass: java.lang.Object
Immediate Subclasses: java.io.BufferedReader, java.io.CharArrayReader,
                         java.io.FilterReader, java.io.InputStreamReader,
                         java.io.PipedReader, java.io.StringReader
Interfaces Implemented: None
Availability: New as of JDK 1.1

Description

The Reader class is an abstract class that is the superclass of all classes that represent input character streams. Reader defines the basic input methods that all character streams provide. A similar hierarchy of classes, based around InputStream, deals with byte streams instead of character streams.

Reader is designed so that read() and read(char[]) both call read(char[], int, int). Thus, a subclass can simply override read(char[], int, int), and all of the read methods will work. Note that this is different from the design of InputStream, where the read() method is the catch-all method. The design of Reader is cleaner and more efficient.

Reader also defines a mechanism for marking a position in the stream and returning to it later, via the mark() and reset() methods. Another method, markSupported(), tells whether or not this mark-and-reset functionality is available in a particular subclass.

Class Summary

```
public abstract class java.io.Reader extends java.lang.Object {
    // Variables
    protected Object lock;

    // Constructors
    protected Reader();
    protected Reader(Object lock);

    // Instance Methods
    public abstract void close();
    public void mark(int readAheadLimit);
    public boolean markSupported();
    public int read();
    public int read(char[] cbuf);
    public abstract int read(char[] cbuf, int off, int len);
    public boolean ready();
```

```
    public void reset();
    public long skip(long n) throws IOException;
}
```

Variables

lock

protected Object lock

> Description   The object used to synchronize operations on this Reader
> object. For efficiency's sake, a particular implementation of a
> character stream can choose to synchronize its operations on
> something other than instances of itself. Thus, any subclass
> should synchronize on the lock object, instead of using a syn-
> chronized method or the this object.

Constructors

Reader

protected Reader()

> Description   This constructor creates a Reader that synchronizes on the
> Reader itself, or in other words, on the this object.

protected Reader(Object lock)

> Parameters   lock   The object to use for synchronization.
> Description   This constructor creates a Reader that synchronizes on the
> given object.

Instance Methods

close

public abstract void close() throws IOException

> Throws   IOException   If any kind of I/O error occurs.
> Description   This method closes the reader and releases any system
> resources associated with it.
>
> A subclass of Reader must implement this method.

mark

public void mark(int readheadLimit) throws IOException

> Parameters   readAheadLimit
>   The maximum number of characters that can be
>   read before the saved position becomes invalid.
> Throws   IOException   If any kind of I/O error occurs.

Description   This method tells this Reader object to remember its current position, so that the position can be restored by a call to the reset() method. The Reader can read readAheadLimit characters beyond the marked position before the mark becomes invalid.

The implementation of the mark() method in Reader simply throws an exception to indicate that the mark-and-reset functionality is not implemented. A subclass must override the method to provide the functionality.

markSupported

public boolean markSupported()

Returns   true if this reader supports mark() and reset(); false otherwise.

Description   This method returns a boolean value that indicates whether or not this object supports mark-and-reset functionality.

The markSupported() method in Reader always returns false. A subclass that implements the mark-and-reset functionality should override the method to return true.

read

public int read() throws IOException

Returns   The next character of data or –1 if the end of the stream is encountered.

Throws   IOException   If any kind of I/O error occurs.

Description   This method reads the next character of input. The character is returned as an integer in the range 0x0000 to 0xFFFF. The method blocks until the character is read, the end of stream is encountered, or an exception is thrown.

The implementation of this method in Reader reads the character by calling read(cb, 0, 1), where cb is a character array, and returning cb[0]. Although it is not strictly necessary, a subclass that wants to provide efficient single-character reads should override this method.

public int read(char[] cbuf) throws IOException

Parameters   cbuf   An array of characters to be filled from the stream.

Returns   The actual number of characters read or –1 if the end of the stream is encountered immediately.

Throws   IOException   If any kind of I/O error occurs.

Description   This method reads characters of input to fill the given array by calling read(cbuf, 0, cbuf.length). The method blocks until some data is available.

A subclass does not usually need to override this method, as it can override read(char[], int, int) and have read(char[]) work automatically.

public abstract int read(char[] cbuf, int off, int len)
              throws IOException

Parameters   cbuf   An array of characters to be filled from the stream.

off   An offset into the array.

len   The number of characters to read.

Returns   The actual number of characters read or –1 if the end of the stream is encountered immediately.

Throws   IOException   If any kind of I/O error occurs.

Description   This method reads up to len characters of input into the given array starting at index off. The method blocks until some data is available.

A subclass of Reader must implement this method.

ready

public boolean ready() throws IOException

Returns   A boolean value that indicates whether the reader is ready to be read.

Throws   IOException   If any kind of I/O error occurs.

Description   This method returns true if the next read() is guaranteed to not block.

The implementation of the ready() method in Reader always returns false. A subclass should override this method as appropriate.

reset

public void reset() throws IOException

Throws   IOException   If there was no previous call to the mark() method or the saved position has been invalidated.

Description   This method restores the position of the stream to the position that was saved by a previous call to mark().

The implementation of the reset() method in Reader throws an exception to indicate that mark-and-reset functionality is not supported by default. A subclass must override the method to provide the functionality.

skip

```
public long skip(long n) throws IOException
```

Parameters   n   The number of characters to skip.

Returns   The actual number of characters skipped.

Throws   IOException   If any kind of I/O error occurs.

Description   This method skips n characters of input. In other words, it moves the position of the stream forward by n characters.

The implementation of the skip() method in Reader simply calls read(cb, 0, n) where cb is a character array that is at least n bytes long. A subclass may want to override this method to implement a more efficient skipping algorithm.

Inherited Methods

Method	Inherited From	Method	Inherited From
clone()	Object	equals(Object)	Object
finalize()	Object	getClass()	Object
hashCode()	Object	notify()	Object
notifyAll()	Object	toString()	Object
wait()	Object	wait(long)	Object
wait(long, int)	Object		

See Also

BufferedReader, CharArrayReader, FilterReader, InputStreamReader, IOException, PipedReader, StringReader

11.58   SequenceInputStream

Synopsis

Class Name: java.io.SequenceInputStream

Superclass: java.io.InputStream

Immediate Subclasses: None
Interfaces Implemented: None
Availability: JDK 1.0 or later

Description

The `SequenceInputStream` class allows a series of `InputStream` objects to be seamlessly concatenated into one stream. In other words, a `SequenceInputStream` appears and functions as a single `InputStream`. Internally, however, the `SequenceInputStream` reads data from each `InputStream` in the specified order. When the end of a stream is encountered, data is automatically read from the next stream.

Class Summary

```
public class java.io.SequenceInputStream extends java.io.InputStream {
    // Constructors
    public SequenceInputStream(Enumeration e);
    public SequenceInputStream(InputStream s1, InputStream s2);

    // Instance Methods
    public int available();                          // New in 1.1
    public void close();
    public int read();
    public int read(byte[] buf, int pos, int len);
}
```

Constructors

SequenceInputStream

public SequenceInputStream(Enumeration e)

    Parameters   e   An `Enumeration` of input streams.

    Description   This constructor creates a `SequenceInputStream` that reads from each of the `InputStream` objects in the given `Enumeration`. Each object in the `Enumeration` must be an `InputStream`.

public SequenceInputStream(InputStream s1, InputStream s2)

    Parameters   s1   An input stream.

                        s2   Another input stream.

    Description   This constructor creates a `SequenceInputStream` that reads first from s1 and then from s2.

Instance Methods

available

public int available() throws IOException

Availability	New as of JDK 1.1
Returns	The number of bytes that can be read without blocking, or 0 if the end of the final stream is encountered.
Throws	IOException If any kind of I/O error occurs.
Overrides	InputStream.available()
Description	This method returns the number of bytes that can be read without having to wait for more data to become available. The method returns the result of calling available() on the current stream. If the end of the final stream is encountered, the method returns 0.

close

public void close() throws IOException

Throws	IOException If any kind of I/O error occurs.
Overrides	InputStream.close()
Description	This method closes the stream and releases the system resources that are associated with it. The method closes all the InputStream objects attached to this object.

read

public int read() throws IOException

Returns	The next byte of data or –1 if the end of the final stream is encountered.
Throws	IOException If any kind of I/O error occurs.
Overrides	InputStream.read()
Description	This method reads the next byte of data from the current stream. When the end of the current stream is encountered, that stream is closed, and the first byte of the next InputStream is read. If there are no more InputStream objects in the SequenceInputStream, –1 is returned to signify the end of the SequenceInputStream. The method blocks until the byte is read, the end of the final stream is encountered, or an exception is thrown.

public int read(byte[] buf, int off, int len) throws IOException

Parameters	buf	An array of bytes to be filled from the stream.

off   An offset into the byte array.

len   The number of bytes to read.

Returns   The actual number of bytes read or −1 if the end of the final
             stream is encountered immediately.

Throws   IOException   If any kind of I/O error occurs.

Overrides   InputStream.read(byte[], int, int)

Description This method reads up to len bytes of input from the current
             stream into the given array starting at index off. When the end
             of the current stream is encountered, that stream is closed, and
             bytes are read from the next InputStream. If there are no more
             InputStream objects in the SequenceInputStream, −1 is
             returned to signify the end of the SequenceInputStream. The
             method blocks until there is some data available.

Inherited Methods

Method	Inherited From	Method	Inherited From
clone()	Object	equals(Object)	Object
finalize()	Object	getClass()	Object
hashCode()	Object	mark(int)	InputStream
markSupported()	InputStream	notify()	Object
notifyAll()	Object	reset()	InputStream
skip(long)	InputStream	toString()	Object
wait()	Object	wait(long)	Object
wait(long, int)	Object		

See Also

InputStream, IOException

11.59   Serializable

Synopsis

Interface Name: java.io.Serializable

Super-interface: None

Immediate Sub-interfaces:

                         java.io.Externalizable

Implemented By:	java.awt.BorderLayout, java.awt.CardLayout,
	java.awt.CheckboxGroup, java.awt.Color,
	java.awt.Component, java.awt.Cursor,
	java.awt.Dimension, java.awt.Event,
	java.awt.FlowLayout, java.awt.Font,
	java.awt.FontMetrics, java.awt.GridBagConstraints,
	java.awt.GridBagLayout, java.awt.GridLayout,
	java.awt.Insets, java.awt.MediaTracker,
	java.awt.MenuComponent, java.awt.MenuShortcut,
	java.awt.Point, java.awt.Polygon,
	java.awt.Rectangle, java.awt.SystemColor,
	java.io.File, java.io.ObjectStreamClass,
	java.lang.Boolean, java.lang.Character,
	java.lang.Class, java.lang.Number,
	java.lang.String, java.lang.StringBuffer,
	java.lang.Throwable, java.net.InetAddress,
	java.net.URL, java.text.BreakIterator,
	java.text.Collator, java.text.DateFormatSymbols,
	java.text.DecimalFormatSymbols, java.text.Format,
	java.util.BitSet, java.util.Calendar,
	java.util.Date, java.util.EventObject,
	java.util.Hashtable, java.util.Locale,
	java.util.Random, java.util.TimeZone,
	java.util.Vector
Availability:	New as of JDK 1.1

Description

The Serializable interface is implemented by classes that allow object instances to be serialized and deserialized. A class uses the default serialization mechanism simply by implementing this interface. A class that wants finer control over serialization and deserialization should implement the following methods (with these exact signatures):

```
private void readObject(ObjectInputStream in)
        throws IOException, ClassNotFoundException;
private void writeObject(ObjectOutputStream out) throws IOException;
```

The ObjectOutputStream and ObjectInputStream classes support serialization and deserialization, respectively.

Interface Declaration

```
public abstract interface java.io.Serializable {
}
```

See Also

BitSet, Boolean, BreakIterator, Calendar, Character, Class, Collator, Date, DateFormatSymbols, DecimalFormatSymbols, EventObject, Externalizable, File, Format, Hashtable, InetAddress, Locale, Number, ObjectInputStream, ObjectOutputStream, ObjectStreamClass, Random, String, StringBuffer, Throwable, TimeZone, URL, Vector

11.60   StreamCorruptedException

Synopsis

Class Name:	java.io.StreamCorruptedException
Superclass:	java.io.ObjectStreamException
Immediate Subclasses:	None
Interfaces Implemented:	None
Availability:	New as of JDK 1.1

Description

A StreamCorruptedException is thrown during object deserialization to indicate that the stream being read is corrupted and doesn't contain valid serialized object data.

Class Summary

```
public class java.io.StreamCorruptedException
            extends java.io.ObjectStreamException {
  // Constructors
  public StreamCorruptedException();
  public StreamCorruptedException(String reason);
}
```

Constructors

StreamCorruptedException

public StreamCorruptedException()

Description   This constructor creates a StreamCorruptedException with no reason string.

```
public StreamCorruptedException(String reason)
```
Parameters   reason   A description of the reason this exception was thrown.

Description   This constructor creates a `StreamCorruptedException` with the specified reason string.

Inherited Methods

Method	Inherited From	Method	Inherited From
clone()	Object	equals(Object)	Object
fillInStackTrace()	Throwable	finalize()	Object
getClass()	Object	getLocalizedMessage()	Throwable
getMessage()	Throwable	hashCode()	Object
notify()	Object	notifyAll()	Object
printStackTrace()	Throwable	printStack-Trace(PrintStream)	Throwable
printStack-Trace(PrintWriter)	Throwable	toString()	Object
wait()	Object	wait(long)	Object
wait(long, int)	Object		

See Also

Exception, ObjectStreamException, Throwable

11.61   StreamTokenizer

Synopsis

Class Name: java.io.StreamTokenizer
Superclass: java.lang.Object
Immediate Subclasses: None
Interfaces Implemented: None
Availability: JDK 1.0 or later

Description

The `StreamTokenizer` class performs a lexical analysis on an `InputStream` object and breaks the stream into tokens. Although `StreamTokenizer` is not a general-purpose parser, it recognizes tokens that are similar to those used in the Java language. A `StreamTokenizer` recognizes identifiers, numbers, quoted strings, and various comment styles.

A StreamTokenizer object can be wrapped around an InputStream. In this case, when the StreamTokenizer reads bytes from the stream, the bytes are converted to Unicode characters by simply zero-extending the byte values to 16 bits. As of Java 1.1, a StreamTokenizer can be wrapped around a Reader to eliminate this problem.

The nextToken() method returns the next token from the stream. The rest of the methods in StreamTokenizer control how the object interprets the characters that it reads and tokenizes them.

The parsing functionality of StreamTokenizer is controlled by a table and a number of flags. Each character that is read from the InputStream is in the range '\u0000' to '\uFFFF'. The character value looks up attributes of the character in the table. A character can have zero or more of the following attributes: whitespace, alphabetic, numeric, string quote, and comment character.

By default, a StreamTokenizer recognizes the following:

- Whitespace characters between '\u0000' and '\u0020'
- Alphabetic characters from 'a' through 'z', 'A' through 'Z', and '\u00A0' and '\u00FF'.
- Numeric characters '1', '2', '3', '4', '5', '6', '7', '8', '9', '0', '.', and '-'
- String quote characters "'" and """
- Comment character "/"

Class Summary

```
public class java.io.StreamTokenizer extends java.lang.Object {
    // Variables
    public double nval;
    public String sval;
    public int ttype;
    public final static int TT_EOF;
    public final static int TT_EOL;
    public final static int TT_NUMBER;
    public final static int TT_WORD;

    // Constructors
    public StreamTokenizer(InputStream in);         // Deprecated in 1.1
    public StreamTokenizer(Reader in);              // New in 1.1

    // Instance Methods
    public void commentChar(int ch);
    public void eolIsSignificant(boolean flag);
    public int lineno();
    public void lowerCaseMode(boolean flag);
    public int nextToken();
```

```
    public void ordinaryChar(int ch);
    public void ordinaryChars(int low, int hi);
    public void parseNumbers();
    public void pushBack();
    public void quoteChar(int ch);
    public void resetSyntax();
    public void slashSlashComments(boolean flag);
    public void slashStarComments(boolean flag);
    public String toString();
    public void whitespaceChars(int low, int hi);
    public void wordChars(int low, int hi);
}
```

Variables

nval

`public double nval`

Description   This variable contains the value of a TT_NUMBER token.

sval

`public String sval`

Description   This variable contains the value of a TT_WORD token.

ttype

`public int ttype`

Description   This variable indicates the token type. The value is either one of the TT_ constants defined below or the character that has just been parsed from the input stream.

TT_EOF

`public final static int TT_EOF = -1`

Description   This token type indicates that the end of the stream has been reached.

TT_EOL

`public final static int TT_EOL = '\n'`

Description   This token type indicates that the end of a line has been reached. The value is not returned by nextToken() unless eolIsSignificant(true) has been called.

TT_NUMBER

    public final static int TT_NUMBER = -2

    Description   This token type indicates that a number has been parsed. The number is placed in nval.

TT_WORD

    public final static int TT_WORD = -3

    Description   This token type indicates that a word has been parsed. The word is placed in sval.

Constructors

StreamTokenizer

    public StreamTokenizer(InputStream in)

    Availability   Deprecated as of JDK 1.1
    Parameters   in   The input stream to tokenize.
    Description   This constructor creates a StreamTokenizer that reads from the given InputStream. As of JDK 1.1, this method is deprecated and StreamTokenizer(Reader) should be used instead.

    public StreamTokenizer(Reader in)

    Availability   New as of JDK 1.1
    Parameters   in   The reader to tokenize.
    Description   This constructor creates a StreamTokenizer that reads from the given Reader.

Instance Methods

commentChar

    public void commentChar(int ch)

    Parameters   ch   The character to use to indicate comments.
    Description   This method tells this StreamTokenizer to treat the given character as the beginning of a comment that ends at the end of the line. The StreamTokenizer ignores all of the characters from the comment character to the end of the line. By default, a StreamTokenizer treats the "/" character as a comment character. This method may be called multiple times if there are multiple characters that begin comment lines.

                     To specify that a character is not a comment character, use ordinaryChar().

eolIsSignificant

public void eolIsSignificant(boolean flag)

Parameters	flag	A boolean value that specifies whether or not this StreamTokenizer returns TT_EOL tokens.
Description		A StreamTokenizer recognizes "\n", "\r", and "\r\n" as the end of a line. By default, end-of-line characters are treated as whitespace and thus, the StreamTokenizer does not return TT_EOL tokens from nextToken(). Call eolIsSignificant(true) to tell the StreamTokenizer to return TT_EOL tokens.

lineo

public int lineno()

Returns	The current line number.
Description	This method returns the current line number. Line numbers begin at 1.

lowerCaseMode

public void lowerCaseMode(boolean flag)

Parameters	flag	A boolean value that specifies whether or not this StreamTokenizer returns TT_WORD tokens in lowercase.
Description		By default, a StreamTokenizer does not change the case of the words that it parses. However if you call lowerCaseMode(true), whenever nextToken() returns a TT_WORD token, the word in sval is converted to lowercase.

nextToken

public int nextToken() throws IOException

Returns		One of the token types (TT_EOF, TT_EOL, TT_NUMBER, or TT_WORD) or a character code.
Throws	IOException	If any kind of I/O error occurs.
Description		This method reads the next token from the stream. The value returned is the same as the value of the variable ttype. The nextToken() method parses the following tokens:
	TT_EOF	The end of the input stream has been reached.
	TT_EOL	The end of a line has been reached. The eolIsSignificant() method controls whether end-of-line characters are treated as whitespace or returned as TT_EOL tokens.

TT_NUMBER	A number has been parsed. The value can be found in the variable nval. The parseNumbers() method tells the StreamTokenizer to recognize numbers distinct from words.
TT_WORD	A word has been parsed. The word can be found in the variable sval.
Quoted string	A quoted string has been parsed. The variable ttype is set to the quote character, and sval contains the string itself. You can tell the StreamTokenizer what characters to use as quote characters using quoteChar().
Character	A single character has been parsed. The variable ttype is set to the character value.

ordinaryChar

public void ordinaryChar(int ch)

Parameters	ch	The character to treat normally.
Description		This method causes this StreamTokenizer to treat the given character as an *ordinary* character. This means that the character has no special significance as a comment, string quote, alphabetic, numeric, or whitespace character. For example, to tell the StreamTokenizer that the slash does not start a single-line comment, use ordinaryChar('/').

ordinaryChars

public void ordinaryChars(int low, int hi)

Parameters	low	The beginning of a range of character values.
	hi	The end of a range of character values.
Description		This method tells this StreamTokenizer to treat all of the characters in the given range as ordinary characters. See the description of ordinaryChar() above for more information.

parseNumbers

public void parseNumbers()

Description	This method tells this StreamTokenizer to recognize numbers. The StreamTokenizer constructor calls this method, so the default behavior of a StreamTokenizer is to recognize numbers. This method modifies the syntax table of the StreamTokenizer so that the following characters have the numeric attribute: '1', '2', '3', '4', '5', '6', '7', '8', '9', '0', '.', and '-'

When the parser encounters a token that has the format of a double-precision floating-point number, the token is treated as a number rather than a word. The `ttype` variable is set to `TT_NUMBER`, and `nval` is set to the value of the number.

To use a `StreamTokenizer` that does not parse numbers, make the above characters ordinary using `ordinaryChar()` or `ordinaryChars()`:

pushBack

`public void pushBack()`

Description   This method has the effect of pushing the current token back onto the stream. In other words, after a call to this method, the next call to the `nextToken()` method returns the same result as the previous call to the `nextToken()`method without reading any input.

quoteChar

`public void quoteChar(int ch)`

Parameters   ch   The character to use as a delimiter for quoted strings.

Description   This method tells this `StreamTokenizer` to treat the given character as the beginning or end of a quoted string. By default, the single-quote character and the double-quote character are string-quote characters. When the parser encounters a string-quote character, the `ttype` variable is set to the quote character, and `sval` is set to the actual string. The string consists of all the characters after (but not including) the string-quote character up to (but not including) the next occurrence of the same string-quote character, a line terminator, or the end of the stream.

To specify that a character is not a string-quote character, use `ordinaryChar()`.

resetSyntax

`public void resetSyntax()`

Description   This method resets this `StreamTokenizer`, which causes it to treat all characters as ordinary characters. See the description of `ordinaryChar()` above for more information.

slashSlashComments

public void slashSlashComments(boolean flag)

Parameters   flag   A boolean value that specifies whether or not
                        this StreamTokenizer recognizes double-slash
                        comments (//).

Description   By default, a StreamTokenizer does not recognize double-slash
              comments. However, if you call slashSlashComments(true), the
              nextToken() method recognizes and ignores double-slash com-
              ments.

slashStarComments

public void slashStarComments(boolean flag)

Parameters   flag   A boolean value that specifies whether or not
                        this StreamTokenizer recognizes slash-star (/*
                        ... */) comments.

Description   By default, a StreamTokenizer does not recognize slash-star
              comments. However, if you call slashStarComments(true), the
              nextToken() method recognizes and ignores slash-star com-
              ments.

toString

public String toString()

Returns   A String representation of the current token.

Overrides   Object.toString()

Description   This method returns a string representation of the current
              token recognized by the nextToken() method. This string rep-
              resentation consists of the value of ttype, the value of sval if
              the token is a word or the value of nval if the token is a num-
              ber, and the current line number.

whitespaceChars

public void whitespaceChars(int low, int hi)

Parameters   low   The beginning of a range of character values.
             hi   The end of a range of character values.

Description   This method causes this StreamTokenizer to treat characters in
              the specified range as whitespace. The only function of whites-
              pace characters is to separate tokens in the stream.

wordChars

public void wordChars(int low, int hi)

Parameters	low	The beginning of a range of character values.
	hi	The end of a range of character values.
Description		This method causes this StreamTokenizer to treat characters in the specified range as characters that are part of a word token, or, in other words, consider the characters to be alphabetic. A word token consists of a sequence of characters that begins with an alphabetic character and is followed by zero or more numeric or alphabetic characters.

Inherited Methods

Method	Inherited From	Method	Inherited From
clone()	Object	equals(Object)	Object
finalize()	Object	getClass()	Object
hashCode()	Object	notify()	Object
notifyAll()	Object	wait()	Object
wait(long)	Object	wait(long, int)	Object

See Also

InputStream, IOException, Reader, StringTokenizer

11.62   StringBufferInputStream

Synopsis

Class Name:	java.io.StringBufferInputStream
Superclass:	java.io.InputStream
Immediate Subclasses:	None
Interfaces Implemented:	None
Availability:	Deprecated as of JDK 1.1

Description

The StringBufferInputStream class represents a byte stream whose data source is a String. This class is similar to the ByteArrayInputStream class, which uses a byte array as its data source.

StringBufferInputStream is deprecated as of JDK 1.1 because it does not correctly convert characters to bytes. The StringReader class should now be used to create a character stream from a String.

Class Summary

```
public class java.io.StringBufferInputStream extends java.io.InputStream {
   // Variables
   protected String buffer;
   protected int count;
   protected int pos;

   // Constructor
   public StringBufferInputStream(String s);

   // Instance Methods
   public synchronized int available();
   public synchronized int read();
   public synchronized int read(byte[] b, int off, int len);
   public synchronized void reset();
   public synchronized long skip(long n);
}
```

Variables

buffer

protected String buffer

   Description   The buffer that stores the data for the input stream.

count

protected int count

   Description   The size of the buffer, or in other words, the length of the
                  string.

pos

protected int pos

   Description   The current stream position.

Constructors

StringBufferInputStream

public StringBufferInputStream(String s)

   Parameters   s   The String to use.

   Description   This constructor creates a StringBufferInputStream that uses
                  the given String as its data source. Note that the data is not
                  copied, so changes made to the String affect the data that the
                  StringBufferInputStream returns.

Instance Methods

available

`public synchronized int available()`

Returns	The number of bytes remaining in the string.
Overrides	`InputStream.available()`
Description	This method returns the number of bytes that are left in the string. This is the length of the string, count, minus the current stream position, pos.

read

`public synchronized int read()`

Returns	The next byte of data or –1 if the end of the string is encountered.
Overrides	`InputStream.read()`
Description	This method returns the next byte from the string. The method takes the next character from the string and returns the low eight bits of that character as a byte, which is not the correct way to convert characters into bytes. The method cannot block.

`public synchronized int read(byte b[], int off, int len)`

Parameters	b	An array of bytes to be filled from the stream.
	off	An offset into the byte array.
	len	The number of bytes to read.
Returns		The actual number of bytes read or –1 if the end of the string is encountered immediately.
Overrides		`InputStream.read(byte[], int, int)`
Description		This method copies bytes from the internal buffer into the given array b, starting at index off and continuing for len bytes. The method takes each character from the string and returns the low eight bits of that character as a byte, which is not the correct way to convert characters into bytes.

reset

`public synchronized void reset()`

Overrides	`InputStream.reset()`
Description	This method sets the position of the StringBufferInputStream back to the beginning of the internal buffer.

skip

```
public synchronized long skip(long n)
```

Parameters	n	The number of bytes to skip.
Returns	The actual number of bytes skipped.	
Overrides	InputStream.skip()	
Description	This method skips n bytes of the string. If you try to skip past the end of the string, the stream is positioned at the end of the string.	

Inherited Methods

Method	Inherited From	Method	Inherited From
clone()	Object	close()	InputStream
equals(Object)	Object	finalize()	Object
getClass()	Object	hashCode()	Object
mark(int)	InputStream	markSupported()	InputStream
notify()	Object	notifyAll()	Object
read(byte[])	InputStream	toString()	Object
wait()	Object	wait(long)	Object
wait(long, int)	Object		

See Also

ByteArrayInputStream, InputStream, IOException, String, StringReader

11.63   StringReader

Synopsis

Class Name:	java.io.StringReader
Superclass:	java.io.Reader
Immediate Subclasses:	None
Interfaces Implemented:	None
Availability:	New as of JDK 1.1

Description

The StringReader class represents a character stream whose data source is a String. This class is similar to the CharArrayReader class, which uses a char array as its data source.

StringReader is meant to replace the StringBufferInputStream class as of JDK 1.1. Unlike StringBufferInputStream, StringReader handles Unicode characters and supports mark() and reset().

Class Summary

```
public class java.io.StringReader extends java.io.Reader {
    // Constructors
    public StringReader(String s);

    // Instance Methods
    public void close();
    public void mark(int readAheadLimit);
    public boolean markSupported();
    public int read();
    public int read(char[] cbuf, int off, int len);
    public boolean ready();
    public void reset();
    public long skip(long ns);
}
```

Constructors

StringReader

public StringReader(String s)

Parameters	s	The String to use.
Description		This constructor creates a StringReader that uses the given String as its data source. The data is not copied, so changes made to the String affect the data that the StringReader returns.

Instance Methods

close

public void close()

Overrides	Reader.close()	
Description	This method closes the reader by removing the link between this StringReader and the String it was created with.	

mark

public void mark(int readAheadLimit) throws IOException

Parameters   readAheadLimit

The maximum number of characters that can be read before the saved position becomes invalid.

Throws   IOException If the stream is closed or any other kind of I/O
                error occurs.

Overrides   Reader.mark()

Description   This method causes the StringReader to remember its current
                position. A subsequent call to reset() causes the object to
                return to that saved position, and thus re-read a portion of the
                string. Because the data for this stream comes from a String,
                there is no limit on reading ahead, so readAheadLimit is
                ignored.

markSupported

public boolean markSupported()

Returns   The boolean value true.

Overrides   Reader.markSupported()

Description   This method returns true to indicate that this class supports
                mark() and reset().

read

public int read() throws IOException

Returns   The next character or –1 if the end of the string is encoun-
                tered.

Throws   IOException If the stream is closed or any other kind of I/O
                error occurs.

Overrides   Reader.read()

Description   This method returns the next character from the string. The
                method cannot block.

public int read(char[] cbuf, int off, int len) throws IOException

Parameters   cbuf   An array of characters to be filled from the
                            stream.

                off   An offset into the character array.

                len   The number of characters to read.

Returns   The actual number of characters read or –1 if the end of the
                string is encountered immediately.

Throws   IOException If the stream is closed or any other kind of I/O
                error occurs.

Overrides   Reader.read(char[], int, int)

Description   This method copies up to len characters from the internal
                buffer into the given array cbuf, starting at index off.

ready

public boolean ready() throws IOException

Returns	A boolean value that indicates whether the stream is ready to be read.
Throws	IOException If the stream is closed or any other kind of I/O error occurs.
Overrides	Reader.ready()
Description	If there is any data left to be read from the string, this method returns true.

reset

public void reset() throws IOException

Throws	IOException If the stream is closed or any other kind of I/O error occurs.
Overrides	Reader.reset()
Description	This method resets the position of the StringReader to the position that was saved by calling the mark() method. If mark() has not been called, the StringReader is reset to read from the beginning of the string.

skip

public long skip(long ns) throws IOException

Parameters	ns The number of bytes to skip.
Returns	The actual number of bytes skipped.
Throws	IOException If the stream is closed or any other kind of I/O error occurs.
Overrides	Reader.skip()
Description	This method skips ns characters of input. If you try to skip past the end of the string, the stream is positioned at the end of the string.

Inherited Methods

Method	Inherited From	Method	Inherited From
clone()	Object	equals (Object)	Object
finalize()	Object	getClass()	Object
hashCode()	Object	notify()	Object
notifyAll()	Object	read(char[])	Reader
toString()	Object	wait()	Object
wait(long)	Object	wait(long, int)	Object

See Also

CharArrayReader, IOException, Reader, String, StringBufferInputStream

11.64   StringWriter

Synopsis

Class Name: java.io.StringWriter
Superclass: java.io.Writer
Immediate Subclasses: None
Interfaces Implemented: None
Availability: New as of JDK 1.1

Description

The StringWriter class represents a stream whose data is written to a string. This class is similar to the CharArrayWriter class, which writes its data to a char array. The StringWriter class uses a StringBuffer to store its data; a String can be retrieved with the toString() method.

Class Summary

```
public class java.io.StringWriter extends java.io.Writer {
    // Constructors
    public StringWriter();
    protected StringWriter(int initialSize);

    // Instance Methods
    public void close();
    public void flush();
    public StringBuffer getBuffer();
    public String toString();
    public void write(int c);
    public void write(char[] cbuf, int off, int len);
    public void write(String str);
    public void write(String str, int off, int len);
}
```

Constructors

StringWriter

public StringWriter()

Description   This constructor creates a StringWriter with an internal buffer that has a default size of 16 characters. The buffer grows automatically as data is written to the stream.

protected StringWriter (int initialSize)

Parameters   initialSize   The initial buffer size.

Description   This constructor creates a StringWriter with an internal buffer that has a size of initialSize characters. The buffer grows automatically as data is written to the stream.

Instance Methods

close

public void close()

Overrides   Writer.close()

Description   This method does nothing. For most subclassesof Writer, this method releases any system resources that are associated with the Writer object. However, the StringWriter's internal buffer may be needed for subsequent calls to toString(). For this reason, close() does nothing, and the internal buffer is not released until the StringWriter is garbage collected.

flush

public void flush()

Overrides   Writer.flush()

Description   This method does nothing. The StringWriter writes data directly into its internal buffer; thus it is never necessary to flush the stream.

getBuffer

public StringBuffer getBuffer()

Returns   A reference to the internal data buffer.

Description   This method returns a reference to the StringBuffer object that is used in this StringWriter.

toString

```
public String toString()
```

Returns   A String constructed from the internal data buffer.

Overrides   Object.toString()

Description   This method returns a reference to a String object created
                from the characters stored in this object's internal buffer.

write

```
public void write(int c)
```

Parameters   c   The value to write.

Overrides   Writer.write(int)

Description   This method writes the given value into the internal buffer. If
                the buffer is full, it is expanded.

```
public void write(char[] cbuf, int off, int len)
```

Parameters   cbuf   An array of characters to write to the stream.

               off   An offset into the character array.

               len   The number of characters to write.

Overrides   Writer.write(char[], int, int)

Description   This method copies len characters to this object's internal
                buffer from cbuf, starting off elements from the beginning of
                the array. If the internal buffer is full, it is expanded.

```
public void write(String str)
```

Parameters   str   A String to write to the stream.

Overrides   Writer.write(String)

Description   This method copies the characters of str into this object's
                internal buffer. If the internal buffer is full, it is expanded.

```
public void write(String str, int off, int len)
```

Parameters   str   A String to write to the stream.

               off   An offset into the string.

               len   The number of characters to write.

Overrides   Writer.write(String, int, int)

Description   This method copies len characters to this object's internal
                buffer from str, starting off characters from the beginning of
                the given string. If the internal buffer is full, it is expanded.

Inherited Methods

Method	Inherited From	Method	Inherited From
clone()	Object	equals(Object)	Object
finalize()	Object	getClass()	Object
hashCode()	Object	notify()	Object
notifyAll()	Object	wait()	Object
wait(long)	Object	wait(long, int)	Object
write(char[])	Writer		

See Also

CharArrayWriter, String, StringBuffer, Writer

11.65   SyncFailedException

Synopsis

Class Name:	java.io.SyncFailedException
Superclass:	java.io.IOException
Immediate Subclasses:	None
Interfaces Implemented:	None
Availability:	New as of JDK 1.1

Description

A SyncFailedException is thrown from when an underlying I/O device cannot be synchronized to a known state. The FileDescriptor.sync() method throws this exception when its synchronization operation fails.

Class Summary

```
public class java.io.SyncFailedException extends java.io.IOException {
   // Constructors
   public SyncFailedException(String desc);
}
```

Constructors

SyncFailedException

```
public SyncFailedException(String desc)
```

Parameters	desc	A description of the reason this exception was thrown.
Description		This constructor creates a SyncFailedException with the specified detail message.

Inherited Methods

Method	Inherited From	Method	Inherited From
clone()	Object	equals(Object)	Object
fillInStackTrace()	Throwable	finalize()	Object
getClass()	Object	getLocalizedMessage()	Throwable
getMessage()	Throwable	hashCode()	Object
notify()	Object	notifyAll()	Object
printStackTrace()	Throwable	printStack-Trace(PrintStream)	Throwable
printStack-Trace(PrintWriter)	Throwable	toString()	Object
wait()	Object	wait(long)	Object
wait(long, int)	Object		

See Also

Exception, FileDescriptor, IOException, Throwable

11.66   UnsupportedEncodingException

Synopsis

Class Name:	java.io.UnsupportedEncodingException
Superclass:	java.io.IOException
Immediate Subclasses:	None
Interfaces Implemented:	None
Availability:	New as of JDK 1.1

Description

An UnsupportedEncodingException is thrown when a character encoding scheme is not available. It can be thrown by methods of classes in java.io and other packages.

Class Summary

```
public class java.io.UnsupportedEncodingException
            extends java.io.IOException {
  // Constructors
  public UnsupportedEncodingException();
  public UnsupportedEncodingException(String s);
}
```

Constructors

UnsupportedEncodingException

public UnsupportedEncodingException()

Description   This constructor creates an UnsupportedEncodingException with no detail message.

public UnsupportedEncodingException(String s)

Parameters   s   The detail message.

Description   This constructor creates an UnsupportedEncodingException with the specified detail message.

Inherited Methods

Method	Inherited From	Method	Inherited From
clone()	Object	equals(Object)	Object
fillInStackTrace()	Throwable	finalize()	Object
getClass()	Object	getLocalizedMessage()	Throwable
getMessage()	Throwable	hashCode()	Object
notify()	Object	notifyAll()	Object
printStackTrace()	Throwable	printStack-Trace(PrintStream)	Throwable
printStack-Trace(PrintWriter)	Throwable	toString()	Object
wait()	Object	wait(long)	Object
wait(long, int)	Object		

See Also

Exception, IOException, Throwable

11.67   UTFDataFormatException

Synopsis

Class Name: java.io.UTFDataFormatException
Superclass: java.io.IOException
Immediate Subclasses: None
Interfaces Implemented: None
Availability: JDK 1.0 or later

Description

A UTFDataFormatException is thrown when there is an attempt to read a UTF
string from a stream that does not contain a properly formatted UTF string. See
Appendix B, for a desciption of the UTF-8 encoding.

Class Summary

```
public class java.io.UTFDataFormatException extends java.io.IOException {
  // Constructors
  public UTFDataFormatException();
  public UTFDataFormatException(String s);
}
```

Constructors

UTFDataFormatException

public UTFDataFormatException()

    Description   This constructor creates a UTFDataFormatException with no
                    detail message.

public UTFDataFormatException(String s)

    Parameters   s   The detail message.
    Description   This constructor creates a UTFDataFormatException with the
                    specified detail message.

Inherited Methods

Method	Inherited From	Method	Inherited From
clone()	Object	equals(Object)	Object
fillInStackTrace()	Throwable	finalize()	Object
getClass()	Object	getLocalizedMessage()	Throwable
getMessage()	Throwable	hashCode()	Object
notify()	Object	notifyAll()	Object
printStackTrace()	Throwable	printStack-Trace(PrintStream)	Throwable
printStack-Trace(PrintWriter)	Throwable	toString()	Object
wait()	Object	wait(long)	Object
wait(long, int)	Object		

See Also

Exception, IOException, Throwable

11.68   WriteAbortedException

Synopsis

Class Name:	java.io.WriteAbortedException
Superclass:	java.io.ObjectStreamException
Immediate Subclasses:	None
Interfaces Implemented:	None
Availability:	New as of JDK 1.1

Description

A WriteAbortedException is thrown during object deserialization when the stream of data is incomplete because an exception was thrown while it was being written. Thus, WriteAbortedException represents an exception that was thrown during object serialization and serialized into the stream.

Class Summary

```
public class java.io.WriteAbortedException
          extends java.io.ObjectStreamException {
   // Variables
   public Exception detail;
```

```
    // Constructors
    public WriteAbortedException(String s, Exception ex);

    // Instance Methods
    public String getMessage();
}
```

Variables

detail

public Exception detail

    Description   The exception that was thrown during serialization; it is a sub-class of ObjectStreamException.

Constructors

WriteAbortedException

public WriteAbortedException(String s, Exception ex)

Parameters	s	A description of the reason this exception was thrown.
	ex	The exception that was thrown during serialization.
Description		This constructor creates a WriteAbortedException with the specified reason string. The created exception wraps the given exception thrown during serialization.

Instance Methods

getMessage

public String getMessage()

    Returns   The detail message for this exception.
    Overrides   Throwable.getMessage()
    Description   This method returns the detail message of this exception, as well the detail message of the nested exception if it exists.

Inherited Methods

Method	Inherited From	Method	Inherited From
clone()	Object	equals(Object)	Object
fillInStackTrace()	Throwable	finalize()	Object
getClass()	Object	getLocalizedMessage()	Throwable
getMessage()	Throwable	hashCode()	Object
notify()	Object	notifyAll()	Object
printStackTrace()	Throwable	printStack-Trace(PrintStream)	Throwable

Method	Inherited From	Method	Inherited From
printStack-Trace(PrintWriter)	Throwable	toString()	Object
wait()	Object	wait(long)	Object
wait(long, int)	Object		

See Also

Exception, ObjectStreamException, Throwable

11.69   Writer

Synopsis

Class Name: java.io.Writer

Superclass: java.lang.Object

Immediate Subclasses: java.io.BufferedWriter, java.io.CharArrayWriter,
java.io.FilterWriter, java.io.OutputStreamWriter,
java.io.PipedWriter, java.io.PrintWriter,
java.io.StringWriter

Interfaces Implemented: None

Availability: New as of JDK 1.1

Description

The Writer class is an abstract class that is the superclass of all classes that represent output character streams. Writer defines the basic output methods that all character streams provide. A similar hierarchy of classes, based around OutputStream, deals with byte streams instead of character streams.

Writer is designed so that write(int b) and write(char[]) both call write(char[], int, int). Thus, a subclass can simply override write(char[], int, int) and all of the write methods will work. Note that this is different from the design of OutputStream, where the write(int b) method is the catch-all method. The design of Writer is cleaner and more efficient.

Some Writer subclasses may implement buffering to increase efficiency. Writer provides a method—flush()—that tells the Writer to write any buffered output to the underlying device, which may be a disk drive or a network.

Class Summary

```
public abstract class java.io.Writer extends java.lang.Object {
    // Variables
    protected Object lock;

    // Constructors
    protected Writer();
    protected Writer(Object lock);

    // Instance Methods
    public abstract void close();
    public abstract void flush();
    public void write(int c);
    public void write(char[] cbuf);
    public abstract void write(char[] cbuf, int off, int len);
    public void write(String str);
    public void write(String str, int off, int len);
}
```

Variables

lock

protected Object lock

> Description   The object used to synchronize operations on this Writer object. For efficiency's sake, a particular implementation of a character stream can choose to synchronize its operations on something other than instances of itself. Thus, any subclass should synchronize on the lock object, instead of using a synchronized method or the this object.

Constructors

Writer

protected Writer()

> Description   This constructor creates a Writer that synchronizes on the Writer itself, or in other words, on the this object.

protected Writer(Object lock)

> Parameters   lock   The object to use for synchronization.
>
> Description   This constructor creates a Writer that synchronizes on the given object.

Instance Methods

close

```
public abstract void close() throws IOException
```
Throws   IOException   If any kind of I/O error occurs.

Description   This method flushes the writer and then closes it, releasing any system resources associated with it.

A subclass of Writer must implement this method.

flush

```
public void flush() throws IOException
```
Throws   IOException   If any kind of I/O error occurs.

Description   This method forces any characters that may be buffered by this Writer to be written to the underlying device.

A subclass of Writer must implement this method.

write

```
public void write(int c) throws IOException
```
Parameters   c   The value to write.

Throws   IOException   If any kind of I/O error occurs.

Description   This method writes a character containing the lowest sixteen bits of the given integer value.

The implementation of this method in Writer writes the character by calling write(cb, 1) where cb is a character array that contains the given value in cb[0]. Although it is not strictly necessary, a subclass that wants to provide efficient single-character writes should override this method.

```
public void write(char[] cbuf) throws IOException
```
Parameters   cbuf   An array of characters to write to the stream.

Throws   IOException   If any kind of I/O error occurs.

Description   This method writes the given array of characters to the stream by calling write(cbuf, 0, cbuf.length).

A subclass does not usually need to override this method, as it can override write(char[], int, int) and have write(char[]) work automatically.

```
public abstract void write(char[] cbuf, int off, int len)
                    throws IOException
```
Parameters   cbuf   An array of characters to write to the stream.

off   An offset into the array.

len   The number of characters to write.

Throws   IOException If any kind of I/O error occurs.

Description This method writes len characters contained in the given array starting at index off.

A subclass of Writer must implement this method.

public void write(String str) throws IOException

Parameters   str   A string to write to the stream.

Throws   IOException If any kind of I/O error occurs.

Description This method writes the given string to the stream by calling write(str,str.length).

A subclass does not usually need to override this method, as it can override write(char[], int, int) and have it work automatically.

public void write(String str, int off, int len) throws IOException

Parameters   str   A string to write to the stream.

off   An offset into the string.

len   The number of characters to write.

Throws   IOException If any kind of I/O error occurs.

Description This method writes len characters contained in the given string starting at index off. The method does this by creating an array of characters for the specified portion of the string and then calling write(cb, 0, cb.length) on the character array cb.

A subclass does not usually need to override this method, as it can override write(char[], int, int) and have it work automatically.

Inherited Methods

Method	Inherited From	Method	Inherited From
clone()	Object	equals(Object)	Object
finalize()	Object	getClass()	Object
hashCode()	Object	notify()	Object
notifyAll()	Object	toString()	Object
wait()	Object	wait(long)	Object
wait(long, int)	Object		

See Also

BufferedWriter, CharArrayWriter, FilterWriter, IOException, Output-StreamWriter, PipedWriter, PrintWriter, StringWriter

12

The java.lang Package

The package `java.lang` contains classes and interfaces that are essential to the Java language. These include:

- `Object`, the ultimate superclass of all classes in Java.
- `Thread`, the class that controls each thread in a multithreaded program.
- `Throwable`, the superclass of all error and exception classes in Java.
- Classes that encapsulate the primitive data types in Java.
- Classes for accessing system resources and other low-level entities.
- `Math`, a class that provides standard mathematical methods.
- `String`, the class that represents strings.

Because the classes in the `java.lang` package are so essential, the `java.lang` package is implicitly imported by every Java source file. In other words, you can refer to all of the classes and interfaces in `java.lang` using their simple names.

Figure 12-1 shows the class hierarchy for the `java.lang` package.

The possible exceptions in a Java program are organized in a hierarchy of exception classes. The `Throwable` class is at the root of the exception hierarchy. `Throwable` has two immediate subclasses: `Exception` and `Error`. Figure 12-2 shows the standard exception classes defined in the `java.lang` package, while Figure 12-3 shows the standard error classes defined in `java.lang`.

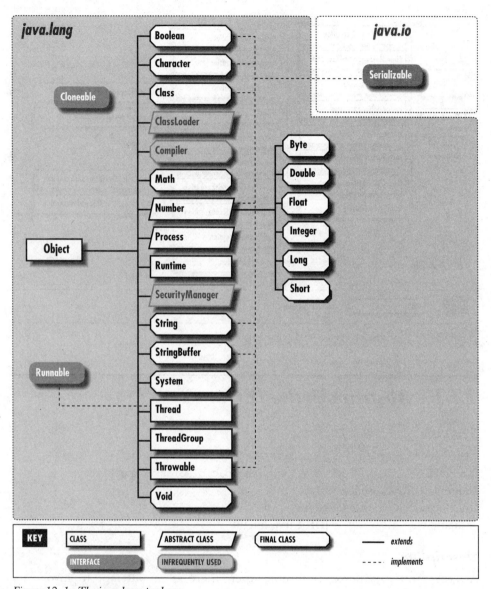

Figure 12–1: The java.lang package

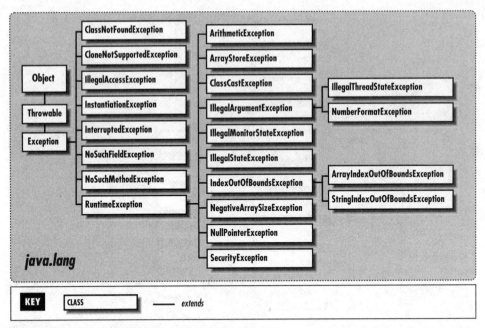

Figure 12–2: The exception classes in the java.lang package

12.1 AbstractMethodError

Synopsis

Class Name:	java.lang.AbstractMethodError
Superclass:	java.lang.IncompatibleClassChangeError
Immediate Subclasses:	None
Interfaces Implemented:	None
Availability:	JDK 1.0 or later

Description

An AbstractMethodError is thrown when there is an attempt to invoke an abstract method.

Class Summary

```
public class java.lang.AbstractMethodError
          extends java.lang.IncompatibleClassChangeError {
  // Constructors
  public AbstractMethodError();
  public AbstractMethodError(String s);
}
```

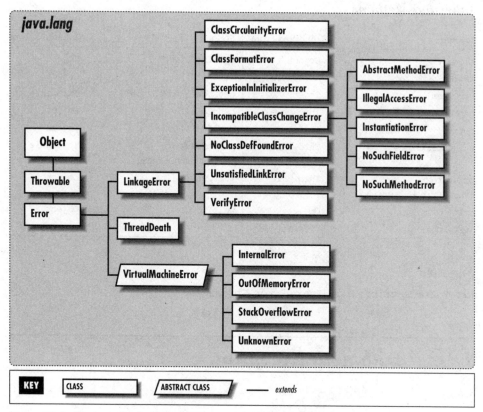

Figure 12–3: The error classes in the java.lang package

Constructors

AbstractMethodError

public AbstractMethodError()

Description   This constructor creates an AbstractMethodError with no associated detail message.

public AbstractMethodError(String s)

Parameters   s   The detail message.

Description   This constructor creates an AbstractMethodError with the specified detail message.

Inherited Methods

Method	Inherited From	Method	Inherited From
clone()	Object	equals(Object)	Object
fillInStackTrace()	Throwable	finalize()	Object
getClass()	Object	getLocalizedMessage()	Throwable
getMessage()	Throwable	hashCode()	Object
notify()	Object	notifyAll()	Object
printStackTrace()	Throwable	printStack-Trace(PrintStream)	Throwable
printStack-Trace(PrintWriter)	Throwable	toString()	Object
wait()	Object	wait(long)	Object
wait(long, int)	Object		

See Also

Error, IncompatibleClassChangeError, Throwable

12.2   ArithmeticException

Synopsis

Class Name: java.lang.ArithmeticException
Superclass: java.lang.RuntimeException
Immediate Subclasses: None
Interfaces Implemented: None
Availability: JDK 1.0 or later

Description

An ArithmeticException is thrown to indicate an exceptional arithmetic condition, such as integer division by zero.

Class Summary

```
public class java.lang.ArithmeticException
        extends java.lang.RuntimeException {
  // Constructors
  public ArithmeticException();
  public ArithmeticException(String s);
}
```

Constructors

ArithmeticException

    public ArithmeticException()

    Description   This constructor creates an ArithmeticException with no associated detail message.

    public ArithmeticException(String s)

    Parameters   s   The detail message.

    Description   This constructor creates ArithmeticException with the specified detail message.

Inherited Methods

Method	Inherited From	Method	Inherited From
clone()	Object	equals(Object)	Object
fillInStackTrace()	Throwable	finalize()	Object
getClass()	Object	getLocalizedMessage()	Throwable
getMessage()	Throwable	hashCode()	Object
notify()	Object	notifyAll()	Object
printStackTrace()	Throwable	printStack-Trace(PrintStream)	Throwable
printStack-Trace(PrintWriter)	Throwable	toString()	Object
wait()	Object	wait(long)	Object
wait(long, int)	Object		

See Also

Exception, RuntimeException, Throwable

12.3 ArrayIndexOutOfBoundsException

Synopsis

Class Name:	java.lang.ArrayIndexOutOfBoundsException
Superclass:	java.lang.IndexOutOfBoundsException
Immediate Subclasses:	None
Interfaces Implemented:	None
Availability:	JDK 1.0 or later

Description

An `ArrayIndexOutOfBoundsException` is thrown when an out-of-range index is detected by an array object. An out-of-range index occurs when the index is less than zero or greater than or equal to the size of the array.

Class Summary

```
public class java.lang.ArrayIndexOutOfBoundsException
            extends java.lang.IndexOutOfBoundsException {
    // Constructors
    public ArrayIndexOutOfBoundsException();
    public ArrayIndexOutOfBoundsException(int index);
    public ArrayIndexOutOfBoundsException(String s);
}
```

Constructors

ArrayIndexOutOfBoundsException

public ArrayIndexOutOfBoundsException()

    Description   This constructor creates an `ArrayIndexOutOfBoundsException` with no associated detail message.

public ArrayIndexOutOfBoundsException(int index)

    Parameters   index   The index value that was out-of-bounds

    Description   This constructor creates an `ArrayIndexOutOfBoundsException` with an associated message that mentions the specified index.

public ArrayIndexOutOfBoundsException(String s)

    Parameters   s   The detail message.

    Description   This constructor creates an `ArrayIndexOutOfBoundsException` with the specified detail message.

Inherited Methods

Method	Inherited From	Method	Inherited From
clone()	Object	equals(Object)	Object
fillInStackTrace()	Throwable	finalize()	Object
getClass()	Object	getLocalizedMessage()	Throwable
getMessage()	Throwable	hashCode()	Object
notify()	Object	notifyAll()	Object
printStackTrace()	Throwable	printStack-Trace(PrintStream)	Throwable
printStack-Trace(PrintWriter)	Throwable	toString()	Object
wait()	Object	wait(long)	Object
wait(long, int)	Object		

See Also

Exception, IndexOutOfBoundsException, RuntimeException, Throwable

---

12.4   ArrayStoreException

Synopsis

Class Name: java.lang.ArrayStoreException
Superclass: java.lang.RuntimeException
Immediate Subclasses: None
Interfaces Implemented: None
Availability: JDK 1.0 or later

Description

An ArrayStoreException is thrown when there is an attempt to store a value in an array element that is incompatible with the type of the array.

Class Summary

```
public class java.lang.ArrayStoreException
           extends java.lang.RuntimeException {
    // Constructors
    public ArrayStoreException();
    public ArrayStoreException(String s);
}
```

Constructors

ArrayStoreException

public ArrayStoreException()

Description   This constructor creates an ArrayStoreException with no asso-
               ciated detail message.

public ArrayStoreException(String s)

Parameters   s   The detail message.

Description   This constructor creates an ArrayStoreException with the
               specified detail message.

Inherited Methods

Method	Inherited From	Method	Inherited From
clone()	Object	equals(Object)	Object
fillInStackTrace()	Throwable	finalize()	Object
getClass()	Object	getLocalizedMessage()	Throwable
getMessage()	Throwable	hashCode()	Object
notify()	Object	notifyAll()	Object
printStackTrace()	Throwable	printStack- Trace(PrintStream)	Throwable
printStack- Trace(PrintWriter)	Throwable	toString()	Object
wait()	Object	wait(long)	Object
wait(long, int)	Object		

See Also

Exception, RuntimeException, Throwable

12.5 Boolean

Synopsis

Class Name:	java.lang.Boolean
Superclass:	java.lang.Object
Immediate Subclasses:	None
Interfaces Implemented:	java.io.Serializable
Availability:	JDK 1.0 or later

Description

The Boolean class provides an object wrapper for a boolean value. This is useful when you need to treat a boolean value as an object. For example, there are a number of utility methods that take a reference to an Object as one of their arguments. You cannot specify a boolean value for one of these arguments, but you can provide a reference to a Boolean object that encapsulates the boolean value. Furthermore, as of JDK 1.1, the Boolean class is necessary to support the Reflection API and class literals.

Class Summary

```
public final class java.lang.Boolean {
    // Constants
    public final static Boolean FALSE;
    public final static Boolean TRUE;
    public final static Class TYPE;                        // New in 1.1

    // Constructors
    public Boolean(boolean value);
    public Boolean(String s);

    // Class Methods
    public static boolean getBoolean(String name);
    public static Boolean valueOf(String s);

    // Instance Methods
    public boolean booleanValue();
    public boolean equals(Object obj);
    public int hashCode();
    public String toString();
}
```

Constants

TRUE

public static final Boolean TRUE

Description   A constant Boolean object that has the value true.

FALSE

public static final Boolean FALSE

Description   A constant Boolean object that has the value false.

TYPE

public static final Class TYPE

Availability   New as of JDK 1.1

Description   The Class object that represents the type boolean. It is always true that Boolean.TYPE == boolean.class.

Constructors

Boolean

public Boolean(boolean value)

Parameters   value   The boolean value to be made into a Boolean object.

Description   Constructs a `Boolean` object with the given value.

`public Boolean(String s)`

Parameters   s   The string to be made into a `Boolean` object.

Description   Constructs a `Boolean` object with the value specified by the given string. If the string equals "`true`" (ignoring case), the value of the object is `true`; otherwise it is `false`.

Class Methods

getBoolean

`public static boolean getBoolean(String name)`

Parameters   name   The name of a system property.

Returns   The `boolean` value of the system property.

Description   This methods retrieves the `boolean` value of a named system property.

valueOf

`public static Boolean valueOf(String s)`

Parameters   s   The string to be made into a `Boolean` object.

Returns   A `Boolean` object with the value specified by the given string.

Description   This method returns a `Boolean` object with the value `true` if the string equals "`true`" (ignoring case); otherwise the value of the object is `false`.

Instance Methods

booleanValue

`public boolean booleanValue()`

Returns   The `boolean` value contained by the object.

equals

`public boolean equals(Object obj)`

Parameters   obj   The object to be compared with this object.

Returns   `true` if the objects are equal; `false` if they are not.

Overrides   `Object.equals()`

Description   This method returns `true` if obj is an instance of `Boolean`, and it contains the same value as the object this method is associated with.

hashCode

public int hashCode()

Returns	A hashcode based on the boolean value of the object.
Overrides	Object.hashCode()

toString

public String toString()

Returns	"true" if the value of the object is true; "false" otherwise.
Overrides	Object.toString()
Description	This method returns a string representation of the Boolean object.

Inherited Methods

Method	Inherited From	Method	Inherited From
clone()	Object	finalize()	Object
getClass()	Object	notify()	Object
notifyAll()	Object	wait()	Object
wait(long)	Object	wait(long, int)	Object

See Also

Class, Object, Serializable, System

12.6   Byte

Synopsis

Class Name:	java.lang.Byte
Superclass:	java.lang.Number
Immediate Subclasses:	None
Interfaces Implemented:	None
Availability:	New as of JDK 1.1

Description

The Byte class provides an object wrapper for a byte value. This is useful when you need to treat a byte value as an object. For example, there are a number of utility methods that take a reference to an Object as one of their arguments. You cannot specify a byte value for one of these arguments, but you can provide a reference to a Byte object that encapsulates the byte value. Furthermore, the Byte class is necessary as of JDK 1.1 to support the Reflection API and class literals.

The Byte class also provides a number of utility methods for converting byte values to other primitive types and for converting byte values to strings and vice versa.

Class Summary

```
public final class java.lang.Byte extends java.lang.Number {
    // Constants
    public static final byte MAX_VALUE;
    public static final byte MIN_VALUE;
    public static final Class TYPE;

    // Constructors
    public Byte(byte value);
    public Byte(String s);

    // Class Methods
    public static Byte decode(String nm);
    public static byte parseByte(String s);
    public static byte parseByte(String s, int radix);
    public static String toString(byte b);
    public static Byte valueOf(String s, int radix);
    public static Byte valueOf(String s);

    // Instance Methods
    public byte byteValue();
    public double doubleValue;
    public boolean equals(Object obj);
    public float floatValue
    public int hashCode();
    public int intValue();
    public long longValue();
    public short shortValue();
    public String toString();
}
```

Constants

MAX_VALUE

```
public static final byte MAX_VALUE= 127
```
The largest value that can be represented by a byte.

MIN_VALUE

```
public static final byte MIN_VALUE= -128
```
The smallest value that can be represented by a byte.

TYPE

```
public static final Class TYPE
```
The Class object that represents the primitive type byte. It is always true that Byte.TYPE == byte.class.

Constructors

Byte

```
public Byte(byte value)
```
Parameters	value	The byte value to be encapsulated by this object.
Description		Creates a Byte object with the specified byte value.

```
public Byte(String s) throws NumberFormatException
```
Parameters	s	The string to be made into a Byte object.
Throws	NumberFormatException	
		If the sequence of characters in the given String does not form a valid byte literal.
Description		Constructs a Byte object with the value specified by the given string. The string should consist of one or more digit characters. The digit characters can be preceded by a single '-' character. If the string contains any other characters, the constructor throws a NumberFormatException.

Class Methods

decode

```
public static Byte decode(String nm) throws NumberFormatException
```
Parameters	nm	A String representation of the value to be encapsulated by a Byte object. If the string begins with # or 0x, it is a radix 16 representation of the value. If the string begins with 0, it is a radix 8 representation of the value. Otherwise, it is assumed to be a radix 10 representation of the value.
Returns		A Byte object that encapsulates the given value.
Throws	NumberFormatException	
		If the String contains any non-digit characters other than a leading minus sign or the value represented by the String is less than Byte.MIN_VALUE or greater than Byte.MAX_VALUE.

Description   This method returns a Byte object that encapsulates the given
                value.

parseByte

public static byte parseByte(String s) throws NumberFormatException

Parameters   s   The String to be converted to a byte value.

Returns   The numeric value of the byte represented by the String
                object.

Throws   NumberFormatException
                                        If the String does not contain a valid represen-
                                        tation of a byte or the value represented by the
                                        String is less than Byte.MIN_VALUE or greater
                                        than Byte.MAX_VALUE.

Description   This method returns the numeric value of the byte represented
                by the contents of the given String object. The String must
                contain only decimal digits, except that the first character may
                be a minus sign.

public static byte parseByte(String s, int radix)
                throws NumberFormatException

Parameters   s   The String to be converted to a byte value.

                radix   The radix used in interpreting the characters in
                                        the String as digits. This value must be in the
                                        range Character.MIN_RADIX to Charac-
                                        ter.MAX_RADIX. If radix is in the range 2
                                        through 10, only characters for which the Char-
                                        acter.isDigit() method returns true are con-
                                        sidered to be valid digits. If radix is in the range
                                        11 through 36, characters in the ranges 'A'
                                        through 'Z' and 'a' through 'z' may be consid-
                                        ered valid digits.

Returns   The numeric value of the byte represented by the String object
                in the specified radix.

Throws   NumberFormatException
                                        If the String does not contain a valid represen-
                                        tation of a byte, radix is not in the appropriate
                                        range, or the value represented by the String is
                                        less than Byte.MIN_VALUE or greater than
                                        Byte.MAX_VALUE.

Description   This method returns the numeric value of the byte represented
                by the contents of the given String object in the specified
                radix. The String must contain only valid digits of the specified
                radix, except that the first character may be a minus sign. The

digits are parsed in the specified radix to produce the numeric value.

toString

`public String toString(byte b)`

Parameters | b | The `byte` value to be converted to a string.
Returns | | The string representation of the given value.
Description | | This method returns a `String` object that contains the decimal representation of the given value.

This method returns a string that begins with '-' if the given value is negative. The rest of the string is a sequence of one or more of the characters '0', '1', '2', '3', '4', '5', '6', '7', '8', and '9'. This method returns "0" if its argument is 0. Otherwise, the string returned by this method does not begin with "0" or "-0".

valueOf

`public static Byte valueOf(String s) throws NumberFormatException`

Parameters | s | The string to be made into a `Byte` object.
Returns | | The `Byte` object constructed from the string.
Throws | NumberFormatException |

If the `String` does not contain a valid representation of a `byte` or the value represented by the `String` is less than `Byte.MIN_VALUE` or greater than `Byte.MAX_VALUE`.

Description | | Constructs a `Byte` object with the value specified by the given string. The string should consist of one or more digit characters. The digit characters can be preceded by a single '-' character. If the string contains any other characters, the method throws a `NumberFormatException`.

`public static Byte valueOf(String s, int radix)`
                `throws NumberFormatException`

Parameters | s | The string to be made into a `Byte` object.
           | radix | The radix used in converting the string to a value. This value must be in the range `Character.MIN_RADIX` to `Character.MAX_RADIX`.
Returns | | The `Byte` object constructed from the string.
Throws | NumberFormatException |

If the `String` does not contain a valid representation of a `byte`, radix is not in the appropriate range, or the value represented by the `String` is less than `Byte.MIN_VALUE` or greater than `Byte.MAX_VALUE`.

Description   Constructs a `Byte` object with the value specified by the given string in the specified radix. The string should consist of one or more digit characters or characters in the range 'A' to 'Z' or 'a' to 'z' that are considered digits in the given radix. The digit characters can be preceded by a single '-' character. If the string contains any other characters, the method throws a `NumberFormatException`.

Instance Methods

byteValue

```
public byte byteValue()
```

Returns   The value of this object as a `byte`.

Overrides   `Number.byteValue()`

Description   This method returns the value of this object as a `byte`.

doubleValue

```
public double doubleValue()
```

Returns   The value of this object as a `double`.

Overrides   `Number.doubleValue()`

Description   This method returns the value of this object as a `double`.

equals

```
public boolean equals(Object obj)
```

Parameters   obj   The object to be compared with this object.

Returns   `true` if the objects are equal; `false` if they are not.

Overrides   `Object.equals()`

Description   This method returns `true` if `obj` is an instance of `Byte` and it contains the same value as the object this method is associated with.

floatValue

```
public float floatValue()
```

Returns   The value of this object as a `float`.

Overrides   `Number.floatValue()`

Description   This method returns the value of this object as a `float`.

hashCode

`public int hashCode()`

Returns	A hashcode based on the byte value of the object.
Overrides	`Object.hashCode()`
Description	This method returns a hashcode computed from the value of this object.

intValue

`public int intValue()`

Returns	The value of this object as an int.
Overrides	`Number.intValue()`
Description	This method returns the value of this object as an int.

longValue

`public long longValue()`

Returns	The value of this object as a long.
Overrides	`Number.longValue()`
Description	This method returns the value of this object as a long.

shortValue

`public short shortValue()`

Returns	The value of this object as a short.
Overrides	`Number.shortValue()`
Description	This method returns the value of this object as a short.

toString

`public String toString()`

Returns	The string representation of the value of this object.
Overrides	`Object.toString()`
Description	This method returns a String object that contains the decimal representation of the value of this object.

This method returns a string that begins with '-' if the given value is negative. The rest of the string is a sequence of one or more of the characters '0', '1', '2', '3', '4', '5', '6', '7', '8', and '9'. This method returns "0" if its argument is 0. Otherwise, the string returned by this method does not begin with "0" or "-0".

Inherited Methods

Method	Inherited From	Method	Inherited From
clone()	Object	finalize()	Object
getClass()	Object	notify()	Object
notifyAll()	Object	wait()	Object
wait(long)	Object	wait(long, int)	Object

See Also

Character, Class, Double, Float, Integer, Long, Number, Short, String

12.7   Character

Synopsis

Class Name:	java.lang.Character
Superclass:	java.lang.Object
Immediate Subclasses:	None
Interfaces Implemented:	java.io.Serializable
Availability:	JDK 1.0 or later

Description

The Character class provides an object wrapper for a char value. This is useful when you need to treat a char value as an object. For example, there are a number of utility methods that take a reference to an Object as one of their arguments. You cannot specify a char value for one of these arguments, but you can provide a reference to a Character object that encapsulates the char value. Furthermore, as of JDK 1.1, the Character class is necessary to support the Reflection API and class literals.

In Java, Character objects represent values defined by the Unicode standard. Unicode is defined by an organization called the Unicode Consortium. The defining document for Unicode is *The Unicode Standard, Version 2.0* (ISBN 0-201-48345-9). More recent information about Unicode is available at *http://unicode.org*. Appendix A, *The Unicode 2.0 Character Set*, contains a table that lists the characters defined by the Unicode 2.0 standard.

The Character class provides some utility methods, such as methods for determining the type (e.g., uppercase or lowercase, digit or letter) of a character and for converting from uppercase to lowercase. The logic for these utility methods is based on a Unicode attribute table that is part of the Unicode standard. That table is available at *ftp://unicode.org/pub/2.0-Update/UnicodeData-2.0.14.txt*.

Some of the methods in the Character class are concerned with characters that are digits; these characters are used by a number of other classes to convert strings that contain numbers into actual numeric values. The digit-related methods all use a radix value to interpret characters. The *radix* is the numeric base used to represent numbers as characters or strings. Octal is a radix 8 representation, while hexadecimal is a radix 16 representation. The methods that require a radix parameter use it to determine which characters should be treated as valid digits. In radix 2, only the characters '0' and '1' are valid digits. In radix 16, the characters '0' through '9', 'a' through 'z', and 'A' through 'Z' are considerd valid digits.

Class Summary

```
public final class java.lang.Character extends java.lang.Object
                            implements java.io.Serializable {
    // Constants
    public final static byte COMBINING_SPACING_MARK;       // New in 1.1
    public final static byte CONNECTOR_PUNCTUATION;        // New in 1.1
    public final static byte CONTROL;                      // New in 1.1
    public final static byte CURRENCY_SYMBOL;              // New in 1.1
    public final static byte DASH_PUNCTUATION;             // New in 1.1
    public final static byte DECIMAL_DIGIT_NUMBER;         // New in 1.1
    public final static byte ENCLOSING_MARK;               // New in 1.1
    public final static byte END_PUNCTUATION;              // New in 1.1
    public final static byte FORMAT;                       // New in 1.1
    public final static byte LETTER_NUMBER;                // New in 1.1
    public final static byte LINE_SEPARATOR;               // New in 1.1
    public final static byte LOWERCASE_LETTER;             // New in 1.1
    public final static byte MATH_SYMBOL;                  // New in 1.1
    public final static int MAX_RADIX;
    public final static char MAX_VALUE;
    public final static int MIN_RADIX;
    public final static char MIN_VALUE;
    public final static byte MODIFIER_LETTER;              // New in 1.1
    public final static byte MODIFIER_SYMBOL;              // New in 1.1
    public final static byte NON_SPACING_MARK;             // New in 1.1
    public final static byte OTHER_LETTER;                 // New in 1.1
    public final static byte OTHER_NUMBER;                 // New in 1.1
    public final static byte OTHER_PUNCTUATION;            // New in 1.1
    public final static byte OTHER_SYMBOL;                 // New in 1.1
    public final static byte PARAGRAPH_SEPARATOR;          // New in 1.1
    public final static byte PRIVATE_USE;                  // New in 1.1
    public final static byte SPACE_SEPARATOR;              // New in 1.1
    public final static byte START_PUNCTUATION;            // New in 1.1
    public final static byte SURROGATE;                    // New in 1.1
    public final static byte TITLECASE_LETTER;             // New in 1.1
    public final static Class TYPE;                        // New in 1.1
```

```
public final static byte UNASSIGNED;                        // New in 1.1
public final static byte UPPERCASE_LETTER;                  // New in 1.1


// Constructors
public Character(char value);


// Class Methods
public static int digit(char ch, int radix);
public static char forDigit(int digit, int radix);
public static int getNumericValue(char ch);                 // New in 1.1
public static int getType(char ch);                         // New in 1.1
public static boolean isDefined(char ch);
public static boolean isDigit(char ch);
public static boolean isIdentifierIgnorable(char ch);       // New in 1.1
public static boolean isISOControl(char ch);                // New in 1.1
public static boolean isJavaIdentifierPart(char ch);        // New in 1.1
public static boolean isJavaIdentifierStart(char ch);       // New in 1.1
public static boolean isJavaLetter(char ch);             // Deprecated in 1.1
public static boolean isJavaLetterOrDigit(char ch);      // Deprecated in 1.1
public static boolean isLetter(char ch);
public static boolean isLetterOrDigit(char ch);
public static boolean isLowerCase(char ch);
public static boolean isSpace(char ch);                  // Deprecated in 1.1
public static boolean isSpaceChar(char ch);                 // New in 1.1
public static boolean isTitleCase(char ch);
public static boolean isUnicodeIdentifierPart(char ch);  // New in 1.1
public static boolean isUnicodeIdentifierStart(char ch); // New in 1.1
public static boolean isUpperCase(char ch);
public static boolean isWhitespace(char ch);                // New in 1.1
public static char toLowerCase(char ch);
public static char toTitleCase(char ch);
public static char toUpperCase(char ch);


// Instance Methods
public char charValue();
public boolean equals(Object obj);
public int hashCode();
public String toString();
}
```

Constants

COMBINING_SPACING_MARK

public final static byte COMBINING_SPACING_MARK

Availability New as of JDK 1.1

Description This constant can be returned by the getType() method as the general category of a Unicode character.

CONNECTOR_PUNCTUATION

`public final static byte CONNECTOR_PUNCTUATION`

Availability   New as of JDK 1.1

Description   This constant can be returned by the `getType()` method as the general category of a Unicode character.

CONTROL

`public final static byte CONTROL`

Availability   New as of JDK 1.1

Description   This constant can be returned by the `getType()` method as the general category of a Unicode character.

CURRENCY_SYMBOL

`public final static byte CURRENCY_SYMBOL`

Availability   New as of JDK 1.1

Description   This constant can be returned by the `getType()` method as the general category of a Unicode character.

DASH_PUNCTUATION

`public final static byte DASH_PUNCTUATION`

Availability   New as of JDK 1.1

Description   This constant can be returned by the `getType()` method as the general category of a Unicode character.

DECIMAL_DIGIT_NUMBER

`public final static byte DECIMAL_DIGIT_NUMBER`

Availability   New as of JDK 1.1

Description   This constant can be returned by the `getType()` method as the general category of a Unicode character.

ENCLOSING_MARK

`public final static byte ENCLOSING_MARK`

Availability   New as of JDK 1.1

Description   This constant can be returned by the `getType()` method as the general category of a Unicode character.

END_PUNCTUATION

`public final static byte END_PUNCTUATION`

Availability   New as of JDK 1.1

Description   This constant can be returned by the getType() method as the general category of a Unicode character.

FORMAT

```
public final static byte FORMAT
```
Availability   New as of JDK 1.1
Description   This constant can be returned by the getType() method as the general category of a Unicode character.

LETTER_NUMBER

```
public final static byte LETTER_NUMBER
```
Availability   New as of JDK 1.1
Description   This constant can be returned by the getType() method as the general category of a Unicode character.

LINE_SEPARATOR

```
public final static byte LINE_SEPARATOR
```
Availability   New as of JDK 1.1
Description   This constant can be returned by the getType() method as the general category of a Unicode character.

LOWERCASE_LETTER

```
public final static byte LOWERCASE_LETTER
```
Availability   New as of JDK 1.1
Description   This constant can be returned by the getType() method as the general category of a Unicode character.

MATH_SYMBOL

```
public final static byte MATH_SYMBOL
```
Availability   New as of JDK 1.1
Description   This constant can be returned by the getType() method as the general category of a Unicode character.

MAX_RADIX

```
public static final int MAX_RADIX = 36
```
Description   The maximum value that can be specified for a radix.

MAX_VALUE

    public final static char MAX_VALUE = '\ufff'f

Description   The largest value that can be represented by a char.

MIN_RADIX

    public static final int MIN_RADIX = 2

Description   The minimum value that can be specified for a radix.

MIN_VALUE

    public final static char MIN_VALUE = '\u0000'

Description   The smallest value that can be represented by a char.

MODIFIER_LETTER

    public final static byte MODIFIER_LETTER

Availability   New as of JDK 1.1

Description   This constant can be returned by the getType() method as the
general category of a Unicode character.

MODIFIER_SYMBOL

    public final static byte MODIFIER_SYMBOL

Availability   New as of JDK 1.1

Description   This constant can be returned by the getType() method as the
general category of a Unicode character.

NON_SPACING_MARK

    public final static byte NON_SPACING_MARK

Availability   New as of JDK 1.1

Description   This constant can be returned by the getType() method as the
general category of a Unicode character.

OTHER_LETTER

    public final static byte OTHER_LETTER

Availability   New as of JDK 1.1

Description   This constant can be returned by the getType() method as the
general category of a Unicode character.

OTHER_NUMBER

    public final static byte OTHER_NUMBER

Availability   New as of JDK 1.1

Description   This constant can be returned by the getType() method as the general category of a Unicode character.

OTHER_PUNCTUATION

public final static byte OTHER_PUNCTUATION

Availability   New as of JDK 1.1

Description   This constant can be returned by the getType() method as the general category of a Unicode character.

OTHER_SYMBOL

public final static byte OTHER_SYMBOL

Availability   New as of JDK 1.1

Description   This constant can be returned by the getType() method as the general category of a Unicode character.

PARAGRAPH_SEPARATOR

public final static byte PARAGRAPH_SEPARATOR

Availability   New as of JDK 1.1

Description   This constant can be returned by the getType() method as the general category of a Unicode character.

PRIVATE_USE

public final static byte PRIVATE_USE

Availability   New as of JDK 1.1

Description   This constant can be returned by the getType() method as the general category of a Unicode character.

SPACE_SEPARATOR

public final static byte SPACE_SEPARATOR

Availability   New as of JDK 1.1

Description   This constant can be returned by the getType() method as the general category of a Unicode character.

START_PUNCTUATION

public final static byte START_PUNCTUATION

Availability   New as of JDK 1.1

Description   This constant can be returned by the getType() method as the general category of a Unicode character.

SURROGATE

```
public final static byte SURROGATE
```
Availability   New as of JDK 1.1

Description   This constant can be returned by the getType() method as the general category of a Unicode character.

TITLECASE_LETTER

```
public final static byte TITLECASE_LETTER
```
Availability   New as of JDK 1.1

Description   This constant can be returned by the getType() method as the general category of a Unicode character.

TYPE

```
public static final Class TYPE
```
Availability   New as of JDK 1.1

Description   The Class object that represents the type char. It is always true that Character.TYPE == char.class.

UNASSIGNED

```
public final static byte UNASSIGNED
```
Availability   New as of JDK 1.1

Description   This constant can be returned by the getType() method as the general category of a Unicode character.

UPPERCASE_LETTER

```
public final static byte UPPERCASE_LETTER
```
Availability   New as of JDK 1.1

Description   This constant can be returned by the getType() method as the general category of a Unicode character.

Constructors

Character

```
public Character(char value)
```
Parameters   value   The char value to be encapsulated by this object.

Description   Creates a Character object with the given char value.

Class Methods

digit

```
public static int digit(char ch, int radix)
```

Parameters	ch	A char value that is a legal digit in the given radix.
	radix	The radix used in interpreting the specified character as a digit. If radix is in the range 2 through 10, only characters for which the isDigit() method returns true are considered to be valid digits. If radix is in the range 11 through 36, characters in the ranges 'A' through 'Z' and 'a' through 'z' may be considered valid digits.
Returns		The numeric value of the digit. This method returns −1 if the value of ch is not considered a valid digit, if radix is less than MIN_RADIX, or if radix is greater than MAX_RADIX.
Description		Returns the numeric value represented by a digit character. For example, digit('7',10) returns 7. If the value of ch is not a valid digit, the method returns −1. For example, digit('7',2) returns −1 because '7' is not a valid digit in radix 2. A number of methods in other classes use this method to convert strings that contain numbers to actual numeric values. The forDigit() method is an approximate inverse of this method.
		If radix is greater than 10, characters in the range 'A' to 'A'+radix-11 are treated as valid digits. Such a character has the numeric value ch-'A'+10. By the same token, if radix is greater than 10, characters in the range 'a' to 'a'+radix-11 are treated as valid digits. Such a character has the numeric value ch-'a'+10.

forDigit

```
public static char forDigit(int digit, int radix)
```

Parameters	digit	The numeric value represented as a digit character.
	radix	The radix used to represent the specified value.
Returns		The character that represents the digit corresponding to the specified numeric value. The method returns '\0' if digit is less than 0, if digit is equal to or greater than radix, if radix is less than MIN_RADIX, or if radix is greater than MAX_RADIX.

Description   This method returns the character that represents the digit corresponding to the specified numeric value. If digit is in the range 0 through 9, the method returns '0'+digit. If digit is in the range 10 through MAX_RADIX-1, the method returns 'a'+digit-10. The method returns '\0' if digit is less than 0, if digit is equal to or greater than radix, if radix is less than MIN_RADIX, or if radix is greater than MAX_RADIX.

getNumericValue

```
public static int getNumericValue(char ch)
```

Availability   New as of JDK 1.1

Parameters   ch   A char value.

Returns   The Unicode numeric value of the character as a nonnegative integer. This method returns -1 if the character has no numeric value; it returns -2 if the character has a numeric value that is not a nonnegative integer, such as $\frac{1}{2}$

Description   This method returns the Unicode numeric value of the specified character as a nonnegative integer.

getType

```
public static int getType(char ch)
```

Availability   New as of JDK 1.1

Parameters   ch   A char value.

Returns   An int value that represents the Unicode general category type of the character.

Description   This method returns the Unicode general category type of the specified character. The value corresponds to one of the general category constants defined by Character.

isDefined

```
public static boolean isDefined(char ch)
```

Parameters   ch   A char value to be tested.

Returns   true if the specified character has an assigned meaning in the Unicode character set; otherwise false.

Description   This method returns true if the specified character value has an assigned meaning in the Unicode character set.

isDigit

public static boolean isDigit(char ch)

Parameters	ch	A char value to be tested.

Returns   true if the specified character is defined as a digit in the Unicode character set; otherwise false.

Description   This method determines whether or not the specified character is a digit, based on the definition of the character in Unicode.

isIdentifierIgnorable

public static boolean isIdentifierIgnorable(char ch)

Availability   New as of JDK 1.1

Parameters   ch   A char value to be tested.

Returns   true if the specified character is ignorable in a Java or Unicode identifier; otherwise false.

Description   This method determines whether or not the specified character is ignorable in a Java or Unicode identifier. The following characters are ignorable in a Java or Unicode identifier:

\u0000 - \u0008 \u000E - \u001B \u007F - \u009F	ISO control characters that aren't whitespace
\u200C - \u200F	Join controls
\u200A - \u200E	Bidirectional controls
\u206A - \u206F	Format controls
\uFEFF	Zero-width no-break space

isISOControl

public static boolean isISOControl(char ch)

Availability   New as of JDK 1.1

Parameters   ch   A char value to be tested.

Returns   true if the specified character is an ISO control character; otherwise false.

Description   This method determines whether or not the specified character is an ISO control character. A character is an ISO control character if it falls in the range \u0000 through \u001F or \u007F through \u009F.

isJavaIdentifierPart

`public static boolean isJavaIdentifierPart(char ch)`

Availability	New as of JDK 1.1
Parameters	ch A char value to be tested.
Returns	true if the specified character can appear after the first character in a Java identifier; otherwise false.
Description	This method returns true if the specified character can appear in a Java identifier after the first character. A character is considered part of a Java identifier if and only if it is a letter, a digit, a currency symbol (e.g., $), a connecting punctuation character (e.g., _), a numeric letter (e.g., a Roman numeral), a combining mark, a nonspacing mark, or an ignorable control character.

isJavaIdentifierStart

`public static boolean isJavaIdentifierStart(char ch)`

Availability	New as of JDK 1.1
Parameters	ch A char value to be tested.
Returns	true if the specified character can appear as the first character in a Java identifier; otherwise false.
Description	This method returns true if the specified character can appear in a Java identifier as the first character. A character is considered a start of a Java identifier if and only if it is a letter, a currency symbol (e.g., $), or a connecting punctuation character (e.g., _).

isJavaLetter

`public static boolean isJavaLetter(char ch)`

Availability	Deprecated as of JDK 1.1
Parameters	ch A char value to be tested.
Returns	true if the specified character can appear as the first character in a Java identifier; otherwise false.
Description	This method returns true if the specified character can appear as the first character in a Java identifier. A character is considered a Java letter if and only if it is a letter, the character $, or the character _. This method returns false for digits because digits are not allowed as the first character of an identifier.
	This method is deprecated as of JDK 1.1. You should use isJavaIdentifierStart() instead.

isJavaLetterOrDigit

    public static boolean isJavaLetterOrDigit(char ch)

Availability	Deprecated as of JDK 1.1
Parameters	ch A char value to be tested.
Returns	true if the specified character can appear after the first character in a Java identifier; otherwise false.
Description	This method returns true if the specified character can appear in a Java identifier after the first character. A character is considered a Java letter or digit if and only if it is a letter, a digit, the character $, or the character _.

This method is deprecated as of JDK 1.1. You should use isJavaIdentifierPart() instead.

isLetter

    public static boolean isLetter(char ch)

Parameters	ch A char value to be tested.
Returns	true if the specified character is defined as a letter in the Unicode character set; otherwise false.
Description	This method determines whether or not the specified character is a letter, based on the definition of the character in Unicode. This method does not consider character values in ranges that have not been assigned meanings by Unicode to be letters.

isLetterOrDigit

    public static boolean isLetterOrDigit(char ch)

Parameters	ch A char value to be tested.
Returns	true if the specified character is defined as a letter in the Unicode character set; otherwise false.
Description	This method determines whether or not the specified character is a letter or a digit, based on the definition of the character in Unicode. There are some ranges that have not been assigned meanings by Unicode. If a character value is in one of these ranges, this method does not consider the character to be a letter.

isLowerCase

    public static boolean isLowerCase (char ch)

Parameters	ch A char value to be tested.

Returns   true if the specified character is defined as lowercase in the Unicode character set; otherwise `false`.

Description   This method determines whether or not the specified character is lowercase. Unicode defines a number of characters that do not have case mappings; if the specified character is one of these characters, the method returns `false`.

isSpace

```
public static boolean isSpace(char ch)
```

Availability   Deprecated as of JDK 1.1

Parameters   ch   A char value to be tested.

Returns   true if the specified character is defined as whitespace in the ISO-Latin-1 character set; otherwise `false`.

Description   This method determines whether or not the specified character is whitespace. This method recognizes the whitespace characters shown in the following table.

\u0009	Horizontal tab
\u000A	Newline
\u000C	Formfeed
\u000D	Carriage return
\u0020 ' '	Space

This method is deprecated as of JDK 1.1. You should use `isWhitespace()` instead.

isSpaceChar

```
public static boolean isSpaceChar(char ch)
```

Availability   New as of JDK 1.1

Parameters   ch   A char value to be tested.

Returns   true if the specified character is a Unicode 2.0 space characters; otherwise `false`.

Description   This method determines if the specified character is a space character according to the Unicode 2.0 specification. A character is considered to be a Unicode space character if and only if it has the general category "Zs", "Zl", or "Zp" in the Unicode specification.

isTitleCase

public static boolean isTitleCase(char ch)

Parameters	ch	A char value to be tested.
Returns		true if the specified character is defined as titlecase in the Unicode character set; otherwise false.
Description		This method determines whether or not the specified character is a titlecase character. Unicode defines a number of characters that do not have case mappings; if the specified character is one of these characters, the method returns false.

Many characters are defined by the Unicode standard as having upper- and lowercase forms. There are some characters defined by the Unicode standard that also have a titlecase form. The glyphs for these characters look like a combination of two Latin letters. The titlecase form of these characters has a glyph that looks like a combination of an uppercase Latin character and a lowercase Latin character; this case should be used when the character appears as the first character of a word in a title. For example, one of the Unicode characters that has a titlecase form looks like the letter 'D' followed by the letter 'Z'. Here is what the three forms of this letter look like:

Uppercase	'DZ'
Titlecase	'Dz'
Lowercase	'dz'

isUnicodeIdentifierPart

public static boolean isUnicodeIdentifierPart(char ch)

Availability		New as of JDK 1.1
Parameters	ch	A char value to be tested.
Returns		true if the specified character can appear after the first character in a Unicode identifier; otherwise false.
Description		This method returns true if the specified character can appear in a Unicode identifier after the first character. A character is considered part of a Unicode identifier if and only if it is a letter, a digit, a connecting punctuation character (e.g., _), a numeric letter (e.g., a Roman numeral), a combining mark, a nonspacing mark, or an ignorable control character.

isUnicodeIdentifierStart

```
public static boolean isUnicodeIdentifierStart(char ch)
```

Availability	New as of JDK 1.1
Parameters	ch A char value to be tested.
Returns	true if the specified character can appear as the first character in a Unicode identifier; otherwise false.
Description	This method returns true if the specified character can appear in a Unicode identifier as the first character. A character is considered a start of a Unicode identifier if and only if it is a letter.

isUpperCase

```
public static boolean isUpperCase(char ch)
```

Parameters	ch A char value to be tested.
Returns	true if the specified character is defined as uppercase in the Unicode character set; otherwise false.
Description	This method determines whether or not the specified character is uppercase. Unicode defines a number of characters that do not have case mappings; if the specified character is one of these characters, the method returns false.

isWhitespace

```
public static boolean isWhitespace(char ch)
```

Availability	New as of JDK 1.1
Parameters	ch A char value to be tested.
Returns	true if the specified character is defined as whitespace according to Java; otherwise false.
Description	This method determines whether or not the specified character is whitespace. This method recognizes the following as whitespace:

Unicode category "Zs" except \u00A0 and \uFEFF	Unicode space separators except no-break spaces
Unicode category "Zl"	Unicode line separators
Unicode category "Zp"	Unicode paragraph separators
\u0009	Horizontal tab
\u000A	Linefeed
\u000B	Vertical tab
\u000C	Formfeed
\u000D	Carriage return
\u001C	File separator
\u001D	Group separator

| \u001E | Record separator |
| \u001F | Unit separator |

toLowerCase

```
public static char toLowerCase(char ch)
```

Parameters   ch   A char value to be converted to lowercase.

Returns   The lowercase equivalent of the specified character, or the character itself if it cannot be converted to lowercase.

Description This method returns the lowercase equivalent of the specified character value. If the specified character is not uppercase or if it has no lowercase equivalent, the character is returned unmodified. The Unicode attribute table determines if a character has a mapping to a lowercase equivalent.

Some Unicode characters in the range \u2000 through \u2FFF have lowercase mappings. For example, \u2160 (Roman numeral one) has a lowercase mapping to \u2170 (small Roman numeral one). The toLowerCase() method maps such characters to their lowercase equivalents even though the method isUpperCase() does not return true for such characters.

toTitleCase

```
public static char toTitleCase(char ch)
```

Parameters   ch   A char value to be converted to titlecase.

Returns   The titlecase equivalent of the specified character, or the character itself if it cannot be converted to titlecase.

Description This method returns the titlecase equivalent of the specified character value. If the specified character has no titlecase equivalent, the character is returned unmodified. The Unicode attribute table is used to determine the character's titlecase equivalent.

Many characters are defined by the Unicode standard as having upper- and lowercase forms. There are some characters defined by the Unicode standard that also have a titlecase form. The glyphs for these characters look like a combination of two Latin letters. The titlecase form of these characters has a glyph that looks like a combination of an uppercase Latin character and a lowercase Latin character; this case should be used when the character appears as the first character of a word in a title. For example, one of the Unicode characters that has a titlecase form looks like the letter 'D' followed by the letter 'Z'. Here is what the three forms of this letter look like:

Uppercase	'DZ'
Titlecase	'Dz'
Lowercase	'dz'

toUpperCase

```
public static char toUpperCase(char ch)
```

Parameters   ch   A char value to be converted to lowercase.

Returns   The uppercase equivalent of the specified character, or the character itself if it cannot be converted to uppercase.

Description   This method returns the uppercase equivalent of the specified character value. If the specified character is not lowercase or if it has no uppercase equivalent, the character is returned unmodified. The Unicode attribute table determines if a character has a mapping to an uppercase equivalent.

Some Unicode characters in the range \u2000 through \u2FFF have uppercase mappings. For example, \u2170 (small Roman numeral one) has a lowercase mapping to \u2160 (Roman numeral one). The toUpperCase() method maps such characters to their uppercase equivalents even though the method isLowerCase() does not return true for such characters.

Instance Methods

charValue

```
public char charValue()
```

Returns   The char value contained by the object.

equals

```
public boolean equals(Object obj)
```

Parameters   The object to be compared with this object.

Returns   true if the objects are equal; false if they are not.

Overrides   Object.equals()

Description   This method returns true if obj is an instance of Character, and it contains the same value as the object this method is associated with.

hashCode

```
public int hashCode()
```
Returns   A hashcode based on the char value of the object.
Overrides   Object.hashCode()

toString

```
public String toString()
```
Returns   A String of length one that contains the character value of the object.
Overrides   Object.toString()
Description This method returns a string representation of the Character object.

Inherited Methods

Method	Inherited From	Method	Inherited From
clone()	Object	finalize()	Object
getClass()	Object	notify()	Object
notifyAll()	Object	wait()	Object
wait(long)	Object	wait(long, int)	Object

See Also

Class, Object, Serializable

12.8   Class

Synopsis

Class Name: java.lang.Class
Superclass: java.lang.Object
Immediate Subclasses: None
Interfaces Implemented: java.io.Seriablizable
Availability: JDK 1.0 or later

Description

As of Java 1.1, instances of the Class class are used as run-time descriptions of all Java data types, both reference types and primitive types. The Class class has also been greatly expanded in 1.1 to provide support for the Reflection API. Prior to 1.1, Class just provided run-time descriptions of reference types.

A Class object provides considerable information about the data type. You can use the isPrimitive() method to find out if a Class object describes a primitive type, while isArray() indicates if the object describes an array type. If a Class object describes a class or interface type, there are numerous methods that return information about the fields, methods, and constructors of the type. This information is returned as java.lang.reflect.Field, java.lang.reflect.Method, and java.lang.reflect.Constructor objects.

There are a number of ways that you can get a Class object for a particular data type:

- If you have an object, you can get the Class object that describes the class of that object by calling the object's getClass() method. Every class inherits this method from the Object class.
- As of Java 1.1, you can get the Class object that describes any Java type using the new class literal syntax. A class literal is simply the name of a type (a class name or a primitive type name) followed by a period and the class keyword. For example:

```
Class s = String.class;
Class i = int.class;
Class v = java.util.Vector.class;
```

- In Java 1.0, you can get the Class object from the name of a data type using the forName() class method of Class. For example:

```
Class v = Class.forName("java.util.Vector");
```

This technique still works in Java 1.1, but it is more cumbersome (and less efficient) than using a class literal.

You can create an instance of a class using the newInstance() method of a Class object, if the class has a constructor that takes no arguments.

The Class class has no public constructors; it cannot be explicitly instantiated. Class objects are normally created by the ClassLoader class or a ClassLoader object.

Class Summary

```
public final class java.lang.Class extends java.lang.Object
                            implements java.io.Serializable {
    // Class Methods
    public static native Class forName(String className);

    // Instance Methods
    public Class[] getClasses();                            // New in 1.1
    public native ClassLoader getClassLoader();
    public native Class getComponentType();                // New in 1.1
    public Constructor
```

```
             getConstructor(Class[] parameterTypes);        // New in 1.1
public Constructor[] getConstructors();                     // New in 1.1
public Class[] getDeclaredClasses();                        // New in 1.1
public Constructor
             getDeclaredConstructor(Class[] parameterTypes); // New in 1.1
public Constructor[] getDeclaredConstructors();             // New in 1.1
public Field getDeclaredField(String name);                // New in 1.1
public Field[] getDeclaredFields();                        // New in 1.1
public Method getDeclaredMethod(String name,
             Class[] parameterTypes)                        // New in 1.1
public Method[] getDeclaredMethods()                       // New in 1.1
public Class getDeclaringClass();                          // New in 1.1
public Field getField(String name);                        // New in 1.1
public Field[] getFields();                                // New in 1.1
public native Class[] getInterfaces();
public Method getMethod(String name,
             Class[] parameterTypes);                       // New in 1.1
public Method[] getMethods();                              // New in 1.1
public native int getModifiers();                          // New in 1.1
public native String getName();
public URL getResource(String name);                       // New in 1.1
public InputStream getResourceAsStream(String name);       // New in 1.1
public native Object[] getSigners();                       // New in 1.1
public native Class getSuperclass();
public native boolean isArray();                           // New in 1.1
public native boolean isAssignableFrom(Class cls);         // New in 1.1
public native boolean isInstance(Object obj);              // New in 1.1
public native boolean isInterface();
public native boolean isPrimitive();                       // New in 1.1
public native Object newInstance();
public String toString();
}
```

Class Methods

forName

```
public static Class forName(String className)
                throws ClassNotFoundException
```

Parameters	className	Name of a class qualified by the name of its package. If the class is defined inside of another class, all dots (.) that separate the top-level class name from the class to load must be changed to dollar signs ($) for the name to be recognized.
Returns		A Class object that describes the named class.
Throws		ClassNotFoundException
		If the class cannot be loaded because it cannot be found.

Description   This method dynamically loads a class if it has not already been loaded. The method returns a Class object that describes the named class.

The most common use of forName() is for loading classes on the fly when an application wants to use classes it wasn't built with. For example, a web browser uses this technique. When a browser needs to load an applet, the browser calls Class.forName() for the applet. The method loads the class if it has not already been loaded and returns the Class object that encapsulates the class. The browser then creates an instance of the applet by calling the Class object's newInstance() method.

When a class is loaded using a ClassLoader object, any classes loaded at the instigation of that class are also loaded using the same ClassLoader object. This method implements that security policy by trying to find a ClassLoader object to load the named class. The method searches the stack for the most recently invoked method associated with a class that was loaded using a ClassLoader object. If such a class is found, the Class-Loader object associated with that class is used.

Instance Methods

getClasses

public Class[] getClasses()

Availability   New as of JDK 1.1

Returns   An array of Class objects that contains the public classes and interfaces that are members of this class.

Description   If this Class object represents a reference type, this method returns an array of Class objects that lists all of the public classes and interfaces that are members of this class or interface. The list includes public classes and interfaces that are inherited from superclasses and that are defined by this class or interface. If there are no public member classes or interfaces, or if this Class represents a primitive type, the method returns an array of length 0.

As of Java 1.1.1, this method always returns an array of length 0, no matter how many public member classes this class or interface actually declares.

getClassLoader

`public native ClassLoader getClassLoader()`

Returns The `ClassLoader` object used to load this class or `null` if this class was not loaded with a `ClassLoader`.

Description This method returns the `ClassLoader` object that was used to load this class. If this class was not loaded with a `ClassLoader`, `null` is returned.

     This method is useful for making sure that a class gets loaded with the same class loader as was used for loading this `Class` object.

getComponentType

`public native Class getComponentType()`

Availability New as of JDK 1.1

Returns A `Class` object that describes the component type of this class if it is an array type.

Description If this `Class` object represents an array type, this method returns a `Class` object that describes the component type of the array. If this `Class` does not represent an array type, the method returns `null`.

getConstructor

`public Constructor getConstructor(Class[] parameterTypes)`
      `throws NoSuchMethodException, SecurityException`

Availability New as of JDK 1.1

Parameters parameterTypes

      An array of `Class` objects that describes the parameter types, in declared order, of the constructor.

Returns A `Constructor` object that reflects the specified public constructor of this class.

Throws NoSuchMethodException

      If the specified constructor does not exist.

    SecurityException

      If the `checkMemberAccess()` method of the `SecurityManager` throws a `SecurityException`.

Description If this `Class` object represents a class, this method returns a `Constructor` object that reflects the specified public constructor of this class. The constructor is located by searching all of the constructors of the class for a public constructor that has exactly the same formal parameters as specified. If this `Class` does not represent a class, the method returns `null`.

getConstructors

```
public Constructor[] getConstructors()
                throws SecurityException
```

Availability   New as of JDK 1.1

Returns   An array of Constructor objects that reflect the public constructors of this class.

Throws   SecurityException

                                If the checkMemberAccess() method of the SecurityManager throws a SecurityException.

Description   If this Class object represents a class, this method returns an array of Constructor objects that reflect the public constructors of this class. If there are no public constructors, or if this Class does not represent a class, the method returns an array of length 0.

getDeclaredClasses

```
public Class[] getDeclaredClasses() throws SecurityException
```

Availability   New as of JDK 1.1

Returns   An array of Class objects that contains all of the declared classes and interfaces that are members of this class.

Throws   SecurityException

                                If the checkMemberAccess() method of the SecurityManager throws a SecurityException.

Description   If this Class object represents a reference type, this method returns an array of Class objects that lists all of the classes and interfaces that are members of this class or interface. The list includes public, protected, default access, and private classes and interfaces that are defined by this class or interface, but it excludes classes and interfaces inherited from superclasses. If there are no such member classes or interfaces, or if this Class represents a primitive type, the method returns an array of length 0.

                As of Java 1.1.1, this method always returns an array of length 0, no matter how many member classes this class or interface declares.

getDeclaredConstructor

```
public Constructor getDeclaredConstructor(Class[] parameterTypes)
            throws NoSuchMethodException, SecurityException
```

Availability	New as of JDK 1.1
Parameters	parameterTypes

        An array of Class objects that describes the parameter types, in declared order, of the constructor.

Returns	A Constructor object that reflects the specified declared constructor of this class.
Throws	NoSuchMethodException

        If the specified constructor does not exist.

        SecurityException

        If the checkMemberAccess() method of the SecurityManager throws a SecurityException.

Description	If this Class object represents a class, this method returns a Constructor object that reflects the specified declared constructor of this class. The constructor is located by searching all of the constructors of the class for a public, protected, default access, or private constructor that has exactly the same formal parameters as specified. If this Class does not represent a class, the method returns null.

getDeclaredConstructors

```
public Constructor[] getDeclaredConstructors()
                    throws SecurityException
```

Availability	New as of JDK 1.1
Returns	An array of Constructor objects that reflect the declared constructors of this class.
Throws	SecurityException

        If the checkMemberAccess() method of the SecurityManager throws a SecurityException.

Description	If this Class object represents a class, this method returns an array of Constructor objects that reflect the public, protected, default access, and private constructors of this class. If there are no declared constructors, or if this Class does not represent a class, the method returns an array of length 0.

getDeclaredField

```
public Field getDeclaredField(String name)
            throws NoSuchFieldException, SecurityException
```

Availability	New as of JDK 1.1

Parameters	name	The simple name of the field.

Returns   A Field object that reflects the specified declared field of this class.

Throws   NoSuchFieldException

         If the specified field does not exist.

         SecurityException

         If the checkMemberAccess() method of the SecurityManager throws a SecurityException.

Description   If this Class object represents a class or interface, this method returns a Field object that reflects the specified declared field of this class. The field is located by searching all of the fields of the class (but not inherited fields) for a public, protected, default access, or private field that has the specified simple name. If this Class does not represent a class or interface, the method returns null.

getDeclaredFields

public Field[] getDeclaredFields() throws SecurityException

Availability   New as of JDK 1.1

Returns   An array of Field objects that reflect the declared fields of this class.

Throws   SecurityException

         If the checkMemberAccess() method of the SecurityManager throws a SecurityException.

Description   If this Class object represents a class or interface, this method returns an array of Field objects that reflect the public, protected, default access, and private fields declared by this class, but excludes inherited fields. If there are no declared fields, or if this Class does not represent a class or interface, the method returns an array of length 0.

         This method does not reflect the implicit length field for array types. The methods of the class Array should be used to manipulate array types.

getDeclaredMethod

public Method getDeclaredMethod(String name, Class[] parameterTypes) throws NoSuchMethodException, SecurityException

Availability   New as of JDK 1.1

Parameters   name   The simple name of the method.

parameterTypes

>An array of Class objects that describes the parameter types, in declared order, of the method.

Returns   A Method object that reflects the specified declared method of this class.

Throws   NoSuchMethodException

>If the specified method does not exist.

SecurityException

>If the checkMemberAccess() method of the SecurityManager throws a SecurityException.

Description   If this Class object represents a class or interface, this method returns a Method object that reflects the specified declared method of this class. The method is located by searching all of the methods of the class (but not inherited methods) for a public, protected, default access, or private method that has the specified simple name and exactly the same formal parameters as specified. If this Class does not represent a class or interface, the method returns null.

getDeclaredMethods

public Method[] getDeclaredMethods() throws SecurityException

Availability   New as of JDK 1.1

Returns   An array of Method objects that reflect the declared methods of this class.

Throws   SecurityException

>If the checkMemberAccess() method of the SecurityManager throws a SecurityException.

Description   If this Class object represents a class or interface, this method returns an array of Method objects that reflect the public, protected, default access, and private methods declared by this class, but excludes inherited methods. If there are no declared methods, or if this Class does not represent a class or interface, the method returns an array of length 0.

getDeclaringClass

public Class getDeclaringClass()

Availability   New as of JDK 1.1

Returns   A Class object that represents the declaring class if this class is a member of another class.

Description   If this Class object represents a class or interface that is a member of another class or interface, this method returns a Class object that describes the declaring class or interface. If this class or interface is not a member of another class or interface, or if it represents a primitive type, the method returns null.

getField

```
public Field getField(String name)
            throws NoSuchFieldException, SecurityException
```

Availability   New as of JDK 1.1

Parameters   name   The simple name of the field.

Returns   A Field object that reflects the specified public field of this class.

Throws   NoSuchFieldException

            If the specified field does not exist.

    SecurityException

            If the checkMemberAccess() method of the SecurityManager throws a SecurityException.

Description   If this Class object represents a class or interface, this method returns a Field object that reflects the specified public field of this class. The field is located by searching all of the fields of the class, including any inherited fields, for a public field that has the specified simple name. If this Class does not represent a class or interface, the method returns null.

getFields

```
public Field[] getFields() throws SecurityException
```

Availability   New as of JDK 1.1

Returns   An array of Field objects that reflect the public fields of this class.

Throws   SecurityException

            If the checkMemberAccess() method of the SecurityManager throws a SecurityException.

Description   If this Class object represents a class or interface, this method returns an array of Field objects that reflect the public fields declared by this class and any inherited public fields. If there are no public fields, or if this Class does not represent a class or interface, the method returns an array of length 0.

This method does not reflect the implicit length field for array types. The methods of the class Array should be used to manipulate array types.

getInterfaces

```
public native Class[] getInterfaces()
```

Returns   An array of the interfaces implemented by this class or extended by this interface.

Description   If the Class object represents a class, this method returns an array that refers to all of the interfaces that the class implements. The order of the interfaces referred to in the array is the same as the order in the class declaration's implements clause. If the class does not implement any interfaces, the length of the returned array is 0.

If the object represents an interface, this method returns an array that refers to all of the interfaces that this interface extends. The interfaces occur in the order they appear in the interface declaration's extends clause. If the interface does not extend any interfaces, the length of the returned array is 0.

If the object represents a primitive or array type, the method returns an array of length 0.

getMethod

```
public Method getMethod(String name, Class[] parameterTypes)
    throws NoSuchMethodException, SecurityException
```

Availability   New as of JDK 1.1

Parameters   name   The simple name of the method.

parameterTypes

An array of Class objects that describes the parameter types, in declared order, of the method.

Returns   A Method object that reflects the specified public method of this class.

Throws   NoSuchMethodException

If the specified method does not exist.

SecurityException

If the checkMemberAccess() method of the SecurityManager throws a SecurityException.

Description   If this Class object represents a class or interface, this method returns a Method object that reflects the specified public method of this class. The method is located by searching all of the methods of the class, including any inherited methods, for a public method that has the specified simple name and exactly the same formal parameters as specified. If this Class does not represent a class or interface, the method returns null.

getMethods

```
public Method[] getMethods() throws SecurityException
```

Availability   New as of JDK 1.1

Returns   An array of Method objects that reflect the public methods of this class.

Throws   SecurityException

If the checkMemberAccess() method of the SecurityManager throws a SecurityException.

Description   If this Class object represents a class or interface, this method returns an array of Method objects that reflect the public methods declared by this class and any inherited public methods. If there are no public methods or if this Class doesn't represent a class or interface, the method returns an array of length 0.

getModifiers

```
public native int getModifiers()
```

Availability   New as of JDK 1.1

Returns   An integer that represents the modifier keywords used to declare this class.

Description   If this Class object represents a class or interface, this method returns an integer value that represents the modifiers used to declare the class or interface. The Modifier class should be used to decode the returned value.

getName

```
public native String getName()
```

Returns   The fully qualified name of this class or interface.

Description   This method returns the fully qualified name of the type represented by this Class object.

If the object represents the class of an array, the method returns a String that contains as many left square brackets as there are dimensions in the array, followed by a code that indicates the type of element contained in the base array. Consider the following:

```
(new int [3][4][5]).getClass().getName()
```

This code returns "[[[I". The codes used to indicate the element type are as follows:

Code	Type
[	array
B	byte
C	char
d	double
F	float
I	int
J	long
L *fully_qualified_class_name*	class or interface
S	short
Z	boolean

getResource

`public URL getResource(String name)`

Availability   New as of JDK 1.1

Parameters   name   A resource name.

Returns   A URL object that is connected to the specified resource or null if the resource cannot be found.

Description   This method finds a resource with the given name for this Class object and returns a URL object that is connected to the resource. The rules for searching for a resource associated with a class are implemented by the ClassLoader for the class; this method simply calls the getResource() method of the Class-Loader. If this class does not have a ClassLoader (i.e., it is a system class), the method calls the Class-Loader.getSystemResource() method.

getResourceAsStream

`public InputStream getResourceAsStream(String name)`

Availability   New as of JDK 1.1

Parameters   name   A resource name.

Returns   An InputStream object that is connected to the specified resource or null if the resource cannot be found.

Description   This method finds a resource with the given name for this Class object and returns an InputStream object that is connected to the resource. The rules for searching for a resource associated with a class are implemented by the ClassLoader for the class; this method simply calls the getResourceAsStream() method of the ClassLoader. If this class does not have a Class-Loader (i.e., it is a system class), the method calls the Class-Loader.getSystemResourceAsStream() method.

getSigners

```
public native Object[] getSigners()
```
Availability   New as of JDK 1.1
Returns   An array of Objects that represents the signers of this class.
Description   This method returns an array of objects that represents the digital signatures for this class.

getSuperclass

```
public native Class getSuperclass()
```
Returns   The superclass of this class or null if there is no superclass.
Description   If the Class object represents a class other than Object, this method returns the Class object that represents its superclass. If the object represents an interface, the Object class, or a primitive type, the method returns null.

isArray

```
public native boolean isArray()
```
Availability   New as of JDK 1.1
Returns   true if this object describes an array type; otherwise false.

isAssignableFrom

```
public native boolean isAssignableFrom(Class cls)
```
Availability   New as of JDK 1.1
Parameters   cls   A Class object to be tested.
Returns   true if the type represented by cls is assignable to the type of this class: otherwise false.
Throws   NullPointerException
                        If cls is null.
Description   This method determines whether or not the type represented by cls is assignable to the type of this class. If this class represents a class, this class must be the same as cls or a superclass of cls. If this class represents an interface, this class must be the same as cls or a superinterface of cls. If this class represents a primitive type, this class must be the same as cls.

isInstance

```
public native boolean isInstance(Object obj)
```
Availability   New as of JDK 1.1
Parameters   obj   An Object to be tested.

Returns	true if obj can be cast to the reference type specified by this class; otherwise false.
Throws	NullPointerException
	If obj is null.
Description	This method determines whether or not the object represented by obj can be cast to the type of this class object without causing a ClassCastException. This method is the dynamic equivalent of the instanceof operator.

isInterface

```
public native boolean isInterface()
```

Returns	true if this object describes an interface; otherwise false.

isPrimitive

```
public native boolean isPrimitive()
```

Availability	New as of JDK 1.1
Returns	true if this object describes a primitive type; otherwise false.

newInstance

```
public native Object newInstance () throws InstantiationException,
            IllegalAccessException
```

Returns	A reference to a new instance of this class.
Throws	InstantiationException
	If the Class object represents an interface or an abstract class.
	IllegalAccessException
	If the class or an initializer is not accessible.
Description	This method creates a new instance of this class by performing these steps:

1. It creates a new object of the class represented by the Class object.
2. It calls the constructor for the class that takes no arguments.
3. It returns a reference to the initialized object.

The newInstance() method is useful for creating an instance of a class that has been dynamically loaded using the forName() method.

The reference returned by this method is usually cast to the type of object that is instantiated.

The newInstance() method can throw objects that are not instances of the classes it is declared to throw. If the constructor invoked by newInstance() throws an exception, the exception is thrown by newInstance() regardless of the class of the object.

toString

public String toString()

Returns   A String that contains the name of the class with either "class" or "interface" prepended as appropriate.

Overrides   Object.toString()

Description   This method returns a string representation of the Class object.

Inherited Methods

Method	Inherited From	Method	Inherited From
clone()	Object	equals()	Object
finalize()	Object	getClass()	Object
hashCode()	Object	notify()	Object
notifyAll()	Object	wait()	Object
wait(long)	Object	wait(long, int)	Object

See Also

Array, ClassLoader, ClassNotFoundException, Constructor, Field, IllegalAccessException, InputStream InstantiationException, Method, Modifier, NoSuchFieldException, NoSuchMethodException, Object, SecurityException, SecurityManager, URL

12.9   ClassCastException

Synopsis

Class Name: java.lang.ClassCastException

Superclass: java.lang.RuntimeException

Immediate Subclasses: None

Interfaces Implemented: None

Availability: JDK 1.0 or later

Description

A ClassCastException is thrown when there is an attempt to cast a reference to an object to an inappropriate type.

Class Summary

```
public class java.lang.ClassCastException
            extends java.lang.RuntimeException {
  // Constructors
  public ClassCastException();
  public ClassCastException(String s);
}
```

Constructors

ClassCastException

public ClassCastException()

Description   This constructor creates a ClassCastException with no associated detail message.

public ClassCastException(String s)

Parameters   s   The detail message.

Description   This constructor creates a ClassCastException with the specified detail message.

Inherited Methods

Method	Inherited From	Method	Inherited From
clone()	Object	equals(Object)	Object
fillInStackTrace()	Throwable	finalize()	Object
getClass()	Object	getLocalizedMessage()	Throwable
getMessage()	Throwable	hashCode()	Object
notify()	Object	notifyAll()	Object
printStackTrace()	Throwable	printStack-Trace(PrintStream)	Throwable
printStack-Trace(PrintWriter)	Throwable	toString()	Object
wait()	Object	wait(long)	Object
wait(long, int)	Object		

See Also

Exception, RuntimeException, Throwable

12.10   ClassCircularityError

Synopsis

Class Name: java.lang.ClassCircularityError
Superclass: java.lang.LinkageError
Immediate Subclasses: None
Interfaces Implemented: None
Availability: JDK 1.0 or later

Description

A ClassCircularityError is thrown when a circular reference among classes is
detected during class initialization.

Class Summary

```
public class java.lang.ClassCircularityError
            extends java.lang.LinkageError {
  // Constructors
  public ClassCircularityError();
  public ClassCircularityError(String s);
}
```

Constructors

ClassCircularityError

public ClassCircularityError()

  Description   This constructor creates a ClassCircularityError with no
                 associated detail message.

public ClassCircularityError(String s)

  Parameters   s   The detail message.
  Description   This constructor creates a ClassCircularityError with the
                 specified detail message.

Inherited Methods

Method	Inherited From	Method	Inherited From
clone()	Object	equals(Object)	Object
fillInStackTrace()	Throwable	finalize()	Object
getClass()	Object	getLocalizedMessage()	Throwable
getMessage()	Throwable	hashCode()	Object
notify()	Object	notifyAll()	Object
printStackTrace()	Throwable	printStack-Trace(PrintStream)	Throwable
printStack-Trace(PrintWriter)	Throwable	toString()	Object
wait()	Object	wait(long)	Object
wait(long, int)	Object		

See Also

Error, LinkageError, Throwable

12.11   ClassFormatError

Synopsis

Class Name: java.lang.ClassFormatError
Superclass: java.lang.LinkageError
Immediate Subclasses: None
Interfaces Implemented: None
Availability: JDK 1.0 or later

Description

A ClassFormatError is thrown when an error is detected in the format of a file that contains a class definition.

Class Summary

```
public class java.lang.ClassFormatError extends java.lang.LinkageError {
    // Constructors
    public ClassFormatError();
    public ClassFormatError(String s);
}
```

Constructors

ClassFormatError

public ClassFormatError()

Description This constructor creates a ClassFormatError with no associated detail message.

public ClassFormatError(String s)

Parameters s The detail message.

Description This constructor creates a ClassFormatError with the specified detail message.

Inherited Methods

Method	Inherited From	Method	Inherited From
clone()	Object	equals(Object)	Object
fillInStackTrace()	Throwable	finalize()	Object
getClass()	Object	getLocalizedMessage()	Throwable
getMessage()	Throwable	hashCode()	Object
notify()	Object	notifyAll()	Object
printStackTrace()	Throwable	printStack-Trace(PrintStream)	Throwable
printStack-Trace(PrintWriter)	Throwable	toString()	Object
wait()	Object	wait(long)	Object
wait(long, int)	Object		

See Also

Error, LinkageError, Throwable

12.12 ClassLoader

Synopsis

Class Name: java.lang.ClassLoader
Superclass: java.lang.Object
Immediate Subclasses: None
Interfaces Implemented: None
Availability: JDK 1.0 or later

Description

The ClassLoader class provides a mechanism for Java to load classes over a network or from any source other than the local filesystem. The default class-loading mechanism loads classes from files found relative to directories specified by the CLASSPATH environment variable. This default mechanism does not use an instance of the ClassLoader class.

An application can implement another mechanism for loading classes by declaring a subclass of the abstract ClassLoader class. A subclass of ClassLoader must override the loadClass() to define a class-loading policy. This method implements any sort of security that is necessary for the class-loading mechanism. The other methods of ClassLoader are final, so they cannot be overridden.

A ClassLoader object is typically used by calling its loadClass() method to explicitly load a top-level class, such as a subclass of Applet. The ClassLoader that loads the class becomes associated with the class; it can be obtained by calling the get-ClassLoader() method of the Class object that represents the class.

Once a class is loaded, it must be resolved before it can be used. Resolving a class means ensuring that all of the other classes it references are loaded. In addition, all of the classes that they reference must be loaded, and so on, until all of the needed classes have been loaded. Classes are resolved using the resolveClass() method of the ClassLoader object that loaded the initial class. This means that when a ClassLoader object is explicitly used to load a class, the same ClassLoader is used to load all of the classes that it references, directly or indirectly.

Classes loaded using a ClassLoader object may attempt to load additional classes without explicitly using a ClassLoader object. They can do this by calling the Class class' forName() method. However, in such a situation, a ClassLoader object is implicitly used. See the description of Class.forName() for more information.

Java identifies a class by a combination of its fully qualified name and the class loader that was used to load the class. If you write a subclass of ClassLoader, it should not attempt to directly load local classes. Instead, it should call findSystemClass(). A local class that is loaded directly by a ClassLoader is considered to be a different class than the same class loaded by findSystemClass(). This can lead to having two copies of the same class loaded, which can cause a number of inconsistencies. For example, the class' equals() method may decide that the same object is not equal to itself.

Class Summary

```
public abstract class java.lang.ClassLoader extends java.lang.Object {
    // Constructors
    protected ClassLoader();

    // Class Methods
    public static final URL
            getSystemResource(String name);               // New in 1.1
    public static final InputStream
            getSystemResourceAsStream(String name);        // New in 1.1

    // Public Instance Methods
    public URL getResource(String name);                   // New in 1.1
    public InputStream getResourceAsStream(String name);   // New in 1.1
    public Class loadClass(String name);                   // New in 1.1

    // Protected Instance Methods
    protected final Class defineClass(byte data[],
            int offset, int length);                       // Deprecated in 1.1
    protected final Class defineClass(String name,
            byte[] data, int offset, int length);          // New in 1.1
    protected final Class findLoadedClass(String name);    // New in 1.1
    protected final Class findSystemClass(String name);
    protected abstract Class loadClass(String name, boolean resolve);
    protected final void resolveClass(Class c);
    protected final void setSigners(Class cl,
            Object[] signers);                             // New in 1.1
}
```

Constructors

ClassLoader

protected ClassLoader()

> Throws   SecurityException
>
> > If there is a SecurityManager object installed
> > and its checkCreateClassLoader() method
> > throws a SecurityException when called by this
> > constructor.
>
> Description   Initializes a ClassLoader object. Because ClassLoader is an
> > abstract class, only subclasses of the class can access this con-
> > structor.

Class Methods

getSystemResource

`public static final URL getSystemResource(String name)`

Availability	New as of JDK 1.1
Parameters	name A system resource name.
Returns	A URL object that is connected to the specified system resource or null if the resource cannot be found.
Description	This method finds a system resource with the given name and returns a URL object that is connected to the resource. The resource name can be any system resource.

getSystemResourceAsStream

`public static final InputStream getSystemResourceAsStream(String name)`

Availability	New as of JDK 1.1
Parameters	name A system resource name.
Returns	An InputStream object that is connected to the specified system resource or null if the resource cannot be found.
Description	This method finds a system resource with the given name and returns an InputStream object that is connected to the resource. The resource name can be any system resource.

Public Instance Methods

getResource

`public URL getResource(String name)`

Availability	New as of JDK 1.1
Parameters	name A resource name.
Returns	A URL object that is connected to the specified resource or null if the resource cannot be found.
Description	This method finds a resource with the given name and returns a URL object that is connected to the resource.
	A resource is a file that contains data (e.g., sound, images, text) and it can be part of a package. The name of a resource is a sequence of identifiers separated by "/". For example, a resource might have the name *help/american/logon.html*. System resources are found on the host machine using the conventions of the host implementation. For example, the "/" in the resource name may be treated as a path separator, with the entire resource name treated as a relative path to be found under a directory in CLASSPATH.

The implementation of getResource() in ClassLoader simply returns null. A subclass can override this method to provide more useful functionality.

getResourceAsStream

`public InputStream getResourceAsStream(String name)`

Availability	New as of JDK 1.1
Parameters	name A resource name.
Returns	An InputStream object that is connected to the specified resource or null if the resource cannot be found.
Description	This method finds a resource with the given name and returns an InputStream object that is connected to the resource.

A resource is a file that contains data (e.g., sound, images, text) and it can be part of a package. The name of a resource is a sequence of identifiers separated by '/'. For example, a resource might have the name *help/american/logon.html*. System resources are found on the host machine using the conventions of the host implementation. For example, the '/' in the resource name may be treated as a path separator, with the entire resource name treated as a relative path to be found under a directory in CLASSPATH.

The implementation of getResourceAsStream() in Class-Loader simply returns null. A subclass can override this method to provide more useful functionality.

loadClass

`public Class loadClass(String name) throws ClassNotFoundException`

Availability	New as of JDK 1.1
Parameters	name The name of the class to be returned. The class name should be qualified by its package name. The lack of an explicit package name specifies that the class is part of the default package.
Returns	The Class object for the specified class.
Throws	ClassNotFoundException
	If it cannot find a definition for the named class.
Description	This method loads the named class by calling loadClass(name, true).

Protected Instance Methods

defineClass

```
protected final Class defineClass(byte data[], int offset,
                                  int length)
```

Availability	Deprecated as of JDK 1.1	
Parameters	data	An array that contains the byte codes that define a class.
	offset	The offset in the array of byte codes.
	length	The number of byte codes in the array.
Returns	The newly created Class object.	
Throws	ClassFormatError	
		If the data array does not constitute a valid class definition.
Description	This method creates a Class object from the byte codes that define the class. Before the class can be used, it must be resolved. The method is intended to be called from an implementation of the loadClass() method.	

Note that this method is deprecated as of Java 1.1. You should use the version of defineClass() that takes a name parameter and is therefore more secure.

```
protected final Class defineClass(String name, byte data[],
                                  int offset, int length)
```

Availability	New as of JDK 1.1	
Parameters	name	The expected name of the class to be defined or null if it is not known. The class name should be qualified by its package name. The lack of an explicit package name specifies that the class is part of the default package.
	data	An array that contains the byte codes that define a class.
	offset	The offset in the array of byte codes.
	length	The number of byte codes in the array.
Returns	The newly created Class object.	
Throws	ClassFormatError	
		If the data array does not constitute a valid class definition.
Description	This method creates a Class object from the byte codes that define the class. Before the class can be used, it must be resolved. The method is intended to be called from an implementation of the loadClass() method.	

findLoadedClass

```
protected final Class findLoadedClass(String name)
```

Availability	New as of JDK 1.1
Parameters	name The name of the class to be returned. The class name should be qualified by its package name. The lack of an explicit package name specifies that the class is part of the default package.
Returns	The Class object for the specified loaded class or null if the class cannot be found.
Description	This method finds the specified class that has already been loaded.

findSystemClass

```
protected final Class findSystemClass(String name)
            throws ClassNotFoundException
```

Parameters	name The name of the class to be returned. The class name should be qualified by its package name. The lack of an explicit package name specifies that the class is part of the default package.
Returns	The Class object for the specified system class.
Throws	ClassNotFoundException If the default class-loading mechanism cannot find a definition for the class.
	NoClassDefFoundError If the default class-loading mechanism cannot find the class.
Description	This method finds and loads a system class if it has not already been loaded. A *system class* is a class that is loaded by the default class-loading mechanism from the local filesystem. An implementation of the loadClass() method typically calls this method to attempt to load a class from the locations specified by the CLASSPATH environment variable.

loadClass

```
protected abstract Class loadClass(String name,
            boolean resolve)
            throws ClassNotFoundException
```

Parameters	name The name of the class to be returned. The class name should be qualified by its package name. The lack of an explicit package name specifies that the class is part of the default package.

resolve   Specifies whether or not the class should be resolved by calling the resolveClass() method.

Returns   The Class object for the specified class.

Throws   ClassNotFoundException

If it cannot find a definition for the named class.

Description   An implementation of this abstract method loads the named class and returns its Class object. It is permitted and encouraged for an implementation to cache the classes it loads, rather than load one each time the method is called. An implementation of this method should do at least the following:

1. Load the byte codes that comprise the class definition into a byte[].
2. Call the defineClass() method to create a Class object to represent the class definition.
3. If the resolve parameter is true, call the resolveClass() method to resolve the class.

If an implementation of this method caches the classes that it loads, it is recommended that it use an instance of the java.util.Hashtable to implement the cache.

resolveClass

protected final void resolveClass(Class c)

Parameters   c   The Class object for the class to be resolved.

Description   This method resolves the given Class object. Resolving a class means ensuring that all of the other classes that the Class object references are loaded. In addition, all of the classes that they reference must be loaded, and so on, until all of the needed classes have been loaded.

The resolveClass() method should be called by an implementation of the loadClass() method when the value of the loadClass() method's resolve parameter is true.

setSigners

protected final void setSigners(Class cl, Object[] signers)

Availability   New as of JDK 1.1

Parameters   cl   The Class object for the class to be signed.

                signers   An array of Objects that represents the signers of this class.

Description   This method specifies the objects that represent the digital signatures for this class.

Inherited Methods

Method	Inherited From	Method	Inherited From
clone()	Object	equals(Object)	Object
finalize()	Object	getClass()	Object
hashCode()	Object	notify()	Object
notifyAll()	Object	toString()	Object
wait()	Object	wait(long)	Object
wait(long, int)	Object		

See Also

Class, ClassNotFoundException, InputStream, NoClassDefFoundError, Object, SecurityException, SecurityManager, URL

12.13   ClassNotFoundException

Synopsis

Class Name:	java.lang.ClassNotFoundException
Superclass:	java.lang.Exception
Immediate Subclasses:	None
Interfaces Implemented:	None
Availability:	JDK 1.0 or later

Description

A ClassNotFoundException is thrown to indicate that a class to be loaded cannot be found.

Class Summary

```
public class java.lang.ClassNotFoundException extends java.lang.Exception {
    // Constructors
    public ClassNotFoundException();
    public ClassNotFoundException(String s);
}
```

Constructors

ClassNotFoundException

```
public ClassNotFoundException()
```
    Description   This constructor creates a `ClassNotFoundException` with no associated detail message.

```
public ClassNotFoundException(String s)
```
    Parameters   s   The detail message.

    Description   This constructor creates a `ClassNotFoundException` with the specified detail message.

Inherited Methods

Method	Inherited From	Method	Inherited From
clone()	Object	equals(Object)	Object
fillInStackTrace()	Throwable	finalize()	Object
getClass()	Object	getLocalizedMessage()	Throwable
getMessage()	Throwable	hashCode()	Object
notify()	Object	notifyAll()	Object
printStackTrace()	Throwable	printStack-Trace(PrintStream)	Throwable
printStack-Trace(PrintWriter)	Throwable	toString()	Object
wait()	Object	wait(long)	Object
wait(long, int)	Object		

See Also

Exception, Throwable

12.14   Cloneable

Synopsis

Interface Name: java.lang.Cloneable
Super-interface: None
Immediate Sub-interfaces:

    java.text.CharacterIterator
Implemented by: java.awt.GridBagConstraints, java.awt.Insets,
    java.awt.image.ImageFilter,
    java.text.BreakIterator,

```
                         java.text.Collator, java.text.DateFormat,
                         java.text.DateFormatSymbols,
                         java.text.DecimalFormatSymbols,
                         java.text.Format, java.text.NumberFormat,
                         java.util.BitSet, java.util.Calendar,
                         java.util.Date, java.util.Hashtable,
                         java.util.Locale, java.util.TimeZone,
                         java.util.Vector
```

Availability: JDK 1.0 or later

Description

The Cloneable interface provides no functionality; it declares no methods or variables. This interface is simply provided as a way of indicating that an object can be cloned (that is, copied). A class that is declared as implementing this interface is assumed to have overridden the Object class' implementation of clone() with an implementation that can successfully clone instances of the class. The implementation of clone() that is provided by the Object class simply throws a CloneNotSupportedException.

Interface Declaration

```
public interface java.lang.Cloneable {
}
```

See Also

BitSet, BreakIterator, Calendar, CloneNoSupportedException, Collator, Date, DateFormat, DateFormatSymbols, DecimalFormatSymbols, Format, Hashtable, Locale, NumberFormat, TimeZone, Vector

---

12.15   CloneNotSupportedException

Synopsis

Class Name: java.lang.CloneNotSupportedException
Superclass: java.lang.Exception
Immediate Subclasses: None
Interfaces Implemented: None
Availability: JDK 1.0 or later

Description

A CloneNotSupportedException is thrown when the clone() method has been called for an object that does not implement the Cloneable interface and thus cannot be cloned.

Class Summary

```
public class java.lang.CloneNotSupportedException
            extends java.lang.Exception {
  // Constructors
  public CloneNotSupportedException();
  public CloneNotSupportedException(String s);
}
```

Constructors

CloneNotSupportedException

public CloneNotSupportedException()

    Description   This constructor creates a CloneNotSupportedException with no associated detail message.

public CloneNotSupportedException(String s)

    Parameters   s   The detail message.

    Description   This constructor creates a CloneNotSupportedException with the specified detail message.

Inherited Methods

Method	Inherited From	Method	Inherited From
clone()	Object	equals(Object)	Object
fillInStackTrace()	Throwable	finalize()	Object
getClass()	Object	getLocalizedMessage()	Throwable
getMessage()	Throwable	hashCode()	Object
notify()	Object	notifyAll()	Object
printStackTrace()	Throwable	printStack-Trace(PrintStream)	Throwable
printStack-Trace(PrintWriter)	Throwable	toString()	Object
wait()	Object	wait(long)	Object
wait(long, int)	Object		

See Also

Exception, Throwable

12.16 Compiler

Synopsis

Class Name: java.lang.Compiler
Superclass: java.lang.Object
Immediate Subclasses: None
Interfaces Implemented: None
Availability: JDK 1.0 or later

Description

The Compiler class encapsulates a facility for compiling Java classes to native code. As provided by Sun, the methods of this class do not actually do anything. However, if the system property java.compiler has been defined and if the method System.loadLibrary() is able to load the library named by the property, the methods of this class use the implementations provided in the library.

The Compiler class has no public constructors, so it cannot be instantiated.

Class Summary

```
public final class java.lang.Compiler extends java.lang.Object {
    // Class Methods
    public static native Object command(Object any);
    public static native boolean compileClass(Class clazz);
    public static native boolean compileClasses(String string);
    public static native void disable();
    public static native void enable();
}
```

Class Methods

command

public static native Object command(Object any)

Parameters   any   The permissible value and its meaning is deter-
                             mined by the compiler library.

Returns   A value determined by the compiler library, or null if no com-
              piler library is loaded.

Description   This method directs the compiler to perform an operation specified by the given argument. The available operations, if any, are determined by the compiler library.

compileClass

```
public static native boolean compileClass(Class clazz)
```
Parameters   clazz   The class to be compiled to native code.
Returns   true if the compilation succeeds, or false if the compilation fails or no compiler library is loaded.
Description   This method requests the compiler to compile the specified class to native code.

compileClasses

```
public static native boolean compileClasses(String string)
```
Parameters   string   A string that specifies the names of the classes to be compiled.
Returns   true if the compilation succeeds or false if the compilation fails or no compiler library is loaded.
Description   This method requests the compiler to compile all of the classes named in the string.

disable

```
public static native void disable()
```
Description   This method disables the compiler if one is loaded.

enable

```
public static native void enable()
```
Description   This method enables the compiler if one is loaded.

Inherited Methods

Method	Inherited From	Method	Inherited From
clone()	Object	equals(Object)	Object
finalize()	Object	getClass()	Object
hashCode()	Object	notify()	Object
notifyAll()	Object	toString()	Object
wait()	Object	wait(long)	Object
wait(long, int)	Object		

See Also

Object, System

12.17   Double

Synopsis

Class Name:	java.lang.Double
Superclass:	java.lang.Number
Immediate Subclasses:	None
Interfaces Implemented:	None
Availability:	JDK 1.0 or later

Description

The Double class provides an object wrapper for a double value. This is useful when you need to treat a double value as an object. For example, there are a number of utility methods that take a reference to an Object as one of their arguments. You cannot specify a double value for one of these arguments, but you can provide a reference to a Double object that encapsulates the double value. Furthermore, as of JDK 1.1, the Double class is necessary to support the Reflection API and class literals.

In Java, double values are represented using the IEEE 754 format. The Double class provides constants for the three special values that are mandated by this format: POSITIVE_INFINITY, NEGATIVE_INFINITY, and NaN (not-a-number).

The Double class also provides some utility methods, such as methods for determining whether a double value is an infinity value or NaN, for converting double values to other primitive types, and for converting a double to a String and vice versa.

Class Summary

```
public final class java.lang.Double extends java.lang.Number {
    // Constants
    public final static double MAX_VALUE;
    public final static double MIN_VALUE;
    public final static double NaN;
    public final static double NEGATIVE_INFINITY;
    public final static double POSITIVE_INFINITY;
    public final static Class TYPE;                    // New in 1.1

    // Constructors
    public Double(double value);
```

```
    public Double(String s);

    // Class Methods
    public static native long doubleToLongBits(double value);
    public static boolean isInfinite(double v);
    public static boolean isNaN(double v);
    public static native double longBitsToDouble(long bits);
    public static String toString(double d);
    public static Double valueOf(String s);

    // Instance Methods
    public byte byteValue();                          // New in 1.1
    public double doubleValue();
    public boolean equals(Object obj);
    public float floatValue();
    public int hashCode();
    public int intValue();
    public boolean isInfinite();
    public boolean isNaN();
    public long longValue();
    public short shortValue();                        // New in 1.1
    public String toString();
}
```

Constants

MAX_VALUE

```
public static final double MAX_VALUE =
                       1.79769313486231570e+308
```

Description   The largest value that can be represented by a double.

MIN_VALUE

```
public static final double MIN_VALUE =
                       4.94065645841246544e-324
```

Description   The smallest value that can be represented by a double.

NaN

```
public static final double NaN = 0.0 / 0.0
```

Description   This variable represents the value not-a-number (NaN), which is a special value produced by double operations such as division of zero by zero. When NaN is one of the operands, most arithmetic operations return NaN as the result.

Most comparison operators (<, <=, ==, >=, >) return false when one of their arguments is NaN. The exception is !=, which returns true when one of its arguments is NaN.

NEGATIVE_INFINITY

`public static final double NEGATIVE_INFINITY = -1.0 / 0.0`

Description   This variable represents the value negative infinity, which is produced when a `double` operation underflows or a negative `double` value is divided by zero. Negative infinity is by definition less than any other `double` value.

POSITIVE_INFINITY

`public static final double POSITIVE_INFINITY = 1.0 / 0.0`

Description   This variable represents the value positive infinity, which is produced when a `double` operation overflows or a positive `double` value is divided by zero. Positive infinity is by definition greater than any other `double` value.

TYPE

`public static final Class TYPE`

Availability   New as of JDK 1.1

Description   The `Class` object that represents the type `double`. It is always true that `Double.TYPE == double.class`.

Constructors

Double

`public Double(double value)`

Parameters   value   The `double` value to be encapsulated by this object.

Description   Creates a `Double` object with the specified `double` value.

`public Double(String s) throws NumberFormatException`

Parameters   s   The string to be made into a `Double` object.

Throws   NumberFormatException

    If the sequence of characters in the given `String` does not form a valid `double` literal.

Description   Constructs a `Double` object with the value specified by the given string. The string must contain a sequence of characters that forms a legal `double` literal.

Class Methods

doubleToLongBits

public static native long doubleToLongBits(double value)

Parameters	value	The double value to be converted.
Returns		The long value that contains the same sequence of bits as the representation of the given double value.
Description		This method returns the long value that contains the same sequence of bits as the representation of the given double value. The meaning of the bits in the result is defined by the IEEE 754 floating-point format: bit 63 is the sign bit, bits 62-52 are the exponent, and bits 51-0 are the mantissa.

An argument of POSITIVE_INFINITY produces the result 0x7ff0000000000000L, an argument of NEGATIVE_INFINITY produces the result 0xfff0000000000000L, and an argument of NaN produces the result 0x7ff8000000000000L.

The value returned by this method can be converted back to the original double value by the longBitsToDouble() method.

isInfinite

static public boolean isInfinite(double v)

Parameters	v	The double value to be tested.
Returns		true if the specified value is equal to POSITIVE_INFINITY or NEGATIVE_INFINITY; otherwise false.
Description		This method determines whether or not the specified value is an infinity value.

isNaN

public static boolean isNaN(double v)

Parameters	v	The double value to be tested.
Returns		true if the specified value is equal to NaN; otherwise false.
Description		This method determines whether or not the specified value is NaN.

longBitsToDouble

public static native double longBitsToDouble(long bits)

Parameters	bits	The long value to be converted.
Returns		The double value whose representation is the same as the bits in the given long value.

Description   This method returns the double value whose representation is
the same as the bits in the given double value. The meaning of
the bits in the long value is defined by the IEEE 754 floating-
point format: bit 63 is the sign bit, bits 62-52 are the exponent,
and bits 51-0 are the mantissa. The argument
0x7f80000000000000L produces the result POSITIVE_INFINITY
and the argument 0xff80000000000000L produces the result
NEGATIVE_INFINITY. Arguments in the ranges
0x7ff0000000000001L through 0x7fffffffffffffffL and
0xfff0000000000001L through 0xffffffffffffffffL all produce the result NaN.

Except for NaN values not normally used by Java, this method is
the inverse of the doubleToLongBits() method.

toString

```
public static String toString(double d)
```
Parameters   d   The double value to be converted.
Returns   A string representation of the given value.
Description   This method returns a String object that contains a representa-
tion of the given double value.

The values NaN, NEGATIVE_INFINITY, POSITIVE_INFINITY, -0.0,
and +0.0 are represented by the strings "NaN", "-Infinity",
"Infinity", "-0.0", and "0.0", respectively.

For other values, the exact string representation depends on
the value being converted. If the absolute value of d is greater
than or equal to 10^{-3} or less than or equal to 10^7, it is converted
to a string with an optional minus sign (if the value is negative)
followed by up to eight digits before the decimal point, a decimal point, and the necessary number of digits after the decimal
point (but no trailing zero if there is more than one significant
digit). There is always a minimum of one digit after the decimal
point.

Otherwise, the value is converted to a string with an optional
minus sign (if the value is negative), followed by a single digit, a
decimal point, the necessary number of digits after the decimal
point (but no trailing zero if there is more than one significant
digit), and the letter E followed by a plus or a minus sign and a
base 10 exponent of at least one digit. Again, there is always a
minimum of one digit after the decimal point.

Note that the definition of this method has changed as of JDK 1.1. Prior to that release, the method provided a string representation that was equivalent to the `%g` format of the `printf` function in C.

valueOf

```
public static Double valueOf(String s)
                      throws NumberFormatException
```

Parameters   s   The string to be made into a `Double` object.

Returns   The `Double` object constructed from the string.

Throws   `NumberFormatException`

If the sequence of characters in the given `String` does not form a valid `double` literal.

Description Constructs a `Double` object with the value specified by the given string. The string must contain a sequence of characters that forms a legal `double` literal. This method ignores leading and trailing white space in the string.

Instance Methods

byteValue

```
public byte byteValue()
```

Availability New as of JDK 1.1

Returns   The value of this object as a `byte`.

Overrides   `Number.byteValue()`

Description   This method returns the truncated value of this object as a `byte`. More specifically, if the value of the object is `NaN`, the method returns 0. If the value is `POSITIVE_INFINITY`, or any other value that is too large to be represented by an `byte`, the method returns `Byte.MAX_VALUE`. If the value is `NEGATIVE_INFINITY`, or any other value that is too small to be represented by an `byte`, the method returns `Byte.MIN_VALUE`. Otherwise, the value is rounded toward zero and returned.

doubleValue

```
public double doubleValue()
```

Returns   The value of this object as a `double`.

Overrides   `Number.doubleValue()`

Description   This method returns the value of this object as a `double`.

equals

```
public boolean equals(Object obj)
```

Parameters   obj   The object to be compared with this object.

Returns   true if the objects are equal; false if they are not.

Overrides   Object.equals()

Description   This method returns true if obj is an instance of Double and it contains the same value as the object this method is associated with. More specifically, the method returns true if the double-ToLongBits() method returns the same result for the values of both objects.

This method produces a different result than the == operator when both values are NaN. In this case, the == operator produces false, while this method returns true. By the same token, the method also produces a different result when the two values are +0.0 and -0.0. In this case, the == operator produces true, while this method returns false.

floatValue

```
public float floatValue()
```

Returns   The value of this object as a float.

Overrides   Number.floatValue()

Description   This method returns this object value as a float. Rounding may occur.

hashCode

```
public int hashCode()
```

Returns   A hashcode based on the double value of the object.

Overrides   Object.hashCode()

Description   This method returns a hashcode computed from the value of this object. More specifically, if d is the value of the object, and bitValue is defined as:

```
long bitValue = Double.doubleToLongBits(d)
```

then the hashcode returned by this method is computed as follows:

```
(int)(bitValue ^ (bitValue>>>32))
```

intValue

public int intValue()

Returns	The value of this object as an int.
Overrides	Number.intValue()
Description	This method returns the truncated value of this object as an int. More specifically, if the value of the object is NaN, the method returns 0. If the value is POSITIVE_INFINITY, or any other value that is too large to be represented by an int, the method returns Integer.MAX_VALUE. If the value is NEGATIVE_INFINITY, or any other value that is too small to be represented by an int, the method returns Integer.MIN_VALUE. Otherwise, the value is rounded toward zero and returned.

isInfinite

public boolean isInfinite()

Returns	true if the value of this object is equal to POSITIVE_INFINITY or NEGATIVE_INFINITY; otherwise false.
Description	This method determines whether or not the value of this object is an infinity value.

isNaN

public boolean isNaN()

Returns	true if the value of this object is equal to NaN; otherwise false.
Description	This method determines whether or not the value of this object is NaN.

longValue

public long longValue()

Returns	The value of this object as a long.
Overrides	Number.longValue()
Description	This method returns the truncated value of this object as a long. More specifically, if the value of the object is NaN, the method returns 0. If the value is POSITIVE_INFINITY, or any other value too large to be represented by a long, the method returns Long.MAX_VALUE. If the value is NEGATIVE_INFINITY, or any other value too small to be represented by a long, the method returns Long.MIN_VALUE. Otherwise, the value is rounded toward zero and returned.

shortValue

public short shortValue()

Availability	New as of JDK 1.1
Returns	The value of this object as a short.
Overrides	Number.shortValue()
Description	This method returns the truncated value of this object as a short. More specifically, if the value of the object is NaN, the method returns 0. If the value is POSITIVE_INFINITY, or any other value that is too large to be represented by an short, the method returns Short.MAX_VALUE. If the value is NEGA-TIVE_INFINITY, or any other value that is too small to be represented by an short, the method returns Short.MIN_VALUE. Otherwise, the value is rounded toward zero and returned.

toString

public String toString()

Returns	A string representation of the value of this object.
Overrides	Object.toString()
Description	This method returns a String object that contains a representation of the value of this object.

The values NaN, NEGATIVE_INFINITY, POSITIVE_INFINITY, -0.0, and +0.0 are represented by the strings "NaN", "-Infinity", "Infinity", "-0.0", and "0.0", respectively.

For other values, the exact string representation depends on the value being converted. If the absolute value of this object is greater than or equal to 10^{-3} or less than or equal to 10^7, it is converted to a string with an optional minus sign (if the value is negative) followed by up to eight digits before the decimal point, a decimal point, and the necessary number of digits after the decimal point (but no trailing zero if there is more than one significant digit). There is always a minimum of one digit after the decimal point.

Otherwise, the value is converted to a string with an optional minus sign (if the value is negative), followed by a single digit, a decimal point, the necessary number of digits after the decimal point (but no trailing zero if there is more than one significant digit), and the letter E followed by a plus or a minus sign and a base 10 exponent of at least one digit. Again, there is always a minimum of one digit after the decimal point.

Note that the definition of this method has changed as of JDK 1.1. Prior to that release, the method provided a string representation that was equivalent to the `%g` format of the `printf` function in C.

Inherited Methods

Method	Inherited From	Method	Inherited From
clone()	Object	finalize()	Object
getClass()	Object	notify()	Object
notifyAll()	Object	wait()	Object
wait(long)	Object	wait(long, int)	Object

See Also

Class, Float, Number, NumberFormatException, String

12.18   Error

Synopsis

Class Name:	java.lang.Error
Superclass:	java.lang.Throwable
Immediate Subclasses:	java.awt.AWTError, java.lang.LinkageError,
	java.lang.ThreadDeath,
	java.lang.VirtualMachineError
Interfaces Implemented:	None
Availability:	JDK 1.0 or later

Description

The `Error` class is the superclass of all of the standard error classes that can be thrown in Java. The subclasses of `Error` are normally thrown by the class loader, the virtual machine, or other support code. Application-specific code should not normally throw any of the standard error classes.

An `Error` or one of its subclasses is typically thrown when an unpredictable run-time error, such as running out of memory, occurs. Because of the unpredictable nature of the events that cause errors to be thrown, a method does not have to declare the `Error` class or any of its subclasses in the `throws` clause of its method declaration.

A Java program should not try to handle the standard error classes. Most of these error classes represent nonrecoverable errors and as such, they cause the Java run-time system to print an error message and terminate program execution.

Class Summary

```
public class java.lang.Error extends java.lang.Throwable {
  // Constructors
  public Error();
  public Error(String s);
}
```

Constructors

Error

public Error()

Description   This constructor creates an Error with no associated detail message.

public Error(String s)

Parameters   s   The detail message.

Description   This constructor creates an Error with the specified detail message.

Inherited Methods

Method	Inherited From	Method	Inherited From
clone()	Object	equals(Object)	Object
fillInStackTrace()	Throwable	finalize()	Object
getClass()	Object	getLocalizedMessage()	Throwable
getMessage()	Throwable	hashCode()	Object
notify()	Object	notifyAll()	Object
printStackTrace()	Throwable	printStack-Trace(PrintStream)	Throwable
printStack-Trace(PrintWriter)	Throwable	toString()	Object
wait()	Object	wait(long)	Object
wait(long, int)	Object		

See Also

LinkageError, ThreadDeath, Throwable, VirtualMachineError

12.19   *Exception*

Synopsis

Class Name:	java.lang.Exception
Superclass:	java.lang.Throwable
Immediate Subclasses:	java.awt.AWTException,
	java.awt.datatransfer.UnsupportedFlavorException,
	java.io.IOException,
	java.lang.ClassNotFoundException,
	java.lang.CloneNotSupportedException,
	java.lang.IllegalAccessException,
	java.lang.InstantiationException,
	java.lang.InterruptedException,
	java.lang.NoSuchMethodException,
	java.lang.RuntimeException,
	java.lang.reflect.InvocationTargetException,
	java.text.FormatException,
	java.util.TooManyListenersException,
	java.util.zip.DataFormatException
Interfaces Implemented:	None
Availability:	JDK 1.0 or later

Description

The Exception class is the superclass of all of the standard exception classes that can be thrown in Java. The subclasses of Exception represent exceptional conditions a normal Java program may want to handle. Any explicitly thrown object in a Java program should be an instance of a subclass of Exception.

Many of the standard exceptions are also subclasses of RuntimeException. Run-time exceptions represent run-time conditions that can occur generally in any Java method, so a method is not required to declare that it throws any of the run-time exceptions. However, if a method can throw any of the other standard exceptions, it must declare them in its throws clause.

A Java program should try to handle all of the standard exception classes, since they represent routine abnormal conditions that should be anticipated and caught to prevent program termination.

Class Summary

```
public class java.lang.Exception extends java.lang.Throwable {
  // Constructors
  public Exception();
  public Exception(String s);
}
```

Constructors

Exception

public Exception()

  Description   This constructor creates an Exception with no associated detail
                 message.

public Exception(String s)

  Parameters   s   The detail message.
  Description   This constructor creates an Exception with the specified mes-
                 sage.

Inherited Methods

Method	Inherited From	Method	Inherited From
clone()	Object	equals(Object)	Object
fillInStackTrace()	Throwable	finalize()	Object
getClass()	Object	getLocalizedMessage()	Throwable
getMessage()	Throwable	hashCode()	Object
notify()	Object	notifyAll()	Object
printStackTrace()	Throwable	printStack-Trace(PrintStream)	Throwable
printStack-Trace(PrintWriter)	Throwable	toString()	Object
wait()	Object	wait(long)	Object
wait(long, int)	Object		

See Also

ClassNotFoundException, CloneNotSupportedException, DataFormatException,
FormatException, IllegalAccessException, InstantiationException, Invoca-
tionTargetException, InterruptedException, NoSuchMethodException, Runtime-
Exception, Throwable, TooManyListenersException

12.20 ExceptionInInitializerError

Synopsis

Class Name:	java.lang.ExceptionInInitializerError
Superclass:	java.lang.LinkageError
Immediate Subclasses:	None
Interfaces Implemented:	None
Availability:	New as of JDK 1.1

Description

A ExceptionInInitializerError is thrown when an unexpected exception has been thrown in a static initializer.

Class Summary

```
public class java.lang.ExceptionInInitializer
            extends java.lang.LinkageError {
  // Constructors
  public ExceptionInInitializerError();
  public ExceptionInInitializerError(Throwable thrown);
  public ExceptionInInitializerError(String s);

  // Instance Methods
  public Throwable getException();
}
```

Constructors

ExceptionInInitializerError

public ExceptionInInitializerError()

  Description   This constructor creates an ExceptionInInitializerError with no associated detail message.

public ExceptionInInitializerError(Throwable thrown)

  Parameters   thrown   The exception that was thrown in the static initializer.

  Description   This constructor creates an ExceptionInInitializerError that refers to the specified exception.

public ExceptionInInitializerError(String s)

  Parameters   s   The detail message.

  Description   This constructor creates an ExceptionInInitializerError with the specified detail message.

Instance Methods

getException

```
public Throwable getException()
```

Returns   The exception object that was thrown in the static initializer.

Description   This methods returns the exception that caused this error to be thrown.

Inherited Methods

Method	Inherited From	Method	Inherited From
clone()	Object	equals(Object)	Object
fillInStackTrace()	Throwable	finalize()	Object
getClass()	Object	getLocalizedMessage()	Throwable
getMessage()	Throwable	hashCode()	Object
notify()	Object	notifyAll()	Object
printStackTrace()	Throwable	printStack-Trace(PrintStream)	Throwable
printStack-Trace(PrintWriter)	Throwable	toString()	Object
wait()	Object	wait(long)	Object
wait(long, int)	Object		

See Also

Error, LinkageError, Throwable

12.21   Float

Synopsis

Class Name: java.lang.Float

Superclass: java.lang.Number

Immediate Subclasses: None

Interfaces Implemented: None

Availability: JDK 1.0 or later

Description

The Float class provides an object wrapper for a float value. This is useful when you need to treat a float value as an object. For example, there are a number of utility methods that take a reference to an Object as one of their arguments. You cannot specify a float value for one of these arguments, but you can provide a reference to a Float object that encapsulates the float value. Furthermore, as of JDK 1.1, the Float class is necessary to support the Reflection API and class literals.

In Java, float values are represented using the IEEE 754 format. The Float class provides constants for the three special values that are mandated by this format: POSITIVE_INFINITY, NEGATIVE_INFINITY, and NaN (not-a-number).

The Float class also provides some utility methods, such as methods for determining whether a floatx value is an infinity value or NaN, for converting float values to other primitive types, and for converting a float to a String and vice versa.

Class Summary

```
public final class java.lang.Float extends java.lang.Number {
    // Constants
    public static final float MIN_VALUE;
    public static final float MAX_VALUE;
    public static final float NaN;
    public static final float NEGATIVE_INFINITY;
    public static final float POSITIVE_INFINITY;
    public final static Class TYPE;                      // New in 1.1

    // Constructors
    public Float(double value);
    public Float(float value);
    public Float(String s);

    // Class Methods
    public static native int floatToIntBits(float value);
    public static native float intBitsToFloat(int bits);
    public static boolean isInfinite(float v);
    public static boolean isNaN(float v);
    public static String toString(float f);
    public static Float valueOf(String s);
    // Instance Methods
    public byte byteValue();                             // New in 1.1
    public double doubleValue();
    public boolean equals(Object obj);
    public float floatValue();
    public int hashCode();
    public int intValue();
    public boolean isInfinite();
    public boolean isNaN();
    public long longValue();
```

```
    public short shortValue();                        // New in 1.1
    public String toString();
}
```

Constants

MAX_VALUE

public static final float MAX_VALUE = 3.40282346638528860e+38f

Description   The largest value that can be represented by a float.

MIN_VALUE

public static final float MIN_VALUE = 1.40129846432481707e-45f

Description   The smallest value that can be represented by a float.

NaN

public static final float NaN = 0.0f / 0.0f

Description   This variable represents the value NaN, a special value produced by float operations such as division of zero by zero. When NaN is one of the operands, most arithmetic operations return NaN as the result. Most comparison operators (<, <=, ==, >=, >) return false when one of their arguments is NaN. The exception is !=, which returns true when one of its arguments is NaN.

NEGATIVE_INFINITY

public static final float NEGATIVE_INFINITY = -1.0f / 0.0f

Description   This variable represents the value negative infinity, which is produced when a float operation underflows or a negative float value is divided by zero. Negative infinity is by definition less than any other float value.

POSITIVE_INFINITY

public static final float POSITIVE_INFINITY = 1.0f / 0.0f

Description   This variable represents the value positive infinity, which is produced when a float operation overflows or a positive float value is divided by zero. Positive infinity is by definition greater than any other float value.

TYPE

> public static final Class TYPE
>
> | | |
> |---|---|
> | Availability | New as of JDK 1.1 |
> | Description | The Class object that represents the type float. It is always true that Float.TYPE == float.class. |

Constructors

Float

> public Float(double value)
>
> | | | |
> |---|---|---|
> | Parameters | value | The double value to be encapsulated by this object. |
> | Description | | Creates a Float object with the specified double value. The value is rounded to float precision. |

> public Float(float value)
>
> | | | |
> |---|---|---|
> | Parameters | value | The float value to be encapsulated by this object. |
> | Description | | Creates a Float object with the specified float value. |

> public Float(String s) throws NumberFormatException
>
> | | | |
> |---|---|---|
> | Parameters | s | The string to be made into a Float object. |
> | Throws | NumberFormatException | |
> | | | If the sequence of characters in the given String does not form a valid float literal. |
> | Description | | Constructs a Float object with the value specified by the given string. The string must contain a sequence of characters that forms a legal float literal. |

Class Methods

floatToIntBits

> public static native int floatToIntBits(float value)
>
> | | | |
> |---|---|---|
> | Parameters | value | The float value to be converted. |
> | Returns | | The int value that contains the same sequence of bits as the representation of the given float value. |
> | Description | | This method returns the int value that contains the same sequence of bits as the representation of the given float value. The meaning of the bits in the result is defined by the IEEE 754 floating-point format: bit 31 is the sign bit, bits 30-23 are the exponent, and bits 22-0 are the mantissa. An argument of POSITIVE_INFINITY produces the result 0x7f800000, an argument of NEGATIVE_INFINITY produces the result 0xff800000, and an argument of NaN produces the result 0x7fc00000. |

The value returned by this method can be converted back to the original float value by the intBitsToFloat() method.

intBitsToFloat

public static native float intBitsToFloat(int bits)

Parameters   bits   The int value to be converted.

Returns   The float value whose representation is the same as the bits in the given int value.

Description   This method returns the float value whose representation is the same as the bits in the given int value. The meaning of the bits in the int value is defined by the IEEE 754 floating-point format: bit 31 is the sign bit, bits 30-23 are the exponent, and bits 22-0 are the mantissa. The argument 0x7f800000 produces the result POSITIVE_INFINITY, and the argument 0xff800000 produces the result NEGATIVE_INFINITY. Arguments in the ranges 0x7f800001 through 0x7f8fffff and 0xff800001 through 0xff8fffffL all produce the result NaN.

Except for NaN values not normally used by Java, this method is the inverse of the floatToIntBits() method.

isInfinite

public static boolean isInfinite(float v)

Parameters   v   The float value to be tested.

Returns   true if the specified value is equal to POSITIVE_INFINITY or NEGATIVE_INFINITY; otherwise false.

Description   This method determines whether or not the specified value is an infinity value.

isNaN

public static boolean isNaN(float v)

Parameters   v   The float value to be tested.

Returns   true if the specified value is equal to NaN; otherwise false.

Description   This method determines whether or not the specified value is NaN.

toString

public static String toString(float f)

Parameters   f   The float value to be converted.

Returns   A string representation of the given value.

Description This method returns a `String` object that contains a representation of the given `float` value.

The values NaN, NEGATIVE_INFINITY, POSITIVE_INFINITY, -0.0, and +0.0 are represented by the strings "NaN", "-Infinity", "Infinity", "-0.0", and "0.0", respectively.

For other values, the exact string representation depends on the value being converted. If the absolute value of f is greater than or equal to 10^{-3} or less than or equal to 10^7, it is converted to a string with an optional minus sign (if the value is negative) followed by up to eight digits before the decimal point, a decimal point, and the necessary number of digits after the decimal point (but no trailing zero if there is more than one significant digit). There is always a minimum of one digit after the decimal point.

Otherwise, the value is converted to a string with an optional minus sign (if the value is negative), followed by a single digit, a decimal point, the necessary number of digits after the decimal point (but no trailing zero if there is more than one significant digit), and the letter E followed by a plus or a minus sign and a base 10 exponent of at least one digit. Again, there is always a minimum of one digit after the decimal point.

Note that the definition of this method has changed as of JDK 1.1. Prior to that release, the method provided a string representation that was equivalent to the %g format of the printf function in C.

valueOf

```
public static Float valueOf(String s)
                    throws NumberFormatException
```

Parameters s The string to be made into a `Float` object.

Returns The `Float` object constructed from the string.

Throws NumberFormatException
If the sequence of characters in the given `String` does not form a valid `float` literal.

Description Constructs a `Float` object with the value specified by the given string. The string must contain a sequence of characters that forms a legal `float` literal. This method ignores leading and trailing whitespace in the string.

Instance Methods

byteValue

public byte byteValue()

Availability	New as of JDK 1.1
Returns	The value of this object as a byte.
Overrides	Number.byteValue()
Description	This method returns the truncated value of this object as a byte. More specifically, if the value of the object is NaN, the method returns 0. If the value is POSITIVE_INFINITY, or any other value that is too large to be represented by an byte, the method returns Byte.MAX_VALUE. If the value is NEGA-TIVE_INFINITY, or any other value that is too small to be represented by an byte, the method returns Byte.MIN_VALUE. Otherwise, the value is rounded toward zero and returned.

doubleValue

public double doubleValue()

Returns	The value of this object as a double.
Overrides	Number.doubleValue()
Description	This method returns the value of this object as a double.

equals

public boolean equals(Object obj)

Parameters	obj The object to be compared with this object.
Returns	true if the objects are equal; false if they are not.
Overrides	Object.equals()
Description	This method returns true if obj is an instance of Float and it contains the same value as the object this method is associated with. More specifically, the method returns true if the float-ToIntBits() method returns the same result for the values of both objects.

This method produces a different result than the == operator when both values are NaN. In this case, the == operator produces false, while this method returns true. By the same token, the method also produces a different result when the two values are +0.0 and -0.0. In this case, the == operator produces true, while this method returns false.

floatValue

```
public float floatValue()
```

Returns	The value of this object as a float.
Overrides	Number.floatValue()
Description	This method returns the value of this object as a float.

hashCode

```
public int hashCode()
```

Returns	A hashcode based on the float value of the object.
Overrides	Object.hashCode()
Description	This method returns a hashcode computed from the value of this object. More specifically, if f is the value of the object, this method returns Float.floatToIntBits(f).

intValue

```
public int intValue()
```

Returns	The value of this object as an int.
Overrides	Number.intValue()
Description	This method returns the truncated value of this object as an int. More specifically, if the value of the object is NaN, the method returns 0. If the value is POSITIVE_INFINITY, or any other value that is too large to be represented by an int, the method returns Integer.MAX_VALUE. If the value is NEGATIVE_INFINITY, or any other value that is too small to be represented by an int, the method returns Integer.MIN_VALUE. Otherwise, the value is rounded toward zero and returned.

isInfinite

```
public boolean isInfinite(float v)
```

Returns	true if the value of this object is equal to POSITIVE_INFINITY or NEGATIVE_INFINITY; otherwise false.
Description	This method determines whether or not the value of this object is an infinity value.

isNaN

```
public boolean isNaN()
```

Returns	true if the value of this object is equal to NaN; otherwise false.
Description	This method determines whether or not the value of this object is NaN.

longValue

public long longValue()

Returns   The value of this object as a long.

Overrides   Number.longValue()

Description   This method returns the truncated value of this object as a long. More specifically, if the value of the object is NaN, the method returns 0. If the value is POSITIVE_INFINITY, or any other value that is too large to be represented by a long, the method returns Long.MAX_VALUE. If the value is NEGATIVE_INFINITY, or any other value that is too small to be represented by a long, the method returns Long.MIN_VALUE. Otherwise, the value is rounded toward zero and returned.

shortValue

public short shortValue()

Availability   New as of JDK 1.1

Returns   The value of this object as a short.

Overrides   Number.shortValue()

Description   This method returns the truncated value of this object as a short. More specifically, if the value of the object is NaN, the method returns 0. If the value is POSITIVE_INFINITY, or any other value that is too large to be represented by an short, the method returns Short.MAX_VALUE. If the value is NEGATIVE_INFINITY, or any other value that is too small to be represented by an short, the method returns Short.MIN_VALUE. Otherwise, the value is rounded toward zero and returned.

toString

public String toString()

Returns   A string representation of the value of this object.

Overrides   Object.toString()

Description   This method returns a String object that contains a representation of the value of this object.

The values NaN, NEGATIVE_INFINITY, POSITIVE_INFINITY, -0.0, and +0.0 are represented by the strings "NaN", "-Infinity", "Infinity", "-0.0", and "0.0", respectively.

For other values, the exact string representation depends on the value being converted. If the absolute value of this object is greater than or equal to 10^{-3} or less than or equal to 10^7, it is converted to a string with an optional minus sign (if the value is negative) followed by up to eight digits before the decimal point, a decimal point, and the necessary number of digits after the decimal point (but no trailing zero if there is more than one significant digit). There is always a minimum of one digit after the decimal point.

Otherwise, the value is converted to a string with an optional minus sign (if the value is negative), followed by a single digit, a decimal point, the necessary number of digits after the decimal point (but no trailing zero if there is more than one significant digit), and the letter E followed by a plus or a minus sign and a base 10 exponent of at least one digit. Again, there is always a minimum of one digit after the decimal point.

Note that the definition of this method has changed as of JDK 1.1. Prior to that release, the method provided a string representation that was equivalent to the %g format of the printf function in C.

Inherited Methods

Method	Inherited From	Method	Inherited From
clone()	Object	finalize()	Object
getClass()	Object	notify()	Object
notifyAll()	Object	wait()	Object
wait(long)	Object	wait(long, int)	Object

See Also

Class, Double, Number, NumberFormatException, String

12.22 IllegalAccessError

Synopsis

Class Name: java.lang.IllegalAccessError
Superclass: java.lang.IncompatibleClassChangeError
Immediate Subclasses: None
Interfaces Implemented: None
Availability: JDK 1.0 or later

Description

An IllegalAccessError is thrown when a class attempts to access a field or call a method it does not have access to. Usually this error is caught by the compiler; this error can occur at run-time if the definition of a class changes after the class that references it was last compiled.

Class Summary

```
public class java.lang.IllegalAccessError
            extends java.lang.IncompatibleClassChangeError {
  // Constructors
  public IllegalAccessError();
  public IllegalAccessError(String s);
}
```

Constructors

IllegalAccessError

public IllegalAccessError()

Description   This constructor creates an IllegalAccessError with no associated detail message.

public IllegalAccessError(String s)

Parameters   s   The detail message.

Description   This constructor creates an IllegalAccessError with the specified detail message.

Inherited Methods

Method	Inherited From	Method	Inherited From
clone()	Object	equals(Object)	Object
fillInStackTrace()	Throwable	finalize()	Object
getClass()	Object	getLocalizedMessage()	Throwable
getMessage()	Throwable	hashCode()	Object
notify()	Object	notifyAll()	Object
printStackTrace()	Throwable	printStack-Trace(PrintStream)	Throwable
printStack-Trace(PrintWriter)	Throwable	toString()	Object
wait()	Object	wait(long)	Object
wait(long, int)	Object		

See Also

Error, IncompatibleClassChangeError, Throwable

12.23   IllegalAccessException

Synopsis

Class Name: java.lang.IllegalAccessException
Superclass: java.lang.Exception
Immediate Subclasses: None
Interfaces Implemented: None
Availability: JDK 1.0 or later

Description

An IllegalAccessException is thrown when a program tries to dynamically load a class (i.e., uses the forName() method of the Class class, or the findSystem-Class() or the loadClass() method of the ClassLoader class) and the currently executing method does not have access to the specified class because it is in another package and not public. This exception is also thrown when a program tries to create an instance of a class (i.e., uses the newInstance() method of the Class class) that does not have a zero-argument constructor accessible to the caller.

Class Summary

```
public class java.lang.IllegalAccessException extends java.lang.Exception {
    // Constructors
    public IllegalAccessException();
    public IllegalAccessException(String s);
}
```

Constructors

IllegalAccessException

public IllegalAccessException()

    Description   This constructor creates an IllegalAccessException with no associated detail message.

public IllegalAccessException(String s)

    Parameters   s   The detail message.

    Description   This constructor creates an IllegalAccessException with the specified detail message.

Inherited Methods

Method	Inherited From	Method	Inherited From
clone()	Object	equals(Object)	Object
fillInStackTrace()	Throwable	finalize()	Object
getClass()	Object	getLocalizedMessage()	Throwable
getMessage()	Throwable	hashCode()	Object
notify()	Object	notifyAll()	Object
printStackTrace()	Throwable	printStack-Trace(PrintStream)	Throwable
printStack-Trace(PrintWriter)	Throwable	toString()	Object
wait()	Object	wait(long)	Object
wait(long, int)	Object		

See Also

Class, ClassLoader, Exception, Throwable

12.24   IllegalArgumentException

Synopsis

Class Name:	java.lang.IllegalArgumentException
Superclass:	java.lang.RuntimeException
Immediate Subclasses:	java.lang.IllegalThreadStateException,
	java.lang.NumberFormatException
Interfaces Implemented:	None
Availability:	JDK 1.0 or later

Description

An IllegalArgumentException is thrown to indicate that an illegal argument has been passed to a method.

Class Summary

```
public class java.lang.IllegalArgumentException
          extends java.lang.RuntimeException {
  // Constructors
  public IllegalArgumentException();
  public IllegalArgumentException(String s);
}
```

Constructors

IllegalArgumentException

public IllegalArgumentException()

Description   This constructor creates an IllegalArgumentException with no associated detail message.

public IllegalArgumentException(String s)

Parameters   s   The detail message.

Description   This constructor creates an IllegalArgumentException with the specified detail message.

Inherited Methods

Method	Inherited From	Method	Inherited From
clone()	Object	equals(Object)	Object
fillInStackTrace()	Throwable	finalize()	Object
getClass()	Object	getLocalizedMessage()	Throwable
getMessage()	Throwable	hashCode()	Object
notify()	Object	notifyAll()	Object
printStackTrace()	Throwable	printStack-Trace(PrintStream)	Throwable
printStack-Trace(PrintWriter)	Throwable	toString()	Object
wait()	Object	wait(long)	Object
wait(long, int)	Object		

See Also

Exception, IllegalThreadStateException, NumberFormatException, RuntimeException, Throwable

12.25   IllegalMonitorStateException

Synopsis

Class Name: java.lang.IllegalMonitorStateException
Superclass: java.lang.RuntimeException
Immediate Subclasses: None
Interfaces Implemented: None
Availability: JDK 1.0 or later

Description

An `IllegalMonitorStateException` is thrown when an object's `wait()`, `notify()`, or `notifyAll()` method is called from a thread that does not own the object's monitor.

Class Summary

```
public class java.lang.IllegalMonitorStateException
          extends java.lang.RuntimeException {
  // Constructors
  public IllegalMonitorStateException();
  public IllegalMonitorStateException(String s);
}
```

Constructors

IllegalMonitorStateException

public IllegalMonitorStateException()

> Description   This constructor creates an `IllegalMonitorStateException` with no associated detail message.

public IllegalMonitorStateException(String s)

> Parameters   s   The detail message.
>
> Description   This constructor creates an `IllegalMonitorStateException` with the specified detail message.

Inherited Methods

Method	Inherited From	Method	Inherited From
clone()	Object	equals(Object)	Object
fillInStackTrace()	Throwable	finalize()	Object
getClass()	Object	getLocalizedMessage()	Throwable
getMessage()	Throwable	hashCode()	Object
notify()	Object	notifyAll()	Object
printStackTrace()	Throwable	printStack-Trace(PrintStream)	Throwable
printStack-Trace(PrintWriter)	Throwable	toString()	Object
wait()	Object	wait(long)	Object
wait(long, int)	Object		

See Also

Exception, Object, RuntimeException, Throwable

12.26   IllegalStateException

Synopsis

Class Name:	java.lang.IllegalStateException
Superclass:	java.lang.RuntimeException
Immediate Subclasses:	None
Interfaces Implemented:	None
Availability:	New as of JDK 1.1

Description

An IllegalStateException is thrown to indicate that a method has been invoked when the run-time environment is in an inappropriate state for the requested operation.

Class Summary

```
public class java.lang.IllegalStateException
            extends java.lang.RuntimeException {
  // Constructors
  public IllegalStateException();
  public IllegalStateException(String s);
}
```

Constructors

IllegalStateException

public IllegalStateException()

Description   This constructor creates an IllegalStateException with no associated detail message.

public IllegalStateException(String s)

Parameters   s   The detail message.

Description   This constructor creates an IllegalStateException with the specified detail message.

Inherited Methods

Method	Inherited From	Method	Inherited From
clone()	Object	equals(Object)	Object
fillInStackTrace()	Throwable	finalize()	Object
getClass()	Object	getLocalizedMessage()	Throwable
getMessage()	Throwable	hashCode()	Object
notify()	Object	notifyAll()	Object
printStackTrace()	Throwable	printStack-Trace(PrintStream)	Throwable
printStack-Trace(PrintWriter)	Throwable	toString()	Object
wait()	Object	wait(long)	Object
wait(long, int)	Object		

See Also

Exception, Object, RuntimeException, Throwable

12.27   IllegalThreadStateException

Synopsis

Class Name:	java.lang.IllegalThreadStateException
Superclass:	java.lang.IllegalArgumentException
Immediate Subclasses:	None
Interfaces Implemented:	None
Availability:	JDK 1.0 or later

Description

An IllegalThreadStateException is thrown to indicate an attempt to perform an operation on a thread that is not legal for the thread's current state, such as attempting to resume a dead thread.

Class Summary

```
public class java.lang.IllegalThreadStateException
            extends java.lang.IllegalArgumentException {
  // Constructors
  public IllegalThreadStateException();
  public IllegalThreadStateException(String s);
}
```

Constructors

IllegalThreadStateException

public IllegalThreadStateException()

Description   This constructor creates an IllegalThreadStateException with no associated detail message.

public IllegalThreadStateException(String s)

Parameters   s   The detail message.

Description   This constructor creates an IllegalThreadStateException with the specified detail message.

Inherited Methods

Method	Inherited From	Method	Inherited From
clone()	Object	equals(Object)	Object
fillInStackTrace()	Throwable	finalize()	Object
getClass()	Object	getLocalizedMessage()	Throwable
getMessage()	Throwable	hashCode()	Object
notify()	Object	notifyAll()	Object
printStackTrace()	Throwable	printStack-Trace(PrintStream)	Throwable
printStack-Trace(PrintWriter)	Throwable	toString()	Object
wait()	Object	wait(long)	Object
wait(long, int)	Object		

See Also

Exception, IllegalArgumentException, RuntimeException, Thread, Throwable

---

12.28   IncompatibleClassChangeError

Synopsis

Class Name: java.lang.IncompatibleClassChangeError

Superclass: java.lang.LinkageError

Immediate Subclasses: java.lang.AbstractMethodError,
                         java.lang.IllegalAccessError,
                         java.lang.InstantiationError,
                         java.lang.NoSuchFieldError,
                         java.lang.NoSuchMethodError

Interfaces Implemented: None
Availability: JDK 1.0 or later

Description

An IncompatibleClassChangeError or one of its subclasses is thrown when a class refers to another class in an incompatible way. This situation occurs when the current definition of the referenced class is incompatible with the definition of the class that was found when the referring class was compiled. For example, say class A refers to a method in class B. Then, after class A is compiled, the method is removed from class B. When class A is loaded, the run-time system discovers that the method in class B no longer exists and throws an error.

Class Summary

```
public class java.lang.IncompatibleClassChangeError
            extends java.lang.LinkageError {
  // Constructors
  public IncompatibleClassChangeError();
  public IncompatibleClassChangeError(String s);
}
```

Constructors

IncompatibleClassChangeError

public IncompatibleClassChangeError()

Description   This constructor creates an IncompatibleClassChangeError with no associated detail message.

public IncompatibleClassChangeError(String s)

Parameters   s   The detail message.
Description   This constructor creates an IncompatibleClassChangeError with the specified detail message.

Inherited Methods

Method	Inherited From	Method	Inherited From
clone()	Object	equals(Object)	Object
fillInStackTrace()	Throwable	finalize()	Object
getClass()	Object	getLocalizedMessage()	Throwable
getMessage()	Throwable	hashCode()	Object
notify()	Object	notifyAll()	Object
printStackTrace()	Throwable	printStack-Trace(PrintStream)	Throwable
printStack-Trace(PrintWriter)	Throwable	toString()	Object

Method	Inherited From	Method	Inherited From
wait()	Object	wait(long)	Object
wait(long, int)	Object		

See Also

AbstractMethodError, Error, IllegalAccessError, InstantiationError, LinkageError, NoSuchFieldError, NoSuchMethodError, Throwable

12.29 IndexOutOfBoundsException

Synopsis

Class Name:	java.lang.IndexOutOfBoundsException
Superclass:	java.lang.RuntimeException
Immediate Subclasses:	java.lang.ArrayIndexOutOfBoundsException,
	java.lang.StringIndexOutOfBoundsException
Interfaces Implemented:	None
Availability:	JDK 1.0 or later

Description

The appropriate subclass of IndexOutOfBoundsException is thrown when an array or string index is out of bounds.

Class Summary

```
public class java.lang.IndexOutOfBoundsException
            extends java.lang.RuntimeException {
  // Constructors
  public IndexOutOfBoundsException();
  public IndexOutOfBoundsException(String s);
}
```

Constructors

IndexOutOfBoundsException

public IndexOutOfBoundsException()

Description   This constructor creates an IndexOutOfBoundsException with no associated detail message.

```
public IndexOutOfBoundsException(String s)
```
Parameters   s   The detail message.

Description   This constructor creates an `IndexOutOfBoundsException` with the specified detail message.

Inherited Methods

Method	Inherited From	Method	Inherited From
clone()	Object	equals(Object)	Object
fillInStackTrace()	Throwable	finalize()	Object
getClass()	Object	getLocalizedMessage()	Throwable
getMessage()	Throwable	hashCode()	Object
notify()	Object	notifyAll()	Object
printStackTrace()	Throwable	printStack-Trace(PrintStream)	Throwable
printStack-Trace(PrintWriter)	Throwable	toString()	Object
wait()	Object	wait(long)	Object
wait(long, int)	Object		

See Also

`ArrayIndexOutOfBoundsException`, `Exception`, `RuntimeException`, `StringIndexOutOfBoundsException`, `Throwable`

12.30 Integer

Synopsis

Class Name: `java.lang.Integer`
Superclass: `java.lang.Number`
Immediate Subclasses: None
Interfaces Implemented: None
Availability: JDK 1.0 or later

Description

The `Integer` class provides an object wrapper for an `int` value. This is useful when you need to treat an `int` value as an object. For example, there are a number of utility methods that take a reference to an `Object` as one of their arguments. You cannot specify an `int` value for one of these arguments, but you can provide a reference to an Integer object that encapsulates the int value. Also, as of JDK 1.1, the Integer class is necessary to support the Reflection API and class literals.

The Integer class also provides a number of utility methods for converting int values to other primitive types and for converting int values to strings and vice versa.

Class Summary

```
public final class java.lang.Integer extends java.lang.Number {
    // Constants
    public static final int MAX_VALUE;
    public static final int MIN_VALUE;
    public final static Class TYPE;                        // New in 1.1


    // Constructors
    public Integer(int value);
    public Integer(String s);


    // Class Methods
    public static Integer decode(String nm)                // New in 1.1
    public static Integer getInteger(String nm);
    public static Integer getInteger(String nm, int val);
    public static Integer getInteger(String nm, Integer val);
    public static int parseInt(String s);
    public static int parseInt(String s, int radix;
    public static String toBinaryString(long i);
    public static String toHexString(long i);
    public static String toOctalString(long i);
    public static String toString(int i);
    public static String toString(int i, int radix);
    public static Integer valueOf(String s);
    public static Integer valueOf(String s, int radix);


    // Instance Methods
    public byte byteValue();                               // New in 1.1
    public double doubleValue();
    public boolean equals(Object obj);
    public float floatValue();
    public int hashCode();
    public int intValue();
    public long longValue();
    public short shortValue();                             // New in 1.1
    public String toString();
}
```

Constants

MAX_VALUE

`public static final int MAX_VALUE = 0x7fffffff // 2147483647`

Description   The largest value that can be represented by an `int`.

MIN_VALUE

`public static final int MIN_VALUE = 0x80000000 // -2147483648`

Description   The smallest value that can be represented by an `int`.

TYPE

`public static final Class TYPE`

Availability   New as of JDK 1.1

Description   The `Class` object that represents the type `int`. It is always true that `Integer.TYPE == int.class`.

Constructors

Integer

`public Integer(int value)`

Parameters   value   The `int` value to be encapsulated by this object.

Description   Creates an `Integer` object with the specified `int` value.

`public Integer(String s) throws NumberFormatException`

Parameters   s   The string to be made into an `Integer` object.

Throws   `NumberFormatException`

            If the sequence of characters in the given `String` does not form a valid `int` literal.

Description   Constructs an `Integer` object with the value specified by the given string. The string should consist of one or more digit characters. The digit characters can be preceded by a single '-' character. If the string contains any other characters, the constructor throws a `NumberFormatException`.

Class Methods

decode

`public static Integer decode(String nm)`

Availability   New as of JDK 1.1

Parameters   nm   A `String` representation of the value to be encapsulated by an `Integer` object. If the string begins with # or 0x, it is a radix 16 representation of the value. If the string begins with 0, it is a radix 8 representation of the value. Otherwise, it is assumed to be a radix 10 representation of the value.

Returns   An `Integer` object that encapsulates the given value.

Throws   `NumberFormatException`

If the `String` contains any nondigit characters other than a leading minus sign or the value represented by the `String` is less than `Integer.MIN_VALUE` or greater than `Integer.MAX_VALUE`.

Description This method returns an `Integer` object that encapsulates the given value.

getInteger

`public static Integer getInteger(String nm)`

Parameters `nm`   The name of a system property.

Returns   The value of the system property as an `Integer` object, or an `Integer` object with the value 0 if the named property does not exist or cannot be parsed.

Description This method retrieves the value of the named system property and returns it as an `Integer` object. The method obtains the value of the system property as a `String` using `System.getProperty()`.

If the value of the property begins with `0x` or `#` and is not followed by a minus sign, the rest of the value is parsed as a hexadecimal integer. If the value begins with 0, it's parsed as an octal integer; otherwise it's parsed as a decimal integer.

`public static Integer getInteger(String nm, int val)`

Parameters `nm`   The name of a system property.

            `val`   A default `int` value for the property.

Returns   The value of the system property as an `Integer` object, or an `Integer` object with the value `val` if the named property does not exist or cannot be parsed.

Description This method retrieves the value of the named system property and returns it as an `Integer` object. The method obtains the value of the system property as a `String` using `System.getProperty()`.

If the value of the property begins with `0x` or `#` and is not followed by a minus sign, the rest of the value is parsed as a hexadecimal integer. If the value begins with 0, it's parsed as an octal integer; otherwise it's parsed as a decimal integer.

`public static Integer getInteger(String nm, Integer val)`

Parameters	nm	The name of a system property.
	val	A default `Integer` value for the property.
Returns		The value of the system property as an `Integer` object, or the `Integer` object `val` if the named property does not exist or cannot be parsed.
Description		This method retrieves the value of the named system property and returns it as an `Integer` object. The method obtains the value of the system property as a `String` using `System.getProperty()`.

If the value of the property begins with `0x` or `#` and is not followed by a minus sign, the rest of the value is parsed as a hexadecimal integer. If the value begins with `0`, it's parsed as an octal integer; otherwise it's as a decimal integer.

parseInt

`public static int parseInt(String s)`
                            `throws NumberFormatException`

Parameters	s	The `String` to be converted to an `int` value.
Returns		The numeric value of the integer represented by the `String` object.
Throws		`NumberFormatException`
		If the `String` does not contain a valid representation of an integer.
Description		This method returns the numeric value of the integer represented by the contents of the given `String` object. The `String` must contain only decimal digits, except that the first character may be a minus sign.

`public static int parseInt(String s, int radix)`
                            `throws NumberFormatException`

Parameters	s	The `String` to be converted to an `int` value.
	radix	The radix used in interpreting the characters in the `String` as digits. This value must be in the range `Character.MIN_RADIX` to `Character.MAX_RADIX`. If `radix` is in the range 2 through 10, only characters for which the `Character.isDigit()` method returns `true` are considered to be valid digits. If `radix` is in the range 11 through 36, characters in the ranges 'A' through 'Z' and 'a' through 'z' may be considered valid digits.

Returns	The numeric value of the integer represented by the String object in the specified radix.
Throws	NumberFormatException
	If the String does not contain a valid representation of an integer, or radix is not in the appropriate range.
Description	This method returns the numeric value of the integer represented by the contents of the given String object in the specified radix. The String must contain only valid digits of the specified radix, except that the first character may be a minus sign. The digits are parsed in the specified radix to produce the numeric value.

toBinaryString

```
public static String toBinaryString(int value)
```

Parameters	value	The int value to be converted to a string.
Returns	A string that contains the binary representation of the given value.
Description	This method returns a String object that contains the representation of the given value as an unsigned binary number. To convert the given value to an unsigned quantity, the method simply uses the value as if it were not negative. In other words, if the given value is negative, the method adds 2^{32} to it. Otherwise the value is used as it is.

The string returned by this method contains a sequence of one or more '0' and '1' characters. The method returns "0" if its argument is 0. Otherwise, the string returned by this method begins with '1'.

toHexString

```
public static String toHexString(int value)
```

Parameters	value	The int value to be converted to a string.
Returns	A string that contains the hexadecimal representation of the given value.
Description	This method returns a String object that contains the representation of the given value as an unsigned hexadecimal number. To convert the given value to an unsigned quantity, the method simply uses the value as if it were not negative. In other words, if the given value is negative, the method adds 2^{32} to it. Otherwise the value is used as it is.

The string returned by this method contains a sequence of one or more of the characters '0', '1', '2', '3', '4', '5', '6', '7', '8', '9', 'a', 'b', 'c', 'd', 'e', and 'f'. The method returns "0" if its argument is 0. Otherwise, the string returned by this method does not begin with '0'.

To produce a string that contains upper- instead of lowercase letters, use the String.toUpperCase() method.

toOctalString

public static String toOctalString(int value)

Parameters	value	The int value to be converted to a string.
Returns		A string that contains the octal representation of the given value.
Description		This method returns a String object that contains a representation of the given value as an unsigned octal number. To convert the given value to an unsigned quantity, the method simply uses the value as if it were not negative. In other words, if the given value is negative, the method adds 2^{32} to it. Otherwise the value is used as it is.

The string returned by this method contains a sequence of one or more of the characters '0', '1', '2', '3', '4', '5', '6', and '7'. The method returns "0" if its argument is 0. Otherwise, the string returned by this method does not begin with '0'.

toString

public static String toString(int i)

Parameters	i	The int value to be converted to a string.
Returns		The string representation of the given value.
Description		This method returns a String object that contains the decimal representation of the given value.

This method returns a string that begins with '-' if the given value is negative. The rest of the string is a sequence of one or more of the characters '0', '1', '2', '3', '4', '5', '6', '7', '8', and '9'. This method returns "0" if its argument is 0. Otherwise, the string returned by this method does not begin with "0" or "-0".

public static String toString(int i, int radix)

Parameters	i	The int value to be converted to a string.
	radix	The radix used in converting the value to a string. This value must be in the range Character.MIN_RADIX to Character.MAX_RADIX.

Returns   The string representation of the given value in the specified radix.

Description   This method returns a `String` object that contains the representation of the given value in the specified radix.

This method returns a string that begins with '-' if the given value is negative. The rest of the string is a sequence of one or more characters that represent the magnitude of the given value. The characters that can appear in the sequence are determined by the value of `radix`. If *N* is the value of `radix`, the first *N* characters on the following line can appear in the sequence:

```
0123456789abcdefghijklmnopqrstuvwxyz
```

The method does not verify that `radix` is in the proper range. If `radix` is less than `Character.MIN_RADIX` or greater than `Character.MAX_RADIX`, the value 10 is used instead of the given value.

This method returns "0" if its argument is 0. Otherwise, the string returned by this method does not begin with "0" or "-0".

valueOf

```
public static Integer valueOf(String s)
               throws NumberFormatException
```

Parameters   s   The string to be made into an `Integer` object.

Returns   The `Integer` object constructed from the string.

Throws   NumberFormatException

If the `String` does not contain a valid representation of an integer.

Description   Constructs an `Integer` object with the value specified by the given string. The string should consist of one or more digit characters. The digit characters can be preceded by a single '-' character. If the string contains any other characters, the method throws a `NumberFormatException`.

```
public static Integer valueOf(String s, int radix)
               throws NumberFormatException
```

Parameters   s   The string to be made into an `Integer` object.

radix   The radix used in converting the string to a value. This value must be in the range `Character.MIN_RADIX` to `Character.MAX_RADIX`.

Returns	The Integer object constructed from the string.
Throws	NumberFormatException
	If the String does not contain a valid representation of an integer or radix is not in the appropriate range.
Description	Constructs an Integer object with the value specified by the given string in the specified radix. The string should consist of one or more digit characters or characters in the range 'A' to 'Z' or 'a' to 'z' that are considered digits in the given radix. The digit characters can be preceded by a single '-' character. If the string contains any other characters, the method throws a NumberFormatException.

Instance Methods

byteValue

```
public byte byteValue()
```

Availability	New as of JDK 1.1
Returns	The value of this object as a byte.
Overrides	Number.byteValue()
Description	This method returns the value of this object as a byte. The high order bits of the value are discarded.

doubleValue

```
public double doubleValue()
```

Returns	The value of this object as a double.
Overrides	Number.doubleValue()
Description	This method returns the value of this object as a double.

equals

```
public boolean equals(Object obj)
```

Parameters	obj	The object to be compared with this object.
Returns	true if the objects are equal; false if they are not.	
Overrides	Object.equals()	
Description	This method returns true if obj is an instance of Integer and it contains the same value as the object this method is associated with.	

floatValue

```
public float floatValue()
```

Returns	The value of this object as a float.
Overrides	Number.floatValue()
Description	This method returns the value of this object as a float. Rounding may occur.

hashCode

```
public int hashCode()
```

Returns	A hashcode based on the int value of the object.
Overrides	Object.hashCode()
Description	This method returns a hashcode computed from the value of this object.

intValue

```
public int intValue()
```

Returns	The value of this object as an int.
Overrides	Number.intValue()
Description	This method returns the value of this object as an int.

longValue

```
public long longValue()
```

Returns	The value of this object as a long.
Overrides	Number.longValue()
Description	This method returns the value of this object as a long.

shortValue

```
public short shortValue()
```

Availability	New as of JDK 1.1
Returns	The value of this object as a short.
Overrides	Number.shortValue()
Description	This method returns the value of this object as a short. The high order bits of the value are discarded.

toString

```
public String toString()
```

Returns	The string representation of the value of this object.
Overrides	Object.toString()
Description	This method returns a String object that contains the decimal representation of the value of this object.

This method returns a string that begins with '–' if the value is negative. The rest of the string is a sequence of one or more of the characters '0', '1', '2', '3', '4', '5', '6', '7', '8', and '9'. This method returns "0" if the value of the object is 0. Otherwise, the string returned by this method does not begin with "0" or "–0".

Inherited Methods

Method	Inherited From	Method	Inherited From
clone()	Object	finalize()	Object
getClass()	Object	notify()	Object
notifyAll()	Object	wait()	Object
wait(long)	Object	wait(long, int)	Object

See Also

Character, Class, Long, Number, NumberFormatException, String, System

12.31 InstantiationError

Synopsis

Class Name: java.lang.InstantiationError
Superclass: java.lang.IncompatibleClassChangeError
Immediate Subclasses: None
Interfaces Implemented: None
Availability: JDK 1.0 or later

Description

An InstantiationError is thrown in response to an attempt to instantiate an abstract class or interface. Usually this error is caught by the compiler; this error can occur at run-time if the definition of a class is changed after the class that references it was last compiled.

Class Summary

```
public class java.lang.InstantiationError
        extends java.lang.IncompatibleClassChangeError {
  // Constructors
  public InstantiationError();
  public InstantiationError(String s);
}
```

Constructors

InstantiationError

public InstantiationError()

Description   This constructor creates an InstantiationError with no associated detail message.

public InstantiationError(String s)

Parameters   s   The detail message.

Description   This constructor creates an InstantiationError with the specified detail message.

Inherited Methods

Method	Inherited From	Method	Inherited From
clone()	Object	equals(Object)	Object
fillInStackTrace()	Throwable	finalize()	Object
getClass()	Object	getLocalizedMessage()	Throwable
getMessage()	Throwable	hashCode()	Object
notify()	Object	notifyAll()	Object
printStackTrace()	Throwable	printStack-Trace(PrintStream)	Throwable
printStack-Trace(PrintWriter)	Throwable	toString()	Object
wait()	Object	wait(long)	Object
wait(long, int)	Object		

See Also

Error, IncompatibleClassChangeError, Throwable

12.32   InstantiationException

Synopsis

Class Name: java.lang.InstantiationException
Superclass: java.lang.Exception
Immediate Subclasses: None
Interfaces Implemented: None
Availability: JDK 1.0 or later

Description

An InstantiationException is thrown in response to an attempt to instantiate an abstract class or an interface using the newInstance() method of the Class class.

Class Summary

```
public class java.lang.InstantiationException extends java.lang.Exception {
    // Constructors
    public InstantiationException();
    public InstantiationException(String s);
}
```

Constructors

InstantiationException

public InstantiationException()

Description   This constructor creates an InstantiationException with no associated detail message.

public InstantiationException(String s)

Parameters   s   The detail message.

Description   This constructor creates an InstantiationException with the specified detail message.

Inherited Methods

Method	Inherited From	Method	Inherited From
clone()	Object	equals(Object)	Object
fillInStackTrace()	Throwable	finalize()	Object
getClass()	Object	getLocalizedMessage()	Throwable
getMessage()	Throwable	hashCode()	Object
notify()	Object	notifyAll()	Object
printStackTrace()	Throwable	printStack-Trace(PrintStream)	Throwable
printStack-Trace(PrintWriter)	Throwable	toString()	Object
wait()	Object	wait(long)	Object
wait(long, int)	Object		

See Also

Class, Exception, Throwable

12.33   *InternalError*

Synopsis

Class Name: java.lang.InternalError
Superclass: java.lang.VirtualMachineError
Immediate Subclasses: None
Interfaces Implemented: None
Availability: JDK 1.0 or later

Description

An InternalError is thrown to signal an internal error within the virtual machine.

Class Summary

```
public class java.lang.InternalError extends java.lang.VirtualMachineError {
    // Constructors
    public InternalError();
    public InternalError(String s);
}
```

Constructors

InternalError

public InternalError()

Description   This constructor creates an InternalError with no associated detail message.

public InternalError(String s)

Parameters   s   The detail message.

Description   This constructor creates an InternalError with the specified detail message.

Inherited Methods

Method	Inherited From	Method	Inherited From
clone()	Object	equals(Object)	Object
fillInStackTrace()	Throwable	finalize()	Object
getClass()	Object	getLocalizedMessage()	Throwable
getMessage()	Throwable	hashCode()	Object
notify()	Object	notifyAll()	Object
printStackTrace()	Throwable	printStack-Trace(PrintStream)	Throwable
printStack-Trace(PrintWriter)	Throwable	toString()	Object

Method	Inherited From	Method	Inherited From
wait()	Object	wait(long)	Object
wait(long, int)	Object		

See Also

Error, Throwable, VirtualMachineError

12.34   *InterruptedException*

Synopsis

Class Name:	java.lang.InterruptedException
Superclass:	java.lang.Exception
Immediate Subclasses:	None
Interfaces Implemented:	None
Availability:	JDK 1.0 or later

Description

An InterruptedException is thrown to signal that a thread that is sleeping, waiting, or otherwise paused, has been interrupted by another thread.

Class Summary

```
public class java.lang.InterruptedException extends java.lang.Exception {
    // Constructors
    public InterruptedException();
    public InterruptedException(String s);
}
```

Constructors

InterruptedException

public InterruptedException()

    Description   This constructor creates an InterruptedException with no associated detail message.

public InterruptedException(String s)

    Parameters   s   The detail message.

    Description   This constructor creates an InterruptedException with the specified detail message.

Inherited Methods

Method	Inherited From	Method	Inherited From
clone()	Object	equals(Object)	Object
fillInStackTrace()	Throwable	finalize()	Object
getClass()	Object	getLocalizedMessage()	Throwable
getMessage()	Throwable	hashCode()	Object
notify()	Object	notifyAll()	Object
printStackTrace()	Throwable	printStack-Trace(PrintStream)	Throwable
printStack-Trace(PrintWriter)	Throwable	toString()	Object
wait()	Object	wait(long)	Object
wait(long, int)	Object		

See Also

Exception, Thread, Throwable

12.35   LinkageError

Synopsis

Class Name:	java.lang.LinkageError
Superclass:	java.lang.Error
Immediate Subclasses:	java.lang.ClassCircularityError,
	java.lang.ClassFormatError,
	java.lang.ExceptionInInitializerError,
	java.lang.IncompatibleClassChangeError,
	java.lang.NoClassDefFoundError,
	java.lang.UnsatisfiedLinkError,
	java.lang.VerifyError
Interfaces Implemented:	None
Availability:	JDK 1.0 or later

Description

The appropriate subclass of LinkageError is thrown when there is a problem resolving a reference to a class. Reasons for this may include a difficulty in finding the definition of the class or an incompatibility between the current definition and the expected definition of the class.

Class Summary

```
public class java.lang.LinkageError extends java.lang.Error {
  // Constructors
  public LinkageError();
  public LinkageError(String s);
}
```

Constructors

LinkageError

public LinkageError()

Description   This constructor creates a LinkageError with no associated detail message.

public LinkageError(String s)

Parameters   s   The detail message.

Description   This constructor create a LinkageError with the specified detail message.

Inherited Methods

Method	Inherited From	Method	Inherited From
clone()	Object	equals(Object)	Object
fillInStackTrace()	Throwable	finalize()	Object
getClass()	Object	getLocalizedMessage()	Throwable
getMessage()	Throwable	hashCode()	Object
notify()	Object	notifyAll()	Object
printStackTrace()	Throwable	printStack-Trace(PrintStream)	Throwable
printStack-Trace(PrintWriter)	Throwable	toString()	Object
wait()	Object	wait(long)	Object
wait(long, int)	Object		

See Also

ClassCircularityError, ClassFormatError, Error, ExceptionInInitializer-Error, IncompatibleClassChangeError, NoClassDefFoundError, Throwable, UnsatisfiedLinkError, VerifyError

12.36 Long

Synopsis

Class Name: java.lang.Long
Superclass: java.lang.Number
Immediate Subclasses: None
Interfaces Implemented: None
Availability: JDK 1.0 or later

Description

The Long class provides an object wrapper for a long value. This is useful when you need to treat a long value as an object. For example, there are a number of utility methods that take a reference to an Object as one of their arguments. You cannot specify a long value for one of these arguments, but you can provide a reference to a Long object that encapsulates the long value. Furthermore, as of JDK 1.1, the Long class is necessary to support the Reflection API and class literals.

The Long class also provides a number of utility methods for converting long values to other primitive types and for converting long values to strings and vice versa.

Class Summary

```
public final class java.lang.Long extends java.lang.Number {
    // Constants
    public static final long MIN_VALUE;
    public static final long MAX_VALUE;
    public final static Class TYPE;                      // New in 1.1

    // Constructors
    public Long(long value);
    public Long(String s);

    // Class Methods
    public static Long getLong(String nm);
    public static Long getLong(String nm, long val);
    public static Long getLong(String nm, Long val);
    public static long parseLong(String s);
    public static long parseLong(String s, int radix);
    public static String toBinaryString(long i);
    public static String toHexString(long i);
    public static String toOctalString(long i);
    public static String toString(long i);
    public static String toString(long i, int radix);
    public static Long valueOf(String s);
    public static Long valueOf(String s, int radix);
```

```
    // Instance Methods
    public byte byteValue();                            // New in 1.1
    public double doubleValue();
    public boolean equals(Object obj);
    public float floatValue();
    public int hashCode();
    public int intValue();
    public long longValue();
    public short shortValue();                          // New in 1.1
    public String toString();
}
```

Constants

MAX_VALUE

public static final long MAX_VALUE = 0x7fffffffffffffffL

Description   The largest value that can be represented by a long.

MIN_VALUE

public static final long MIN_VALUE = 0x8000000000000000L

Description   The smallest value that can be represented by a long.

TYPE

public static final Class TYPE

Availability   New as of JDK 1.1

Description   The Class object that represents the type long. It is always true that Long.TYPE == long.class.

Constructors

Long

public Long(long value)

Parameters   value   The long value to be encapsulated by this object.

Description   Creates a Long object with the specified long value.

public Long(String s) throws NumberFormatException

Parameters   s   The string to be made into a Long object.

Throws   NumberFormatException

                           If the sequence of characters in the given String does not form a valid long literal.

Description   Constructs a Long object with the value specified by the given string. The string should consist of one or more digit characters. The digit characters can be preceded by a single '–' character. If the string contains any other characters, the constructor throws a NumberFormatException.

Class Methods

getLong

`public static Integer getLong(String nm)`

Parameters	nm	The name of a system property.

Returns The value of the system property as a Long object or a Long object with the value 0 if the named property does not exist or cannot be parsed.

Description This method retrieves the value of the named system property and returns it as a Long object. The method obtains the value of the system property as a String using `System.getProperty()`.

If the value of the property begins with 0x or # and is not followed by a minus sign, the rest of the value is parsed as a hexadecimal integer. If the value begins with 0, it's parsed as an octal integer; otherwise it's parsed as a decimal integer.

`public static Long getLong(String nm, long val)`

Parameters	nm	The name of a system property.
	val	A default value for the property.

Returns The value of the system property as a Long object or a Long object with the value val if the named property does not exist or cannot be parsed.

Description This method retrieves the value of the named system property and returns it as a Long object. The method obtains the value of the system property as a String using `System.getProperty()`.

If the value of the property begins with 0x or # and is not followed by a minus sign, the rest of the value is parsed as a hexadecimal integer. If the value begins with 0, it's parsed as an octal integer; otherwise it's parsed as a decimal integer.

`public static Long getLong(String nm, Long val)`

Parameters	nm	The name of a system property.
	val	A default value for the property.

Returns The value of the system property as a Long object, or the Long object val if the named property does not exist or cannot be parsed.

Description This method retrieves the value of the named system property and returns it as a Long object. The method obtains the value of the system property as a String using `System.getProperty()`.

If the value of the property begins with 0x or # and is not followed by a minus sign, the rest of the value is parsed as a hexadecimal integer. If the value begins with 0, it's parsed as an octal integer; otherwise it's parsed as a decimal integer.

parseLong

```
public static long parseLong(String s)
                        throws NumberFormatException
```

Parameters	s	The String to be converted to a long value.

Returns   The numeric value of the long represented by the String object.

Throws   NumberFormatException

If the String does not contain a valid representation of a long value.

Description This method returns the numeric value of the long represented by the contents of the given String object. The String must contain only decimal digits, except that the first character may be a minus sign.

```
public static long parseLong(String s, int radix)
                        throws NumberFormatException
```

Parameters	s	The String to be converted to a long value.
	radix	The radix used in interpreting the characters in the String as digits. It must be in the range Character.MIN_RADIX to Character.MAX_RADIX. If radix is in the range 2 through 10, only characters for which the Character.isDigit() method returns true are considered valid digits. If radix is in the range 11 through 36, characters in the ranges 'A' through 'Z' and 'a' through 'z' may be considered valid digits.

Returns   The numeric value of the long represented by the String object in the specified radix.

Throws   NumberFormatException

If the String does not contain a valid representation of a long or radix is not in the appropriate range.

Description This method returns the numeric value of the long represented by the contents of the given String object in the specified radix. The String must contain only valid digits of the specified radix, except that the first character may be a minus sign. The digits are parsed in the specified radix to produce the numeric value.

toBinaryString

```
public static String toBinaryString(long value)
```

Parameters value The long value to be converted to a string.

Returns A string that contains the binary representation of the given value.

Description This method returns a String object that contains the representation of the given value as an unsigned binary number. To convert the given value to an unsigned quantity, the method simply uses the value as if it were not negative. In other words, if the given value is negative, the method adds 2^{64} to it. Otherwise the value is used as it is.

The string returned by this method contains a sequence of one or more '0' and '1' characters. The method returns "0" if its argument is 0. Otherwise, the string returned by this method begins with '1'.

toHexString

```
public static String toHexString(long value)
```

Parameters value The long value to be converted to a string.

Returns A string that contains the hexadecimal representation of the given value.

Description This method returns a String object that contains the representation of the given value as an unsigned hexadecimal number. To convert the given value to an unsigned quantity, the method simply uses the value as if it were not negative. In other words, if the given value is negative, the method adds 2^{64} to it. Otherwise the value is used as it is.

The string returned by this method contains a sequence of one or more of the characters '0', '1', '2', '3', '4', '5', '6', '7', '8', '9', 'a', 'b', 'c', 'd', 'e', and 'f'. The method returns "0" if its argument is 0. Otherwise, the string returned by this method does not begin with '0'.

To produce a string that contains upper- instead of lowercase letters, use the String.toUpperCase() method.

toOctalString

```
public static String toOctalString(long value)
```

Parameters value The long value to be converted to a string.

Returns	A string that contains the octal representation of the given value.
Description	This method returns a String object that contains a representation of the given value as an unsigned octal number. To convert the given value to an unsigned quantity, the method simply uses the value as if it were not negative. In other words, if the given value is negative, the method adds 2^{64} to it. Otherwise the value is used as it is.

The string returned by this method contains a sequence of one or more of the characters '0', '1', '2', '3', '4', '5', '6', and '7'. The method returns "0" if its argument is 0. Otherwise, the string returned by this method does not begin with '0'.

toString

```
public static String toString(long i)
```

Parameters	i	The long value to be converted to a string.
Returns	The string representation of the given value.	
Description	This method returns a String object that contains the decimal representation of the given value.	

This method returns a string that begins with '–' if the given value is negative. The rest of the string is a sequence of one or more of the characters '0', '1', '2', '3', '4', '5', '6', '7', '8', and '9'. This method returns "0" if its argument is 0. Otherwise, the string returned by this method does not begin with "0" or "–0".

```
public static String toString(long i, int radix)
```

Parameters	i	The long value to be converted to a string.
	radix	The radix used in converting the value to a string. This value must be in the range Character.MIN_RADIX to Character.MAX_RADIX.
Returns	The string representation of the given value in the specified radix.	
Description	This method returns a String object that contains the representation of the given value in the specified radix.	

This method returns a string that begins with '–' if the given value is negative. The rest of the string is a sequence of one or more characters that represent the magnitude of the given value. The characters that can appear in the sequence are determined by the value of radix. If N is the value of radix, the first N characters on the following line can appear in the sequence:

```
0123456789abcdefghijklmnopqrstuvwxyz
```

The method does not verify that radix is in the proper range. If radix is less than Character.MIN_RADIX or greater than Character.MAX_RADIX, the value 10 is used instead of the given value.

This method returns "0" if its argument is 0. Otherwise, the string returned by this method does not begin with "0" or "-0".

valueOf

```
public static Long valueOf(String s)
                  throws NumberFormatException
```

Parameters   s   The string to be made into a Long object.

Returns   The Long object constructed from the string.

Throws   NumberFormatException

                   If the String does not contain a valid representation of a long.

Description   Constructs a Long object with the value specified by the given string. The string should consist of one or more digit characters. The digit characters can be preceded by a single - character. If the string contains any other characters, the method throws a NumberFormatException.

```
public static Long valueOf(String s, int radix)
                  throws NumberFormatException
```

Parameters   s   The string to be made into a Long object.

             radix   The radix used in converting the string to a value. This value must be in the range Character.MIN_RADIX to Character.MAX_RADIX.

Returns   The Long object constructed from the string.

Throws   NumberFormatException

                   If the String does not contain a valid representation of a long.

Description   Constructs a Long object with the value specified by the given string in the specified radix. The string should consist of one or more digit characters or characters in the range 'A' to 'Z' or 'a' to 'z' that are considered digits in the given radix. The digit characters can be preceded by a single '-' character. If the string contains any other characters, the method throws a NumberFormatException.

The method does not verify that radix is in the proper range. If radix is less than Character.MIN_RADIX or greater than Character.MAX_RADIX, the value 10 is used instead of the given value.

Instance Methods

byteValue

```
public byte byteValue()
```
Availability   New as of JDK 1.1

Returns   The value of this object as a byte.

Overrides   Number.byteValue()

Description   This method returns the value of this object as a byte. The high order bits of the value are discarded.

doubleValue

```
public double doubleValue()
```
Returns   The value of this object as a double.

Overrides   Number.doubleValue()

Description   This method returns the value of this object as a double. Rounding may occur.

equals

```
public boolean equals(Object obj)
```
Parameters   obj   The object to be compared with this object.

Returns   true if the objects are equal; false if they are not.

Overrides   Object.equals()

Description   This method returns true if obj is an instance of Long and it contains the same value as the object this method is associated with.

floatValue

```
public float floatValue()
```
Returns   The value of this object as a float.

Overrides   Number.floatValue()

Description   This method returns the value of this object as a float. Rounding may occur.

hashCode

```
public int hashCode()
```
Returns   A hashcode based on the long value of the object.

Overrides   Object.hashCode()

Description   This method returns a hashcode computed from the value of this object. More specifically, the result is the exclusive OR of the two halves of the long value represented by the object. If value is the value of the object, the method returns a result equivalent to the following expression:

```
(int)(value^(value>>>32))
```

intValue

`public int intValue()`

Returns   The value of this object as an int.

Overrides   `Number.intValue()`

Description   This method returns the value of this object as an int. The high-order bits of the value are discarded.

longValue

`public long longValue()`

Returns   The value of this object as a long.

Overrides   `Number.longValue()`

Description   This method returns the value of this object as a long.

shortValue

`public short shortValue()`

Availability   New as of JDK 1.1

Returns   The value of this object as a short.

Overrides   `Number.shortValue()`

Description   This method returns the value of this object as a short. The high-order bits of the value are discarded.

toString

`public String toString()`

Returns   The string representation of the value of this object.

Overrides   `Object.toString()`

Description   This method returns a String object that contains the decimal representation of the value of this object.

This method returns a string that begins with '–' if the value is negative. The rest of the string is a sequence of one or more of the characters '0', '1', '2', '3', '4', '5', '6', '7', '8', and '9'. This method returns "0" if the value of the object is 0. Otherwise, the string returned by this method does not begin with "0" or "–0".

Inherited Methods

Method	Inherited From	Method	Inherited From
clone()	Object	finalize()	Object
getClass()	Object	notify()	Object
notifyAll()	Object	wait()	Object
wait(long)	Object	wait(long, int)	Object

See Also

Character, Class, Integer, Number, NumberFormatException, String, System

12.37 Math

Synopsis

Class Name:	java.lang.Math
Superclass:	java.lang.Object
Immediate Subclasses:	None
Interfaces Implemented:	None
Availability:	JDK 1.0 or later

Description

The Math class contains constants for the mathematical values π and e. The class also defines methods that compute various mathematical functions, such as trigonometric and exponential functions. All of these constants and methods are static. In other words, it is not necessary to create an instance of the Math class in order to use its constants and methods. In fact, the Math class does not define any public constructors, so it cannot be instantiated.

To ensure that the methods in this class return consistent results under different implementations of Java, all of the methods use the algorithms from the well-known Freely-Distributable Math Library package, *fdlibm*. This package is part of the network library *netlib*. The library can be obtained through the URL *http://netlib.att.com*. The algorithms used in this class are from the version of *fdlibm* dated January 4, 1995. *fdlibm* provides more than one definition for some functions. In those cases, the "IEEE 754 core function" version is used.

Class Summary

```
public final class java.lang.Math extends java.lang.Object {
    // Constants
    public static final double E;
    public static final double PI;

    // Class Methods
    public static int abs(int a);
    public static long abs(long a);
    public static float abs(float a);
    public static double abs(double a);
    public static native double acos(double a);
    public static native double asin(double a);
    public static native double atan(double a);
    public static native double atan2(double a, double b);
    public static native double ceil(double a);
    public static native double cos(double a);
    public static native double exp(double a);
    public static native double floor(double a);
    public static native double IEEEremainder(double f1, double f2);
    public static native double log(double a);
    public static int max(int a, int b);
    public static long max(long a, long b);
    public static float max(float a, float b);
    public static double max(double a, double b);
    public static int min(int a, int b);
    public static long min(long a, long b);
    public static float min(float a, float b);
    public static double min(double a, double b);
    public static native double pow(double a, double b);
    public static synchronized double random();
    public static native double rint(double a);
    public static int round(float a);
    public static long round(double a);
    public static native double sin(double a);
    public static native double sqrt(double a);
    public static native double tan(double a);
}
```

Constants

E

```
public static final double E = 2.7182818284590452354
```
Description   The value of this constant is e, the base for natural logarithms.

PI

> public static final double PI = 3.14159265358979323846
> Description   The value for this constant is π.

Class Methods

abs

> public static double abs(double a)
> | | | |
> |---|---|---|
> | Parameters | a | A double value. |
> | Returns | The absolute value of its argument. | |
> | Description | This method returns the absolute value of its argument. | |
>
> If the argument to this method is negative or positive zero, the method should return positive zero. If the argument is positive or negative infinity, the method returns positive infinity. If the argument is NaN, the method returns NaN.

> public static float abs(float a)
> | | | |
> |---|---|---|
> | Parameters | a | A float value. |
> | Returns | The absolute value of its argument. | |
> | Description | This method returns the absolute value of its argument. | |
>
> If the argument to this method is negative or positive zero, the method should return positive zero. If the argument is positive or negative infinity, the method returns positive infinity. If the argument is NaN, the method returns NaN.

> public static int abs(int a)
> | | | |
> |---|---|---|
> | Parameters | a | An int value. |
> | Returns | The absolute value of its argument. | |
> | Description | This method returns the absolute value of its argument. | |
>
> If the argument is Integer.MIN_VALUE, the method actually returns Integer.MIN_VALUE because the true absolute value of Integer.MIN_VALUE is one greater than the largest positive value that can be represented by an int.

> public static long abs(long a)
> | | | |
> |---|---|---|
> | Parameters | a | A long value. |
> | Returns | The absolute value of its argument. | |
> | Description | This method returns the absolute value of its argument. | |
>
> If the argument is Long.MIN_VALUE, the method actually returns Long.MIN_VALUE because the true absolute value of Long.MIN_VALUE is one greater than the largest positive value represented by a long.

acos

```
public static native double acos(double a)
```

Parameters   a   A double value greater than or equal to -1.0 and less than or equal to 1.0.

Returns   The arc cosine measured in radians; the result is greater than or equal to 0.0 and less than or equal to π.

Description   This method returns the arc cosine of the given value.

If the value is NaN or its absolute value is greater than 1.0, the method returns NaN.

asin

```
public static native double asin(double a)
```

Parameters   a   A double value greater than or equal to -1.0 and less than or equal to 1.0.

Returns   The arc sine measured in radians; the result is greater than or equal to $-\pi/2$ and less than or equal to $\pi/2$.

Description   This method returns the arc sine of the given value.

If the value is NaN or its absolute value is greater than 1.0, the method returns NaN. If the value is positive zero, the method returns positive zero. If the value is negative zero, the method returns negative zero.

atan

```
public static native double atan(double a)
```

Parameters   a   A double value greater than or equal to -1.0 and less than or equal to 1.0.

Returns   The arc tangent measured in radians; the result is greater than or equal to $-\pi/2$ and less than or equal to $\pi/2$.

Description   This method returns the principle value of the arc tangent of the given value.

If the value is NaN, the method returns NaN. If the value is positive zero, the method returns positive zero. If the value is negative zero, the method returns negative zero.

atan2

```
public static native double atan2(double a, double b)
```

Parameters   a   A double value.
                   b   A double value.

Returns

The θ component of the polar coordinate (r,θ) that corresponds to the cartesian coordinate (a,b); the result is measured in radians and is greater than or equal to -π and less than or equal to π.

Description

This method returns the θ component of the polar coordinate (r,θ) that corresponds to the cartesian coordinate (a,b). It computes θ as the principle value of the arc tangent of b/a, using the signs of both arguments to determine the quadrant (and sign) of the return value.

If either argument is NaN, the method returns NaN.

If the first argument is positive zero and the second argument is positive, then the method returns positive zero. If the first argument is positive zero and the second argument is negative, then the method returns the double value closest to π.

If the first argument is negative zero and the second argument is positive, the method returns negative zero. If the first argument is negative zero and the second argument is negative, the method returns the double value closest to -π.

If the first argument is positive and finite and the second argument is positive infinity, the method returns positive zero. If the first argument is positive and finite and the second argument is negative infinity, the method returns the double value closest to π.

If the first argument is negative and finite and the second argument is positive infinity, the method returns negative zero. If the first argument is negative and finite and the second argument is negative infinity, the method returns the double value closest to -π.

If the first argument is positive and the second argument is positive zero or negative zero, the method returns the double value closest to π/2. If the first argument is negative and the second argument is positive or negative zero, the method returns the double value closest to -π/2.

If the first argument is positive infinity and the second argument is finite, the method returns the double value closest to π/2. If the first argument is negative infinity and the second argument is finite, the method returns the double value closest to -π/2.

If both arguments are positive infinity, the method returns the double value closest to π/4. If the first argument is positive infinity and the second argument is negative infinity, the method returns the double value closest to 3π/4. If the first argument is negative infinity and the second argument is positive infinity, the method returns the double value closest to -π/4. If both arguments are negative infinity, the method returns the double value closest to -3π/4.

ceil

```
public static native double ceil(double a)
```

Parameters	a	A double value.
Returns		The smallest integer greater than or equal to the given value.
Description		This method performs the ceiling operation. It returns the smallest integer that is greater than or equal to its argument.

If the argument is NaN, an infinity value, or a zero value, the method returns that same value. If the argument is less than zero but greater than –1.0, the method returns negative zero.

cos

```
public static native double cos(double a)
```

Parameters	a	A double value that's an angle measured in radians.
Returns		The cosine of the given angle.
Description		This method returns the cosine of the given angle measured in radians.

If the angle is NaN or an infinity value, the method returns NaN.

exp

```
public static native double exp(double a)
```

Parameters	a	A double value.
Returns		e^a
Description		This method returns the exponential function of a. In other words, *e* is raised to the value specified by the parameter a, where *e* is the base of the natural logarithms.

If the value is NaN, the method returns NaN. If the value is positive infinity, the method returns positive infinity. If the value is negative infinity, the method returns positive zero.

floor

public static native double floor(double a)

Parameters   a   A double value.

Returns   The greatest integer less than or equal to the given value.

Description   This method performs the floor operation. It returns the largest integer that is less than or equal to its argument.

If the argument is NaN, an infinity value, or a zero value, the method returns that same value.

IEEEremainder

public static native double IEEEremainder(double a, double b)

Parameters   a   A double value.
                 b   A double value.

Returns   The remainder of a divided by b as defined by the IEEE 754 standard.

Description   This method returns the remainder of a divided by b as defined by the IEEE 754 standard. This operation involves first determining the mathematical quotient of a/b rounded to the nearest integer. If the quotient is equally close to two integers, it is rounded to the even integer. The method then returns a-(b×Q), where Q is the rounded quotient.

If either argument is NaN, the method returns NaN. If the first argument is positive or negative infinity and the second argument is positive or negative zero, the method also returns NaN. If the first argument is a finite value and the second argument is positive or negative infinity, the method returns its first argument.

log

public static native double log(double a)

Parameters   a   A double value that is greater than 0.0.

Returns   The natural logarithm of a.

Description   This method returns the natural logarithm (base e) of its argument.

In particular, if the argument is positive infinity, the method returns positive infinity. If the argument is positive or negative zero, the method returns negative infinity. If the argument is less than zero, the method returns NaN. If the argument is NaN, the method returns NaN.

max

```
public static double max(double a, double b)
```
Parameters   a   A double value.

                  b   A double value.

Returns   The greater of a and b.

Description   This method returns the greater of its two arguments. In other words, it returns the one that is closer to positive infinity.

               If one argument is positive zero and the other is negative zero, the method returns positive zero. If either argument is NaN, the method returns NaN.

```
public static float max(float a, float b)
```
Parameters   a   A float value.

                  b   A float value.

Returns   The greater of a and b.

Description   This method returns the greater of its two arguments. In other words, it returns the one that is closer to positive infinity.

               If one argument is positive zero and the other is negative zero, the method returns positive zero. If either argument is NaN, the method returns NaN.

```
public static int max(int a, int b)
```
Parameters   a   An int value.

                  b   An int value.

Returns   The greater of a and b.

Description   This method returns the greater of its two arguments. In other words, it returns the one that is closer to Integer.MAX_VALUE.

```
public static long max(long a, long b)
```
Parameters   a   A long value.

                  b   A long value.

Returns   The greater of a and b.

Description   This method returns the greater of its two arguments. In other words, it returns the one that is closer to Long.MAX_VALUE.

min

```
public static double min(double a, double b)
```
Parameters   a   A double value.

                  b   A double value.

Returns   The lesser of a and b.

Description   This method returns the lesser of its two arguments. In other words, it returns the one that is closer to negative infinity.

If one argument is positive zero and the other is negative zero, the method returns negative zero. If either argument is NaN, the method returns NaN.

`public static float min(float a, float b)`

Parameters   a   A float value.
              b   A float value.
Returns   The lesser of a and b.
Description   This method returns the lesser of its two arguments. In other words, it returns the one that is closer to negative infinity.

If one argument is positive zero and the other is negative zero, the method returns negative zero. If either argument is NaN, the method returns NaN.

`public static int min(int a, int b)`

Parameters   a   An int value.
              b   An int value.
Returns   The lesser of a and b.
Description   This method returns the lesser of its two arguments. In other words, it returns the one that is closer to `Integer.MIN_VALUE`.

`public static long min(long a, long b)`

Parameters   a   A long value.
              b   A long value.
Returns   The lesser of a and b.
Description   This method returns the lesser of its two arguments. In other words, it returns the one that is closer to `Long.MIN_VALUE`.

pow

`public static native double pow(double a, double b)`

Parameters   a   A double value.
              b   A double value.
Returns a^b
Description   This method computes the value of raising a to the power of b.

If the second argument is positive or negative zero, the method returns `1.0`. If the second argument is `1.0`, the method returns its first argument. If the second argument is NaN, the method returns NaN. If the first argument is NaN and the second argument is nonzero, the method returns NaN.

If the first argument is positive zero and the second argument is greater than zero, the method returns positive zero. If the first argument is positive zero and the second argument is less than zero, the method returns positive infinity.

If the first argument is positive infinity and the second argument is less than zero, the method returns positive zero. If the first argument is positive infinity and the second argument is greater than zero, the method returns positive infinity.

If the absolute value of the first argument is greater than 1 and the second argument is positive infinity, the method returns positive infinity. If the absolute value of the first argument is greater than 1 and the second argument is negative infinity, the method returns positive zero. If the absolute value of the first argument is less than 1 and the second argument is negative infinity, the method returns positive infinity. If the absolute value of the first argument is less than 1 and the second argument is positive infinity, the method returns positive zero. If the absolute value of the first argument is 1 and the second argument is positive or negative infinity, the method returns NaN.

If the first argument is negative zero and the second argument is greater than zero but not a finite odd integer, the method returns positive zero. If the first argument is negative zero and the second argument is a positive finite odd integer, the method returns negative zero. If the first argument is negative zero and the second argument is less than zero but not a finite odd integer, the method returns positive infinity. If the first argument is negative zero and the second argument is a negative finite odd integer, the method returns negative infinity.

If the first argument is negative infinity and the second argument is less than zero but not a finite odd integer, the method returns positive zero. If the first argument is negative infinity and the second argument is a negative finite odd integer, the method returns negative zero. If the first argument is negative infinity and the second argument is greater than zero but not a finite odd integer, the method returns positive infinity. If the first argument is negative infinity and the second argument is a positive finite odd integer, the method returns negative infinity.

If the first argument is less than zero and the second argument is a finite even integer, the method returns the result of the absolute value of the first argument raised to the power of the second argument. If the first argument is less than zero and the second argument is a finite odd integer, the method returns the negative of the result of the absolute value of the first argument raised to the power of the second argument. If the first argument is finite and less than zero and the second argument is finite and not an integer, the method returns NaN.

If both arguments are integer values, the method returns the first argument raised to the power of the second argument.

random

```
public static synchronized double random()
```
Returns   A random number between 0.0 and 1.0.

Description   This method returns a random number greater than or equal to 0.0 and less than 1.0. The implementation of this method uses the java.util.Random class. You may prefer to use the Random class directly, in order to gain more control over the distribution, type, and repeatability of the random numbers you are generating.

rint

```
public static native double rint(double a)
```
Parameters   a   A double value.

Returns   The value of its argument rounded to the nearest integer.

Description   This method returns its argument rounded to the nearest integer; the result is returned as a double value. If the argument is equidistant from two integers (e.g., 1.5), the method returns the even integer.

If the argument is an infinity value, a zero value, or NaN, the method returns that same value.

round

```
public static long round(double a)
```
Parameters   a   A double value.

Returns   The value of its argument rounded to the nearest long.

Description   This method returns its double argument rounded to the nearest integral value and converted to a long. If the argument is equidistant from two integers, the method returns the greater of the two integers.

If the argument is positive infinity or any other value greater than Long.MAX_VALUE, the method returns Long.MAX_VALUE. If the argument is negative infinity or any other value less than Long.MIN_VALUE, the method returns Long.MIN_VALUE. If the argument is NaN, the method returns 0.

```
public static int round(float a)
```
Parameters   a   A float value.

Returns   The value of its argument rounded to the nearest int.

Description   This method returns its float argument rounded to the near-
              est integral value and converted to an int. If the argument is
              equidistant from two integers, the method returns the greater
              of the two integers.

              If the argument is positive infinity or any other value greater
              than the Integer.MAX_VALUE, the method returns Inte-
              ger.MAX_VALUE. If the argument is negative infinity or any
              other value less than Integer.MIN_VALUE, the method returns
              Integer.MIN_VALUE. If the argument is NaN, the method
              returns 0.

sin

```
public static native double sin(double a)
```
Parameters   a   A double value that's an angle measured in radi-
                           ans.

Returns   The sine of the given angle.

Description   This method returns the sine of the given angle measured in
              radians.

              If the angle is NaN or an infinity value, the method returns
              NaN. If the angle is positive zero, the method returns positive
              zero. If the angle is negative zero, the method returns negative
              zero.

sqrt

```
public static native double sqrt(double a)
```
Parameters   a   A double value.

Returns   The square root of its argument.

Description   This method returns the square root of its argument.

              If the argument is negative or NaN, the method returns NaN.
              If the argument is positive infinity, the method returns positive
              infinity. If the argument is positive or negative zero, the method
              returns that same value.

tan

    public static native double tan(double a)

Parameters	a	A double value that is an angle measured in radians.
Returns		The tangent of the given angle.
Description		This method returns the tangent of the given angle measured in radians.

If the angle is NaN or an infinity value, the method returns NaN. If the angle is positive zero, the method returns positive zero. If the angle is negative zero, the method returns negative zero.

Inherited Methods

Method	Inherited From	Method	Inherited From
clone()	Object	equals(Object)	Object
finalize()	Object	getClass()	Object
hashCode()	Object	notify()	Object
notifyAll()	Object	toString()	Object
wait()	Object	wait(long)	Object
wait(long, int)	Object		

See Also

Double, Float, Integer, Long, Object

12.38   *NegativeArraySizeException*

Synopsis

Class Name:	java.lang.NegativeArraySizeException
Superclass:	java.lang.RuntimeException
Immediate Subclasses:	None
Interfaces Implemented:	None
Availability:	JDK 1.0 or later

Description

A NegativeArraySizeException is thrown in response to an attempt to create an array with a negative size.

Class Summary

```
public class java.lang.NegativeArraySizeException
          extends java.lang.RuntimeException {
  // Constructors
  public NegativeArraySizeException();
  public NegativeArraySizeException(String s);
}
```

Constructors

NegativeArraySizeException

```
public NegativeArraySizeException()
```

Description | This constructor creates a NegativeArraySizeException with no associated detail message.

```
public NegativeArraySizeException(String s)
```

Parameters | s | The detail message.

Description | This constructor creates a NegativeArraySizeException with the specified detail message.

Inherited Methods

Method	Inherited From	Method	Inherited From
clone()	Object	equals(Object)	Object
fillInStackTrace()	Throwable	finalize()	Object
getClass()	Object	getLocalizedMessage()	Throwable
getMessage()	Throwable	hashCode()	Object
notify()	Object	notifyAll()	Object
printStackTrace()	Throwable	printStack-Trace(PrintStream)	Throwable
printStack-Trace(PrintWriter)	Throwable	toString()	Object
wait()	Object	wait(long)	Object
wait(long, int)	Object		

See Also

Exception, RuntimeException, Throwable

12.39   NoClassDefFoundError

Synopsis

Class Name: java.lang.NoClassDefFoundError
Superclass: java.lang.LinkageError
Immediate Subclasses: None
Interfaces Implemented: None
Availability: JDK 1.0 or later

Description

A NoClassDefFoundError is thrown when the definition of a class cannot be found.

Class Summary

```
public class java.lang.NoClassDefFoundError extends java.lang.LinkageError {
    // Constructors
    public NoClassDefFoundError();
    public NoClassDefFoundError(String s);
}
```

Constructors

NoClassDefFoundError

public NoClassDefFoundError()

    Description   This constructor creates a NoClassDefFoundError with no asso-
                 ciated detail message.

public NoClassDefFoundError(String s)

    Parameters   s   The detail message.
    Description   This constructor creates a NoClassDefFoundError with the spec-
                 ified detail message.

Inherited Methods

Method	Inherited From	Method	Inherited From
clone()	Object	equals(Object)	Object
fillInStackTrace()	Throwable	finalize()	Object
getClass()	Object	getLocalizedMessage()	Throwable
getMessage()	Throwable	hashCode()	Object

Method	Inherited From	Method	Inherited From
notify()	Object	notifyAll()	Object
printStackTrace()	Throwable	printStack-Trace(PrintStream)	Throwable
printStack-Trace(PrintWriter)	Throwable	toString()	Object
wait()	Object	wait(long)	Object
wait(long, int)	Object		

See Also

Error, LinkageError, Throwable

12.40   NoSuchFieldError

Synopsis

Class Name:	java.lang.NoSuchFieldError
Superclass:	java.lang.IncompatibleClassChangeError
Immediate Subclasses:	None
Interfaces Implemented:	None
Availability:	JDK 1.0 or later

Description

A NoSuchFieldError is thrown in response to an attempt to reference an instance or class variable that is not defined in the current definition of a class. Usually this error is caught by the compiler; it can occur at run-time if the definition of a class is changed after the class that references it was last compiled.

Class Summary

```
public class java.lang.NoSuchFieldError
          extends java.lang.IncompatibleClassChangeError {
   // Constructors
   public NoSuchFieldError();
   public NoSuchFieldError(String s);
}
```

Constructors

NoSuchFieldError

public NoSuchFieldError()

Description	This constructor creates a NoSuchFieldError with no associated detail message.

public NoSuchFieldError(String s)

Parameters	s The detail message.
Description	This constructor creates a NoSuchFieldError with the specified detail message.

Inherited Methods

Method	Inherited From	Method	Inherited From
clone()	Object	equals(Object)	Object
fillInStackTrace()	Throwable	finalize()	Object
getClass()	Object	getLocalizedMessage()	Throwable
getMessage()	Throwable	hashCode()	Object
notify()	Object	notifyAll()	Object
printStackTrace()	Throwable	printStack-Trace(PrintStream)	Throwable
printStack-Trace(PrintWriter)	Throwable	toString()	Object
wait()	Object	wait(long)	Object
wait(long, int)	Object		

See Also

Error, IncompatibleClassChangeError, Throwable

12.41   NoSuchFieldException

Synopsis

Class Name:	java.lang.NoSuchFieldException
Superclass:	java.lang.Exception
Immediate Subclasses:	None
Interfaces Implemented:	None
Availability:	New as of JDK 1.1

Description

A NoSuchFieldException is thrown when a specified variable cannot be found.

Class Summary

```
public class java.lang.NoSuchFieldException extends java.lang.Exception {
  // Constructors
  public NoSuchFieldException();
  public NoSuchFieldException(String s);
}
```

Constructors

NoSuchFieldException

public NoSuchFieldException()

    Description   This constructor creates a NoSuchFieldException with no associated detail message.

public NoSuchFieldException(String s)

    Parameters   s   The detail message.

    Description   This constructor creates a NoSuchFieldException with the specified detail message.

Inherited Methods

Method	Inherited From	Method	Inherited From
clone()	Object	equals(Object)	Object
fillInStackTrace()	Throwable	finalize()	Object
getClass()	Object	getLocalizedMessage()	Throwable
getMessage()	Throwable	hashCode()	Object
notify()	Object	notifyAll()	Object
printStackTrace()	Throwable	printStack-Trace(PrintStream)	Throwable
printStack-Trace(PrintWriter)	Throwable	toString()	Object
wait()	Object	wait(long)	Object
wait(long, int)	Object		

See Also

Exception, Throwable

12.42   NoSuchMethodError

Synopsis

Class Name: `java.lang.NoSuchMethodError`
Superclass: `java.lang.IncompatibleClassChangeError`
Immediate Subclasses: None
Interfaces Implemented: None
Availability: JDK 1.0 or later

Description

A `NoSuchMethodError` is thrown in response to an attempt to reference a method that is not defined in the current definition of a class. Usually this error is caught by the compiler; it can occur at run-time if the definition of a class is changed after the class that references it was last compiled.

Class Summary

```
public class java.lang.NoSuchMethodError
            extends java.lang.IncompatibleClassChangeError {
  // Constructors
  public NoSuchMethodError();
  public NoSuchMethodError(String s);
}
```

Constructors

NoSuchMethodError

`public NoSuchMethodError()`

Description   This constructor creates a `NoSuchMethodError` with no associated detail message.

`public NoSuchMethodError(String s)`

Parameters   s   The detail message.
Description   This constructor creates a `NoSuchMethodError` with the specified detail message.

Inherited Methods

Method	Inherited From	Method	Inherited From
clone()	Object	equals(Object)	Object
fillInStackTrace()	Throwable	finalize()	Object
getClass()	Object	getLocalizedMessage()	Throwable
getMessage()	Throwable	hashCode()	Object
notify()	Object	notifyAll()	Object

Method	Inherited From	Method	Inherited From
printStackTrace()	Throwable	printStack-Trace(PrintStream)	Throwable
printStack-Trace(PrintWriter)	Throwable	toString()	Object
wait()	Object	wait(long)	Object
wait(long, int)	Object		

See Also

Error, IncompatibleClassChangeError, Throwable

12.43   NoSuchMethodException

Synopsis

Class Name:	java.lang.NoSuchMethodException
Superclass:	java.lang.Exception
Immediate Subclasses:	None
Interfaces Implemented:	None
Availability:	JDK 1.0 or later

Description

A NoSuchMethodException is thrown when a specified method cannot be found.

Class Summary

```
public class java.lang.NoSuchMethodException extends java.lang.Exception {
    // Constructors
    public NoSuchMethodException();
    public NoSuchMethodException(String s);
}
```

Constructors

NoSuchMethodException

public NoSuchMethodException()

Description   This constructor creates a NoSuchMethodException with no associated detail message.

public NoSuchMethodException(String s)

Parameters   s   The detail message.

Description   This constructor creates a NoSuchMethodException with the specified detail message.

Inherited Methods

Method	Inherited From	Method	Inherited From
clone()	Object	equals(Object)	Object
fillInStackTrace()	Throwable	finalize()	Object
getClass()	Object	getLocalizedMessage()	Throwable
getMessage()	Throwable	hashCode()	Object
notify()	Object	notifyAll()	Object
printStackTrace()	Throwable	printStack-Trace(PrintStream)	Throwable
printStack-Trace(PrintWriter)	Throwable	toString()	Object
wait()	Object	wait(long)	Object
wait(long, int)	Object		

See Also

Exception, Throwable

12.44   NullPointerException

Synopsis

Class Name: java.lang.NullPointerException
Superclass: java.lang.RuntimeException
Immediate Subclasses: None
Interfaces Implemented: None
Availability: JDK 1.0 or later

Description

A NullPointerException is thrown when there is an attempt to access an object through a null object reference. This can occur when there is an attempt to access an instance variable or call a method through a null object or when there is an attempt to subscript an array with a null object.

Class Summary

```
public class java.lang.NullPointerException
            extends java.lang.RuntimeException {
  // Constructors
  public NullPointerException();
  public NullPointerException(String s);
}
```

Constructors

NullPointerException

public NullPointerException()

Description	This constructor creates a NullPointerException with no associated detail message.

public NullPointerException(String s)

Parameters	s	The detail message.
Description	This constructor creates a NullPointerException with the specified detail message.	

Inherited Methods

Method	Inherited From	Method	Inherited From
clone()	Object	equals(Object)	Object
fillInStackTrace()	Throwable	finalize()	Object
getClass()	Object	getLocalizedMessage()	Throwable
getMessage()	Throwable	hashCode()	Object
notify()	Object	notifyAll()	Object
printStackTrace()	Throwable	printStack-Trace(PrintStream)	Throwable
printStack-Trace(PrintWriter)	Throwable	toString()	Object
wait()	Object	wait(long)	Object
wait(long, int)	Object		

See Also

Exception, RuntimeException, Throwable

12.45   Number

Synopsis

Class Name:	java.lang.Number
Superclass:	java.lang.Object
Immediate Subclasses:	java.lang.Byte, java.lang.Double,
	java.lang.Float, java.lang.Integer,
	java.lang.Long, java.lang.Short,
	java.math.BigDecimal,
	java.math.BigInteger
Interfaces Implemented:	java.io.Serializable
Availability:	JDK 1.0 or later

Description

The Number class is an abstract class that serves as the superclass for all of the classes that provide object wrappers for primitive numeric values: byte, short, int, long, float, and double. Wrapping a primitive value is useful when you need to treat such a value as an object. For example, there are a number of utility methods that take a reference to an Object as one of their arguments. You cannot specify a primitive value for one of these arguments, but you can provide a reference to an object that encapsulates the primitive value. Furthermore, as of JDK 1.1, these wrapper classes are necessary to support the Reflection API and class literals.

The Number class defines six methods that must be implemented by its subclasses: byteValue(), shortValue(), intValue(), longValue(), floatValue(), and doubleValue(). This means that a Number object can be fetched as an byte, short, int, long, float, or double value, without regard for its actual class.

Class Summary

```
public abstract class java.lang.Number extends java.lang.Number
                                implements java.io.Serializable {
    // Instance Methods
    public abstract byte byteValue();                   // New in 1.1
    public abstract double doubleValue();
    public abstract float floatValue();
    public abstract int intValue();
    public abstract long longValue();
    public abstract short shortValue();                 // New in 1.1
}
```

Instance Methods

byteValue

```
public abstract byte byteValue()
```

Availability   New as of JDK 1.1

Returns   The value of this object as a byte.

Description   This method returns the value of this object as a byte. If the
                data type of the value is not byte, rounding may occur.

doubleValue

```
public abstract double doubleValue()
```

Returns   The value of this object as a double.

Description   This method returns the value of this object as a double. If the
                data type of the value is not double, rounding may occur.

floatValue

```
public abstract float floatValue()
```

Returns   The value of this object as a float.

Description   This method returns the value of this object as a float. If the
                data type of the value is not float, rounding may occur.

intValue

```
public abstract int intValue()
```

Returns   The value of this object as an int.

Description   This method returns the value of this object as an int. If the
                type of value is not an int, rounding may occur.

longValue

```
public abstract long longValue()
```

Returns   The value of this object as a long.

Description   This method returns the value of this object as a long. If the
                type of value is not a long, rounding may occur.

shortValue

```
public abstract short shortValue()
```

Availability   New as of JDK 1.1

Returns   The value of this object as a short.

Description   This method returns the value of this object as a short. If the
                type of value is not a short, rounding may occur.

Inherited Methods

Method	Inherited From	Method	Inherited From
clone()	Object	equals(Object)	Object
finalize()	Object	getClass()	Object
hashCode()	Object	notify()	Object
notifyAll()	Object	toString()	Object
wait()	Object	wait(long)	Object
wait(long, int)	Object		

See Also

Byte, Double, Float, Integer, Long, Object, Short

12.46   *NumberFormatException*

Synopsis

Class Name: java.lang.NumberFormatException
Superclass: java.lang.IllegalArgumentException
Immediate Subclasses: None
Interfaces Implemented: None
Availability: JDK 1.0 or later

Description

A NumberFormatException is thrown to indicate that an attempt to parse numeric information in a string has failed.

Class Summary

```
public class java.lang.NumberFormatException
            extends java.lang.IllegalArgumentException {
  // Constructors
  public NumberFormatException();
  public NumberFormatException(String s);
}
```

Constructors

NumberFormatException

`public NumberFormatException()`

Description   This constructor creates a NumberFormatException with no associated detail message.

`public NumberFormatException(String s)`

Parameters   s   The detail message.

Description   This constructor creates a NumberFormatException with the specified detail message.

Inherited Methods

Method	Inherited From	Method	Inherited From
clone()	Object	equals(Object)	Object
fillInStackTrace()	Throwable	finalize()	Object
getClass()	Object	getLocalizedMessage()	Throwable
getMessage()	Throwable	hashCode()	Object
notify()	Object	notifyAll()	Object
printStackTrace()	Throwable	printStack-Trace(PrintStream)	Throwable
printStack-Trace(PrintWriter)	Throwable	toString()	Object
wait()	Object	wait(long)	Object
wait(long, int)	Object		

See Also

Exception, IllegalArgumentException, RuntimeException, Throwable

12.47   Object

Synopsis

Class Name: java.lang.Object
Superclass: None
Immediate Subclasses: Too many to be listed here
Interfaces Implemented: None
Availability: JDK 1.0 or later

Description

The Object class is the ultimate superclass of all other classes in Java. Because every other class is a subclass of Object, all of the methods accessible from Object are inherited by every other class. In other words, all objects in Java, including arrays, have access to implementations of the methods in Object.

The methods of Object provide some basic object functionality. The equals() method compares two objects for equality, while the hashCode() method returns a hashcode for an object. The getClass() method returns the Class object associated with an object. The wait(), notify(), and notifyAll() methods support thread synchronization for an object. The toString() method provides a string representation of an object.

Some of these methods should be overridden by subclasses of Object. For example, every class should provide its own implementation of the toString() method, so that it can provide an appropriate string representation.

Although it is possible to create an instance of the Object class, this is rarely done because it is more useful to create specialized objects. However, it is often useful to declare a variable that contains a reference to an Object because such a variable can contain a reference to an object of any other class.

Class Summary

```
public class java.lang.Object {
    // Constructors
    public Object();

    // Public Instance Methods
    public boolean equals(Object obj);
    public final native Class getClass();
    public native int hashCode();
    public final native void notify();
    public final native void notifyAll();
    public String toString();
    public final native void wait();
    public final native void wait(long millis);
    public final native void wait(long millis, int nanos);

    // Protected Instance Methods
    protected native Object clone();
    protected void finalize() throws Throwable;
}
```

Constructors

Object

> public Object()
>
> Description   Creates an instance of the Object class.

Public Instance Methods

equals

> public boolean equals(Object obj)
>
> Parameters   obj   The object to be compared with this object.
>
> Returns   true if the objects are equal; false if they are not.
>
> Description   The equals() method of Object returns true if the obj parameter refers to the same object as the object this method is associated with. This is equivalent to using the == operator to compare two objects.
>
> Some classes, such as String, override the equals() method to provide a comparison based on the contents of the two objects, rather than on the strict equality of the references. Any subclass can override the equals() method to implement an appropriate comparison, as long as the overriding method satisfies the following rules for an equivalence relation:
>
> - The method is *reflexive*: given a reference x, x.equals(x) returns true.
> - The method is *symmetric*: given references x and y, x.equals(y) returns true if and only if y.equals(x) returns true.
> - The method is *transitive*: given references x, y, and z, if x.equals(y) returns true and y.equals(z) returns true, then x.equals(z) returns true.
> - The method is *consistent*: given references x and y, multiple invocations of x.equals(y) consistently return true or consistently return false, provided that no information contained by the objects referenced by x or y changes.
> - A comparison with null returns false: given a reference x that is non-null, x.equals(null) returns false.

getClass

> public final native Class getClass()
>
> Returns   A reference to the Class object that describes the class of this object.

Description   The getClass() method of Object returns the Class object that describes the class of this object. This method is final, so it cannot be overridden by subclasses.

hashCode

public native int hashCode()

Returns   A relatively unique value that should be the same for all objects that are considered equal.

Description   The hashCode() method of Object calculates a hashcode value for this object. The method returns an integer value that should be relatively unique to the object. If the equals() method for the object bases its result on the contents of the object, the hashcode() method should also base its result on the contents. The hashCode() method is provided for the benefit of hashtables, which store and retrieve elements using key values called *hashcodes*. The internal placement of a particular piece of data is determined by its hashcode; hashtables are designed to use hashcodes to provide efficient retrieval.

The java.util.Hashtable class provides an implementation of a hashtable that stores values of type Object. Each object is stored in the hashtable based on the hash code of its key object. It is important that each object have the most unique hash code possible. If two objects have the same hash code but they are not equal (as determined by equals()), a Hashtable that stores these two objects may need to spend additional time searching when it is trying to retrieve objects. The implementation of hashCode() in Object tries to make sure that every object has a distinct hash code by basing its result on the internal representation of a reference to the object.

Some classes, such as String, override the hashCode() method to produce values based on the contents of individual objects, instead of the objects themselves. In other words, two String objects that contain the exact same strings have the same hash code. If String did not override the hashCode() method inherited from Object, these two String objects would have different hash code values and it would be impossible to use String objects as keys for hashtables.

Any subclass can override the hashCode() method to implement an appropriate way of producing hash code values, as long as the overriding method satisfies the following rules:

- If the hashCode() method is called on the same object more than once during the execution of a Java application, it must consistently return the same integer value. The integer does not, however, need to be consistent between Java applications, or from one execution of an application to another execution of the same application.
- If two objects compare as equal according to their equals() methods, calls to the hashCode() methods for the objects must produce the same result.
- If two objects compare as not equal according to their equals() methods, calls to the hashCode() methods for the two objects are not required to produce distinct results. However, implementations of hashCode() that produce distinct results for unequal objects may improve the performance of hashtables.

In general, if a subclass overrides the equals() method of Object, it should also override the hashCode() method.

notify

public final native void notify()

Throws	IllegalMonitorStateException
	If the method is called from a thread that does not hold this object's lock.
Description	The notify() method wakes up a thread that is waiting to return from a call to this object's wait() method. The awakened thread can resume executing as soon as it regains this object's lock. If more than one thread is waiting, the notify() method arbitrarily awakens just one of the threads.

The notify() method can be called only by a thread that is the current owner of this object's lock. A thread holds the lock on this object while it is executing a synchronized instance method of the object or executing the body of a synchronized statement that synchronizes on the object. A thread can also hold the lock for a Class object if it is executing a synchronized static method of that class.

This method is final, so it cannot be overridden by subclasses.

notifyAll

public final native void notifyAll()

Throws	IllegalMonitorStateException
	If the method is called from a thread that does not hold this object's lock.
Description	The notifyAll() method wakes up all the threads that are waiting to return from a call to this object's wait() method. Each awakened thread can resume executing as soon as it regains this object's lock.
	The notifyAll() method can be called only by a thread that is the current owner of this object's lock. A thread holds the lock on this object while it is executing a synchronized instance method of the object or executing the body of a synchronized statement that synchronizes on the object. A thread can also hold the lock for a Class object if it is executing a synchronized static method of that class.
	This method is final, so it cannot be overridden by subclasses.

toString

public String toString()

Returns	The string representation of this object.
Description	The toString() method of Object returns a generic string representation of this object. The method returns a String that consists of the object's class name, an "at" sign, and the unsigned hexadecimal representation of the value returned by the object's hashCode() method.
	Many classes override the toString() method to provide a string representation that is specific to that type of object. Any subclass can override the toString() method; the overriding method should simply return a String that represents the contents of the object with which it is associated.

wait

public final native void wait() throws InterruptedException

Throws	IllegalMonitorStateException
	If the method is called from a thread that does not hold this object's lock.
	InterruptedException
	If another thread interrupted this thread.

Description   The wait() method causes a thread to wait until it is notified by another thread to stop waiting. When wait() is called, the thread releases its lock on this object and waits until another thread notifies it to wake up through a call to either notify() or notifyAll(). After the thread is awakened, it has to regain the lock on this object before it can resume executing.

The wait() method can be called only by a thread that is the current owner of this object's lock. A thread holds the lock on this object while it is executing a synchronized instance method of the object or executing the body of a synchronized statement that synchronizes on the object. A thread can also hold the lock for a Class object if it is executing a synchronized static method of that class.

This method is final, so it cannot be overridden by subclasses.

```
public final native void wait(long timeout)
                      throws InterruptedException
```

Parameters   timeout   The maximum number of milliseconds to wait.

Throws   IllegalMonitorStateException

If the method is called from a thread that does not hold this object's lock.

InterruptedException

If another thread interrupted this thread.

Description   The wait() method causes a thread to wait until it is notified by another thread to stop waiting or until the specified amount of time has elapsed, whichever comes first. When wait() is called, the thread releases its lock on this object and waits until another thread notifies it to wake up through a call to either notify() or notifyAll(). If the thread is not notified within the specified timeout period, it is automatically awakened when that amount of time has elapsed. If timeout is zero, the thread waits indefinitely, just as if wait() had been called without a timeout argument. After the thread is awakened, it has to regain the lock on this object before it can resume executing.

The wait() method can be called only by a thread that is the current owner of this object's lock. A thread holds the lock on this object while it is executing a synchronized instance method of the object or executing the body of a synchronized statement that synchronizes on the object. A thread can also hold the lock for a Class object if it is executing a synchronized static method of that class.

This method is final, so it cannot be overridden by subclasses.

```
public final native void wait(long timeout, int nanos)
                      throws InterruptedException
```

Parameters	timeout	The maximum number of milliseconds to wait.
	nanos	An additional number of nanoseconds to wait.
Throws	IllegalMonitorStateException	
		If the method is called from a thread that does not hold this object's lock.
	InterruptedException	
		If another thread interrupted this thread.
Description		The wait() method causes a thread to wait until it is notified by another thread to stop waiting or until the specified amount of time has elapsed, whichever comes first. When wait() is called, the thread releases its lock on this object and waits until another thread notifies it to wake up through a call to either notify() or notifyAll(). If the thread is not notified within the specified time period, it is automatically awakened when that amount of time has elapsed. If timeout and nanos are zero, the thread waits indefinitely, just as if wait() had been called without any arguments. After the thread is awakened, it has to regain the lock on this object before it can resume executing.

The wait() method can be called only by a thread that is the current owner of this object's lock. A thread holds the lock on this object while it is executing a synchronized instance method of the object or executing the body of a synchronized statement that synchronizes on the object. A thread can also hold the lock for a Class object if it is executing a synchronized static method of that class.

Note that Sun's reference implementation of Java does not attempt to implement the precision implied by this method. Instead, it rounds to the nearest millisecond (unless timeout is 0, in which case it rounds up to 1 millisecond) and calls wait(long).

This method is final, so it cannot be overridden by subclasses.

Protected Instance Methods

clone

```
protected native Object clone() throws CloneNotSupportedException
```

Returns   A clone of this object.

Throws   OutOfMemoryError

> If there is not enough memory to create the new object.

CloneNotSupportedException

> If the object is of a class that does not support clone().

Description   A *clone* of an object is another object of the same type that has all of its instance variables set to the same values as the object being cloned. In other words, a clone is an exact copy of the original object.

The clone() method of Object creates a new object that is a clone of this object. No constructor is used in creating the clone. The clone() method only clones an object if the class of that object indicates that its instances can be cloned. A class indicates that its objects can be cloned by implementing the Cloneable interface.

Although array objects do not implement the Cloneable interface, the clone() method works for arrays. The clone of an array is an array that has the same number of elements as the original array, and each element in the clone array has the same value as the corresponding element in the original array. Note that if an array element contains an object reference, the clone array contains a reference to the same object, not a copy of the object.

A subclass of Object can override the clone() method in Object to provide any additional functionality that is needed. For example, if an object contains references to other objects, the clone() method should recursively call the clone() methods of all the referenced objects. An overriding clone() method can throw a CloneNotSupportedException to indicate that particular objects cannot be cloned.

finalize

protected void finalize() throws Throwable

Throws   Throwable   For any reason that suits an overriding implementation of this method.

Description   The finalize() method is called by the garbage collector when it decides that an object can never be referenced again. The method gives an object a chance to perform any cleanup operations that are necessary before it is destroyed by the garbage collector.

The finalize() method of Object does nothing. A subclass overrides the finalize() method to perform any necessary cleanup operations. The overriding method should call super.finalize() as the very last thing it does, so that any finalize() method in the superclass is called.

When the garbage collector calls an object's finalize() method, the garbage collector does not immediately destroy the object because the finalize() method might do something that results in a reference to the object. Thus the garbage collector waits to destroy the object until it can again prove it is safe to do so. The next time the garbage collector decides it is safe to destroy the object, it does so without calling finalize() again. In other words, the garbage collector never calls the finalize() method more than once for a particular object.

A finalize() method can throw any kind of exception. An exception causes the finalize() method to stop running. The garbage collector then catches and ignores the exception, so it has no further effect on a program.

See Also

CloneNotSupportedException, IllegalMonitorStateException, InterruptedException, OutOfMemoryError, Throwable

12.48   OutOfMemoryError

Synopsis

Class Name:	java.lang.OutOfMemoryError
Superclass:	java.lang.VirtualMachineError
Immediate Subclasses:	None
Interfaces Implemented:	None
Availability:	JDK 1.0 or later

Description

An OutOfMemoryError is thrown when an attempt to allocate memory fails.

Class Summary

```
public class java.lang.OutOfMemoryError
            extends java.lang.VirtualMachineError {
  // Constructors
  public OutOfMemoryError();
  public OutOfMemoryError(String s);
}
```

Constructors

OutOfMemoryError

public OutOfMemoryError()

   Description   This constructor creates an OutOfMemoryError with no associated detail message.

public OutOfMemoryError(String s)

   Parameters   s   The detail message.

   Description   This constructor creates an OutOfMemoryError with the specified detail message.

Inherited Methods

Method	Inherited From	Method	Inherited From
clone()	Object	equals(Object)	Object
fillInStackTrace()	Throwable	finalize()	Object
getClass()	Object	getLocalizedMessage()	Throwable
getMessage()	Throwable	hashCode()	Object
notify()	Object	notifyAll()	Object
printStackTrace()	Throwable	printStack-Trace(PrintStream)	Throwable
printStack-Trace(PrintWriter)	Throwable	toString()	Object

Method	Inherited From	Method	Inherited From
wait()	Object	wait(long)	Object
wait(long, int)	Object		

See Also

Error, Throwable, VirtualMachineError

12.49   Process

Synopsis

Class Name: java.lang.Process
Superclass: java.lang.Object
Immediate Subclasses: None that are provided on all platforms. However, a platform-specific version of Java should include at least one operating-system-specific subclass.
Interfaces Implemented: None
Availability: JDK 1.0 or later

Description

The Process class describes processes that are started by the exec() method in the Runtime class. A Process object controls a process and gets information about it.

The Process class is an abstract class; therefore, it cannot be instantiated. The actual Process objects created by the exec() method belong to operating-system-specific subclasses of Process that implement the Process methods in platform-dependent ways.

Note that losing all references to a Process object, thereby making it garbage collectable, does not result in the underlying Process object dying. It merely means that there is no longer a Java object to control the process. The process itself continues to run asynchronously. In addition, no guarantees are made as to whether a controlled process will be able to continue after its parent process dies.

Class Summary

```
public abstract class java.lang.Process extends java.lang.Object {
    // Constructors
    public Process();

    // Instance Methods
    public abstract void destroy();
    public abstract int exitValue();
```

```
public abstract InputStream getErrorStream();
public abstract InputStream getInputStream();
public abstract OutputStream getOutputStream();
public abstract int waitFor();
}
```

Constructors

Process

```
public Process()
```
Description   Creates a Process object.

Instance Methods

destroy

```
abstract public void destroy()
```
Description   This method kills the process controlled by this object.

exitValue

```
abstract public int exitValue()
```
Returns   The exit value of the process controlled by this object.

Throws   IllegalThreadStateException

If the process is still running and the exit value is not yet available.

Description   This method returns the exit value of the process that this object is controlling.

The waitFor() method is a similar method that waits for the controlled process to terminate and then returns its exit value.

getErrorStream

```
abstract public InputStream getErrorStream()
```
Returns   An InputStream object connected to the error stream of the process.

Description   This method returns an InputStream object that can read from the error stream of the process.

Although it is suggested that this InputStream not be buffered, the Java specification does not forbid such an implementation. In other words, although error output from programs is traditionally unbuffered, there is no guarantee that it won't be buffered. This means that error output written by the process may not be received immediately.

getInputStream

abstract public InputStream getInputStream()

Returns	An InputStream object that is connected to the standard output stream of the process.
Description	This method returns an InputStream object that can read from the standard output stream of the process.

This InputStream is likely to be buffered, which means that output written by the process may not be received immediately.

getOutputStream

abstract public OutputStream getOutputStream()

Returns	An OutputStream object that is connected to the standard input stream of the process.
Description	This method returns an OutputStream object that can write to the standard input stream of the process.

This OutputStream is likely to be buffered, which means that input sent to the process may not be received until the buffer fills up or a new line or carriage-return character is sent.

waitFor

abstract public int waitFor()

Returns	The exit value of the process controlled by this object.
Throws	InterruptedException
	If another thread interrupts this thread while it is waiting for the process to exit.
Description	This method returns the exit value of the process that this object is controlling. If the process is still running, the method waits until the process terminates and its exit value is available.

The exitValue() method is a similar method that does not wait for the controlled process to terminate.

Inherited Methods

Method	Inherited From	Method	Inherited From
clone()	Object	equals(Object)	Object
finalize()	Object	getClass()	Object
hashCode()	Object	notify()	Object
notifyAll()	Object	toString()	Object
wait()	Object	wait(long)	Object
wait(long, int)	Object		

See Also

InterruptedException, Object, Runtime

12.50   Runnable

Synopsis

Interface Name: java.lang.Runnable
Super-interface: None
Immediate Sub-interfaces:
                         None
Implemented By: java.lang.Thread
Availability: JDK 1.0 or later

Description

The Runnable interface declares the run() method that is required for use with the Thread class. Any class that implements the Runnable interface must define a run() method. This method is the top-level code that is run by a thread.

Interface Declaration

```
public interface java.lang.Runnable {
    // Methods
    public abstract void run();
}
```

Methods

run

public abstract void run()

Description   When a Thread object starts running a thread, it associates executable code with the thread by calling a Runnable object's run() method. The subsequent behavior of the thread is controlled by the run() method. Thus, a class that wants to perform certain operations in a separate thread should implement the Runnable interface and define an appropriate run() method. When the run() method called by a Thread object returns or throws an exception, the thread dies.

See Also

Thread, ThreadGroup

12.51   Runtime

Synopsis

Class Name:	java.lang.Runtime
Superclass:	java.lang.Object
Immediate Subclasses:	None
Interfaces Implemented:	None
Availability:	JDK 1.0 or later

Description

The Runtime class provides access to various information about the environment in which a program is running. The Java run-time environment creates a single instance of this class that is associated with a program. The Runtime class does not have any public constructors, so a program cannot create its own instances of the class. A program must call the getRuntime() method to get a reference to the current Runtime object.

Information about operating system features is accessible through the System class.

Class Summary

```
public class java.lang.Runtime extends java.lang.Object {
    // Class Methods
    public static Runtime getRuntime();
    public static void runFinalizersOnExit(boolean value);   // New in 1.1

    // Instance Methods
    public Process exec(String command);
    public Process exec(String command, String envp[]);
    public Process exec(String cmdarray[]);
    public Process exec(String cmdarray[], String envp[]);
    public void exit(int status);
    public native long freeMemory();
    public native void gc();
    public InputStream
        getLocalizedInputStream(InputStream in);     // Deprecated in 1.1
    public OutputStream
        getLocalizedOutputStream(OutputStream out);   // Deprecated in 1.1
    public synchronized void load(String filename);
    public synchronized void loadLibrary(String libname);
    public native void runFinalization();
```

```
public native long totalMemory();
public native void traceInstructions(boolean on);
public native void traceMethodCalls(boolean on);
}
```

Class Methods

getRuntime

`public static Runtime getRuntime()`

Returns	A reference to the current Runtime object.
Description	This method returns a reference to the current Runtime object. Because the other methods of the Runtime class are not static, a program must call this method first in order to get a reference to a Runtime object that can be used in calling the other methods.

runFinalizersOnExit

`public static void runFinalizersOnExit(boolean value)`

Availability	New as of JDK 1.1	
Parameters	value	A boolean value that specifies whether or not finalization occurs on exit.
Throws	SecurityException	
		If the checkExit() method of the SecurityManager throws a SecurityException.
Description	This method specifies whether or not the finalize() methods of all objects that have finalize() methods are run before the Java virtual machine exits. By default, the finalizers are not run on exit.	

Instance Methods

exec

`public Process exec(String command) throws IOException`

Parameters	command	A string that contains the name of an external command and any arguments to be passed to it.
Returns		A Process object that controls the process started by this method.
Throws	IOException	If there is a problem finding or accessing the specified external command.
	SecurityException	
		If the checkExec() method of the SecurityManager throws a SecurityException.

Description	This method starts a new process to execute the given external command. The standard input, standard output, and standard error streams from the process are redirected to OutputStream and InputStream objects that are accessible through the Process object returned by this method.

Calling this method is equivalent to:

```
exec(command, null)
```

public Process exec(String command, String[] envp)
throws IOException

Parameters	command	A string that contains the name of an external command and any arguments to be passed to it.
	envp	An array of strings that specifies the values for the environment variables of the new process. Each String in the array should be of the form *variableName=value*. If envp is null, the values of the environment variables in the current process are copied to the new process.
Returns	A Process object that controls the process started by this method.	
Throws	IOException	If there is a problem finding or accessing the specified external command.
	SecurityException	
		If the checkExec() method of the SecurityManager throws a SecurityException.
Description	This method starts a new process to execute the given external command. The standard input, standard output, and standard error streams from the process are redirected to OutputStream and InputStream objects that are accessible through the Process object returned by this method.	

The method parses the command string into words that are separated by whitespace. It creates a String object for each word and places word String objects into an array. If that array is called commandArray, calling this method is equivalent to:

```
exec(commandArray, envp)
```

public Process exec(String[] commandArray) throws IOException

Parameters	commandArray	
		An array of strings that contains separate strings for the name of an external command and any arguments to be passed to it. The first string in the array must be the command name.

Returns	A Process object that controls the process started by this method.
Throws	IOException If there is a problem finding or accessing the specified external command.
	SecurityException
	If the checkExec() method of the SecurityManager throws a SecurityException.
Description	This method starts a new process to execute the given external command. The standard input, standard output, and standard error streams from the process are redirected to OutputStream and InputStream objects that are accessible through the Process object returned by this method.

Calling this method is equivalent to:

```
exec(commandArray, null)
```

public Process exec(String[] commandArray, String[] envp)
                throws IOException

Parameters	commandArray
	An array of strings that contains separate strings for the name of an external command and any arguments to be passed to it. The first string in the array must be the command name.
	envp
	An array of strings that specifies the values for the environment variables of the new process. Each String in the array should be of the form *variableName=value*. If envp is null, the values of the environment variables in the current process are copied to the new process.
Returns	A Process object that controls the process started by this method.
Throws	IOException If there is a problem finding or accessing the specified external command.
	SecurityException
	If the checkExec() method of the SecurityManager throws a SecurityException.
Description	This method starts a new process to execute the given external command. The standard input, standard output, and standard error streams from the process are redirected to OutputStream and InputStream objects that are accessible through the Process object returned by this method.

exit

public void exit(int status)

Parameters	status	The exit status code to use.
Throws	SecurityException	
		If the checkExit() method of the SecurityManager throws a SecurityException.
Description		This method causes the Java virtual machine to exit with the given status code. By convention, a nonzero status code indicates abnormal termination. This method never returns.

freeMemory

public native long freeMemory()

Returns	An estimate of the number of free bytes in system memory.
Description	This method returns an estimate of the number of free bytes in system memory. The value returned by this method is always less than the value returned by totalMemory(). Additional memory may be freed by calling the gc() method.

gc

public native void gc()

Description	This method causes the Java virtual machine to run the garbage collector in the current thread.
	The garbage collector finds objects that will never be used again because there are no live references to them. After it finds these objects, the garbage collector frees the storage occupied by these objects.
	The garbage collector is normally run continuously in a thread with the lowest possible priority, so that it works intermittently to reclaim storage. The gc() method allows a program to invoke the garbage collector explicitly when necessary.

getLocalizedInputStream

public InputStream getLocalizedInputStream(InputStream in)

Availability	Deprecated as of JDK 1.1	
Parameters	in	An InputStream object that is to be localized.
Returns	The localized InputStream.	
Description	This method returns an InputStream object that converts characters from the local character set to Unicode. For example, if the InputStream uses an 8-bit character set with values less than 128 representing Cyrillic letters, this method maps those char-	

acters to the corresponding Unicode characters in the range
'\u0400' to '\u04FF'.

This method is deprecated as of JDK 1.1. You should instead
use the new InputStreamReader and BufferedReader classes to
convert characters from the local character set to Unicode.

getLocalizedOutputStream

public OutputStream getLocalizedOutputStream(OutputStream out)

Availability	Deprecated as of JDK 1.1
Parameters	out An OutputStream object that is to be localized.
Returns	The localized OutputStream.
Description	This method returns an OutputStream object that converts characters from Unicode to the local character set. For example, if the local character set is an 8-bit character set with values less than 128 representing Cyrillic letters, this method maps Unicode characters in the range '\u0400' to '\u04FF' to the appropriate characters in the local character set.

This method is deprecated as of JDK 1.1. You should instead
use the new OutputStreamWriter and BufferedWriter classes
to convert characters from Unicode to the local character set.

load

public synchronized void load(String filename)

Parameters	filename A string that specifies the complete path of the file to be loaded.
Throws	SecurityException
	If the checkLink() method of the SecurityManager throws a SecurityException.
	UnsatisfiedLinkError
	If the method is unsuccessful in loading the specified dynamically linked library.
Description	This method loads the specified dynamically linked library.

It is often more convenient to call the load() method of the
System class because it does not require getting a Runtime
object.

loadLibrary

public synchronized void loadLibrary(String libname)

Parameters   libname   A string that specifies the name of a dynamically linked library.

Throws   SecurityException

If the checkLink() method of the SecurityManager throws a SecurityException.

UnsatisfiedLinkError

If the method is unsuccessful in loading the specified dynamically linked library.

Description   This method loads the specified dynamically linked library. It looks for the specified library in a platform-specific way.

It is often more convenient to call the loadLibrary() method of the System class because it does not require getting a Runtime object.

runFinalization

public native void runFinalization()

Description   This method causes the Java virtual machine to run the finalize() methods of any objects in the finalization queue in the current thread.

When the garbage collector discovers that there are no references to an object, it checks to see if the object has a finalize() method that has never been called. If the object has such a finalize() method, the object is placed in the finalization queue. While there is a reference to the object in the finalization queue, the object is no longer considered garbage-collectable.

Normally, the objects in the finalization queue are handled by a separate finalization thread that runs continuously at a very low priority. The finalization thread removes an object from the queue and calls its finalize() method. As long as the finalize() method does not generate a reference to the object, the object again becomes available for garbage collection.

Because the finalization thread runs at a very low priority, there may be a long delay from the time that an object is put on the finalization queue until the time that its finalize() method is called. The runFinalization() method allows a program to run the finalize() methods explicitly. This can be useful when there is a shortage of some resource that is released by a finalize() method.

totalMemory

```
public native long totalMemory()
```

Returns   The total number of bytes in system memory.

Description   This method returns the total number of bytes in system memory in the Java virtual machine. The total includes the number of bytes of memory being used by allocated objects, as well as the number of free bytes available for allocating additional objects. An estimate of the number of free bytes in system memory is available through the freeMemory() method.

traceInstructions

```
public native void traceInstructions(boolean on)
```

Parameters   on   A boolean value that specifies if instructions are to be traced. true if instructions are to be traced; otherwise false.

Description   This method controls whether or not the Java virtual machine outputs a detailed trace of each instruction that is executed. The boolean parameter causes tracing to be turned on or off. The tracing of instructions is only possible in a Java virtual machine that was compiled with the tracing option enabled. Production releases of the Java virtual machine are generally not compiled with tracing enabled.

traceMethodCalls

```
public native void traceMethodCalls(boolean on)
```

Parameters   on   A boolean value that specifies if method calls are to be traced. true if instructions are to be traced; otherwise false.

Description   This method controls whether or not the Java virtual machine outputs a detailed trace of each method that is invoked. The boolean parameter causes tracing to be turned on or off. The tracing of instructions is only possible in a Java virtual machine that was compiled with the tracing option enabled. Production releases of the Java virtual machine are generally not compiled with tracing enabled.

Inherited Methods

Method	Inherited From	Method	Inherited From
clone()	Object	equals(Object)	Object
finalize()	Object	getClass()	Object
hashCode()	Object	notify()	Object
notifyAll()	Object	toString()	Object
wait()	Object	wait(long)	Object
wait(long, int)	Object		

See Also

IOException, Object, Process, SecurityException, SecurityManager, System, UnsatisfiedLinkError

12.52   RuntimeException

Synopsis

Class Name:	java.lang.RuntimeException
Superclass:	java.lang.Exception
Immediate Subclasses:	java.lang.ArithmeticException,
	java.lang.ArrayStoreException,
	java.lang.ClassCastException,
	java.lang.IllegalArgumentException,
	java.lang.IllegalMonitorStateException,
	java.lang.IllegalStateException,
	java.lang.IndexOutOfBoundsException,
	java.lang.NegativeArraySizeException,
	java.lang.NullPointerException,
	java.lang.SecurityException,
	java.util.EmptyStackException,
	java.util.MissingResourceException,
	java.util.NoSuchElementException
Interfaces Implemented:	None
Availability:	JDK 1.0 or later

Description

The RuntimeException class is the superclass of the standard run-time exceptions that can be thrown in Java. The appropriate subclass of RuntimeException is thrown in response to a run-time error detected at the virtual machine level. A run-time exception represents a run-time condition that can occur generally in any Java method, so a method is not required to declare that it throws any of the run-time exceptions.

A Java program should try to handle all of the standard run-time exception classes, since they represent routine abnormal conditions that should be anticipated and caught to prevent program termination.

Class Summary

```
public class java.lang.RuntimeException extends java.lang.Exception {
    // Constructors
    public RuntimeException();
    public RuntimeException(String s);
}
```

Constructors

RuntimeException

public RuntimeException()

    Description   This constructor creates a RuntimeException with no associated detail message.

public RuntimeException(String s)

    Parameters   s   The detail message.

    Description   This constructor creates a RuntimeException with the specified detail message.

Inherited Methods

Method	Inherited From	Method	Inherited From
clone()	Object	equals(Object)	Object
fillInStackTrace()	Throwable	finalize()	Object
getClass()	Object	getLocalizedMessage()	Throwable
getMessage()	Throwable	hashCode()	Object
notify()	Object	notifyAll()	Object
printStackTrace()	Throwable	printStack-Trace(PrintStream)	Throwable
printStack-Trace(PrintWriter)	Throwable	toString()	Object
wait()	Object	wait(long)	Object
wait(long, int)	Object		

See Also

ArithmeticException, ArrayStoreException, ClassCastException, EmptyStack-Exception, IllegalArgumentException, IllegalMonitorStateException, IllegalStateException, IndexOutOfBoundsException, MissingResourceException, NegativeArraySizeException, NoSuchElementException, NullPointerException, SecurityException, Throwable

12.53   SecurityException

Synopsis

Class Name:	java.lang.SecurityException
Superclass:	java.lang.RuntimeException
Immediate Subclasses:	None
Interfaces Implemented:	None
Availability:	JDK 1.0 or later

Description

A SecurityException is thrown in response to an attempt to perform an operation that violates the security policy implemented by the installed SecurityManager object.

Class Summary

```
public class java.lang.SecurityException
          extends java.lang.RuntimeException {
    // Constructors
    public SecurityException();
    public SecurityException(String s);
}
```

Constructors

SecurityException

public SecurityException()

Description   This constructor creates a SecurityException with no associated detail message.

public SecurityException(String s)

Parameters   s   The detail message.

Description   This constructor creates a SecurityException with the specified detail message.

Inherited Methods

Method	Inherited From	Method	Inherited From
clone()	Object	equals(Object)	Object
fillInStackTrace()	Throwable	finalize()	Object
getClass()	Object	getLocalizedMessage()	Throwable
getMessage()	Throwable	hashCode()	Object
notify()	Object	notifyAll()	Object
printStackTrace()	Throwable	printStack- Trace(PrintStream)	Throwable
printStack- Trace(PrintWriter)	Throwable	toString()	Object
wait()	Object	wait(long)	Object
wait(long, int)	Object		

See Also

Exception, RuntimeException, SecurityManager, Throwable

12.54   SecurityManager

Synopsis

Class Name:	java.lang.SecurityManager
Superclass:	java.lang.Object
Immediate Subclasses:	None
Interfaces Implemented:	None
Availability:	JDK 1.0 or later

Description

The SecurityManager class provides a way of implementing a comprehensive security policy for a Java program. As of this writing, SecurityManager objects are used primarily by Web browsers to establish security policies for applets. However, the use of a SecurityManager object is appropriate in any situation where a hosting environment wants to limit the actions of hosted programs.

The SecurityManager class contains methods that are called by methods in other classes to ask for permission to do something that can affect the security of the system. These permission methods all have names that begin with check. If a check method does not permit an action, it throws a SecurityException or returns a value that indicates the lack of permission. The SecurityManager class provides default implementations of all of the check methods. These default implementations are the most restrictive possible implementations; they simply deny permission to do anything that can affect the security of the system.

The SecurityManager class is an abstract class. A hosting environment should define a subclass of SecurityManager that implements an appropriate security policy. To give the subclass of SecurityManager control over security, the hosting environment creates an instance of the class and installs it by passing it to the setSecurityManager() method of the System class. Once a SecurityManager object is installed, it cannot be changed. If the setSecurityManager() method is called any additional times, it throws a SecurityException.

The methods in other classes that want to ask the SecurityManager for permission to do something are able to access the SecurityManager object by calling the get-SecurityManager() method of the System class. This method returns the SecurityManager object, or null to indicate that there is no SecurityManager installed.

Class Summary

```
public abstract class java.lang.SecurityManager extends java.lang.Object {
    // Constructors
    protected SecurityManager();

    // Variables
    protected boolean inCheck;

    // Instance Methods
    public void checkAccept(String host, int port);
    public void checkAccess(Thread t);
    public void checkAccess(ThreadGroup g);
    public void checkAwtEventQueueAccess();                      // New in 1.1
    public void checkConnect(String host, int port);
    public void checkConnect(String host, int port, Object context);
    public void checkCreateClassLoader();
    public void checkDelete(String file);
    public void checkExec(String cmd);
    public void checkExit(int status);
    public void checkLink(String libname);
    public void checkListen(int port);
    public void checkMemberAccess(Class clazz, int which);   // New in 1.1
    public void checkMulticast(InetAddress maddr);           // New in 1.1
    public void checkMulticast(InetAddress maddr, byte ttl); // New in 1.1
    public void checkPackageAccess();
    public void checkPackageDefinition();
    public void checkPrintJobAccess();                       // New in 1.1
    public void checkPropertiesAccess();
```

```
            public void checkPropertyAccess(String key);
            public void checkRead(int fd);
            public void checkRead(String file);
            public void checkRead(String file, Object context);
            public void checkSecurityAccess(String action);        // New in 1.1
            public void checkSetFactory();
            public void checkSystemClipboardAccess();               // New in 1.1
            public boolean checkTopLevelWindow();
            public void checkWrite(int fd);
            public void checkWrite(String file);
            public boolean getInCheck();
            public Object getSecurityContext();
            public ThreadGroup getThreadGroup();                    // New in 1.1


            // Protected Instance Methods
            protected int classDepth(String name);
            protected int classLoaderDepth();
            protected ClassLoader currentClassLoader();
            protected Class currentLoadedClass();                   // New in 1.1
            protected Class[] getClassContext();
            protected boolean inClass(String name);
            protected boolean inClassLoader();
    }
```

Variables

inCheck

`protected boolean inCheck = false`

Description   This variable indicates whether or not a security check is in progress. A subclass of SecurityManager should set this variable to true while a security check is in progress.

This variable can be useful for security checks that require access to resources that a hosted program may not be permitted to access. For example, a security policy might be based on the contents of a permissions file. This means that the various check methods need to read information from a file to decide what to do. Even though a hosted program may not be allowed to read files, the check methods can allow such reads when inCheck is true to support this style of security policy.

Constructors

SecurityManager

protected SecurityManager()

Throws	SecurityException
	If a SecurityManager object already exists. In other words, if System.getSecurityManager() returns a value other than null.
Description	Creates a new SecurityManager object. This constructor cannot be called if there is already a current SecurityManager installed for the program.

Public Instance Methods

checkAccept

public void checkAccept(String host, int port)

Parameters	host	The name of the host machine.
	port	A port number.
Throws	SecurityException	
	If the caller does not have permission to accept the connection.	
Description	This method decides whether or not to allow a connection from the given host on the given port to be accepted. An implementation of the method should throw a SecurityException to deny permission to accept the connection. The method is called by the accept() method of the java.net.ServerSocket class.	
	The checkAccept() method of SecurityManager always throws a SecurityException.	

checkAccess

public void checkAccess(Thread g)

Parameters	g	A reference to a Thread object.
Throws	SecurityException	
	If the current thread does not have permission to modify the specified thread.	
Description	This method decides whether or not to allow the current thread to modify the specified Thread. An implementation of the method should throw a SecurityException to deny permission to modify the thread. Methods of the Thread class that call this method include stop(), suspend(), resume(), setPriority(), setName(), and setDaemon().	

The `checkAccess()` method of `SecurityManager` always throws a `SecurityException`.

public void checkAccess(ThreadGroup g)

Parameters	g	A reference to a `ThreadGroup` object.
Throws	SecurityException	
		If the current thread does not have permission to modify the specified thread group.
Description		This method decides whether or not to allow the current thread to modify the specified `ThreadGroup`. An implementation of the method should throw a `SecurityException` to deny permission to modify the thread group. Methods of the `ThreadGroup` class that call this method include `setDaemon()`, `setMaxPriority()`, `stop()`, `suspend()`, `resume()`, and `destroy()`.

The `checkAccess()` method of `SecurityManager` always throws a `SecurityException`.

checkAwtEventQueueAccess

public void checkAwtEventQueueAccess()

Availability	New as of JDK 1.1	
Throws	SecurityException	
		If the caller does not have permission to access the AWT event queue.
Description		This method decides whether or not to allow access to the AWT event queue. An implementation of the method should throw a `SecurityException` to deny permission to access the event queue. The method is called by the `getSystemEventQueue()` method of the `java.awt.Toolkit` class.

The `checkAwtEventQueueAccess()` method of `SecurityManager` always throws a `SecurityException`.

checkConnect

public void checkConnect(String host, int port)

Parameters	host	The name of the host.
	port	A port number. A value of -1 indicates an attempt to determine the IP address of given hostname.
Throws	SecurityException	
		If the caller does not have permission to open the socket connection.

Description This method decides whether or not to allow a socket connection to the given host on the given port to be opened. An implementation of the method should throw a SecurityException to deny permission to open the connection. The method is called by the constructors of the java.net.Socket class, the send() and receive() methods of the java.net.DatagramSocket class, and the getByName() and getAllByName() methods of the java.net.InetAddress class.

The checkConnect() method of SecurityManager always throws a SecurityException.

```
public void checkConnect(String host, int port,
                Object context)
```

Parameters host The name of the host.

port A port number. A value of -1 indicates an attempt to determine the IP address of given host name.

context A security context object returned by this object's getSecurityContext() method.

Throws SecurityException

If the specified security context does not have permission to open the socket connection.

Description This method decides whether or not to allow a socket connection to the given host on the given port to be opened for the specified security context. An implementation of the method should throw a SecurityException to deny permission to open the connection.

The checkConnect() method of SecurityManager always throws a SecurityException.

checkCreateClassLoader

```
public void checkCreateClassLoader()
```

Throws SecurityException

If the caller does not have permission to create a ClassLoader object.

Description This method decides whether or not to allow a ClassLoader object to be created. An implementation of the method should throw a SecurityException to deny permission to create a ClassLoader. The method is called by the constructor of the ClassLoader class.

The checkCreateClassLoader() method of SecurityManager always throws a SecurityException.

checkDelete

public void checkDelete(String file)

Parameters	file	The name of a file.
Throws	SecurityException	
		If the caller does not have permission to delete the specified file.
Description		This method decides whether or not to allow a file to be deleted. An implementation of the method should throw a SecurityException to deny permission to delete the specified file. The method is called by the delete() method of the java.io.File class.

The checkDelete() method of SecurityManager always throws a SecurityException.

checkExec

public void checkExec(String cmd)

Parameters	cmd	The name of an external command.
Throws	SecurityException	
		If the caller does not have permission to execute the specified command.
Description		This method decides whether or not to allow an external command to be executed. An implementation of the method should throw a SecurityException to deny permission to execute the specified command. The method is called by the exec() methods of the Runtime and System classes.

The checkExec() method of SecurityManager always throws a SecurityException.

checkExit

public void checkExit(int status)

Parameters	status	An exit status code.
Throws	SecurityException	
		If the caller does not have permission to exit the Java virtual machine with the given status code.
Description		This method decides whether or not to allow the Java virtual machine to exit with the given status code. An implementation of the method should throw a SecurityException to deny permission to exit with the specified status code. The method is called by the exit() methods of the Runtime and System classes.

The checkExit() method of SecurityManager always throws a SecurityException.

checkLink

public void checkLink(String lib)

Parameters	lib	The name of a library.
Throws	SecurityException	
		If the caller does not have permission to load the specified library.
Description		This method decides whether to allow the specified library to be loaded. An implementation of the method should throw a SecurityException to deny permission to load the specified library. The method is called by the load() and loadLibrary() methods of the Runtime and System classes.

The checkLink() method of SecurityManager always throws a SecurityException.

checkListen

public void checkListen(int port)

Parameters	port	A port number.
Throws	SecurityException	
		If the caller does not have permission to listen on the specified port.
Description		This method decides whether or not to allow the caller to listen on the specified port. An implementation of the method should throw a SecurityException to deny permission to listen on the specified port. The method is called by the constructors of the java.net.ServerSocket class and by the constructor of the java.net.DatagramSocket class that takes one argument.

The checkListen() method of SecurityManager always throws a SecurityException.

checkMemberAccess

public void checkMemberAccess(Class clazz, int which)

Availability	New as of JDK 1.1	
Parameters	clazz	A Class object.
	which	The value Member.PUBLIC for the set of all public members including inherited members or the value Member.DECLARED for the set of all declared members of the specified class or interface.

Throws   SecurityException

                If the caller does not have permission to access
                the members of the specified class or interface.

Description   This method decides whether or not to allow access to the
                members of the specified Class object. An implementation of
                the method should throw a SecurityException to deny permis-
                sion to access the members. Methods of the Class class that call
                this method include getField(), getFields(), getDeclared-
                Field(), getDeclaredFields(), getMethod(), getMethods(),
                getDeclaredMethod(), getDeclaredMethods(), getConstruc-
                tor(), getConstructors(), getDeclaredConstructor(), getDe-
                claredConstructors(), and getDeclaredClasses().

                The checkMemberAccess() method of SecurityManager always
                throws a SecurityException.

checkMulticast

public void checkMulticast(InetAddress maddr)

Availability   New as of JDK 1.1

Parameters   maddr   An InetAddress object that represents a multi-
                             cast address.

Throws   SecurityException

                             If the current thread does not have permission
                             to use the specified multicast address.

Description   This method decides whether or not to allow the current
                thread to use the specified multicast InetAddress. An imple-
                mentation of the method should throw a SecurityException to
                deny permission to use the multicast address. The method is
                called by the send() method of java.net.DatagramSocket if
                the packet is being sent to a multicast address. The method is
                also called by the joinGroup() and leaveGroup() methods of
                java.net.MulticastSocket.

                The checkMulticast() method of SecurityManager always
                throws a SecurityException.

public void checkMulticast(InetAddress maddr, byte ttl)

Availability   New as of JDK 1.1

Parameters   maddr   An InetAddress object that represents a multi-
                             cast address.

                ttl   The time-to-live (TTL) value.

Throws   SecurityException

> If the current thread does not have permission to use the specified multicast address and TTL value.

Description   This method decides whether or not to allow the current thread to use the specified multicast `InetAddress` and TTL value. An implementation of the method should throw a `SecurityException` to deny permission to use the multicast address. The method is called by the `send()` method of `java.net.MulticastSocket`.

The `checkMulticast()` method of `SecurityManager` always throws a `SecurityException`.

checkPackageAccess

```
public void checkPackageAccess(String pkg)
```
Parameters   pkg   The name of a package.
Throws   SecurityException

> If the caller does not have permission to access the specified package.

Description   This method decides whether or not to allow the specified package to be accessed. An implementation of the method should throw a `SecurityException` to deny permission to access the specified package. The method is intended to be called by implementations of the `loadClass()` method in subclasses of the `ClassLoader` class.

The `checkPackageAccess()` method of `SecurityManager` always throws a `SecurityException`.

checkPackageDefinition

```
public void checkPackageDefinition(String pkg)
```
Parameters   pkg   The name of a package.
Throws   SecurityException

> If the caller does not have permission to define classes in the specified package.

Description   This method decides whether or not to allow the caller to define classes in the specified package. An implementation of the method should throw a `SecurityException` to deny permission to create classes in the specified package. The method is intended to be called by implementations of the `loadClass()` method in subclasses of the `ClassLoader` class.

The checkPackageDefinition() method of SecurityManager always throws a SecurityException.

checkPrintJobAccess

public void checkPrintJobAccess()
Availability	New as of JDK 1.1
Throws	SecurityException

If the caller does not have permission to initiate a print job request.

Description	This method decides whether or not to allow the caller to initiate a print job request. An implementation of the method should throw a SecurityException to deny permission to initiate the request.

The checkPrintJobAccess() method of SecurityManager always throws a SecurityException.

checkPropertiesAccess

public void checkPropertiesAccess()
Throws	SecurityException

If the caller does not have permission to access the system properties.

Description	This method decides whether or not to allow the caller to access and modify the system properties. An implementation of the method should throw a SecurityException to deny permission to access and modify the properties. Methods of the System class that call this method include getProperties() and setProperties().

The checkPropertiesAccess() method of SecurityManager always throws a SecurityException.

checkPropertyAccess

public void checkPropertyAccess(String key)
Parameters	key	The name of an individual system property.
Throws	SecurityException	

If the caller does not have permission to access the specified system property.

Description	This method decides whether or not to allow the caller to access the specified system property. An implementation of the method should throw a SecurityException to deny permission to access the property. The method is called by the getProperty() method of the System class.

The checkPropertyAccess() method of SecurityManager always throws a SecurityException.

checkRead

public void checkRead(FileDescriptor fd)

Parameters	fd	A reference to a FileDescriptor object.
Throws	SecurityException	
		If the caller does not have permission to read from the given file descriptor.
Description		This method decides whether or not to allow the caller to read from the specified file descriptor. An implementation of the method should throw a SecurityException to deny permission to read from the file descriptor. The method is called by the constructor of the java.io.FileInputStream class that takes a FileDescriptor argument.

The checkRead() method of SecurityManager always throws a SecurityException.

public void checkRead(String file)

Parameters	file	The name of a file.
Throws	SecurityException	
		If the caller does not have permission to read from the named file.
Description		This method decides whether or not to allow the caller to read from the named file. An implementation of the method should throw a SecurityException to deny permission to read from the file. The method is called by constructors of the java.io.FileInputStream and java.io.RandomAccessFile classes, as well as by the canRead(), exists(), isDirectory(), isFile(), lastModified(), length(), and list() methods of the java.io.File class.

The checkRead() method of SecurityManager always throws a SecurityException.

public void checkRead(String file, Object context)

Parameters	file	The name of a file.
	context	A security context object returned by this object's getSecurityContext() method.
Throws	SecurityException	
		If the specified security context does not have permission to read from the named file.

Description   This method decides whether or not to allow the specified secu-
                  rity context to read from the named file. An implementation of
                  the method should throw a SecurityException to deny permis-
                  sion to read from the file.

                  The checkRead() method of SecurityManager always throws a
                  SecurityException.

checkSecurityAccess

    public void checkSecurityAccess(String action)
        Availability   New as of JDK 1.1
        Parameters   action   A string that specifies a security action.
        Throws   SecurityException
                        If the caller does not have permission to per-
                        form the specified security action.
        Description   This method decides whether to allow the caller to perform the
                        specified security action. An implementation of the method
                        should throw a SecurityException to deny permission to per-
                        form the action. The method is called by many of the methods
                        in the java.security.Identity and java.security.Security
                        classes.

                        The checkSecurityAccess() method of SecurityManager
                        always throws a SecurityException.

checkSetFactory

    public void checkSetFactory()
        Throws   SecurityException
                        If the caller does not have permission to set the
                        factory class to be used by another class.
        Description   This method decides whether to allow the caller to set the fac-
                        tory class to be used by another class. An implementation of the
                        method should throw a SecurityException to deny permission
                        to set the factory class. The method is called by the setSocket-
                        Factory() method of the java.net.ServerSocket class, the
                        setSocketImplFactory() method of the java.net.Socket
                        class, the setURLStreamHandlerFactory() method of the
                        java.net.URL class, and the setContentHandlerFactory()
                        method of the java.net.URLConnection class.

                        The checkSetFactory() method of SecurityManager always
                        throws a SecurityException.

checkSystemClipboardAccess

public void checkSystemClipboardAccess()

Availability	New as of JDK 1.1
Throws	SecurityException
	If the caller does not have permission to access the system clipboard.
Description	This method decides whether or not to allow the caller to access the system clipboard. An implementation of the method should throw a SecurityException to deny permission to access the system clipboard.

The checkSystemClipboardAccess() method of SecurityManager always throws a SecurityException.

checkTopLevelWindow

public boolean checkTopLevelWindow(Object window)

Parameters	window A window object.
Returns	true if the caller is trusted to put up the specified top-level window; otherwise false.
Description	This method decides whether or not to trust the caller to put up the specified top-level window. An implementation of the method should return false to indicate that the caller is not trusted. In this case, the hosting environment can still decide to display the window, but the window should include a visual indication that it is not trusted. If the caller is trusted, the method should return true, and the window can be displayed without any special indication.

The checkTopLevelWindow() method of SecurityManager always returns false.

checkWrite

public void checkWrite(FileDescriptor fd)

Parameters	fd A FileDescriptor object.
Throws	SecurityException
	If the caller does not have permission to write to the given file descriptor.
Description	This method decides whether or not to allow the caller to write to the specified file descriptor. An implementation of the method should throw a SecurityException to deny permission to write to the file descriptor. The method is called by the constructor of the java.io.FileOutputStream class that takes a FileDescriptor argument.

The checkWrite() method of SecurityManager always throws a SecurityException.

public void checkWrite(String file)

Parameters   file   The name of a file.

Throws   SecurityException

        If the caller does not have permission to read from the named file.

Description   This method decides whether or not to allow the caller to write to the named file. An implementation of the method should throw a SecurityException to deny permission to write to the file. The method is called by constructors of the java.io.FileOutputStream and java.io.RandomAccessFile classes, as well as by the canWrite(), mkdir(), and renameTo() methods of the java.io.File class.

The checkWrite() method of SecurityManager always throws a SecurityException.

getInCheck

public boolean getInCheck()

Returns   true if a security check is in progress; otherwise false.

Description   This method returns the value of the SecurityManager object's inCheck variable, which is true if a security check is in progress and false otherwise.

getSecurityContext

public Object getSecurityContext()

Returns   An implementation-dependent object that contains enough information about the current execution environment to perform security checks at a later time.

Description   This method is meant to create an object that encapsulates information about the current execution environment. The resulting security context object is used by specific versions of the checkConnect() and checkRead() methods. The intent is that such a security context object can be used by a trusted method to determine whether or not another, untrusted method can perform a particular operation.

The getSecurityContext() method of SecurityManager simply returns null. This method should be overridden to return an appropriate security context object for the security policy that is being implemented.

getThreadGroup

public ThreadGroup getThreadGroup()

Availability	New as of JDK 1.1
Returns	A ThreadGroup in which to place any threads that are created when this method is called.
Description	This method returns the appropriate parent ThreadGroup for any threads that are created when the method is called. The getThreadGroup() method of SecurityManager simply returns the ThreadGroup of the current thread. This method should be overridden to return an appropriate ThreadGroup.

Protected Instance Methods

classDepth

protected native int classDepth(String name)

Parameters	name The fully qualified name of a class.
Returns	The number of pending method invocations from the top of the stack to a call to a method of the given class; –1 if no stack frame in the current thread is associated with a call to a method in the given class.
Description	This method returns the number of pending method invocations between this method invocation and an invocation of a method associated with the named class.

classLoaderDepth

protected native int classLoaderDepth()

Returns	The number of pending method invocations from the top of the stack to a call to a method that is associated with a class that was loaded by a ClassLoader object; –1 if no stack frame in the current thread is associated with a call to such a method.
Description	This method returns the number of pending method invocations between this method invocation and an invocation of a method associated with a class that was loaded by a Class-Loader object.

currentClassLoader

protected native ClassLoader currentClassLoader()

Returns	The most recent ClassLoader object executing on the stack.
Description	This method finds the most recent pending invocation of a method associated with a class that was loaded by a Class-Loader object. The method then returns the ClassLoader object that loaded that class.

currentLoadedClass

protected Class currentLoadedClass()

Availability	New as of JDK 1.1
Returns	The most recent Class object loaded by a ClassLoader.
Description	This method finds the most recent pending invocation of a method associated with a class that was loaded by a ClassLoader object. The method then returns the Class object for that class.

getClassContext

protected native Class[] getClassContext()

Returns	An array of Class objects that represents the current execution stack.
Description	This method returns an array of Class objects that represents the current execution stack. The length of the array is the number of pending method calls on the current thread's stack, not including the call to getClassContext(). Each element of the array references a Class object that describes the class associated with the corresponding method call. The first element of the array corresponds to the most recently called method, the second element is that method's caller, and so on.

inClass

protected boolean inClass(String name)

Parameters	name	The fully qualified name of a class.
Returns		true if there is a pending method invocation on the stack for a method of the given class; otherwise false.
Description		This method determines whether or not there is a pending method invocation that is associated with the named class.

inClassLoader

protected boolean inClassLoader()

Returns	true if there is a pending method invocation on the stack for a method of a class that was loaded by a ClassLoader object; otherwise false.
Description	This method determines whether or not there is a pending method invocation that is associated with a class that was loaded by a ClassLoader object. The method returns true only if the currentClassLoader() method does not return null.

Inherited Methods

Method	Inherited From	Method	Inherited From
clone()	Object	equals(Object)	Object
finalize()	Object	getClass()	Object
hashCode()	Object	notify()	Object
notifyAll()	Object	toString()	Object
wait()	Object	wait(long)	Object
wait(long, int)	Object		

See Also

Class, ClassLoader, DatagramSocket, File, FileDescriptor, FileInputStream, FileOutputStream, InetAddress, MulticastSocket, Object, RandomAccessFile, Runtime, SecurityException, ServerSocket, Socket, System, Thread, ThreadGroup, Toolkit, URL, URLConnection

12.55   Short

Synopsis

Class Name:	java.lang.Short
Superclass:	java.lang.Number
Immediate Subclasses:	None
Interfaces Implemented:	None
Availability:	New as of JDK 1.1

Description

The Short class provides an object wrapper for a short value. This is useful when you need to treat a short value as an object. For example, there are a number of utility methods that take a reference to an Object as one of their arguments. You cannot specify a short value for one of these arguments, but you can provide a reference to a Short object that encapsulates the byte value. Furthermore, the Short class is necessary as of JDK 1.1 to support the Reflection API and class literals.

The Short class also provides a number of utility methods for converting short values to other primitive types and for converting short values to strings and vice-versa.

Class Summary

```
public final class java.lang.Short extends java.lang.Number {
  // Constants
  public static final short MAX_VALUE;
  public static final short MIN_VALUE;
  public static final Class TYPE;

  // Constructors
  public Short(short value);
  public Short(String s);

  // Class Methods
  public static Short decode(String nm);
  public static short parseShort(String s);
  public static short parseShort(String s, int radix);
  public static String toString(short s);
  public static Short valueOf(String s, int radix);
  public static Short valueOf(String s);

  // Instance Methods
  public byte byteValue();
  public double doubleValue();
  public boolean equals(Object obj);
  public float floatValue();
  public int hashCode();
  public int intValue();
  public long longValue();
  public short shortValue();
  public String toString();
}
```

Constants

MAX_VALUE

```
public static final short MAX_VALUE= 32767
```
The largest value that can be represented by a short.

MIN_VALUE

```
public static final byte MIN_VALUE= -32768
```
The smallest value that can be represented by a short.

TYPE

```
public static final Class TYPE
```
The Class object that represents the primitive type short. It is always true that Short.TYPE == short.class.

Constructors

Short

public Short(short value)

Parameters	value	The short value to be encapsulated by this object.
Description		Creates a Short object with the specified short value.

public Short(String s) throws NumberFormatException

Parameters	s	The string to be made into a Short object.
Throws		NumberFormatException
		If the sequence of characters in the given String does not form a valid short literal.
Description		Constructs a Short object with the value specified by the given string. The string should consist of one or more digit characters. The digit characters can be preceded by a single '–' character. If the string contains any other characters, the constructor throws a NumberFormatException.

Class Methods

decode

public static Short decode(String nm) throws NumberFormatException

Parameters	nm	A String representation of the value to be encapsulated by a Short object. If the string begins with # or 0x, it is a radix 16 representation of the value. If the string begins with 0, it is a radix 8 representation of the value. Otherwise, it is assumed to be a radix 10 representation of the value.
Returns		A Short object that encapsulates the given value.
Throws		NumberFormatException
		If the String contains any non-digit characters other than a leading minus sign or the value represented by the String is less than Short.MIN_VALUE or greater than Short.MAX_VALUE.
Description		This method returns a Short object that encapsulates the given value.

parseByte

```
public static short parseShort(String s)
                throws NumberFormatException
```

Parameters   s   The String to be converted to a short value.

Returns   The numeric value of the short represented by the String object.

Throws   NumberFormatException

              If the String does not contain a valid representation of a short or the value represented by the String is less than Short.MIN_VALUE or greater than Short.MAX_VALUE.

Description   This method returns the numeric value of the short represented by the contents of the given String object. The String must contain only decimal digits, except that the first character may be a minus sign.

```
public static short parseShort(String s, int radix)
                throws NumberFormatException
```

Parameters   s   The String to be converted to a short value.

              radix   The radix used in interpreting the characters in the String as digits. This value must be in the range Character.MIN_RADIX to Character.MAX_RADIX. If radix is in the range 2 through 10, only characters for which the Character.isDigit() method returns true are considered to be valid digits. If radix is in the range 11 through 36, characters in the ranges 'A' through 'Z' and 'a' through 'z' are considered valid digits.

Returns   The numeric value of the short represented by the String object in the specified radix.

Throws   NumberFormatException

              If the String does not contain a valid representation of a short, radix is not in the appropriate range, or the value represented by the String is less than Short.MIN_VALUE or greater than Short.MAX_VALUE.

Description   This method returns the numeric value of the short represented by the contents of the given String object in the specified radix. The String must contain only valid digits of the specified radix, except that the first character may be a minus sign. The digits are parsed in the specified radix to produce the numeric value.

toString

`public String toString(short s)`

Parameters	s	The short value to be converted to a string.
Returns	The string representation of the given value.	
Description	This method returns a String object that contains the decimal representation of the given value.	

This method returns a string that begins with '-' if the given value is negative. The rest of the string is a sequence of one or more of the characters '0', '1', '2', '3', '4', '5', '6', '7', '8', and '9'. This method returns "0" if its argument is 0. Otherwise, the string returned by this method does not begin with "0" or "-0".

valueOf

`public static Short valueOf(String s) throws NumberFormatException`

Parameters   s   The string to be made into a Short object.

Returns   The Short object constructed from the string.

Throws   NumberFormatException

If the String does not contain a valid representation of a short or the value represented by the String is less than Short.MIN_VALUE or greater than Short.MAX_VALUE.

Description   Constructs a Short object with the value specified by the given string. The string should consist of one or more digit characters. The digit characters can be preceded by a single '-'. If the string contains any other characters, the method throws a NumberFormatException.

`public static Short valueOf(String s, int radix)`
`                 throws NumberFormatException`

Parameters   s   The string to be made into a Short object.

              radix   The radix used in converting the string to a value. This value must be in the range Character.MIN_RADIX to Character.MAX_RADIX.

Returns   The Short object constructed from the string.

Throws   NumberFormatException

If the String does not contain a valid representation of a short, radix is not in the appropriate range, or the value represented by the String is less than Short.MIN_VALUE or greater than Short.MAX_VALUE.

Description   Constructs a Short object with the value specified by the given string in the specified radix. The string should consist of one or more digit characters or characters in the range 'A' to 'Z' or 'a' to 'z' that are considered digits in the given radix. The digit characters can be preceded by a single '-' character. If the string contains any other characters, the method throws a NumberFormatException.

Instance Methods

byteValue

```
public byte byteValue()
```

Returns   The value of this object as a byte. The high order bits of the value are discarded.

Overrides   Number.byteValue()

Description   This method returns the value of this object as a byte.

doubleValue

```
public double doubleValue()
```

Returns   The value of this object as a double.

Overrides   Number.doubleValue()

Description   This method returns the value of this object as a double.

equals

```
public boolean equals(Object obj)
```

Parameters   obj   The object to be compared with this object.

Returns   true if the objects are equal; false if they are not.

Overrides   Object.equals()

Description   This method returns true if obj is an instance of Short and it contains the same value as the object this method is associated with.

floatValue

```
public float floatValue()
```

Returns   The value of this object as a float.

Overrides   Number.floatValue()

Description   This method returns the value of this object as a float.

hashCode

```
public int hashCode()
```

Returns	A hashcode based on the short value of the object.
Overrides	Object.hashCode()
Description	This method returns a hash code computed from the value of this object.

intValue

```
public int intValue()
```

Returns	The value of this object as an int.
Overrides	Number.intValue()
Description	This method returns the value of this object as an int.

longValue

```
public long longValue()
```

Returns	The value of this object as a long.
Overrides	Number.longValue()
Description	This method returns the value of this object as a long.

shortValue

```
public short shortValue()
```

Returns	The value of this object as a short.
Overrides	Number.shortValue()
Description	This method returns the value of this object as a short.

toString

```
public String toString()
```

Returns	The string representation of the value of this object.
Overrides	Object.toString()
Description	This method returns a String object that contains the decimal representation of the value of this object.
	This method returns a string that begins with '-' if the value is negative. The rest of the string is a sequence of one or more of the characters '0', '1', '2', '3', '4', '5', '6', '7', '8', and '9'. This method returns "0" if the value of the object is 0. Otherwise, the string returned by this method does not begin with "0" or "-0".

Inherited Methods

Method	Inherited From	Method	Inherited From
clone()	Object	finalize()	Object
getClass()	Object	notify()	Object
notifyAll()	Object	wait()	Object
wait(long)	Object	wait(long, int)	Object

See Also

Byte, Character, Class, Double, Float, Integer, Long, Number, String

12.56   StackOverflowError

Synopsis

Class Name:	java.lang.StackOverflowError
Superclass:	java.lang.VirtualMachineError
Immediate Subclasses:	None
Interfaces Implemented:	None
Availability:	JDK 1.0 or later

Description

A StackOverflowError is thrown when a stack overflow error occurs within the virtual machine.

Class Summary

```
public class java.lang.StackOverflowError
          extends java.lang.VirtualMachineError {
  // Constructors
  public StackOverflowError();
  public StackOverflowError(String s);
}
```

Constructors

StackOverflowError

public StackOverflowError()

Description   This constructor creates a StackOverflowError with no associated detail message.

```
public StackOverflowError(String s)<
```
Parameters   s   The detail message.

Description   This constructor creates a StackOverflowError with the speci-
              fied detail message.

Inherited Methods

Method	Inherited From	Method	Inherited From
clone()	Object	equals(Object)	Object
fillInStackTrace()	Throwable	finalize()	Object
getClass()	Object	getLocalizedMessage()	Throwable
getMessage()	Throwable	hashCode()	Object
notify()	Object	notifyAll()	Object
printStackTrace()	Throwable	printStack-Trace(PrintStream)	Throwable
printStack-Trace(PrintWriter)	Throwable	toString()	Object
wait()	Object	wait(long)	Object
wait(long, int)	Object		

See Also

Error, Throwable, VirtualMachineError

12.57   String

Synopsis

Class Name: java.lang.String
Superclass: java.lang.Object
Immediate Subclasses: None
Interfaces Implemented: java.io.Serializable
Availability: JDK 1.0 or later

Description

The String class represents sequences of characters. Once a String object is created, it is immutable. In other words, the sequence of characters that a String represents cannot be changed after it is created. The StringBuffer class, on the other
hand, represents a sequence of characters that can be changed. StringBuffer
objects are used to perform computations on String objects.

The String class includes a number of utility methods, such as methods for fetching individual characters or ranges of contiguous characters, for translating characters to upper- or lowercase, for searching strings, and for parsing numeric values in strings.

String literals are compiled into String objects. Where a String literal appears in an expression, the compiled code contains a String object. If s is declared as String, the following two expressions are identical:

```
s.equals("ABC")
"ABC".equals(s)
```

The string concatenation operator implicitly creates String objects.

Class Summary

```
public final class java.lang.String extends java.lang.Object {
    // Constructors
    public String();
    public String(byte[] bytes);                         // New in 1.1
    public String(byte[] bytes, String enc);             // New in 1.1
    public String(byte[] bytes, int offset, int length); // New in 1.1
    public String(byte[] bytes, int offset,
                  int length, String enc);               // New in 1.1
    public String(byte[] lowbytes, int hibyte);          // Deprecated in 1.1
    public String(byte[] lowbytes, int hibyte,
                  int offset, int count);                // Deprecated in 1.1
    public String(char[] value);
    public String(char[] value, int offset, int;
    public String(String value);
    public String(StringBuffer buffer);

    // Class Methods
    public static String copyValueOf(char data[]);
    public static String copyValueOf(char data[], int offset, int count);
    public static String valueOf(boolean b);
    public static String valueOf(char c);
    public static String valueOf(char[] data);
    public static String valueOf(char[] data, int offset, int count);
    public static String valueOf(double d);
    public static String valueOf(float f);
    public static String valueOf(int i);
    public static String valueOf(long l);
    public static String valueOf(Object obj);

    // Instance Methods
    public char charAt(int index);
    public int compareTo(String anotherString);
    public String concat(String str);
    public boolean endsWith(String suffix);
```

```
    public boolean equals(Object anObject);
    public boolean equalsIgnoreCase(String anotherString);
    public byte[] getBytes();                              // New in 1.1
    public byte[] getBytes(String enc);                    // New in 1.1
    public void getBytes(int srcBegin, int srcEnd,
                         byte[] dst, int dstBegin);        // Deprecated in 1.1
    public void getChars(int srcBegin, int srcEnd, char[] dst, int dstBegin);
    public int hashCode();
    public int indexOf(int ch);
    public int indexOf(int ch, int fromIndex);
    public int indexOf(String str);
    public int indexOf(String str, int fromIndex);
    public native String intern();
    public int lastIndexOf(int ch);
    public int lastIndexOf(int ch, int fromIndex);
    public int lastIndexOf(String str);
    public int lastIndexOf(String str, int fromIndex;
    public int length();
    public boolean regionMatches(boolean ignoreCase, int toffset,
                                 String other, int ooffset, int len);
    public boolean regionMatches(int toffset, String other,
                                 int ooffset, int len);
    public String replace(char oldChar, char newChar);
    public boolean startsWith(String prefix);
    public boolean startsWith(String prefix, int toffset);
    public String substring(int beginIndex);
    public String substring(int beginIndex, int endIndex);
    public char[] toCharArray();
    public String toLowerCase();
    public String toLowerCase(Locale locale);              // New in 1.1
    public String toString();
    public String toUpperCase();
    public String toUpperCase(Locale locale);              // New in 1.1
    public String trim();
}
```

Constructors

String

```
    public String()
```

Description   Creates a new String object that represents the empty string (i.e., a string with zero characters).

```
    public String(byte[] bytes)
```

Availability   New as of JDK 1.1

Parameters   bytes   An array of byte values.

Description Creates a new String object that represents the sequence of characters stored in the given bytes array. The bytes in the array are converted to characters using the system's default character encoding scheme.

public String(byte[] bytes, String enc)

Availability New as of JDK 1.1

Parameters bytes   An array of byte values.

enc   The name of an encoding scheme.

Throws   UnsupportedEncodingException

If enc is not a supported encoding scheme.

Description Creates a new String object that represents the sequence of characters stored in the given bytes array. The bytes in the array are converted to characters using the specified character encoding scheme.

public String(byte[] bytes, int offset, int length)

Availability New as of JDK 1.1

Parameters bytes   An array of byte values.

offset   An offset into the array.

length   The number of bytes to be included.

Throws   StringIndexOutOfBoundsException

If offset or length indexes an element that is outside the bounds of the bytes array.

Description Creates a new String object that represents the sequence of characters stored in the specified portion of the given bytes array. The bytes in the array are converted to characters using the system's default character encoding scheme.

public String(byte[] bytes, int offset, int length, String enc)

Availability New as of JDK 1.1

Parameters bytes   An array of byte values.

offset   An offset into the array.

length   The number of bytes to be included.

enc   The name of an encoding scheme.

Throws   StringIndexOutOfBoundsException

If offset or length indexes an element that is outside the bounds of the bytes array.

UnsupportedEncodingException

If enc is not a supported encoding scheme.

Description   Creates a new String object that represents the sequence of characters stored in the specified portion of the given bytes array. The bytes in the array are converted to characters using the specified character encoding scheme.

`public String(byte[] lowbytes, int hibyte)`

Availability   Deprecated as of JDK 1.1

Parameters   lowbytes   An array of byte values.

hibyte   The value to be put in the high-order byte of each 16-bit character.

Description   Creates a new String object that represents the sequence of characters stored in the given lowbytes array. The type of the array elements is byte, which is an 8-bit data type, so each element must be converted to a char, which is a 16-bit data type. The value of the hibyte argument is used to provide the value of the high-order byte when the byte values in the array are converted to char values.

More specifically, for each element i in the array lowbytes, the character at position i in the created String object is:

```
((hibyte & 0xff)<<8) | lowbytes[i]
```

This method is deprecated as of JDK 1.1 because it does not convert bytes into characters properly. You should instead use one of the constructors that takes a specific character encoding argument or that uses the default encoding.

`public String(byte[] lowbytes, int hibyte, int offset, int count)`

Availability   Deprecated as of JDK 1.1

Parameters   lowbytes   An array of byte values.

hibyte   The value to be put in the high-order byte of each 16-bit character.

offset   An offset into the array.

count   The number of bytes from the array to be included in the string.

Throws   StringIndexOutOfBoundsException

If offset or count indexes an element that is outside the bounds of the lowbytes array.

Description   Creates a new String object that represents the sequence of characters stored in the specified portion of the lowbytes array. That is, the portion of the array that starts at offset elements from the beginning of the array and is count elements long.

The type of the array elements is byte, which is an 8-bit data type, so each element must be converted to a char, which is a 16-bit data type. The value of the hibyte argument is used to provide the value of the high-order byte when the byte values in the array are converted to char values.

More specifically, for each element i in the array lowbytes that is included in the String object, the character at position i in the created String is:

```
((hibyte & 0xff)<<8) | lowbytes[I]
```

This method is deprecated as of JDK 1.1 because it does not convert bytes into characters properly. You should instead use one of the constructors that takes a specific character encoding argument or that uses the default encoding.

public String(char[] value)

Parameters	value	An array of char values.
Description		Creates a new String object that represents the sequence of characters stored in the given array.

public String(char[] value, int offset, int count)

Parameters	value	An array of char values.
	offset	An offset into the array.
	count	The number of characters from the array to be included in the string.
Throws	StringIndexOutOfBoundsException	
		If offset or count indexes an element that is outside the bounds of the value array.
Description		Creates a new String object that represents the sequence of characters stored in the specified portion of the given array. That is, the portion of the given array that starts at offset elements from the beginning of the array and is count elements long.

public String(String value)

Parameters	value	A String object.
Description		Creates a new String object that represents the same sequence of characters as the given String object.

public String(StringBuffer value)

Parameters	value	A StringBuffer object.
Description		Creates a new String object that represents the same sequence of characters as the given object.

Class Methods

copyValueOf

public static String copyValueOf(char data[])

Parameters	data	An array of char values.

Returns   A new String object that represents the sequence of characters stored in the given array.

Description   This method returns a new String object that represents the character sequence contained in the given array. The String object produced by this method is guaranteed not to refer to the given array, but instead to use a copy. Because the String object uses a copy of the array, subsequent changes to the array do not change the contents of this String object.

This method is now obsolete. The same result can be obtained using the valueOf() method that takes an array of char values.

public static String copyValueOf(char data[], int offset,
                               int count)

Parameters	data	An array of char values.
	offset	An offset into the array.
	count	The number of characters from the array to be included in the string.

Returns   A new String object that represents the sequence of characters stored in the specified portion of the given array.

Throws   StringIndexOutOfBoundsException
           If offset or count indexes an element that is outside the bounds of the data array.

Description   This method returns a new String object that represents the character sequence contained in the specified portion of the given array. That is, the portion of the given array that starts at offset elements from the beginning of the array and is count elements long. The String object produced by this method is guaranteed not to refer to the given array, but instead to use a copy. Because the String object uses a copy of the array, subsequent changes to the array do not change the contents of this String object.

This method is obsolete. The same result can be obtained by using the valueOf() method that takes an array of char values, an offset, and a count.

valueOf

```
public static String valueOf(boolean b)
```

Parameters	b	A boolean value.

Returns   A new String object that contains "true" if b is true or "false" if b is false.

Description   This method returns a string representation of a boolean value. In other words, it returns "true" if b is true or "false" if b is false.

```
public static String valueOf(char c)
```

Parameters	c	A char value.

Returns   A new String object that contains just the given character.

Description   This method returns a string representation of a char value. In other words, it returns a String object that contains just the given character.

```
public static String valueOf(char[] data)
```

Parameters	data	An array of char values.

Returns   A new String object that contains the sequence of characters stored in the given array.

Description   This method returns a string representation of an array of char values. In other words, it returns a String object that contains the sequence of characters stored in the given array.

```
public static String valueOf(char[] data, int offset,
                             int count)
```

Parameters	data	An array of char values.
	offset	An offset into the array.
	count	The number of characters from the array to be included in the string.

Returns   A new String object that contains the sequence of characters stored in the specified portion of the given array.

Throws   StringIndexOutOfBoundsException

                If offset or count indexes an element that is outside the bounds of the data array.

Description   This method returns a string representation of the specified portion of an array of char values. In other words, it returns a String object that contains the sequence of characters in the given array that starts offset elements from the beginning of the array and is count elements long.

```
public static String valueOf(double d)
```
Parameters | d | A double value.

Returns | A new String object that contains a string representation of the given double value.

Description | This method returns a string representation of a double value. In other words, it returns the String object returned by Double.toString(d).

```
public static String valueOf(float f)
```
Parameters | f | A float value.

Returns | A new String object that contains a string representation of the given float value.

Description | This method returns a string representation of a float value. In other words, it returns the String object returned by Float.toString(f).

```
public static String valueOf(int i)
```
Parameters | i | An int value.

Returns | A new String object that contains a string representation of the given int value.

Description | This method returns a string representation of an int value. In other words, it returns the String object returned by Integer.toString(i).

```
public static String valueOf(long l)
```
Parameters | l | A long value.

Returns | A new String object that contains a string representation of the given long value.

Description | This method returns a string representation of a long value. In other words, it returns the String object returned by Long.toString(l).

```
public static String valueOf (Object obj)
```
Parameters | obj | A reference to an object.

Returns | A new String that contains a string representation of the given object.

Description | This method returns a string representation of the given object. If obj is null, the method returns"null". Otherwise, the method returns the String object returned by the toString() method of the object.

Instance Methods

charAt

```
public char charAt(int index)
```

Parameters	index	An index into the string.
Returns		The character at the specified position in this string.
Throws		StringIndexOutOfBoundsException
		If index is less than zero or greater than or equal to the length of the string.
Description		This method returns the character at the specified position in the String object; the first character in the string is at position 0.

compareTo

```
public int compareTo(String anotherString)
```

Parameters　anotherString

The String object to be compared.

Returns　A positive value if this string is greater than anotherString, 0 if the two strings are the same, or a negative value if this string is less than anotherString.

Description　This method lexicographically compares this String object to anotherString.

Here is how the comparison works: the two String objects are compared character-by-character, starting at index 0 and continuing until a position is found in which the two strings contain different characters or until all of the characters in the shorter string have been compared. If the characters at k are different, the method returns:

```
this.charAt(k)-anotherString.charAt(k)
```

Otherwise, the comparison is based on the lengths of the strings and the method returns:

```
this.length()-anotherString.length()
```

concat

```
public String concat(String str)
```

Parameters　str　　　The String object to be concatenated.

Returns　A new String object that contains the character sequences of this string and str concatenated together.

Description   This method returns a new String object that concatenates the characters from the argument string str onto the characters from this String object. Although this is a good way to concatenate two strings, concatenating more than two strings can be done more efficiently using a StringBuffer object.

endsWith

public boolean endsWith(String suffix)

Parameters   suffix   The String object suffix to be tested.

Returns   true if this string ends with the sequence of characters specified by suffix; otherwise false.

Description   This method determines whether or not this String object ends with the specified suffix.

equals

public boolean equals(Object anObject)

Parameters   anObject   The Object to be compared.

Returns   true if the objects are equal; false if they are not.

Overrides   Object.equals()

Description   This method returns true if anObject is an instance of String and it contains the same sequence of characters as this String object.

Note the difference between this method and the == operator, which only returns true if both of its arguments are references to the same object.

equalsIgnoreCase

public boolean equalsIgnoreCase(String anotherString)

Parameters   anotherString

                The String object to be compared.

Returns   true if the strings are equal, ignoring case; otherwise false.

Description   This method determines whether or not this String object contains the same sequence of characters, ignoring case, as anotherString. More specifically, corresponding characters in the two strings are considered equal if any of the following conditions are true:

- The two characters compare as equal using the == operator.
- The Character.toUppercase() method returns the same result for both characters.

- The `Character.toLowercase()` method returns the same result for both characters.

getBytes

`public byte[] getBytes()`

Availability	New as of JDK 1.1
Returns	A byte array that contains the characters of this `String`.
Description	This method converts the characters in this `String` object to an array of byte values. The characters in the string are converted to bytes using the system's default character encoding scheme.

`public byte[] getBytes(String enc)`

Availability	New as of JDK 1.1	
Parameters	enc	The name of an encoding scheme.
Returns	A byte array that contains the characters of this `String`.	
Throws	`UnsupportedEncodingException`	
		If enc is not a supported encoding scheme.
Description	This method converts the characters in this `String` object to an array of byte values. The characters in the string are converted to bytes using the specified character encoding scheme.	

`public void getBytes(int srcBegin, int srcEnd,`
`                      byte[] dst, int dstBegin)`

Availability	Deprecated as of JDK 1.1	
Parameters	srcBegin	The index of the first character to be copied.
	srcEnd	The index after the last character to be copied.
	dst	The destination byte array.
	dstBegin	An offset into the destination array.
Throws	`StringIndexOutOfBoundsException`	
		If srcBegin, srcEnd, or dstBegin is out of range.
Description	This method copies the low-order byte of each character in the specified range of this `String` object to the given array of byte values. More specifically, the first character to be copied is at index srcBegin; the last character to be copied is at index srcEnd-1. The low-order bytes of these characters are copied into dst, starting at index dstBegin and ending at index:	

```
dstBegin + (srcEnd-srcBegin) - 1
```

This method is deprecated as of JDK 1.1 because it does not convert characters into bytes properly. You should instead use the `getBytes()` method that takes a specific character encoding argument or the one that uses the default encoding.

getChars

```
public void getChars(int srcBegin, int srcEnd,
              char[] dst, int dstBegin)
```

Parameters	srcBegin	The index of the first character to be copied.
	srcEnd	The index after the last character to be copied.
	dst	The destination char array.
	dstBegin	An offset into the destination array.

Throws	StringIndexOutOfBoundsException
	If srcBegin, srcEnd, or dstBegin is out of range.

Description	This method copies each character in the specified range of this String object to the given array of char values. More specifically, the first character to be copied is at index srcBegin; the last character to be copied is at index srcEnd-1. These characters are copied into dst, starting at index dstBegin and ending at index:

```
dstBegin + (srcEnd-srcBegin) - 1
```

hashCode

```
public int hashCode()
```

Returns	A hashcode based on the sequence of characters in this string.
Overrides	Object.hashCode()
Description	This method returns a hashcode based on the sequence of characters this String object represents.

More specifically, one of two algorithms is used to compute a hash code for the string, depending on its length. If n is the length of the string and S_i is the character at position i in the string, then if $n = 15$ the method returns:

$$\sum_{i=0}^{n-1} 37^i \cdot S_i$$

If $n > 15$, the method returns:

$$\sum_{i=0}^{\left\lceil \frac{n}{k} \right\rceil} 39^i \cdot S_{i \cdot k} \ \text{where} \ k = \left\lfloor \frac{n}{8} \right\rfloor$$

indexOf

```
public int indexOf(int ch)
```

Parameters	ch	A char value.

Returns   The index of the first occurrence of the given character in this
                 string or -1 if the character does not occur.

Description   This method returns the index of the first occurrence of the
                 given character in this String object. If there is no such occur-
                 rence, the method returns the value -1.

`public int indexOf(int ch, int fromIndex)`

Parameters   ch   A char value.

                 fromIndex   The index where the search is to begin.

Returns   The index of the first occurrence of the given character in this
                 string after fromIndex or -1 if the character does not occur.

Description   This method returns the index of the first occurrence of the
                 given character in this String object after ignoring the first
                 fromIndex characters. If there is no such occurrence, the
                 method returns the value -1.

`public int indexOf(String str)`

Parameters   str   A String object.

Returns   The index of the first occurrence of str in this string or -1 if
                 the substring does not occur.

Description   This method returns the index of the first character of the first
                 occurrence of the substring str in this String object. If there is
                 no such occurrence, the method returns the value -1.

`public int indexOf(String str, int fromIndex)`

Parameters   str   A String object.

                 fromIndex   The index where the search is to begin.

Returns   The index of the first occurrence of str in this string after
                 fromIndex or -1 if the substring does not occur.

Description   This method returns the index of the first character of the first
                 occurrence of the substring str in this String object after
                 ignoring the first fromIndex characters. If there is no such
                 occurrence, the method returns the value -1.

intern

`public native String intern()`

Returns   A String object that is guaranteed to be the same object for
                 every String that contains the same character sequence.

Description   This method returns a canonical representation for this String
                 object. The returned String object is guaranteed to be the
                 same String object for every String object that contains the
                 same character sequence. In other words, if:

```
s1.equals(s2)
```

then:

```
s1.intern() == s2.intern()
```

The intern() method is used by the Java environment to ensure that String literals and constant-value String expressions that contain the same sequence of characters are all represented by a single String object.

lastIndexOf

public int lastIndexOf(int ch)

Parameters	ch	A char value.
Returns		The index of the last occurrence of the given character in this string or –1 if the character does not occur.
Description		This method returns the index of the last occurrence of the given character in this String object. If there is no such occurrence, the method returns the value –1.

public int lastIndexOf(int ch, int fromIndex)

Parameters	ch	A char value.
	fromIndex	The index where the search is to begin.
Returns		The index of the last occurrence of the given character in this string after fromIndex or –1 if the character does not occur.
Description		This method returns the index of the last occurrence of the given character in this String object after ignoring the first fromIndex characters. If there is no such occurrence, the method returns the value –1.

public int lastIndexOf(String str)

Parameters	str	A String object.
Returns		The index of the last occurrence of str in this string or –1 if the substring does not occur.
Description		This method returns the index of the first character of the last occurrence of the substring str in this String object. If there is no such occurrence, the method returns the value –1.

public int lastIndexOf(String str, int fromIndex)

Parameters	str	A String object.
	fromIndex	The index where the search is to begin.
Returns		The index of the last occurrence of str in this string after fromIndex or –1 if the substring does not occur.

Description This method returns the index of the first character of the last occurrence of the substring str in this String object after ignoring the first fromIndex characters. If there is no such occurrence, the method returns the value -1.

length

```
public int length()
```

Returns The length of the character sequence represented by this string.

Description This method returns the number of characters in the character sequence represented by this String object.

regionMatches

```
public boolean regionMatches(int toffset, String other,
                             int ooffset, int len)
```

Parameters toffset The index of the first character in this string.

other The String object to be used in the comparison.

ooffset The index of the first character in other.

len The length of the sub-sequences to be compared.

Returns true if the sub-sequences are identical; otherwise false.

Description This method determines whether or not the specified sub-sequences in this String object and other are identical. The method returns false if toffset is negative, if ooffset is negative, if toffset+len is greater than the length of this string, or if ooffset+len is greater than the length of other. Otherwise, the method returns true if for all nonnegative integers k less than len it is true that:

```
this.charAt(toffset+k) == other.charAt(ooffset+k)
```

```
public boolean regionMatches(boolean ignoreCase, int toffset,
                             String other, int ooffset,
                             int len)
```

Parameters ignoreCase A boolean value that indicates whether case should be ignored.

toffset The index of the first character in this string.

other The String object to be used in the comparison.

ooffset The index of the first character in other.

len The length of the sub-sequences to be compared.

Returns	true if the sub-sequences are identical; otherwise false. The ignoreCase argument controls whether or not case is ignored in the comparison.
Description	This method determines whether or not the specified sub-sequences in this String object and other are identical. The method returns false if toffset is negative, if ooffset is negative, if toffset+len is greater than the length of this string, or if ooffset+len is greater than the length of other. Otherwise, if ignoreCase is false, the method returns true if for all nonnegative integers k less than len it is true that:

```
this.charAt(toffset+k) == other.charAt(ooffset+k)
```

If ignoreCase is true, the method returns true if for all nonnegative integers k less than len it is true that:

```
Character.toLowerCase(this.charAt(toffset+k))
== Character.toLowerCase(other.charAt(ooffset+k))
```

or:

```
Character.toUpperCase(this.charAt(toffset+k))
== Character.toUpperCase(other.charAt(ooffset+k))
```

replace

```
public String replace(char oldChar, char newChar)
```

Parameters	oldChar	The character to be replaced.
	newChar	The replacement character.
Returns		A new String object that results from replacing every occurrence of oldChar in the string with newChar.
Description		This method returns a new String object that results from replacing every occurrence of oldChar in this String object with newChar. If there are no occurrences of oldChar, the method simply returns this String object.

startsWith

```
public boolean startsWith(String prefix)
```

Parameters	prefix	The String object prefix to be tested.
Returns		true if this string begins with the sequence of characters specified by prefix; otherwise false.
Description		This method determines whether or not this String object begins with the specified prefix.

```
public boolean startsWith(String prefix, int toffset)
```
Parameters   prefix   The String object prefix to be tested.

                toffset   The index where the search is to begin.

Returns   true if this string contains the sequence of characters specified by prefix starting at the index toffset; otherwise false.

Description   This method determines whether or not this String object contains the specified prefix at the index specified by toffset.

substring

```
public String substring(int beginIndex)
```
Parameters   beginIndex   The index of the first character in the substring.

Returns   A new String object that contains the sub-sequence of this string that starts at beginIndex and extends to the end of the string.

Throws   StringIndexOutOfBoundsException

                     If beginIndex is less than zero or greater than or equal to the length of the string.

Description   This method returns a new String object that represents a sub-sequence of this String object. The sub-sequence consists of the characters starting at beginIndex and extending through the end of this String object.

```
public String substring(int beginIndex, int endIndex)
```
Parameters   beginIndex   The index of the first character in the substring.

                endIndex   The index after the last character in the substring.

Returns   A new String object that contains the sub-sequence of this string that starts at beginIndex and extends to the character at endindex-1.

Throws   StringIndexOutOfBoundsException

                     If beginIndex or endIndex is less than zero or greater than or equal to the length of the string.

Description   This method returns a new String object that represents a sub-sequence of this String object. The sub-sequence consists of the characters starting at beginIndex and extending through endIndex-1 of this String object.

toCharArray

```
public char[] toCharArray()
```
Returns   A new char array that contains the same sequence of characters as this string.

Description   This method returns a new char array that contains the same
sequence of characters as this Stringobject. The length of the
array is the same as the length of this String object.

toLowerCase

public String toLowerCase()
Returns   A new String object that contains the characters of this string
converted to lowercase.
Description   This method returns a new String that represents a character
sequence of the same length as this String object, but with
each character replaced by its lowercase equivalent if it has one.
If no character in the string has a lowercase equivalent, the
method returns this String object.

public String toLowerCase(Locale locale)
Availability   New as of JDK 1.1
Parameters   locale   The Locale to use.
Returns   A new String object that contains the characters of this string
converted to lowercase using the rules of the specified locale.
Description   This method returns a new String that represents a character
sequence of the same length as this String object, but with
each character replaced by its lowercase equivalent if it has one
according to the rules of the specified locale. If no character in
the string has a lowercase equivalent, the method returns this
String object.

toString

public String toString()
Returns   This String object.
Overrides   Object.toString()
Description   This method returns this String object.

toUpperCase

public String toUpperCase()
Returns   A new String object that contains the characters of this string
converted to uppercase.
Description   This method returns a new String that represents a character
sequence of the same length as this String object, but with
each character replaced by its uppercase equivalent if it has
one. If no character in the string has an uppercase equivalent,
the method returns this String object.

`public String toUpperCase(Locale locale)`

Availability   New as of JDK 1.1

Parameters   locale   The Locale to use.

Returns   A new String object that contains the characters of this string converted to uppercase using the rules of the specified locale.

Description   This method returns a new String that represents a character sequence of the same length as this String object, but with each character replaced by its uppercase equivalent if it has one according to the rules of the specified locale. If no character in the string has an uppercase equivalent, the method returns this String object.

trim

`public String trim()`

Returns   A new String object that represents the same character sequence as this string, but with leading and trailing whitespace and control characters removed.

Description   If the first and last character in this String object are greater than '\u0020' (the space character), the method returns this String object. Otherwise, the method returns a new String object that contains the same character sequence as this String object, but with leading and trailing characters that are less than '\u0020'' removed.

Inherited Methods

Method	Inherited From	Method	Inherited From
clone()	Object	finalize()	Object
getClass()	Object	notify()	Object
notifyAll()	Object	wait()	Object
wait(long)	Object	wait(long, int)	Object

See Also

Class, Character, Double, Float, Integer, Locale, Long, Object, StringBuffer, StringIndexOutOfBoundsException, UnsupportedEncodingException

12.58   StringBuffer

Synopsis

Class Name:	`java.lang.StringBuffer`
Superclass:	`java.lang.Object`
Immediate Subclasses:	None
Interfaces Implemented:	`java.io.Serializable`
Availability:	JDK 1.0 or later

Description

The `StringBuffer` class represents a variable-length sequence of characters. `StringBuffer` objects are used in computations that involve creating new `String` objects. The `StringBuffer` class provides a number of utility methods for working with `StringBuffer` objects, including `append()` and `insert()` methods that add characters to a `StringBuffer` and methods that fetch the contents of `String-Buffer` objects.

When a `StringBuffer` object is created, the constructor determines the initial contents and capacity of the `StringBuffer`. The capacity of a `StringBuffer` is the number of characters that its internal data structure can hold. This is distinct from the length of the contents of a `StringBuffer`, which is the number of characters that are actually stored in the `StringBuffer` object. The capacity of a `String-Buffer` can vary. When a `StringBuffer` object is asked to hold more characters than its current capacity allows, the `StringBuffer` enlarges its internal data structure. However, it is more costly in terms of execution time and memory when a `StringBuffer` has to repeatedly increase its capacity than when a `StringBuffer` object is created with sufficient capacity.

Because the intended use of `StringBuffer` objects involves modifying their contents, all methods of the `StringBuffer` class that modify `StringBuffer` objects are synchronized. This means that is it safe for multiple threads to try to modify a `StringBuffer` object at the same time.

`StringBuffer` objects are used implicitly by the string concatenation operator. Consider the following code:

```
String s, s1, s2;
s = s1 + s2;
```

To compute the string concatenation, the Java compiler generates code like:

```
s = new StringBuffer().append(s1).append(s2).toString();
```

Class Summary

```
public class java.lang.StringBuffer extends java.lang.Object {
    // Constructors
    public StringBuffer();
    public StringBuffer(int length);
    public StringBuffer(String str);

    // Instance Methods
    public StringBuffer append(boolean b);
    public synchronized StringBuffer append(char c);
    public synchronized StringBuffer append(char[] str);
    public synchronized StringBuffer append(char[] str, int offset, int len);
    public StringBuffer append(double d);
    public StringBuffer append(float f);
    public StringBuffer append(int i);
    public StringBuffer append(long l);
    public synchronized StringBuffer append(Object obj);
    public synchronized StringBuffer append(String str);
    public int capacity();
    public synchronized char charAt(int index);
    public synchronized void ensureCapacity(int minimumCapacity);
    public synchronized void getChars(int srcBegin, int srcEnd,
                            char[] dst, int dstBegin);
    public StringBuffer insert(int offset, boolean b);
    public synchronized StringBuffer insert(int offset, char c);
    public synchronized StringBuffer insert(int offset, char[] str);
    public StringBuffer insert(int offset, double d);
    public StringBuffer insert(int offset, float f);
    public StringBuffer insert(int offset, int i);
    public StringBuffer insert(int offset, long l);
    public synchronized StringBuffer insert(int offset, Object obj);
    public synchronized StringBuffer insert(int offset, String str);
    public int length();
    public synchronized StringBuffer reverse();
    public synchronized void setCharAt(int index, char ch);
    public synchronized void setLength(int newLength);
    public String toString();
}
```

Constructors

StringBuffer

public StringBuffer()

Description   Creates a StringBuffer object that does not contain any characters and has a capacity of 16 characters.

`public StringBuffer(int capacity)`

Parameters	capacity	The initial capacity of this StringBufffer object.
Throws	NegativeArraySizeException	
		If capacity is negative.
Description		Creates a StringBuffer object that does not contain any characters and has the specified capacity.

`public StringBuffer(String str)`

Parameters	str	A String object.
Description		Creates a StringBuffer object that contains the same sequence of characters as the given String object and has a capacity 16 greater than the length of the String.

Instance Methods

append

`public StringBuffer append(boolean b)`

Parameters	b	A boolean value.
Returns		This StringBuffer object.
Description		This method appends either "true" or "false" to the end of the sequence of characters stored in ths StringBuffer object, depending on the value of b.

`public synchronized StringBuffer append(char c)`

Parameters	c	A char value.
Returns		This StringBuffer object.
Description		This method appends the given character to the end of the sequence of characters stored in this StringBuffer object.

`public synchronized StringBuffer append(char str[])`

Parameters	str	An array of char values.
Returns		This StringBuffer object.
Description		This method appends the characters in the given array to the end of the sequence of characters stored in this StringBuffer object.

`public synchronized StringBuffer append(char str[], int offset, int len)`

Parameters	str	An array of char values.
	offset	An offset into the array.
	len	The number of characters from the array to be appended.
Returns		This StringBuffer object.

Throws	`StringIndexOutOfBoundsException` If `offset` or `len` are out of range.
Description	This method appends the specified portion of the given array to the end of the character sequence stored in this `String-Buffer` object. The portion of the array that is appended starts `offset` elements from the beginning of the array and is `len` elements long.

public StringBuffer append(double d)

Parameters	`d` A `double` value.
Returns	This `StringBuffer` object.
Description	This method converts the given `double` value to a string using `Double.toString(d)` and appends the resulting string to the end of the sequence of characters stored in this `StringBuffer` object.

public StringBuffer append(float f)

Parameters	`f` A `float` value.
Returns	This `StringBuffer` object.
Description	This method converts the given `float` value to a string using `Float.toString(f)` and appends the resulting string to the end of the sequence of characters stored in this `StringBuffer` object.

public StringBuffer append(int i)

Parameters	`i` An `int` value.
Returns	This `StringBuffer` object.
Description	This method converts the given `int` value to a string using `Integer.toString(i)` and appends the resulting string to the end of the sequence of characters stored in this `StringBuffer` object.

public StringBuffer append(long l)

Parameters	`l` A `long` value.
Returns	This `StringBuffer` object.
Description	This method converts the given `long` value to a string using `Long.toString(l)` and appends the resulting string to the end of the sequence of characters stored in this `StringBuffer` object.

public synchronized StringBuffer append(Object obj)

Parameters	`obj` A reference to an object.
Returns	This `StringBuffer` object.

Description   This method gets the string representation of the given object by calling `String.valueOf(obj)` and appends the resulting string to the end of the character sequence stored in this `StringBuffer` object.

`public synchronized StringBuffer append(String str)`

Parameters   str   A `String` object.

Returns   This `StringBuffer` object.

Description   This method appends the sequence of characters represented by the given `String` to the characters in this `StringBuffer` object. If `str` is `null`, the string `"null"` is appended.

capacity

`public int capacity()`

Returns   The capacity of this `StringBuffer` object.

Description   This method returns the current capacity of this object. The capacity of a `StringBuffer` object is the number of characters that its internal data structure can hold. A `StringBuffer` object automatically increases its capacity when it is asked to hold more characters than its current capacity allows.

charAt

`public synchronized char charAt(int index)`

Parameters   index   An index into the `StringBuffer`.

Returns   The character stored at the specified position in this `String-Buffer` object.

Throws   `StringIndexOutOfBoundsException`
                              If `index` is less than zero or greater than or equal to the length of the `StringBuffer` object.

Description   This method returns the character at the specified position in the `StringBuffer` object. The first character in the `String-Buffer` is at index 0.

ensureCapacity

`public synchronized void ensureCapacity(int minimumCapacity)`

Parameters   minimumCapacity
                              The minimum desired capacity.

Description   This method ensures that the capacity of this `StringBuffer` object is at least the specified number of characters. If necessary, the capacity of this object is increased to the greater of `minimumCapacity` or double its current capacity plus two.

It is more efficient to ensure that the capacity of a String-Buffer object is sufficient to hold all of the additions that will be made to its contents, rather than let the StringBuffer increase its capacity in multiple increments.

getChars

```
public synchronized void getChars(int srcBegin, int srcEnd,
                                  char dst[], int dstBegin)
```

Parameters	srcBegin	The index of the first character to be copied.
	srcEnd	The index after the last character to be copied.
	dst	The destination char array.
	dstBegin	An offset into the destination array.
Throws	StringIndexOutOfBoundsException	
		If srcBegin, srcEnd, or dstBegin is out of range.

Description   This method copies each character in the specified range of this StringBuffer object to the given array of char values. More specifically, the first character to be copied is at index srcBegin; the last character to be copied is at index srcEnd-1.

These characters are copied into dst, starting at index dstBegin and ending at index:

```
dstBegin + (srcEnd-srcBegin) - 1
```

insert

```
public StringBuffer insert(int offset, boolean b)
```

Parameters	offset	An offset into the StringBuffer.
	b	A boolean value.
Returns	This StringBuffer object.	
Throws	StringIndexOutOfBoundsException	
		If offset is out of range.

Description   This method inserts either "true" or "false" into the sequence of characters stored in this StringBuffer object, depending on the value of b. The string is inserted at a position offset characters from the beginning of the sequence. If offset is 0, the string is inserted before the first character in the StringBuffer.

```
public synchronized StringBuffer insert(int offset, char c)
```

Parameters	offset	An offset into the StringBuffer.
	c	A char value.

Returns   This StringBuffer object.

Throws   StringIndexOutOfBoundsException

If offset is less than zero or greater than or equal to the length of the StringBuffer object.

Description This method inserts the given character into the sequence of characters stored in this StringBuffer object. The character is inserted at a position offset characters from the beginning of the sequence. If offset is 0, the character is inserted before the first character in the StringBuffer.

```
public synchronized StringBuffer insert(int offset, char str[])
```

Parameters   offset   An offset into the StringBuffer.

str   An array of char values.

Returns   This StringBuffer object.

Throws   StringIndexOutOfBoundsException

If offset is less than zero or greater than or equal to the length of the StringBuffer object.

Description This method inserts the characters in the given array into the sequence of characters stored in this StringBuffer object. The characters are inserted at a position offset characters from the beginning of the sequence. If offset is 0, the characters are inserted before the first character in the StringBuffer.

```
public StringBuffer insert(int offset, double d)
```

Parameters   offset   An offset into the StringBuffer.

d   A double value.

Returns   This StringBuffer object.

Throws   StringIndexOutOfBoundsException

If offset is less than zero or greater than or equal to the length of the StringBuffer object.

Description This method converts the given double value to a string using Double.toString(d) and inserts the resulting string into the sequence of characters stored in this StringBuffer object. The string is inserted at a position offset characters from the beginning of the sequence. If offset is 0, the string is inserted before the first character in the StringBuffer.

```
public StringBuffer insert(int offset, float f)
```

Parameters   offset   An offset into the StringBuffer.

f   A float value.

Returns   This StringBuffer object.

Throws	StringIndexOutOfBoundsException
	If offset is less than zero or greater than or equal to the length of the StringBuffer object.
Description	This method converts the given float value to a string using Float.toString(f) and inserts the resulting string into the sequence of characters stored in this StringBuffer object. The string is inserted at a position offset characters from the beginning of the sequence. If offset is 0, the string is inserted before the first character in the StringBuffer.

public StringBuffer insert(int offset, int i)

Parameters	offset	An offset into the StringBuffer.
	i	An int value.
Returns	This StringBuffer object.	
Throws	StringIndexOutOfBoundsException	
	If offset is less than zero or greater than or equal to the length of the StringBuffer object.	
Description	This method converts the given int value to a string using Integer.toString(i) and inserts the resulting string into the sequence of characters stored in this StringBuffer object. The string is inserted at a position offset characters from the beginning of the sequence. If offset is 0, the string is inserted before the first character in the StringBuffer.	

public StringBuffer insert(int offset, long l)

Parameters	offset	An offset into the StringBuffer.
	l	A long value.
Returns	This StringBuffer object.	
Throws	StringIndexOutOfBoundsException	
	If offset is less than zero or greater than or equal to the length of the StringBuffer object.	
Description	This method converts the given long value to a string using Long.toString(l) and inserts the resulting string into the sequence of characters stored in this StringBuffer object. The string is inserted at a position offset characters from the beginning of the sequence. If offset is 0, the string is inserted before the first character in the StringBuffer.	

public synchronized StringBuffer insert(int offset, Object obj)

Parameters	offset	An offset into the StringBuffer.
	obj	A reference to an object.

Returns	This StringBuffer object.
Throws	StringIndexOutOfBoundsException
	If offset is less than zero or greater than or equal to the length of the StringBuffer object.
Description	This method gets the string representation of the given object by calling String.valueOf(obj) and inserts the resulting string into the sequence of characters stored in this StringBuffer object. The string is inserted at a position offset characters from the beginning of the sequence. If offset is 0, the string is inserted before the first character in the StringBuffer.

```
public synchronized StringBuffer insert(int offset, String str)
```

Parameters	offset	An offset into the StringBuffer.
	str	A String object.
Returns	This StringBuffer object.	
Throws	StringIndexOutOfBoundsException	
	If offset is less than zero or greater than or equal to the length of the StringBuffer object.	
Description	This method inserts the sequence of characters represented by the given String into the sequence of characters stored in this StringBuffer object. If str is null, the string "null" is inserted. The string is inserted at a position offset characters from the beginning of the sequence. If offset is 0, the string is inserted before the first character in the StringBuffer.	

length

```
public int length()
```

Returns	The number of characters stored in this StringBuffer object.
Description	This method returns the number of characters stored in this StringBuffer object. The length is distinct from the capacity of a StringBuffer, which is the number of characters that its internal data structure can hold.

reverse

```
public synchronized StringBuffer reverse()
```

Returns	This StringBuffer object.
Description	This method reverses the sequence of characters stored in this StringBuffer object.

setCharAt

`public synchronized void setCharAt(int index, char ch)`

Parameters	index	The index of the character to be set.
	ch	A char value.
Throws	StringIndexOutOfBoundsException	
		If index is less than zero or greater than or equal to the length of the StringBuffer object.
Description		This method modifies the character located index characters from the beginning of the sequence of characters stored in this StringBuffer object. The current character at this position is replaced by the character ch.

setLength

`public synchronized void setLength(int newLength)`

Parameters	newLength	The new length for this StringBuffer.
Throws	StringIndexOutOfBoundsException	
		If index is less than zero.
Description		This method sets the length of the sequence of characters stored in this StringBuffer object. If the length is set to be less than the current length, characters are lost from the end of the character sequence. If the length is set to be more than the current length, NUL characters (\u0000) are added to the end of the character sequence.

toString

`public String toString()`

Returns	A new String object that represents the same sequence of characters as the sequence of characters stored in this StringBuffer object.
Overrides	Object.toString()
Description	This method returns a new String object that represents the same sequence of characters as the sequence of characters stored in this StringBuffer object. Note that any subsequent changes to the contents of this StringBuffer object do not affect the contents of the String object created by this method.

Inherited Methods

Method	Inherited From	Method	Inherited From
clone()	Object	equals(Object)	Object
finalize()	Object	getClass()	Object
hashCode()	Object	notify()	Object
notifyAll()	Object	wait()	Object
wait(long)	Object	wait(long, int)	Object

See Also

Class, Double, Float, Integer, Long, Object, String, StringIndexOutOfBoundsException

12.59   StringIndexOutOfBoundsException

Synopsis

Class Name:	java.lang.StringIndexOutOfBoundsException
Superclass:	java.lang.IndexOutOfBoundsException
Immediate Subclasses:	None
Interfaces Implemented:	None
Availability:	JDK 1.0 or later

Description

A StringIndexOutOfBoundsException is thrown when a String or StringBuffer object detects an out-of-range index. An out-of-range index occurs when the index is less than zero, or greater than or equal to the length of the string.

Class Summary

```
public class java.lang.StringIndexOutOfBoundsException
        extends java.lang.IndexOutOfBoundsException {
  // Constructors
  public StringIndexOutOfBoundsException();
  public StringIndexOutOfBoundsException(int index);
  public StringIndexOutOfBoundsException(String s);
}
```

Constructors

StringIndexOutOfBoundsException

public StringIndexOutOfBoundsException()

Description   This constructor creates a StringIndexOutOfBoundsException with no associated detail message.

public StringIndexOutOfBoundsException(int index)

Parameters   index   The index value that was out of bounds

Description   This constructor creates an StringIndexOutOfBoundsException with an associated message that mentions the specified index.

public StringIndexOutOfBoundsException(String s)

Parameters   s   The detail message.

Description   This constructor creates a StringIndexOutOfBoundsException with the specified detail message.

Inherited Methods

Method	Inherited From	Method	Inherited From
clone()	Object	equals(Object)	Object
fillInStackTrace()	Throwable	finalize()	Object
getClass()	Object	getLocalizedMessage()	Throwable
getMessage()	Throwable	hashCode()	Object
notify()	Object	notifyAll()	Object
printStackTrace()	Throwable	printStack-Trace(PrintStream)	Throwable
printStack-Trace(PrintWriter)	Throwable	toString()	Object
wait()	Object	wait(long)	Object
wait(long, int)	Object		

See Also

Exception, IndexOutOfBoundsException, RuntimeException, Throwable

12.60   System

Synopsis

Class Name:	`java.lang.System`
Superclass:	`java.lang.Object`
Immediate Subclasses:	None
Interfaces Implemented:	None
Availability:	JDK 1.0 or later

Description

The System class provides access to various information about the operating system environment in which a program is running. For example, the System class defines variables that allow access to the standard I/O streams and methods that allow a program to run the garbage collector and stop the Java virtual machine.

All of the variables and methods in the System class are static. In other words, it is not necessary to create an instance of the System class in order to use its variables and methods. In fact, the System class does not define any public constructors, so it cannot be instantiated.

The System class supports the concept of system properties that can be queried and set. The following properties are guaranteed always to be defined:

Property Name	Description
`file.encoding`	The character encoding for the default locale (Java 1.1 only)
`file.encoding.pkg`	The package that contains converters between local encodings and Unicode (Java 1.1 only)
`file.separator`	File separator ("/" on UNIX, "\" on Windows)
`java.class.path`	The class path
`java.class.version`	Java class version number
`java.compiler`	The just-in-time compiler to use, if any (Java 1.1 only)
`java.home`	Java installation directory
`java.vendor`	Java vendor-specific string
`java.vendor.url`	Java vendor URL
`java.version`	Java version number
`line.separator`	Line separator(" \n" on UNIX, " \r\n" on Windows)
`os.arch`	Operating system architecture
`os.name`	Operating system name
`os.version`	Operating system version
`path.separator`	Path separator (":" on UNIX, "," on Windows)
`user.dir`	User's current working directory when the properties were initialized
`user.home`	User's home directory

Property Name	Description
user.language	The two-letter language code of the default locale (Java 1.1 only)
user.name	User's account name
user.region	The two-letter country code of the default locale (Java 1.1 only)
user.timezone	The default time zone (Java 1.1 only)

Additional properties may be defined by the run-time environment. The -D command-line option can be used to define system properties when a program is run.

The Runtime class is related to the System class; it provides access to information about the environment in which a program is running.

Class Summary

```
public final class java.lang.System extends java.lang.Object {
    // Constants
    public static final PrintStream err;
    public static final InputStream in;
    public static final PrintStream out;

    // Class Methods
    public static void arraycopy(Object src, int srcOffset,
                                 Object dst, int dstOffset, int length);
    public static long currentTimeMillis();
    public static void exit(int status);
    public static void gc();
    public static Properties getProperties();
    public static String getProperty(String key);
    public static String getProperty(String key, String default);
    public static SecurityManager getSecurityManager();
    public static String getenv(String name);            // Deprecated in 1.1
    public static native int identityHashCode(Object x);   // New in 1.1
    public static void load(String filename);
    public static void loadLibrary(String libname);
    public static void runFinalization();
    public static void runFinalizersOnExit(boolean value); // New in 1.1
    public static void setErr(PrintStream err);            // New in 1.1
    public static void setIn(InputStream in);              // New in 1.1
    public static void setOut(PrintStream out);            // New in 1.1
    public static void setProperties(Properties props);
    public static void setSecurityManager(SecurityManager s);
}
```

Variables

err

public static final PrintStream err

Description   The standard error stream. In an application environment, this variable refers to a java.io.PrintStream object that is associated with the standard error output for the process running the Java virtual machine. In an applet environment, the PrintStream is likely to be associated with a separate window, although this is not guaranteed.

The value of err can be set using the setErr() method. The value of err can only be set if the currently installed Security-Manager does not throw a SecurityException when the request is made.

Prior to to Java 1.1, err was not final. It has been made final as of Java 1.1 because the unchecked ability to set err is a security hole.

in

public static final InputStream in

Description   The standard input stream. In an application environment, this variable refers to a java.io.InputStream object that is associated with the standard input for the process running the Java virtual machine.

The value of in can be set using the setIn() method. The value of in can only be set if the currently installed Security-Manager does not throw a SecurityException when the request is made.

Prior to to Java 1.1, in was not final. It has been made final as of Java 1.1 because the unchecked ability to set in is a security hole.

out

public static final PrintStream out

Description   The standard output stream. In an application environment, this variable refers to a java.io.PrintStream object that is associated with the standard output for the process running the Java virtual machine. In an applet environment, the PrintStream is likely to be associated with a separate window, although this is not guaranteed.

out is the most commonly used of the three I/O streams provided by the System class. Even in GUI-based applications, sending output to this stream can be useful for debugging. The
usual idiom for sending output to this stream is:

```
System.out.println("Some text");
```

The value of out can be set using the setOut() method. The
value of out can only be set if the currently installed Security-
Manager does not throw a SecurityException when the request
is made.

Prior to to Java 1.1, out was not final. It has been made final
as of Java 1.1 because the unchecked ability to set out is a security hole.

Class Methods

arraycopy

```
public static void arraycopy(Object src, int src_position,
                             Object dst, int dst_position,
                             int length)
```

Parameters	src	The source array.
	src_position	
		An index into the source array.
	dst	The destination array.
	dst_position	
		An index into the destination array.
	length	The number of elements to be copied.
Throws	ArrayIndexOutOfBoundsException	
		If the values of the src_position, dst_position, and length arguments imply accessing either array with an index that is less than zero or an index greater than or equal to the number of elements in the array.
	ArrayStoreException	
		If the type of value stored in the src array cannot be stored in the dst array.
	NullPointerException	
		If src or dst is null.
Description		This method copies a range of array elements from the src array to the dst array. The number of elements that are copied is specified by length. The elements at positions src_position through src_position+length-1 in src are copied to the posi-

tions dst_position through dst_position+length-1 in dst, respectively.

If src and dst refer to the same array, the copying is done as if the array elements were first copied to a temporary array and then copied to the destination array.

Before this method does any copying, it performs a number of checks. If either src or dst are null, the method throws a NullPointerException and dst is not modified.

If any of the following conditions are true, the method throws an ArrayStoreException, and dst is not modified:

- Either src or dst refers to an object that is not an array.
- src and dst refer to arrays whose element types are different primitive types.
- src refers to an array that has elements that contain a primitive type, while dst refers to an array that has elements that contain a reference type, or vice versa.

If any of the following conditions are true, the method throws an ArrayIndexOutOfBoundsException, and dst is not modified:

- srcOffset, dstOffset, or length is negative.
- srcOffset+length is greater than src.length().
- dstOffset+length is greater than dst.length().

Otherwise, if an element in the source array being copied cannot be converted to the type of the destination array using the rules of the assignment operator, the method throws an ArrayStoreException when the problem occurs. Since the problem is discovered during the copy operation, the state of the dst array reflects the incomplete copy operation.

currentTimeMillis

public static native long currentTimeMillis()

Returns   The current time as the number of milliseconds since 00:00:00 UTC, January 1, 1970.

Description   This method returns the current time as the number of milliseconds since 00:00:00 UTC, January 1, 1970. It will not overflow until the year 292280995.

The java.util.Date class provides more extensive facilities for dealing with times and dates.

exit

    public static void exit(int status)

Parameters	status	The exit status code to use.
Throws	SecurityException	
		If the checkExit() method of the SecurityMan-ager throws a SecurityException.

Description   This method causes the Java virtual machine to exit with the given status code. This method works by calling the exit() method of the current Runtime object. By convention, a nonzero status code indicates abnormal termination. This method never returns.

gc

    public static void gc()

Description   This method causes the Java virtual machine to run the garbage collector in the current thread. This method works by calling the gc() method of the current Runtime object.

The garbage collector finds objects that will never be used again because there are no live references to them. After it finds these objects, the garbage collector frees the storage occupied by these objects.

The garbage collector is normally run continuously in a thread with the lowest possible priority, so that it works intermittently to reclaim storage. The gc() method allows a program to invoke the garbage collector explicitly when necessary.

getProperties

    public static Properties getProperties()

Returns	A Properties object that contains the values of all the system properies.
Throws	SecurityException
	If the checkPropertiesAccess() method of the SecurityManager throws a SecurityException.

Description   This method returns all of the defined system properties encapsulated in a java.util.Properties object. If there are no system properties currently defined, a set of default system properties is created and initialized. As discussed in the description of the System class, some system properties are guaranteed always to be defined.

getProperty

public static String getProperty(String key)

Parameters	key	The name of a system property.
Returns		The value of the named system property or null if the named property is not defined.
Throws		SecurityException
		If the checkPropertyAccess() method of the SecurityManager throws a SecurityException.
Description		This method returns the value of the named system property. If there is no definition for the named property, the method returns null. If there are no system properties currently defined, a set of default system properties is created and initialized. As discussed in the description of the System class, some system properties are guaranteed always to be defined.

public static String getProperty(String key, String def)

Parameters	key	The name of a system property.
	def	A default value for the property.
Returns		The value of the named system property, or the default value if the named property is not defined.
Throws		SecurityException
		If the checkPropertyAccess() method of the SecurityManager throws a SecurityException.
Description		This method returns the value of the named system property. If there is no definition for the named property, the method returns the default value as specified by the def parameter. If there are no system properties currently defined, a set of default system properties is created and initialized. As discussed earlier in the description of the System class, some system properties are guaranteed to always be defined.

getSecurityManager

public static SecurityManager getSecurityManager()

Returns	A reference to the installed SecurityManager object or null if there is no SecurityManager object installed.
Description	This method returns a reference to the installed SecurityManager object. If there is no SecurityManager object installed, the method returns null.

getenv

`public static String getenv(String name)`

Availability	Deprecated as of JDK 1.1	
Parameters	name	The name of a system-dependent environment variable.
Returns	The value of the environment variable or null if the variable is not defined.	
Description	This method is obsolete; it always throws an error. Use getProperties() and the -D option instead.	

identityHashCode

`public static native int identityHashCode(Object x)`

Availability	New as of JDK 1.1	
Parameters	x	An object.
Returns	The identity hashcode value for the specified object.	
Description	This method returns the same hashcode value for the specified object as would be returned by the default hashCode() method of Object, regardless of whether or not the object's class overrides hashCode().	

load

`public void load(String filename)`

Parameters	filename	A string that specifies the complete path of the file to be loaded.
Throws	SecurityException	
		If the checkLink() method of the SecurityManager throws a SecurityException.
	UnsatisfiedLinkError	
		If the method is unsuccessful in loading the specified dynamically linked library.
Description	This method loads the specified dynamically linked library. This method works by calling the load() method of the current Runtime object.	

loadLibrary

`public void loadLibrary(String libname)`

Parameters	libname	A string that specifies the name of a dynamically linked library.
Throws	SecurityException	
		If the checkLink() method of the SecurityManager throws a SecurityException.

UnsatisfiedLinkError

> If the method is unsuccessful in loading the specified dynamically linked library.

Description This method loads the specified dynamically linked library. It looks for the specified library in a platform-specific way. This method works by calling the loadLibrary() method of the current Runtime object.

runFinalization

public static void runFinalization()

Description This method causes the Java virtual machine to run the finalize() methods of any objects in the finalization queue in the current thread. This method works by calling the runFinalization() method of the current Runtime object.

When the garbage collector discovers that there are no references to an object, it checks to see if the object has a finalize() method that has never been called. If the object has such a finalize() method, the object is placed in the finalization queue. While there is a reference to the object in the finalization queue, the object is no longer considered garbage collectable.

Normally, the objects in the finalization queue are handled by a separate finalization thread that runs continuously at a very low priority. The finalization thread removes an object from the queue and calls its finalize() method. As long as the finalize() method does not generate a reference to the object, the object again becomes available for garbage collection.

Because the finalization thread runs at a very low priority, there may be a long delay from the time that an object is put on the finalization queue until the time that its finalize() method is called. The runFinalization() method allows a program to run the finalize() methods explicitly. This can be useful when there is a shortage of some resource that is released by a finalize() method.

runFinalizersOnExit

public static void runFinalizersOnExit(boolean value)

Availability New as of JDK 1.1

Parameters   value   A boolean value that specifies whether or not finalization occurs on exit.

Throws   SecurityException

                    If the checkExit() method of the SecurityManager throws a SecurityException.

Description   This method specifies whether or not the finalize() methods of all objects that have finalize() methods are run before the Java virtual machine exits. By default, the finalizers are not run on exit. This method works by calling the runFinalizersOnExit() method of the current Runtime object.

setErr

```
public static void setErr(PrintStream err)
```

Availability New as of JDK 1.1

Parameters   err   A PrintStream object to use for the standard error stream.

Throws   SecurityException

                    If the checkExec() method of the SecurityManager throws a SecurityException.

Description   This method sets the standard error stream to be this PrintStream object.

setIn

```
public static void setIn(InputStream in)
```

Availability New as of JDK 1.1

Parameters   in   A InputStream object to use for the standard input stream.

Throws   SecurityException

                    If the checkExec() method of the SecurityManager throws a SecurityException.

Description   This method sets the standard input stream to be this InputStream object.

setOut

```
public static void setOut(PrintStream out)
```

Availability New as of JDK 1.1

Parameters   out   A PrintStream object to use for the standard output stream.

Throws   SecurityException

                    If the checkExec() method of the SecurityManager throws a SecurityException.

Description   This method sets the standard output stream to be this
               PrintStream object.

setProperties

public static void setProperties(Properties props)

Parameters   props   A reference to a Properties object.

Throws   SecurityException

               If the checkPropertiesAccess() method of the
               SecurityManager throws a SecurityException.

Description   This method replaces the current set of system property defini-
               tions with a new set of system property definitions that are
               encapsulated by the given Properties object. As discussed in
               the description of the System class, some system properties are
               guaranteed to always be defined.

setSecurityManager

public static void setSecurityManager(SecurityManager s)

Parameters   s   A reference to a SecurityManager object.

Throws   SecurityException

               If a SecurityManager object has already been
               installed.

Description   This method installs the given SecurityManager object. If s is
               null, then no SecurityManager object is installed. Once a
               SecurityManager object is installed, any subsequent calls to this
               method throw a SecurityException.

Inherited Methods

Method	Inherited From	Method	Inherited From
clone()	Object	equals(Object)	Object
finalize()	Object	getClass()	Object
hashCode()	Object	notify()	Object
notifyAll()	Object	toString()	Object
wait()	Object	wait(long)	Object
wait(long, int)	Object		

See Also

ArrayIndexOutOfBoundsException, ArrayStoreException, InputStream, Null-
PointerException, Object, PrintStream, Process, Runtime, SecurityException,
SecurityManager, UnsatisfiedLinkError

12.61   Thread

Synopsis

Class Name:	java.lang.Thread
Superclass:	java.lang.Object
Immediate Subclasses:	None
Interfaces Implemented:	java.lang.Runnable
Availability:	JDK 1.0 or later

Description

The Thread class encapsulates all of the information about a single thread of control running in a Java environment. Thread objects are used to control threads in a
multithreaded program.

The execution of Java code is always under the control of a Thread object. The
Thread class provides a static method called currentThread() that can be used to
get a reference to the Thread object that controls the current thread of execution.

In order for a Thread object to be useful, it must be associated with a method that
it is supposed to run. Java provides two ways of associating a Thread object with a
method:

- Declare a subclass of Thread that defines a run() method. When such a class is
  instantiated and the object's start() method is called, the thread invokes this
  run() method.
- Pass a reference to an object that implements the Runnable interface to a
  Thread constructor. When the start() method of such a Thread object is
  called, the thread invokes the run() method of the Runnable object.

After a thread is started, it dies when one of the following things happens:

- The run() method called by the Thread returns.
- An exception is thrown that causes the run() method to be exited.
- The stop() method of the Thread is called.

Class Summary

```
public class java.lang.Thread extends java.lang.Object
                        implements java.lang.Runnable {
    // Constants
    public final static int MAX_PRIORITY;
    public final static int MIN_PRIORITY;
    public final static int NORM_PRIORITY;


    // Constructors
    public Thread();
    public Thread(Runnable target);
    public Thread(Runnable target, String name);
    public Thread(String name);
    public Thread(ThreadGroup group, Runnable target);
    public Thread(ThreadGroup group, Runnable target, String name);
    public Thread(ThreadGroup group, String name);


    // Class Methods
    public static int activeCount();
    public static native Thread currentThread();
    public static void dumpStack();
    public static int enumerate(Thread tarray[]);
    public static boolean interrupted();
    public static native void sleep(long millis);
    public static void sleep(long millis, int nanos);
    public static native void yield();


    // Instance Methods
    public void checkAccess();
    public native int countStackFrames();
    public void destroy();
    public final String getName();
    public final int getPriority();
    public final ThreadGroup getThreadGroup();
    public void interrupt();
    public final native boolean isAlive();
    public final boolean isDaemon();
    public boolean isInterrupted();
    public final void join();
    public final synchronized void join(long millis);
    public final synchronized void join(long millis, int nanos);
    public final void resume();
    public void run();
    public final void setDaemon(boolean on);
    public final void setName(String name);
    public final void setPriority(int newPriority);
    public synchronized native void start();
    public final void stop();
    public final synchronized void stop(Throwable o);
```

```
    public final void suspend();
    public String toString();
}
```

Constants

MAX_PRIORITY

public final static int MAX_PRIORITY = 10

Description   The highest priority a thread can have.

MIN_PRIORITY

public final static int MIN_PRIORITY = 1

Description   The lowest priority a thread can have.

NORM_PRIORITY

public final static int NORM_PRIORITY = 5

Description   The default priority assigned to a thread.

Constructors

Thread

public Thread()

Throws   SecurityException

If the checkAccess() method of the Security-
Manager throws a SecurityException.

Description   Creates a Thread object that belongs to the same ThreadGroup
object as the current thread, has the same daemon attribute as
the current thread, has the same priority as the current thread,
and has a default name.

A Thread object created with this constructor invokes its own
run() method when the Thread object's start() method is
called. This is not useful unless the object belongs to a subclass
of the Thread class that overrides the run() method.

Calling this constructor is equivalent to:

```
Thread(null, null, genName)
```

genName is an automatically generated name of the form
"Thread-"+n, where n is an integer incremented each time a
Thread object is created.

`public Thread(String name)`

Parameters	name	The name of this `Thread` object.
Throws	SecurityException	
		If the `checkAccess()` method of the `Security-Manager` throws a `SecurityException`.
Description		Creates a `Thread` object that belongs to the same `ThreadGroup` object as the current thread, has the same daemon attribute as the current thread, has the same priority as the current thread, and has the specified name.

A `Thread` object created with this constructor invokes its own `run()` method when the `Thread` object's `start()` method is called. This is not useful unless the object belongs to a subclass of the `Thread` class that overrides the `run()` method.

Calling this constructor is equivalent to:

```
Thread(null, null, name)
```

The uniqueness of the specified `Thread` object's name is not checked, which may be a problem for programs that attempt to identify `Thread` objects by their name.

`public Thread(ThreadGroup group, Runnable target)`

Parameters	group	The `ThreadGroup` object that this `Thread` object is to be added to.
	target	A reference to an object that implements the `Runnable` interface.
Throws	SecurityException	
		If the `checkAccess()` method of the `Security-Manager` throws a `SecurityException`.
Description		Creates a `Thread` object that belongs to the specified `ThreadGroup` object, has the same daemon attribute as the current thread, has the same priority as the current thread, and has a default name.

A `Thread` object created with this constructor invokes the `run()` method of the specified `Runnable` object when the `Thread` object's `start()` method is called.

Calling this constructor is equivalent to:

```
Thread(group, target, genName)
```

`genName` is an automatically generated name of the form `"Thread-"+n`, where n is an integer that is incremented each time a `Thread` object is created.

```
public Thread(ThreadGroup group, Runnable target, String name)
```
Parameters   group   The ThreadGroup object that this Thread object
                                is to be added to.

                target   A reference to an object that implements the
                                Runnable interface.

                name   The name of this Thread object.

Throws   SecurityException

                                If the checkAccess() method of the Security-
                                Manager throws a SecurityException.

Description   Creates a Thread object that belongs to the specified Thread-
                Group object, has the same daemon attribute as the current
                thread, has the same priority as the current thread, and has the
                specified name.

                A Thread object created with this constructor invokes the run()
                method of the specified Runnable object when the Thread
                object's start() method is called.

                The uniqueness of the specified Thread object's name is not
                checked, which may be a problem for programs that attempt to
                identify Thread objects by their names.

```
public Thread(ThreadGroup group, String name)
```
Parameters   group   The ThreadGroup object that this Thread object
                                is to be added to.

                name   The name of this Thread object.

Throws   SecurityException

                                If the checkAccess() method of the Security-
                                Manager throws a SecurityException.

Description   Creates a Thread object that belongs to the specified Thread-
                Group object, has the same daemon attribute as the current
                thread, has the same priority as the current thread, and has the
                specified name.

                A Thread object created with this constructor invokes its own
                run() method when the Thread object's start() method is
                called. This is not useful unless the object belongs to a subclass
                of the Thread class that overrides the run() method. Calling
                this constructor is equivalent to:

```
Thread(group, null, name)
```

                The uniqueness of the specified Thread object's name is not
                checked, which may be a problem for programs that attempt to
                identify Thread objects by their name.

Class Methods

activeCount

public static int activeCount()

Returns   The current number of threads in the ThreadGroup of the currently running thread.

Description   This method returns the number of threads in the ThreadGroup of the currently running thread for which the isAlive() method returns true.

currentThread

public static native Thread currentThread()

Returns   A reference to the Thread object that controls the currently executing thread.

Description   This method returns a reference to the Thread object that controls the currently executing thread.

dumpStack

public static void dumpStack()

Description   This method outputs a stack trace of the currently running thread.

enumerate

public static int enumerate(Thread tarray[])

Parameters   tarray   A reference to an array of Thread objects.

Returns   The number of Thread objects stored in the array.

Description   This method stores a reference in the array for each of the Thread objects in the ThreadGroup of the currently running thread for which the isAlive() method returns true.

Calling this method is equivalent to:

```
currentThread().getThreadGroup().enumerate(tarray)
```

If the array is not big enough to contain references to all the Thread objects, only as many references as will fit are put into the array. No indication is given that some Thread objects were left out, so it is a good idea to call activeCount() before calling this method, to get an idea of how large to make the array.

interrupted

`public static boolean interrupted()`

Returns   true if the currently running thread has been interrupted; otherwise false.

Description This method determines whether or not the currently running thread has been interrupted.

sleep

`public static native void sleep(long millis)`

Parameters `millis` The number of milliseconds that the currently running thread should sleep.

Throws   `InterruptedException`
            If another thread interrupts the currently running thread.

Description This method causes the currently running thread to sleep. The method does not return until at least the specified number of milliseconds have elapsed.

            While a thread is sleeping, it retains ownership of all locks. The `Object` class defines a method called `wait()` that is similar to `sleep()` but causes the currently running thread to temporarily relinquish its locks.

`public static void sleep(long millis, int nanos)`

Parameters `millis` The number of milliseconds that the currently running thread should sleep.

            `nanos`   An additional number of nanoseconds to sleep.

Throws   `InterruptedException`
            If another thread interrupts the currently running thread.

Description This method causes the currently running thread to sleep. The method does not return until at least the specified number of milliseconds have elapsed.

            While a thread is sleeping, it retains ownership of all locks. The `Object` class defines a method called `wait()` that is similar to `sleep()` but causes the currently running thread to temporarily relinquish its locks.

            Note that Sun's reference implementation of Java does not attempt to implement the precision implied by this method. Instead, it rounds to the nearest millisecond (unless `millis` is 0, in which case it rounds up to 1 millisecond) and calls `sleep(long)`.

yield

> public static native void yield()
>> Description   This method causes the currently running thread to yield control of the processor so that another thread can be scheduled.

Instance Methods

checkAccess

> public void checkAccess()
>> Throws   SecurityException
>>> If the `checkAccess()` method of the `Security-Manager` throws a `SecurityException`.
>> Description   This method determines if the currently running thread has permission to modify this Thread object.

countStackFrames

> public native int countStackFrames()
>> Returns   The number of pending method invocations on this thread's stack.
>> Description   This method returns the number of pending method invocations on this thread's stack.

destroy

> public void destroy()
>> Description   This method is meant to terminate this thread without any of the usual cleanup (i.e., any locks held by the thread are not released). This method provides a last-resort way to terminate a thread. While a thread can defeat its `stop()` method by catching objects thrown from it, there is nothing that a thread can do to stop itself from being destroyed.
>>
>> Note that Sun's reference implementation of Java does not implement the documented functionality of this method. Instead, the implementation of this method just throws a `NoSuchMethodError`.

getName

```
public final String getName()
```
Returns   The name of this thread.

Description   This method returns the name of this Thread object.

getPriority

```
public final int getPriority()
```
Returns   The priority of this thread.

Description   This method returns the priority of this Thread object.

getThreadGroup

```
public final ThreadGroup getThreadGroup()
```
Returns   The ThreadGroup of this thread.

Description   This method returns a reference to the ThreadGroup that this Thread object belongs to.

interrupt

```
public void interrupt()
```
Description   This method interrupts this Thread object.

Note that prior to version 1.1, Sun's reference implementation of Java does not implement the documented functionality of this method. Instead, the method just sets a private flag that indicates that an interrupt has been requested. None of the methods that should throw an InterruptedException currently do. However, the interrupted() and isInterrupted() methods do return true after this method has been called.

isAlive

```
public final native boolean isAlive()
```
Returns   true if this thread is alive; otherwise false.

Description   This method determines whether or not this Thread object is alive. A Thread object is alive if it has been started and has not yet died. In other words, it has been scheduled to run before and can still be scheduled to run again. A thread is generally alive after its start() method is called and until its stop() method is called.

isDaemon

`public final boolean isDaemon()`

Returns   true if the thread is a daemon thread; otherwise false.

Description This method determines whether or not this thread is a daemon thread, based on the value of the daemon attribute of this Thread object.

isInterrupted

`public boolean isInterrupted()`

Returns   true if this thread has been interrupted; otherwise false.

Description This method determines whether or not this Thread object has been interrupted.

join

`public final void join()`

Throws   InterruptedException

             If another thread interrupts this thread.

Description This method allows the thread that calls it to wait for the Thread associated with this method to die. The method returns when the Thread dies. If this thread is already dead, then this method returns immediately.

`public final synchronized void join(long millis)`

Parameters   millis   The maximum number of milliseconds to wait for this thread to die.

Throws   InterruptedException

             If another thread interrupts this thread.

Description This method causes a thread to wait to die. The method returns when this Thread object dies or after the specified number of milliseconds has elapsed, whichever comes first. However, if the specified number of milliseconds is zero, the method will wait forever for this thread to die. If this thread is already dead, the method returns immediately.

`public final synchronized void join(long millis, int nanos)`

Parameters   millis   The maximum number of milliseconds to wait for this thread to die.

             nanos   An additional number of nanoseconds to wait.

Throws   InterruptedException

             If another thread interrupts this thread.

Description   This method causes a thread to wait to die. The method returns when this Thread object dies or after the specified amount of time has elapsed, whichever comes first. However, if millis and nanos are zero, the method will wait forever for this thread to die. If this thread is already dead, the method returns immediately.

Note that Sun's reference implementation of Java does not attempt to implement the precision implied by this method. Instead, it rounds to the nearest millisecond (unless millis is 0, in which case it rounds up to 1 millisecond) and calls join(long).

resume

```
public final void resume()
```
Throws   SecurityException
                        If the checkAccess() method of the Security-
                        Manager throws a SecurityException.
Description   This method resumes a suspended thread. The method causes this Thread object to once again be eligible to be run. Calling this method for a thread that is not suspended has no effect.

run

```
public void run()
```
Implements   Runnable.run()
Description   A Thread object's start() method causes the thread to invoke a run() method. If this Thread object was created without a specified Runnable object, the Thread object's own run() method is executed. This behavior is only useful in a subclass of Thread that overrides this run() method, since the run() method of the Thread class does not do anything.

setDaemon

```
public final void setDaemon(boolean on)
```
Parameters   on   The new value for this thread's daemon attribute.
Throws   IllegalThreadStateException
                        If this method is called after this thread has been started and while it is still alive.
               SecurityException
                        If the checkAccess() method of the Security-
                        Manager throws a SecurityException.

Description   This method sets the daemon attribute of this Thread object to the given value. This method must be called before the thread is started. If a thread dies and there are no other threads except daemon threads alive, the Java virtual machine stops.

setName

public final void setName(String name)

Parameters   name   The new name for this thread.

Throws   SecurityException

If the checkAccess() method of the Security-Manager throws a SecurityException.

Description   This method sets the name of this Thread object to the given value. The uniqueness of the specified Thread object's name is not checked, which may be a problem for programs that attempt to identify Thread objects by their name.

setPriority

public final void setPriority(int newPriority)

Parameters   newPriority   The new priority for this thread.

Throws   IllegalArgumentException

If the given priority is less than MIN_PRIORITY or greater than MAX_PRIORITY.

SecurityException

If the checkAccess() method of the Security-Manager throws a SecurityException.

Description   This method sets the priority of this Thread to the given value.

start

public synchronized native void start()

Throws   IllegalThreadStateException

If this Thread object's start() method has been called before.

Description   This method starts this Thread object, allowing it to be scheduled for execution. The top-level code that is executed by the thread is the run() method of the Runnable object specified in the constructor that was used to create this object. If no such object was specified, the top-level code executed by the thread is this object's run() method.

It is not permitted to start a thread more than once.

stop

public final void stop()

Throws   SecurityException

If the checkAccess() method of the Security-Manager throws a SecurityException.

Description   This method causes this Thread object to stop executing by throwing a ThreadDeath object. The object is thrown in this thread, even if the method is called from a different thread. This thread is forced to stop whatever it is doing and throw a newly created ThreadDeath object. If this thread was suspended, it is resumed; if it was sleeping, it is awakened. Normally, you should not catch ThreadDeath objects in a try statement. If you need to catch ThreadDeath objects to detect a Thread is about to die, the try statement that catches ThreadDeath objects should rethrow them.

When an object is thrown out of the run() method associated with a Thread, the uncaughtException() method of the ThreadGroup for that Thread is called. The uncaughtException() method normally outputs a stack trace. However, uncaughtException() treats a ThreadDeath object as a special case by not outputting a stack trace. When the uncaughtException() method returns, the thread is dead. The thread is never scheduled to run again.

If this Thread object's stop() method is called before this thread is started, the ThreadDeath object is thrown as soon as the thread is started.

public final synchronized void stop(Throwable o)

Parameters   o   The object to be thrown.

Throws   SecurityException

If the checkAccess() method of the Security-Manager throws a SecurityException.

Description   This method causes this Thread object to stop executing by throwing the given object. Normally, the stop() method that takes no arguments and throws a ThreadDeath object should be called instead of this method. However, if it is necessary to stop a thread by throwing some other type of object, this method can be used.

The object is thrown in this thread, even if the method is called from a different thread. This thread is forced to stop whatever it is doing and throw the Throwable object o. If this thread was suspended, it is resumed; if it was sleeping, it is awakened.

When an object is thrown out of the run() method associated with a Thread, the uncaughtException() method of the ThreadGroup for that Thread is called. If the thrown object is not an instance of the ThreadDeath class, uncaughtException() calls the thrown object's printStackTrace() method and then the thread dies. The thread is never scheduled to run again.

If this Thread object's stop() method is called before this thread is started, the ThreadDeath object is thrown as soon as the thread is started.

suspend

public final void suspend()

Throws	SecurityException
	If the checkAccess() method of the Security-Manager throws a SecurityException.
Description	This method suspends a thread. The method causes this Thread object to temporarily be ineligible to be run. The thread becomes eligible to be run again after its resume() method is called. Calling this method for a thread that is already suspended has no effect.

toString

public String toString()

Returns	A string representation of this Thread object.
Overrides	Object.toString()
Description	This method returns a string representation of this Thread object.

Inherited Methods

Method	Inherited From	Method	Inherited From
clone()	Object	equals(Object)	Object
finalize()	Object	getClass()	Object
hashCode()	Object	notify()	Object
notifyAll()	Object	wait()	Object
wait(long)	Object	wait(long, int)	Object

See Also

IllegalThreadStateException, InterruptedException, Object, Runnable, SecurityException, SecurityManager, ThreadGroup

---

12.62   ThreadDeath

Synopsis

Class Name:	java.lang.ThreadDeath
Superclass:	java.lang.Error
Immediate Subclasses:	None
Interfaces Implemented:	None
Availability:	JDK 1.0 or later

Description

A ThreadDeath object is thown by the stop() method of a Thread object to kill the thread. Catching ThreadDeath objects is not recommended. If it is necessary to catch a ThreadDeath object, it is important to rethrow the object so that it is possible to cleanly stop the catching thread.

Class Summary

```
public class java.lang.ThreadDeath extends java.lang.Error {
    // Constructors
    public ThreadDeath();
}
```

Constructors

ThreadDeath

public ThreadDeath()

Description   This constructor creates a ThreadDeath object with no associated detail message.

Inherited Methods

Method	Inherited From	Method	Inherited From
clone()	Object	equals(Object)	Object
fillInStackTrace()	Throwable	finalize()	Object
getClass()	Object	getLocalizedMessage()	Throwable
getMessage()	Throwable	hashCode()	Object
notify()	Object	notifyAll()	Object

Method	Inherited From	Method	Inherited From
printStackTrace()	Throwable	printStack-Trace(PrintStream)	Throwable
printStack-Trace(PrintWriter)	Throwable	toString()	Object
wait()	Object	wait(long)	Object
wait(long, int)	Object		

See Also

Error, Thread, Throwable

12.63   ThreadGroup

Synopsis

Class Name:	java.lang.ThreadGroup
Superclass:	java.lang.Object
Immediate Subclasses:	None
Interfaces Implemented:	None
Availability:	JDK 1.0 or later

Description

The ThreadGroup class implements a grouping scheme for threads. A ThreadGroup object can own Thread objects and other ThreadGroup objects. The ThreadGroup class provides methods that allow a ThreadGroup object to control its Thread and ThreadGroup objects as a group. For example, suspend() and resume() methods of a ThreadGroup object call the suspend() and resume() methods of each of the Thread and ThreadGroup objects that belong to the particular ThreadGroup.

When a Java program starts, a ThreadGroup object is created to own the first Thread. Any additional ThreadGroup objects are explicitly created by the program.

Class Summary

```
public class java.lang.ThreadGroup extends java.lang.Object {
    // Constructors
    public ThreadGroup(String name);
    public ThreadGroup(ThreadGroup parent, String name;

    // Instance Methods
    public int activeCount();
    public int activeGroupCount();
    public boolean allowThreadSuspension(boolean b);        // New in 1.1
```

```
    public final void checkAccess();
    public final void destroy();
    public int enumerate(Thread list[]);
    public int enumerate(Thread list[], boolean recurse);
    public int enumerate(ThreadGroup list[]);
    public int enumerate(ThreadGroup list[], boolean recurse);
    public final int getMaxPriority();
    public final String getName();
    public final ThreadGroup getParent();
    public final boolean isDaemon();
    public synchronized boolean isDestroyed();        // New in 1.1
    public void list();
    public final boolean parentOf(ThreadGroup g);
    public final void resume();
    public final void setDaemon(boolean daemon);
    public final void setMaxPriority(int pri);
    public final void stop();
    public final void suspend();
    public String toString();
    public void uncaughtException(Thread t, Throwable e);
}
```

Constructors

ThreadGroup

`public ThreadGroup(String name)`

Parameters	name	The name of this ThreadGroup object.
Throws	SecurityException	
		If the checkAccess() method of the Security-Manager throws a SecurityException.
Description		Creates a ThreadGroup object that has the specified name and the same parent ThreadGroup as the current thread.

`public ThreadGroup(ThreadGroup parent, String name)`

Parameters	parent	The ThreadGroup object that this ThreadGroup object is to be added to.
	name	The name of this ThreadGroup object.
Throws	SecurityException	
		If the checkAccess() method of the Security-Manager throws a SecurityException.
Description		Creates a ThreadGroup object with the specified name and parent ThreadGroup object.

Instance Methods

activeCount

```
public int activeCount()
```

Returns   An approximation of the current number of threads in this
                 ThreadGroup object and any child ThreadGroup objects.

Description   This method returns an approximation of the number of
                 threads that belong to this ThreadGroup object and any child
                 ThreadGroup objects. The count is approximate because a
                 thread can die after it is counted, but before the complete
                 count is returned. Also, after a child ThreadGroup is counted
                 but before the total count is returned, additional Thread and
                 ThreadGroup objects can be added to a child ThreadGroup.

activeGroupCount

```
public int activeGroupCount()
```

Returns   An approximation of the current number of child ThreadGroup
                 objects in this ThreadGroup object.

Description   This method returns an approximation of the number of child
                 ThreadGroup objects that belong to this ThreadGroup object.
                 The count is approximate because after a child ThreadGroup is
                 counted but before the total count is returned, additional
                 ThreadGroup objects can be added to a child ThreadGroup.

allowThreadSuspension

```
public boolean allowThreadSuspension(boolean b)
```

Availability   New as of JDK 1.1

Parameters   b   A boolean value that specifies whether or not
                                   the run-time system is allowed to suspend
                                   threads due to low memory.

Returns   The boolean value true.

Description   This method specifies whether or not the Java virtual machine
                 is allowed to suspend threads due to low memory.

checkAccess

```
public final void checkAccess()
```

Throws   SecurityException
                                   If the checkAccess() method of the Security-
                                   Manager throws a SecurityException.

Description   This method determines if the currently running thread has
                 permission to modify this ThreadGroup object.

destroy

public final void destroy()

Throws	IllegalThreadStateException
	If this ThreadGroup object is not empty, or if it has already been destroyed.
	SecurityException
	If the checkAccess() method of the Security-Manager throws a SecurityException.
Description	This method destroys this ThreadGroup object and any child ThreadGroup objects. The ThreadGroup must not contain any Thread objects. This method also removes the ThreadGroup object from its parent ThreadGroup object.

enumerate

public int enumerate(Thread list[])

Parameters	list	A reference to an array of Thread objects.
Returns		The number of Thread objects stored in the array.
Description		This method stores a reference in the array for each of the Thread objects that belongs to this ThreadGroup or any of its child ThreadGroup objects.

If the array is not big enough to contain references to all the Thread objects, only as many references as will fit are put into the array. No indication is given that some Thread objects were left out, so it is a good idea to call activeCount() before calling this method, to get an idea of how large to make the array.

public int enumerate(Thread list[], boolean recurse)

Parameters	list	A reference to an array of Thread objects.
	recurse	A boolean value that specifies whether or not to include Thread objects that belong to child ThreadGroup objects of this ThreadGroup object.
Returns		The number of Thread objects stored in the array.
Description		This method stores a reference in the array for each of the Thread objects that belongs to this ThreadGroup object. If recurse is true, the method also stores a reference for each of the Thread objects that belongs to a child ThreadGroup object of this ThreadGroup.

If the array is not big enough to contain references to all the Thread objects, only as many references as will fit are put into the array. No indication is given that some Thread objects were left out, so it is a good idea to call activeCount() before calling this method, to get an idea of how large to make the array.

`public int enumerate(ThreadGroup list[])`

Parameters	list	A reference to an array of ThreadGroup objects.
Returns		The number of ThreadGroup objects stored in the array.
Description		This method stores a reference in the array for each Thread-Group object that belongs to this ThreadGroup or any of its child ThreadGroup objects.

If the array is not big enough to contain references to all the ThreadGroup objects, only as many references as will fit are put into the array. No indication is given that some ThreadGroup objects were left out, so it is a good idea to call activeGroup-Count() before calling this method, to get an idea of how large to make the array.

`public int enumerate(Thread list[], boolean recurse)`

Parameters	list	A reference to an array of ThreadGroup objects.
	recurse	A boolean value that specifies whether or not to include ThreadGroup objects that belong to child ThreadGroup objects of this ThreadGroup object.
Returns		The number of ThreadGroup objects stored in the array.
Description		This method stores a reference in the array for each of the ThreadGroup objects that belongs to this ThreadGroup object. If recurse is true, the method also stores a reference for each of the ThreadGroup objects that belongs to a child ThreadGroup object of this ThreadGroup.

If the array is not big enough to contain references to all the ThreadGroup objects, only as many references as will fit are put into the array. No indication is given that some ThreadGroup objects were left out, so it is a good idea to call activeGroup-Count() before calling this method, to get an idea of how large to make the array.

getMaxPriority

`public final int getMaxPriority()`

Returns	The maximum priority that can be assigned to Thread objects that belong to this ThreadGroup object.
Description	This method returns the maximum priority that can be assigned to Thread objects that belong to this ThreadGroup object.

It is possible for a ThreadGroup to contain Thread objects that have higher priorities than this maximum, if they were given that higher priority before the maximum was set to a lower value.

getName

```
public final String getName()
```

Returns   The name of this ThreadGroup object.

Description   This method returns the name of this ThreadGroup object.

getParent

```
public final ThreadGroup getParent()
```

Returns   The parent ThreadGroup object of this ThreadGroup, or null if
               this ThreadGroup is the root of the thread group hierarchy.

Description   This method returns the parent ThreadGroup object of this
               ThreadGroup object. If this ThreadGroup is at the root of the
               thread group hierarchy and has no parent, the method returns
               null.

isDaemon

```
public final boolean isDaemon()
```

Returns   true if this ThreadGroup is a daemon thread group; otherwise
               false.

Description   This method determines whether or not this ThreadGroup is a
               daemon thread group, based on the value of daemon attribute
               of this ThreadGroup object. A daemon thread group is
               destroyed when the last Thread in it is stopped, or the last
               ThreadGroup in it is destroyed.

isDestroyed

```
public synchronized boolean isDestroyed()
```

Availability   New as of JDK 1.1

Returns   true if this ThreadGroup has been destroyed; otherwise false.

Description   This method determines whether or not this ThreadGroup has
               been destroyed.

list

```
public void list()
```

Description   This method outputs a listing of the contents of this Thread-
               Group object to System.out.

parentOf

```
public final boolean parentOf(ThreadGroup g)
```

Parameters   g   A ThreadGroup object.

Returns   true if this ThreadGroup object is the same ThreadGroup, or a direct or indirect parent of the specified ThreadGroup; otherwise false.

Description   This method determines if this ThreadGroup object is the same as the specified ThreadGroup or one of its ancestors in the thread-group hierarchy.

resume

```
public final void resume()
```

Throws   SecurityException

If the checkAccess() method of the Security-Manager throws a SecurityException.

Description   This method resumes each Thread object that directly or indirectly belongs to this ThreadGroup object by calling its resume() method.

setDaemon

```
public final void setDaemon(boolean daemon)
```

Parameters   daemon   The new value for this ThreadGroup object's daemon attribute.

Throws   SecurityException

If the checkAccess() method of the Security-Manager throws a SecurityException.

Description   This method sets the daemon attribute of this ThreadGroup object to the given value. A daemon thread group is destroyed when the last Thread in it is stopped, or the last ThreadGroup in it is destroyed.

setMaxPriority

```
public final void setMaxPriority(int pri)
```

Parameters   pri   The new maximum priority for Thread objects that belong to this ThreadGroup object.

Description   This method sets the maximum priority that can be assigned to Thread objects that belong to this ThreadGroup object.

It is possible for a ThreadGroup to contain Thread objects that have higher priorities than this maximum, if they were given that higher priority before the maximum was set to a lower value.

stop

`public final void stop()`

Throws   `SecurityException`

If the `checkAccess()` method of the Security-
Manager throws a `SecurityException`.

Description   This method stops each `Thread` object that directly or indirectly
belongs to this `ThreadGroup` object by calling its `stop()`
method.

suspend

`public final void suspend()`

Throws   `SecurityException`

If the `checkAccess()` method of the Security-
Manager throws a `SecurityException`.

Description   This method suspends each `Thread` object that directly or indirectly belongs to this `ThreadGroup` object by calling its sus-
pend() method.

toString

`public String toString()`

Returns   A string representation of this `ThreadGroup` object.

Overrides   `Object.toString()`

Description   This method returns a string representation of this Thread-
Group object.

uncaughtException

`public void uncaughtException(Thread t, Throwable e)`

Parameters   t   A reference to a `Thread` that just died because of
an uncaught exception.

e   The uncaught exception.

Description   This method is called when a `Thread` object that belongs to this
`ThreadGroup` object dies because of an uncaught exception. If
this `ThreadGroup` object has a parent `ThreadGroup` object, this
method just calls the parent's `uncaughtException()` method.
Otherwise, this method must determine whether the uncaught
exception is an instance of `ThreadDeath`. If it is, nothing is
done. If it is not, the method calls the `printStackTrace()`
method of the exception object.

If this method is overridden, the overriding method should end
with a call to `super.uncaughtException()`.

Inherited Methods

Method	Inherited From	Method	Inherited From
clone()	Object	equals(Object)	Object
finalize()	Object	getClass()	Object
hashCode()	Object	notify()	Object
notifyAll()	Object	wait()	Object
wait(long)	Object	wait(long, int)	Object

See Also

IllegalThreadStateException, Object, Runnable, SecurityException, Security-Manager, Thread, Throwable

12.64   Throwable

Synopsis

Class Name: java.lang.Throwable
Superclass: java.lang.Object
Immediate Subclasses: java.lang.Error, java.lang.Exception
Interfaces Implemented: java.io.Serializable
Availability: JDK 1.0 or later

Description

The Throwable class is the superclass of all objects that can be thrown by the throw statement in Java. This is a requirement of the throw statement.

A Throwable object can have an associated message that provides more detail about the particular error or exception that is being thrown.

The Throwable class provides a method that outputs information about the state of the system when an exception object is created. This method can be useful in debugging Java programs.

The subclasses of Throwable that are provided with Java do not add functionality to Throwable. Instead, they offer more specific classifications of errors and exceptions.

Class Summary

```
public class java.lang.Throwable extends java.lang.Object
                              implements java.lang.Serializable {
    // Constructors
    public Throwable();
    public Throwable(String message);

    // Instance Methods
    public native Throwable fillInStackTrace();
    public String getLocalizedMessage();           // New in 1.1
    public String getMessage();
    public void printStackTrace();
    public void printStackTrace(PrintStream s);
    public void printStackTrace(PrintWriter s);     // New in 1.1
    public String toString();
}
```

Constructors

Throwable

public Throwable()

Description	Creates a Throwable object with no associated message. This constructor calls fillInStackTrace() so that information is available for printStackTrace().

public Throwable(String message)

Parameters	message	A message string to be associated with the object.
Description		Create a Throwable object with an associated message. This constructor calls fillInStackTrace() so that information is available for printStackTrace().

Instance Methods

fillInStackTrace

public native Throwable fillInStackTrace()

Returns	A reference to this object.
Description	This method puts stack trace information in this Throwable object. It is not usually necessary to explicitly call this method, since it is called by the constructors of the class. However, this method can be useful when rethrowing an object. If the stack trace information in the object needs to reflect the location that the object is rethrows from, fillInStackTrace() should be called.

getLocalizedMessage

`public String getLocalizedMessage()`

Availability   New as of JDK 1.1

Returns   A localized version of the `String` object associated with this `Throwable` object, or `null` if there is no message associated with this object.

Description   This method creates a localized version of the message that was associated with this object by its constructor.

The `getLocalizedMessage()` method in `Throwable` always returns the same result as `getMessage()`. A subclass must override this method to produce a locale-specific message.

getMessage

`public String getMessage()`

Returns   The `String` object associated with this `Throwable` object, or `null` if there is no message associated with this object.

Description   This method returns any string message that was associated with this object by its constructor.

printStackTrace

`public void printStackTrace()`

Description   This method outputs the string representation of this `Throwable` object and a stack trace to `System.err`.

`public void printStackTrace(PrintStream s)`

Parameters   s   A `java.io.PrintStream` object.

Description   This method outputs the string representation of this `Throwable` object and a stack trace to the specified `PrintStream` object.

`public void printStackTrace(PrintStream w)`

Availability   New as of JDK 1.1

Parameters   s   A `java.io.PrintWriter` object.

Description   This method outputs the string representation of this `Throwable` object and a stack trace to the specified `PrintWriter` object.

toString

`public String toString()`

Returns   A string representation of this object.

Overrides	Object.toString()
Description	This method returns a string representation of this Throwable object.

Inherited Methods

Method	Inherited From	Method	Inherited From
clone()	Object	equals(Object)	Object
finalize()	Object	getClass()	Object
hashCode()	Object	notify()	Object
notifyAll()	Object	wait()	Object
wait(long)	Object	wait(long, int)	Object

See Also

Error, Exception, Object

12.65   UnknownError

Synopsis

Class Name:	java.lang.UnknownError
Superclass:	java.lang.VirtualMachineError
Immediate Subclasses:	None
Interfaces Implemented:	None
Availability:	JDK 1.0 or later

Description

An UnknownError is thrown when an error of unknown origins is detected in the run-time system.

Class Summary

```
public class java.lang.UnknownError
        extends java.lang.VirtualMachineError {
  // Constructors
  public UnknownError();
  public UnknownError(String s);
}
```

Constructors

UnknownError

public UnknownError()

Description   This constructor creates an UnknownError with no associated detail message.

public UnknownError(String s)

Parameters   s   The detail message.

Description   This constructor creates an UnknownError with the specified detail message.

Inherited Methods

Method	Inherited From	Method	Inherited From
clone()	Object	equals(Object)	Object
fillInStackTrace()	Throwable	finalize()	Object
getClass()	Object	getLocalizedMessage()	Throwable
getMessage()	Throwable	hashCode()	Object
notify()	Object	notifyAll()	Object
printStackTrace()	Throwable	printStack-Trace(PrintStream)	Throwable
printStack-Trace(PrintWriter)	Throwable	toString()	Object
wait()	Object	wait(long)	Object
wait(long, int)	Object		

See Also

Error, Throwable, VirtualMachineError

12.66   UnsatisfiedLinkError

Synopsis

Class Name: java.lang.UnsatisfiedLinkError
Superclass: java.lang.LinkageError
Immediate Subclasses: None
Interfaces Implemented: None
Availability: JDK 1.0 or later

Description

An UnsatisfiedLinkError is thrown when the implementation of a native method cannot be found.

Class Summary

```
public class java.lang.UnsatisfiedLinkError
            extends java.lang.LinkageError {
  // Constructors
  public UnsatisfiedLinkError();
  public UnsatisfiedLinkError(String s);
}
```

Constructors

UnsatisfiedLinkError

   public UnsatisfiedLinkError()

      Description   This constructor creates an UnsatisfiedLinkError with no associated detail message.

   public UnsatisfiedLinkError(String s)

      Parameters   s   The detail message.

      Description   This constructor creates an UnsatisfiedLinkError with the specified detail message.

Inherited Methods

Method	Inherited From	Method	Inherited From
clone()	Object	equals(Object)	Object
fillInStackTrace()	Throwable	finalize()	Object
getClass()	Object	getLocalizedMessage()	Throwable
getMessage()	Throwable	hashCode()	Object
notify()	Object	notifyAll()	Object
printStackTrace()	Throwable	printStack-Trace(PrintStream)	Throwable
printStack-Trace(PrintWriter)	Throwable	toString()	Object
wait()	Object	wait(long)	Object
wait(long, int)	Object		

See Also

Error, LinkageError, Throwable

12.67 VerifyError

Synopsis

Class Name:	java.lang.VerifyError
Superclass:	java.lang.LinkageError
Immediate Subclasses:	None
Interfaces Implemented:	None
Availability:	JDK 1.0 or later

Description

A VerifyError is thrown when the byte-code verifier detects that a class file, though well-formed, contains some sort of internal inconsistency or security problem.

As part of loading the byte-codes for a class, the Java virtual machine may run the *.class* file through the byte-code verifier. The default mode of the virtual machine causes it not to verify classes that are found locally, however. Thus, after compiling an applet and running it locally, you may still get a VerifyError when you put it on a web server.

Class Summary

```
public class java.lang.VerifyError extends java.lang.LinkageError {
    // Constructors
    public VerifyError();
    public VerifyError(String s);
}
```

Constructors

VerifyError

public VerifyError()

Description   This constructor creates a VerifyError with no associated detail message.

public VerifyError(String s)

Parameters   s   The detail message.

Description   This constructor creates a `VerifyError` with the specified detail message.

Inherited Methods

Method	Inherited From	Method	Inherited From
clone()	Object	equals(Object)	Object
fillInStackTrace()	Throwable	finalize()	Object
getClass()	Object	getLocalizedMessage()	Throwable
getMessage()	Throwable	hashCode()	Object
notify()	Object	notifyAll()	Object
printStackTrace()	Throwable	printStack-Trace(PrintStream)	Throwable
printStack-Trace(PrintWriter)	Throwable	toString()	Object
wait()	Object	wait(long)	Object
wait(long, int)	Object		

See Also

Error, LinkageError, Throwable

12.68   VirtualMachineError

Synopsis

Class Name: java.lang.VirtualMachineError
Superclass: java.lang.Error
Immediate Subclasses: java.lang.InternalError,
                       java.lang.OutOfMemoryError,
                       java.lang.StackOverflowError,
                       java.lang.UnknownError
Interfaces Implemented: None
Availability: JDK 1.0 or later

Description

The appropriate subclass of `VirtualMachineError` is thrown to indicate that the Java virtual machine has encountered an error.

Class Summary

```
public class java.lang.VirtualMachineError extends java.lang.Error {
  // Constructors
  public VirtualMachineError();
  public VirtualMachineError(String s);
}
```

Constructors

VirtualMachineError

public VirtualMachineError()

Description   This constructor creates a VirtualMachineError with no associated detail message.

public VirtualMachineError(String s)

Parameters   s   The detail message.

Description   This constructor creates a VirtualMachineError with the specified detail message.

Inherited Methods

Method	Inherited From	Method	Inherited From
clone()	Object	equals(Object)	Object
fillInStackTrace()	Throwable	finalize()	Object
getClass()	Object	getLocalizedMessage()	Throwable
getMessage()	Throwable	hashCode()	Object
notify()	Object	notifyAll()	Object
printStackTrace()	Throwable	printStack-Trace(PrintStream)	Throwable
printStack-Trace(PrintWriter)	Throwable	toString()	Object
wait()	Object	wait(long)	Object
wait(long, int)	Object		

See Also

Error, InternalError, OutOfMemoryError, StackOverflowError, Throwable, UnknownError

12.69 Void

Synopsis

Class Name:	java.lang.Void
Superclass:	java.lang.Object
Immediate Subclasses:	None
Interfaces Implemented:	None
Availability	New as of JDK 1.1

Description

The Void class is an uninstantiable wrapper for the primitive type void. The class contains simply a reference to the Class object that represents the primitive type void. The Void class is necessary as of JDK 1.1 to support the Reflection API and class literals.

Class Summary

```
public final class java.lang.Void extends java.lang.Object {
    // Constants
    public static final Class TYPE;
}
```

Constants

TYPE

```
public static final Class TYPE
```

The Class object that represents the primitive type void. It is always true that Void.TYPE == void.class.

Inherited Methods

Method	Inherited From	Method	Inherited From
clone()	Object	equals(Object)	Object
finalize()	Object	getClass()	Object
hashCode()	Object	notify()	Object
notifyAll()	Object	toString()	Object
wait()	Object	wait(long)	Object
wait(long, int)	Object		

See Also

Byte, Character, Class, Double, Float, Integer, Long, Short

13

The java.lang.reflect Package

The package `java.lang.reflect` is new as of Java 1.1. It contains classes and interfaces that support the Reflection API. Reflection refers to the ability of a class to reflect upon itself, or look inside of itself, to see what it can do. The Reflection API makes it possible to:

- Discover the variables, methods, and constructors of any class.
- Create an instance of any class using any available constructor of that class, even if the class initiating the creation was not compiled with any information about the class to be instantiated.
- Access the variables of any object, even if the accessing class was not compiled with any information about the class to be accessed.
- Call the methods of any object, even if the calling class was not compiled with any information about the class that contains the methods.
- Create an array of objects that are instances of any class, even if the creating class was not compiled with any information about the class.

These capabilities are implemented by the `java.lang.Class` class and the classes in the `java.lang.reflect` package. Figure 13-1 shows the class hierarchy for the `java.lang.reflect` package.

Java 1.1 currently uses the Reflection API for two purposes:

- The JavaBeans API supports a mechanism for customizing objects that is based on being able to discover their public variables, methods, and constructors. See the forthcoming *Developing Java Beans* from O'Reilly & Associates for more information about the JavaBeans API.
- The object serialization functionality in `java.io` is built on top of the Reflection API. Object serialization allows arbitrary objects to be written to a stream of bytes and then read back later as objects.

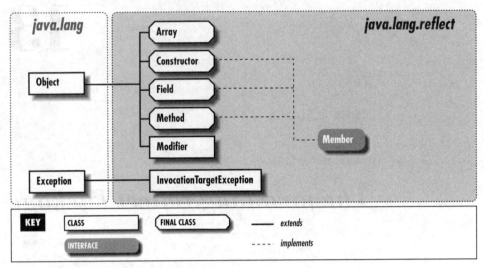

Figure 13–1: The java.lang.reflect package

13.1 Array

Synopsis

Class Name:	`java.lang.reflect.Array`
Superclass:	`java.lang.Object`
Immediate Subclasses:	None
Interfaces Implemented:	`java.lang.Cloneable`, `java.io.Serializable`
Availability:	New as of JDK 1.1

Description

The `Array` class provides static methods to manipulate arbitrary arrays in Java. There are methods to set and retrieve elements in an array, determine the size of an array, and create a new instance of an array.

The `Array` class is used to create array objects and manipulate their elements. The `Array` class is not used to represent array types. Because arrays in Java are objects, array types are represented by `Class` objects.

Class Summary

```
public final class java.lang.reflect.Array extends java.lang.Object {
    // Class Methods
    public static native Object get(Object array, int index);
    public static native boolean getBoolean(Object array, int index);
    public static native byte getByte(Object array, int index);
    public static native char getChar(Object array, int index);
    public static native double getDouble(Object array, int index);
    public static native float getFloat(Object array, int index);
    public static native int getInt(Object array, int index);
    public static native int getLength(Object array);
    public static native long getLong(Object array, int index);
    public static native short getShort(Object array, int index);
    public static Object newInstance(Class componentType, int length);
    public static Object newInstance(Class componentType, int[] dimensions);
    public static native void set(Object array, int index, Object value);
    public static native void setBoolean(Object array, int index, boolean z);
    public static native void setByte(Object array, int index, byte b);
    public static native void setChar(Object array, int index, char c);
    public static native void setDouble(Object array, int index, double d);
    public static native void setFloat(Object array, int index, float f);
    public static native void setInt(Object array, int index, int i);
    public static native void setLong(Object array, int index, long l);
    public static native void setShort(Object array, int index, short s);
}
```

Class Methods

get

```
public static native Object get(Object array, int index)
                          throws IllegalArgumentException,
                              ArrayIndexOutOfBoundsException
```

Parameters	array	An array object.
	index	An index into the array.
Returns		The object at the given index in the specified array.
Throws	IllegalArgumentException	
		If the given object is not an array.
	ArrayIndexOutOfBoundsException	
		If the given index is invalid.
	NullPointerException	
		If array is null.
Description		This method returns the object at the given index in the array. If the array contains values of a primitive type, the value at the given index is wrapped in an appropriate object, and the object is returned.

getBoolean

```
public static native boolean getBoolean(Object array, int index)
                    throws IllegalArgumentException,
                            ArrayIndexOutOfBoundsException
```

Parameters	array	An array object.
	index	An index into the array.

Returns   The boolean value at the given index in the specified array.

Throws   IllegalArgumentException

If the given object is not an array, or the object at the given index cannot be converted to a boolean.

ArrayIndexOutOfBoundsException

If the given index is invalid.

NullPointerException

If array is null.

Description This method returns the object at the given index in the array as a boolean value.

getByte

```
public static native byte getByte(Object array, int index)
                    throws IllegalArgumentException,
                            ArrayIndexOutOfBoundsException
```

Parameters	array	An array object.
	index	An index into the array.

Returns   The byte value at the given index in the specified array.

Throws   IllegalArgumentException

If the given object is not an array, or the object at the given index cannot be converted to a byte.

ArrayIndexOutOfBoundsException

If the given index is invalid.

NullPointerException

If array is null.

Description This method returns the object at the given index in the array as a byte value.

getChar

```
public static native char getChar(Object array, int index)
                    throws IllegalArgumentException,
                            ArrayIndexOutOfBoundsException
```

Parameters   `array`   An array object.

                        `index`   An index into the array.

Returns   The `char` value at the given index in the specified array.

Throws   `IllegalArgumentException`

                                If the given object is not an array, or the object at the given index cannot be converted to a char.

               `ArrayIndexOutOfBoundsException`

                                If the given index is invalid.

               `NullPointerException`

                                If `array` is `null`.

Description   This method returns the object at the given index in the array as a `char` value.

getDouble

```
public static native double getDouble(Object array, int index)
                        throws IllegalArgumentException,
                                ArrayIndexOutOfBoundsException
```

Parameters   `array`   An array object.

                        `index`   An index into the array.

Returns   The `double` value at the given index in the specified array.

Throws   `IllegalArgumentException`

                                If the given object is not an array, or the object at the given index cannot be converted to a double.

               `ArrayIndexOutOfBoundsException`

                                If the given index is invalid.

               `NullPointerException`

                                If `array` is `null`.

Description   This method returns the object at the given index in the array as a `double` value.

getFloat

```
public static native float getFloat(Object array, int index)
                        throws IllegalArgumentException,
                                ArrayIndexOutOfBoundsException
```

Parameters   `array`   An array object.

                        `index`   An index into the array.

Returns   The `float` value at the given index in the specified array.

Throws	IllegalArgumentException
	If the given object is not an array, or the object at the given index cannot be converted to a float.
	ArrayIndexOutOfBoundsException
	If the given index is invalid.
	NullPointerException
	If array is null.
Description	This method returns the object at the given index in the array as a float value.

getInt

```
public static native int getInt(Object array, int index)
                    throws IllegalArgumentException,
                            ArrayIndexOutOfBoundsException
```

Parameters	array	An array object.
	index	An index into the array.
Returns	The int value at the given index in the specified array.	
Throws	IllegalArgumentException	
	If the given object is not an array, or the object at the given index cannot be converted to a int.	
	ArrayIndexOutOfBoundsException	
	If the given index is invalid.	
	NullPointerException	
	If array is null.	
Description	This method returns the object at the given index in the array as a int value.	

getLength

```
public static native int getLength(Object array)
                    throws IllegalArgumentException
```

Parameters	array	An array object.
Returns	The length of the specified array.	
Throws	IllegalArgumentException	
	If the given object is not an array.	
Description	This method returns the length of the array.	

getLong

```
public static native long getLong(Object array, long index)
                    throws IllegalArgumentException,
                        ArrayIndexOutOfBoundsException
```

Parameters	array	An array object.
	index	An index into the array.
Returns		The long value at the given index in the specified array.
Throws	IllegalArgumentException	

> If the given object is not an array, or the object at the given index cannot be converted to a long.

ArrayIndexOutOfBoundsException

> If the given index is invalid.

NullPointerException

> If array is null.

Description   This method returns the object at the given index in the array as a long value.

getShort

```
public static native short getShort(Object array, short index)
                    throws IllegalArgumentException,
                        ArrayIndexOutOfBoundsException
```

Parameters	array	An array object.
	index	An index into the array.
Returns		The short value at the given index in the specified array.
Throws	IllegalArgumentException	

> If the given object is not an array, or the object at the given index cannot be converted to a short.

ArrayIndexOutOfBoundsException

> If the given index is invalid.

NullPointerException

> If array is null.

Description   This method returns the object at the given index in the array as a short value.

newInstance

```
public static Object newInstance(Class componentType, int length)
            throws NegativeArraySizeException
```

Parameters   componentType
               The type of each element in the array.
             length   The length of the array.
Returns   An array object that contains elements of the given component
             type and has the specified length.
Throws   NegativeArraySizeException
               If length is negative.
             NullPointerException
               If componentType is null.
Description This method creates a single-dimension array with the given
             length and component type.

```
public static Object newInstance(Class componentType,
                                 int[] dimensions)
                throws IllegalArgumentException,
                       NegativeArraySizeException
```

Parameters   componentType
               The type of each element in the array.
             dimensions   An array that specifies the dimensions of the
                          array to be created.
Returns   An array object that contains elements of the given component
             type and has the specified number of dimensions.
Throws   IllegalArgumentException
               If dimensions has zero dimensions itself, or if it
               has too many dimensions (typically 255 array
               dimensions are supported).
             NegativeArraySizeException
               If length is negative.
             NullPointerException
               If componentType is null.
Description This method creates a multidimensional array with the given
             dimensions and component type.

set

```
public static native void set(Object array, int index,
                              Object value)
                throws IllegalArgumentException,
                       ArrayIndexOutOfBoundsException
```

Parameters   array   An array object.
             index   An index into the array.
             value   The new value.

Throws   IllegalArgumentException

                           If the given object is not an array, or if it repre-
                           sents an array of primitive values, and the given
                           value cannot be unwrapped and converted to
                           that primitive type.

                ArrayIndexOutOfBoundsException

                           If the given index is invalid.

                NullPointerException

                           If array is null.

Description   This method sets the object at the given index in the array to
                the specified value. If the array contains values of a primitive
                type, the given value is automatically unwrapped before it is put
                in the array.

setBoolean

```
public static native void setBoolean(Object array, int index,
                                     boolean z)
                throws IllegalArgumentException,
                       ArrayIndexOutOfBoundsException
```

Parameters   array   An array object.
                index   An index into the array.
                z   The new value.

Throws   IllegalArgumentException

                           If the given object is not an array, or if the given
                           value cannot be converted to the component
                           type of the array.

                ArrayIndexOutOfBoundsException

                           If the given index is invalid.

                NullPointerException

                           If array is null.

Description   This method sets the element at the given index in the array to
                the given boolean value.

setByte

```
public static native void setByte(Object array, int index, byte b)
                throws IllegalArgumentException,
                       ArrayIndexOutOfBoundsException
```

Parameters   array   An array object.
                index   An index into the array.
                b   The new value.

Throws   IllegalArgumentException

If the given object is not an array, or if the given value cannot be converted to the component type of the array.

ArrayIndexOutOfBoundsException

If the given index is invalid.

NullPointerException

If array is null.

Description   This method sets the element at the given index in the array to the given byte value.

setChar

```
public static native void setChar(Object array, int index, char c)
                   throws IllegalArgumentException,
                           ArrayIndexOutOfBoundsException
```

Parameters   array   An array object.
                index   An index into the array.
                c   The new value.

Throws   IllegalArgumentException

If the given object is not an array, or if the given value cannot be converted to the component type of the array.

ArrayIndexOutOfBoundsException

If the given index is invalid.

NullPointerException

If array is null.

Description   This method sets the element at the given index in the array to the given char value.

setDouble

```
public static native void setDouble(Object array, int index,
                   double d)
                   throws IllegalArgumentException,
                           ArrayIndexOutOfBoundsException
```

Parameters   array   An array object.
                index   An index into the array.
                d   The new value.

Throws   IllegalArgumentException

If the given object is not an array, or if the given value cannot be converted to the component type of the array.

ArrayIndexOutOfBoundsException
>   If the given index is invalid.
NullPointerException
>   If array is null.

Description   This method sets the element at the given index in the array to the given double value.

setFloat

```
public static native void setFloat(Object array, int index,
                                    float f)
                   throws IllegalArgumentException,
                          ArrayIndexOutOfBoundsException
```

Parameters   array   An array object.
              index   An index into the array.
              f   The new value.

Throws   IllegalArgumentException
>   If the given object is not an array, or if the given value cannot be converted to the component type of the array.
              ArrayIndexOutOfBoundsException
>   If the given index is invalid.
              NullPointerException
>   If array is null.

Description   This method sets the element at the given index in the array to the given float value.

setInt

```
public static native void setInt(Object array, int index, int i)
                   throws IllegalArgumentException,
                          ArrayIndexOutOfBoundsException
```

Parameters   array   An array object.
              index   An index into the array.
              i   The new value.

Throws   IllegalArgumentException
>   If the given object is not an array, or if the given value cannot be converted to the component type of the array.
              ArrayIndexOutOfBoundsException
>   If the given index is invalid.

NullPointerException
If array is null.

Description   This method sets the element at the given index in the array to the given int value.

setLong

```
public static native void setLong(Object array, int index, long l)
                throws IllegalArgumentException,
                    ArrayIndexOutOfBoundsException
```

Parameters   array   An array object.
              index   An index into the array.
              l   The new value.

Throws   IllegalArgumentException
              If the given object is not an array, or if the given value cannot be converted to the component type of the array.

              ArrayIndexOutOfBoundsException
              If the given index is invalid.

              NullPointerException
              If array is null.

Description   This method sets the element at the given index in the array to the given long value.

setShort

```
public static native void setShort(Object array, int index,
                    short s)
                throws IllegalArgumentException,
                    ArrayIndexOutOfBoundsException
```

Parameters   array   An array object.
              index   An index into the array.
              s   The new value.

Throws   IllegalArgumentException
              If the given object is not an array, or if the given value cannot be converted to the component type of the array.

              ArrayIndexOutOfBoundsException
              If the given index is invalid.

              NullPointerException
              If array is null.

Description   This method sets the element at the given index in the array to the given short value.

Inherited Methods

Method	Inherited From	Method	Inherited From
clone()	Object	equals(Object)	Object
finalize()	Object	getClass()	Object
hashCode()	Object	notify()	Object
notifyAll()	Object	toString()	Object
wait()	Object	wait(long)	Object
wait(long, int)	Object		

See Also

ArrayIndexOutOfBoundsException, Class, IllegalArgumentException, NegativeArraySizeException, NullPointerException, Object

13.2   Constructor

Synopsis

Class Name: java.lang.reflect.Constructor
Superclass: java.lang.Object
Immediate Subclasses: None
Interfaces Implemented: java.lang.reflect.Member
Availability: New as of JDK 1.1

Description

The Constructor class represents a constructor of a class. A Constructor object can be obtained by calling the getConstructor() method of a Class object. Constructor provides methods for getting the name, modifiers, parameters, exceptions, and declaring class of a constructor. The newInstance() method can create a new instance of the class that declares a constructor.

Class Summary

```
public final class java.lang.reflect.Constructor extends java.lang.Object
                implements java.lang.reflect.Member {
   // Instance Methods
   public boolean equals(Object obj);
   public Class getDeclaringClass();
   public Class[] getExceptionTypes();
```

```
public native int getModifiers();
public String getName();
public Class[] getParameterTypes();
public int hashCode();
public native Object newInstance(Object[] initargs);
public String toString();
}
```

Instance Methods

equals

`public boolean equals(Object obj)`

Parameters	`obj` The object to be compared with this object.
Returns	`true` if the objects are equal; `false` if they are not.
Overrides	`Object.equals()`
Description	This method returns `true` if `obj` is an instance of `Constructor`, and it is equivalent to this `Constructor`.

getDeclaringClass

`public Class getDeclaringClass()`

Returns	The `Class` object that represents the class that declared this constructor.
Implements	`Member.getDeclaringClass()`
Description	This method returns the `Class` object for the class in which this constructor is declared.

getExceptionTypes

`public Class[] getExceptionTypes()`

Returns	An array that contains the `Class` objects that describe the exceptions that can be thrown by this constructor.
Description	This method returns an array of `Class` objects that represents the `throws` clause of this constructor. If the constructor does not throw any exceptions, an array of length 0 is returned. As of Java 1.1.2, this method is not properly supported: it always returns an empty array.

getModifiers

`public native int getModifiers()`

Returns	An integer that represents the modifier keywords used to declare this constructor.
Implements	`Member.getModifiers()`

Description   This method returns an integer value that represents the modifiers of this constructor. The `Modifier` class should decode the returned value.

getName

`public String getName()`

Returns   The name of this constructor as a `String`.

Implements   `Member.getName()`

Description   This method returns the name of this constructor, which is always the same as the name of the declaring class.

getParameterTypes

`public Class[] getParameterTypes()`

Returns   An array that contains the `Class` objects that describe the parameter types that this constructor accepts.

Description   This method returns an array of `Class` objects that represents the parameter types this constructor accepts. The parameter types are listed in the order in which they are declared. If the constructor does not take any parameters, an array of length 0 is returned.

hashCode

`public int hashCode()`

Returns   A hashcode for this object.

Overrides   `Object.hashCode()`

Description   This method returns a hashcode for this `Constructor`.

newInstance

```
public native Object newInstance(Object[] initargs)
                    throws InstantiationException,
                           IllegalAccessException,
                           IllegalArgumentException,
                           InvocationTargetException
```

Parameters   initargs   An array of arguments to be passed to this constructor.

Returns   The newly created object.

Throws   `InstantiationException`

                    If the declaring class of this constructor is abstract.

IllegalAccessException
>   If the constructor is inaccessible.

IllegalArgumentException
>   If initargs is the wrong length or contains any value of the wrong type.

InvocationTargetException
>   If the constructor itself throws an exception.

Description   This method executes the constructor represented by this object using the given array of arguments. Thus, it creates and initializes a new instance of the declaring class of the constructor. If a particular parameter is of a primitive type, the corresponding argument is automatically unwrapped and converted to the appropriate type, if possible. If that is not possible, an IllegalArgumentException is thrown. If the constructor itself throws an exception, the exception is placed in an Invocation-TargetException, which is then thrown to the caller of newInstance(). If the constructor completes normally, the newly created instance is returned.

toString

```
public String toString()
```

Returns   A string representation of this object.

Overrides   Object.toString()

Description   This method returns a string representation of this Constructor. This string contains the access modifiers of the constructor, if any, followed by the fully qualified name of the declaring class and a list of the parameters of the constructor, if any. The list is enclosed by parentheses, and the individual parameters are separated by commas. If the constructor does not have any parameters, just the parentheses are included in the string.

Inherited Methods

Method	Inherited From	Method	Inherited From
clone()	Object	finalize()	Object
getClass()	Object	notify()	Object
notifyAll()	Object	wait()	Object
wait(long)	Object	wait(long, int)	Object

See Also

Class, Field, InstantiationException, IllegalAccessException, IllegalArgumentException, InvocationTargetException, Member, Method, Modifier, Object

13.3 Field

Synopsis

Class Name: java.lang.reflect.Field
Superclass: java.lang.Object
Immediate Subclasses: None
Interfaces Implemented: java.lang.reflect.Member
Availability: New as of JDK 1.1

Description

The Field class represents a variable or constant in a class. A Field object can be obtained by calling the getField() method of a Class object. Field includes methods for getting the name, modifiers, type, and declaring class of a field. The class also provides methods that can set and retrieve the value of a field for a particular object.

Class Summary

```
public final class java.lang.reflect.Field extends java.lang.Object
                implements java.lang.reflect.Member {
  // Instance Methods
  public boolean equals(Object obj);
  public native Object get(Object obj);
  public native boolean getBoolean(Object obj);
  public native byte getByte(Object obj);
  public native char getChar(Object obj);
  public Class getDeclaringClass();
  public native double getDouble(Object obj);
  public native float getFloat(Object obj);
  public native int getInt(Object obj);
  public native long getLong(Object obj);
  public native int getModifiers();
  public String getName();
  public native short getShort(Object obj);
  public Class getType();
  public int hashCode();
  public native void set(Object obj, Object value);
  public native void setBoolean(Object obj, boolean z);
  public native void setByte(Object obj, byte b);
  public native void setChar(Object obj, char c);
```

```
public native void setDouble(Object obj, double d);
public native void setFloat(Object obj, float f);
public native void setInt(Object obj, int i);
public native void setLong(Object obj, long l);
public native void setShort(Object obj, short s);
public String toString();
}
```

Instance Methods

equals

public boolean equals(Object obj)

Parameters	obj	The object to be compared with this object.
Returns	true if the objects are equal; false if they are not.	
Overrides	Object.equals()	
Description	This method returns true if obj is an instance of Field, and it is equivalent to this Field.	

get

public native Object get(Object obj)
                    throws IllegalArgumentException,
                           IllegalAccessException

Parameters	obj	The instance whose field value is to be retrieved.
Returns	The value of this field in the given object.	
Throws	IllegalArgumentException	
	If obj is not the correct type.	
	IllegalAccessException	
	If the field is not accessible.	
	NullPointerException	
	If obj is null.	
Description	This method returns the value of this field in the given object. If the field is declared static, the obj parameter is ignored. Otherwise, the object supplied must be an instance of the class that declares this field. If the field contains a value of a primitive type, the value is wrapped in an appropriate object, and the object is returned.	

getBoolean

public native boolean getBoolean(Object obj)
                    throws IllegalArgumentException,
                           IllegalAccessException

Parameters	obj	The instance whose field value is to be retrieved.
Returns	The boolean value of this field in the given object.
Throws	IllegalArgumentException

> If obj is not the correct type, or the field cannot be converted to a boolean.

IllegalAccessException

> If the field is not accessible.

NullPointerException

> If obj is null.

| Description | This method returns the value of this field in the given object as a boolean. If the field is declared static, the obj parameter is ignored. Otherwise, the object supplied must be an instance of the class that declares this field. |

getByte

```
public native byte getByte(Object obj)
            throws IllegalArgumentException,
                   IllegalAccessException
```

Parameters	obj	The instance whose field value is to be retrieved.
Returns	The byte value of this field in the given object.
Throws	IllegalArgumentException

> If obj is not the correct type, or the field cannot be converted to a byte.

IllegalAccessException

> If the field is not accessible.

NullPointerException

> If obj is null.

| Description | This method returns the value of this field in the given object as a byte. If the field is declared static, the obj parameter is ignored. Otherwise, the object supplied must be an instance of the class that declares this field. |

getChar

```
public native char getChar(Object obj)
            throws IllegalArgumentException,
                   IllegalAccessException
```

Parameters	obj	The instance whose field value is to be retrieved.
Returns	The char value of this field in the given object.
Throws	IllegalArgumentException

> If obj is not the correct type, or the field cannot be converted to a char.

IllegalAccessException
>If the field is not accessible.

NullPointerException
>If obj is null.

Description   This method returns the value of this field in the given object as a char. If the field is declared static, the obj parameter is ignored. Otherwise, the object supplied must be an instance of the class that declares this field.

getDeclaringClass

public Class getDeclaringClass()

Returns   The Class object that represents the class that declared this field.

Implements   Member.getDeclaringClass()

Description   This method returns the Class object for the class in which this field is declared.

getDouble

public native double getDouble(Object obj)
>throws IllegalArgumentException,
>IllegalAccessException

Parameters   obj   The instance whose field value is to be retrieved.

Returns   The double value of this field in the given object.

Throws   IllegalArgumentException
>If obj is not the correct type, or the field cannot be converted to a double.

IllegalAccessException
>If the field is not accessible.

NullPointerException
>If obj is null.

Description   This method returns the value of this field in the given object as a double. If the field is declared static, the obj parameter is ignored. Otherwise, the object supplied must be an instance of the class that declares this field.

getFloat

public native float getFloat(Object obj)
>throws IllegalArgumentException,
>IllegalAccessException

Parameters   obj   The instance whose field value is to be retrieved.

Returns   The float value of this field in the given object.

Throws   IllegalArgumentException

If obj is not the correct type, or the field cannot be converted to a float.

IllegalAccessException

If the field is not accessible.

NullPointerException

If obj is null.

Description   This method returns the value of this field in the given object as a float. If the field is declared static, the obj parameter is ignored. Otherwise, the object supplied must be an instance of the class that declares this field.

getInt

```
public native int getInt(Object obj)
            throws IllegalArgumentException,
                    IllegalAccessException
```

Parameters   obj   The instance whose field value is to be retrieved.

Returns   The int value of this field in the given object.

Throws   IllegalArgumentException

If obj is not the correct type, or the field cannot be converted to a int.

IllegalAccessException

If the field is not accessible.

NullPointerException

If obj is null.

Description   This method returns the value of this field in the given object as an int. If the field is declared static, the obj parameter is ignored. Otherwise, the object supplied must be an instance of the class that declares this field.

getLong

```
public native long getLong(Object obj)
            throws IllegalArgumentException,
                    IllegalAccessException
```

Parameters   obj   The instance whose field value is to be retrieved.

Returns   The long value of this field in the given object.

Throws   IllegalArgumentException

If obj is not the correct type, or the field cannot be converted to a long.

```
IllegalAccessException
```
　　　　　　　If the field is not accessible.
```
NullPointerException
```
　　　　　　　If obj is null.

Description　　This method returns the value of this field in the given object as a long. If the field is declared static, the obj parameter is ignored. Otherwise, the object supplied must be an instance of the class that declares this field.

getModifiers

```
public native int getModifiers()
```

Returns　　　　An integer that represents the modifier keywords used to declare this field.

Implements　　`Member.getModifiers()`

Description　　This method returns an integer value that represents the modifiers of this field. The `Modifier` class should decode the returned value.

getName

```
public String getName()
```

Returns　　　　The name of this field as a `String`.

Implements　　`Member.getName()`

Description　　This method returns the name of this field.

getShort

```
public native short getShort(Object obj)
                throws IllegalArgumentException,
                       IllegalAccessException
```

Parameters　　obj　　　　　The instance whose field value is to be retrieved.

Returns　　　　The short value of this field in the given object.

Throws　　　　`IllegalArgumentException`
　　　　　　　If obj is not the correct type, or the field cannot be converted to a short.
```
IllegalAccessException
```
　　　　　　　If the field is not accessible.
```
NullPointerException
```
　　　　　　　If obj is null.

Description　　This method returns the value of this field in the given object as a short. If the field is declared static, the obj parameter is ignored. Otherwise, the object supplied must be an instance of the class that declares this field.

getType

```
public Class getType()
```

Returns   The Class object that represents the type of this field.

Description   This method returns the Class object for the type of this field.

hashCode

```
public int hashCode()
```

Returns   A hashcode for this object.

Overrides   Object.hashCode()

Description   This method returns a hashcode for this Field.

set

```
public native void set(Object obj, Object value)
                  throws IllegalArgumentException,
                         IllegalAccessException
```

Parameters   obj   The instance whose field value is to be set.

              value   The new value.

Throws   IllegalArgumentException

                            If obj is not an instance of the correct class, or
                            value cannot be converted to the correct type.

              IllegalAccessException

                            If the field is not accessible or declared final.

              NullPointerException

                            If obj is null.

Description   This method sets the value of this field in the given object to
              the given value. If the field is declared static, the obj parame-
              ter is ignored. Otherwise, the object supplied must be an
              instance of the class that declares this field. If the field contains
              a value of a primitive type, the given value is automatically
              unwrapped before it is used to set the value of the field.

setBoolean

```
public native void setBoolean(Object obj, boolean z)
                  throws IllegalArgumentException,
                         IllegalAccessException
```

Parameters   obj   The instance whose field value is to be set.

              z   The new value.

Throws   IllegalArgumentException

                            If obj is not an instance of the correct class, or z
                            cannot be converted to the correct type.

IllegalAccessException

> If the field is not accessible or declared final.

NullPointerException

> If obj is null.

Description   This method sets the value of this field in the given object to the given boolean value. If the field is declared static, the obj parameter is ignored. Otherwise, the object supplied must be an instance of the class that declares this field.

setByte

```
public native void setByte(Object obj, byte b)
            throws IllegalArgumentException,
            IllegalAccessException
```

Parameters   obj   The instance whose field value is to be set.

b   The new value.

Throws   IllegalArgumentException

> If obj is not an instance of the correct class, or b cannot be converted to the correct type.

IllegalAccessException

> If the field is not accessible or declared final.

NullPointerException

> If obj is null.

Description   This method sets the value of this field in the given object to the given byte value. If the field is declared static, the obj parameter is ignored. Otherwise, the object supplied must be an instance of the class that declares this field.

setChar

```
public native void setChar(Object obj, char c)
            throws IllegalArgumentException,
            IllegalAccessException
```

Parameters   obj   The instance whose field value is to be set.

c   The new value.

Throws   IllegalArgumentException

> If obj is not an instance of the correct class, or c cannot be converted to the correct type.

IllegalAccessException

> If the field is not accessible or declared final.

NullPointerException

> If obj is null.

Description   This method sets the value of this field in the given object to the given char value. If the field is declared static, the obj parameter is ignored. Otherwise, the object supplied must be an instance of the class that declares this field.

setDouble

```
public native void setDouble(Object obj, double d)
              throws IllegalArgumentException,
              IllegalAccessException
```

Parameters   obj   The instance whose field value is to be set.
              d   The new value.

Throws   IllegalArgumentException
                      If obj is not an instance of the correct class, or d cannot be converted to the correct type.
          IllegalAccessException
                      If the field is not accessible or declared final.
          NullPointerException
                      If obj is null.

Description   This method sets the value of this field in the given object to the given double value. If the field is declared static, the obj parameter is ignored. Otherwise, the object supplied must be an instance of the class that declares this field.

setFloat

```
public native void setFloat(Object obj, float f)
              throws IllegalArgumentException,
              IllegalAccessException
```

Parameters   obj   The instance whose field value is to be set.
              f   The new value.

Throws   IllegalArgumentException
                      If obj is not an instance of the correct class, or f cannot be converted to the correct type.
          IllegalAccessException
                      If the field is not accessible or declared final.
          NullPointerException
                      If obj is null.

Description   This method sets the value of this field in the given object to the given float value. If the field is declared static, the obj parameter is ignored. Otherwise, the object supplied must be an instance of the class that declares this field.

setInt

```
public native void setInt(Object obj, int i)
                throws IllegalArgumentException,
                IllegalAccessException
```

| Parameters | obj | The instance whose field value is to be set. |
| | i | The new value. |

Throws   IllegalArgumentException

If obj is not an instance of the correct class, or i cannot be converted to the correct type.

IllegalAccessException

If the field is not accessible or declared final.

NullPointerException

If obj is null.

Description   This method sets the value of this field in the given object to the given int value. If the field is declared static, the obj parameter is ignored. Otherwise, the object supplied must be an instance of the class that declares this field.

setLong

```
public native void setLong(Object obj, long 1)
                throws IllegalArgumentException,
                IllegalAccessException
```

| Parameters | obj | The instance whose field value is to be set. |
| | 1 | The new value. |

Throws   IllegalArgumentException

If obj is not an instance of the correct class, or 1 cannot be converted to the correct type.

IllegalAccessException

If the field is not accessible or declared final.

NullPointerException

If obj is null.

Description   This method sets the value of this field in the given object to the given long value. If the field is declared static, the obj parameter is ignored. Otherwise, the object supplied must be an instance of the class that declares this field.

setShort

```
public native void setShort(Object obj, short s)
                throws IllegalArgumentException,
                IllegalAccessException
```

| Parameters | obj | The instance whose field value is to be set. |
| | s | The new value. |

Throws   IllegalArgumentException

If obj is not an instance of the correct class, or s cannot be converted to the correct type.

IllegalAccessException

If the field is not accessible or declared final.

NullPointerException

If obj is null.

Description   This method sets the value of this field in the given object to the given short value. If the field is declared static, the obj parameter is ignored. Otherwise, the object supplied must be an instance of the class that declares this field.

toString

public String toString()

Returns   A string representation of this object.

Overrides   Object.toString()

Description   This method returns a string representation of this Field. This string contains the access modifiers of the field, if any, followed by the type, the fully qualified name of the declaring class, a period, and the name of the field.

Inherited Methods

Method	Inherited From	Method	Inherited From
clone()	Object	finalize()	Object
getClass()	Object	notify()	Object
notifyAll()	Object	wait()	Object
wait(long)	Object	wait(long, int)	Object

See Also

Class, Constructor, IllegalAccessException, IllegalArgumentException, Member, Method, Modifier, NullPointerException, Object

13.4   InvocationTargetException

Synopsis

Class Name:	java.lang.reflect.InvocationTargetException
Superclass:	java.lang.Exception
Immediate Subclasses:	None
Interfaces Implemented:	None
Availability:	New as of JDK 1.1

Description

An InvocationTargetException is thrown when a constructor called through Constructor.newInstance(), or a method called through Method.invoke() throws an exception. The InvocationTargetException encapsulates the thrown exception, which can be retrieved using getTargetException().

Class Summary

```
public class java.lang.reflect.InvocationTargetException
           extends java.lang.Exception {
// Constructors
   protected InvocationTargetException();
   public InvocationTargetException(Throwable target);
   public InvocationTargetException(Throwable target, String s);


// Instance Methods
   public Throwable getTargetException();
}
```

Constructors

InvocationTargetException

protected InvocationTargetException()

Description   This constructor creates an InvocationTargetException.

public InvocationTargetException(Throwable target)

Parameters   target   The exception thrown by the target constructor or method.

Description   This constructor creates an InvocationTargetException around the given exception with no associated detail message.

public InvocationTargetException(Throwable target, String s)

Parameters   target   The exception thrown by the target constructor or method.

s   A detail message.

Description   This constructor creates an `InvocationTargetException` around the given exception with the given detail message.

Instance Methods

getName

```
public Throwable getTargetException()
```
Returns   The exception thrown by the target constructor or method.

Description   This method returns the exception that was originally thrown by the constructor or method.

Inherited Methods

Method	Inherited From	Method	Inherited From
clone()	Object	equals(Object)	Object
fillInStackTrace()	Throwable	finalize()	Object
getClass()	Object	getLocalizedMessage()	Throwable
getMessage()	Throwable	hashCode()	Object
notify()	Object	notifyAll()	Object
printStackTrace()	Throwable	printStack- Trace(PrintStream)	Throwable
printStack- Trace(PrintWriter)	Throwable	toString()	Throwable
wait()	Object	wait(long)	Object
wait(long, int)	Object		

See Also

`Constructor, Method, Throwable`

13.5   Member

Synopsis

Interface Name:	`java.lang.reflect.Member`
Super-interface:	None
Immediate Sub-interfaces:	None

Implemented By:	`java.lang.reflect.Constructor,`
	`java.lang.reflect.Field,`
	`java.lang.reflect.Method`

Availability:	New as of JDK 1.1

Description

The Member interface defines methods shared by members of a class: fields, methods, and constructors.

Class Summary

```
public abstract interface java.lang.reflect.Member {
    // Constants
    public final static int DECLARED;
    public final static int PUBLIC;

    // Methods
    public abstract Class getDeclaringClass();
    public abstract int getModifiers();
    public abstract String getName();
}
```

Constants

DECLARED

public final static int DECLARED

　　Description　　A constant that represents the set of all declared members of a class or interface. This set does not include inherited members. The set can be used in calls to SecurityManager.checkMemberAccess().

PUBLIC

public final static int PUBLIC

　　Description　　A constant that represents the set of all public members of a class or interface, including inherited members. The set can be used in calls to SecurityManager.checkMemberAccess().

Methods

getDeclaringClass

public abstract Class getDeclaringClass()

　　Returns　　The Class object that represents the class that declared this member.

　　Description　　This method returns the Class object for the class in which this member is declared.

getModifiers

```
public abstract int getModifiers()
```

Returns   An integer that represents the modifier keywords used to
            declare this member.

Description   This method returns an integer value that represents the modi-
            fiers of this member. The `Modifier` class should be used to
            decode the returned value.

getName

```
public abstract String getName()
```

Returns   The name of this member as a `String`.

Description   This method returns the name of this member.

See Also

`Class`, `Constructor`, `Field`, `Method`, `Modifier`, `SecurityManager`

13.6   Method

Synopsis

Class Name: `java.lang.reflect.Method`
Superclass: `java.lang.Object`
Immediate Subclasses: None
Interfaces Implemented: `java.lang.reflect.Member`
Availability: New as of JDK 1.1

Description

The `Method` class represents a method of a class. A `Method` object can be obtained
by calling the `getMethod()` method of a `Class` object. `Method` provides methods for
getting the name, modifiers, return type, parameters, exceptions, and declaring
class of a method. The `invoke()` method can be used to run the method.

Class Summary

```
public final class java.lang.reflect.Method extends java.lang.Object
                implements java.lang.reflect.Member {
  // Instance Methods
  public boolean equals(Object obj);
  public Class getDeclaringClass();
  public Class[] getExceptionTypes();
  public native int getModifiers();
  public String getName();
  public Class[] getParameterTypes();
```

```
    public Class getReturnType();
    public int hashCode();
    public native Object invoke(Object obj, Object[] args);
    public String toString();
}
```

Instance Methods

equals

public boolean equals(Object obj)

Parameters	obj	The object to be compared with this object.
Returns		true if the objects are equal; false if they are not.
Overrides		Object.equals()
Description		This method returns true if obj is an instance of Method, and it is equivalent to this Method.

getDeclaringClass

public Class getDeclaringClass()

Returns	The Class object that represents the class that declared this method.
Implements	Member.getDeclaringClass()
Description	This method returns the Class object for the class in which this method is declared.

getExceptionTypes

public Class[] getExceptionTypes()

Returns	An array that contains the Class objects that describe the exceptions that can be thrown by this method.
Description	This method returns an array of Class objects that represents the throws clause of this method. If the method does not throw any exceptions, an array of length 0 is returned. As of Java 1.1.2, this method is not properly supported: it always returns an empty array.

getModifiers

public native int getModifiers()

Returns	An integer that represents the modifier keywords used to declare this method.
Implements	Member.getModifiers()
Description	This method returns an integer value that represents the modifiers of this method. The Modifier class should be used to decode the returned value.

getName

public String getName()

Returns	The name of this method as a String.
Implements	Member.getName()
Description	This method returns the name of this method.

getParameterTypes

public Class[] getParameterTypes()

Returns	An array that contains the Class objects that describe the parameter types that this method accepts.
Description	This method returns an array of Class objects that represents the parameter types this method accepts. The parameter types are listed in the order in which they are declared. If the method does not take any parameters, an array of length 0 is returned.

getReturnType

public Class getReturnType()

Returns	The Class object that represents the return type of this method.
Description	This method returns the Class object for the type that this method returns.

hashCode

public int hashCode()

Returns	A hashcode for this object.
Overrides	Object.hashCode()
Description	This method returns a hashcode for this Method.

invoke

public native Object invoke(Object obj, Object[] args)
                throws IllegalAccessException,
                       IllegalArgumentException,
                       InvocationTargetException

Parameters	obj	The instance upon which this method is invoked.
	args	An array of arguments to be passed to this method.
Returns		A Object that contains the return value of the invoked method.

Throws	`IllegalAccessException`
	If the method is inaccessible.
	`IllegalArgumentException`
	If `obj` is not the correct type, or if `args` is the wrong length or contains the wrong types.
	`InvocationTargetException`
	If the method itself throws an exception.
	`NullPointerException`
	If `obj` is `null`.
Description	This method executes the method represented by this object on the given object using the given array of arguments. If the method is declared `static`, the `obj` parameter is ignored. Otherwise, the object supplied must be an instance of the class that declares this method.

If a particular parameter is of a primitive type, the corresponding argument is automatically unwrapped and converted to the appropriate type, if possible. If that is not possible, an `IllegalArgumentException` is thrown. If the method itself throws an exception, the exception is placed in an `InvocationTargetException`, which is then thrown to the caller of `invoke()`.

If the method completes normally, the value it returns is returned. If the value is of a primitive type, the value is wrapped in an appropriate object and the object is returned. If the return type is `void`, `null` is returned.

toString

`public String toString()`

Returns	A string representation of this object.
Overrides	`Object.toString()`
Description	This method returns a string representation of this `Method`. This string contains the access modifiers of the method, if any, followed by the return type, the fully qualified name of the declaring class, a period, the name of the method, and a list of the parameters of the method, if any. The list is enclosed by parentheses and the individual parameters are separated by commas. If the method does not have any parameters, just the parentheses are included in the string.

Inherited Methods

Method	Inherited From	Method	Inherited From
clone()	Object	finalize()	Object
getClass()	Object	notify()	Object
notifyAll()	Object	wait()	Object
wait(long)	Object	wait(long, int)	Object

See Also

Class, Constructor, Field, IllegalAccessException, IllegalArgumentException, InvocationTargetException, Member, Modifier, NullPointerException, Object

13.7   Modifier

Synopsis

Class Name:	java.lang.reflect.Modifier
Superclass:	java.lang.Object
Immediate Subclasses:	None
Interfaces Implemented:	None
Availability:	New as of JDK 1.1

Description

The Modifier class defines a number of constants and static methods that can decode the modifier values returned by the getModifiers() methods of the Class, Constructor, Field, and Method classes. In other words, you can use the methods in this class to determine the modifiers used to declare a class or a member of a class. The constants in the Modifier class specify the bit values used to represent the various modifiers in a modifier value. You can use these constants to test for modifiers if you want to handle the boolean algebra yourself.

Class Summary

```
public class java.lang.reflect.Modifier extends java.lang.Object {
    // Constants
    public final static int ABSTRACT;
    public final static int FINAL;
    public final static int INTERFACE;
    public final static int NATIVE;
    public final static int PRIVATE;
    public final static int PROTECTED;
    public final static int PUBLIC;
```

```
    public final static int STATIC;
    public final static int SYNCHRONIZED;
    public final static int TRANSIENT;
    public final static int VOLATILE;

    // Class Methods
    public static boolean isAbstract(int mod);
    public static boolean isFinal(int mod);
    public static boolean isInterface(int mod);
    public static boolean isNative(int mod);
    public static boolean isPrivate(int mod);
    public static boolean isProtected(int mod);
    public static boolean isPublic(int mod);
    public static boolean isStatic(int mod);
    public static boolean isSynchronized(int mod);
    public static boolean isTransient(int mod);
    public static boolean isVolatile(int mod);
    public static String toString(int mod);
}
```

Constants

ABSTRACT

   public final static int ABSTRACT
     Description   A constant that represents the abstract modifier.

FINAL

   public final static int FINAL
     Description   A constant that represents the final modifier.

INTERFACE

   public final static int INTERFACE
     Description   A constant that represents the interface keyword.

NATIVE

   public final static int NATIVE
     Description   A constant that represents the native modifier.

PRIVATE

   public final static int PRIVATE
     Description   A constant that represents the private modifier.

PROTECTED

public final static int PROTECTED

Description   A constant that represents the protected modifier.

PUBLIC

public final static int PUBLIC

Description   A constant that represents the public modifier.

STATIC

public final static int STATIC

Description   A constant that represents the static modifier.

SYNCHRONIZED

public final static int SYNCHRONIZED

Description   A constant that represents the synchronized modifier.

TRANSIENT

public final static int TRANSIENT

Description   A constant that represents the transient modifier.

VOLATILE

public final static int VOLATILE

Description   A constant that represents the volatile modifier.

Class Methods

isAbstract

public static boolean isAbstract(int mod)

Parameters   mod   The modifier value to test.

Returns   true if the given modifier value includes the abstract modifier; false otherwise.

Description   This method tests the given modifier value for the ABSTRACT constant.

isFinal

public static boolean isFinal(int mod)

Parameters   mod   The modifier value to test.

Returns   true if the given modifier value includes the final modifier; false otherwise.

Description   This method tests the given modifier value for the FINAL constant.

isInterface

    public static boolean isInterface(int mod)

Parameters	mod	The modifier value to test.
Returns		true if the given modifier value includes the interface keyword; false otherwise.
Description		This method tests the given modifier value for the INTERFACE constant.

isNative

    public static boolean isNative(int mod)

Parameters	mod	The modifier value to test.
Returns		true if the given modifier value includes the native modifier; false otherwise.
Description		This method tests the given modifier value for the NATIVE constant.

isPrivate

    public static boolean isPrivate(int mod)

Parameters	mod	The modifier value to test.
Returns		true if the given modifier value includes the private modifier; false otherwise.
Description		This method tests the given modifier value for the PRIVATE constant.

isProtected

    public static boolean isProtected(int mod)

Parameters	mod	The modifier value to test.
Returns		true if the given modifier value includes the protected modifier; false otherwise.
Description		This method tests the given modifier value for the PROTECTED constant.

isPublic

    public static boolean isPublic(int mod)

Parameters	mod	The modifier value to test.
Returns		true if the given modifier value includes the public modifier; false otherwise.
Description		This method tests the given modifier value for the PUBLIC constant.

isStatic

`public static boolean isStatic(int mod)`

Parameters	mod	The modifier value to test.
Returns		true if the given modifier value includes the static modifier; false otherwise.
Description		This method tests the given modifier value for the STATIC constant.

isSynchronized

`public static boolean isSynchronized(int mod)`

Parameters	mod	The modifier value to test.
Returns		true if the given modifier value includes the synchronized modifier; false otherwise.
Description		This method tests the given modifier value for the SYNCHRONIZED constant.

isTransient

`public static boolean isTransient(int mod)`

Parameters	mod	The modifier value to test.
Returns		true if the given modifier value includes the transient modifier; false otherwise.
Description		This method tests the given modifier value for the TRANSIENT constant.

isVolatile

`public static boolean isVolatile(int mod)`

Parameters	mod	The modifier value to test.
Returns		true if the given modifier value includes the volatile modifier; false otherwise.
Description		This method tests the given modifier value for the VOLATILE constant.

toString

`public static String toString(int mod)`

Parameters	mod	The modifier value to represent as a string.
Returns		A string representation of the given modifier value.
Description		This method returns a string that represents the given modifier value. This string contains all of the modifiers specified by the given modifier value.

Inherited Methods

Method	Inherited From	Method	Inherited From
clone()	Object	equals(Object)	Object
finalize()	Object	getClass()	Object
hashCode()	Object	notify()	Object
notifyAll()	Object	toString()	Object
wait()	Object	wait(long)	Object
wait(long, int)	Object		

See Also

Class, Constructor, Field, Member

14

The java.math Package

The package `java.math` is new as of Java 1.1. It contains two classes that support arithmetic on arbitrarily large integers and floating-point numbers. Figure 14-1 shows the class hierarchy for the `java.math` package.

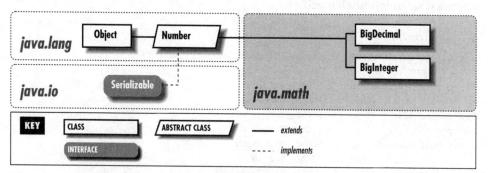

Figure 14–1: The java.math package

14.1 BigDecimal

Synopsis

Class Name:	`java.math.BigDecimal`
Superclass:	`java.lang.Number`
Immediate Subclasses:	None

Interfaces Implemented: None
Availability: New as of JDK 1.1

Description

The BigDecimal class represents arbitrary-precision rational numbers. A BigDecimal object provides a good way to represent a real number that exceeds the range or precision that can be represented by a double value or the rounding that is done on a double value is unacceptable.

The representation for a BigDecimal consists of an unlimited precision integer value and an integer scale factor. The scale factor indicates a power of 10 that the integer value is implicitly divided by. For example, a BigDecimal would represent the value 123.456 with an integer value of 123456 and the scale factor of 3. Note that the scale factor cannot be negative and a BigDecimal cannot overflow.

Most of the methods in BigDecimal perform mathematical operations or make comparisons with other BigDecimal objects. Operations that result in some loss of precision, such as division, require a rounding method to be specified. The BigDecimal class defines constants to represent the different rounding methods. The rounding method determines if the digit before a discarded fraction is rounded up or left unchanged.

Class Summary

```
public class java.math.BigDecimal extends java.lang.Number {
    // Constants
    public static final int ROUND_CEILING;
    public static final int ROUND_DOWN;
    public static final int ROUND_FLOOR;
    public static final int ROUND_HALF_DOWN;
    public static final int ROUND_HALF_EVEN;
    public static final int ROUND_HALF_UP;
    public static final int ROUND_UNNECESSARY;
    public static final int ROUND_UP;

    // Constructors
    public BigDecimal(double val);
    public BigDecimal(String val);
    public BigDecimal(BigInteger val);
    public BigDecimal(BigInteger val, int scale);

    // Class Methods
    public static BigDecimal valueOf(long val);
    public static BigDecimal valueOf(long val, int scale);

    // Instance Methods
    public BigDecimal abs();
    public BigDecimal add(BigDecimal val);
```

```
public int compareTo(BigDecimal val);
public BigDecimal divide(BigDecimal val, int roundingMode);
public BigDecimal divide(BigDecimal val, int scale, int roundingMode);
public double doubleValue();
public boolean equals(Object x);
public float floatValue();
public int hashCode();
public int intValue();
public long longValue();
public BigDecimal max(BigDecimal val);
public BigDecimal min(BigDecimal val);
public BigDecimal movePointLeft(int n);
public BigDecimal movePointRight(int n);
public BigDecimal multiply(BigDecimal val);
public BigDecimal negate();
public int scale();
public BigDecimal setScale(int scale);
public BigDecimal setScale(int scale, int roundingMode);
public int signum();
public BigDecimal subtract(BigDecimal val);
public BigInteger toBigInteger();
public String toString();
}
```

Constants

ROUND_CEILING

public static final int ROUND_CEILING

Description   A rounding method that rounds towards positive infinity. Under this method, the value is rounded to the least integer greater than or equal to its value. For example, 2.5 rounds to 3 and -2.5 rounds to -2.

ROUND_DOWN

public static final int ROUND_DOWN

Description   A rounding method that rounds towards zero by truncating. For example, 2.5 rounds to 2 and -2.5 rounds to -2.

ROUND_FLOOR

public static final int ROUND_FLOOR

Description   A rounding method that rounds towards negative infinity. Under this method, the value is rounded to the greatest integer less than or equal to its value. For example, 2.5 rounds to 2 and -2.5 rounds to -3.

ROUND_HALF_DOWN

`public static final int ROUND_HALF_DOWN`

Description   A rounding method that increments the digit prior to a discarded fraction if the fraction is greater than 0.5; otherwise, the digit is left unchanged. For example, 2.5 rounds to 2, 2.51 rounds to 3, -2.5 rounds to -2, and -2.51 rounds to -3.

ROUND_HALF_EVEN

`public static final int ROUND_HALF_EVEN`

Description   A rounding method that behaves like ROUND_HALF_UP if the digit prior to the discarded fraction is odd; otherwise it behaves like ROUND_HALF_DOWN. For example, 2.5 rounds to 2, 3.5 rounds to 4, -2.5 rounds to -2, and -3.5 rounds to -4.

ROUND_HALF_UP

`public static final int ROUND_HALF_UP`

Description   A rounding method that increments the digit prior to a discarded fraction if the fraction is greater than or equal to 0.5; otherwise, the digit is left unchanged. For example, 2.5 rounds to 3, 2.49 rounds to 2, -2.5 rounds to -3, and -2.49 rounds to -2.

ROUND_UNNECESSARY

`public static final int ROUND_UNNECESSARY`

Description   A constant that specifies that rounding is not necessary. If the result really does require rounding, an `ArithmeticException` is thrown.

ROUND_UP

`public static final int ROUND_UP`

Description   A rounding method that rounds away from zero by truncating. For example, 2.5 rounds to 3 and -2.5 rounds to -3.

Constructors

BigDecimal

`public BigDecimal(double val) throws NumberFormatException`

Parameters   val   The initial value.

Throws   NumberFormatException

If the double has any of the special values: `Double.NEGATIVE_INFINITY`, `Double.POSITIVE_INFINITY`, or `Double.NaN`.

Description   This constructor creates a `BigDecimal` with the given initial value. The scale of the `BigDecimal` that is created is the smallest value such that ($10^{scale} \times$ val) is an integer.

`public BigDecimal(String val) throws NumberFormatException`

Parameters   val   The initial value.

Throws   `NumberFormatException`

                              If the string cannot be parsed into a valid `BigDecimal`.

Description   This constructor creates a `BigDecimal` with the initial value specified by the `String`. The string can contain an optional minus sign, followed by zero or more decimal digits, followed by an optional fraction. The fraction must contain a decimal point and zero or more decimal digits. The string must contain as least one digit in the integer or fractional part. The scale of the `BigDecimal` that is created is equal to the number of digits to the right of the decimal point or 0 if there is no decimal point. The mapping from characters to digits is provided by the `Character.digit()` method.

`public BigDecimal(BigInteger val)`

Parameters   val   The initial value.

Description   This constructor creates a `BigDecimal` whose initial value comes from the given `BigInteger`. The scale of the `BigDecimal` that is created is 0.

`public BigDecimal(BigInteger val, int scale)`
`        throws NumberFormatException`

Parameters   val   The initial value.
              scale   The initial scale.

Throws   `NumberFormatException`
                              If scale is negative.

Description   This constructor creates a `BigDecimal` from the given parameters. The scale parameter specifies how many digits of the supplied `BigInteger` fall to the right of the decimal point.

Class Methods

valueOf

`public static BigDecimal valueOf(long val)`

Parameters   val   The initial value.

Returns   A `BigDecimal` that represents the given value.

Description   This method creates a `BigDecimal` from the given `long` value. The scale of the `BigDecimal` that is created is 0.

`public static BigDecimal valueOf(long val, int scale)`
                    `throws NumberFormatException`

Parameters   `val`   The initial value.

              `scale`   The initial scale.

Returns   A `BigDecimal` that represents the given value and scale.

Throws   `NumberFormatException`
                    If `scale` is negative.

Description   This method creates a `BigDecimal` from the given parameters. The `scale` parameter specifies how many digits of the supplied `long` fall to the right of the decimal point.

Instance Methods

abs

`public BigDecimal abs()`

Returns   A `BigDecimal` that contains the absolute value of this number.

Description   This method returns the absolute value of this `BigDecimal`. If this `BigDecimal` is nonnegative, it is returned. Otherwise, a new `BigDecimal` that contains the absolute value of this `BigDecimal` is returned. The scale of the new `BigDecimal` is the same as that of this `BigDecimal`.

add

`public BigDecimal add(BigDecimal val)`

Parameters   `val`   The number to be added.

Returns   A new `BigDecimal` that contains the sum of this number and the given value.

Description   This method returns the sum of this `BigDecimal` and the given `BigDecimal` as a new `BigDecimal`. The value of the new `BigDecimal` is the sum of the values of the two `BigDecimal` objects being added; the scale is the maximum of their two scales.

compareTo

`public int compareTo(BigDecimal val)`

Parameters   `val`   The number to be compared.

Returns   -1 if this number is less than `val`, 0 if this number is equal to `val`, or 1 if this number is greater than `val`.

Description   This method compares this `BigDecimal` to the given `BigDecimal` and returns a value that indicates the result of the comparison. The method considers two `BigDecimal` objects that have the same values but different scales to be equal. This method can be used to implement all six of the standard boolean comparison operators: ==, !=, <=, <, >=, and >.

divide

```
public BigDecimal divide(BigDecimal val, int roundingMode)
                throws ArithmeticException,
                        IllegalArgumentException
```

Parameters   val   The divisor.

                    roundingMode

                          The rounding mode.

Returns   A new BigDecimal that contains the result (quotient) of dividing this number by the supplied value.

Throws   ArithmeticException

                          If val is 0, or if ROUND_UNNECESSARY is specified for the rounding mode but rounding is necessary.

                  IllegalArgumentException

                          If roundingMode is not a valid value.

Description   This method returns the quotient that results from dividing this BigDecimal by the given BigDecimal and applying the specified rounding mode. The quotient is returned as a new BigDecimal that has the same scale as the scale of this BigDecimal scale. One of the rounding constants must be specified for the rounding mode.

```
public BigDecimal divide(BigDecimal val, int scale,
                    int roundingMode)
                throws ArithmeticException,
                        IllegalArgumentException
```

Parameters   val   The divisor.

                    scale   The scale for the result.

                    roundingMode

                          The rounding mode.

Returns   A new BigDecimal that contains the result (quotient) of dividing this number by the supplied value.

Throws   ArithmeticException

                          If val is 0, if scale is less than zero, or if ROUND_UNNECESSARY is specified for the rounding mode but rounding is necessary.

                  IllegalArgumentException

                          If roundingMode is not a valid value.

Description   This method returns the quotient that results from dividing
                   dividing this BigDecimal by the given BigDecimal and applying
                   the specified rounding mode. The quotient is returned as a
                   new BigDecimal that has the given scale. One of the rounding
                   constants must be specified for the rounding mode.

doubleValue

public double doubleValue()

Returns   The value of this BigDecimal as a double.
Overrides   Number.doubleValue()
Description   This method returns the value of this BigDecimal as a double. If
                   the   value   exceeds   the   limits   of   a   double,
                   Double.POSITIVE_INFINITY or Double.NEGATIVE_INFINITY is
                   returned.

equals

public boolean equals(Object x)

Parameters   x   The object to be compared with this object.
Returns   true if the objects are equal; false if they are not.
Overrides   Object.equals()
Description   This method returns true if x is an instance of BigDecimal, and
                   it represents the same value as this BigDecimal. In order to be
                   considered equal using this method, two BigDecimal objects
                   must have the same values and scales.

floatValue

public float floatValue()

Returns   The value of this BigDecimal as a float.
Overrides   Number.floatValue()
Description   This method returns the value of this BigDecimal as a float. If
                   the   value   exceeds   the   limits   of   a   float,
                   Float.POSITIVE_INFINITY or Float.NEGATIVE_INFINITY is
                   returned.

hashCode

public int hashCode()

Returns   A hashcode for this object.
Overrides   Object.hashCode()
Description   This method returns a hashcode for this BigDecimal.

intValue

```
public int intValue()
```

Returns	The value of this BigDecimal as an int.
Overrides	Number.intValue()
Description	This method returns the value of this BigDecimal as an int. If the value exceeds the limits of an int, the excessive high-order bits are discarded. Any fractional part of this BigDecimal is truncated.

longValue

```
public long longValue()
```

Returns	The value of this BigDecimal as a long.
Overrides	Number.longValue()
Description	This method returns the value of this BigDecimal as a long. If the value exceeds the limits of a long, the excessive high-order bits are discarded. Any fractional part of this BigDecimal is also truncated.

max

```
public BigDecimal max(BigDecimal val)
```

Parameters	val	The number to be compared.
Returns	The BigDecimal that represents the greater of this number and the given value.	
Description	This method returns the greater of this BigDecimal and the given BigDecimal.	

min

```
public BigDecimal min(BigDecimal val)
```

Parameters	val	The number to be compared.
Returns	The BigDecimal that represents the lesser of this number and the given value.	
Description	This method returns the lesser of this BigDecimal and the given BigDecimal.	

movePointLeft

```
public BigDecimal movePointLeft(int n)
```

Parameters	n	The number of digits to move the decimal point to the left.
Returns	A new BigDecimal that contains the adjusted number.	

Description   This method returns a BigDecimal that is computed by shifting the decimal point of this BigDecimal left by the given number of digits. If n is nonnegative, the value of the new BigDecimal is the same as the current value, and the scale is increased by n. If n is negative, the method call is equivalent to move-PointRight(-n).

movePointRight

    public BigDecimal movePointRight(int n)

Parameters   n   The number of digits to move the decimal point to the right.

Returns   A new BigDecimal that contains the adjusted number.

Description   This method returns a BigDecimal that is computed by shifting the decimal point of this BigDecimal right by the given number of digits. If n is nonnegative, the value of the new BigDecimal is the same as the current value, and the scale is decreased by n. If n is negative, the method call is equivalent to move-PointLeft(-n).

multiply

    public BigDecimal multiply(BigDecimal val)

Parameters   val   The number to be multiplied.

Returns   A new BigDecimal that contains the product of this number and the given value.

Description   This method multiplies this BigDecimal and the given BigDecimal, and returns the result as a new BigDecimal. The value of the new BigDecimal is the product of the values of the two BigDecimal objects being added; the scale is the sum of their two scales.

negate

    public BigDecimal negate()

Returns   A new BigDecimal that contains the negative of this number.

Description   This method returns a new BigDecimal that is identical to this BigDecimal except that its sign is reversed. The scale of the new BigDecimal is the same as the scale of this BigDecimal.

scale

```
public int scale()
```
Returns   The scale of this number.

Description   This method returns the scale of this BigDecimal.

setScale

```
public BigDecimal setScale(int scale)
               throws ArithmeticException,
                    IllegalArgumentException
```
Parameters   scale   The new scale.

Returns   A new BigDecimal that is identical to this number, except that is has the given scale.

Throws   ArithmeticException

               If the new number cannot be calculated without rounding.

               IllegalArgumentException

               This exception is never thrown.

Description   This method creates a new BigDecimal that has the given scale and a value that is calculated by multiplying or dividing the value of this BigDecimal by the appropriate power of 10 to maintain the overall value. The method is typically used to increase the scale of a number, not decrease it. It can decrease the scale, however, if there are enough zeros in the fractional part of the value to allow for rescaling without loss of precision.

               Calling this method is equivalent to calling setScale(scale, BigDecimal.ROUND_UNNECESSARY).

```
public BigDecimal setScale(int scale, int roundingMode)
               throws ArithmeticException,
                    IllegalArgumentException
```
Parameters   scale   The new scale.

               roundingMode

               The rounding mode.

Returns   A new BigDecimal that contains this number adjusted to the given scale.

Throws   ArithmeticException

               If scale is less than zero, or if ROUND_UNNECESSARY is specified for the rounding mode but rounding is necessary.

               IllegalArgumentException

               If roundingMode is not a valid value.

Description   This method creates a new `BigDecimal` that has the given scale
                and a value that is calculated by multiplying or dividing the
                value of this `BigDecimal` by the appropriate power of 10 to
                maintain the overall value. When the scale is reduced, the value
                must be divided, so precision may be lost. In this case, the spec-
                ified rounding mode is used.

signum

`public int signum()`

Returns   −1 if this number is negative, 0 if this number is zero, or 1 if this
                number is positive.

Description   This method returns a value that indicates the sign of this
                `BigDecimal`.

subtract

`public BigDecimal subtract(BigDecimal val)`

Parameters   val   The number to be subtracted.

Returns   A new `BigDecimal` that contains the result of subtracting the
                given number from this number.

Description   This method subtracts the given `BigDecimal` from this `BigDeci-`
                `mal` and returns the result as a new `BigDecimal`. The value of
                the new `BigDecimal` is the result of subtracting the value of the
                given `BigDecimal` from this `BigDecimal`; the scale is the maxi-
                mum of their two scales.

toBigInteger

`public BigInteger toBigInteger()`

Returns   The value of this `BigDecimal` as a `BigInteger`.

Description   This method returns the value of this `BigDecimal` as a `BigInte-`
                `ger`. The fractional part of this number is truncated.

toString

`public String toString()`

Returns   A string representation of this object.

Overrides   `Object.toString()`

Description   This method returns a string representation of this `BigDecimal`.
                A minus sign represents the sign, and a decimal point is used to
                represent the scale. The mapping from digits to characters is
                provided by the `Character.forDigit()` method.

Inherited Methods

Method	Inherited From	Method	Inherited From
byteValue()	Number	clone()	Object
getClass()	Object	finalize()	Object
notify()	Object	notifyAll()	Object
shortValue()	Number	wait()	Object
wait(long)	Object	wait(long, int)	Object

See Also

ArithmeticException, BigInteger, Character, Double, Float, IllegalArgumentException, Integer, Long, Number, NumberFormatException

---

14.2   BigInteger

Synopsis

Class Name:	java.math.BigInteger
Superclass:	java.lang.Number
Immediate Subclasses:	None
Interfaces Implemented:	None
Availability:	New as of JDK 1.1

Description

The BigInteger class represents an arbitrary-precision integer value. You should use this class if a long is not big enough for your purposes. The number in a BigInteger is represented by a sign value and a magnitude, which is an arbitrarily large array of bytes. A BigInteger cannot overflow.

Most of the methods in BigInteger perform mathematical operations or make comparisons with other BigInteger objects. BigInteger also defines some methods for handling modular arithmetic and determining primality that are needed for cryptographic purposes.

Class Summary

```
public class java.math.BigInteger extends java.lang.Number {
    // Constructors
    public BigInteger(byte[] val);
    public BigInteger(int signum, byte[] magnitude);
    public BigInteger(String val);
    public BigInteger(String val, int radix);
```

```
    public BigInteger(int numBits, Random rndSrc);
    public BigInteger(int bitLength, int certainty, Random rnd);

    // Class Methods
    public static BigInteger valueOf(long val);

    // Instance Methods
    public BigInteger abs();
    public BigInteger add(BigInteger val);
    public BigInteger and(BigInteger val);
    public BigInteger andNot(BigInteger val);
    public int bitCount();
    public int bitLength();
    public BigInteger clearBit(int n);
    public int compareTo(BigInteger val);
    public BigInteger divide(BigInteger val);
    public BigInteger[] divideAndRemainder(BigInteger val);
    public double doubleValue();
    public boolean equals(Object x);
    public BigInteger flipBit(int n);
    public float floatValue();
    public BigInteger gcd(BigInteger val);
    public int getLowestSetBit();
    public int hashCode();
    public int intValue();
    public boolean isProbablePrime(int certainty);
    public long longValue();
    public BigInteger max(BigInteger val);
    public BigInteger min(BigInteger val);
    public BigInteger mod(BigInteger m);
    public BigInteger modInverse(BigInteger m);
    public BigInteger modPow(BigInteger exponent, BigInteger m);
    public BigInteger multiply(BigInteger val);
    public BigInteger negate();
    public BigInteger not();
    public BigInteger or(BigInteger val);
    public BigInteger pow(int exponent);
    public BigInteger remainder(BigInteger val);
    public BigInteger setBit(int n);
    public BigInteger shiftLeft(int n);
    public BigInteger shiftRight(int n);
    public int signum();
    public BigInteger subtract(BigInteger val);
    public boolean testBit(int n);
    public byte[] toByteArray();
    public String toString();
    public String toString(int radix);
    public BigInteger xor(BigInteger val);
}
```

Constructors

BigInteger

public BigInteger(byte[] val) throws NumberFormatException

Parameters | val | The initial value.
Throws | NumberFormatException |
| | If the array does not contain any bytes.
Description | This constructor creates a BigInteger with the given initial value. The value is expressed as a two's complement signed integer, with the most significant byte in the first position (val[0]) of the array (big-endian). The most significant bit of the most significant byte is the sign bit.

public BigInteger(int signum, byte[] magnitude)
    throws NumberFormatException

Parameters | signum | The sign of the value: -1 indicates negative, 0 indicates zero, and 1 indicates positive.
| magnitude | The initial magnitude of the value.
Throws | NumberFormatException |
| | If signum is invalid or if signum is 0 but magnitude is not 0.
Description | This constructor creates a BigInteger with the given initial value and sign. The magnitude is expressed as a big-endian byte array.

public BigInteger(String val) throws NumberFormatException

Parameters | val | The initial value.
Throws | NumberFormatException |
| | If the string cannot be parsed into a valid BigInteger.
Description | This constructor creates a BigInteger with the initial value specified by the String. The string can contain an optional minus sign followed by zero or more decimal digits. The mapping from characters to digits is provided by the Character.digit() method.

public BigInteger(String val, int radix)
    throws NumberFormatException

Parameters | val | The initial value.
| radix | The radix to use to parse the given string.
Throws | NumberFormatException |
| | If the string cannot be parsed, or if the radix is not in the allowed range (Character.MIN_RADIX through Character.MAX_RADIX).

Description   This constructor creates a `BigInteger` with the initial value specified by the `String` using the given radix. The string can contain an optional minus sign followed by zero or more digits in the specified radix. The mapping from characters to digits is provided by the `Character.digit()` method.

`public BigInteger(int numBits, Random rndSrc)`
    `throws IllegalArgumentException`

Parameters   `numBits`   The maximum number of bits in the returned number.

                    `rndSrc`   The source of the random bits.

Throws   `IllegalArgumentException`
                    If `numBits` is less than zero.

Description   This constructor creates a random `BigInteger` in the range 0 to $2^{numBits} - 1$.

`public BigInteger(int bitLength, int certainty, Random rnd)`

Parameters   `bitLength`   The maximum number of bits in the returned number.

                    `certainty`   The certainty that the returned value is a prime number.

                    `rnd`   The source of the random bits.

Throws   `ArithmeticException`
                    If `numBits` is less than 2.

Description   This constructor creates a random `BigInteger` in the range 0 to $2^{numBits} - 1$ that is probably a prime number. The probability that the returned number is prime is greater than $1 - .5^{certainty}$. In other words, the higher the value of `certainty`, the more likely the `BigInteger` is to be prime, and also the longer it takes for the constructor to create the `BigInteger`.

Class Methods

valueOf

`public static BigInteger valueOf(long val)`

Parameters   `val`   The initial value.

Returns   A `BigInteger` that represents the given value.

Description   This method creates a `BigInteger` from the given `long` value.

Instance Methods

abs

public BigInteger abs()

Returns   A BigInteger that contains the absolute value of this number.

Description   This method returns the absolute value of this BigInteger. If
               this BigInteger is nonnegative, it is returned. Otherwise, a new
               BigInteger that contains the absolute value of this BigInteger
               is returned.

add

public BigInteger add(BigInteger val) throws ArithmeticException

Parameters   val   The number to be added.

Returns   A new BigInteger that contains the sum of this number and
               the given value.

Throws   ArithmeticException
                             If any kind of arithmetic error occurs.

Description   This method returns the sum of this BigInteger and the given
               BigInteger as a new BigInteger.

and

public BigInteger and(BigInteger val)

Parameters   val   The number to be ANDed.

Returns   A new BigInteger that contains the bitwise AND of this num-
               ber and the given value.

Description   This method returns the bitwise AND of this BigInteger and
               the supplied BigInteger as a new BigInteger.

andNot

public BigInteger andNot(BigInteger val)

Parameters   val   The number to be combined with this BigInte-
                             ger.

Returns   A new BigInteger that contains the bitwise AND of this num-
               ber and the bitwise negation of the given value.

Description   This method returns the bitwise AND of this BigInteger and
               the bitwise negation of the given BigInteger as a new BigInte-
               ger. Calling this method is equivalent to calling
               and(val.not()).

bitCount

```
public int bitCount()
```

Returns   The number of bits that differ from this BigInteger's sign bit.

Description This method returns the number of bits in the two's comple-
             ment representation of this BigInteger that differ from the
             sign bit of this BigInteger.

bitLength

```
public int bitLength()
```

Returns   The number of bits needed to represent this number, exclud-
             ing a sign bit.

Description This method returns the minimum number of bits needed to
             represent this number, not counting a sign bit.

clearBit

```
public BigInteger clearBit(int n) throws ArithmeticException
```

Parameters   n   The bit to clear.

Returns   A new BigInteger that contains the value of this BigInteger
             with the given bit cleared.

Throws   ArithmeticException
                            If n is less than 0.

Description This method returns a new BigInteger that is equal to this
             BigInteger, except that the given bit is cleared, or set to zero.

compareTo

```
public int compareTo(BigInteger val)
```

Parameters   val   The value to be compared.

Returns   -1 if this number is less than val, 0 if this number is equal to
             val, or 1 if this number is greater than val.

Description This method compares this BigInteger to the given BigInte-
             ger and returns a value that indicates the result of the compari-
             son. This method can be used to implement all six of the stan-
             dard boolean comparison operators: ==, !=, <=, <, >=, and >.

divide

```
public BigInteger divide(BigInteger val) throws ArithmeticException
```

Parameters   val   The divisor.

Returns   A new BigInteger that contains the result (quotient) of divid-
             ing this number by the given value.

Throws   ArithmeticException

                If val is zero.

Description   This method returns the quotient that results from dividing this
                BigInteger by the given BigInteger as a new BigInteger. Any
                fractional remainder is discarded.

divideAndRemainder

public BigInteger[] divideAndRemainder(BigInteger val)
                throws ArithmeticException

Parameters   val   The divisor.

Returns   An array of BigInteger objects that contains the quotient and
                remainder (in that order) that result from dividing this number
                by the given value.

Throws   ArithmeticException

                If val is zero.

Description   This method returns the quotient and remainder that results
                from dividing this BigInteger by the given BigInteger as an
                array of new BigInteger objects. The first element of the array
                is equal to divide(val); the second element is equal to
                remainder(val).

doubleValue

public double doubleValue()

Returns   The value of this BigInteger as a double.

Overrides   Number.doubleValue()

Description   This method returns the value of this BigInteger as a double. If
                the   value   exceeds   the   limits   of   a   double,
                Double.POSITIVE_INFINITY or Double.NEGATIVE_INFINITY is
                returned.

equals

public boolean equals(Object x)

Parameters   x   The object to be compared with this object.

Returns   true if the objects are equal; false if they are not.

Overrides   Object.equals()

Description   This method returns true if x is an instance of BigInteger, and
                it represents the same value as this BigInteger.

flipBit

public BigInteger flipBit(int n)

Parameters	n The bit to toggle.
Returns	A new BigInteger that contains the value of this BigInteger with the given bit toggled.
Throws	ArithmeticException
	If n is less than 0.
Description	This method returns a new BigInteger that is equal to this BigInteger, except that the given bit is toggled. In other words, if the given bit is 0, it is set to one, or if it is 1, it is set to zero.

floatValue

public float floatValue()

Returns	The value of this BigInteger as a float.
Overrides	Number.floatValue()
Description	This method returns the value of this BigInteger as a float. If the value exceeds the limits of a float, Float.POSITIVE_INFINITY or Float.NEGATIVE_INFINITY is returned.

gcd

public BigInteger gcd(BigInteger val)

Parameters	val The number to be compared.
Returns	A new BigInteger that contains the greatest common denominator of this number and the given number.
Description	This method calculates the greatest common denominator of the absolute value of this BigInteger and the absolute value of the given BigInteger, and returns it as a new BigInteger. If both values are 0, the method returns a BigInteger that contains the value 0.

getLowestSetBit

public int getLowestSetBit()

Returns	The index of the lowest-order bit with a value of 1, or -1 if there are no bits that are 1.
Description	This method returns the index of the lowest-order, or right-most, bit with a value of 1.

hashCode

```
public int hashCode()
```
Returns   A hashcode for this object.
Overrides   Object.hashCode()
Description   This method returns a hashcode for this BigInteger.

intValue

```
public int intValue()
```
Returns   The value of this BigInteger as an int.
Overrides   Number.intValue()
Description   This method returns the value of this BigInteger as an int. If
                  the value exceeds the limits of an int, the excessive high-order
                  bits are discarded.

isProbablePrime

```
public boolean isProbablePrime(int certainty)
```
Parameters   certainty   The "certainty" that this number is prime, where
                              a higher value indicates more certainty.
Returns   true if this number is probably prime; false if it is definitely
                 not prime.
Description   This method returns true if this number has a probability of
                 being prime that is greater than $1-.5^{certainty}$. If the number is
                 definitely not prime, false is returned.

longValue

```
public long longValue()
```
Returns   The value of this BigInteger as a long.
Overrides   Number.longValue()
Description   This method returns the value of this BigInteger as a long. If
                  the value exceeds the limits of a long, the excessive high-order
                  bits are discarded.

max

```
public BigInteger max(BigInteger val)
```
Parameters   val   The number to be compared.
Returns   The BigInteger that represents the greater of this number and
                 the given value.
Description   This method returns the greater of this BigInteger and the
                 given BigInteger.

min

```
public BigInteger min(BigInteger val)
```

Parameters	val The number to be compared.
Returns	The BigInteger that represents the lesser of this number and the given value.
Description	This method returns the lesser of this BigInteger and the given BigInteger.

mod

```
public BigInteger mod(BigInteger m)
```

Parameters	m The number to use.
Returns	A new BigInteger that contains the modulus of this number and the given number.
Throws	ArithmeticException
	If m is less than or equal to zero.
Description	This method returns a new BigInteger that contains the value of this BigInteger mod m.

modInverse

```
public BigInteger modInverse(BigInteger m)
          throws ArithmeticException
```

Parameters	m The number to use.
Returns	A new BigInteger that contains the multiplicative inverse of the modulus of this number and the given number.
Throws	ArithmeticException
	If m is less than or equal to zero, or if the result cannot be calculated.
Description	This method returns a new BigInteger that contains the multiplicative inverse of the value of this BigInteger mod m.

modPow

```
public BigInteger modInverse(BigInteger exponent, BigInteger m)
```

Parameters	exponent The exponent.
	m The number to use.
Returns	A new BigInteger that contains the modulus of this number raised to the given power and the given number.
Throws	ArithmeticException
	If m is less than or equal to zero.
Description	This method returns a new BigInteger that contains the value of this BigInteger raised to the given power mod m.

multiply

`public BigInteger multiply(BigInteger val)`

Parameters	val	The number to be multiplied.
Returns		A new `BigInteger` that contains the product of this number and the given number.
Description		This method multiplies this `BigInteger` by the given `BigInteger` and returns the product as a new `BigInteger`.

negate

`public BigInteger negate()`

Returns	A new `BigInteger` that contains the negative of this number.
Description	This method returns a new `BigInteger` that is identical to this `BigInteger` except that its sign is reversed.

not

`public BigInteger not()`

Returns	A new `BigInteger` that contains the bitwise negation of this number.
Description	This method returns a new `BigInteger` that is calculated by inverting every bit of this `BigInteger`.

or

`public BigInteger or(BigInteger val)`

Parameters	val	The value to be ORed.
Returns		A new `BigInteger` that contains the bitwise OR of this number and the given value.
Description		This method returns the bitwise OR of this `BigInteger` and the given `BigInteger` as a new `BigInteger`.

pow

`public BigInteger pow(int exponent) throws ArithmeticException`

Parameters	exponent	The exponent.
Returns		A new `BigInteger` that contains the result of raising this number to the given power.
Throws	ArithmeticException	
		If exponent is less than zero.
Description		This method raises this `BigInteger` to the given power and returns the result as a new `BigInteger`.

remainder

```
public BigInteger remainder(BigInteger val)
             throws ArithmeticException
```

Parameters	val	The divisor.
Returns		A new BigInteger that contains the remainder that results from dividing this number by the given value.
Throws	ArithmeticException	
		If val is zero.
Description		This method returns the remainder that results from dividing this BigInteger by the given BigInteger as a new BigInteger.

setBit

```
public BigInteger setBit(int n) throws ArithmeticException
```

Parameters	n	The bit to set.
Returns		A new BigInteger that contains the value of this BigInteger with the given bit set.
Throws	ArithmeticException	
		If n is less than zero.
Description		This method returns a new BigInteger that is equal to this BigInteger, except that the given bit is set to 1.

shiftLeft

```
public BigInteger shiftLeft(int n)
```

Parameters	n	The number of bits to shift.
Returns		A new BigInteger that contains the result of shifting the bits of this number left by the given number of bits.
Description		This method returns a new BigInteger that contains the value of this BigInteger left-shifted by the given number of bits.

shiftRight

```
public BigInteger shiftRight(int n)
```

Parameters	n	The number of bits to shift.
Returns		A new BigInteger that contains the result of shifting the bits of this number right by the given number of bits with sign extension.
Description		This method returns a new BigInteger that contains the value of this BigInteger right-shifted by the given number of bits with sign extension.

signum

> public int signum()

Returns	-1 is this number is negative, 0 if this number is zero, or 1 if this number is positive.
Description	This method returns a value that indicates the sign of this BigInteger.

subtract

> public BigInteger subtract(BigInteger val)

Parameters	val The number to be subtracted.
Returns	A new BigDecimal that contains the result of subtracting the given number from this number.
Description	This method subtracts the given BigInteger from this BigInteger and returns the result as a new BigInteger.

testBit

> public boolean testBit(int n) throws ArithmeticException

Parameters	n The bit to test.
Returns	true if the specified bit is 1; false if the specified bit is 0.
Throws	ArithmeticException
	If n is less than zero.
Description	This method returns true if the specified bit in this BigInteger is 1. Otherwise the method returns false.

toByteArray

> public byte[] toByteArray()

Returns	An array of bytes that represents this object.
Description	This method returns an array of bytes that contains the two's complement representation of this BigInteger. The most significant byte is in the first position (val[0]) of the array. The array can be used with the BigInteger(byte[]) constructor to reconstruct the number.

toString

> public String toString()

Returns	A string representation of this object in decimal form.
Overrides	Object.toString()
Description	This method returns a string representation of this BigInteger in decimal form. A minus sign represents the sign if necessary. The mapping from digits to characters is provided by the Character.forDigit() method.

```
public String toString(int radix)
```
Parameters   `radix`   The radix to use.

Returns   A string representation of this object in the given radix.

Overrides   `Object.toString()`

Description   This method returns a string representation of this `BigInteger` for the given radix. A minus sign is used to represent the sign if necessary. The mapping from digits to characters is provided by the `Character.forDigit()` method.

xor

```
public BigInteger xor(BigInteger val)
```
Parameters   `val`   The value to be XORed.

Returns   A new `BigInteger` that contains the bitwise XOR of this number and the given value.

Description   This method returns the bitwise XOR of this `BigInteger` and the given `BigInteger` as a new `BigInteger`.

Inherited Methods

Method	Inherited From	Method	Inherited From
byteValue()	Number	clone()	Object
getClass()	Object	finalize()	Object
notify()	Object	notifyAll()	Object
shortValue()	Number	wait()	Object
wait(long)	Object	wait(long, int)	Object

See Also

`ArithmeticException`, `BigDecimal`, `Character`, `Double`, `Float`, `IllegalArgumentException`, `Integer`, `Long`, `Number`, `NumberFormatException`

15

The java.net Package

The package `java.net` contains classes and interfaces that provide a powerful infrastructure for networking in Java. These include:

- The `URL` class for basic access to Uniform Resource Locators (URLs).
- The `URLConnection` class, which supports more complex operations on URLs.
- The `Socket` class for connecting to particular ports on specific Internet hosts and reading and writing data using streams.
- The `ServerSocket` class for implementing servers that accept connections from clients.
- The `DatagramSocket`, `MulticastSocket`, and `DatagramPacket` classes for implementing low-level networking.
- The `InetAddress` class, which represents Internet addresses.

Figure 15-1 shows the class hierarchy for the `java.net` package.

15.1   *BindException*

Synopsis

Class Name: `java.net.BindException`
Superclass: `java.net.SocketException`
Immediate Subclasses: None
Interfaces Implemented: None
Availability: New as of JDK 1.1

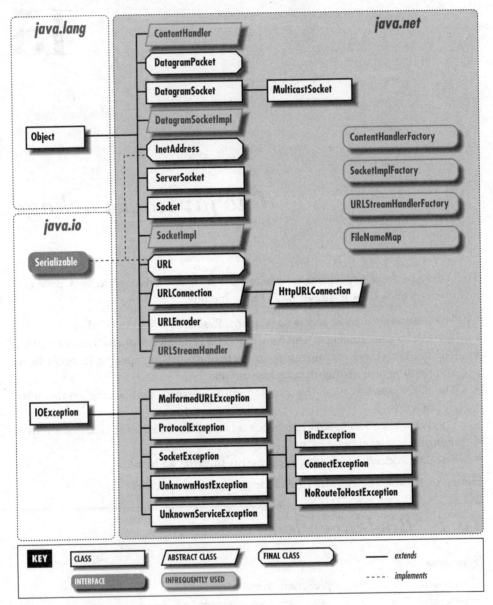

Figure 15–1: The java.net package

Description

A BindException is thrown when a socket cannot be bound to a local address and port, which can occur if the port is already in use or the address is unavailable.

Class Summary

```
public class java.net.BindException extends java.net.SocketException {
  // Constructors
  public BindException();
  public BindException(String msg);
}
```

Constructors

BindException

public BindException()

    Description   This constructor creates a BindException with no associated detail message.

public BindException(String msg)

    Parameters   msg   The detail message.

    Description   This constructor creates a BindException with the specified detail message.

Inherited Methods

Method	Inherited From	Method	Inherited From
clone()	Object	equals(Object)	Object
fillInStackTrace()	Throwable	finalize()	Object
getClass()	Object	getLocalizedMessage()	Throwable
getMessage()	Throwable	hashCode()	Object
notify()	Object	notifyAll()	Object
printStackTrace()	Throwable	printStack-Trace(PrintStream)	Throwable
printStack-Trace(PrintWriter)	Throwable	toString()	Throwable
wait()	Object	wait(long)	Object
wait(long, int)	Object		

See Also

Exception, IOException, RuntimeException, SocketException

15.2   ConnectException

Synopsis

Class Name:	java.net.ConnectException
Superclass:	java.net.SocketException
Immediate Subclasses:	None
Interfaces Implemented:	None
Availability:	New as of JDK 1.1

Description

A ConnectException is thrown when a socket connection cannot be established with a remote machine. This type of exception usually indicates that there is no listening process on the remote machine.

Class Summary

```
public class java.net.ConnectException extends java.net.SocketException {
    // Constructors
    public ConnectException();
    public ConnectException(String msg);
}
```

Constructors

ConnectException

public ConnectException()

Description   This constructor creates a ConnectException with no associated detail message.

public ConnectException(String msg)

Parameters   msg   The detail message.

Description   This constructor create a ConnectException with the specified detail message.

Inherited Methods

Method	Inherited From	Method	Inherited From
clone()	Object	equals(Object)	Object
fillInStackTrace()	Throwable	finalize()	Object
getClass()	Object	getLocalizedMessage()	Throwable
getMessage()	Throwable	hashCode()	Object
notify()	Object	notifyAll()	Object
printStackTrace()	Throwable	printStack-Trace(PrintStream)	Throwable

Method	Inherited From	Method	Inherited From
printStack-Trace(PrintWriter)	Throwable	toString()	Throwable
wait()	Object	wait(long)	Object
wait(long, int)	Object		

See Also

Exception, IOException, SocketException

15.3   ContentHandler

Synopsis

Class Name: java.net.ContentHandler
Superclass: java.lang.Object
Immediate Subclasses: None
Interfaces Implemented: None
Availability: JDK 1.0 or later

Description

The ContentHandler class is an abstract class that defines a method to read data from a URLConnection and then create an Object appropriate for the type of content it has read. Each subclass of ContentHandler handles a specific type of content (i.e., MIME type).

You do not create ContentHandler objects directly; they are created by an object that implements the ContentHandlerFactory interface. A ContentHandlerFactory object selects and creates an appropriate ContentHandler for the content type. If you write your own ContentHandler subclasses, you should also write your own ContentHandlerFactory. The content handler factory for an application is set by a call to URLConnection.setContentHandlerFactory().

An application does not normally call the getContent() method of a ContentHandler directly; it should call URL.getContent() or URLConnection.getContent() instead.

A ContentHandler works in conjunction with a URLStreamHandler, but their roles do not overlap. The URLStreamHandler deals with the specifics of a protocol, such as negotiating with a server to retrieve a resource, while the ContentHandler expects a data stream from which it can construct an object.

Class Summary

```
public abstract class java.net.ContentHandler extends java.lang.Object {
  // Instance Methods
  public abstract Object getContent(URLConnection urlc) throws IOException;
}
```

Instance Methods

getContent

```
public abstract Object getContent(URLConnection urlc)
                     throws IOException
```

Parameters   urlc   A URLConnection that is the data source.
Returns   The Object created from the data source.
Throws   IOException If any kind of I/O error occurs.
Description   This method reads data from the given URLConnection and
             returns the object that is represented by the data.

Inherited Methods

Method	Inherited From	Method	Inherited From
clone()	Object	equals(Object)	Object
finalize()	Object	getClass()	Object
int hashCode()	Object	notify()	Object
notifyAll()	Object	toString()	Object
wait()	Object	wait(long)	Object
wait(long, int)	Object		

See Also

ContentHandlerFactory, IOException, URL, URLConnection, URLStreamHandler

15.4   ContentHandlerFactory

Synopsis

Interface Name: java.net.ContentHandlerFactory
Super-interface: None
Immediate Sub-interfaces:
                          None

Implemented By: None
Availability: JDK 1.0 or later

Description

The ContentHandlerFactory interface defines a method that creates and returns an appropriate ContentHandler object for a given MIME type. The interface is implemented by classes that select ContentHandler subclasses to process content.

The URLStreamHandler class uses a ContentHandlerFactory to create ContentHandler objects. The content type is usually implied by the portion of the URL following the last period. For example, given the following URL:

```
http://www.tolstoi.org/anna.html
```

the MIME content type is text/html. A ContentHandlerFactory that recognizes text/html returns a ContentHandler object that can process that kind of content.

Interface Declaration

```
public abstract interface java.net.ContentHandlerFactory {
    // Methods
    public abstract ContentHandler createContentHandler(String mimetype);
}
```

Methods

createContentHandler

```
public abstract ContentHandler createContentHandler(
                            String mimetype)
```

Parameters   mimetype   A String that represents a MIME type.

Returns   A ContentHandler object that can read the specified type of content.

Description   This method creates an object of the appropriate subclass of ContentHandler that can read and process data for the given MIME type.

See Also

ContentHandler, URLStreamHandler

15.5 DatagramPacket

Synopsis

Class Name: java.net.DatagramPacket
Superclass: java.lang.Object
Immediate Subclasses: None
Interfaces Implemented: None
Availability: JDK 1.0 or later

Description

The DatagramPacket class represents a packet of data that can be sent and received over the network using a DatagramSocket. The class is used to implement connectionless data communication.

Class Summary

```
public final class java.net.DatagramPacket extends java.lang.Object {
    // Constructors
    public DatagramPacket(byte[] ibuf, int ilength);
    public DatagramPacket(byte[] ibuf, int ilength,
                          InetAddress iaddr, int iport);

    // Instance Methods
    public synchronized InetAddress getAddress();
    public synchronized byte[] getData();
    public synchronized int getLength();
    public synchronized int getPort();
    public synchronized void setAddress(InetAddress iaddr);   // New in 1.1
    public synchronized void setData(byte[] ibuf);            // New in 1.1
    public synchronized void setLength(int ilength);          // New in 1.1
    public synchronized void setPort(int iport);              // New in 1.1
}
```

Constructors

DatagramPacket

public DatagramPacket(byte ibuf[], int ilength)

Parameters   ibuf   The data buffer for receiving incoming bytes.
                ilength   The number of bytes to read.

Description   This constructor creates a DatagramPacket that receives data. The value of ilength must be less than or equal to ibuf.length. This DatagramPacket can be passed to Datagram-Socket.receive().

```
public DatagramPacket(byte ibuf[], int ilength,
                      InetAddress iaddr, int iport)
```

Parameters	ibuf	The data buffer for the packet.
	ilength	The number of bytes to send.
	iaddr	The destination address.
	iport	The destination port number.
Description		This constructor creates a DatagramPacket that sends packets of length ilength to the given port of the specified address. The value of ilength must be less than or equal to ibuf.length. The packets are sent using DatagramSocket.send().

Instance Methods

getAddress

```
public synchronized InetAddress getAddress()
```

Returns	The IP address of the packet.
Description	If this packet has been received, the method returns the address of the machine that sent it. If the packet is being sent, the method returns the destination address.

getData

```
public synchronized byte[] getData()
```

Returns	The packet data.
Description	This method returns the data buffer associated with this DatagramPacket object. This data is either the data being sent or the data that has been received.

getLength

```
public synchronized int getLength()
```

Returns	The packet length.
Description	This method returns the length of the message in the buffer associated with this DatagramPacket. This length is either the length of the data being sent or the length of the data that has been received.

getPort

```
public synchronized int getPort()
```

Returns	The port number of the packet.
Description	If this packet has been received, the method returns the port number of the machine that sent it. If the packet is being sent, the method returns the destination port number.

setAddress

`public synchronized void setAddress(InetAddress iaddr)`

Availability	New as of JDK 1.1
Parameters	`iaddr` The destination address for the packet.
Description	This method sets the destination address for this packet. When the packet is sent using `DatagramSocket.send()`, it is sent to the specified address.

setData

`public synchronized void setData(byte[] ibuf)`

Availability	New as of JDK 1.1
Parameters	`ibuf` The data buffer for the packet.
Description	This method sets the data for this packet. When the packet is sent using `DatagramSocket.send()`, the specified data is sent.

setLength

`public synchronized void setLength(int ilength)`

Availability	New as of JDK 1.1
Parameters	`ilength` The number of bytes to send.
Description	This method sets the length of the data to be sent for this packet. When the packet is sent using `DatagramSocket.send()`, the specified amount of data is sent.

setPort

`public synchronized void setPort(int iport)`

Availability	New as of JDK 1.1
Parameters	`iport` The port number for the packet.
Description	This method sets the destination port number for this packet. When the packet is sent using `DatagramSocket.send()`, it is sent to the specified port.

Inherited Methods

Method	Inherited From	Method	Inherited From
`clone()`	Object	`equals(Object)`	Object
`finalize()`	Object	`getClass()`	Object
`hashCode()`	Object	`notify()`	Object
`notifyAll()`	Object	`toString()`	Object
`wait()`	Object	`wait(long)`	Object
`wait(long, int)`	Object		

See Also

DatagramSocket, InetAddress

15.6   DatagramSocket

Synopsis

Class Name:	java.net.DatagramSocket
Superclass:	java.lang.Object
Immediate Subclasses:	java.net.MulticastSocket
Interfaces Implemented:	None
Availability:	JDK 1.0 or later

Description

The DatagramSocket class implements packet-oriented, connectionless data communication. In Internet parlance, this is the User Datagram Protocol, commonly known as UDP (see RFC 768). Each packet wanders through the network, routed by its destination address. Different packets can take different paths through the network and may arrive in a different order than they were sent. Furthermore, packets are not even guaranteed to reach their destination. It is up to an application that uses DatagramSocket to determine if data is out of order or missing. While these features may seem like disadvantages of DatagramSocket, there is also some advantage to using this class. Primarily, communication using DatagramSocket is faster than Socket stream communication because of the lack of overhead involved.

Class Summary

```
public class java.net.DatagramSocket extends java.lang.Object {
   // Constructors
   public DatagramSocket();
   public DatagramSocket(int port);
   public DatagramSocket(int port, InetAddress laddr);      // New in 1.1

   // Instance Methods
   public void close();
   public InetAddress getLocalAddress();                    // New in 1.1
   public int getLocalPort();
   public synchronized int getSoTimeout();                  // New in 1.1
   public synchronized void receive(DatagramPacket p);
   public void send(DatagramPacket p);
   public synchronized void setSoTimeout(int timeout);      // New in 1.1
}
```

Constructors

DatagramSocket

```
public DatagramSocket() throws SocketException
```
Throws   SocketException
                    If any kind of socket error occurs.

                SecurityException
                    If the application is not allowed to listen on the
                    port.

Description   This constructor creates a DatagramSocket that is bound to any
                available port on the local host machine.

```
public DatagramSocket(int port) throws SocketException
```
Parameters   port   A port number.
Throws   SocketException
                    If any kind of socket error occurs.

                SecurityException
                    If the application is not allowed to listen on the
                    given port.

Description   This constructor creates a DatagramSocket that is bound to the
                given port on the local host machine.

```
public DatagramSocket(int port, InetAddress laddr)
        throws SocketException
```
Availability   New as of JDK 1.1
Parameters   port   A port number.
                laddr   A local address.
Throws   SocketException
                    If any kind of socket error occurs.

                SecurityException
                    If the application is not allowed to listen on the
                    given port on the specified host.

Description   This constructor creates a DatagramSocket that is bound to the
                given port on the specified local host machine.

Instance Methods

close

```
public void close()
```
Description   This method closes the socket, releasing any system resources it
                holds.

getLocalAddress

`public InetAddress getLocalAddress()`

Availability	New as of JDK 1.1
Returns	The local address of the socket.
Throws	`SecurityException`
	If the application is not allowed to retrieve the address.
Description	This method returns the local address to which this `Datagram-Socket` is bound.

getLocalPort

`public int getLocalPort()`

Returns	The port number of the socket.
Description	This method returns the local port to which this `Datagram-Socket` is bound.

getSoTimeout

`public synchronized int getSoTimeout() throws SocketException`

Availability	New as of JDK 1.1
Returns	The receive time-out value for the socket.
Throws	`SocketException`
	If any kind of socket error occurs.
Description	This method returns the receive time-out value for this socket. A value of zero indicates that the socket waits indefinitely for an incoming packet, while a non-zero value indicates the number of milliseconds it waits.

receive

`public synchronized void receive(DatagramPacket p)`
`                        throws IOException`

Parameters	`p`	The `DatagramPacket` that receives incoming data.
Throws	`IOException`	If any kind of I/O error occurs.
	`SecurityException`	
		If the application is not allowed to receive data from the packet's source.
	`InterruptedIOException`	
		If a packet does not arrive before the time-out period expires.

Description   This method receives a datagram packet on this socket. After this method returns, the given `DatagramPacket` contains the packet's data and length, and the sender's address and port number. If the data that was sent is longer that the given packet's data buffer, the data is truncated.

If a time-out value is specified using the `setSoTimeout()` method, the method either returns with the received packet or times out, throwing an `InterruptedIOException`. If no time-out value is specified, the method blocks until it receives a packet.

send

```
public void send(DatagramPacket p)
throws IOException
```

Parameters   p   The `DatagramPacket` to be sent.

Throws   IOException   If any kind of I/O error occurs.

                SecurityException

                If the application is not allowed to send data to the packet's destination.

Description   This method sends a packet from this socket. The packet data, packet length, destination address, and destination port number are specified by the given `DatagramPacket`.

setSoTimeout

```
public synchronized void setSoTimeout(int timeout)
                    throws SocketException
```

Availability   New as of JDK 1.1

Parameters   timeout   The new time-out value, in milliseconds, for this socket.

Throws   SocketException

                If any kind of socket error occurs.

Description   This method is used to set the time-out value that is used for `receive()`. A non-zero value specifies the length of time, in milliseconds, that the `DatagramSocket` should wait for an incoming packet. A value of zero indicates that the `DatagramSocket` should wait indefinitely for an incoming packet. If a time-out value is needed, this method must be called before `receive()`.

Inherited Methods

Method	Inherited From	Method	Inherited From
clone()	Object	equals(Object)	Object
finalize()	Object	getClass()	Object
hashCode()	Object	notify()	Object
notifyAll()	Object	toString()	Object
wait()	Object	wait(long)	Object
wait(long, int)	Object		

See Also

DatagramPacket, DatagramSocketImpl, InetAddress, InterruptedIOException, IOException, MulticastSocket, SecurityException, Socket, SocketException

15.7   DatagramSocketImpl

Synopsis

Class Name:	java.net.DatagramSocketImpl
Superclass:	java.lang.Object
Immediate Subclasses:	None
Interfaces Implemented:	None
Availability:	New as of JDK 1.1

Description

The DatagramSocketImpl class is an abstract class that defines the bulk of the methods that make the DatagramSocket and MulticastSocket classes work. Non-public subclasses of DatagramSocketImpl provide platform-specific implementations of datagram socket communication.

Class Summary

```
public abstract class java.net.DatagramSocketImpl
                  extends java.lang.Object {
  // Variables
  protected FileDescriptor fd;
  protected int localPort;

  // Protected Instance Methods
  protected abstract void bind(int lport, InetAddress laddr);
  protected abstract void close();
  protected abstract void create();
```

```
    protected FileDescriptor getFileDescriptor();
    protected int getLocalPort();
    protected abstract byte getTTL();
    protected abstract void join(InetAddress inetaddr);
    protected abstract void leave(InetAddress inetaddr);
    protected abstract int peek(InetAddress i);
    protected abstract void receive(DatagramPacket p);
    protected abstract void send(DatagramPacket p);
    protected abstract void setTTL(byte ttl);
}
```

Variables

fd

protected FileDescriptor fd

Description   The file descriptor that represents this socket.

localPort

protected int localPort

Description   The local port number of this socket.

Protected Instance Methods

bind

protected abstract void bind(int lport, InetAddress laddr)
                    throws SocketException

Parameters   lport   A port number.
              laddr   A local address.
Throws   SocketException
                           If any kind of socket error occurs.
Description   This method binds the socket to the given address and port. If
               the address or the port is unavailable, an exception is thrown.

close

protected void close()

Description   This method closes the socket, releasing any system resources it
               holds.

create

protected abstract void create() throws SocketException

Throws   SocketException
                           If a socket error occurs.

Description   This method creates a socket that is not bound to an address and port.

getFileDescriptor

`protected FileDescriptor getFileDescriptor()`

Returns   The file descriptor for this socket.

Description   This method returns the file descriptor associated with this `DatagramSocketImpl`.

getLocalPort

`protected int getLocalPort()`

Returns   The port number for this socket.

Description   This method returns the local port to which this `DatagramSock-etImpl` is bound.

getTTL

`protected abstract byte getTTL() throws IOException`

Returns   The time-to-live (TTL) value for this socket.

Throws   `IOException` If any kind of I/O error occurs.

Description   This method returns the TTL value for this socket. This value is the number of hops that an outgoing packet can traverse before it is discarded.

join

`protected abstract void join(InetAddress inetaddr)`
                    `throws IOException`

Parameters   `inetaddr`   The IP address of the group to join.

Throws   `IOException` If any kind of I/O error occurs.

Description   This method is used by `MulticastSocket` to join a multicast group. An exception is thrown if the given address is not a multicast address. While the socket is part of a group, it receives all packets that are sent to the group.

leave

`protected abstract void leave(InetAddress inetaddr)`
                    `throws IOException`

Parameters   `inetaddr`   The IP address of the group to leave.

Throws   `IOException` If any kind of I/O error occurs.

Description   This method is used by `MulticastSocket` to leave a multicast group. An exception is thrown if the given address is not a multicast address.

peek

```
protected abstract int peek(InetAddress i) throws IOException
```

Parameters   i   A reference to an `InetAddress` object.

Returns   The port number of the next incoming packet.

Throws   `IOException`   If any kind of I/O error occurs.

Description   This method places the address of the next incoming packet in the given `InetAddress` object. The method also returns the port number of the next incoming packet. The method looks at the address of an incoming packet to determine if it should be accepted.

receive

```
protected abstract void receive(DatagramPacket p)
                    throws IOException
```

Parameters   p   The `DatagramPacket` that receives incoming data.

Throws   `IOException`   If any kind of I/O error occurs.

Description   This method receives a datagram packet on this socket. After this method returns, the given `DatagramPacket` contains the packet's data and length, and the sender's address and port number. If the data that was sent is longer that the given packet's data buffer, the data is truncated.

send

```
protected abstract void send(DatagramPacket p) throws IOException
```

Parameters   p   The `DatagramPacket` to be sent.

Throws   `IOException`   If any kind of I/O error occurs.

Description   This method sends a packet from this socket. The packet data, packet length, destination address, and destination port number are specified by the given `DatagramPacket`.

setTTL

```
protected abstract void setTTL(byte ttl) throws IOException
```

Parameters   ttl   The new TTL value for this socket.

Throws   `IOException`   If any kind of I/O error occurs.

Description   This method is used to set the TTL value of the socket. The TTL value is the number of hops that an outgoing packet can traverse before it is discarded.

Inherited Methods

Method	Inherited From	Method	Inherited From
clone()	Object	equals(Object)	Object
finalize()	Object	getClass()	Object
hashCode()	Object	notify()	Object
notifyAll()	Object	toString()	Object
wait()	Object	wait(long)	Object
wait(long, int)	Object		

See Also

DatagramPacket, DatagramSocket, FileDescriptor, InetAddress, IOException, MulticastSocket

15.8   FileNameMap

Synopsis

Interface Name: java.net.FileNameMap
Super-interface: None
Immediate Sub-interfaces:
                          None
Implemented By: None
Availability: New as of JDK 1.1

Description

The FileNameMap interface defines a method that maps filenames to MIME types. The interface is implemented by classes that provide this mapping. The mapping is typically done by examining the file extension of the filename, or in other words, the part of the filename that follows the final period.

Interface Declaration

```
public abstract interface java.net.FileNameMap {
  // Methods
  public abstract String getContentTypeFor(String fileName);
}
```

Methods

getContentTypeFor

public abstract String getContentTypeFor(String fileName)

Parameters	fileName	A String that contains a filename.
Returns		The String that contains the MIME type that corresponds to the filename.
Description		This method attempts to determine the MIME type of a file by examining its filename.

See Also

ContentHandler, ContentHandlerFactory

15.9   HttpURLConnection

Synopsis

Class Name:	java.net.HttpURLConnection
Superclass:	java.net.URLConnection
Immediate Subclasses:	None
Interfaces Implemented:	None
Availability:	New as of JDK 1.1

Description

The HttpURLConnection class is an abstract class that is a subclass of URLConnection. HttpURLConnection defines many of the HTTP server response codes as constants and provides methods for parsing server responses.

An HttpURLConnection object defines a network connection to a resource specified by a URL. Essentially, the HttpURLConnection object represents the HTTP request for that resource.

Class Summary

```
public abstract class java.net.HttpURLConnection
                   extends java.net.URLConnection {
    // Constants
    public final static int HTTP_ACCEPTED;
    public final static int HTTP_BAD_GATEWAY;
    public final static int HTTP_BAD_METHOD;
    public final static int HTTP_BAD_REQUEST;
    public final static int HTTP_CLIENT_TIMEOUT;
    public final static int HTTP_CONFLICT;
    public final static int HTTP_CREATED;
```

```
public final static int HTTP_ENTITY_TOO_LARGE;
public final static int HTTP_FORBIDDEN;
public final static int HTTP_GATEWAY_TIMEOUT;
public final static int HTTP_GONE;
public final static int HTTP_INTERNAL_ERROR;
public final static int HTTP_LENGTH_REQUIRED;
public final static int HTTP_MOVED_PERM;
public final static int HTTP_MOVED_TEMP;
public final static int HTTP_MULT_CHOICE;
public final static int HTTP_NOT_ACCEPTABLE;
public final static int HTTP_NOT_AUTHORITATIVE;
public final static int HTTP_NOT_FOUND;
public final static int HTTP_NOT_MODIFIED;
public final static int HTTP_NO_CONTENT;
public final static int HTTP_OK;
public final static int HTTP_PARTIAL;
public final static int HTTP_PAYMENT_REQUIRED;
public final static int HTTP_PRECON_FAILED;
public final static int HTTP_PROXY_AUTH;
public final static int HTTP_REQ_TOO_LONG;
public final static int HTTP_RESET;
public final static int HTTP_SEE_OTHER;
public final static int HTTP_SERVER_ERROR;
public final static int HTTP_UNAUTHORIZED;
public final static int HTTP_UNAVAILABLE;
public final static int HTTP_UNSUPPORTED_TYPE;
public final static int HTTP_USE_PROXY;
public final static int HTTP_VERSION;

// Variables
protected String method;
protected int responseCode;
protected String responseMessage;

// Constructors
protected HttpURLConnection(URL u);

// Class Methods
public static boolean getFollowRedirects();
public static void setFollowRedirects(boolean set);

// Instance Methods
public abstract void disconnect();
public String getRequestMethod();
public int getResponseCode();
public String getResponseMessage();
public void setRequestMethod(String method);
public abstract boolean usingProxy();
}
```

Constants

HTTP_ACCEPTED

public final static int HTTP_ACCEPTED = 202

Description   The HTTP response code that means the request has been accepted by the server.

HTTP_BAD_GATEWAY

public final static int HTTP_BAD_GATEWAY = 502

Description   The HTTP response code that means the server, acting as a gateway, has received a bad response from another server.

HTTP_BAD_METHOD

public final static int HTTP_BAD_METHOD = 405

Description   The HTTP response code that means the requested method is not allowed for the requested resource.

HTTP_BAD_REQUEST

public final static int HTTP_BAD_REQUEST = 400

Description   The HTTP response code that means the request was syntactically incorrect.

HTTP_CLIENT_TIMEOUT

public final static int HTTP_CLIENT_TIMEOUT = 408

Description   The HTTP response code that means the server has not received a request from the client in the time it expected.

HTTP_CONFLICT

public final static int HTTP_CONFLICT = 409

Description   The HTTP response code that means there is a conflict with the state of the requested resource.

HTTP_CREATED

public final static int HTTP_CREATED = 201

Description   The HTTP response code that means a new resource has been created as the result of the request.

HTTP_ENTITY_TOO_LARGE

public final static int HTTP_ENTITY_TOO_LARGE = 413

Description   The HTTP response code that means the request contains an entity that is too large for the server.

HTTP_FORBIDDEN

public final static int HTTP_FORBIDDEN = 403

Description   The HTTP response code that means the client does not have permission to access the requested resource.

HTTP_GATEWAY_TIMEOUT

public final static int HTTP_GATEWAY_TIMEOUT = 504

Description   The HTTP response code that means the server, acting as a gateway, has not received a response from an upstream server in the time it expected.

HTTP_GONE

public final static int HTTP_GONE = 410

Description   The HTTP response code that means the requested resource is no longer available.

HTTP_INTERNAL_ERROR

public final static int HTTP_INTERNAL_ERROR = 501

Description   The HTTP response code that means the server does not or cannot support the client's request.

HTTP_LENGTH_REQUIRED

public final static int HTTP_LENGTH_REQUIRED = 411

Description   The HTTP response code that means the server won't accept the request without a length indication.

HTTP_MOVED_PERM

public final static int HTTP_MOVED_PERM = 301

Description   The HTTP response code that means the requested resource has moved permanently.

HTTP_MOVED_TEMP

public final static int HTTP_MOVED_TEMP = 302

Description   The HTTP response code that means the requested resource has moved temporarily.

HTTP_MULT_CHOICE

public final static int HTTP_MULT_CHOICE = 300

Description   The HTTP response code that means the requested resource is available in multiple representations.

HTTP_NOT_ACCEPTABLE

public final static int HTTP_NOT_ACCEPTABLE = 406

Description   The HTTP response code that means the requested resource is not available in a representation that is acceptable to the client.

HTTP_NOT_AUTHORITATIVE

public final static int HTTP_NOT_AUTHORITATIVE = 203

Description   The HTTP response code that means the information returned may be a copy.

HTTP_NOT_FOUND

public final static int HTTP_NOT_FOUND = 404

Description   The HTTP response code that means the server could not find the requested resource.

HTTP_NOT_MODIFIED

public final static int HTTP_NOT_MODIFIED = 304

Description   The HTTP response code that means the requested resource has not been modified.

HTTP_NO_CONTENT

public final static int HTTP_NO_CONTENT = 204

Description   The HTTP response code that means the request has been processed, but there is no new information.

HTTP_OK

public final static int HTTP_OK = 200

Description   The HTTP response code that means the request succeeded.

HTTP_PARTIAL

public final static int HTTP_PARTIAL = 206

Description   The HTTP response code that means the partial request has been fulfilled.

HTTP_PAYMENT_REQUIRED

public final static int HTTP_PAYMENT_REQUIRED = 402

Description   An HTTP response code that is reserved for future use.

HTTP_PRECON_FAILED

    public final static int HTTP_PRECON_FAILED = 412
      Description   The HTTP response code that means the precondition in the
                     request has failed.

HTTP_PROXY_AUTH

    public final static int HTTP_PROXY_AUTH = 407
      Description   The HTTP response code that means the client needs to
                     authenticate itself with the proxy.

HTTP_REQ_TOO_LONG

    public final static int HTTP_REQ_TOO_LONG = 414
      Description   The HTTP response code that means the client request is too
                     long.

HTTP_RESET

    public final static int HTTP_RESET = 205
      Description   The HTTP response code that means the request has been ful-
                     filled, and the client should reset its view.

HTTP_SEE_OTHER

    public final static int HTTP_SEE_OTHER = 303
      Description   The HTTP response code that means the requested resource is
                     available at another URL.

HTTP_SERVER_ERROR

    public final static int HTTP_SERVER_ERROR = 500
      Description   The HTTP response code that means the server encountered a
                     problem and could not fulfill the request.

HTTP_UNAUTHORIZED

    public final static int HTTP_UNAUTHORIZED = 401
      Description   The HTTP response code that means the client is not authenti-
                     cated for the requested resource.

HTTP_UNAVAILABLE

    public final static int HTTP_UNAVAILABLE = 503
      Description   The HTTP response code that means the server is temporarily
                     unable to fulfill the request.

HTTP_UNSUPPORTED_TYPE

public final static int HTTP_UNSUPPORTED_TYPE = 415

Description   The HTTP response code that means the server cannot process the type of the request.

HTTP_USE_PROXY

public final static int HTTP_USE_PROXY = 305

Description   The HTTP response code that means a proxy must be used to access the requested resource.

HTTP_VERSION

public final static int HTTP_VERSION = 505

Description   The HTTP response code that means the server does not support the HTTP version used in the request.

Variables

method

protected String method = "GET"

Description   The method of this request. Valid values are: "DELETE", "GET", "HEAD", "OPTIONS", "POST", "PUT", and "TRACE".

responseCode

protected int responseCode = -1

Description   The response code from the server, which may be one of the HTTP_ constants.

responseMessage

protected String responseMessage = null

Description   The response message from the server that corresponds to responseCode.

Constructors

HttpURLConnection

protected HttpURLConnection(URL u)

Parameters   u   A URL object that represents a resource.

Description   This constructor creates an HttpURLConnection for the given URL object.

Class Methods

getFollowRedirects

public static boolean getFollowRedirects()

Returns   A boolean value that indicates whether or not HTTP redirect codes are automatically followed.

Description   This method indicates whether or not this HttpURLConnection follows HTTP redirects. The default value is false.

setFollowRedirects

public static void setFollowRedirects(boolean set)

Parameters   set   A boolean value that specifies whether or not HTTP redirects should be followed.

Throws   SecurityException

                         If there is a SecurityManager installed and its checkSetFactory() method throws a SecurityException.

Description   This method specifies whether or not this HttpURLConnection follows HTTP redirects.

Instance Methods

disconnect

public abstract void disconnect()

Description   This method closes the connection to the server.

getRequestMethod

public String getRequestMethod()

Returns   The method of this request.

Description   This method returns the method of this request.

getResponseCode

public int getResponseCode() throws IOException

Returns   The response code from the server.

Throws   IOException   If any kind of I/O error occurs.

Description   This method returns the code the server sent in response to this request. For example, suppose the server response is:

HTTP/1.0 404 Not Found

In this case, the method returns integer value 404.

getResponseMessage

```
public int getResponseMessage() throws IOException
```

Returns   The response message from the server.

Throws   IOException   If any kind of I/O error occurs.

Description   This method returns the message the server sent in response to
              this request. For example, suppose the server response is:

```
HTTP/1.0 404 Not Found
```

In this case, the method returns the string "Not Found".

setRequestMethod

```
public void setRequestMethod(String method)
          throws ProtocolException
```

Parameters   method   The new method for this request.

Throws   ProtocolException

              If the connection has already been made or if
              method is invalid.

Description   This method sets the method of this request. Valid values are:
              "DELETE", "GET", "HEAD", "OPTIONS", "POST", "PUT", and
              "TRACE".

usingProxy

```
public abstract boolean usingProxy()
```

Returns   A boolean value that indicates whether or not this HttpURLCon-
             nection is using a proxy.

Throws   IOException   If any kind of I/O error occurs.

Description   This method returns a flag that indicates if this connection is
              going through a proxy or not.

Inherited Variables

Variable	Inherited From	Variable	Inherited From
allowUserInteraction	URLConnection	connected	URLConnection
doInput	URLConnection	doOutput	URLConnection
ifModifiedSince	URLConnection	url	URLConnection
useCaches	URLConnection		

Inherited Methods

Method	Inherited From	Method	Inherited From
clone()	Object	connect()	URLConnection
equals(Object)	Object	finalize()	Object
getAllowUserInteraction()	URLConnection	getClass()	Object
getContent()	URLConnection	getContentEncoding()	URLConnection
getContentLength()	URLConnection	getContentType()	URLConnection
getDate()	URLConnection	getDefaultUseCaches()	URLConnection
getDoInput()	URLConnection	getDoOutput()	URLConnection
getExpiration()	URLConnection	getHeaderField(String)	URLConnection
getHeaderField(int)	URLConnection	getHeaderFieldDate(String, long)	URLConnection
getHeaderFieldInt(String, int)	URLConnection	getHeaderFieldKey(int)	URLConnection
getIfModifiedSince()	URLConnection	getInputStream()	URLConnection
getLastModified()	URLConnection	getOutputStream()	URLConnection
getRequestProperty(String)	URLConnection	getURL()	URLConnection
getUseCaches()	URLConnection	hashCode()	Object
notify()	Object	notifyAll()	Object
setAllowUserInteraction(boolean)	URLConnection	setDefaultUseCaches(boolean)	URLConnection
setDoInput(boolean)	URLConnection	setDoOutput(boolean)	URLConnection
setIfModifiedSince(long)	URLConnection	setRequestProperty(String, String)	URLConnection
setUseCaches(boolean)	URLConnection	toString()	URLConnection
wait()	Object	wait(long)	Object
wait(long, int)	Object		

See Also

IOException, ProtocolException, SecurityException, SecurityManager, URL, URLConnection

15.10   InetAddress

Synopsis

Class Name: java.net.InetAddress
Superclass: java.lang.Object
Immediate Subclasses: None
Interfaces Implemented: java.io.Serializable
Availability: JDK 1.0 or later

Description

The InetAddress class encapsulates an Internet Protocol (IP) address. InetAddress objects are used by the various classes that are responsible for specifying the destination addresses of outbound network packets, such as DatagramSocket, MulticastSocket, and Socket. InetAddress does not provide any public constructors. Instead, you must use the static methods getAllByName(), getByName(), and getLocalHost() to create InetAddress objects.

Class Summary

```
public final class java.net.InetAddress extends java.lang.Object
                    implements java.io.Serializable {
  // Class Methods
  public static InetAddress[] getAllByName(String host);
  public static InetAddress getByName(String host);
  public static InetAddress getLocalHost();

  // Instance Methods
  public boolean equals(Object obj);
  public byte[] getAddress();
  public String getHostAddress();                  // New in 1.1
  public String getHostName();
  public int hashCode();
  public boolean isMulticastAddress();             // New in 1.1
  public String toString();
}
```

Class Methods

getAllByName

```
public static InetAddress[] getAllByName(String host)
                            throws UnknownHostException
```

Parameters	host	A String that contains a hostname.
Returns		An array of InetAddress objects that corresponds to the given name.

Throws   SecurityException

                      If the application is not allowed to connect to
                      host.

                UnknownHostException

                      If host cannot be resolved.

Description   This method finds all of the IP addresses that correspond to the
                given hostname. The hostname can be a machine name, such
                as "almond.nuts.com", or a string representation of an IP
                address, such as "208.25.146.1".

getByName

```
public static InetAddress getByName(String host)
                    throws UnknownHostException
```

Parameters   host   A String that contains a host name.

Returns   An InetAddress that corresponds to the given name.

Throws   SecurityException

                      If the application is not allowed to connect to
                      host.

                UnknownHostException

                      If host cannot be resolved.

Description   This method returns the primary IP address that correspond to
                the given hostname. The hostname can be a machine name,
                such as "almond.nuts.com", or a string representation of an IP
                address, such as "208.25.146.1".

getLocalHost

```
public static InetAddress getLocalHost()
                    throws UnknownHostException
```

Returns   An InetAddress that corresponds to the name of the local
                machine.

Throws   SecurityException

                      If the application is not allowed to connect to
                      host.

                UnknownHostException

                      If host cannot be resolved.

Description   This method finds the IP address of the local machine.

Instance Methods

equals

    public boolean equals(Object obj)

Parameters	obj	The object to be compared with this object.
Returns		true if the objects are equivalent; false if they are not.
Overrides		Object.equals()
Description		This method returns true if obj is an instance of InetAddress that specifies the same IP address as the object this method is associated with.

getAddress

    public byte[] getAddress()

Returns	A byte array with elements that correspond to the bytes of the IP address that this object represents.
Description	This method returns the IP address associated with this object as an array of bytes in network order. That means that the first element of the array contains the highest order byte, and the last element of the array contains the lowest order byte.

getHostAddress

    public String getHostAddress()

Availability	New as of JDK 1.1
Returns	A String that contains the IP address of this object.
Description	This method returns a string representation of the IP address associated with this object. For example: "206.175.64.78".

getHostName

    public String getHostName()

Returns	The hostname associated with this object.
Description	In most cases, this method returns the hostname that corresponds to the IP address associated with this object. However, there are a few special cases:

- If the address associated with this object is address of the local machine, the method may return null.
- If the method cannot determine a home name to go with the address associated with this object, the method returns a string representation of the address.
- If the application is not allowed to know the hostname, the method returns a string representation of the address.

hashCode

public int hashCode()

Returns	The hashcode based on the IP address of the object.
Overrides	Object.hashCode()
Description	This method returns a hashcode for this object, based on the IP address associated with this object.

isMulticastAddress

public boolean isMulticastAddress()

Availability	New as of JDK 1.1
Returns	true if this object represents a multicast address; false otherwise.
Description	This method returns a flag that indicates if this object represents an IP multicast address. A multicast address is a Class D address, which means that its four highest-order bits are set to 1110. In other words, multicast addresses are in the range 224.0.0.1 through 239.255.255.255 inclusive.

toString

public String toString()

Returns	The string representation of this InetAddress.
Overrides	Object.toString()
Description	This method returns a String that contains both the hostname and IP address of this object.

Inherited Methods

Method	Inherited From	Method	Inherited From
clone()	Object	finalize()	Object
getClass()	Object	notify()	Object
notifyAll()	Object	wait()	Object
wait(long)	Object	wait(long, int)	Object

See Also

DatagramSocket, MulticastSocket, SecurityException, Serializable, Socket, UnknownHostException

15.11 MalformedURLException

Synopsis

Class Name: java.net.MalformedURLException
Superclass: java.io.IOException
Immediate Subclasses: None
Interfaces Implemented: None
Availability: JDK 1.0 or later

Description

A MalformedURLException is thrown when a malformed URL is encountered, which can occur if a URL does not contain a valid protocol or if the string is unparsable.

Class Summary

```
public class java.net.MalformedURLException extends java.io.IOException {
    // Constructors
    public MalformedURLException();
    public MalformedURLException(String msg);
}
```

Constructors

MalformedURLException

public MalformedURLException()

> Description   This constructor creates a MalformedURLException with no associated detail message.

public MalformedURLException(String msg)

> Parameters   msg   The detail message.
> Description   This constructor creates a MalformedURLException with the specified detail message.

Inherited Methods

Method	Inherited From	Method	Inherited From
clone()	Object	equals(Object)	Object
fillInStackTrace()	Throwable	finalize()	Object
getClass()	Object	getLocalizedMessage()	Throwable
getMessage()	Throwable	hashCode()	Object
notify()	Object	notifyAll()	Object
printStackTrace()	Throwable	printStack-Trace(PrintStream)	Throwable

Method	Inherited From	Method	Inherited From
printStack- Trace(PrintWriter)	Throwable	toString()	Throwable
wait()	Object	wait(long)	Object
wait(long, int)	Object		

See Also

Exception, IOException, RuntimeException

15.12   MulticastSocket

Synopsis

Class Name: java.net.MulticastSocket
Superclass: java.net.DatagramSocket
Immediate Subclasses: None
Interfaces Implemented: None
Availability: New as of JDK 1.1

Description

The MulticastSocket class implements packet-oriented, connectionless, multicast data communication. In Internet parlance, this is the User Datagram Protocol (UDP) with additional functionality for joining and leaving groups of other multicast hosts on the Internet. A multicast group is specified by a Class D address, which means that the four highest-order bits are set to 1110. In other words, multicast addresses are in the range 224.0.0.1 through 239.255.255.255 inclusive.

MulticastSocket inherits most of its functionality from DatagramSocket; it adds the ability to join and leave multicast groups. When a MulticastSocket joins a group, it receives all of the packets destined for the group. Any DatagramSocket or MulticastSocket can send packets to a multicast group.

Class Summary

```
public final class java.net.MulticastSocket
                extends java.net.DatagramSocket {
    // Constructors
    public MulticastSocket();
    public MulticastSocket(int port);

    // Instance Methods
    public InetAddress getInterface();
    public byte getTTL();
```

```
    public void joinGroup(InetAddress mcastaddr);
    public void leaveGroup(InetAddress mcastaddr)
    public synchronized void send(DatagramPacket p, byte ttl);
    public void setInterface(InetAddress inf);
    public void setTTL(byte ttl);
}
```

Constructors

MulticastSocket

public MulticastSocket()
throws IOException

Throws	IOException	If any kind of I/O error occurs.
	SecurityException	
		If the application is not allowed to listen on the port.
Description	This constructor creates a MulticastSocket that is bound to any available port on the local host machine.	

public MulticastSocket(int port)
throws IOException

Parameters	port	A port number.
Throws	IOException	If any kind of I/O error occurs.
	SecurityException	
		If the application is not allowed to listen on the given port.
Description	This constructor creates a MulticastSocket that is bound to the given port on the local host machine.	

Instance Methods

getInterface

public InetAddress getInterface() throws SocketException

Returns	The address of the network interface used for outgoing multicast packets.
Throws	SocketException
	If any kind of socket error occurs.
Description	This method returns the IP address that this MulticastSocket uses to send out packets to multicast destinations.

getTTL

```
public byte getTTL() throws IOException
```

Returns	The time-to-live (TTL) value for this socket.
Throws	IOException If any kind of I/O error occurs.
Description	This method returns the TTL value for this socket. This value is the number of hops an outgoing packet can traverse before it is discarded.

joinGroup

```
public void joinGroup(InetAddress mcastaddr) throws IOException
```

Parameters	mcastaddr	The IP address of the group to join.
Throws	IOException	If any kind of I/O error occurs.
	SecurityException	
		If the application is not allowed to access the given multicast address.
Description		This method is used to join a multicast group. An exception is thrown if the given address is not a multicast address. While the socket is part of a group, it receives all the packets that are sent to the group.

leaveGroup

```
public void leaveGroup(InetAddress mcastaddr) throws IOException
```

Parameters	mcastaddr	The IP address of the group to leave.
Throws	IOException	If any kind of I/O error occurs.
	SecurityException	
		If the application is not allowed to access the given multicast address.
Description		This method is used to leave a multicast group. An exception is thrown if the given address is not a multicast address.

send

```
public synchronized void send(DatagramPacket p, byte ttl)
                    throws IOException
```

Parameters	p	The DatagramPacket to be sent.
	ttl	The time-to-live (TTL) value for this packet.
Throws	IOException	If any kind of I/O error occurs.
	SecurityException	
		If the application is not allowed to send data to the packet's destination.

Description   This method sends a packet from this socket using the given TTL value. The packet data, packet length, destination address, and destination port number are specified by the given `DatagramPacket`.

Generally, it is easier to use `setTTL()` to set the TTL value for the socket, then use `send(DatagramPacket)` to send data. This method is provided for special cases.

setInterface

`public void setInterface(InetAddress inf) throws SocketException`

Parameters   inf   The new address of the network interface for multicast packets.

Throws   SocketException   If any kind of socket error occurs.

Description   This method is used to set the address that is used for outgoing multicast packets.

setTTL

`public void setTTL(byte ttl) throws IOException`

Parameters   ttl   The new time-to-live (TTL) value for this socket.

Throws   IOException   If any kind of I/O error occurs.

Description   This method is used to set the TTL value of the socket. The TTL value is the number of hops an outgoing packet can traverse before it is discarded.

Inherited Methods

Method	Inherited From	Method	Inherited From
clone()	Object	close()	Datagram-Socket
equals(Object)	Object	finalize()	Object
getClass()	Object	getLocalAddress()	Datagram-Socket
getLocalPort()	Datagram-Socket	getSoTimeout()	Datagram-Socket
hashCode()	Object	notify()	Object
notifyAll()	Object	receive(DatagramPacket)	Datagram-Socket
send(DatagramPacket)	Datagram-Socket	setSoTimeout(int)	Datagram-Socket
toString()	Object	wait()	Object
wait(long)	Object	wait(long, int)	Object

See Also

DatagramPacket, DatagramSocket, DatagramSocketImpl, InetAddress, IOException, SecurityException, SocketException

15.13   NoRouteToHostException

Synopsis

Class Name: java.net.NoRouteToHostException
Superclass: java.net.SocketException
Immediate Subclasses: None
Interfaces Implemented: None
Availability: New as of JDK 1.1

Description

A NoRouteToHostException is thrown when a socket connection cannot be established with a remote host. This type of exception usually indicates that a firewall is blocking access to the host, or that an intermediate router is down.

Class Summary

```
public class java.net.NoRouteToHostException
            extends java.net.SocketException {
  // Constructors
  public NoRouteToHostException();
  public NoRouteToHostException(String msg);
}
```

Constructors

NoRouteToHostException

public NoRouteToHostException()

Description   This constructor creates a NoRouteToHostException with no associated detail message.

public NoRouteToHostException(String msg)

Parameters   msg   The detail message.
Description   This constructor creates a NoRouteToHostException with the specified detail message.

Inherited Methods

Method	Inherited From	Method	Inherited From
clone()	Object	equals(Object)	Object
fillInStackTrace()	Throwable	finalize()	Object
getClass()	Object	getLocalizedMessage()	Throwable
getMessage()	Throwable	hashCode()	Object
notify()	Object	notifyAll()	Object
printStackTrace()	Throwable	printStack- Trace(PrintStream)	Throwable
printStack- Trace(PrintWriter)	Throwable	toString()	Throwable
wait()	Object	wait(long)	Object
wait(long, int)	Object		

See Also

Exception, IOException, RuntimeException, SocketException

15.14   ProtocolException

Synopsis

Class Name: java.net.ProtocolException
Superclass: java.io.IOException
Immediate Subclasses: None
Interfaces Implemented: None
Availability: JDK 1.0 or later

Description

A ProtocolException is thrown to indicate that there has been an error in an underlying protocol, such as an HTTP or TCP protocol error.

Class Summary

```
public class java.net.ProtocolException extends java.io.IOException {
    // Constructors
    public ProtocolException();
    public ProtocolException(String host);
}
```

Constructors

ProtocolException

public ProtocolException()

Description This constructor creates a ProtocolException with no associated detail message.

public ProtocolException(String host)

Parameters host The detail message.

Description This constructor creates a ProtocolException with the specified detail message, which should be the host that caused the underlying protocol error.

Inherited Methods

Method	Inherited From	Method	Inherited From
clone()	Object	equals(Object)	Object
fillInStackTrace()	Throwable	finalize()	Object
getClass()	Object	getLocalizedMessage()	Throwable
getMessage()	Throwable	hashCode()	Object
notify()	Object	notifyAll()	Object
printStackTrace()	Throwable	printStack-Trace(PrintStream)	Throwable
printStack-Trace(PrintWriter)	Throwable	toString()	Throwable
wait()	Object	wait(long)	Object
wait(long, int)	Object		

See Also

Exception, IOException, RuntimeException

15.15 ServerSocket

Synopsis

Class Name:	java.net.ServerSocket
Superclass:	java.lang.Object
Immediate Subclasses:	None
Interfaces Implemented:	None
Availability:	JDK 1.0 or later

Description

The ServerSocket class represents a socket that listens for connection requests from clients on a specified port. When a connection is requested, a Socket object is created to handle the communication.

The low-level network access in ServerSocket is provided by a subclass of the abstract class SocketImpl. An application can change the server socket factory that creates the SocketImpl subclass by supplying a SocketImplFactory using the setSocketFactory() method. This feature allows an application to create sockets that are appropriate for the local network configuration and accommodate such things as firewalls.

Class Summary

```
public class java.net.ServerSocket extends java.lang.Object {
    // Constructors
    public ServerSocket(int port);
    public ServerSocket(int port, int backlog);
    public ServerSocket(int port, int backlog,
                        InetAddress bindAddr);              // New in 1.1

    // Class Methods
    public static synchronized void setSocketFactory(SocketImplFactory fac);

    // Instance Methods
    public Socket accept();
    public void close();
    public InetAddress getInetAddress();
    public int getLocalPort();
    public synchronized int getSoTimeout()                 // New in 1.1
    public synchronized void setSoTimeout(int timeout);    // New in 1.1
    public String toString();

    // Protected Instance Methods
    protected final void implAccept(Socket s);             // New in 1.1
}
```

Constructors

ServerSocket

public ServerSocket(int port) throws IOException

Parameters	port	A port number, or 0 for any available port.
Throws	IOException	If any kind of I/O error occurs.
	SecurityException	
		If the application is not allowed to listen on the given port.

Description   This method creates a server socket that listens for a connection on the given port. A default of 50 pending connections can be queued by the `ServerSocket`. Calling `accept()` removes a pending connections from the queue. If the queue is full, additional connection requests are refused.

If an application has specified a server socket factory, the `createSocketImpl()` method of that factory is called to create the actual socket implementation. Otherwise, the constructor creates a plain socket.

public ServerSocket(int port, int backlog) throws IOException
   Parameters   port   A port number, or 0 for any available port.
                  backlog   The maximum length of the pending connections queue.

   Throws   IOException   If any kind of I/O error occurs.
                  SecurityException
                        If the application is not allowed to listen on the given port.

Description   This method creates a server socket that listens for a connection on the given port. The `backlog` parameter specifies how many pending connections can be queued by the `ServerSocket`. Calling `accept()` removes a pending connection from the queue. If the queue is full, additional connection requests are refused.

If an application has specified a server socket factory, the `createSocketImpl()` method of that factory is called to create the actual socket implementation. Otherwise, the constructor creates a plain socket.

public ServerSocket(int port, int backlog, InetAddress bindAddr)
    throws IOException
   Availability   New as of JDK 1.1
   Parameters   port   A port number, or 0 for any available port.
                  backlog   The maximum length of the pending connections queue.
                  bindAddr   A local address.
   Throws   IOException   If any kind of I/O error occurs.
                  SecurityException
                        If the application is not allowed to listen on the given port.

Description   This method creates a server socket that listens for a connection on the given port of bindAddr. On machines with multiple addresses, bindAddr specifies the address on which this Server-Socket listens. The backlog parameter specifies how many pending connections can be queued by the ServerSocket. Calling accept() removes pending connections from the queue. If the queue is full, additional connection requests are refused.

If an application has specified a server socket factory, the createSocketImpl() method of that factory is called to create the actual socket implementation. Otherwise, the constructor creates a plain socket.

Class Methods

setSocketFactory

```
public static synchronized void setSocketFactory(
                          SocketImplFactory fac)
                          throws IOException
```

Parameters   fac   An object that implements SocketImplFactory.
Throws   IOException   If the factory has already been defined.
              SecurityException
                            If the application does not have permission to set the factory.
Description   This method is used to set the SocketImplFactory. This factory object produces instances of subclasses of SocketImpl that do the low-level work of server sockets. When a ServerSocket constructor is called, the createSocketImpl() method of the factory is called to create the server socket implementation.

Instance Methods

accept

```
public Socket accept() throws IOException
```

Returns   A Socket object for the connection.
Throws   IOException   If any kind of I/O error occurs.
              SecurityException
                            If the application is not allowed to accept the connection.
Description   This method accepts a connection and returns a Socket object to handle communication. If there are pending connections, the method accepts a pending connection from the queue and returns immediately. Otherwise, the method may block until a

connection is requested. If a time-out value has been specified using the setSoTimeout() method, accept() may time out and throw an InterruptedIOException if no connection is requested in the time-out period.

close

public void close() throws IOException

Throws	IOException If any kind of I/O error occurs.
Description	This method closes this server socket, releasing any system resources it holds.

getInetAddress

public InetAddress getInetAddress()

Returns	The IP address to which this ServerSocket is listening.
Description	Generally, this method returns the address of the local host. However, a ServerSocket can be constructed with an alternate address using ServerSocket(int, int, InetAddress). The method returns null if the socket is not yet connected.

getLocalPort

public int getLocalPort()

Returns	The port number to which this ServerSocket is listening.
Description	This method returns the port number to which this object is connected.

getSoTimeout

public synchronized int getSoTimeout() throws IOException

Availability	New as of JDK 1.1
Returns	The receive timeout value for the socket.
Throws	IOException If any kind of I/O error occurs.
Description	This method returns the receive time-out value for this socket. A value of zero indicates that accept() waits indefinitely for an incoming packet, while a non-zero value indicates the number of milliseconds it waits.

setSoTimeout

public synchronized void setSoTimeout(int timeout)
                         throws SocketException

Availability	New as of JDK 1.1

| Parameters | timeout | The new time-out value, in milliseconds, for this socket. |

| Throws | SocketException | |
| | | If any kind of socket error occurs. |

| Description | | This method is used to set the time-out value that is used for accept(). A nonzero value is the length of time, in milliseconds, the ServerSocket should wait for a connection. A value of zero indicates that the ServerSocket should wait indefinitely. If a time-out value is needed, this method must be called before accept(). |

toString

```
public String toString()
```

Returns	The string representation of this ServerSocket.
Overrides	Object.toString()
Description	This method returns a String that contains the address and port of this ServerSocket.

Protected Instance Methods

implAccept

```
protected final void implAccept(Socket s) throws IOException
```

Availability	New as of JDK 1.1
Parameters	s	The Socket object to be connected.
Throws	IOException	If any kind of I/O error occurs.
	SecurityException	
		If the application is not allowed to accept the connection.
Description		This method is a helper method for accept(). It can be overridden in subclasses of ServerSocket to support new subclasses of Socket.

Inherited Methods

Method	Inherited From	Method	Inherited From
clone()	Object	equals(Object)	Object
finalize()	Object	getClass()	Object
hashCode()	Object	notify()	Object
notifyAll()	Object	wait()	Object
wait(long)	Object	wait(long, int)	Object

See Also

InetAddress, IOException, SecurityException, Socket, SocketException, SocketImpl, SocketImplFactory

---

15.16   Socket

Synopsis

Class Name:	java.net.Socket
Superclass:	java.lang.Object
Immediate Subclasses:	None
Interfaces Implemented:	None
Availability:	JDK 1.0 or later

Description

The Socket class implements stream-based, connection-oriented, reliable data communication. Although Socket objects are often used with the Transmission Control Protocol, commonly known as TCP, they are independent of the actual protocol being used. The Socket class encapsulates client logic that is common to connection-oriented protocols. Sockets are two-way data pipes that are connected on either end to an address and port number. As of JDK 1.1, new constructors allow you to specify the local address and port as well as the remote address and port.

A Socket object uses an object that belongs to a subclass of the abstract class SocketImpl to access protocol-specific logic. A program can specify the subclass of SocketImpl that is used by passing an appropriate SocketImplFactory object to the setSocketImplFactory() method before any Socket objects are created. This feature allows a program to create sockets that are able to accommodate such things as firewalls or even work with different protocols.

Class Summary

```
public class java.net.Socket extends java.lang.Object {
  // Constructors
  public Socket(String host, int port);
  public Socket(InetAddress address, int port);
  public Socket(String host, int port,
                InetAddress localAddr, int localPort);     // New in 1.1
  public Socket(InetAddress address, int port,
                InetAddress localAddr, int localPort);     // New in 1.1
  public Socket(String host, int port,
                boolean stream);                           // Deprecated in 1.1
  public Socket(InetAddress host, int port,
```

```
                    boolean stream);              // Deprecated in 1.1
    protected Socket();                           // New in 1.1
    protected Socket(SocketImpl impl);            // New in 1.1


    // Class Methods
    public static synchronized void setSocketImplFactory(
                            SocketImplFactory fac);


    // Instance Methods
    public synchronized void close();
    public InetAddress getInetAddress();
    public InputStream getInputStream();
    public InetAddress getLocalAddress();         // New in 1.1
    public int getLocalPort();
    public OutputStream getOutputStream();
    public int getPort();
    public int getSoLinger();                     // New in 1.1
    public synchronized int getSoTimeout();       // New in 1.1
    public boolean getTcpNoDelay();               // New in 1.1
    public void setSoLinger(boolean on, int val); // New in 1.1
    public synchronized void setSoTimeout(int timeout);  // New in 1.1
    public void setTcpNoDelay(boolean on);        // New in 1.1
    public String toString();
}
```

Constructors

Socket

```
public Socket(String host, int port)
        throws IOException, UnknownHostException
```

Parameters	host	The name of a remote machine.
	port	A port on a remote machine.
Throws	IOException	If any kind of I/O error occurs.
	SecurityException	
		If the application is not allowed to connect to the given host and port.
	UnknownHostException	
		If the IP address of the given hostname cannot be determined.
Description		This constructor creates a Socket and connects it to the specified port on the given host.

If a program has specified a socket factory, the createSocketImpl() method of that factory is called to create the actual socket implementation. Otherwise, the constructor creates a plain socket.

```
public Socket(InetAddress address, int port) throws IOException
```
Parameters address The IP address of a remote machine.

      port   A port on a remote machine.

Throws   IOException If any kind of I/O error occurs.

      SecurityException

          If the application is not allowed to connect to the given address and port.

Description This constructor creates a Socket and connects it to the specified port on the host at the given address.

     If a program has specified a socket factory, the createSocketImpl() method of that factory is called to create the actual socket implementation. Otherwise, the constructor creates a plain socket.

```
public Socket(String host, int port, InetAddress localAddr,
              int localPort) throws IOException
```
Availability New as of JDK 1.1

Parameters host   The name of a remote machine.

      port   A port on a remote machine.

      localAddr An IP address on the local host.

      localPort A port on the local host.

Throws   IOException If any kind of I/O error occurs.

      SecurityException

          If the application is not allowed to connect to the given host and port.

Description This constructor creates a Socket and connects it to the specified port on the given host. The constructor also binds the Socket to the specified local address and port.

     If a program has specified a socket factory, the createSocketImpl() method of that factory is called to create the actual socket implementation. Otherwise, the constructor creates a plain socket.

```
public Socket(InetAddress address, int port,
              InetAddress localAddr, int localPort)
         throws IOException
```
Availability New as of JDK 1.1

Parameters address The IP address of a remote machine.

      port   A port on a remote machine.

      localAddr An IP address on the local host.

```
                    localPort    A port on the local host.
```

Throws   `IOException` If any kind of I/O error occurs.

                     `SecurityException`

                               If the application is not allowed to connect to the given address and port.

Description   This constructor creates a `Socket` and connects it to the specified port on the host at the given address. The constructor also binds the `Socket` to the specified local address and port.

               If a program has specified a socket factory, the `createSocketImpl()` method of that factory is called to create the actual socket implementation. Otherwise, the constructor creates a plain socket.

`public Socket(String host, int port, boolean stream)`
       `throws IOException`

Availability   Deprecated as of JDK 1.1

Parameters   `host`   The name of a remote machine.

              `port`   A port on a remote machine.

              `stream`   A `boolean` value that indicates if this socket is a stream socket.

Throws   `IOException` If any kind of I/O error occurs.

                     `SecurityException`

                               If the application is not allowed to connect to the given host and port.

Description   This constructor creates a `Socket` and connects it to the specified port on the given host.

               If the `stream` argument is `true`, a stream socket is created. Otherwise, a datagram socket is created. This constructor is deprecated as of JDK 1.1; use `DatagramSocket` for datagrams.

               If a program has specified a socket factory, the `createSocketImpl()` method of that factory is called to create the actual socket implementation. Otherwise, the constructor creates a plain socket.

`public Socket(InetAddress address, int port, boolean stream)`
       `throws IOException`

Availability   Deprecated as of JDK 1.1

Parameters   `address`   The IP address of a remote machine.

              `port`   A port on a remote machine.

              `stream`   A `boolean` value that indicates if this socket is a stream socket.

Throws   `IOException`   If any kind of I/O error occurs.

                `SecurityException`

                        If the application is not allowed to connect to the given host and port.

Description   This constructor creates a `Socket` and connects it to the specified port on the host at the given address.

                If the `stream` argument is `true`, a stream socket is created. Otherwise, a datagram socket is created. This constructor is deprecated as of JDK 1.1; use `DatagramSocket` for datagrams.

                If a program has specified a socket factory, the `createSocketImpl()` method of that factory is called to create the actual socket implementation. Otherwise, the constructor creates a plain socket.

protectedSocket()

Availability   New as of JDK 1.1

Description   This constructor creates a `Socket` that uses an instance of the system default `SocketImpl` subclass for its low-level network access.

protectedSocket(SocketImpl impl) throws SocketException

Availability   New as of JDK 1.1

Parameters   `impl`   The socket implementation to use.

Throws   `SocketException`

                        This exception is never thrown by this constructor.

Description   This constructor creates a `Socket` that uses the given object for its low-level network access.

Class Methods

setSocketImplFactory

```
public static synchronized void setSocketImplFactory(
                        SocketImplFactory fac)
                        throws IOException
```

Parameters   `fac`   An object that implements `SocketImplFactory`.

Throws   `IOException`   If the factory has already been defined.

                `SecurityException`

                        If the application does not have permission to set the factory.

Description   This method sets the `SocketImplFactory`. This factory produces instances of subclasses of `SocketImpl` that do the low-level work of sockets. When a `Socket` constructor is called, the createSocketImpl() method of the factory is called to create the socket implementation.

Instance Methods

close

public synchronized void close() throws IOException

Throws	IOException If any kind of I/O error occurs.
Description	This method closes this socket, releasing any system resources it holds.

getInetAddress

public InetAddress getInetAddress()

Returns	The remote IP address to which this Socket is connected.
Description	This method returns the IP address of the remote host to which this socket is connected.

getInputStream

public InputStream getInputStream() throws IOException

Returns	An InputStream that wraps this socket.
Throws	IOException If any kind of I/O error occurs.
Description	This method returns an InputStream that reads data from the socket.

getLocalAddress

public InetAddress getLocalAddress()

Availability	New as of JDK 1.1
Returns	The local IP address from which this Socket originates.
Description	This method returns the local address that is the origin of the socket.

getLocalPort

public int getLocalPort()

Returns	The local port number from which this Socket originates.
Description	This method returns the local port number that is the origin of the socket.

getOutputStream

public OutputStream getOutputStream() throws IOException

Returns	An OutputStream that wraps this socket.

Throws   IOException   If any kind of I/O error occurs.

Description   This method returns an OutputStream that sends data through the socket.

getPort

public int getPort()

Returns   The remote port number to which this Socket is connected.

Description   This method returns the port number of the remote host to which this socket is connected.

getSoLinger

public int getSoLinger() throws SocketException

Availability   New as of JDK 1.1

Returns   The close time-out value for the socket.

Throws   SocketException

                If any kind of socket error occurs.

Description   This method returns the close time-out value for this socket. A value of –1 or 0 indicates that close() closes the socket immediately. A value greater than 0 indicates the amount of time, in seconds, that close() blocks, waiting for unsent data to be sent.

getSoTimeout

public synchronized int getSoTimeout() throws SocketException

Availability   New as of JDK 1.1

Returns   The read time-out value for the socket.

Throws   SocketException

                If any kind of socket error occurs.

Description   This method returns the read time-out value for this socket. A value of zero indicates that the read() method of the associated InputStream waits indefinitely for an incoming packet, while a non-zero value indicates the number of milliseconds it waits before throwing an InterruptedIOException.

getTcpNoDelay

public boolean getTcpNoDelay() throws SocketException

Availability   New as of JDK 1.1

Returns   true if Nagle's algorithm is disabled for this connection; false otherwise.

Throws   SocketException

                If any kind of socket error occurs.

Description   This method indicates whether Nagle's algorithm is disabled for this socket or not. Said another way, it indicates whether the `TCPNODELAY` option is enabled or not.

In essence, Nagle's algorithm takes small outgoing packets that are closely spaced in time and combines them into larger packets. This improves overall efficiency, since each packet has a certain amount of overhead; however, it does so at the expense of immediacy.

setSoLinger

```
public void setSoLinger(boolean on, int val)
        throws SocketException
```

Availability   New as of JDK 1.1

Parameters   on   A `boolean` value that specifies whether or not `close()` blocks

val   The new close time-out value, in seconds, for this socket.

Throws   SocketException
         If any kind of socket error occurs.

Description   This method sets the close timeout value for this socket. If `val` is –1 or 0, or if on is `false`, `close()` closes the socket immediately. If on is `true` and `val` is greater than 0, `val` indicates the amount of time, in seconds, that `close()` blocks, waiting for unsent data to be sent.

setSoTimeout

```
public synchronized void setSoTimeout(int timeout)
                throws SocketException
```

Availability   New as of JDK 1.1

Parameters   timeout   The new read time-out value, in milliseconds, for the socket.

Throws   SocketException
         If any kind of socket error occurs.

Description   This method is used to set the time-out value that is used for the `read()` method of the corresponding `InputStream`. A non-zero value is the length of time, in milliseconds, that the `Socket` should wait for data before throwing an `InterruptedIOException`. A value of zero indicates that the `Socket` should wait indefinitely. If a timeout value is needed, this method must be called before `read()`.

setTcpNoDelay

public void setTcpNoDelay(boolean on) throws SocketException

Availability	New as of JDK 1.1
Parameters	on A boolean value that specifies whether or not to disable Nagle's algorithm.
Throws	SocketException
	If any kind of socket error occurs.
Description	This method specifies whether Nagle's algorithm is disabled for this socket or not. Said another way, it determines whether the TCPNODELAY option is enabled or not.

In essence, Nagle's algorithm takes small outgoing packets that are closely spaced in time and combines them into larger packets. This improves overall efficiency, since each packet has a certain amount of overhead; however, it does so at the expense of immediacy.

toString

public String toString()

Returns	The string representation of this Socket.
Overrides	Object.toString()
Description	This method returns a String that contains the address and port of this Socket.

Inherited Methods

Method	Inherited From	Method	Inherited From
clone()	Object	equals(Object)	Object
finalize()	Object	getClass()	Object
hashCode()	Object	notify()	Object
notifyAll()	Object	wait()	Object
wait(long)	Object	wait(long, int)	Object

See Also

DatagramSocket, InetAddress, InputStream, IOException, OutputStream, SecurityException, SocketException, SocketImpl, SocketImplFactory, UnknownHostException

15.17   SocketException

Synopsis

Class Name:	java.net.SocketException
Superclass:	java.io.IOException
Immediate Subclasses:	java.net.BindException,
	java.net.ConnectException,
	java.net.NoRouteToHostException
Interfaces Implemented:	None
Availability:	JDK 1.0 and later

Description

A SocketException is thrown when an error occurs while a socket is being used. As of JDK 1.1, there are some more specific subclasses of SocketException, namely BindException, ConnectException, and NoRouteToHostException.

Class Summary

```
public class java.net.SocketException extends java.io.IOException {
    // Constructors
    public SocketException();
    public SocketException(String msg);
}
```

Constructors

SocketException

public SocketException()

   Description   This constructor creates a SocketException with no associated detail message.

public SocketException(String msg)

   Parameters   msg   The detail message.

   Description   This constructor creates a SocketException with the specified detail message.

Inherited Methods

Method	Inherited From	Method	Inherited From
clone()	Object	equals(Object)	Object
fillInStackTrace()	Throwable	finalize()	Object
getClass()	Object	getLocalizedMessage()	Throwable
getMessage()	Throwable	hashCode()	Object
notify()	Object	notifyAll()	Object

Method	Inherited From	Method	Inherited From
printStackTrace()	Throwable	printStack-Trace(PrintStream)	Throwable
printStack-Trace(PrintWriter)	Throwable	toString()	Throwable
wait()	Object	wait(long)	Object
wait(long, int)	Object		

See Also

BindException, ConnectException, Exception, IOException, NoRouteToHostException, RuntimeException

15.18   SocketImpl

Synopsis

Class Name: java.net.SocketImpl
Superclass: java.lang.Object
Immediate Subclasses: None
Interfaces Implemented: None
Availability: JDK 1.0 or later

Description

The SocketImpl class is an abstract class that defines the bulk of the methods that make the Socket and ServerSocket classes work. Thus, SocketImpl is used to create both client and server sockets. Non-public subclasses of SocketImpl provide platform-specific implementations of stream-based socket communication. A plain socket implements the methods in SocketImpl as described; other implementations could provide socket communication through a proxy or firewall.

Class Summary

```
public abstract class java.net.SocketImpl extends java.lang.Object {
    // Variables
    protected InetAddress address;
    protected FileDescriptor fd;
    protected int localport;
    protected int port;

    // Instance Methods
    public String toString();
```

```
// Protected Instance Methods
protected abstract void accept(SocketImpl s);
protected abstract int available();
protected abstract void bind(InetAddress host, int port);
protected abstract void close();
protected abstract void connect(String host, int port);
protected abstract void connect(InetAddress address, int port);
protected abstract void create(boolean stream);
protected FileDescriptor getFileDescriptor();
protected InetAddress getInetAddress();
protected abstract InputStream getInputStream();
protected int getLocalPort();
protected abstract OutputStream getOutputStream();
protected int getPort();
protected abstract void listen(int backlog);
}
```

Variables

address

```
protected InetAddress address
```
    Description   The remote IP address to which this socket is connected.

fd

```
protected FileDescriptor fd
```
    Description   The file descriptor that represents this socket.

localPort

```
protected int localPort
```
    Description   The local port number of this socket.

port

```
protected int port
```
    Description   The remote port number of this socket.

Instance Methods

toString

```
public String toString()
```
    Returns   The string representation of this `SocketImpl`.
    Overrides   `Object.toString()`
    Description This method returns a `String` that contains a representation of this object.

Protected Instance Methods

accept

protected abstract void accept(SocketImpl s) throws IOException

Parameters	s	A SocketImpl to connect.
Throws	IOException	If any kind of I/O error occurs.
Description		This method accepts a connection. The method connects the given socket s to a remote host in response to the remote host's connection request on this SocketImpl.

available

protected abstract int available() throws IOException

Returns	The number of bytes that can be read without blocking.
Throws	IOException If any kind of I/O error occurs.
Description	This method returns the number of bytes that can be read from the socket without waiting for more data to arrive.

bind

protected abstract void bind(InetAddress host, int port)
                          throws IOException

Parameters	host	An IP address.
	port	A port number.
Throws	IOException	If any kind of I/O error occurs.
Description		This method binds the socket to the given address and port. If the address or the port is unavailable, an exception is thrown.

close

protected abstract void close() throws IOException

Throws	IOException If any kind of I/O error occurs.
Description	This method closes the socket, releasing any system resources it holds.

connect

protected abstract void connect(String host, int port)
                          throws IOException

Parameters	host	A remote hostname.
	port	A port number on the remote host.
Throws	IOException	If any kind of I/O error occurs.
Description		This method connects this socket to the specified port on the given host.

```
protected abstract void connect(InetAddress address, int port)
                          throws IOException
```

Parameters	address	A remote IP address.
	port	A port number on the remote host.
Throws	IOException	If any kind of I/O error occurs.
Description		This method connects this socket to the specified port on the host at the given address.

create

```
protected abstract void create(boolean stream) throws IOException
```

Parameters	stream	A boolean value that indicates if this socket is a stream socket.
Throws	IOException	If any kind of I/O error occurs.
Description		This method creates a socket that is not bound and not connected. If the stream argument is true, a stream socket is created. Otherwise, a datagram socket is created.

getFileDescriptor

```
protected final FileDescriptor getFileDescriptor
```

Returns	The file descriptor for this socket.
Description	This method returns the file descriptor associated with this SocketImpl.

getInetAddress

```
protected InetAddress getInetAddress()
```

Returns	The remote IP address to which this SocketImpl is connected.
Description	This method returns the IP address of the remote host to which this SocketImpl is connected.

getInputStream

```
protected abstract InputStream getInputStream() throws IOException
```

Returns	An InputStream that wraps this socket.
Throws	IOException If any kind of I/O error occurs.
Description	This method returns an InputStream that reads data from the socket.

getLocalPort

```
protected int getLocalPort()
```

Returns	The local port number from which this SocketImpl originates.

Description   This method returns the local port number that is the origin of
               the socket.

getOutputStream

```
protected abstract OutputStream getOutputStream()
                              throws IOException
```
Returns   An OutputStream that wraps this socket.
Throws   IOException   If any kind of I/O error occurs.
Description   This method returns an OutputStream that sends data through
               the socket.

getPort

```
protected int getPort()
```
Returns   The remote port number to which this SocketImpl is con-
               nected.
Description   This method returns the port number of the remote host to
               which this socket is connected.

listen

```
protected abstract void listen(int backlog) throws IOException
```
Parameters   backlog   The maximum length of pending connections
                             queue.
Throws   IOException   If any kind of I/O error occurs.
Description   This object can directly accept a connection if its accept()
               method has been called and is waiting for a connection. Other-
               wise, the local system rejects connections to this socket unless
               listen() has been called.

               This method requests that the local system listen for connec-
               tions and accept them on behalf of this object. The accepted
               connections are placed in a queue of the specified length.
               When there are connections in the queue, a call to this object's
               accept() method removes a connection from the queue and
               immediately returns. If the queue is full, additional connection
               requests are refused.

Inherited Methods

Method	Inherited From	Method	Inherited From
clone()	Object	equals(Object)	Object
finalize()	Object	getClass()	Object
hashCode()	Object	notify()	Object

Method	Inherited From	Method	Inherited From
notifyAll()	Object	wait()	Object
wait(long)	Object	wait(long, int)	Object

See Also

FileDescriptor, InetAddress, InputStream, IOException, OutputStream, Server-Socket, Socket, SocketImplFactory

15.19   *SocketImplFactory*

Synopsis

Interface Name:	java.net.SocketImplFactory
Super-interface:	None
Immediate Sub-interfaces:	
	None
Implemented By:	None
Availability:	JDK 1.0 or later

Description

The SocketImplFactory interface defines a method that creates a SocketImpl object. The interface is implemented by classes that select SocketImpl subclasses to support the Socket and ServerSocket classes.

Interface Declaration

```
public abstract interface java.net.SocketImplFactory {
    // Methods
    public abstract SocketImpl createSocketImpl();
}
```

Methods

createSocketImpl

public abstract SocketImpl createSocketImpl()

Returns   A SocketImpl object.

Description   This method creates an instance of a subclass of SocketImpl that is appropriate for the environment.

See Also

ServerSocket, Socket, SocketImpl

15.20   URL

Synopsis

Class Name:	java.net.URL
Superclass:	java.lang.Object
Immediate Subclasses:	None
Interfaces Implemented:	java.io.Serializable
Availability:	JDK 1.0 or later

Description

The URL class represents a Uniform Resource Locator, or URL. The class provides methods for retrieving the various parts of a URL and also access to the resource itself.

An absolute URL consists of a protocol, a hostname, a port number, a filename, and an optional reference, or anchor. For example, consider the following URL:

    http://www.woolf.net:81/books/Orlando/chapter4.html#p6

This URL consists of the following parts:

Part	Value
Protocol	http
Hostname	www.woolf.net
Port number	81
Filename	/books/Orlando/chapter4.html
Reference	p6

A relative URL specifies only enough information to locate the resource relative to another URL. The filename component is the only part that must be specified for a relative URL. If the protocol, hostname, or port number is not specified, the value is taken from a fully specified URL. For example, the following is a relative URL based on the absolute URL above:

    chapter6.html

This relative URL is equivalent to the following absolute URL:

```
http://www.woolf.net:81/books/Orlando/chapter6.html
```

The URL class also provides access to the resource itself, through the getContent(), openConnection(), and openStream() methods. However, these are all convenience functions: other classes do the actual work of accessing the resource.

A protocol handler is an object that knows how to deal with a specific protocol. For example, an http protocol handler opens a connection to an http host. In java.net, subclasses of URLStreamHandler deal with different protocols. A URLStreamHandlerFactory selects a subclass of URLStreamHandler based on a MIME type. Once the URLStreamHandler has established a connection with a host using a specific protocol, a subclass of ContentHandler retrieves resource data from the host and creates an object from it.

Class Summary

```
public final class java.net.URL extends java.lang.Object
                                implements java.io.Serializable {
    // Constructors
    public URL(String spec);
    public URL(URL context, String spec);
    public URL(String protocol, String host, String file);
    public URL(String protocol, String host, int port, String file);

    // Class Methods
    public static synchronized void setURLStreamHandlerFactory(
                            URLStreamHandlerFactory fac);

    // Instance Methods
    public boolean equals(Object obj);
    public final Object getContent();
    public String getFile();
    public String getHost();
    public int getPort();
    public String getProtocol();
    public String getRef();
    public int hashCode();
    public URLConnection openConnection();
    public final InputStream openStream();
    public boolean sameFile(URL other);
    public String toExternalForm();
    public String toString();

    // Protected Instance Methods
    protected void set(String protocol, String host, int port,
                    String file, String ref);
}
```

Constructors

URL

public URL(String spec) throws MalformedURLException

Parameters   spec   A String that represents a URL.

Throws   MalformedURLException

If the string is incorrectly constructed or specifies an unknown protocol.

Description   This constructor creates a URL by parsing the given string. The string should specify an absolute URL. Calling this constructor is equivalent to calling URL(null, spec).

public URL(URL context, String spec) throws MalformedURLException

Parameters   context   A base URL that provides the context for parsing spec.

spec   A String that represents a URL.

Throws   MalformedURLException

If the string is incorrectly constructed or specifies an unknown protocol.

Description   This constructor creates a URL relative to the base URL specified by context. If context is not null, and spec specifies a partial URL, the missing parts of spec are inherited from context.

The given string is first parsed to see if it specifies a protocol. If the string contains a colon (:) before the first occurrence of a slash (/), the characters before the colon comprise the protocol.

If spec does not specify a protocol, and context is not null, the protocol is inherited from context, as are the hostname, port number, and filename. If context is null in this situation, the constructor throws a MalformedURLException.

If spec does specify a protocol, and context is null or specifies a different protocol, the context argument is ignored and spec should specify an absolute URL. If context specifies the same protocol as spec, the hostname, port number, and filename from context are inherited.

Once the constructor has created a fully specified URL object, it searches for an appropriate protocol handler of type URL-StreamHandler, as described for URL(String, String, int, String). Then the parseURL() method of the URLStreamHandleris called to parse the remainder of the URL so that the fields in spec can override any values inherited from context.

```
public URL(String protocol, String host, String file)
     throws MalformedURLException
```
Parameters protocol A protocol.

      host   A hostname.

      file   A filename.

Throws   MalformedURLException

      If an unknown protocol is specified.

Description This constructor creates a URL with the given protocol, host-name, and filename. The port number is set to the default port for the given protocol. Calling this constructor is equivalent to calling URL(protocol, host, -1, file).

```
public URL(String protocol, String host, int port, String file)
     throws MalformedURLException
```
Parameters protocol A protocol.

      host   A hostname.

      port   A port number or –1 to use the default port for the protocol.

      file   A filename.

Throws   MalformedURLException

      If an unknown protocol is specified.

Description This constructor creates a URL with the given protocol, host-name, port number, and filename.

If this is the first URL object being created with the specified protocol, a protocol handler of type URLStreamHandler is created for the protocol. Here are the steps that are taken to create a protocol handler:

1. If an application has set up a URLStreamHandlerFactory by calling setURLStreamHandlerFactory(), the constructor calls the createURLStreamHandler() method of that object to create the protocol handler. The protocol is passed as a String argument to that method.

2. If no URLStreamHandlerFactory has been established, or the createURLStreamHandler() method returns null, the constructor retrieves the value of the system property java.protocol.handler.pkgs. If this value is not null, it is interpreted as a list of packages separated by vertical bar (|) characters. The constructor then tries to load the class named *package*.*protocol*.Handler, where *package* is the name of the first package in the list and *protocol* is the name of the protocol. If the class exists, and is a subclass of URL-StreamHandler, it is used as the URLStreamHandler for the

protocol. If the class does not exist, or if it exists but is not a subclass of URLStreamHandler, the constructor tries the next package in the list.

3. If the previous step fails to find an appropriate protocol handler, the constructor tries to load the class named sun.net.www.protocol.*protocol*.Handler, where *protocol* is the name of the protocol. If the class exists and is a subclass of URLStreamHandler, it is used as the URLStreamHandler for the protocol. If the class does not exist, or if it exists but is not a subclass of URLStreamHandler, a MalformedURLException is thrown.

Class Methods

setURLStreamHandlerFactory

public static synchronized void
      setURLStreamHandlerFactory(URLStreamHandlerFactory fac)

Parameters	fac	An object that implements URLStreamHandler-Factory.
Throws	Error	If the factory has already been defined.
	SecurityException	
		If the application does not have permission to set the factory.
Description		This method tells the URL class to use the given URLStreamHandlerFactory object for handling all URL objects. The purpose of this mechanism is to allow a program that hosts applets, such as a web browser, control over the creation of URLStreamHandler objects.

Instance Methods

equals

public boolean equals(Object obj)

Parameters	obj	The object to be compared with this object.
Returns	true	if the objects are equivalent;
	false	if they are not.
Overrides	Object.equals()	
Description		This method returns true if obj is an instance of URL with the same protocol, hostname, port number, and filename as this URL. The reference is only compared if it is not null in this URL.

getContent

```
public Object getContent() throws IOException
```

Returns   The Object created from the resource represented by this URL.

Throws   IOException If any kind of I/O error occurs.

Description   This method returns the content of the URL, encapsulated in an object that is appropriate for the type of the content. The method is shorthand for calling openConnection().getContent(), which uses a ContentHandler object to retrieve the content.

getFile

```
public String getFile()
```

Returns   The filename of the URL.

Description   This method returns the name of the file of this URL. Note that the file can be misleading; although the resource represented by this URL may be a file, it can also be generated on the fly by the server.

getHost

```
public String getHost()
```

Returns   The hostname of the URL.

Description   This method returns the hostname from this URL.

getPort

```
public int getPort()
```

Returns   The port number of the URL.

Description   This method returns the port number of this URL. If a port number is not specified for this URL, meaning it uses the default port for the protocol, -1 is returned.

getProtocol

```
public String getProtocol()
```

Returns   The protocol of the URL.

Description   This method returns the protocol of this URL. Some examples of protocols are: http, ftp, and mailto.

getRef

```
public String getRef()
```

Returns   The reference of the URL.

Description   This method returns the reference, or anchor, of this URL.

hashCode

`public int hashCode()`

Returns   The hashcode of the URL.

Overrides   `Object.hashCode()`

Description   This method returns a hashcode for this object.

openConnection

`public URLConnection openConnection() throws IOException`

Returns   A `URLConnection` object for the URL.

Throws   `IOException`   If any kind of I/O error occurs.

Description   This method returns a `URLConnection` than manages a connection to the resource represented by this URL. If there is not already an open connection, the method opens a connection by calling the `openConnection()` method of the `URLStreamHandler` for this URL. A `URLStreamHandler` for the protocol of the URL is created by the constructor of the URL.

openStream

`public final InputStream openStream() throws IOException`

Returns   A `InputStream` that reads from this URL.

Throws   `IOException`   If any kind of I/O error occurs.

Description   This method returns an `InputStream` object that reads the content of the given URL. The method is shorthand for calling `openConnection().getInputStream()`.

sameFile

`public boolean sameFile(URL other)`

Parameters   other   The URL to compare.

Returns   A `boolean` value that indicates if this URL is equivalent to other with the exception of references.

Description   This method returns true if this object and the given URL object specify the same protocol, specify hosts that have the same IP address, specify the same port number, and specify the same filename. The filename comparison is case-sensitive. References specified by the URLs are not considered by this method. This method is a helper method for `equals()`.

toExternalForm

```
public String toExternalForm)
```
    Returns   A string representation of the URL.

    Description   This method returns a string representation of this URL. The string representation is determined by the protocol of the URL. The method calls the toExternalForm() method of the URL-StreamHandler for this URL. A URLStreamHandler for the protocol of the URL is created by the constructor of the URL.

toString

```
public String toString()
```
    Returns   A string representation of the URL.

    Overrides   Object.toString()

    Description   This method returns a string representation of this URL by calling toExternalForm().

Protected Instance Methods

set

```
protected void set(String protocol, String host, int port,
                   String file, String ref)
```
    Parameters   protocol   A protocol.

                host   A hostname.

                port   A port number.

                file   A filename.

                ref   A reference.

    Description   This method sets the protocol, hostname, port number, filename, and reference of this URL. The method is called by a URL-StreamHandler to set the parts of the URL. A URLStreamHandler for the protocol of the URL is created by the constructor of the URL. It is this URLStreamHandler that parses the URL string. This method is used after parsing to set the values of the URL.

Inherited Methods

Method	Inherited From	Method	Inherited From
clone()	Object	finalize()	Object
getClass()	Object	notify()	Object
notifyAll()	Object	wait()	Object
wait(long)	Object	wait(long, int)	Object

See Also

ContentHandler, Error, InputStream, IOException, MalformedURLException, SecurityException, URLConnection, URLStreamHandler, URLStreamHandlerFactory

15.21   URLConnection

Synopsis

Class Name: java.net.URLConnection
Superclass: java.lang.Object
Immediate Subclasses: java.net.HttpURLConnection
Interfaces Implemented: None
Availability: JDK 1.0 or later

Description

The URLConnection class is an abstract class that represents a connection to a URL. A subclass of URLConnection supports a protocol-specific connection. A URLConnection can both read from and write to a URL.

A URLConnection object is created when the openConnection() method is called for a URL object. At this point, the actual connection has not yet been made, so setup parameters and general request properties can be modified for the specific connection. The various set methods control the setup parameters and request properties. Then the actual connection is made by calling the connect() method. Finally, the remote object becomes available, and the header fields and the content are accessed using various get methods.

The URLConnection class defines quite a few methods for setting parameters and retrieving information. Fortunately, for simple connections, all of the setup parameters and request properties can be left alone, as they all have reasonable default values. In most cases, you'll only be interested in the getInputStream() and getContent() methods. getInputStream() provides an InputStream that reads from the URL, while getContent() uses a ContentHandler to return an Object that represents the content of the resource. These methods are mirrored by the openStream() and getContent() convenience methods in the URL class.

Class Summary

```
public abstract class java.net.URLConnection extends java.lang.Object {
  // Variables
  protected boolean allowUserInteraction;
  protected boolean connected;
  protected boolean doInput;
  protected boolean doOutput;
  public static FileNameMap fileNameMap;               // New in 1.1
  protected long ifModifiedSince;
  protected URL url;
  protected boolean useCaches;

  // Constructors
  protected URLConnection(URL url);

  // Class Methods
  public static boolean getDefaultAllowUserInteraction();
  public static String getDefaultRequestProperty(String key);
  protected static String guessContentTypeFromName(String fname);
  public static String guessContentTypeFromStream(InputStream is);
  public static synchronized void setContentHandlerFactory(
                                ContentHandlerFactory fac);
  public static void setDefaultAllowUserInteraction(
                    boolean defaultallowuserinteraction);
  public static void setDefaultRequestProperty(String key,
                    String value);

  // Instance Methods
  public abstract void connect();
  public boolean getAllowUserInteraction();
  public Object getContent()
  public String getContentEncoding();
  public int getContentLength();
  public String getContentType();
  public long getDate();
  public boolean getDefaultUseCaches();
  public boolean getDoInput();
  public boolean getDoOutput();
  public long getExpiration();
  public String getHeaderField(int n);
  public String getHeaderField(String name);
  public long getHeaderFieldDate(String name, long default);
  public int getHeaderFieldInt(String name, int default);
  public String getHeaderFieldKey(int n);
  public long getIfModifiedSince();
  public InputStream getInputStream();
  public long getLastModified();
  public OutputStream getOutputStream();
  public String getRequestProperty(String key);
```

```
    public URL getURL();
    public boolean getUseCaches();
    public void setAllowUserInteraction(boolean allowuserinteraction);
    public void setDefaultUseCaches(boolean defaultusecaches);
    public void setDoInput(boolean doinput);
    public void setDoOutput(boolean dooutput);
    public void setIfModifiedSince(long ifmodifiedsince);
    public void setRequestProperty(String key, String value);
    public void setUseCaches(boolean usecaches);
    public String toString();
}
```

Variables

allowUserInteraction

protected boolean allowUserInteraction

Description   A flag that indicates whether or not user interaction is enabled for this connection. If this variable is true, it is possible to allow user interactions such as popping up dialog boxes. If it is false, no user interaction is allowed. The variable can be set by setAllowUserInteraction() and retrieved by getAllowUserInteraction(). The default value is false, unless the setDefaultAllowUserInteraction() method has been called, in which case that method call controls the default value.

connected

protected boolean connected

Description   A flag that indicates whether or not this object has established a connection to a remote host.

doInput

protected boolean doInput

Description   A flag that indicates whether or not this connection is enabled for input. Setting this variable to true indicates that the connection is going to read data. The variable can be set by setDoInput() and retrieved by getDoInput(). The default value is true.

doOutput

protected boolean doOutput

Description   A flag that indicates whether or not this connection is enabled for output. Setting this variable to true indicates that the connection is going to write data. The variable can be set by set-

DoOutput() and retrieved by getDoOutput(). The default value is false.

fileNameMap

public static FileNameMap fileNameMap

Availability   New as of JDK 1.1

Description   A reference to the object that maps filename extensions to MIME type strings. This variable is used in guessContentType-FromName().

ifModifiedSince

protected long ifModifiedSince

Description   A time value, specified as the number of seconds since January 1, 1970, that controls whether or not a resource is fetched based on its last modification time. Some protocols do not bother to retrieve a resource if there is a current local cached copy. However, if the resource has been modified more recently than ifModifiedSince, it is retrieved. If ifModifiedSince is 0, the resource is always retrieved. The variable can be set by setIfModifiedSince() and retrieved by getIfModifiedSince(). The default value is 0, which means that the resource must always be retrieved.

url

protected URL url

Description   The resource to which this URLConnection connects. This variable is set to the value of the URL argument in the URLConnection constructor. It can be retrieved by getURL().

useCaches

protected boolean useCaches

Description   A flag that indicates whether or not locally cached resources are used. Some protocols cache documents. If this variable is true, the protocol is allowed to use caching whenever possible. If it is false, the protocol must always try to retrieve the resource. The variable can be set by setUseCaches() and retrieved by getUseCaches(). The default value is true, unless the setDefaultUseCaches() method has been called, in which case that method call controls the default value.

Constructors

URLConnection

protected URLConnection(URL url)

Parameters	url	The URL to access.
Description		This constructor creates a URLConnection object to manage a connection to the destination specified by the given URL. The actual connection is not created, however.

Class Methods

getDefaultAllowUserInteraction

public static boolean getDefaultAllowUserInteraction()

Returns	true if user interaction is allowed by default; false otherwise.
Description	This method returns the default value of the allowUserInteraction variable for all instances of URLConnection. The default value is false, unless the setDefaultAllowUserInteraction() method has been called, in which case that method call controls the default value.

getDefaultRequestProperty

public static String getDefaultRequestProperty(String key)

Parameters	key	The name of a request property.
Returns		The default value of the named request property.
Description		This method returns the default value for the request property named by the key parameter.

guessContentTypeFromName

protected static String guessContentTypeFromName(String fname)

Parameters	fname	A String that contains the name of a file.
Returns		A guess at the MIME type of the given file, or null if a guess cannot be made.
Description		This method uses the FileNameMap specified by the variable fileNameMap to return a MIME content type for the given filename.

guessContentTypeFromStream

protected static String guessContentTypeFromStream(InputStream is)
                        throws IOException

Parameters	is	The input stream to inspect.
Returns		A guess at the MIME type of the given input stream, or null if a guess cannot be made.

Throws   IOException   If any kind of I/O error occurs.

Description   This method looks at the first few bytes of an InputStream and
                 returns a guess of the MIME content type. Note that the Input-
                 Stream must support marks, which usually means that there is a
                 BufferedInputStream at some level. Here are some strings that
                 are recognized and the inferred content type:

String	MIME Type Guess
#def	image/x-bitmap
<!	text/html
<body	text/html
<head>	text/html
<html>	text/html
! XPM2	image/x-pixmap
GIF8	image/gif

setContentHandlerFactory

```
public static synchronized void
       setContentHandlerFactory(ContentHandlerFactory fac)
```

Parameters   fac   An object that implements ContentHandlerFac-
                                tory.

Throws   Error   If the factory has already been defined.

                SecurityException

                                If the application does not have permission to
                                set the factory.

Description   This method tells the URLConnection class to use the given Con-
                 tentHandlerFactory object for all URLConnection objects. The
                 purpose of this mechanism is to allow a program that hosts
                 applets, such as a web browser, control over the creation of
                 ContentHandler objects.

setDefaultAllowUserInteraction

```
public static void setDefaultAllowUserInteraction(
                   boolean defaultallowuserinteraction)
```

Parameters   defaultallowuserinteraction
                                The new default value.

Description   This method sets the default value of the allowUserInterac-
                 tion variable for all new instances of URLConnection.

setDefaultRequestProperty

```
public static void setDefaultRequestProperty(String key,
                                              String value)
```

Parameters   key   The name of a request property.

              value   The new default value.

Description   This method sets the default value of the request property
              named by the key parameter.

Instance Methods

connect

```
public abstract void connect() throws IOException
```

Throws   IOException   If any kind of I/O error occurs.

Description   When a URLConnection object is created, it is not immediately
              connected to the resource specified by its associated URL object.
              This method actually establishes the connection. If this method
              is called after the connection has been established, it does
              nothing.

              Before the connection is established, various parameters can be
              set with the set methods. After the connection has been estab-
              lished, it is an error to try to set these parameters.

              As they retrieve information about the resource specified by the
              URL object, many of the get methods require that the connec-
              tion be established. If the connection has not been established
              when one of these methods is called, the connection is estab-
              lished implicitly.

getAllowUserInteraction

```
public boolean getAllowUserInteraction()
```

Returns   true if user interaction is allowed for this connection; false
              otherwise.

Description   This method returns the value of the allowUserInteraction
              variable for this URLConnection.

getContent

```
public Object getContent()
              throws IOException, UnknownServiceException
```

Returns   An Object created from this URLConnection.

Throws   IOException   If any kind of I/O error occurs.

UnknownServiceException

If the protocol cannot support the content type.

Description   This method retrieves the content of the resource specified by the URL object associated with this URLConnection. If the connection for this object has not been established, the method implicitly establishes it.

The method returns an object that encapsulates the content of the connection. For example, for a connection that has content type image/jpeg, the method might return a object that belongs to subclass of Image, or for content type text/plain, it might return a String. The instanceof operator should determine the specific type of object that is returned.

The method first determines the content type of the connection by calling getContentType(). If this is the first time the content type has been seen, a content handler of type ContentHandler is created for the content type. Here are the steps that are taken to create a content handler:

1. If an application has set up a ContentHandlerFactory by calling setContentHandlerFactory(), the method calls the createContentHandler() method of that object to create the content handler. The content type is passed as a String argument to that method.

2. If no ContentHandlerFactory has been established, or the createContentHandler() method returns null, the method retrieves the value of the system property java.content.handler.pkgs. If this value is not null, it is interpreted as a list of packages separated by vertical bar (|) characters. The method then tries to load the class named *package.contentType*, where *package* is the name of the first package in the list and *contentType* is formed by taking the content-type string and replacing every slash (/) character with a period (.) and every other nonalphanumeric character with an underscore (_). If the class exists and is a subclass of ContentHandler, it is used as the ContentHandler for the content type. If the class does not exist, or if it exists but is not a subclass of ContentHandler, the method tries the next package in the list.

3. If the previous step fails to find an appropriate content handler, the method tries to load the class named sun.net.www.content.*contentType*, where *contentType* is formed by taking the content-type string and replacing

every slash (/) character with a period (.) and every other nonalphanumeric character with an underscore (_). If the class exists and is a subclass of ContentHandler, it is used as the ContentHandler for the content type. If the class does not exist, or if it exists but is not a subclass of ContentHandler, a UnknownServiceException is thrown.

getContentEncoding

public String getContentEncoding()

Returns	The content encoding, or null if it is not known.
Description	This method retrieves the content encoding of the resource specified by the URL object associated with this URLConnection. In other words, the method returns the value of the content-encoding header field. If the connection for this object has not been established, the method implicitly establishes it.

getContentLength

public int getContentLength()

Returns	The content length or –1 if it is not known.
Description	This method retrieves the content length of the resource specified by the URL object associated with this URLConnection. In other words, the method returns the value of the content-length header field. If the connection for this object has not been established, the method implicitly establishes it.

getContentType

public String getContentType()

Returns	The content type, or null if it is not known.
Description	This method retrieves the content type of the resource specified by the URL object associated with this URLConnection. In other words, the method returns the value of the content-type header field. This string is generally be a MIME type, such as image/jpeg or text/html. If the connection for this object has not been established, the method implicitly establishes it.

getDate

public long getDate()

Returns	The content date, or 0 if it is not known.

Description   This method retrieves the date of the resource specified by the
URL object associated with this URLConnection. In other words,
the method returns the value of the date header field. The date
is returned as the number of seconds since January 1, 1970. If
the connection for this object has not been established, the
method implicitly establishes it.

getDefaultUseCaches

```
public boolean getDefaultUseCaches()
```

Returns   true if the use of caches is allowed by default; false otherwise.

Description   This method returns the default value of the useCaches variable for all instances of URLConnection. The default value is
true, unless the setDefaultUseCaches() method has been
called, in which case that method call controls the default
value.

getDoInput

```
public boolean getDoInput()
```

Returns   true if this URLConnection is to be used for input; false otherwise.

Description   This method returns the value of the doInput variable for this
URLConnection.

getDoOutput

```
public boolean getDoOutput()
```

Returns   true if this URLConnection is to be used for output; false otherwise.

Description   This method returns the value of the doOutput variable for this
URLConnection.

getExpiration

```
public long getExpiration()
```

Returns   The content expiration date, or if it is not known.

Description   This method retrieves the expiration date of the resource specified by the URL object associated with this URLConnection. In
other words, the method returns the value of the expires
header field. The date is returned as the number of seconds
since January 1, 1970. If the connection for this object has not
been established, the method implicitly establishes it.

getHeaderField

`public String getHeaderField(int n)`

Parameters	n	A header field index.
Returns		The value of the header field with the given index, or `null` if n is greater than the number of fields in the header.
Description		This method retrieves the value of the header field at index n of the resource specified by the URL object associated with this URLConnection. If the connection for this object has not been established, the method implicitly establishes it.

`public String getHeaderField(String name)`

Parameters	name	A header field name.
Returns		The value of the named header field, or `null` if the header field is not known or its value cannot be determined.
Description		This method retrieves the value of the named header field of the resource specified by the URL object associated with this URLConnection. This method is a helper for methods like getContentEncoding() and getContentType(). If the connection for this object has not been established, the method implicitly establishes it.

getHeaderFieldDate

`public long getHeaderFieldDate(String name, long default)`

Parameters	name	A header field name.
	default	A default date value.
Returns		The value of the named header field parsed as a date value, or default if the field is missing or cannot be parsed.
Description		This method retrieves the value of the named header field of the resource specified by the URL object associated with this URLConnection and parses it as a date value. The date is returned as the number of seconds since January 1, 1970. If the value of the header field cannot be determined or it is not a properly formed date, the given default value is returned. If the connection for this object has not been established, the method implicitly establishes it.

getHeaderFieldInt

`public int getHeaderFieldInt(String name, int default)`

Parameters	name	A header field name.
	default	A default value.

Returns	The value of the named header field parsed as a number, or default if the field is missing or cannot be parsed.
Description	This method retrieves the value of the named header field of the resource specified by the URL object associated with this URLConnection and parses it as a number. If the value of the header field cannot be determined or it is not a properly formed integer, the given default value is returned. If the connection for this object has not been established, the method implicitly establishes it.

getHeaderFieldKey

public String getHeaderFieldKey(int n)

Parameters	n	A header field index.
Returns		The name of the header field at the given index, or null if n is greater than the number of fields in the header.
Description		This method retrieves the name of the header field at index n of the resource specified by the URL object associated with this URLConnection. If the connection for this object has not been established, the method implicitly establishes it.

getIfModifiedSince

public long getIfModifiedSince()

Returns	The value of the ifModifiedSince variable.
Description	This method returns the value of the ifModifiedSince variable for this URLConnection.

getInputStream

public InputStream getInputStream()
                    throws IOException, UnknownServiceException

Returns	An InputStream that reads data from this connection.
Throws	IOException If any kind of I/O error occurs.
	UnknownServiceException
	If this protocol does not support input.
Description	This method returns an InputStream that reads the contents of the resource specified by the URL object associated with this URLConnection.

getLastModified

`public long getLastModified()`

Returns   The content last-modified date, or if it is not known.

Description   This method retrieves the last-modified date of the resource specified by the URL object associated with this URLConnection. In other words, the method returns the value of the last-modified header field. The date is returned as the number of seconds since January 1, 1970. If the connection for this object has not been established, the method implicitly establishes it.

getOutputStream

`public OutputStream getOutputStream()`
                     `throws IOException, UnknownServiceException`

Returns   An OutputStream that writes data to this connection.

Throws   IOException   If any kind of I/O error occurs.

                 UnknownServiceException

                       If this protocol does not support output.

Description   This method returns an OutputStream that writes to the resource specified by the URL object associated with this URL-Connection.

getRequestProperty

`public String getRequestProperty(String key)`

Parameters   key   The name of a request property.

Returns   The value of the named request property.

Description   This method returns the value of the request property named by the key parameter.

getURL

`public URL getURL()`

Returns   The URL that this connection accesses.

Description   This method returns a reference to the URL associated with this object. This is the value of the url variable for this URLConnection.

getUseCaches

`public boolean getUseCaches()`

Returns   true if this URLConnection uses caches; false otherwise.

Description   This method returns the value of the useCaches variable for this URLConnection.

setAllowUserInteraction

`public void setAllowUserInteraction(boolean allowuserinteraction)`

Parameters	allowuserinteraction	
		A boolean value that indicates whether user interaction is allowed or not.
Throws	IllegalAccessError	
		If this method is called after the connection has been established.
Description		This method sets the value of the allowUserInteraction variable for this URLConnection. This method must be called before this object establishes a connection.

setDefaultUseCaches

`public void setDefaultUseCaches(boolean defaultusecaches)`

Parameters	defaultusecaches	
		The new default value.
Description		This method sets the default value of the useCaches variable for all new instances of URLConnection.

setDoInput

`public void setDoInput(boolean doinput)`

Parameters	doinput	A boolean value that indicates if this connection is to be used for input.
Throws	IllegalAccessError	
		If this method is called after the connection has been established.
	Description	This method sets the value of the doInput variable for this URLConnection. This method must be called before this object establishes a connection.

setDoOutput

`public void setDoOutput(boolean dooutput)`

Parameters	dooutput	A boolean value that indicates if this connection is to be used for output.
Throws	IllegalAccessError	
		If this method is called after the connection has been established.
Description		This method sets the value of the doOutput variable for this URLConnection. This method must be called before this object establishes a connection.

setIfModifiedSince

```
public void setIfModifiedSince(long ifmodifiedsince)
```

Parameters   ifmodifiedsince

A time value, specified as the number of seconds since January 1, 1970.

Throws   IllegalAccessError

If this method is called after the connection has been established.

Description   This method sets the value of the ifModifiedSince variable for this URLConnection. This method must be called before this object establishes a connection.

setRequestProperty

```
public void setRequestProperty(String key, String value)
```

Parameters   key   The name of a request property.

value   The new value.

Throws   IllegalAccessError

If this method is called after the connection has been established.

Description   This method sets the value of the request property named by the key parameter.

setUseCaches

```
public void setUseCaches(boolean defaultusecaches)
```

Parameters   defaultusecaches

A boolean value that indicates if this connection uses caches.

Throws   IllegalAccessError

If this method is called after the connection has been established.

Description   This method sets the value of the useCaches variable for this URLConnection. This method must be called before this object establishes a connection.

toString

```
public String toString()
```

Returns   A string representation of the URLConnection.

Overrides   Object.toString()

Description   This method returns a string representation of this URLConnection.

Inherited Methods

Method	Inherited From	Method	Inherited From
clone()	Object	equals(Object)	Object
finalize()	Object	getClass()	Object
hashCode()	Object	notify()	Object
notifyAll()	Object	wait()	Object
wait(long)	Object	wait(long, int)	Object

See Also

ContentHandler, ContentHandlerFactory, Error, FileNameMap, HttpURLConnection, IllegalAccessError, InputStream, IOException, OutputStream, SecurityException, UnknownServiceException, URL, URLStreamHandler, URLStreamHandlerFactory

15.22   URLEncoder

Synopsis

Class Name:	java.net.URLEncoder
Superclass:	java.lang.Object
Immediate Subclasses:	None
Interfaces Implemented:	None
Availability:	JDK 1.0 or later

Description

The URLEncoder class defines a single static method that converts a String to its URL-encoded form. More precisely, the String is converted to a MIME type called x-www-form-urlencoded.

This is the format used when posting forms on the Web. The algorithm leaves letters, numbers, and the dash (-), underscore (_), period (.), and asterisk (*) characters unchanged. Space characters are converted to plus signs (+). All other characters are encoded with a percent sign (%) followed by the character code represented as a two-digit hexadecimal number. For example, consider the following string:

Jean-Louis Gassée

This string gets encoded as:

```
Jean-Louis+Gas%8ee
```

The point of the URLEncoder class is to provide a way to canonicalize a string into an extremely portable subset of ASCII that can be handled properly by computers around the world.

Class Summary

```
public class java.net.URLEncoder extends java.lang.Object {
  // Class Methods
  public static String encode(String s);
}
```

Class Methods

encode

public static String encode(String s)

Parameters	s	The string to encode.
Returns		A URL-encoded string.
Description		This method returns the contents of the String in the x-www-form-urlencoded format.

Inherited Methods

Method	Inherited From	Method	Inherited From
clone()	Object	equals(Object)	Object
finalize()	Object	getClass()	Object
hashCode()	Object	notify()	Object
notifyAll()	Object	toString()	Object
wait()	Object	wait(long)	Object
wait(long timeout, int nanos)	Object		

See Also

String, URL

15.23 *URLStreamHandler*

Synopsis

Class Name:	`java.net.URLStreamHandler`
Superclass:	`java.lang.Object`
Immediate Subclasses:	None
Interfaces Implemented:	None
Availability:	JDK 1.0 or later

Description

The `URLStreamHandler` class is an abstract class that defines methods that encapsulate protocol-specific behavior. A stream handler protocol knows how to establish a connection for a particular protocol and how to parse the protocol-specific portion of a URL. An application does not normally create a `URLStreamHandler` directly; the appropriate subclass of `URLStreamHandler` is created by a `URL-StreamHandlerFactory`.

The main purpose of a subclass of `URLStreamHandler` is to create a `URLConnection` object for a given `URL`. The `URLStreamHandler` object creates an object of the appropriate subclass of `URLConnection` for the protocol type specified by the URL. In order for a `URL` object to handle a protocol type such as http, ftp, or nntp, it needs an object of the appropriate subclass of `URLStreamHandler` to handle the protocol-specific details.

Class Summary

```
public abstract class java.net.URLStreamHandler extends java.lang.Object {
    // Protected Instance Methods
    protected abstract URLConnection openConnection(URL u);
    protected void parseURL(URL u, String spec, int start, int limit);
    protected void setURL(URL u, String protocol, String host,
                            int port, String file, String ref);
    protected String toExternalForm(URL u);
}
```

Protected Instance Methods

openConnection

```
protected abstract URLConnection openConnection(URL u)
                                        throws IOException
```

Parameters	u	The URL being connected to.
Returns		The URLConnection object for the given URL.

Throws   `IOException` If any kind of I/O error occurs.

Description   This method handles the protocol-specific details of establishing a connection to a remote resource specified by the URL. The connection should be handled just up to the point where the resource data can be downloaded. A `ContentHandler` then takes care of downloading the data and creating an appropriate object.

A subclass of `URLStreamHandler` must implement this method.

parseURL

`protected void parseURL(URL u, String spec, int start, int limit)`

Parameters   u   A reference to a URL object that receives the results of parsing.

spec   The string representation of a URL to be parsed.

start   The offset at which to begin parsing the protocol-specific portion of the URL.

limit   The offset of the last character that is to be parsed.

Description   This method parses the string representation of a URL into a URL object.

Some parts of the URL object may already be specified if spec specifies a relative URL. However, values for those parts in spec can override the inherited context.

The method only parses the protocol-specific portion of the URL. In other words, start should specify the character immediately after the first colon (:), which marks the termination of the protocol type, and limit should either be the last character in the string or the first pound sign (#), which marks the beginning of a protocol-independent anchor. Rather than return a result, the method calls the set() method of the specified URL object to set its fields to the appropriate values.

The implementation of the parseURL() method in URLStreamHandler parses the string representation as if it were an http specification. A subclass that implements a protocol stream handler for a different protocol must override this method to properly parse the URL.

setURL

```
protected void setURL(URL u, String protocol, String host,
                      int port, String file, String ref)
```

Parameters	u	A reference to a URL object to be modified.
	protocol	A protocol.
	host	A hostname.
	port	A port number.
	file	A filename.
	ref	A reference.

Description   This method sets the protocol, hostname, port number, file-name, and reference of the given URL to the specified values by calling the set() method of the URL. Only subclasses of URL-StreamHandler are allowed to call the set() method of a URL object.

toExternalForm

```
protected String toExternalForm(URL u)
```

Parameters   u   The URL object to convert to a string representation.

Returns   A string representation of the given URL.

Description   This method unparses a URL object and returns a string representation of the URL.

The implementation of the toExternalForm() method in URL-StreamHandler returns a string representation that is appropriate for an http specification. A subclass that implements a protocol stream handler for a different protocol must override this method to create a correct string representation.

Inherited Methods

Method	Inherited From	Method	Inherited From
clone()	Object	equals(Object)	Object
finalize()	Object	getClass()	Object
hashCode()	Object	notify()	Object
notifyAll()	Object	toString()	Object
wait()	Object	wait(long)	Object
wait(long, int)	Object		

See Also

ContentHandler, IOException, URL, URLConnection, URLStreamHandlerFactory

15.24   URLStreamHandlerFactory

Synopsis

Interface Name:	java.net.StreamHandlerFactory
Super-interface:	None
Immediate Sub-interfaces:	
	None
Implemented By:	None
Availability:	JDK 1.0 or later

Description

The URLStreamHandlerFactory interface defines a method that creates a URLStreamHandler object for a specific protocol. The interface is implemented by classes that select URLStreamHandler subclasses to process particular protocol types.

The URL class uses a URLStreamHandlerFactory to create URLStreamHandler objects. The protocol type is determined by the portion of the URL up to the first colon. For example, given the following URL:

```
http://www.tolstoi.org/ilych.html
```

the protocol type is http. A URLStreamHandlerFactory that recognizes http returns a URLStreamHandler that can process the URL.

Interface Declaration

```
public abstract interface java.net.URLStreamHandlerFactory {
  // Methods
   public abstract URLStreamHandler createURLStreamHandler(String protocol);
}
```

Methods

createURLStreamHandler

public abstract URLStreamHandler createURLStreamHandler
(String protocol)

    Parameters   protocol   A String that represents a protocol.

Description   This method creates an object of the appropriate subclass of
URLStreamHandler that can process a URL using the named
protocol.

See Also

URL, URLStreamHandler

15.25   UnknownHostException

Synopsis

Class Name: java.net.UnknownHostException
Superclass: java.io.IOException
Immediate Subclasses: None
Interfaces Implemented: None
Availability: JDK 1.0 or later

Description

A UnknownHostException is thrown when a hostname cannot be resolved to an IP
address.

Class Summary

```
public class java.net.UnknownHostException extends java.io.IOException {
  // Constructors
  public UnknownHostException();
  public UnknownHostException(String host);
}
```

Constructors

UnknownHostException

public UnknownHostException()

Description   This constructor creates an UnknownHostException with no
associated detail message.

public UnknownHostException(String host)

Parameters   host   The detail message.

Description   This constructor creates an UnknownHostException with the
specified detail message, which should be the hostname that
cannot be resolved.

Inherited Methods

Method	Inherited From	Method	Inherited From
clone()	Object	equals(Object)	Object
fillInStackTrace()	Throwable	finalize()	Object
getClass()	Object	getLocalizedMessage()	Throwable
getMessage()	Throwable	hashCode()	Object
notify()	Object	notifyAll()	Object
printStackTrace()	Throwable	printStack- Trace(PrintStream)	Throwable
printStack- Trace(PrintWriter)	Throwable	toString()	Throwable
wait()	Object	wait(long)	Object
wait(long, int)	Object		

See Also

Exception, IOException, RuntimeException

15.26   UnknownServiceException

Synopsis

Class Name:	java.net.UnknownServiceException
Superclass:	java.io.IOException
Immediate Subclasses:	None
Interfaces Implemented:	None
Availability:	JDK 1.0 or later

Description

A UnknownServiceException is thrown when an unrecognized service is requested, which can occur when the MIME type returned by a URLConnection does not match any recognized types.

Class Summary

```
public class java.net.UnknownServiceException
          extends java.io.IOException {
  // Constructors
  public UnknownServiceException();
  public UnknownServiceException(String msg);
}
```

Constructors

UnknownServiceException

public UnknownServiceException()

    Description   This constructor creates an UnknownServiceException with no associated detail message.

public UnknownServiceException(String msg)

    Parameters   msg   The detail message.

    Description   This constructor creates an UnknownServiceException with the specified detail message.

Inherited Methods

Method	Inherited From	Method	Inherited From
clone()	Object	equals(Object)	Object
fillInStackTrace()	Throwable	finalize()	Object
getClass()	Object	getLocalizedMessage()	Throwable
getMessage()	Throwable	hashCode()	Object
notify()	Object	notifyAll()	Object
printStackTrace()	Throwable	printStack-Trace(PrintStream)	Throwable
printStack-Trace(PrintWriter)	Throwable	toString()	Throwable
wait()	Object	wait(long)	Object
wait(long, int)	Object		

See Also

Exception, IOException, RuntimeException

16

The java.text Package

The package `java.text` is new as of Java 1.1. It contains classes that support the internationalization of Java programs. The internationalization classes can be grouped as follows:

- Classes for formatting string representations of dates, times, numbers, and messages based on the conventions of a locale.
- Classes that collate strings according to the rules of a locale.
- Classes for finding boundaries in text according to the rules of a locale.

Many of the classes in `java.text` rely upon a `java.util.Locale` object to provide information about the locale that is in use.

The `Format` class is the superclass of all of the classes that generate and parse string representations of various types of data. The `DateFormat` class formats and parses dates and times according to the customs and language of a particular locale. Similarly, the `NumberFormat` class formats and parses numbers, including currency values, in a locale-dependent manner.

The `MessageFormat` class can create a textual message from a pattern string, while `ChoiceFormat` maps numerical ranges to strings. By themselves, these classes do not provide different results for different locales. However, they can be used in conjunction with `java.util.ResourceBundle` objects that generate locale-specific pattern strings.

The `Collator` class handles collating strings according to the rules of a particular locale. Different languages have different characters and different rules for sorting those characters; `Collator` and its subclass, `RuleBasedCollator`, are designed to take those differences into account when collating strings. In addition, the `CollationKey` class can be used to optimize the sorting of a large collection of strings.

The `BreakIterator` class finds various boundaries, such as word boundaries and line boundaries, in textual data. Again, `BreakIterator` locates these boundaries according to the rules of a particular locale.

Figure 16-1 shows the class hierarchy for the `java.text` package.

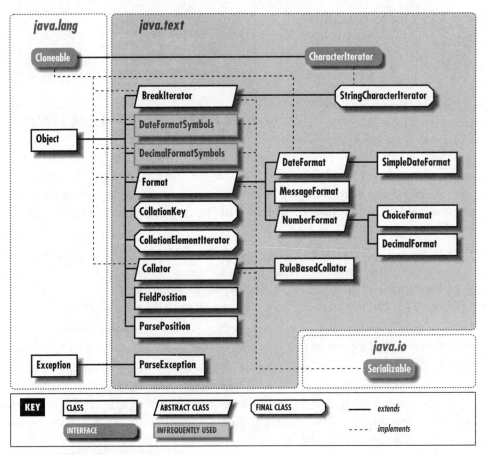

Figure 16–1: The java.text package

16.1 *BreakIterator*

Synopsis

Class Name: `java.text.BreakIterator`
Superclass: `java.lang.Object`
Immediate Subclasses: None
Interfaces Implemented: `java.lang.Cloneable`, `java.io.Serializable`
Availability: New as of JDK 1.1

Description

The `BreakIterator` class is an abstract class that defines methods that find the locations of boundaries in text, such as word boundaries and sentence boundaries. A `BreakIterator` operates on the object passed to its `setText()` method; that object must implement the `CharacterIterator` interface or be a `String` object. When a `String` is passed to `setText()`, the `BreakIterator` creates an internal `StringCharacterIterator` to iterate over the `String`.

When you use a `BreakIterator`, you call `first()` to get the location of the first boundary and then repeatedly call `next()` to iterate through the subsequent boundaries.

The `BreakIterator` class defines four static factory methods that return instances of `BreakIterator` that locate various kinds of boundaries. Each of these factory methods selects a concrete subclass of `BreakIterator` based either on the default locale or a specified locale. You must create a separate instance of `BreakIterator` to handle each kind of boundary you are trying to locate:

- `getWordInstance()` returns an iterator that locates word boundaries, which is useful for search-and-replace operations. A word iterator correctly handles punctuation marks.
- `getSentenceInstance()` returns an iterator that locates sentence boundaries, which is useful for textual selection. A sentence iterator correctly handle punctuation marks.
- `getLineInstance()` returns an iterator that locates line boundaries, which is useful in line wrapping. A line iterator correctly handles hyphenation and punctuation.
- `getCharacterInstance()` returns an iterator that locates boundaries between characters, which is useful for allowing the cursor to interact with characters appropriately, since some characters are stored as a base character and a diacritical mark, but only represent one display character.

Class Summary

```
public abstract class java.util.BreakIterator extends java.lang.Object
                    implements java.lang.Cloneable,
                                   java.io.Serializable {

    // Constants
    public final static int DONE;


    // Constructors
    protected BreakIterator();


    // Class Methods
    public static synchronized Locale[] getAvailableLocales();
    public static BreakIterator getCharacterInstance();
    public static BreakIterator getCharacterInstance(Locale where);
    public static BreakIterator getLineInstance();
    public static BreakIterator getLineInstance(Locale where);
    public static BreakIterator getSentenceInstance();
    public static BreakIterator getSentenceInstance(Locale where);
    public static BreakIterator getWordInstance();
    public static BreakIterator getWordInstance(Locale where);


    // Instance Methods
    public Object clone();
    public abstract int current();
    public abstract int first();
    public abstract int following(int offset);
    public abstract CharacterIterator getText();
    public abstract int last();
    public abstract int next();
    public abstract int next(int n);
    public abstract int previous();
    public abstract void setText(CharacterIterator newText);
    public void setText(String newText);
}
```

Constants

DONE

```
public final static int DONE
```

Description   A constant that is returned by next() or previous() if there are
no more breaks to be returned.

Constructors

BreakIterator

protected BreakIterator()

> Description   This constructor should be called only from constructors of subclasses.

Class Methods

getAvailableLocales

public static synchronized Locale[] getAvailableLocales()

> Returns   An array of Locale objects.
>
> Description   This method returns an array of the Locale objects that can be passed to getCharacterInstance(), getLineInstance(), get-SentenceInstance(), or getWordInstance().

getCharacterInstance

public static BreakIterator getCharacterInstance()

> Returns   A BreakIterator appropriate for the default Locale.
>
> Description   This method creates a BreakIterator that can locate character boundaries in the default Locale.

public static BreakIterator getCharacterInstance(Locale where)

> Parameters   where   The Locale to use.
>
> Returns   A BreakIterator appropriate for the given Locale.
>
> Description   This method creates a BreakIterator that can locate character boundaries in the given Locale.

getLineInstance

public static BreakIterator getLineInstance()

> Returns   A BreakIterator appropriate for the default Locale.
>
> Description   This method creates a BreakIterator that can locate line boundaries in the default Locale.

public static BreakIterator getLineInstance(Locale where)

> Parameters   where   The Locale to use.
>
> Returns   A BreakIterator appropriate for the given Locale.
>
> Description   This method creates a BreakIterator that can locate line boundaries in the given Locale.

getSentenceInstance

`public static BreakIterator getSentenceInstance()`

Returns | A BreakIterator appropriate for the default Locale.

Description | This method creates a BreakIterator that can locate sentence boundaries in the default Locale.

`public static BreakIterator getSentenceInstance(Locale where)`

Parameters | where | The Locale to use.

Returns | A BreakIterator appropriate for the given Locale.

Description | This method creates a BreakIterator that can locate sentence boundaries in the given Locale.

getWordInstance

`public static BreakIterator getWordInstance()`

Returns | A BreakIterator appropriate for the default Locale.

Description | This method creates a BreakIterator that can locate word boundaries in the default Locale.

`public static BreakIterator getWordInstance(Locale where)`

Parameters | where | The Locale to use.

Returns | A BreakIterator appropriate for the given Locale.

Description | This method creates a BreakIterator that can locate word boundaries in the given Locale.

Instance Methods

clone

`public Object clone()`

Returns | A copy of this BreakIterator.

Overrides | Object.clone()

Description | This method creates a copy of this BreakIterator and then returns it.

current

`public abstract int current()`

Returns | The current position of this BreakIterator.

Description | This method returns the current position of this BreakIterator. The current position is the character index of the most recently returned boundary.

first

public abstract int first()

Returns	The position of the first boundary of this BreakIterator.
Description	This method finds the first boundary in this BreakIterator and returns its character index. The current position of the iterator is set to this boundary.

following

public abstract int following(int offset)

Parameters	offset	An offset into this BreakIterator.
Returns		The position of the first boundary after the given offset of this BreakIterator or DONE if there are no more boundaries.
Throws		IllegalArgumentException
		If offset is not a valid value for the CharacterIterator of this BreakIterator.
Description		This method finds the first boundary after the given offset in this BreakIterator and returns its character index.

getText

public abstract CharacterIterator getText()

Returns	The CharacterIterator that this BreakIterator uses.
Description	This method returns a CharacterIterator that represents the text this BreakIterator examines.

last

public abstract int last()

Returns	The position of the last boundary of this BreakIterator.
Description	This method finds the last boundary in this BreakIterator and returns its character index. The current position of the iterator is set to this boundary.

next

public abstract int next()

Returns	The position of the next boundary of this BreakIterator or DONE if there are no more boundaries.
Description	This method finds the next boundary in this BreakIterator after the current position and returns its character index. The current position of the iterator is set to this boundary.

```
public abstract int next(int n)
```
    Parameters   n   The boundary to return. A positive value moves
                               to a later boundary a negative value moves to a
                               previous boundary; the value 0 does nothing.
    Returns   The position of the requested boundary of this `BreakIterator`.
    Description   This method finds the nth boundary in this `BreakIterator`,
                  starting from the current position, and returns its character
                  index. The current position of the iterator is set to this bound-
                  ary.

                  For example, `next(-2)` finds the third previous boundary. Thus
                  `next(1)` is equivalent to `next()`, `next(-1)` is equivalent to `pre-
                  vious()`, and `next(0)` does nothing.

previous

```
public abstract int previous()
```
    Returns   The position of the previous boundary of this `BreakIterator`.
    Description   This method finds the previous boundary in this `BreakItera-
                  tor`, starting from the current position, and returns its charac-
                  ter index. The current position of the iterator is set to this
                  boundary.

setText

```
public abstract void setText(CharacterIterator newText)
```
    Parameters   newText   The `CharacterIterator` that contains the text to
                               be examined.
    Description   This method tells this `BreakIterator` to examine the piece of
                  text specified by the `CharacterIterator`. This current position
                  of this `BreakIterator` is set to `first()`.

```
public void setText(String newText)
```
    Parameters   newText   The `String` that contains the text to be exam-
                               ined.
    Description   This method tells this `BreakIterator` to examine the piece of
                  text specified by the `String`, using a `StringCharacterIterator`
                  created from the given string. This current position of this
                  `BreakIterator` is set to `first()`.

Inherited Methods

Method	Inherited From	Method	Inherited From
equals(Object)	Object	finalize()	Object
getClass()	Object	hashCode()	Object
notify()	Object	notifyAll()	Object
toString()	Object	wait()	Object
wait(long)	Object	wait(long, int)	Object

See Also

CharacterIterator, Locale, String, StringCharacterIterator

16.2   CharacterIterator

Synopsis

Interface Name: java.text.CharacterIterator
Super-interface: java.lang.Cloneable
Immediate Sub-interfaces:

                            None
Implemented By: java.text.StringCharacterIterator
Availability: New as of JDK 1.1

Description

The CharacterIterator interface defines methods that support bidirectional movement through a sequence of text. The interface is implemented by classes that maintain a current position in a sequence of characters. The interface provides methods for moving to the first, last, next, and previous characters in the sequence. The BreakIterator classes uses this interface to locate boundaries in textual sequences.

Class Summary

```
public abstract interface java.text.CharacterIterator
                       extends java.lang.Cloneable {
   // Constants
   public static final char DONE;

   // Methods
   public abstract Object clone();
   public abstract char current();
   public abstract char first();
```

```
    public abstract int getBeginIndex();
    public abstract int getEndIndex();
    public abstract int getIndex();
    public abstract char last();
    public abstract char next();
    public abstract char previous();
    public abstract char setIndex(int position);
}
```

Constants

DONE

public final static char DONE

Description   A constant that indicates that the beginning or end of the text has been reached. It can be returned by next() or previous().

Methods

clone

public abstract Object clone()

Returns   A copy of this CharacterIterator.

Overrides   Object.clone()

Description   This method creates a copy of this CharacterIterator and returns it.

current

public abstract char current()

Returns   The character at the current position of this CharacterIterator or DONE if the current position is not within the text sequence.

Description   This method returns the character at the current position of this CharacterIterator. The current position is returned by getIndex().

first

public abstract char first()

Returns   The first character in this CharacterIterator.

Description   This method returns the character at the first position in this CharacterIterator. The first position is returned by getBeginIndex(). The current position of the iterator is set to this position.

getBeginIndex

```
public abstract int getBeginIndex()
```

Returns   The index of the first character in this CharacterIterator.

Description   This method returns the index of the beginning of the text for this CharacterIterator.

getEndIndex

```
public abstract int getEndIndex()
```

Returns   The index after the last character in this CharacterIterator.

Description   This method returns the index of the character following the end of the text for this CharacterIterator.

getIndex

```
public abstract int getIndex()
```

Returns   The index of the current character in this CharacterIterator.

Description   This method returns the current position, or index, of this CharacterIterator.

last

```
public abstract char last()
```

Returns   The last character in this CharacterIterator.

Description   This method returns the character at the ending position of this CharacterIterator. The last position is the value of getEndIndex()-1. The current position of the iterator is set to this position.

next

```
public abstract char next()
```

Returns   The next character in this CharacterIterator or DONE if the current position is already at the end of the text.

Description   This method increments the current position of this CharacterIterator by one and returns the character at the new position. If the current position is already at getEndIndex(), the position is not changed, and DONE is returned.

previous

```
public abstract char previous()
```

Returns   The previous character in this CharacterIterator or DONE if the current position is already at the beginning of the text.

Description   This method decrements the current position of this CharacterIterator by one and returns the character at the new position. If the current position is already at getBeginIndex(), the
position is not changed, and DONE is returned.

setIndex

public abstract char setIndex(int position)

Parameters   position   The new position.

Returns   The character at the specified position in this CharacterIterator.

Throws   IllegalArgumentException

If the given position is not between getBeginIn-
dex() and getEndIndex()-1.

Description   This method sets the current position, or index, of this CharacterIterator to the given position.

See Also

BreakIterator, StringCharacterIterator

16.3 ChoiceFormat

Synopsis

Class Name: java.text.ChoiceFormat
Superclass: java.text.NumberFormat
Immediate Subclasses: None
Interfaces Implemented: None
Availability: New as of JDK 1.1

Description

The ChoiceFormat class is a concrete subclass of NumberFormat that maps numerical ranges to strings, or formats. ChoiceFormat objects are used most often by MessageFormat objects to handle plurals, verb agreement, and other such issues.

The ranges in a ChoiceFormat are specified as an ascending array of double values,
where each number is the bottom end of a range. A value is mapped to a format
when it falls within the range for that format. If the value does not fall in any of the
ranges, it is mapped to the first or the last format, depending on whether the value
is too low or too high. For example, consider the following code:

```
double[] limits = {1, 10, 100};
String[] labels = {"small", "medium", "large"}
ChoiceFormat cf = new ChoiceFormat(limits, labels);
```

Any number greater than or equal to one and less than 10 is mapped to the format "small". Any number greater than or equal to 10 and less than 100 is mapped to "medium". Numbers greater than or equal to 100 are mapped to "large". Furthermore, numbers less than one are also mapped to "small".

The nextDouble() and previousDouble() methods can generate double values that are higher or lower than other double values. These methods provide another way to specify the limits used by a ChoiceFormat object.

As shown above, you can create a ChoiceFormat object by specifying the limits and formats in two separate arrays. You can also create a ChoiceFormat object using a pattern string that specifies the limits and formats. The string is of the form:

```
[limit1]#[format1]|[limit2]#[format2]|...
```

A < character can be used in place of the # to indicate that the next higher number, as determined by nextDouble(), should be used as the limit. The toPattern() method can be used to generate the pattern string for an existing ChoiceFormat object.

Note that you create ChoiceFormat objects directly, rather than through factory methods. This is because ChoiceFormat does not implement any locale-specific behavior. To produce properly internationalized output, the formats for a Choice-Format should come from a ResourceBundle instead of being embedded in the code.

Class Summary

```
public class java.text.ChoiceFormat extends java.text.NumberFormat {
    // Constructors
    public ChoiceFormat(String newPattern);
    public ChoiceFormat(double[] limits, String[] formats);

    // Class Methods
    public static final double nextDouble(double d);
    public static double nextDouble(double d, boolean positive);
    public static final double previousDouble(double d);

    // Instance Methods
    public void applyPattern(String newPattern);
    public Object clone();
    public boolean equals(Object obj);
    public StringBuffer format(double number,
                    StringBuffer toAppendTo, FieldPosition status);
    public StringBuffer format(long number,
                    StringBuffer toAppendTo, FieldPosition status);
```

```
    public Object[] getFormats();
    public double[] getLimits();
    public int hashCode();
    public Number parse(String text, ParsePosition status);
    public void setChoices(double[] limits, String[] formats);
    public String toPattern();
}
```

Constructors

ChoiceFormat

public ChoiceFormat(String newPattern)

Parameters	newPattern	The pattern string.
Description		This constructor creates a ChoiceFormat that uses the limits and formats represented by the given pattern string.

public ChoiceFormat(double[] limits, String[] formats)

Parameters	limits	An array of limits. Each element is the lower end of a range that runs up through, but not including, the next element.
	formats	An array of format strings that correspond to the limit ranges.
Description		This constructor creates a ChoiceFormat that uses the given limits and format strings

Class Methods

nextDouble

public static final double nextDouble(double d)

Parameters	d	A double value.
Returns		The least double that is greater than d.
Description		This method returns the least double greater than d. Calling this method is equivalent to nextDouble(d, true).

public static double nextDouble(double d, boolean positive)

Parameters	d	A double value.
	positive	A boolean value that specifies whether to return the next higher or next lower value.
Returns		If positive is true, the least double that is greater than d. If positive is false, the greatest double that is less than d.
Description		This method finds the next higher or next lower double value from d, depending on the value of positive. If positive is true, the method returns the least double greater than d. Otherwise, the method returns the greatest double less than d.

previousDouble

public static final double previousDouble(double d)

Parameters	d	A double value.
Returns		The greatest double that is less than d.
Description		This method returns the greatest double less than d. Calling this method is equivalent to nextDouble(d, false).

Instance Methods

applyPattern

public void applyPattern(String newPattern)

Parameters	newPattern	The pattern string.
Description		This method tells this ChoiceFormat to use the limits and formats represented by the given formatting pattern string. Pattern strings for ChoiceFormat objects are described above in the class description.

clone

public Object clone()

Returns	A copy of this ChoiceFormat.
Overrides	NumberFormat.clone()
Description	This method creates a copy of this ChoiceFormat and returns it.

equals

public boolean equals(Object obj)

Parameters	obj	The object to be compared with this object.
Returns		true if the objects are equal; false if they are not.
Overrides		Format.equals()
Description		This method returns true if obj is an instance of ChoiceFormat and is equivalent to this ChoiceFormat.

format

public StringBuffer format(double number, StringBuffer toAppendTo, FieldPosition status)

Parameters	number	The double value to be formatted.
	toAppendTo	A StringBuffer on which to append the formatted information.
	status	Ignored.
Returns		The given StringBuffer with the String corresponding to the given number appended to it.

Overrides	`NumberFormat.format(double, StringBuffer, FieldPosition)`	
Description	This method formats the given number and appends the result to the given `StringBuffer`.	

`public StringBuffer format(long number, StringBuffer toAppendTo,`
                        `FieldPosition status)`

Parameters	number	The `long` value to be formatted.
	toAppendTo	A `StringBuffer` on which to append the formatted information.
	status	Ignored.
Returns	The given `StringBuffer` with the `String` corresponding to the given number appended to it.	
Overrides	`NumberFormat.format(long, StringBuffer, FieldPosition)`	
Description	This method formats the given number and appends the result to the given `StringBuffer`.	

getFormats

`public Object[] getFormats()`

Returns	An array that contains the format strings.
Description	This method returns an array containing the current set of format strings.

getLimits

`public double[] getLimits()`

Returns	An array that contains the limit values.
Description	This method returns an array that contains the current set of limits.

hashCode

`public int hashCode()`

Returns	A hashcode for this object.
Overrides	`NumberFormat.hashCode()`
Description	This method returns a hashcode for this `ChoiceFormat`.

parse

`public Number parse(String text, ParsePosition status)`

Parameters	text	The string to be parsed.
	status	A `ParsePosition` object that can specify a position in the string.
Returns	A `Number` object that encapsulates the value that corresponds to the longest format string that matches the text that starts at the given position. If there is no matching format string, the value `Double.NaN` is returned.	

Overrides   `NumberFormat.parse(String, ParsePosition)`

Description   This method parses a number from the given string, starting from the given position. The method returns a `Number` object that encapsulates the value that corresponds to the longest format string that matches the text starting at the given position. If there is no matching format string, the method returns the value `Double.NaN`.

If there is a matching format string, the index value of the given `ParsePosition` object is incremented by the length of that format string.

setChoices

`public void setChoices(double[] limits, String[] formats)`

Parameters   limits   An array of limits. Each element is the lower end of a range that runs up through, but not including, the next element.

formats   An array of format strings that correspond to the limit ranges.

Description   This method sets the limits and format strings that this `Choice-Format` uses.

toPattern

`public String toPattern()`

Returns   The pattern string of this `ChoiceFormat`.

Description   This method returns a string that represents the limits and format strings of this `ChoiceFormat`. Pattern strings for `ChoiceFormat` objects are described above in the class description.

Inherited Methods

Method	Inherited From	Method	Inherited From
finalize()	Object	format(double)	NumberFormat
format(long number)	NumberFormat	format(Object, String-Buffer, FieldPosition)	NumberFormat
getClass()	Object	getMaximumFractionDig-its()	NumberFormat
getMaximumIntegerDigits()	NumberFormat	getMinimumFractionDig-its()	NumberFormat
getMinimumIntegerDigits()	NumberFormat	isGroupingUsed()	NumberFormat
isParseIntegerOnly()	NumberFormat	notify()	Object
notifyAll()	Object	parse(String)	NumberFormat

Method	Inherited From	Method	Inherited From
parseObject(String)	Format	parseObject(String, ParsePosition)	NumberFormat
setGroupingUsed(boolean)	NumberFormat	setMaximumFractionDig-its(int)	NumberFormat
setMaximumIntegerDig-its(int)	NumberFormat	setMinimumFractionDig-its(int)	NumberFormat
setMinimumIntegerDig-its(int)	NumberFormat	setParseInte-gerOnly(boolean)	NumberFormat
toString()	Object	wait()	Object
wait(long)	Object	wait(long, int)	Object

See Also

FieldPosition, MessageFormat, Number, NumberFormat, ParsePosition, Resource-Bundle, String, StringBuffer

16.4   CollationElementIterator

Synopsis

Class Name: java.text.CollationElementIterator
Superclass: java.lang.Object
Immediate Subclasses: None
Interfaces Implemented: None
Availability: New as of JDK 1.1

Description

A RuleBasedCollator object creates an instance of the CollationElementIterator class to iterate through the characters of a string and determine their relative collation sequence. A CollationElementIterator object performs callbacks to the RuleBasedCollator that created it to get the information it needs to recognize groups of characters that are treated as single collation characters. For example, a RuleBasedCollator for a Spanish language locale would be set up to treat 'ch' as a single letter. A CollationElementIterator object also gets information from its RuleBasedCollator that is used to determine the collation ordering priority for characters.

A collation-ordering priority of a character is a composite integer value that determines how the character is collated. This priority is comprised of:

- A primary order that distinguishes between different letters. Characters that are considered to be different letters, such as 'e' and 'f', have different primary orders. Different forms of the same letter, such as 'e' and 'E', or an accented form of 'e', have the same primary order. Primary orders are short values.

- A secondary order that distinguishes between accented forms of the same letter. An unaccented 'e' has a different secondary order than forms of 'e' that have different accents. 'E' and 'e' have the same secondary order, as do upper- and lowercase forms of 'e' that have the same accent. Secondary orders are byte values.

- A tertiary order that distinguishes between case differences. 'E' and 'e' have different tertiary orders. Tertiary orders are byte values.

The next() method returns the collation-ordering priority of the next logical character. Primary, secondary, and tertiary orders are extracted from an ordering priority with the primaryOrder(), secondaryOrder(), and tertiaryOrder() methods.

Class Summary

```
public final class java.text.CollationElementIterator
                extends java.lang.Object {
    // Constants
    public static final int NULLORDER;

    // Class Methods
    public static final int primaryOrder(int order);
    public static final short secondaryOrder(int order);
    public static final short tertiaryOrder(int order);

    // Instance Methods
    public int next();
    public void reset();
}
```

Constants

NULLORDER

```
public final static int NULLORDER
```

   Description   A constant that is returned by next() if the end of the string has been reached.

Class Methods

primaryOrder

public static final int primaryOrder(int order)

Returns	The primary order component of the given order key.
Description	This method extracts the primary order value from the given order key.

secondaryOrder

public static final short secondaryOrder(int order)

Returns	The secondary order component of the given order key.
Description	This method extracts the secondary order value from the given order key.

tertiaryOrder

public static final short tertiaryOrder(int order)

Returns	The tertiary order component of the given order key.
Description	This method extracts the tertiary order value from the given order key.

Instance Methods

next

public int next()

Returns	The order value of the next character in the string.
Description	This method returns the order key for the next character in the string. The returned value can be broken apart using the primaryOrder(), secondaryOrder(), and tertiaryOrder() methods.

reset

public void reset()

Description	This method resets the position of this CollationElementIterator to the beginning of the string.

Inherited Methods

Method	Inherited From	Method	Inherited From
clone()	Object	equals(Object)	Object
finalize()	Object	getClass()	Object
hashCode()	Object	notify()	Object
notifyAll()	Object	toString()	Object
wait()	Object	wait(long)	Object
wait(long, int)	Object		

See Also

Collator, RuleBasedCollator, String

16.5   CollationKey

Synopsis

Class Name: java.text.CollationKey
Superclass: java.lang.Object
Immediate Subclasses: None
Interfaces Implemented: None
Availability: New as of JDK 1.1

Description

The CollationKey class optimizes the sorting of many strings. The easiest way to compare strings is using Collator.compare(), but this can be inefficient, especially if the same strings are compared many times. Instead, you can create a Collation-Key for each of your strings and compare the CollationKey objects to each other using the compareTo() method. A CollationKey is essentially a bit representation of a String object. Two CollationKey objects can be compared bitwise, which allows for a fast comparison.

You cannot create CollationKey objects directly; you must create them through a specific Collator object using Collator.getCollationKey(). You can only compare CollationKey objects that have been generated from the same Collator.

Class Summary

```
public final class java.text.CollationKey extends java.lang.Object {
    // Instance Methods
    public int compareTo(CollationKey target);
    public boolean equals(Object target);
    public String getSourceString();
    public int hashCode();
    public byte[] toByteArray();
}
```

Instance Methods

compareTo

```
public int compareTo(CollationKey target)
```

Parameters	target	The key to compare with this CollationKey.
Returns		-1 if this CollationKey is less than target, 0 if this Collation-Key is equal to target, or 1 if this CollationKey is greater than target.
Description		This method returns an integer that indicates the ordering of this CollationKey and the given CollationKey. Only CollationKey objects generated by the same Collator should be compared.

equals

```
public boolean equals(Object target)
```

Parameters	target	The object to be compared with this object.
Returns		true if the objects are equal; false if they are not.
Overrides		Object.equals()
Description		This method returns true if obj is an instance of CollationKey and is equivalent to this CollationKey.

getSourceString

```
public String getSourceString()
```

Returns	The string that generated this CollationKey.
Description	This method returns the string that was passed to Collator.getCollationKey() to create this CollationKey.

hashCode

```
public int hashCode()
```

Returns	A hashcode for this object.
Overrides	Object.hashCode()
Description	This method returns a hashcode for this CollationKey.

toByteArray

```
public byte[] toByteArray()
```

Returns	A byte array that represents this CollationKey.
Description	This method returns a byte array that represents the value of this CollationKey, with the most significant byte first.

Inherited Methods

Method	Inherited From	Method	Inherited From
clone()	Object	finalize()	Object
getClass()	Object	notify()	Object
notifyAll()	Object	toString()	Object
wait()	Object	wait(long)	Object
wait(long, int)	Object		

See Also

Collator, RuleBasedCollator, String

16.6   Collator

Synopsis

Class Name:	java.text.Collator
Superclass:	java.lang.Object
Immediate Subclasses:	java.text.RuleBasedCollator
Interfaces Implemented:	java.lang.Cloneable, java.io.Serializable
Availability:	New as of JDK 1.1

Description

The Collator class compares strings in a manner that is appropriate for a particular locale. Although Collator is an abstract class, the getInstance() factory methods can be used to get a usable instance of a Collator subclass that implements a particular collation strategy. One subclass, RuleBasedCollator, is provided as part of the JDK.

A Collator object has a *strength* property that controls the level of difference that is considered significant for comparison purposes. The Collator class provides four strength values: PRIMARY, SECONDARY, TERTIARY, and IDENTICAL. Although the interpretation of these strengths is locale-dependent, they generally have the following meanings:

PRIMARY   The comparison considers letter differences, but ignores case and diacriticals.

SECONDARY   The comparison considers letter differences and diacriticals, but ignores case.

TERTIARY   The comparison considers letter differences, case, and diacriticals.

IDENTICAL   The comparison considers all differences.

The default comparison strength is TERTIARY.

If you only need to compare two String objects once, the compare() method of the Collator class provides the best performance. However, if you need to compare the same String objects multiple times, such as when you are sorting, you should use CollationKey objects instead. A CollationKey object contains a String that has been converted into a series of bits that can be compared in a bitwise fashion against other CollationKey objects. You use a Collator object to create a CollationKey for a given String.

Class Summary

```
public abstract class java.text.Collator extends java.lang.Object
                      implements java.io.Serializable,
                                 java.lang.Cloneable {

   // Constants
   public static final int CANONICAL_DECOMPOSITION;
   public static final int FULL_DECOMPOSITION;
   public static final int IDENTICAL;
   public static final int NO_DECOMPOSITION;
   public static final int PRIMARY;
   public static final int SECONDARY;
   public static final int TERTIARY;


   // Constructors
   protected Collator();


   // Class Methods
   public static synchronized Locale[] getAvailableLocales();
   public static synchronized Collator getInstance();
   public static synchronized Collator getInstance(Locale desiredLocale);


   // Instance Methods
   public Object clone();
   public abstract int compare(String source, String target);
   public boolean equals(Object that);
   public boolean equals(String source, String target);
   public abstract CollationKey getCollationKey(String source);
   public synchronized int getDecomposition();
   public synchronized int getStrength();
   public abstract synchronized int hashCode();
   public synchronized void setDecomposition(int decompositionMode);
   public synchronized void setStrength(int newStrength);
}
```

Constants

CANONICAL_DECOMPOSITION

`public final static int CANONICAL_DECOMPOSITION`

Description   A decomposition constant that specifies that Unicode 2.0 characters which are canonical variants are decomposed for collation. This is the default decomposition setting.

FULL_DECOMPOSITION

`public final static int FULL_DECOMPOSITION`

Description   A decomposition constant that specifies that Unicode 2.0 canonical variants and compatibility variants are decomposed for collation. This is the most complete decomposition setting, and thus the slowest setting.

IDENTICAL

`public final static int IDENTICAL`

Description   A strength constant that specifies that all differences are considered significant for comparison purposes.

NO_DECOMPOSITION

`public final static int NO_DECOMPOSITION`

Description   A decomposition setting that specifies that no Unicode characters are decomposed for collation. This is the least complete decomposition setting, and thus the fastest setting. It only works correctly for languages that do not use diacriticals.

PRIMARY

`public final static int PRIMARY`

Description   A strength constant that specifies that only primary differences are considered significant for comparison purposes. Primary differences are typically letter differences.

SECONDARY

`public final static int SECONDARY`

Description   A strength constant that specifies that only secondary differences and above are considered significant for comparison purposes. Secondary differences are typically differences in diacriticals, or accents.

TERTIARY

public final static int TERTIARY

Description A strength constant that specifies that only tertiary differences and above are considered significant for comparison purposes. Tertiary differences are typically differences in case. This is the default strength setting.

Constructors

Collator

protected Collator()

Description This constructor creates a Collator with the default strength of TERTIARY and default decomposition mode of CANONI-CAL_DECOMPOSITION.

Class Methods

getAvailableLocales

public static synchronized Locale[] getAvailableLocales()

Returns An array of Locale objects.

Description This method returns an array of the Locale objects for which this class can create Collator objects.

getInstance

public static synchronized Collator getInstance()

Returns A Collator appropriate for the default Locale.

Description This method creates a Collator that compares strings in the default Locale.

public static synchronized Collator getInstance(
                              Locale desiredLocale)

Parameters desiredLocale
                  The Locale to use.

Returns A Collator appropriate for the given Locale.

Description This method creates a Collator that compares strings in the given Locale.

Instance Methods

clone

public Object clone()

Returns A copy of this Collator.

Overrides   `Object.clone()`

Description   This method creates a copy of this `Collator` and returns it.

compare

`public abstract int compare(String source, String target)`

Parameters   `source`   The source string.

              `target`   The target string.

Returns   −1 if `source` is less than `target`, 0 if the strings are equal, or 1 if source is greater than `target`.

Description   This method compares the given strings according to the collation rules for this `Collator` and returns a value that indicates their relationship. If either of the strings are compared more than once, a `CollationKey` should be used instead.

equals

`public boolean equals(Object that)`

Parameters   `that`   The object to be compared with this object.

Returns   `true` if the objects are equal; `false` if they are not.

Overrides   `Object.equals()`

Description   This method returns `true` if `obj` is an instance of `Collator` and is equivalent to this `Collator`.

`public boolean equals(String source, Source target)`

Parameters   `source`   The source string.

              `target`   The target string.

Returns   `true` if the given strings are equal; `false` otherwise.

Description   This method compares the given strings for equality using the collation rules for this `Collator`. Note that this method applies locale-specific rules and is thus not the same as `String.equals()`.

getCollationKey

`public abstract CollationKey getCollationKey(String source)`

Parameters   `source`   The string to use when generating the CollationKey.

Returns   A `CollationKey` for the given string.

Description   This method generates a `CollationKey` for the given string. The returned object can be compared with other `CollationKey` objects using `CollationKey.compareTo()`. This comparison is faster than using `Collator.compare()`, so if the same string is used for many comparisons, you should use `CollationKey` objects.

getDecomposition

public synchronized int getDecomposition()

Returns   The decomposition mode for this Collator.

Description   This method returns the current decomposition mode for this
               Collator. The decomposition mode specifies how composed
               Unicode characters are handled during collation. You can
               adjust the decomposition mode to choose between faster and
               more complete collation. The returned value is one of the fol-
               lowing values: NO_DECOMPOSITION, CANONICAL_DECOMPOSITION,
               or FULL_DECOMPOSITION.

getStrength

public synchronized int getStrength()

Returns   The strength setting for this Collator.

Description   This method returns the current strength setting for this Col-
               lator. The strength specifies the minimum level of difference
               that is considered significant during collation. The returned
               value is one of the following values: PRIMARY, SECONDARY, TER-
               TIARY, or IDENTICAL.

hashCode

public abstract synchronized int hashCode()

Returns   A hashcode for this object.

Overrides   Object.hashCode()

Description   This method returns a hashcode for this Collator.

setDecomposition

public synchronized void setDecomposition(int decompositionMode)

Parameters   decompositionMode

               The decomposition mode: NO_DECOMPOSITION,
               CANONICAL_DECOMPOSITION,
               or FULL_DECOMPOSITION.

Description   This method sets the decomposition mode for this Collator.
               The decomposition mode specifies how composed Unicode
               characters are handled during collation. You can adjust the
               decomposition mode to choose between faster and more com-
               plete collation.

setStrength

public synchronized void setStrength(int newStrength)

Parameters   newStrength   The new strength setting: PRIMARY, SECONDARY, TERTIARY, or IDENTICAL.

Description   This method sets the strength of this Collator. The strength specifies the minimum level of difference that is considered significant during collation.

Inherited Methods

Method	Inherited From	Method	Inherited From
finalize()	Object	getClass()	Object
notify()	Object	notifyAll()	Object
toString()	Object	wait()	Object
wait(long)	Object	wait(long, int)	Object

See Also

CollationKey, Locale, RuleBasedCollator, String

16.7 DateFormat

Synopsis

Class Name:	java.text.DateFormat
Superclass:	java.text.Format
Immediate Subclasses:	java.text.SimpleDateFormat
Interfaces Implemented:	java.lang.Cloneable
Availability:	New as of JDK 1.1

Description

The DateFormat class formats and parses dates and times in a locale-specific manner. DateFormat is an abstract class, but it provides factory methods that return useful instances of DateFormat subclasses. These factory methods come in three groups:

- The getDateInstance() methods return objects that format and parse only dates.
- The getDateTimeInstance() methods return objects that format and parse date and time combinations.

- The getTimeInstance() methods return objects that format only times.

Certain of these factory methods allow you to specify the style, or length, of the resulting date and time strings. The interpretation of the style parameter is locale-specific. For the locale Locale.US, the styles and their results are as follows:

FULL	Tuesday, March 04, 1997 12:00:00 o'clock AM EST
LONG	March 04, 1997 12:00:00 AM EST
MEDIUM	04-Mar-97 12:00:00 AM
SHORT	3/4/97 12:00 AM

There is also a DEFAULT style, which is equivalent to MEDIUM.

The DateFormat class defines a number of field constants that represent the various fields in formatted date and time strings. These field constants can create FieldPosition objects.

Class Summary

```
public abstract class java.text.DateFormat extends java.text.Format
                    implements java.lang.Cloneable {
    // Constants
    public static final int AM_PM_FIELD;
    public static final int DATE_FIELD;
    public static final int DAY_OF_WEEK_FIELD;
    public static final int DAY_OF_WEEK_IN_MONTH_FIELD;
    public static final int DAY_OF_YEAR_FIELD;
    public static final int DEFAULT;
    public static final int ERA_FIELD;
    public static final int FULL;
    public static final int HOUR0_FIELD;
    public static final int HOUR1_FIELD;
    public static final int HOUR_OF_DAY0_FIELD;
    public static final int HOUR_OF_DAY1_FIELD;
    public static final int LONG;
    public static final int MEDIUM;
    public static final int MILLISECOND_FIELD;
    public static final int MINUTE_FIELD;
    public static final int MONTH_FIELD;
    public static final int SECOND_FIELD;
    public static final int SHORT;
    public static final int TIMEZONE_FIELD;
    public static final int WEEK_OF_MONTH_FIELD;
    public static final int WEEK_OF_YEAR_FIELD;
    public static final int YEAR_FIELD;

    // Variables
    protected Calendar calendar;
    protected NumberFormat numberFormat;
```

```
// Constructors
protected DateFormat();

// Class Methods
public static Locale[] getAvailableLocales();
public static final DateFormat getDateInstance();
public static final DateFormat getDateInstance(int style);
public static final DateFormat getDateInstance(int style, Locale aLocale);
public static final DateFormat getDateTimeInstance();
public static final DateFormat getDateTimeInstance(int dateStyle,
                            int timeStyle);
public static final DateFormat getDateTimeInstance(int dateStyle,
                            int timeStyle, Locale aLocale);
public static final DateFormat getInstance();
public static final DateFormat getTimeInstance();
public static final DateFormat getTimeInstance(int style);
public static final DateFormat getTimeInstance(int style, Locale aLocale);

// Instance Methods
public Object clone();
public boolean equals(Object obj);
public final String format(Date date);
public final StringBuffer format(Object obj, StringBuffer toAppendTo,
                    FieldPosition fieldPosition);
public abstract StringBuffer format(Date date, StringBuffer toAppendTo,
                    FieldPosition fieldPosition);
public Calendar getCalendar();
public NumberFormat getNumberFormat();
public TimeZone getTimeZone();
public int hashCode();
public boolean isLenient();
public Date parse(String text);
public abstract Date parse(String text, ParsePosition pos);
public Object parseObject(String source, ParsePosition pos);
public void setCalendar(Calendar newCalendar);
public void setLenient(boolean lenient);
public void setNumberFormat(NumberFormat newNumberFormat);
public void setTimeZone(TimeZone zone);
}
```

Constants

AM_PM_FIELD

```
public final static int AM_PM_FIELD
```
   Description   A field constant that represents the A.M./P.M. field.

DATE_FIELD

public final static int DATE_FIELD

Description   A field constant that represents the date (day of month) field.

DAY_OF_WEEK_FIELD

public final static int DAY_OF_WEEK_FIELD

Description   A field constant that represents the day-of-the-week field.

DAY_OF_WEEK_IN_MONTH_FIELD

public final static int DAY_OF_WEEK_IN_MONTH_FIELD

Description   A field constant that represents the day of the week in the current month field.

DAY_OF_YEAR_FIELD

public final static int DAY_OF_YEAR_FIELD

Description   A field constant that represents the day-of-the-year field.

DEFAULT

public final static int DEFAULT

Description   A constant that specifies the default style.

ERA_FIELD

public final static int ERA_FIELD

Description   A field constant that represents the era field.

FULL

public final static int FULL

Description   A constant that specifies the most complete style.

HOUR0_FIELD

public final static int HOUR0_FIELD

Description   A field constant that represents the zero-based hour field.

HOUR1_FIELD

public final static int HOUR1_FIELD

Description   A field constant that represents the one-based hour field.

HOUR_OF_DAY0_FIELD

public final static int HOUR_OF_DAY0_FIELD

Description   A field constant that represents the zero-based hour of the day field.

HOUR_OF_DAY1_FIELD

public final static int HOUR_OF_DAY1_FIELD

Description   A field constant that represents the one-based hour of the day field.

LONG

public final static int LONG

Description   A constant that specifies the long style.

MEDIUM

public final static int MEDIUM

Description   A constant that specifies the medium style.

MILLISECOND_FIELD

public final static int MILLISECOND_FIELD

Description   A field constant that represents the millisecond field.

MINUTE_FIELD

public final static int MINUTE_FIELD

Description   A field constant that represents the minute field.

MONTH_FIELD

public final static int MONTH_FIELD

Description   A field constant that represents the month field.

SECOND_FIELD

public final static int SECOND_FIELD

Description   A field constant that represents the second field.

SHORT

public final static int SHORT

Description   A constant that specifies the short style.

TIMEZONE_FIELD

    `public final static int TIMEZONE_FIELD`

      Description   A field constant that represents the time-zone field.

WEEK_OF_MONTH_FIELD

    `public final static int WEEK_OF_MONTH_FIELD`

      Description   A field constant that represents the week-of-the-month field.

WEEK_OF_YEAR_FIELD

    `public final static int WEEK_OF_YEAR_FIELD`

      Description   A field constant that represents the week-of-the-year field.

YEAR_FIELD

    `public final static int YEAR_FIELD`

      Description   A field constant that represents the year field.

Variables

calendar

    `protected Calendar calendar`

      Description   A `Calendar` object that internally generates the field values for formatting dates and times.

numberFormat

    `protected NumberFormat numberFormat`

      Description   A `NumberFormat` object that internally formats the numbers in dates and times.

Constructors

DateFormat

    `protected DateFormat()`

      Description   This constructor creates a `DateFormat`.

Class Methods

getAvailableLocales

    `public static Locale[] getAvailableLocales()`

      Returns   An array of `Locale` objects.

      Description   This method returns an array of the `Locale` objects for which this class can create `DateFormat` objects.

getDateInstance

```
public static final DateFormat getDateInstance()
```

Returns   A DateFormat appropriate for the default Locale that uses the default style.

Description   This method creates a DateFormat that formats and parses dates in the default locale with the default style.

```
public static final DateFormat getDateInstance(int style)
```

Parameters   style   A style constant.

Returns   A DateFormat appropriate for the default Locale that uses the given style.

Description   This method creates a DateFormat that formats and parses dates in the default locale with the given style.

```
public static final DateFormat getDateInstance(int style,
                                      Locale aLocale)
```

Parameters   style   A style constant.

                aLocale   The Locale to use.

Returns   A DateFormat appropriate for the given Locale that uses the given style.

Description   This method creates a DateFormat that formats and parses dates in the given locale with the given style.

getDateTimeInstance

```
public static final DateFormat getDateTimeInstance()
```

Returns   A DateFormat appropriate for the default Locale that uses the default date and time styles.

Description   This method creates a DateFormat that formats and parses dates and times in the default locale with the default date and time styles.

```
public static final DateFormat getDateTimeInstance(int dateStyle,
                                        int timeStyle)
```

Parameters   dateStyle   A style constant.

                timeStyle   A style constant.

Returns   A DateFormat appropriate for the default Locale that uses the given data and time styles.

Description   This method creates a DateFormat that formats and parses dates and times in the default locale with the given date and time styles.

```
public static final DateFormat getDateTimeInstance(int dateStyle,
                                    int timeStyle, Locale aLocale)
```

Parameters	dateStyle	A style constant.
	timeStyle	A style constant.
	aLocale	The Locale to use.

Returns   A DateFormat appropriate for the given Locale that uses the given date and time styles.

Description   This method creates a DateFormat that formats and parses dates and times in the given locale with the given date and time styles.

getInstance

```
public static final DateFormat getInstance()
```

Returns   A DateFormat appropriate for the default Locale.

Description   This method creates a general purpose DateFormat by calling `getDateTimeInstance(DateFormat.SHORT, DateFormat.SHORT)`.

getTimeInstance

```
public static final DateFormat getTimeInstance()
```

Returns   A DateFormat appropriate for the default Locale that uses the default style.

Description   This method creates a DateFormat that formats and parses times in the default locale with the default style.

```
public static final DateFormat getTimeInstance(int style)
```

Parameters   style   A style constant.

Returns   A DateFormat appropriate for the default Locale that uses the given style.

Description   This method creates a DateFormat that formats and parses times in the default locale with the given style.

```
public static final DateFormat getTimeInstance(int style,
                                             Locale aLocale)
```

Parameters	style	A style constant.
	aLocale	The Locale to use.

Returns   A DateFormat appropriate for the given Locale that uses the given style.

Description   This method creates a DateFormat that formats and parses times in the given locale with the given style.

Instance Methods

clone

```
public Object clone()
```

Returns   A copy of this DateFormat.

Overrides   Format.clone()

Description   This method creates a copy of this DateFormat and returns it.

equals

```
public boolean equals(Object obj)
```

Parameters   obj   The object to be compared with this object.

Returns   true if the objects are equal; false if they are not.

Overrides   Object.equals()

Description   This method returns true if obj is an instance of DateFormat
             and is equivalent to this DateFormat.

format

```
public final String format(Date date)
```

Parameters   date   The Date object to be formatted.

Returns   A string that contains a formatted representation of the date.

Description   This method formats the given date and returns the result as a
             string.

```
public final StringBuffer format(Object obj, StringBuffer toAppendTo,
                                 FieldPosition fieldPosition)
```

Parameters   obj   The object to be formatted.

             toAppendTo   A StringBuffer on which to append the format-
                            ted information.

             fieldPosition
                            A date or time field.

Returns   The given buffer toAppendTo with the formatted representation
             of the object appended to it.

Overrides   Format.format(Object, StringBuffer, FieldPosition)

Description   This method formats the given object and appends the result to
             the given StringBuffer. If fieldPosition refers to one of the
             time or date fields, its beginning and ending indices are filled
             with the beginning and ending positions of the given field in
             the resulting formatted string.

```
public abstract StringBuffer format(Date date, StringBuffer toAppendTo,
                                    FieldPosition fieldPosition)
```

Parameters date   The Date object to be formatted.

      toAppendTo A StringBuffer on which to append the format-ted information.

      fieldPosition

          A date or time field.

Returns The given buffer toAppendTo with the formatted representation of the date appended to it.

Description This method formats the given date and appends the result to the given StringBuffer. If fieldPosition refers to one of the time or date fields, its beginning and ending indices are filled with the beginning and ending positions of the given field in the resulting formatted string.

getCalendar

public Calendar getCalendar()

Returns The internal Calendar object of this DateFormat.

Description This method returns the Calendar object that this DateFormat uses internally.

getNumberFormat

public NumberFormat getNumberFormat()

Returns The internal NumberFormat object of this DateFormat.

Description This method returns the NumberFormat object that this Date-Format uses internally.

getTimeZone

public TimeZone getTimeZone()

Returns The internal TimeZone object of this DateFormat.

Description This method returns the TimeZone object that this DateFormat uses internally.

hashCode

public int hashCode()

Returns A hashcode for this object.

Overrides Object.hashCode()

Description This method returns a hashcode for this DateFormat.

isLenient

public boolean isLenient()

Returns   A boolean value that indicates the leniency of this DateFormat.

Description   This method returns the current leniency of this DateFormat. A value of false indicates that the DateFormat throws exceptions when it tries to parse questionable data, while a value of true indicates that the DateFormat makes its best guess to interpret questionable data. For example, if the DateFormat is being lenient, a date such as March 135, 1997 is interpreted as the 135th day after March 1, 1997.

parse

public Date parse(String text) throws ParseException

Parameters   text   The string to be parsed.

Returns   The Date object represented by the given string.

Throws   ParseException

                             If the text cannot be parsed as a date.

Description   This method parses a date from the given string, starting from the beginning of the string.

public abstract Date parse(String text, ParsePosition pos)

Parameters   text   The string to be parsed.

               pos   A ParsePosition object that can specify a position in the string.

Returns   The Date object represented by the text starting at the given position.

Description   This method parses a date from the given string, starting from the given position. After the string has been parsed, the given ParsePosition object is updated so that its index is after the parsed text.

parseObject

public Object parseObject(String source, ParsePosition pos)

Parameters   source   The string to be parsed.

               pos   A ParsePosition object that can specify a position in the string.

Returns   The object represented by the text starting at the given position.

Overrides   Format.parseObject(String, ParsePosition)

Description   This method parses a date from the given string, starting from the given position. After the string has been parsed, the given ParsePosition object is updated so that its index is after the parsed text.

setCalendar

public void setCalendar(Calendar newCalendar)

Parameters   newCalendar   The new Calendar to use.

Description   This method sets the Calendar that this DateFormat uses internally.

setLenient

public void setLenient(boolean lenient)

Parameters   lenient   A boolean value that specifies the leniency of this DateFormat.

Description   This method sets the leniency of this DateFormat. A value of false specifies that the DateFormat throws exceptions when it tries to parse questionable data, while a value of true indicates that the DateFormat makes its best guess to interpret questionable data. For example, if the Calendar is being lenient, a date such as March 135, 1997 is interpreted as the 135th day after March 1, 1997.

setNumberFormat

public void setNumberFormat(NumberFormat newNumberFormat)

Parameters   newNumberFormat

The new NumberFormat to use.

Description   This method sets the NumberFormat that this DateFormat uses internally.

setTimeZone

public void setTimeZone(TimeZone zone)

Parameters   zone   The new TimeZone to use.

Description   This method sets the TimeZone that this DateFormat uses internally.

Inherited Methods

Method	Inherited From	Method	Inherited From
finalize()	Object	format(Object)	Format
getClass()	Object	notify()	Object
notifyAll()	Object	parseObject(String)	Format
toString()	Object	wait()	Object
wait(long)	Object	wait(long, int)	Object

See Also

Calendar, Cloneable, Date, FieldPosition, Format, Locale, NumberFormat, Parse-
Position, String, StringBuffer, TimeZone

16.8   DateFormatSymbols

Synopsis

Class Name:	java.text.DateFormatSymbols
Superclass:	java.lang.Object
Immediate Subclasses:	None
Interfaces Implemented:	java.lang.Cloneable, java.io.Serializable
Availability:	New as of JDK 1.1

Description

The DateFormatSymbols class encapsulates date and time formatting data that is
locale-specific, like the names of the days of the week and the names of the
months. Typically, you do not need to instantiate DateFormatSymbols yourself.
Instead, an instance is automatically created for you, behind the scenes, when you
use one of the factory methods in DateFormat to create a DateFormat object. You
can retrieve a DateFormatSymbols object by calling the getDateFormatSymbols()
method of SimpleDateFormat. Once you have a DateFormatSymbols object, you
can modify the strings it uses if you want to change them.

Class Summary

```
public class java.text.DateFormatSymbols extends java.lang.Object
            implements java.io.Serializable, java.lang.Cloneable {
    // Constructors
    public DateFormatSymbols();
    public DateFormatSymbols(Locale locale);

    // Instance Methods
    public Object clone();
    public boolean equals(Object obj);
    public String[] getAmPmStrings();
    public String[] getEras();
    public String getLocalPatternChars();
    public String[] getMonths();
    public String[] getShortMonths();
    public String[] getShortWeekdays();
    public String[] getWeekdays();
    public String[][] getZoneStrings();
    public int hashCode();
```

```
    public void setAmPmStrings(String[] newAmpms);
    public void setEras(String[] newEras);
    public void setLocalPatternChars(String newLocalPatternChars);
    public void setMonths(String[] newMonths);
    public void setShortMonths(String[] newShortMonths);
    public void setShortWeekdays(String[] newShortWeekdays);
    public void setWeekdays(String[] newWeekdays);
    public void setZoneStrings(String[][] newZoneStrings);
}
```

Constructors

DateFormatSymbols

public DateFormatSymbols()

Throws	MissingResourceException
	If the resources for the default locale cannot be found or loaded.
Description	This constructor creates a DateFormatSymbols object for the default locale.

public DateFormatSymbols(Locale locale)

Parameters	locale	The Locale to use.
Throws	MissingResourceException	
	If the resources for the given locale cannot be found or loaded.	
Description	This constructor creates a DateFormatSymbols object for the given locale.	

Instance Methods

clone

public Object clone()

Returns	A copy of this DateFormatSymbols.
Overrides	Object.clone()
Description	This method creates a copy of this DateFormatSymbols and returns it.

equals

public boolean equals(Object obj)

Parameters	obj	The object to be compared with this object.
Returns	true if the objects are equal; false if they are not.	
Overrides	Object.equals()	
Description	This method returns true if obj is an instance of DecimalFormatSymbols and is equivalent to this DateFormatSymbols.	

getAmPmStrings

`public String[] getAmPmStrings()`

Returns	An array of strings used for the A.M./P.M. field for this Date-FormatSymbols.
Description	This method returns the strings that are used for the A.M./P.M. field (e.g., "AM", "PM").

getEras

`public String[] getEras()`

Returns	An array of strings used for the era field for this DateFormat-Symbols.
Description	This method returns the strings that are used for the era field (e.g., "BC", "AD").

getLocalPatternChars

`public String getLocalPatternChars()`

Returns	A string that contains the data-time pattern characters for this DateFormatSymbols.
Description	This method returns the data-time pattern characters for the locale of this object.

getMonths

`public String[] getMonths()`

Returns	An array of strings used for the month field for this DateFormatSymbols.
Description	This method returns the strings that are used for the month field (e.g., "January", "February").

getShortMonths

`public String[] getShortMonths()`

Returns	An array of strings used for the short month field for this Date-FormatSymbols.
Description	This method returns the strings that are used for the short (i.e., three-character) month field (e.g., "Jan", "Feb").

getShortWeekdays

`public String[] getShortWeekdays()`

Returns	An array ofstrings used for the short weekday field for this DateFormatSymbols.

Description   This method returns the strings that are used for the short (i.e., three-character) weekday field (e.g., "Mon", "Tue").

getWeekdays

public String[] getWeekdays()

Returns   An array of strings used for the weekday field for this DateFormatSymbols.

Description   This method returns the strings that are used for the weekday field (e.g., "Monday", "Tuesday").

getZoneStrings

public String[][] getZoneStrings()

Returns   An array of arrays of strings used for the time zones for this DateFormatSymbols.

Description   This method returns the time-zone strings. Each subarray is an array of six strings that specify a time-zone ID, its long name, its short name, its daylight-savings-time name, its short daylight-savings-time name, and a major city in the time zone. For example, an entry for Mountain Standard Time is:

```
{"MST", "Mountain Standard Time", "MST",
 "Mountain Daylight Time", "MDT", "Denver"}
```

hashCode

public int hashCode()

Returns   A hashcode for this object.

Overrides   Object.hashCode()

Description   This method returns a hashcode for this DateFormatSymbols object.

setAmPmStrings

public void setAmPmStrings(String[] newAmpms)

Parameters   newAmpms   The new strings.

Description   This method sets the strings that are used for the A.M./P.M. field for this DateFormatSymbols.

setEras

public void setEras(String[] newEras)

Parameters   newEras   The new strings.

Description   This method sets the strings that are used for the era field for this DateFormatSymbols.

setLocalPatternChars

public void setLocalPatternChars(String newLocalPatternChars)

Parameters   newLocalPatternChars

           The new date-time pattern characters.

Description   This method sets the date-time pattern characters of this Date-FormatSymbols object.

setMonths

public void setMonths(String[] newMonths)

Parameters   newMonths   The new strings.

Description   This method sets the strings that are used for the month field for this DateFormatSymbols.

setShortMonths

public void setShortMonths(String[] newShortMonths)

Parameters   newShortMonths

           The new strings.

Description   This method sets the strings that are used for the short (i.e., three-character) month field for this DateFormatSymbols.

setShortWeekdays

public void setShortWeekdays(String[] newShortWeekdays)

Parameters   newShortWeekdays

           The new strings.

Description   This method sets the strings that are used for the short (i.e., three-character) weekday field for this DateFormatSymbols.

setWeekdays

public void setWeekdays(String[] newWeekdays)

Parameters   newWeekdays   The new strings.

Description   This method sets the strings that are used for the weekday field for this DateFormatSymbols.

setZones

public void setZones(String[][] newZoneStrings)

Parameters   newZoneStrings

           The new strings.

Description   This method sets the strings that are used for the time-zone field for this DateFormatSymbols.

Inherited Methods

Method	Inherited From	Method	Inherited From
finalize()	Object	getClass()	Object
notify()	Object	notifyAll()	Object
toString()	Object	wait()	Object
wait(long)	Object	wait(long, int)	Object

See Also

Calendar, DateFormat, Locale, SimpleDateFormat, TimeZone

16.9   DecimalFormat

Synopsis

Class Name: java.text.DecimalFormat
Superclass: java.text.NumberFormat
Immediate Subclasses: None
Interfaces Implemented: None
Availability: New as of JDK 1.1

Description

The DecimalFormat class is a concrete subclass of NumberFormat that formats and
parses numbers using a formatting pattern. Typically, you do not need to instantiate DecimalFormat yourself. Instead, the factory methods of NumberFormat return
instances of DecimalFormat that are appropriate for particular locales.

However, if you need a specialized number format, you can instantiate your own
DecimalFormat using a pattern string. You can also modify the formatting pattern
of an existing DecimalFormat object using the applyPattern() method. A pattern
string has the following form:

```
positive-pattern[;negative-pattern]
```

If the negative pattern is omitted, negative numbers are formatted using the positive pattern with a – character prepended to the result. Each pattern has the following form:

```
[prefix]integer[.fraction][suffix]
```

The following symbols are significant in the pattern string.

Symbol	Description
0	A digit
#	A digit where 0 is not shown
.	A placeholder for a decimal separator
,	A placeholder for a grouping separator
;	The format separator
−	The default negative prefix
%	Divides value by 100 and shows as a percentage

Any characters other than these special characters can appear in the prefix or the suffix. A single quote can be used to escape a special character, if you need to use one of these symbols in a prefix or a suffix.

For example, the pattern string for U.S. currency values is:

```
$#,##0.00;($#,##0.00)
```

This indicates that a $ character is prepended to all formatted values. The grouping separator character , is inserted every three digits. Exactly two digits after the decimal place are always shown. Negative values are shown in parentheses. Thus, the value −1234.56 produces output like:

```
($1,234.56)
```

Internally, the DecimalFormat class uses a DecimalFormatSymbols object to get the numerical strings that are appropriate for a particular locale. If you want to modify these strings, you can get the DecimalFormatSymbols object by calling getDecimal-FormatSymbols().

Class Summary

```
public class java.text.DecimalFormat extends java.text.NumberFormat {
    // Constructors
    public DecimalFormat();
    public DecimalFormat(String pattern);
    public DecimalFormat(String pattern, DecimalFormatSymbols symbols);

    // Instance Methods
    public void applyLocalizedPattern(String pattern);
    public void applyPattern(String pattern);
    public Object clone();
    public boolean equals(Object obj);
    public StringBuffer format(double number, StringBuffer result,
                        FieldPosition fieldPosition);
    public StringBuffer format(long number, StringBuffer result,
                        FieldPosition fieldPosition);
    public DecimalFormatSymbols getDecimalFormatSymbols();
    public int getGroupingSize();
    public int getMultiplier();
```

```
public String getNegativePrefix();
public String getNegativeSuffix();
public String getPositivePrefix();
public String getPositiveSuffix();
public int hashCode();
public boolean isDecimalSeparatorAlwaysShown();
public Number parse(String text, ParsePosition status);
public void setDecimalFormatSymbols(DecimalFormatSymbols newSymbols);
public void setDecimalSeparatorAlwaysShown(boolean newValue);
public void setGroupingSize(int newValue);
public void setMultiplier(int newValue);
public void setNegativePrefix(String newValue);
public void setNegativeSuffix(String newValue);
public void setPositivePrefix(String newValue);
public void setPositiveSuffix(String newValue);
public String toLocalizedPattern();
public String toPattern();
}
```

Constructors

DecimalFormat

public DecimalFormat()

Description   This constructor creates a DecimalFormat that uses the default
                formatting pattern and DecimalFormatSymbols that are appro-
                priate for the default locale.

public DecimalFormat(String pattern)

Parameters   pattern   The pattern string.

Description   This constructor creates a DecimalFormat that uses the given
                formatting pattern and a DecimalFormatSymbols that is appro-
                priate for the default locale.

public DecimalFormat(String pattern, DecimalFormatSymbols symbols)

Parameters   pattern   The pattern string.

                symbols   The DecimalFormatSymbols to use.

Description   This constructor creates a DecimalFormat that uses the given
                formatting pattern and DecimalFormatSymbols object.

Instance Methods

applyLocalizedPattern

public void applyLocalizedPattern(String pattern)

Parameters   pattern   The pattern string.

Description   This method tells this DecimalFormat to use the given format-
                ting pattern to format and parse numbers. The pattern string is
                assumed to have been localized to the DecimalFormatSymbols
                object this DecimalFormat uses.

applyPattern

```
public void applyPattern(String pattern)
```

Parameters	pattern	The pattern string.

Description   This method tells this DecimalFormat to use the given formatting pattern to format and parse numbers. The pattern string is localized to the DecimalFormatSymbols object this DecimalFormat uses.

clone

```
public Object clone()
```

Returns   A copy of this DecimalFormat.

Overrides   NumberFormat.clone()

Description   This method creates a copy of this DecimalFormat and then returns it.

equals

```
public boolean equals(Object obj)
```

Parameters   obj   The object to be compared with this object.

Returns   true if the objects are equal; false if they are not.

Overrides   NumberFormat.equals()

Description   This method returns true if obj is an instance of DecimalFormat and is equivalent to this DecimalFormat.

format

```
public StringBuffer format(double number, StringBuffer result,
                           FieldPosition fieldPosition)
```

Parameters   number   The double value to be formatted.

result   A StringBuffer on which to append the formatted information.

fieldPosition

A number field.

Returns   The given buffer result with the formatted representation of the number appended to it.

Overrides   NumberFormat.format(double, StringBuffer, FieldPosition)

Description   This method formats the given number and appends the result to the given StringBuffer. If fieldPosition refers to one of the number fields, its beginning and ending indices are filled with the beginning and ending positions of the given field in the resulting formatted string.

```
public StringBuffer format(long number, StringBuffer result,
                           FieldPosition fieldPosition)
```

Parameters   `number`   The `long` value to be formatted.

                `result`   A `StringBuffer` on which to append the formatted information.

                `fieldPosition`

                            A number field.

Returns   The given buffer `result` with the formatted representation of the number appended to it.

Overrides   `NumberFormat.format(double, StringBuffer, FieldPosition)`

Description   This method formats the given number and appends the result to the given `StringBuffer`. If `fieldPosition` refers to one of the number fields, its beginning and ending indices are filled with the beginning and ending positions of the given field in the resulting formatted string.

getDecimalFormatSymbols

```
public DecimalFormatSymbols getDecimalFormatSymbols()
```

Returns   The `DecimalFormatSymbols` object used by this `DecimalFormat`.

Description   This method returns the `DecimalFormatSymbols` object that this `DecimalFormat` uses internally.

getGroupingSize

```
public int getGroupingSize()
```

Returns   The grouping size of this `DecimalFormat`.

Description   This method returns the grouping size of this `DecimalFormat`. The grouping size is the number of digits between grouping separators in the integer portion of a number. For example, in the number `1,234.56`, the grouping size is 3 (and the grouping symbol is ",").

getMultiplier

```
public int getMultiplier()
```

Returns   The multiplier of this `DecimalFormat`.

Description   This method returns the multiplier of this `DecimalFormat`. The multiplier is used to adjust a number before it is formatted or after it is parsed. For example, a percent format has a multiplier of 100 and a suffix of '`%`'. Thus, a value of `.42` could be formatted as `42%`.

getNegativePrefix

public String getNegativePrefix()

Returns	The string that is prepended to negative values.
Description	This method returns the prefix string for negative numbers.

getNegativeSuffix

public String getNegativeSuffix()

Returns	The string that is appended to negative values.
Description	This method returns the suffix string for negative numbers.

getPositivePrefix

public String getPositivePrefix()

Returns	The string that is prepended to positive values.
Description	This method returns the prefix string for positive numbers.

getPositiveSuffix

public String getPositiveSuffix()

Returns	The string that is appended to positive values.
Description	This method returns the suffix string for positive numbers.

hashCode

public int hashCode()

Returns	A hashcode for this object.
Overrides	NumberFormat.hashCode()
Description	This method returns a hashcode for this DecimalFormat.

isDecimalSeparatorAlwaysShown

public boolean isDecimalSeparatorAlwaysShown()

Returns	A boolean value that indicates whether or not the decimal separator symbol is always shown.
Description	This method returns true if this DecimalFormat always shows the decimal separator. The method returns false if the decimal separator is only shown if there is a fractional portion of the number being formatted.

parse

public Number parse(String text, ParsePosition status)

Parameters	text	The string to be parsed.
	status	A ParsePosition object that specifies a position in the string.

Returns   The Number object represented by the text starting at the given position.

Overrides   NumberFormat.parse(String, ParsePosition)

Description   This method parses a number from the given string, starting from the given position. After the string has been parsed, the given ParsePosition object is updated so that its index is after the parsed text.

setDecimalFormatSymbols

```
public void setDecimalFormatSymbols(
        DecimalFormatSymbols newSymbols)
```

Parameters   newSymbols   The new DecimalFormatSymbols object to use.

Description   This method sets the DecimalFormatSymbols object that this DecimalFormat uses internally.

setDecimalSeparatorAlwaysShown

```
public void setDecimalSeparatorAlwaysShown(boolean newValue)
```

Parameters   newValue   The new decimal separator value.

Description   This method specifies whether or not the decimal separator symbol is always shown in formatted numbers. If newValue is false, the separator is only shown for numbers that have a fractional part. Otherwise, the separator is always shown.

setGroupingSize

```
public void setGroupingSize(int newValue)
```

Parameters   newValue   The new grouping size.

Description   This method sets the grouping size of this DecimalFormat. The grouping size is the number of digits between grouping separators in the integer portion of a number. For example, in the number 1,234.56, the grouping size is 3 (and the grouping symbol is ",").

setMultiplier

```
public void setMultiplier(int newValue)
```

Parameters   newValue   The new multiplier.

Description   This method sets the multiplier of this DecimalFormat. The multiplier is used to adjust a number before it is formatted or after it is parsed. For example, a percent format has a multiplier of 100 and a suffix of %. Thus, a value of .42 could be formatted as 42%.

setNegativePrefix

```
public void setNegativePrefix(String newValue)
```
    Parameters   newValue   The new prefix.

    Description   This method sets the prefix string for negative values.

setNegativeSuffix

```
public void setNegativeSuffix(String newValue)
```
    Parameters   newValue   The new suffix.

    Description   This method sets the suffix string for negative values.

setPositivePrefix

```
public void setPositivePrefix(String newValue)
```
    Parameters   newValue   The new prefix.

    Description   This method sets the prefix string for positive values.

setPositiveSuffix

```
public void setPositiveSuffix(String newValue)
```
    Parameters   newValue   The new suffix.

    Description   This method sets the suffix string for positive values.

toLocalizedPattern

```
public String toLocalizedPattern()
```
    Returns   The pattern string of this DecimalFormat.

    Description   This method returns the pattern string of this DecimalFormat, localized with the DecimalFormatSymbols object of this DecimalFormat.

toPattern

```
public String toPattern()
```
    Returns   The pattern string of this DecimalFormat.

    Description   This method returns the pattern string of this DecimalFormat.

Inherited Methods

Method	Inherited From	Method	Inherited From
finalize()	Object	format(double)	NumberFormat
format(long)	NumberFormat	format(Object, String-Buffer, FieldPosition)	NumberFormat
getClass()	Object	getMaximumFractionDig-its()	NumberFormat

Method	Inherited From	Method	Inherited From
getMaximumIntegerDigits()	NumberFormat	getMinimumFractionDig-its()	NumberFormat
getMinimumIntegerDigits()	NumberFormat	isGroupingUsed()	NumberFormat
isParseIntegerOnly()	NumberFormat	notify()	Object
notifyAll()	Object	parse(String)	NumberFormat
parseObject(String)	Format	parseObject(String, ParsePosition)	NumberFormat
setGroupingUsed(boolean)	NumberFormat	setMaximumFractionDig-its(int)	NumberFormat
setMaximumIntegerDig-its(int)	NumberFormat	setMinimumFractionDig-its(int)	NumberFormat
setMinimumIntegerDig-its(int)	NumberFormat	setParseInte-gerOnly(boolean)	NumberFormat
toString()	Object	wait()	Object
wait(long)	Object	wait(long, int)	Object

See Also

DecimalFormatSymbols, FieldPosition, Number, NumberFormat, ParsePosition, String, StringBuffer

16.10   DecimalFormatSymbols

Synopsis

Class Name: java.text.DecimalFormatSymbols
Superclass: java.lang.Object
Immediate Subclasses: None
Interfaces Implemented: java.lang.Cloneable, java.io.Serializable
Availability: New as of JDK 1.1

Description

The DecimalFormatSymbols class encapsulates number-formatting data that is locale-specific, like grouping separators and decimal separators. Typically, you do not need to instantiate DecimalFormatSymbols yourself. Instead, an instance is automatically created for you, behind the scenes, when you use one of the factory methods in NumberFormat to create a DecimalFormat object. You can retrieve a DecimalFormatSymbols object by calling the getDecimalFormatSymbols() method of DecimalFormat. Once you have a DecimalFormatSymbols object, you can modify the strings it uses if you want to change them.

Class Summary

```
public final class java.text.DecimalFormatSymbols extends java.lang.Object
                implements java.io.Serializable, java.lang.Cloneable {
    // Constructors
    public DecimalFormatSymbols();
    public DecimalFormatSymbols(Locale locale);

    // Instance Methods
    public Object clone();
    public boolean equals(Object obj);
    public char getDecimalSeparator();
    public char getDigit();
    public char getGroupingSeparator();
    public String getInfinity();
    public char getMinusSign();
    public String getNaN();
    public char getPatternSeparator();
    public char getPerMill();
    public char getPercent();
    public char getZeroDigit();
    public int hashCode();
    public void setDecimalSeparator(char decimalSeparator);
    public void setDigit(char digit);
    public void setGroupingSeparator(char groupingSeparator);
    public void setInfinity(String infinity);
    public void setMinusSign(char minusSign);
    public void setNaN(String NaN);
    public void setPatternSeparator(char patternSeparator);
    public void setPerMill(char perMill);
    public void setPercent(char percent);
    public void setZeroDigit(char zeroDigit);
}
```

Constructors

DecimalFormatSymbols

public DecimalFormatSymbols()

Description	This constructor creates a DecimalFormatSymbols object for the default locale.

public DecimalFormatSymbols(Locale locale)

Parameters	locale	The Locale to use.
Description	This constructor creates a DecimalFormatSymbols object for the given locale.

Instance Methods

clone

```
public Object
clone()
```

Returns	A copy of this DecimalFormatSymbols.
Overrides	Object.clone()
Description	This method creates a copy of this DecimalFormatSymbols and returns it.

equals

```
public boolean equals(Object obj)
```

Parameters	obj	The object to be compared with this object.
Returns		true if the objects are equal; false if they are not.
Overrides		Object.equals()
Description		This method returns true if obj is an instance of DateFormat-Symbols and is equivalent to this DecimalFormatSymbols.

getDecimalSeparator

```
public char getDecimalSeparator()
```

Returns	The character used to separate the integer and fractional parts of a number for this DecimalFormatSymbols.
Description	This method returns the decimal separator character (e.g., ".", ",").

getDigit

```
public char getDigit()
```

Returns	The character used to represent a digit in a pattern string for this DecimalFormatSymbols.
Description	This method returns the digit pattern character, which represents a digit that is not shown if it is zero.

getGroupingSeparator

```
public char getGroupingSeparator()
```

Returns	The character used to separate long numbers for this Decimal-FormatSymbols.
Description	This method returns the grouping separator character (e.g., ",", ".").

getInfinity

```
public String getInfinity()
```

Returns   The string used to represent infinity for this DecimalFormat-Symbols.

Description This method returns the string that represents infinity.

getMinusSign

```
public char getMinusSign()
```

Returns   The character used to signify negative numbers for this DecimalFormatSymbols.

Description This method returns the character that signifies negative numbers.

getNaN

```
public String getNaN()
```

Returns   The string used to represent the value not-a-number for this DecimalFormatSymbols.

Description This method returns the string that represents not-a-number.

getPatternSeparator

```
public char getPatternSeparator()
```

Returns   The pattern separator character for this DecimalFormatSymbols.

Description This method returns the character used in pattern strings to separate the positive subpattern and negative subpattern.

getPerMill

```
public char getPerMill()
```

Returns   The character used to represent the per mille sign for this DecimalFormatSymbols.

Description This method returns the character that represents a per mille value.

getPercent

```
public char getPercent()
```

Returns   The character used to represent the percent sign for this DecimalFormatSymbols.

Description This method returns the character that represents a percent value (e.g., %).

getZeroDigit

```
public char getZeroDigit()
```

Returns   The character used to represent a digit in a pattern string for this DecimalFormatSymbols.

Description This method returns the zero-digit pattern character, which represents a digit that is shown even if it is zero.

hashCode

```
public int hashCode()
```

Returns   A hashcode for this object.

Overrides   Object.hashCode()

Description This method returns a hashcode for this DecimalFormatSymbols object.

setDecimalSeparator

```
public void setDecimalSeparator(char decimalSeparator)
```

Parameters decimalSeparator
                 The new decimal separator.

Description This method sets the decimal separator character for this DecimalFormatSymbols.

setDigit

```
public void setDigit(char digit)
```

Parameters digit   The new digit pattern character.

Description This method sets the digit pattern character, which represents a digit that is not shown if it is zero, for this DecimalFormatSymbols.

setGroupingSeparator

```
public void setGroupingSeparator(char groupingSeparator)
```

Parameters groupingSeparator
                 The new grouping separator.

Description This method sets the grouping separator character for this DecimalFormatSymbols.

setInfinity

```
public Void setInfinity(String infinity)
```

Parameters infinity   The new infinity string.

Description This method sets the string that represents infinity for this DecimalFormatSymbols.

setMinusSign

public void setMinusSign(char minusSign)

Parameters   minusSign   The new minus sign.

Description   This method sets the character that signifies negative numbers for this DecimalFormatSymbols.

setNaN

public Void setNaN(String NaN)

Parameters   NaN   The new non-a-number string.

Description   This method sets the string that represents not-a-number for this DecimalFormatSymbols.

setPatternSeparator

public void setPatternSeparator(char patternSeparator)

Parameters   patternSeparator

   The new pattern separator.

Description   This method sets the character that is used in pattern strings to separate the positive subpattern and negative subpattern for this DecimalFormatSymbols.

setPerMill

public void setPerMill(char perMill)

Parameters   perMill   The new per mille sign.

Description   This method sets the character that represents the per mille sign for this DecimalFormatSymbols.

setPercent

public void setPercent(char percent)

Parameters   percent   The new percent sign.

Description   This method sets the character that represents the percent sign for this DecimalFormatSymbols.

setZeroDigit

public void setZeroDigit(char zeroDigit)

Parameters   zeroDigit   The new zero-digit pattern character.

Description   This method sets the zero-digit pattern character, which represents a digit that is shown even if it is zero, for this DecimalFormatSymbols.

Inherited Methods

Method	Inherited From	Method	Inherited From
finalize()	Object	getClass()	Object
notify()	Object	notifyAll()	Object
toString()	Object	wait()	Object
wait(long)	Object	wait(long, int)	Object

See Also

DecimalFormat, NumberFormat, Locale

16.11   FieldPosition

Synopsis

Class Name:	java.text.FieldPosition
Superclass:	java.lang.Object
Immediate Subclasses:	None
Interfaces Implemented:	None
Availability:	New as of JDK 1.1

Description

The FieldPosition class encapsulates information about fields in formatted output. The fields in a particular type of formatted output are identified by constants. A FieldPosition object contains its field type and the field's position within the formatted output. The field position is specified by the index of the first character in the field and the index of the last character in the field.

You can use a FieldPosition object to find the position of a particular field in a formatted string. Consider the following code:

```
NumberFormat nf = NumberFormat.getInstance();
StringBuffer sb = new StringBuffer();
FieldPosition fp = new FieldPosition(NumberFormat.FRACTION_FIELD);
nf.format(-1234.56, sb, fp);
System.out.println(new String(sb));
System.out.println("FRACTION_FIELD goes from " + fp.getBeginIndex()
                + " to " + fp.getEndIndex() + ".");
```

This code produces the following output:

```
-1,234.56
FRACTION_FIELD goes from 7 to 9.
```

Class Summary

```
public class java.text.FieldPosition extends java.lang.Object {
    // Constructors
    public FieldPosition(int field);

    // Instance Methods
    public int getBeginIndex();
    public int getEndIndex();
    public int getField();
}
```

Constructors

FieldPosition

```
public FieldPosition(int field)
```

Parameters	field	A field constant.
Description		This constructor creates a `FieldPosition` object that represents the given field.

Instance Methods

getBeginIndex

```
public int getBeginIndex()
```

Returns	The beginning index.
Description	This method returns the beginning index of the field that is represented by this `FieldPosition`.

getEndIndex

```
public int getEndIndex()
```

Returns	The ending index of this `FieldPosition`.
Description	This method returns the ending index of the field that is represented by this `FieldPosition`.

getField

```
public int getField()
```

Returns	The field constant of this `FieldPosition`.
Description	This method returns the field constant of this `FieldPosition`.

Inherited Methods

Method	Inherited From	Method	Inherited From
clone()	Object	equals(Object)	Object
finalize()	Object	getClass()	Object
hashCode()	Object	notify()	Object
notifyAll()	Object	toString()	Object
wait()	Object	wait(long)	Object
wait(long, int)	Object		

See Also

DateFormat, Format, MessageFormat, NumberFormat, ParsePosition, String

16.12   Format

Synopsis

Class Name:	java.text.Format
Superclass:	java.lang.Object
Immediate Subclasses:	java.text.DateFormat, java.text.MessageFormat, java.text.NumberFormat
Interfaces Implemented:	java.lang.Cloneable, java.io.Serializable
Availability:	New as of JDK 1.1

Description

The Format class is an abstract class that is the superclass of all classes that handle locale-sensitive parsing and formatting of dates, numbers, and messages. The two format() methods take the information in a supplied object and convert it to a string. The two parseObject() methods do the reverse; they take the information from a string and construct an appropriate object.

Class Summary

```
public abstract class java.text.Format extends java.lang.Object
                    implements java.io.Serializable, java.lang.Cloneable {
    // Instance Methods
    public Object clone();
    public final String format(Object obj);
    public abstract StringBuffer format(Object obj, StringBuffer toAppendTo,
                            FieldPosition pos);
    public Object parseObject(String source);
    public abstract Object parseObject(String source, ParsePosition status);
}
```

Instance Methods

clone

```
public Object clone()
```
Returns   A copy of this Format.

Overrides   Object.clone()

Description   This method creates a copy of this Format and returns it.

format

```
public final String format(Object obj)
```
Parameters   obj   The object to be formatted.

Returns   A string that contains a formatted representation of the object.

Throws   IllegalArgumentException

                    If the given object cannot be formatted.

Description   This method formats the given object by calling format-(Object, StringBuffer, FieldPosition) with an empty StringBuffer and a FieldPosition that has a value of 0.

```
public abstract StringBuffer format(Object obj,
                                    StringBuffer toAppendTo,
                                    FieldPosition pos)
```
Parameters   obj   The object to be formatted.

             toAppendTo A StringBuffer on which to append the formatted information.

             pos   A field.

Returns   The given buffer toAppendTo with the formatted representation of the object appended to it.

Throws   IllegalArgumentException

                    If the given object cannot be formatted.

Description   This method formats the given object and appends the result to the given StringBuffer. After the object has been formatted, the beginning and ending indices of the given FieldPosition are updated to reflect the field's position in the formatted output.

              A subclass of Format must implement this method.

parseObject

```
public Object parseObject(String source) throws ParseException
```
Parameters   source   The string to be parsed.

Returns   The object represented by the given string.

Throws	ParseException
	If the text cannot be parsed by this Format.
Description	This method parses the given text and returns an appropriate object. It does this by calling parseObject(String, ParsePosition) with a ParsePosition that has an index of 0.

```
public abstract Object parseObject(String source,
                                   ParsePosition status)
```

Parameters	source	The string to be parsed.
	status	A ParsePosition object that specifies a position in the string.
Returns	The object represented by the text starting at the given position.	
Description	This method parses the given text, starting at the specified position, and returns an object created from the data. After the string has been parsed, the given ParsePosition object is updated so that its index is after the parsed text.	
	A subclass of Format must implement this method.	

Inherited Methods

Method	Inherited From	Method	Inherited From
equals(Object)	Object	finalize()	Object
getClass()	Object	hashCode()	Object
notify()	Object	notifyAll()	Object
toString()	Object	wait()	Object
wait(long)	Object	wait(long, int)	Object

See Also

DateFormat, FieldPosition, MessageFormat, NumberFormat, ParseException, ParsePosition, String, StringBuffer

16.13 MessageFormat

Synopsis

Class Name:	java.text.MessageFormat
Superclass:	java.text.Format

Immediate Subclasses: None
Interfaces Implemented: None
Availability: New as of JDK 1.1

Description

The MessageFormat class constructs textual messages using a formatting pattern
string. Conceptually, the class functions much like printf() in C. Syntactically,
however, it is quite different. A MessageFormat object uses a pattern string; formatted arguments are placed into the pattern string to produce a resulting string.
Arguments are delimited by matching sets of curly braces and may include additional information about how that data should be formatted. For example, consider the following code:

```
String message =
   "Boot of server {0}began at {1, time}on {1, date, full}.";
MessageFormat boot = new MessageFormat(message);
Date now = new Date();
Object[] arguments = {"luna3", now};
System.out.println(boot.format(arguments));
```

This code produces the following output:

```
Boot of server luna3 began at 11:13:22 AM on Monday, March 03, 1997.
```

Each of the arguments is numbered and includes an optional type and an optional
style. In the example above, {1, date, full} indicates that the argument at index
1 in the argument array should be formatted using a DateFormat object with the
FULL style. The allowed types and styles are:

Type	Object	Styles
choice	ChoiceFormat	*pattern*
date	DateFormat	short, medium, long, full, *pattern*
number	NumberFormat	integer, percent, currency, *pattern*
time	DateFormat	short, medium, long, full, *pattern*

For the date and time types, the styles correspond to the styles, or lengths, of the
resulting date and time strings. You can also specify a date or time pattern string as
you would for creating a SimpleDateFormat object. For the number type, the styles
correspond to formatting normal numbers, percentage values, and currency values. You can also specify a number pattern string as you would for creating a DecimalFormat object. For the choice type, you can specify a choice pattern as you
would for creating a ChoiceFormat object. If no type is specified, the argument
should be a string.

The following example shows how to use a choice format pattern with a Message-
Format:

```
Object[] arguments = {new Integer(1)};
String grammar = "At last count, {0}server{0, choice, 0#s|1#|1<s}
 {0, choice, 0#were|1#was|1<were}booted.";
MessageFormat booted = new MessageFormat(grammar);
System.out.println(booted.format(arguments));
arguments[0] = new Integer(2);
System.out.println(booted.format(arguments));
```

This example produces the following output:

```
At last count, 1 server was booted.
At last count, 2 servers were booted.
```

As an alternative to specifying all of the formatting in the pattern string, you can use an array of Format objects to format the arguments. You can specify this array using setFormats().

Note that you create MessageFormat objects directly, rather than through factory methods. This is because MessageFormat does not implement any locale-specific behavior. To produce properly internationalized output, the pattern string that is used to construct a MessageFormat should come from a ResourceBundle instead of being embedded in the code.

Class Summary

```
public class java.text.MessageFormat extends java.text.Format {
  // Constructors
  public MessageFormat(String pattern);

  // Class Methods
  public static String format(String pattern, Object[] arguments);

  // Instance Methods
  public void applyPattern(String newPattern);
  public Object clone();
  public boolean equals(Object obj);
  public final StringBuffer format(Object source, StringBuffer result,
                      FieldPosition ignore);
  public final StringBuffer format(Object[] source, StringBuffer result,
                      FieldPosition ignore);
  public Format[] getFormats();
  public Locale getLocale();
  public int hashCode();
  public Object[] parse(String source);
  public Object[] parse(String source, ParsePosition status);
  public Object parseObject(String text, ParsePosition status);
  public void setFormat(int variable, Format newFormat);
  public void setFormats(Format[] newFormats);
  public void setLocale(Locale theLocale);
  public String toPattern();
}
```

Constructors

MessageFormat

> public MessageFormat(String pattern)
>
> | | | |
> |---|---|---|
> | Parameters | pattern | The pattern string. |
> | Description | This constructor creates a MessageFormat with the given formatting pattern string. | |

Class Methods

format

> public static String format(String pattern, Object[] arguments)
>
> | | | |
> |---|---|---|
> | Parameters | pattern | The pattern string. |
> | | arguments | An array of arguments. |
> | Description | Calling this static method is equivalent to constructing a MessageFormat using the given formatting pattern string and asking it to format the given arguments with the format() method. | |

Instance Methods

applyPattern

> public void applyPattern(String pattern)
>
> | | | |
> |---|---|---|
> | Parameters | pattern | The pattern string. |
> | Description | This method tells this MessageFormat to use the given formatting pattern to format and parse arguments. | |

clone

> public Object clone()
>
> | | |
> |---|---|
> | Returns | A copy of this MessageFormat. |
> | Overrides | Format.clone() |
> | Description | This method creates a copy of this MessageFormat and then returns it. |

equals

> public boolean equals(Object obj)
>
> | | | |
> |---|---|---|
> | Parameters | obj | The object to be compared with this object. |
> | Returns | true if the objects are equal; false if they are not. | |
> | Overrides | Format.equals() | |
> | Description | This method returns true if obj is an instance of MessageFormat and is equivalent to this MessageFormat. | |

format

```
public StringBuffer format(Object source, StringBuffer result,
                           FieldPosition ignore)
```

Parameters	source	The object to be formatted.
	result	A StringBuffer on which to append the formatted information.
	ignore	Ignored.
Returns		The given buffer result with the formatted representation of the object appended to it.
Overrides		Format.format(Object, StringBuffer, FieldPosition)
Description		This method formats the given object and appends the result to the given StringBuffer. The method assumes that the given object is an array of arguments.

```
public StringBuffer format(Object[] source, StringBuffer result,
                           FieldPosition ignore)
```

Parameters	source	The object array to be formatted.
	result	A StringBuffer on which to append the formatted information.
	ignore	Ignored.
Returns		The given buffer result with the formatted representation of the object array appended to it.
Description		This method formats the given arguments in the object array and appends the result to the given StringBuffer.

getFormats

```
public Format[] getFormats()
```

Returns	An array of the formats used by this MessageFormat.
Description	This method returns the format objects that this MessageFormat uses. Note that formats are numbered according to the order in which they appear in the formatting pattern string, not according to their specified argument numbers.

getLocale

```
public Locale getLocale()
```

Returns	The Locale of this MessageFormat.
Description	This method returns the locate for this MessageFormat. This locale is used to get default date, time, and number formatters.

hashCode

`public int hashCode()`

Returns   A hashcode for this object.

Overrides   `Object.hashCode()`

Description   This method returns a hashcode for this `MessageFormat`.

parse

`public Object[] parse(String source) throws ParseException`

Parameters   source   The string to be parsed.

Returns   An array of objects represented by the given string.

Throws   `ParseException`

                If the text cannot be parsed.

Description   This method parses arguments from the given string, which
                should be in the format given by the formatting pattern string
                of this `MessageFormat`. If the string is not correctly formatted,
                an exception is thrown.

`public Object[] parse(String source, ParsePosition status)`

Parameters   source   The string to be parsed.

                status   A `ParsePosition` object that specifies a position
                                in the string.

Returns   An array of objects represented by the test starting at the given
                position.

Description   This method parses arguments from the given string, starting at
                the specified position. The string should be in the format given
                by the formatting pattern string of this `MessageFormat`.

parseObject

`public Object parseObject(String text, ParsePosition status)`

Parameters   text   The string to be parsed.

                status   A `ParsePosition` object that specifies a position
                                in the string.

Returns   The object represented by the test starting at the given posi-
                tion.

Overrides   `Format.parseObject(String, ParsePosition)`

Description   This method parses arguments from the given string, starting at
                the specified position. The string should be in the format given
                by the formatting pattern string of this `MessageFormat`.

setFormat

public void setFormat(int variable, Format newFormat)

Parameters   variable   The index of an argument in the pattern string.

                 newFormat   The format object to use.

Description   This method sets the Format object that is used for the given argument in the formatting pattern string.

setFormats

public void setFormats(Format[] newFormats)

Parameters   newFormats   The format objects to use.

Description   This method sets the Format objects that format the arguments of this MessageFormat. Note that formats are numbered according to the order in which they appear in the formatting pattern string, not according to their specified argument numbers.

setLocale

public void setLocale(Locale theLocale)

Parameters   theLocale   The new locale.

Description   This method sets the Locale object that generates the default date, time, and number format objects.

toPattern

public String toPattern()

Returns   The pattern string of this MessageFormat.

Description   This method returns the pattern string of this MessageFormat.

Inherited Methods

Method	Inherited From	Method	Inherited From
finalize()	Object	format(Object)	Format
getClass()	Object	notify()	Object
notifyAll()	Object	parseObject(String)	Format
toString()	Object	wait()	Object
wait(long)	Object	wait(long, int)	Object

See Also

ChoiceFormat, DateFormat, FieldPosition, Format, Locale, NumberFormat, Parse-
Exception, ParsePosition, ResourceBundle, String, StringBuffer

---

16.14 NumberFormat

Synopsis

Class Name:	java.text.NumberFormat
Superclass:	java.text.Format
Immediate Subclasses:	java.text.ChoiceFormat, java.text.DecimalFormat
Interfaces Implemented:	java.lang.Cloneable
Availability:	New as of JDK 1.1

Description

The NumberFormat class formats and parses numbers in a locale-specific manner.
NumberFormat is an abstract class, but it provides factory methods that return useful instances of NumberFormat subclasses. These factory methods come in three
groups:

- The getCurrencyInstance() methods return objects that format and parse
  currency values.
- The getNumberInstance() methods return objects that format and parse normal numbers.
- The getPercentInstance() methods return objects that format percentage
  values.

For example, to format a number as an Italian currency value, you can use this
code:

```
double salary = 1234.56;
System.out.println
  (NumberFormat.getCurrencyInstance(Locale.ITALY).format(salary));
```

This produces the following output:

```
L 1.234,56
```

The NumberFormat class defines two field constants that represent the integer and
fractional fields in a formatted number. These field constants create FieldPosition objects.

Class Summary

```
public abstract class java.text.NumberFormat extends java.text.Format
                       implements java.lang.Cloneable {

// Constants
public static final int FRACTION_FIELD;
public static final int INTEGER_FIELD;

// Class Methods
public static Locale[] getAvailableLocales();
public static final NumberFormat getCurrencyInstance();
public static NumberFormat getCurrencyInstance(Locale inLocale);
public static final NumberFormat getInstance();
public static NumberFormat getInstance(Locale inLocale);
public static final NumberFormat getNumberInstance();
public static NumberFormat getNumberInstance(Locale inLocale);
public static final NumberFormat getPercentInstance();
public static NumberFormat getPercentInstance(Locale inLocale);

// Instance Methods
public Object clone();
public boolean equals(Object obj);
public final String format(double number);
public final String format(long number);
public final StringBuffer format(Object number, StringBuffer toAppendTo,
                       FieldPosition pos);
public abstract StringBuffer format(double number,
                            StringBuffer toAppendTo, FieldPosition pos);
public abstract StringBuffer format(long number, StringBuffer toAppendTo,
                       FieldPosition pos);
public int getMaximumFractionDigits();
public int getMaximumIntegerDigits();
public int getMinimumFractionDigits();
public int getMinimumIntegerDigits();
public int hashCode();
public boolean isGroupingUsed();
public boolean isParseIntegerOnly();
public Number parse(String text);
public abstract Number parse(String text, ParsePosition parsePosition);
public final Object parseObject(String source,
                       ParsePosition parsePosition);
public void setGroupingUsed(boolean newValue);
public void setMaximumFractionDigits(int newValue);
public void setMaximumIntegerDigits(int newValue);
public void setMinimumFractionDigits(int newValue);
public void setMinimumIntegerDigits(int newValue);
public void setParseIntegerOnly(boolean value);
}
```

Constants

FRACTION_FIELD

public final static int FRACTION_FIELD

Description   A field constant that represents the fractional part of the number.

INTEGER_FIELD

public final static int INTEGER_FIELD

Description   A field constant that represents the integer part of the number.

Class Methods

getAvailableLocales

public static Locale[] getAvailableLocales()

Returns   An array of Locale objects.

Description   This method returns an array of the Locale objects for which this class can create NumberFormat objects.

getCurrencyInstance

public static final NumberFormat getCurrencyInstance()

Returns   A NumberFormat appropriate for the default Locale that formats currency values.

Description   This method creates a NumberFormat that formats and parses currency values in the default locale.

public static NumberFormat getCurrencyInstance(Locale inLocale)

Parameters   inLocale   The Locale to use.

Returns   A NumberFormat appropriate for the given Locale that formats currency values.

Description   This method creates a NumberFormat that formats and parses currency values in the given locale.

getInstance

public static final NumberFormat getInstance()

Returns   A default NumberFormat appropriate for the default Locale.

Description   This method creates a default NumberFormat that formats and parses values in the default locale.

public static NumberFormat getInstance(Locale inLocale)

Parameters   inLocale   The Locale to use.

Returns   A default NumberFormat appropriate for the given Locale.

Description   This method creates a NumberFormat that formats and parses values in the given locale.

getNumberInstance

public static final NumberFormat getNumberInstance()

Returns   A NumberFormat appropriate for the default Locale that formats normal numbers.

Description   This method creates a NumberFormat that formats and parses number values in the default locale.

public static NumberFormat getNumberInstance(Locale inLocale)

Parameters   inLocale   The Locale to use.

Returns   A NumberFormat appropriate for the given Locale that formats normal numbers.

Description   This method creates a NumberFormat that formats and parses number values in the given locale.

getPercentInstance

public static final NumberFormat getPercentInstance()

Returns   A NumberFormat appropriate for the default Locale that formats percentage values.

Description   This method creates a NumberFormat that formats and parses percent values in the default locale.

public static NumberFormat getPercentInstance(Locale inLocale)

Parameters   inLocale   The Locale to use.

Returns   A NumberFormat appropriate for the given Locale that formats percentage values.

Description   This method creates a NumberFormat that formats and parses percent values in the given locale.

Instance Methods

clone

public Object clone()

Returns   A copy of this NumberFormat.

Overrides   Format.clone()

Description   This method creates a copy of this NumberFormat and returns it.

equals

```
public boolean equals(Object obj)
```

Parameters	obj The object to be compared with this object.
Returns	true if the objects are equal; false if they are not.
Overrides	Object.equals()
Description	This method returns true if obj is an instance of NumberFormat and is equivalent to this NumberFormat.

format

```
public final String format(double number)
```

Parameters	number The double value to be formatted.
Returns	A string that contains a formatted representation of the value.
Description	This method formats the given number and returns the result as a string.

```
public final String format(long number)
```

Parameters	number The long value to be formatted.
Returns	A string that contains a formatted representation of the value.
Description	This method formats the given number and returns the result as a string.

```
public final StringBuffer format(Object number,
                          StringBuffer toAppendTo,
                          FieldPosition pos)
```

Parameters	number The object to be formatted.
	toAppendTo A StringBuffer on which to append the formatted information.
	pos A number field.
Returns	The given buffer toAppendTo with the formatted representation of the object appended to it.
Overrides	Format.format(Object, StringBuffer, FieldPosition)
Description	This method formats the given object and appends the result to the given StringBuffer. If pos refers to one of the number fields, its beginning and ending indices are filled with the beginning and ending positions of the given field in the resulting formatted string.

```
public abstract StringBuffer format(double number,
                          StringBuffer toAppendTo,
                          FieldPosition pos)
```

Parameters	number The double value to be formatted.

	toAppendTo	A StringBuffer on which to append the formatted information.
	pos	A number field.
Returns		The given buffer toAppendTo with the formatted representation of the object appended to it.
Description		This method formats the given number and appends the result to the given StringBuffer. If pos refers to one of the number fields, its beginning and ending indices are filled with the beginning and ending positions of the given field in the resulting formatted string.

```
public abstract StringBuffer format(long number,
                          StringBuffer toAppendTo,
                          FieldPosition pos)
```

Parameters	number	The long value to be formatted.
	toAppendTo	A StringBuffer on which to append the formatted information.
	pos	A number field.
Returns		The given buffer toAppendTo with the formatted representation of the object appended to it.
Description		This method formats the given number and appends the result to the given StringBuffer. If pos refers to one of the number fields, its beginning and ending indices are filled with the beginning and ending positions of the given field in the resulting formatted string.

getMaximumFractionDigits

```
public int getMaximumFractionDigits()
```

Returns	The maximum number of digits allowed in the fraction portion.
Description	This method returns the maximum number of digits that can be in the fraction part of the number.

getMaximumIntegerDigits

```
public int getMaximumIntegerDigits()
```

Returns	The maximum number of digits allowed in the integer portion.
Description	This method returns the maximum number of digits that can be in the integer part of the number.

getMinimumFractionDigits

public int getMinimumFractionDigits()

Returns   The minimum number of digits allowed in the fraction portion.

Description   This method returns the minimum number of digits that can be in the fraction part of the number.

getMinimumIntegerDigits

public int getMinimumIntegerDigits()

Returns   The minimum number of digits allowed in the integer portion.

Description   This method returns the minimum number of digits that can be in the integer part of the number.

hashCode

public int hashCode()

Returns   A hashcode for this object.

Overrides   Object.hashCode()

Description   This method returns a hashcode for this NumberFormat.

isGroupingUsed

public boolean isGroupingUsed()

Returns   A boolean value that indicates whether or not this NumberFormat uses a grouping character to break up long sequences of digits in the integer part of a number.

Description   This method returns true if this NumberFormat uses a grouping character. For example, it is common in the United States to use a comma as a grouping character: 1,234.56.

isParseIntegerOnly

public boolean isParseIntegerOnly()

Returns   A boolean value that indicates whether or not this NumberFormat parses only integers.

Description   This method returns true if this NumberFormat parses only integers.

parse

public Number parse(String text) throws ParseException

Parameters   text   The string to be parsed.

Returns   The Number object represented by the given string.

Throws   ParseException

                If the text cannot be parsed as a number.

Description | This method parses a number from the given string, starting from the beginning of the string.

```
public abstract Number parse(String text,
                             ParsePosition parsePosition)
```

Parameters | text | The string to be parsed.
| parsePosition |
| | A ParsePosition object that specifies a position in the string.

Returns | The Number object represented by the text starting at the given position.

Description | This method parses a number from the given string, starting from the given position. After the string has been parsed, the given ParsePosition object is updated so that its index is after the parsed text.

parseObject

```
public final Object parseObject(String source,
                                ParsePosition parsePosition)
```

Parameters | source | The string to be parsed.
| parsePosition |
| | A ParsePosition object that specifies a position in the string.

Returns | The object represented by the text starting at the given position.

Overrides | Format.parseObject(String, ParsePosition)

Description | This method parses a number from the given string, starting from the given position. After the string has been parsed, the given ParsePosition object is updated so that its index is after the parsed text.

setGroupingUsed

```
public void setGroupingUsed(boolean newValue)
```

Parameters | newValue | The new grouping flag.

Description | This method sets whether or not this NumberFormat uses a grouping character to break up long sequences of digits in the integer part of a number. For example, it is common in the United States to use a comma as a grouping character: 1,234.56.

setMaximumFractionDigits

```
public void setMaximumFractionDigits(int newValue)
```

Parameters   newValue   The new maximum number of fraction digits.

Description   This method sets the maximum number of digits that may be present in the fraction part of the number. The maximum value must be greater than the minimum number of fraction digits allowed. If the value is less than the current minimum, the minimum is also set to this value.

setMaximumIntegerDigits

```
public void setMaximumIntegerDigits(int newValue)
```

Parameters   newValue   The new maximum number of integer digits.

Description   This method sets the maximum number of digits that may be present in the integer part of the number. The maximum value must be greater than the minimum number of integer digits allowed. If the value is less than the current minimum, the minimum is also set to this value.

setMinimumFractionDigits

```
public void setMinimumFractionDigits(int newValue)
```

Parameters   newValue   The new minimum number of fraction digits.

Description   This method sets the minimum number of digits that may be present in the fraction part of the number. The minimum value must be less than the maximum number of fraction digits allowed. If the value is greater than the current maximum, the maximum is also set to this value.

setMinimumIntegerDigits

```
public void setMinimumIntegerDigits(int newValue)
```

Parameters   newValue   The new minimum number of integer digits.

Description   This method sets the minimum number of digits that may be present in the integer part of the number. The minimum value must be less than the maximum number of integer digits allowed. If the value is greater than the current maximum, the maximum is also set to this value.

setParseIntegerOnly

```
public void setParseIntegerOnly(boolean value)
```

Parameters   value   The new parsing flag.

Description   This method sets whether or not this NumberFormat parses only integers. If the value is true, this NumberFormat only parse integers. Otherwise it parses both the integer and fractional parts of numbers.

Inherited Methods

Method	Inherited From	Method	Inherited From
finalize()	Object	format(Object)	Format
getClass()	Object	notify()	Object
notifyAll()	Object	parseObject(String)	Format
toString()	Object	wait()	Object
wait(long)	Object	wait(long, int)	Object

See Also

ChoiceFormat, DecimalFormat, FieldPosition, Format, Number, ParseException, ParsePosition, String, StringBuffer

16.15   ParseException

Synopsis

Class Name: java.text.ParseException
Superclass: java.lang.Exception
Immediate Subclasses: None
Interfaces Implemented: None
Availability: New as of JDK 1.1

Description

A ParseException is thrown when the text in a string that is being parsed is not in the correct format.

Class Summary

```
public class java.text.ParseException extends java.lang.Exception {
    // Constructors
    public ParseException(String s, int errorOffset);

    // Instance Methods
    public int getErrorOffset();
}
```

Constructors

ParseException

public ParseException(String s, int errorOffset)

Parameters	s	The detail message.
	errorOffset	The offset at which the parsing error occurred.
Description		This constructor creates a ParseException with the given detail message and offset.

Instance Methods

getErrorOffset

public int getErrorOffset()

Returns	The error offset.
Description	This method returns the offset at which the parsing error occurred.

Inherited Methods

Method	Inherited From	Method	Inherited From
clone()	Object	equals(Object)	Object
fillInStackTrace()	Throwable	finalize()	Object
getClass()	Object	getLocalizedMessage()	Throwable
getMessage()	Throwable	hashCode()	Object
notify()	Object	notifyAll()	Object
printStackTrace()	Throwable	printStack-Trace(PrintStream)	Throwable
printStack-Trace(PrintWriter)	Throwable	toString()	Throwable
wait()	Object	wait(long)	Object
wait(long, int)	Object		

See Also

DateFormat, Exception, Format, MessageFormat, NumberFormat

16.16   ParsePosition

Synopsis

Class Name: java.text.ParsePosition
Superclass: java.lang.Object
Immediate Subclasses: None
Interfaces Implemented: None
Availability: New as of JDK 1.1

Description

The ParsePosition class encapsulates information about the current position in a text string. A ParsePosition can be passed to the parse() method of a Format subclass to cause parsing to start at the index of the ParsePosition. After an object has been parsed from the string, the index of the ParsePosition is updated to point to just after the text that was parsed. Thus, the same ParsePosition can be passed to multiple Format objects to parse through a complex string.

Class Summary

```
public class java.text.ParsePosition extends java.lang.Object {
    // Constructors
    public ParsePosition(int index);

    // Instance Methods
    public int getIndex();
    public void setIndex(int index);
}
```

Constructors

ParsePosition

public ParsePosition(int index)

    Parameters   index   The initial position.

    Description   This constructor creates a ParsePosition object that is initialized to the given position.

Instance Methods

getIndex

public int getIndex()

    Returns   The current position of this ParsePosition.

    Description   This method returns the current position of this ParsePosition.

setIndex

```
public void setIndex(int index)
```
Parameters   index   The new position of this `ParsePosition`.

Description   This method sets the current position of this `ParsePosition`.

Inherited Methods

Method	Inherited From	Method	Inherited From
clone()	Object	equals(Object)	Object
finalize()	Object	getClass()	Object
hashCode()	Object	notify()	Object
notifyAll()	Object	toString()	Object
wait()	Object	wait(long)	Object
wait(long, int)	Object		

See Also

DateFormat, FieldPosition, Format, MessageFormat, NumberFormat, String

16.17   *RuleBasedCollator*

Synopsis

Class Name: java.text.RuleBasedCollator

Superclass: java.text.Collator

Immediate Subclasses: None

Interfaces Implemented: None

Availability: New as of JDK 1.1

Description

The `RuleBasedCollator` class is a concrete subclass of `Collator` that can compare strings using a table of rules. The rules for many locales already exist. To get a useful `Collator` for a given locale, use the `getInstance(Locale)` factory method of `Collator`.

If you need a special-purpose `Collator` or a `Collator` for a new locale, you can create your own `RuleBasedCollator` from a string that represents the rules. The rules are expressed in three primary forms:

```
[relation] [text]
[reset] [text]
[modifier]
```

The rules can be chained together. The only modifier is the @ character, which specifies that all diacriticals are sorted backwards, as in French.

The valid relations are:

> Greater than as a primary difference
; Greater than as a secondary difference or difference in accent
, Greater than as a tertiary difference or difference in case
= Equal

For example "<a<b" is two chained rules that state that 'a' is greater than all ignorable characters, and 'b' is greater than 'a'. To expand this rule to include capitals, use "<a,A<b,B".

A reset, specified by the & character, is used to insert rules in an existing list of chained rules. For example, we can add a rule to sort 'e' with an umlaut (Unicode 0308) after plain 'e'. The existing rules might look like "<a<b<c<d<e<f". We can add the following reset, "&e;e\u0308", so that the complete rule table looks like "<a<b<c<d<e<f&e;e\u0308".

Class Summary

```
public class java.text.RuleBasedCollator extends java.text.Collator {
    // Constructors
    public RuleBasedCollator(String rules);

    // Instance Methods
    public Object clone();
    public int compare(String source, String target);
    public boolean equals(Object obj);
    public CollationElementIterator
        getCollationElementIterator( String source);
    public CollationKey getCollationKey(String source);
    public String getRules();
    public int hashCode();
}
```

Constructors

RuleBasedCollator

public RuleBasedCollator(String rules) throws ParseException

Parameters	rules	A string that contains the rules.
Throws	ParseException	
		If the given rules are incorrectly formed.
Description		This constructor creates a RuleBasedCollator with the given rules.

Instance Methods

clone

public Object clone()

Returns	A copy of this RuledBasedCollator.
Overrides	Collator.clone()
Description	This method creates a copy of this RuledBasedCollator and returns it.

compare

public int compare(String source, String target)

Parameters	source	The source string.
	target	The target string.
Returns	-1 if source is less than target, 0 if the strings are equal, or 1 if source is greater than target.	
Overrides	Collator.compare()	
Description	This method compares the given strings according to the rules for this RuleBasedCollator and returns a value that indicates their relationship. If either of the strings are compared more than once, a CollationKey should be used instead.	

equals

public boolean equals(Object obj)

Parameters	obj	The object to be compared with this object.
Returns	true if the objects are equal; false if they are not.	
Overrides	Collator.equals()	
Description	This method returns true if obj is an instance of RuleBased-Collator and is equivalent to this RuleBasedCollator.	

getCollationElementIterator

public CollationElementIterator getCollationElementIterator(
                                    String source)

Parameters	source	The source string.
Returns	A CollationElementIterator for the given string.	
Description	This method generates a CollationElementIterator for the given string.	

getCollationKey

public CollationKey getCollationKey(String source)

Parameters	source	The source string.

Returns	A CollationKey for the given string.
Overrides	Collator.getCollationKey()
Description	This method generates a CollationKey for the given string. The returned object can be compared with other CollationKey objects using CollationKey.compareTo(). This comparison is faster than using RuleBasedCollator.compare(), so if the same string is used for many comparisons, you should use CollationKey objects.

getRules

public String getRules()

Returns	The rules string for this RuleBasedCollator.
Description	This method returns a string that contains the rules that this RuleBasedCollator is using.

hashCode

public int hashCode()

Returns	A hashcode for this object.
Overrides	Collator.hashCode()
Description	This method returns a hashcode for this RuleBasedCollator.

Inherited Methods

Method	Inherited From	Method	Inherited From
equals(String, String)	Collator	finalize()	Object
getClass()	Object	getDecomposition()	Collator
getStrength()	Collator	notify()	Object
notifyAll()	Object	setDecomposition(int)	Collator
setStrength(int)	Collator	toString()	Object
wait()	Object	wait(long)	Object
wait(long, int)	Object		

See Also

CollationKey, CollationElementIterator, Collator, Locale, ParseException, String

16.18   *SimpleDateFormat*

Synopsis

Class Name: `java.text.SimpleDateFormat`
Superclass: `java.text.DateFormat`
Immediate Subclasses: None
Interfaces Implemented: None
Availability: New as of JDK 1.1

Description

The `SimpleDateFormat` class is a concrete subclass of `DateFormat` that formats and parses dates and times using a formatting pattern. Typically, you do not need to instantiate `SimpleDateFormat` yourself. Instead, the factory methods of `DateFormat` return instances of `SimpleDateFormat` that are appropriate for particular locales.

However, if you need a specialized date and time format, you can instantiate your own `SimpleDateFormat` using a pattern string. You can also modify the formatting pattern of an existing `SimpleDateFormat` object using the `applyPattern()` method. The following symbols are significant in the pattern string.

Symbol	Description	Example	Type
G	Era	AD	Text
y	Year	1997	Numeric
M	Month in year	3 or March	Text or numeric
d	Day in month	4	Numeric
h	Hour in A.M./P.M. (1-12)	2	Numeric
H	Hour in day (0-23)	14	Numeric
m	Minute in hour	33	Numeric
s	Second in minute	21	Numeric
S	Milliseconds	333	Numeric
E	Day of week	Thursday	Text
D	Day in year	63	Numeric
F	Day of week of month	1	Numeric
w	Week in year	9	Numeric
W	Week in month	1	Numeric
a	A.M./P.M.	P.M.	Text
k	Hour in day (1-24)	14	Numeric
K	Hour in A.M./P.M. (0-11)	2	Numeric
z	Time zone	EST	Text

Symbols that are numeric can be repeated to specify a minimum number of digits. For example, "hh" produces an hour field that is always at least two digits, like

`"02"`. Symbols that are textual can be repeated to specify whether the short form or the long form of the text string is used, if there are both short and long forms. If four or more symbols are specified, the long form is used; otherwise the short form is used. For example, `"E"` produces a short form of the day of the week, such as `"Tue"`, while `"EEEE"` produces the long form, such as `"Tuesday"`. For the month of the year, if one or two `"M"` symbols are used, the field is numeric. If three or more `"M"` symbols are used, the field is textual.

Single quotes can be used to specify literal text that should be included in the formatted output, and any unrecognized symbol is treated as literal text. For example, the following pattern:

```
hh:mm a 'in the' zzzz 'zone.'
```

produces output like:

```
02:33 PM in the Eastern Standard Time zone.
```

Internally, the `SimpleDataFormat` class uses a `DateFormatSymbols` object to get the date and time strings that are appropriate for a particular locale. If you want to modify these strings, you can get the `DateFormatSymbols` object by calling `get-DateFormatSymbols()`.

Class Summary

```
public class java.text.SimpleDateFormat  extends java.text.DateFormat {
    // Constructors
    public SimpleDateFormat();
    public SimpleDateFormat(String pattern);
    public SimpleDateFormat(String pattern, Locale loc);
    public SimpleDateFormat(String pattern, DateFormatSymbols formatData);

    // Instance Methods
    public void applyLocalizedPattern(String pattern);
    public void applyPattern(String pattern);
    public Object clone();
    public boolean equals(Object obj);
    public StringBuffer format(Date date, StringBuffer toAppendTo,
                    FieldPosition pos);
    public DateFormatSymbols getDateFormatSymbols();
    public int hashCode();
    public Date parse(String text, ParsePosition pos);
    public void setDateFormatSymbols(DateFormatSymbols newFormatSymbols);
    public String toLocalizedPattern();
    public String toPattern();
}
```

Constructors

SimpleDateFormat

public SimpleDateFormat()

Description   This constructor creates a SimpleDateFormat that uses a default
formatting pattern and DateFormatSymbols that are appropri-
ate for the default locale. It produces the same result as calling
DateFormat.getDateTimeInstance(DateFormat.SHORT, Date-
Format.SHORT).

public SimpleDateFormat(String pattern)

Parameters   pattern   The pattern string.

Description   This constructor creates a SimpleDateFormat that uses the
given formatting pattern and a DateFormatSymbols object that
is appropriate for the default locale.

public SimpleDateFormat(String pattern, Locale loc)

Parameters   pattern   The pattern string.
loc   The Locale to use.

Description   This constructor creates a SimpleDateFormat that uses the
given formatting pattern and a DateFormatSymbols object that
is appropriate for the given locale.

public SimpleDateFormat(String pattern,
                        DateFormatSymbols formatData)

Parameters   pattern   The pattern string.
formatData   The DateFormatSymbols to use.

Description   This constructor creates a SimpleDateFormat that uses the
given formatting pattern and DateFormatSymbols object.

Instance Methods

applyLocalizedPattern

public void applyLocalizedPattern(String pattern)

Parameters   pattern   The pattern string.

Description   This method tells this SimpleDateFormat to use the given for-
mating pattern to format and parse dates and times. The pattern string is assumed to have been localized to the DateFormatSymbols object this SimpleDateFormat uses.

applyPattern

public void applyPattern(String pattern)

Parameters   pattern   The pattern string.

Description   This method tells this SimpleDateFormat to use the given formatting pattern to format and parse dates and times. The pattern string is localized to the DateFormatSymbols object this SimpleDateFormat uses.

clone

```
public Object clone()
```
Returns   A copy of this SimpleDateFormat.

Overrides   DateFormat.clone()

Description   This method creates a copy of this SimpleDateFormat and returns it.

equals

```
public boolean equals(Object obj)
```
Parameters   obj   The object to be compared with this object.

Returns   true if the objects are equal; false if they are not.

Overrides   DateFormat.equals()

Description   This method returns true if obj is an instance of SimpleDateFormat and is equivalent to this SimpleDateFormat.

format

```
public StringBuffer format(Date date, StringBuffer toAppendTo,
                FieldPosition pos)
```
Parameters   date   The Date object to be formatted.

toAppendTo   A StringBuffer on which to append the formatted information.

pos   A date or time field.

Returns   The given buffer toAppendTo with the formatted representation of the object appended to it.

Overrides   DateFormat.format(Date, StringBuffer, FieldPosition)

Description   This method formats the given date and appends the result to the given StringBuffer. If pos refers to one of the time or date fields, its beginning and ending indexes are filled with the beginning and ending positions of the given field in the resulting formatted string.

getDateFormatSymbols

```
public DateFormatSymbols getDateFormatSymbols()
```
Returns   The DateFormatSymbols object used by this SimpleDateFormat.

Description   This method returns the DateFormatSymbols object that this SimpleDateFormat uses internally.

hashCode

`public int hashCode()`

Returns   A hashcode for this object.

Overrides   `DateFormat.hashCode()`

Description   This method returns a hashcode for this SimpleDateFormat.

parse

`public Date parse(String text, ParsePosition pos)`

Parameters   text   The string to be parsed.

pos   A ParsePosition object that specifies a position in the string.

Returns   The Date object represented by the text starting at the given position.

Overrides   `DateFormat.parse(String, ParsePosition)`

Description   This method parses a date from the given string, starting from the given position. After the string has been parsed, the given ParsePosition object is updated so that its index is after the parsed text.

setDateFormatSymbols

`public void setDateFormatSymbols(`
`        DateFormatSymbols newFormatSymbols)`

Parameters   newFormatSymbols

The new DateFormatSymbols object to use.

Description   This method sets the DateFormatSymbols object that this SimpleDateFormat uses internally.

toLocalizedPattern

`public String toLocalizedPattern()`

Returns   The pattern string of this SimpleDateFormat.

Description   This method returns the pattern string of this SimpleDateFormat, localized with the DateFormatSymbols object of this SimpleDateFormat.

toPattern

```
public String toPattern()
```

Returns   The pattern string of this SimpleDateFormat.

Description   This method returns the pattern string of this SimpleDateFormat.

Inherited Methods

Method	Inherited From	Method	Inherited From
finalize()	Object	format(Object)	Format
format(Date)	DateFormat	format(Object, String-Buffer, FieldPosition)	DateFormat
getCalendar()	DateFormat	getClass()	Object
getNumberFormat()	DateFormat	getTimeZone()	DateFormat
isLenient()	DateFormat	notify()	Object
notifyAll()	Object	parse(String)	DateFormat
parseObject(String)	Format	parseObject(String, ParsePosition)	DateFormat
setCalendar(Calendar)	DateFormat	setLenient(boolean)	DateFormat
setNumberFormat(NumberFormat)	DateFormat	setTimeZone(TimeZone)	DateFormat
toString()	Object	wait()	Object
wait(long)	Object	wait(long, int)	Object

See Also

Calendar, Date, DateFormat, DateFormatSymbols, FieldPosition, Format, Locale, ParsePosition, String, StringBuffer, TimeZone

16.19   *StringCharacterIterator*

Synopsis

Class Name: java.text.StringCharacterIterator

Superclass: java.lang.Object

Immediate Subclasses: None

Interfaces Implemented: java.text.CharacterIterator

Availability: New as of JDK 1.1

Description

The StringCharacterIterator class can move bidirectionally through a character string. In other words, the class iterates through the characters in a String. The class implements the CharacterIterator interface. The class is used by BreakIterator to find boundaries in text strings.

Class Summary

```
public final class java.text.StringCharacterIterator
                extends java.lang.Object
                implements java.text.CharacterIterator {
// Constructors
public StringCharacterIterator(String text);
public StringCharacterIterator(String text, int pos);
public StringCharacterIterator(String text, int begin, int end, int pos);

// Instance Methods
public Object clone();
public char current();
public boolean equals(Object obj);
public char first();
public int getBeginIndex();
public int getEndIndex();
public int getIndex();
public int hashCode();
public char last();
public char next();
public char previous();
public char setIndex(int p);
}
```

Constructors

StringCharacterIterator

public StringCharacterIterator(String text)

Parameters	text	The String to use.
Description		This constructor creates a StringCharacterIterator that uses the given string. The initial index of the iterator is at the beginning of the string, or in other words, at index 0.

public StringCharacterIterator(String text, int pos)

Parameters	text	The String to use.
	pos	The initial position.
Description		This constructor creates a StringCharacterIterator that uses the given string. The initial index of the iterator is set to the given initial position.

```
public StringCharacterIterator(String text, int begin,
                               int end, int pos)
```
Parameters   text   The String to use.

begin   The beginning index.

end   The ending index.

pos   The initial position.

Description   This constructor creates a StringCharacterIterator that uses the specified range of the given string. In other words, the iterator uses the sequence of text from the specified beginning index to the specified ending index. The initial index of the iterator is set to the given initial position.

Instance Methods

clone

```
public Object clone()
```
Returns   A copy of this StringCharacterIterator.

Implements   CharacterIterator.clone()

Overrides   Object.clone()

Description   This method creates a copy of this StringCharacterIterator and returns it.

current

```
public char current()
```
Returns   The character at the current position of this StringCharacterIterator or DONE if the current position is not within the text sequence.

Implements   CharacterIterator.current()

Description   This method returns the character at the current position of this CharacterIterator. The current position is returned by getIndex().

equals

```
public boolean equals(Object obj)
```
Parameters   obj   The object to be compared with this object.

Returns   true if the objects are equal; false if they are not.

Overrides   Object.equals()

Description   This method returns true if obj is an instance of StringCharacterIterator and is equivalent to this StringCharacterIterator.

first

```
public char first()
```

Returns	The first character in this StringCharacterIterator.
Implements	CharacterIterator.first()
Description	This method returns the character at the first position in this StringCharacterIterator. The first position is returned by getBeginIndex(). The current position of the iterator is set to this position.

getBeginIndex

```
public int getBeginIndex()
```

Returns	The index of the first character in this StringCharacterIterator.
Implements	CharacterIterator.getBeginIndex()
Description	This method returns the index of the beginning of the text for this StringCharacterIterator.

getEndIndex

```
public int getEndIndex()
```

Returns	The index after the last character in this StringCharacterIterator.
Implements	CharacterIterator.getEndIndex()
Description	This method returns the index of the character following the end of the text for this StringCharacterIterator.

getIndex

```
public int getIndex()
```

Returns	The index of the current character in this StringCharacterIterator.
Description	This method returns the current position, or index, of this StringCharacterIterator.

hashCode

```
public int hashCode()
```

Returns	A hashcode for this object.
Overrides	Object.hashCode()
Description	This method returns a hashcode for this StringCharacterIterator.

last

public char last()

Returns	The last character in this StringCharacterIterator.
Implements	CharacterIterator.last()
Description	This method returns the character at the ending position of this StringCharacterIterator. The last position is the value of getEndIndex()-1. The current position of the iterator is set to this position.

next

public char next()

Returns	The next character in this StringCharacterIterator or DONE if the current position is already at the end of the text.
Implements	CharacterIterator.next()
Description	This method increments the current position of this StringCharacterIterator by 1 and returns the character at the new position. If the current position is already at getEndIndex(), the position is not changed and DONE is returned.

previous

public char previous()

Returns	The previous character in this StringCharacterIterator or DONE if the current position is already at the beginning of the text.
Implements	CharacterIterator.previous()
Description	This method decrements the current position of this StringCharacterIterator by 1 and returns the character at the new position. If the current position is already at getBeginIndex(), the position is not changed and DONE is returned.

setIndex

public char setIndex(int p)

Parameters	p	The new position.
Returns		The character at the specified position in this StringCharacterIterator.
Throws		IllegalArgumentException
		If the given position is not between getBeginIndex() and getEndIndex()-1.
Implements		CharacterIterator.setIndex()

Description   This method sets the current position, or index, of this StringCharacterIterator to the given position.

Inherited Methods

Method	Inherited From	Method	Inherited From
finalize()	Object	getClass()	Object
notify()	Object	notifyAll()	Object
toString()	Object	wait()	Object
wait(long)	Object	wait(long, int)	Object

See Also

BreakIterator, CharacterIterator, String

17

The java.util Package

The package `java.util` contains a number of useful classes and interfaces. Although the name of the package might imply that these are utility classes, they are really more important than that. In fact, Java depends directly on several of the classes in this package, and many programs will find these classes indispensable. The classes and interfaces in `java.util` include:

- The `Hashtable` class for implementing hashtables, or associative arrays.
- The `Vector` class, which supports variable-length arrays.
- The `Enumeration` interface for iterating through a collection of elements.
- The `StringTokenizer` class for parsing strings into distinct tokens separated by delimiter characters.
- The `EventObject` class and the `EventListener` interface, which form the basis of the new AWT event model in Java 1.1.
- The `Locale` class in Java 1.1, which represents a particular locale for internationalization purposes.
- The `Calendar` and `TimeZone` classes in Java. These classes interpret the value of a `Date` object in the context of a particular calendar system.
- The `ResourceBundle` class and its subclasses, `ListResourceBundle` and `PropertyResourceBundle`, which represent sets of localized data in Java 1.1.

Figure 17-1 shows the class hierarchy for the `java.util` package.

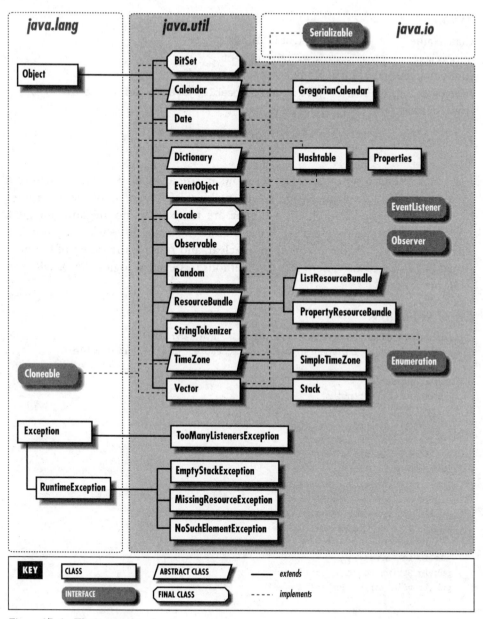

Figure 17–1: The java.util package

17.1   BitSet

Synopsis

Class Name: java.util.BitSet

Superclass: java.lang.Object

Immediate Subclasses: None

Interfaces Implemented: java.lang.Cloneable, java.io.Serializable

Availability: JDK 1.0 or later

Description

The BitSet
 class implements a set of bits. The set grows in size as needed. Each element of a BitSet has a boolean value. When a BitSet object is created, all of the bits are set to false by default. The bits in a BitSet are indexed by nonnegative integers, starting at 0. The size of a BitSet is the number of bits that it currently contains. The BitSet class provides methods to set, clear, and retrieve the values of the individual bits in a BitSet. There are also methods to perform logical AND, OR, and XOR operations.

Class Summary

```
public final class java.util.BitSet extends java.lang.Object
                    implements java.lang.Cloneable, java.io.Serializable {
    // Constructors
    public BitSet();
    public BitSet(int nbits);

    // Instance Methods
    public void and(BitSet set);
    public void clear(int bit);
    public Object clone();
    public boolean equals(Object obj);
    public boolean get(int bit);
    public int hashCode();
    public void or(BitSet set);
    public void set(int bit);
    public int size();
    public String toString();
    public void xor(BitSet set);
}
```

Constructors

BitSet

public BitSet()

Description   This constructor creates a BitSet with a default size of 64 bits. All of the bits in the BitSet are initially set to false.

public BitSet(int nbits)

Parameters   nbits   The initial number of bits.

Description   This constructor creates a BitSet with a size of nbits. All of the bits in the BitSet are initially set to false.

Instance Methods

and

public void and(BitSet set)

Parameters   set   The BitSet to AND with this BitSet.

Description   This method computes the logical AND of this BitSet and the specified BitSet and stores the result in this BitSet. In other words, for each bit in this BitSet, the value is set to only true if the bit is already true in this BitSet and the corresponding bit in set is true.

If the size of set is greater than the size of this BitSet, the extra bits in set are ignored. If the size of set is less than the size of this BitSet, the extra bits in this BitSet are set to false.

clear

public void clear(int bit)

Parameters   bit   The index of the bit to clear.

Description   This method sets the bit at the given index to false. If bit is greater than or equal to the number of bits in the BitSet, the size of the BitSet is increased so that it contains bit values. All of the additional bits are set to false.

clone

public Object clone()

Returns   A copy of this BitSet.

Overrides   Object.clone()

Description   This method creates a copy of this BitSet and returns it. In other words, the returned BitSet has the same size as this BitSet, and it has the same bits set to true.

equals

`public boolean equals(Object obj)`

Parameters	obj	The object to be compared with this object.
Returns	true if the objects are equal; false if they are not.	
Overrides	Object.equals()	
Description	This method returns true if obj is an instance of BitSet and it contains the same bit values as the object this method is associated with. In other words, this method compares each bit of this BitSet with the corresponding bit of obj. If any bits do not match, the method returns false. If the size of this BitSet is different than obj, the extra bits in either this BitSet or in obj must be false for this method to return true.	

get

`public boolean get(int bit)`

Parameters	bit	The index of the bit to retrieve.
Returns	The boolean value of the bit at the given index.	
Description	This method returns the value of the given bit. If bit is greater than or equal to the number of bits in the BitSet, the method returns false.	

hashCode

`public int hashCode()`

Returns	The hashcode for this BitSet.
Overrides	Object.hashCode()
Description	This method returns a hashcode for this object.

or

`public void or(BitSet set)`

Parameters	set	The BitSet to OR with this BitSet.
Description	This method computes the logical OR of this BitSet and the specified BitSet, and stores the result in this BitSet. In other words, for each bit in this BitSet, the value is set to true if the bit is already true in this BitSet or the corresponding bit in set is true.	

If the size of set is greater than the size of this BitSet, this BitSet is first increased in size to accommodate the additional bits. All of the additional bits are initially set to false.

set

```
public void set(int bit)
```
Parameters   bit   The index of the bit to set.

Description   This method sets the bit at the given index to true. If bit is greater than or equal to the number of bits in the BitSet, the size of the BitSet is increased so that it contains bit values. All of the additional bits except the last one are set to false.

size

```
public int size()
```
Returns   The size of this BitSet.

Description   This method returns the size of this BitSet, which is the number of bits currently in the set.

toString

```
public String toString()
```
Returns   A string representation of this BitSet.

Overrides   Object.toString()

Description   This method returns a string representation of this BitSet. The string lists the indexes of all the bits in the BitSet that are true.

xor

```
public void xor(BitSet set)
```
Parameters   set   The BitSet to XOR with this BitSet.

Description   This method computes the logical XOR (exclusive OR) of this BitSet and the specified BitSet and stores the result in this BitSet. In other words, for each bit in this BitSet, the value is set to true only if the bit is already true in this BitSet, and the corresponding bit in set is false, or if the bit is false in this BitSet and the corresponding bit in set is true.

If the size of set is greater than the size of this BitSet, this BitSet is first increased in size to accommodate the additional bits. All of the additional bits are initially set to false.

Inherited Methods

Method	Inherited From	Method	Inherited From
finalize()	Object	getClass()	Object
notify()	Object	notifyAll()	Object
wait()	Object	wait(long)	Object
wait(long, int)	Object		

See Also

Cloneable, Serializable

17.2   Calendar

Synopsis

Class Name:	java.util.Calendar
Superclass:	java.lang.Object
Immediate Subclasses:	java.util.GregorianCalendar
Interfaces Implemented:	java.lang.Cloneable, java.io.Serializable
Availability:	New as of JDK 1.1

Description

The Calendar class is an abstractclass that is used to convert between Date objects, which represent points in time, and calendar fields, like months or days of the week. The JDK 1.0 Date class included calendar and text-formatting methods. As of JDK 1.1, both of these functions have been split off from Date in order to support internationalization. As of JDK 1.1, Date represents only a point in time, measured in milliseconds. A subclass of Calendar examines the Date in the context of a particular calendar system; a Calendar instance is a locale-sensitive object. Also as of JDK 1.1, the java.text.DateFormat class generates and parses strings representing points in time.

Calendar defines a number of symbolic constants. They represent either fields or values. For example, MONTH is a field constant. It can be passed to get() and set() to retrieve and adjust the month. AUGUST, on the other hand, represents a particular month value. Calling get(Calendar.MONTH) could return Calendar.AUGUST.

Internally, Calendar keeps track of a point in time in two ways. First, a "raw" value is maintained, which is simply a count of milliseconds since midnight, January 1, 1970 GMT, or, in other words, a Date object. Second, the calendar keeps track of a number of fields, which are the values that are specific to the Calendar type. These are values such as day of the week, day of the month, and month. The raw millisecond value can be calculated from the field values, or vice versa.

When a Date object is computed from the time fields, there may be insufficient information to compute the raw millisecond value. For example, the year and the month could be set, but not the day of the month. In this case, Calendar uses default information to fill in the missing fields. For GregorianCalendar, the default field values are taken from the date of the epoch, or midnight, January 1, 1970 GMT.

Another problem that can arise when computing a Date object from the time fields is that of inconsistent information in the fields. For example, the time fields could specify "Sunday, March 8, 1997" when in fact March 8, 1997 is a Saturday. If the time fields contain inconsistent information, Calendar gives preference to the combinations of fields in the following order:

1. month and day of the week
2. month, week of the month, and day of the week
3. month, day of the week in the month, and day of the week
4. day of the year
5. day of the week and week of the year
6. hour of the day
7. A.M./P.M. and hour of A.M./P.M.

There is also the possibility of ambiguity for certain points in time, so the following rules apply. The time 24:00:00 belongs to the next day and midnight is an A.M. time, while noon is a P.M. time.

Class Summary

```
public abstract class java.util.Calendar extends java.lang.Object
                      implements java.lang.Cloneable, java.io.Serializable {
    // Constants
    public final static int AM;
    public final static int AM_PM;
    public final static int APRIL;
    public final static int AUGUST;
    public final static int DATE;
    public final static int DAY_OF_MONTH;
    public final static int DAY_OF_WEEK;
    public final static int DAY_OF_WEEK_IN_MONTH;
    public final static int DAY_OF_YEAR;
    public final static int DECEMBER;
    public final static int DST_OFFSET;
    public final static int ERA;
    public final static int FEBRUARY;
    public final static int FIELD_COUNT;
    public final static int FRIDAY;
```

```
public final static int HOUR;
public final static int HOUR_OF_DAY;
public final static int JANUARY;
public final static int JULY;
public final static int JUNE;
public final static int MARCH;
public final static int MAY;
public final static int MILLISECOND;
public final static int MINUTE;
public final static int MONDAY;
public final static int MONTH;
public final static int NOVEMBER;
public final static int OCTOBER;
public final static int PM;
public final static int SATURDAY;
public final static int SECOND;
public final static int SEPTEMBER;
public final static int SUNDAY;
public final static int THURSDAY;
public final static int TUESDAY;
public final static int UNDECIMBER;
public final static int WEDNESDAY;
public final static int WEEK_OF_MONTH;
public final static int WEEK_OF_YEAR;
public final static int YEAR;
public final static int ZONE_OFFSET;

// Variables
protected boolean areFieldsSet;
protected int[] fields;
protected boolean[] isSet;
protected boolean isTimeSet;
protected long time;

// Constructors
protected Calendar();
protected Calendar(TimeZone zone, Locale aLocale);

// Class Methods
public static synchronized Locale[] getAvailableLocales();
public static synchronized Calendar getInstance();
public static synchronized Calendar getInstance(TimeZone zone);
public static synchronized Calendar getInstance(Locale aLocale);
public static synchronized Calendar getInstance(TimeZone zone,
                                    Locale aLocale);

// Instance Methods
public abstract void add(int field, int amount);
public abstract boolean after(Object when);
```

```
public abstract boolean before(Object when);
public final void clear();
public final void clear(int field);
public Object clone();
public abstract boolean equals(Object when);
public final int get(int field);
public int getFirstDayOfWeek();
public abstract int getGreatestMinimum(int field);
public abstract int getLeastMaximum(int field);
public abstract int getMaximum(int field);
public int getMinimalDaysInFirstWeek();
public abstract int getMinimum(int field);
public final Date getTime();
public TimeZone getTimeZone();
public boolean isLenient();
public final boolean isSet(int field);
public abstract void roll(int field, boolean up);
public final void set(int field, int value);
public final void set(int year, int month, int date);
public final void set(int year, int month, int date,
                      int hour, int minute);
public final void set(int year, int month, int date, int hour,
                      int minute, int second);
public void setFirstDayOfWeek(int value);
public void setLenient(boolean lenient);
public void setMinimalDaysInFirstWeek(int value);
public final void setTime(Date date);
public void setTimeZone(TimeZone value);

// Protected Instance Methods
protected void complete();
protected abstract void computeFields();
protected abstract void computeTime();
protected long getTimeInMillis();
protected final int internalGet(int field);
protected void setTimeInMillis(long millis);
}
```

Constants

AM

```
public final static int AM
```

> Description   A constant value that represents morning times.

AM_PM

> public final static int AM_PM
>> Description   A field constant that represents the A.M./P.M. flag of this object.

APRIL

> public final static int APRIL
>> Description   A constant value that represents the month of April.

AUGUST

> public final static int AUGUST
>> Description   A constant value that represents the month of August.

DATE

> public final static int DATE
>> Description   A field constant that represents the day of the month of this object.

DAY_OF_MONTH

> public final static int DAY_OF_MONTH
>> Description   A field constant that represents the day of the month of this object. This field is synonymous with DATE.

DAY_OF_WEEK

> public final static int DAY_OF_WEEK
>> Description   A field constant that represents the day of the week of this object.

DAY_OF_WEEK_IN_MONTH

> public final static int DAY_OF_WEEK_IN_MONTH
>> Description   A field constant that represents the day of the week in the current month. For example, February 10, 1997, has a DAY_OF_WEEK_IN_MONTH value of 2 because it is the second Monday in February for that year.

DAY_OF_YEAR

> public final static int DAY_OF_YEAR
>> Description   A field constant that represents the day of the year of this object. January 1 is the first day of the year.

DECEMBER

public final static int DECEMBER

Description   A constant value that represents the month of December.

DST_OFFSET

public final static int DST_OFFSET

Description   A field constant that represents the offset due to daylight savings time, in milliseconds, of this object.

ERA

public final static int ERA

Description   A field constant that represents the era of this object. A Gregorian calendar has two eras, BC and AD.

FEBRUARY

public final static int FEBRUARY

Description   A constant value that represents the month of February.

FIELD_COUNT

public final static int FIELD_COUNT

Description   A constant that represents the number of attribute fields for Calendar objects.

FRIDAY

public final static int FRIDAY

Description   A constant value that represents the day Friday.

HOUR

public final static int HOUR

Description   A field constant that represents the hour of this object.

HOUR_OF_DAY

public final static int HOUR_OF_DAY

Description   A field constant that represents the hour of the day of this object. A time of 1:00 P.M. has an HOUR value of 1, but an HOUR_OF_DAY value of 13.

JANUARY

`public final static int JANUARY`
  Description   A constant value that represents the month of January.

JULY

`public final static int JULY`
  Description   A constant value that represents the month of July.

JUNE

`public final static int JUNE`
  Description   A constant value that represents the month of June.

MARCH

`public final static int MARCH`
  Description   A constant value that represents the month of March.

MAY

`public final static int MAY`
  Description   A constant value that represents the month of May.

MILLISECOND

`public final static int MILLISECOND`
  Description   A field constant that represents the milliseconds of this object.

MINUTE

`public final static int MINUTE`
  Description   A field constant that represents the minutes of this object.

MONDAY

`public final static int MONDAY`
  Description   A constant value that represents the day Monday.

MONTH

`public final static int MONTH`
  Description   A field constant that represents the month of this object.

NOVEMBER

`public final static int NOVEMBER`
  Description   A constant value that represents the month of November.

OCTOBER

public final static int OCTOBER

Description   A constant value that represents the month of October.

PM

public final static int PM

Description   A constant value that represents afternoon and evening times.

SATURDAY

public final static int SATURDAY

Description   A constant value that represents the day Saturday.

SECOND

public final static int SECOND

Description   A field constant that represents the seconds of this object.

SEPTEMBER

public final static int SEPTEMBER

Description   A constant value that represents the month of September.

SUNDAY

public final static int SUNDAY

Description   A constant value that represents the day Sunday.

THURSDAY

public final static int THURSDAY

Description   A constant value that represents the day Thursday.

TUESDAY

public final static int TUESDAY

Description   A constant value that represents the day Tuesday.

UNDECIMBER

public final static int UNDECIMBER

Description   A constant value that represents the thirteenth month used in lunar calendars.

WEDNESDAY

```
public final static int WEDNESDAY
```
    Description   A constant value that represents the day Wednesday.

WEEK_OF_MONTH

```
public final static int WEEK_OF_MONTH
```
    Description   A field constant that represents the week of the month of this object.

WEEK_OF_YEAR

```
public final static int WEEK_OF_YEAR
```
    Description   A field constant that represents the week of the year of this object.

YEAR

```
public final static int YEAR
```
    Description   A field constant that represents the year of this object.

ZONE_OFFSET

```
public final static int ZONE_OFFSET
```
    Description   A field constant that represents the raw time zone offset, in milliseconds, of this object. The value should be added to GMT to get local time.

Variables

areFieldsSet

```
protected boolean areFieldsSet
```
    Description   A boolean value that indicates if the time fields of this Calendar have been set. These fields can be computed from the raw millisecond time value.

fields

```
protected int[] fields
```
    Description   An array that stores the time field values for this Calendar.

isSet

```
protected boolean[] isSet
```
    Description   An array that contains a flag for each entry in the fields array. The value of each flag indicates if the corresponding entry in fields has been set for this Calendar.

isTimeSet

protected boolean isTimeSet

Description   A boolean value that indicates if the raw millisecond time value of this Calendar has been set. The value can be computed from the time fields.

time

protected long time

Description   The raw time value for this Calendar. The value is the number of milliseconds since midnight, January 1, 1970 GMT.

Constructors

Calendar

protected Calendar()

Description   This constructor creates a Calendar that uses the system's default time zone and locale. The default time zone is that returned by TimeZone.getDefault(). The default locale is that returned by Locale.getDefault().

protected Calendar(TimeZone zone, Locale aLocale)

Parameters   zone   The TimeZone to use.

aLocale   The Locale to use.

Description   This constructor creates a Calendar that uses the supplied time zone and locale.

Class Methods

getAvailableLocales

public static synchronized Locale[] getAvailableLocales()

Returns   An array of Locale objects for which Calendar objects are installed.

Description   This method returns an array of locales that have corresponding Calendar objects.

getInstance

public static synchronized Calendar getInstance()

Returns   A Calendar for the default time zone and locale.

Description   This method returns a newly constructed Calendar for the default time zone and locale. Future implementations of this method may infer the subclass of Calendar to instantiate based on the default locale. However, the current implementation always returns a GregorianCalendar. The default time zone is that returned by `TimeZone.getDefault()`. The default locale is that returned by `Locale.getDefault()`.

public static synchronized Calendar getInstance(TimeZone zone)

Parameters	zone	The `TimeZone` to use.
Returns		A `Calendar` for the given time zone and the default locale.
Description		This method returns a newly constructed `Calendar` for the given time zone and the default locale. Future implementations of this method may infer the subclass of `Calendar` to instantiate based on the default locale. However, the current implementation always returns a `GregorianCalendar`. The default locale is that returned by `Locale.getDefault()`.

public static synchronized Calendar getInstance(Locale aLocale)

Parameters	aLocale	The `Locale` to use.
Returns		A `Calendar` for the given locale and the default time zone.
Description		This method returns a newly constructed `Calendar` for the given locale and the default time zone. Future implementations of this method may infer the subclass of `Calendar` to instantiate based on the given locale. However, the current implementation always returns a `GregorianCalendar`. The default time zone is that returned by `TimeZone.getDefault()`.

public static synchronized Calendar getInstance(TimeZone zone, Locale aLocale)

Parameters	zone	The `TimeZone` to use.
	aLocale	The `Locale` to use.
Returns		A `Calendar` for the given time zone and locale.
Description		This method returns a newly constructed `Calendar` for the given time zone and locale. Future implementations of this method may infer the subclass of `Calendar` to instantiate based on the given locale. However, the current implementation always returns a `GregorianCalendar`.

Instance Methods

add

public abstract void add(int field, int amount)

Parameters	field	The time field to be modified.
	amount	The amount to add to the specified field value. This value can be negative.
Description		This method adds the given amount to the specified time field. For example, you can compute a date 90 days beyond the current date of this `Calendar` by calling `add(Calendar.DATE, 90)`.

after

public abstract boolean after(Object when)

Parameters	when	The object to compare to this Calendar.
Returns	true if this object is after when; false otherwise.	
Description	This method returns true if when is a Calendar object whose value falls before the value of this Calendar.	

before

public abstract boolean before(Object when)

Parameters	when	The object to compare to this Calendar.
Returns	true if this object is before when; false otherwise.	
Description	This method returns true if when is a Calendar object whose value falls after the value of this Calendar.	

clear

public final void clear()

Description	This method clears the values of all of the time fields of this Calendar.

public final void clear(int field)

Parameters	field	The time field to be cleared.
Description	This method clears the specified time field by setting its value to 0.	

clone

public Object clone()

Returns	A copy of this Calendar.
Overrides	Object.clone()
Description	This method creates a copy of this Calendar and returns it. In other words, the returned Calendar has the same time field values and raw time value as this Calendar.

equals

public abstract boolean equals(Object when)

Parameters	when	The object to be compared with this object.
Returns	true if the objects are equal; false if they are not.	
Overrides	Object.equals()	
Description	This method returns true if when is an instance of Calendar and it contains the same value as the object this method is associated with.	

get

```
public final int get(int field)
```

Parameters	field	The time field to be retrieved.
Returns	The value of the given time field.	
Description	This method returns the value of the specified time field. If the fields of this Calendar have not been set, they are set from the raw time value before the requested field is returned.	

getFirstDayOfWeek

```
public int getFirstDayOfWeek()
```

Returns	The first day of the week for this Calendar.
Description	This method returns the day that is considered the beginning of the week for this Calendar. This value is determined by the Locale of this Calendar. For example, the first day of the week in the United States is Sunday, while in France it is Monday.

getGreatestMinimum

```
public abstract int getGreatestMinimum(int field)
```

Parameters	field	A time field constant.
Returns	The highest minimum value for the given time field.	
Description	This method returns the highest minimum value for the given time field, if the field has a range of minimum values. If the field does not have a range of minimum values, this method is equivalent to getMinimum().	

getLeastMaximum

```
public abstract int getLeastMaximum(int field)
```

Parameters	field	A time field constant.
Returns	The lowest maximum value for the given time field.	
Description	This method returns the lowest maximum value for the given time field, if the field has a range of maximum values. If the field does not have a range of maximum values, this method is equivalent to getMaximum(). For example, for a GregorianCalendar, the lowest maximum value of DATE_OF_MONTH is 28.	

getMaximum

```
public abstract int getMaximum(int field)
```

Parameters	field	A time field constant.
Returns	The maximum value for the given time field.	

Description   This method returns the maximum value for the given time field. For example, for a GregorianCalendar, the maximum value of DATE_OF_MONTH is 31.

getMinimalDaysInFirstWeek

public int getMinimalDaysInFirstWeek()

Returns   The number of days that must be in the first week of the year.

Description   This method returns the number of days that must be in the first week of the year. For example, a value of 7 indicates that the first week of the year must be a full week, while a value of 1 indicates that the first week of the year can contain a single day. This value is determined by the Locale of this Calendar.

getMinimum

public abstract int getMinimum(int field)

Parameters   field   A time field constant.

Returns   The minimum value for the given time field.

Description   This method returns the minimum value for the given time field. For example, for a GregorianCalendar, the minimum value of DATE_OF_MONTH is 1.

getTime

public final Date getTime()

Returns   A Date object that represents the point in time represented by this Calendar.

Description   This method returns a newly created Date object that is constructed from the value returned by getTimeInMillis().

getTimeZone

public TimeZone getTimeZone()

Returns   The TimeZone of this Calendar.

Description   This method returns the TimeZone object for this Calendar.

isLenient

public boolean isLenient()

Returns   A boolean value that indicates the leniency of this Calendar.

Description   This method returns the current leniency of this Calendar. A value of false indicates that the Calendar throws exceptions when questionable data is passed to it, while a value of true indicates that the Calendar makes its best guess to interpret questionable data. For example, if the Calendar is being lenient, a date such as March 135, 1997 is interpreted as the 134th day after March 1, 1997.

isSet

```
public final boolean isSet(int field)
```

Parameters	field	A time field constant.
Returns		true if the time field has been set; false otherwise.
Description		This method returns a boolean value that indicates whether or not the specified time field has been set.

roll

```
public abstract void roll(int field, boolean up)
```

Parameters	field	The time field to be adjusted.
	up	A boolean value that indicates if the given field should be incremented.
Description		This method adds or subtracts one time unit from the given time field. For example, to increase the current date by one day, you can call roll(Calendar.DATE, true).

The method maintains the field being rolled within its valid range. For example, in a calendar system that uses hours and minutes to measure time, rolling the minutes up from 59 sets that field to 0. By the same token, rolling that field down from 0 sets it to 59.

The roll() method does not adjust the value of any other field than the one specified by its field argument. In particular, for calendar systems that have months with different numbers of days, it may be necessary to adjust the month and also year when the day of the month is rolled up. It is the responsibility of the caller of roll() to perform that adjustment.

set

```
public final void set(int field, int value)
```

Parameters	field	The time field to be set.
	value	The new value.
Description		This method sets the value of the specified time field.

```
public final void set(int year, int month, int date)
```

Parameters	year	The value for the year field.

month	The value for the month field, where 0 represents the first month.
date	The value for the day-of-the-month field.
Description	This method sets the values of the year, month, and day-of-the-month fields of this `Calendar`.

```
public final void set(int year, int month, int date,
                      int hour, int minute)
```

Parameters
year	The value for the year field.
month	The value for the month field, where 0 represents the first month.
date	The value for the day-of-the-month field.
hour	The value for the hour field.
minute	The value for the minute field.

Description   This method sets the values of the year, month, day-of-the-month, hour, and minute fields of this `Calendar`.

```
public final void set(int year, int month, int date,
                      int hour, int minute, int second)
```

Parameters
year	The value for the year field.
month	The value for the month field, where 0 represents the first month.
date	The value for the day-of-the-month field.
hour	The value for the hour field.
minute	The value for the minute field.
second	The value for the second field.

Description   This method sets the values of the year, month, day-of-the-month, hour, minute, and second fields of this `Calendar`.

setFirstDayOfWeek

```
public void setFirstDayofWeek(int value)
```

Parameters   value   The value for the first day of the week.

Description   This method sets the day that is considered the beginning of the week for this `Calendar`. This value should be determined by the `Locale` of this `Calendar`. For example, the first day of the week in the United States is Sunday; in France it's Monday.

setLenient

```
public void setLenient(boolean lenient)
```

Parameters   lenient   A boolean value that specifies the leniency of this `Calendar`.

Description   This method sets the leniency of this Calendar. A value of false specifies that the Calendar throws exceptions when questionable data is passed to it, while a value of true indicates that the Calendar makes its best guess to interpret questionable data. For example, if the Calendar is being lenient, a date such as March 135, 1997 is interpreted as the 135th day after March 1, 1997.

setMinimalDaysInFirstWeek

public void setMinimalDaysInFirstWeek(int value)

Parameters   value   The value for the minimum number of days in the first week of the year.

Description   This method sets the minimum number of days in the first week of the year. For example, a value of 7 indicates the first week of the year must be a full week, while a value of 1 indicates the first week of the year can contain a single day. This value should be determined by the Locale of this Calendar.

setTime

public final void setTime(Date date)

Parameters   date   A Date object that represents the new time value.

Description   This method sets the point in time that is represented by this Calendar.

setTimeZone

public void setTimeZone(TimeZone value)

Parameters   value   A TimeZone object that represents the new time zone.

Description   This method is used to set the time zone of this Calendar.

Protected Instance Methods

complete

protected void complete()

Description   This method fills out the fields of this Calendar as much as possible by calling computeTime() and computeFields().

computeFields

protected abstract void computeFields()

Description   This method calculates the time fields of this Calendar from its raw time value.

computeTime

protected abstract void computeTime()

Description   This method calculates the raw time value of this Calendar from its time field values.

getTimeInMillis

protected long getTimeInMillis()

Returns   The raw time value of this Calendar.

Description   This method returns the raw time value of this Calendar. The value is measured as the number of milliseconds since midnight, January 1, 1970 GMT.

internalGet

protected final int internalGet(int field)

Parameters   field   A time field constant.

Returns   The value of the given time field.

Description   This method returns the value of the specified time field without first checking to see if it needs to be computed from the raw time value.

setTimeInMillis

protected void setTimeInMillis(long millis)

Parameters   millis   The new raw time value for this Calendar.

Description   This method sets the raw time value of this Calendar. The value is measured as the number of milliseconds since midnight, January 1, 1970 GMT.

Inherited Methods

Method	Inherited From	Method	Inherited From
finalize()	Object	getClass()	Object
hashCode()	Object	notify()	Object
notifyAll()	Object	toString()	Object
wait()	Object	wait(long)	Object
wait(long, int)	Object		

See Also

Cloneable, Date, DateFormat, GregorianCalendar, Locale, Serializable, Time-Zone

---

17.3   Date

Synopsis

Class Name:	java.util.Date
Superclass:	java.lang.Object
Immediate Subclasses:	None
Interfaces Implemented:	java.lang.Cloneable, java.io.Serializable
Availability:	JDK 1.0 or later

Description

The Date class encapsulates a point in time with millisecond precision. The value of a Date is represented internally by a long value that contains the number of milliseconds since midnight, January 1, 1970 GMT.

Prior to JDK 1.1, the Date class was used for two purposes that are now encapsulated by other classes. First, the Date class included methods for calculating calendar values, like months and days of the week. This functionality is now embedded in the Calendar class. Second, the Date class included methods for generating and parsing a string representation of a date. This functionality is now provided by java.text.DateFormat. Thus, as of JDK 1.1, most of the methods of Date are deprecated; the class is used only to represent a point in time.

The accurate measurement of time is a subject of considerable complexity and multifarious acronyms. There are two main methods of measuring time, atomic and astronomical. The U.S. Naval Observatory (*http://tycho.usno.navy.mil*) maintains a set of atomic clocks that provide the basis for Coordinated Universal Time (UTC). These clocks adhere to precise definitions of the second based on atomic decay.

Outside of the U.S. Navy, people tend to measure time in terms of Greenwich Mean Time (GMT). In the scientific community, GMT is called UT, which is a system of time predicated on the assumption that each rotation of the earth is exactly 24 * 60 * 60 seconds long. Because the earth's rotation is gradually slowing down, the seconds in UT are a little bit longer than the seconds in UTC. Now and then a "leap second" is added in UTC to keep it close to UT. Because the Date class simply measures milliseconds since a point in time, without regard for leap seconds, it is a good representation of UT or GMT.

Class Summary

```
public class java.util.Date extends java.lang.Object
            implements java.lang.Cloneable, java.io.Serializable {
   // Constructors
   public Date();
   public Date(long date);
   public Date(int year, int month, int date);          // Deprecated in 1.1
   public Date(int year, int month, int date,
               int hrs, int min);                        // Deprecated in 1.1
   public Date(int year, int month, int date,
               int hrs, int min, int sec);               // Deprecated in 1.1
   public Date(String s);                                // Deprecated in 1.1

   // Class Methods
   public static long parse(String s);                  // Deprecated in 1.1
   public static long UTC(int year, int month,
                     int date, int hrs,
                     int min, int sec);                  // Deprecated in 1.1

   // Instance Methods
   public boolean after(Date when);
   public boolean before(Date when);
   public boolean equals(Object obj);
   public int getDate();                                // Deprecated in 1.1
   public int getDay();                                 // Deprecated in 1.1
   public int getHours();                               // Deprecated in 1.1
   public int getMinutes();                             // Deprecated in 1.1
   public int getMonth();                               // Deprecated in 1.1
   public int getSeconds();                             // Deprecated in 1.1
   public long getTime();
   public int getTimezoneOffset();                      // Deprecated in 1.1
   public int getYear();                                // Deprecated in 1.1
   public int hashCode();
   public void setDate(int date);                       // Deprecated in 1.1
   public void setHours(int hours);                     // Deprecated in 1.1
   public void setMinutes(int minutes);                 // Deprecated in 1.1
   public void setMonth(int month);                     // Deprecated in 1.1
   public void setSeconds(int seconds);                 // Deprecated in 1.1
   public void setTime(long time);
   public void setYear(int year);                       // Deprecated in 1.1
   public String toGMTString();                         // Deprecated in 1.1
   public String toLocaleString();                      // Deprecated in 1.1
   public String toString();
}
```

Constructors

Date

public Date()

Description This constructor creates a Date object that is initialized to the current time.

public Date(long date)

Parameters	date	A time value, measured as the number of milliseconds since midnight, January 1, 1970 GMT.
Description		This constructor creates a Date object that represents the given time.

public Date(int year, int month, int day)

Availability	Deprecated as of JDK 1.1	
Parameters	year	The year specified as a value that is added to 1900 to get the actual year.
	month	The month specified in the range 0 to 11.
	day	The day of the month specified in the range 1 to 31.
Description		This constructor creates a Date that represents midnight local time on the specified date.

public Date(int year, int month, int day, int hrs, int min)

Availability	Deprecated as of JDK 1.1	
Parameters	year	The year specified as a value that is added to 1900 to get the actual year.
	month	The month specified in the range 0 to 11.
	day	The day of the month specified in the range 1 to 31.
	hrs	The hours specified in the range 0 to 23.
	min	The minutes specified in the range 0 to 59.
Description		This constructor creates a Date that represents the given date and time.

public Date(int year, int month, int day, int hrs,
    int min, int sec)

Availability	Deprecated as of JDK 1.1	
Parameters	year	The year specified as a value that is added to 1900 to get the actual year.
	month	The month specified in the range 0 to 11.
	day	The day of the month specified in the range 1 to 31.

hrs	The hours specified in the range 0 to 23.
min	The minutes specified in the range 0 to 59.
sec	The seconds specified in the range 0 to 59.

Description   This constructor creates a Date that represents the given date and time.

public Date(String s)

Availability   Deprecated as of JDK 1.1

Parameters   s   The string to parse.

Description   This constructor creates a Date that represents the date and time specified by the given string. The syntax of the date in the string must satisfy the requirements of the parse() method. The following is an example of a string that this constructor can understand:

```
Sat, 8 Feb 1997 13:30:00 GMT
```

Class Methods

parse

public static long parse(String s)

Availability   Deprecated as of JDK 1.1

Parameters   s   The string to parse.

Returns   A time value represented as the number of milliseconds since midnight, January 1, 1970 GMT.

Throws   IllegalArgumentException

If the string cannot be parsed.

Description   This method returns the raw time value specified by the given string. This method understands a number of different formats. The following are examples of strings that this method can understand:

```
Sat, 8 Feb 1997 13:30:00 GMT
4/6/97
4/6/1997
January 5, 1997
2/4/97 11:03 AM
2/4/97 10:25 PM
2/4/97 17:03 GMT-6
2/4/97 17:03:24
March 16, 97 17:03 EST
March (comment)16, 97 (comment) 17:03 EST
16 march 1996 17:03 pdt
Sat 16 march 97 17:03 cst
```

The JDK 1.0.2 implementation of parse() has a serious bug. It incorrectly interprets date formats that specify the month as a number by making the month one greater than it should be. So 2/4/97 is incorrectly interpreted as March 4, 1997.

For the purposes of this method, UTC and GMT are considered equivalent.

UTC

```
public static long UTC(int year, int month, int date,
                       int hrs, int min, int sec)
```

Availability	Deprecated as of JDK 1.1	
Parameters	year	The year specified as a value that is added to 1900 to get the actual year.
	month	The month specified in the range 0 to 11.
	day	The day of the month specified in the range 1 to 31.
	hrs	The hours specified in the range 0 to 23.
	min	The minutes specified in the range 0 to 59.
	sec	The seconds specified in the range 0 to 59.
Returns	A time value represented as the number of milliseconds since midnight, January 1, 1970 GMT.	
Description	This method returns a raw time value that corresponds to the given parameters. Computations are based on GMT, not the local time zone.	

Instance Methods

after

```
public boolean after(Date when)
```

Parameters	when	The object to compare to this Date.
Returns	true if this object is after when; false otherwise.	
Description	This method returns true if the value of when falls before the value of this Date.	

before

```
public boolean before(Date when)
```

Parameters	when	The object to compare to this Date.
Returns	true if this object is before when; false otherwise.	
Description	This method returns true if the value of when falls after the value of this Date.	

equals

    public boolean equals(Object obj)

Parameters	obj	The object to be compared with this object.
Returns		true if the objects are equal; false if they are not.
Overrides		Object.equals()
Description		This method returns true if when is an instance of Date and it contains the same value as the object this method is associated with. In other words, the two Date objects are equal only if they both represent the same point in time, to the millisecond.

getDate

    public int getDate()

Availability	Deprecated as of JDK 1.1
Returns	The day of the month of this Date.
Description	This method returns the day of the month represented by this Date object. The value is in the range 1 to 31.

getDay

    public int getDay()

Availability	Deprecated as of JDK 1.1
Returns	The day of the week of this Date.
Description	This method returns the day of the week represented by this Date object. The value is in the range 0 to 6, where 0 means Sunday.

getHours

    public int getHours()

Availability	Deprecated as of JDK 1.1
Returns	The hour value of this Date.
Description	This method returns the hour represented by this Date object. The value is in the range 0 to 23, where 0 means midnight.

getMinutes

    public int getMinutes()

Availability	Deprecated as of JDK 1.1
Returns	The minute value of this Date.
Description	This method returns the number of minutes after the hour represented by this Date object. The value is in the range 0 to 59.

getMonth

public int getMonth()

Availability	Deprecated as of JDK 1.1
Returns	The month of this Date.
Description	This method returns the month represented by this Date object. The value is in the range 0 to 11, where 0 means January.

getSeconds

public int getSeconds()

Availability	Deprecated as of JDK 1.1
Returns	The second value of this Date.
Description	This method returns the number of seconds after the minute represented by this Date object. The value is in the range 0 to 59.

getTime

public long getTime()

Returns	The raw time value of this Date.
Description	This method returns the date and time of this Date as the number of milliseconds since midnight, January 1, 1970 GMT.

getTimezoneOffset

public int getTimezoneOffset()

Availability	Deprecated as of JDK 1.1
Returns	The time zone offset for this Date.
Description	This method returns the number of minutes between the local time zone and GMT for this Date object.

getYear

public int getYear()

Availability	Deprecated as of JDK 1.1
Returns	The year of this Date.
Description	This method returns the year represented by this Date object. The value is the number of years since 1990.

hashCode

public int hashCode()

Returns	The hashcode for this Date.

Overrides   `Object.hashCode()`

Description   This method returns a hashcode for this object.

setDate

`public void setDate(int date)`

Availability   Deprecated as of JDK 1.1

Parameters   date   The day of the month specified in the range 1 to
                                31.

Description   This method sets the day of the month of this Date object.

setHours

`public void setHours(int hours)`

Availability   Deprecated as of JDK 1.1

Parameters   hours   The hours specified in the range 0 to 23.

Description   This method sets the hour of this Date object.

setMinutes

`public void setMinutes(int minutes)`

Availability   Deprecated as of JDK 1.1

Parameters   minutes   The minutes specified in the range 0 to 59.

Description   This method sets the minute value of this Date object.

setMonth

`public void setMonth(int month)`

Availability   Deprecated as of JDK 1.1

Parameters   month   The month specified in the range 0 to 11.

Description   This method sets the month of this Date object

setSeconds

`public void setSeconds(int seconds)`

Availability   Deprecated as of JDK 1.1

Parameters   seconds   The seconds specified in the range 0 to 59.

Description   This method sets the second value of this Date object.

setTime

`public void setTime(long time)`

Parameters   time   A time value specified as the number of millisec-
                                onds since midnight, January 1, 1970 GMT.

Description   This method sets the date and time represented by this Date to
               the given raw time value.

setYear

`public void setYear(int year)`

Availability	Deprecated as of JDK 1.1
Parameters	year The year specified as a value that is added to 1900 to get the actual year.
Description	This method sets the year of this Date object.

toGMTString

`public String toGMTString()`

Availability	Deprecated as of JDK 1.1
Returns	A string that represents this Date.
Description	The method returns a string representation of this Date object based on Internet GMT conventions. The string is of the form:

```
Sat, 8 Feb 1997 13:30:00 GMT
```

The date is the string is either one or two digits; the rest of the fields always have the width shown. The time zone is always GMT.

toLocaleString

`public String toLocaleString()`

Availability	Deprecated as of JDK 1.1
Returns	A string that represents this Date.
Description	The method returns a string representation of this Date based on the conventions of the current locale.

toString

`public String toString()`

Returns	A string that represents this Date.
Overrides	Object.toString()
Description	This method returns a string representation of this Date. The string is of the form:

```
Sat Feb 8 2:30:00 MST 1997
```

Inherited Methods

Method	Inherited From	Method	Inherited From
clone()	Object	finalize()	Object
getClass()	Object	notify()	Object
notifyAll()	Object	wait()	Object
wait(long)	Object	wait(long, int)	Object

See Also

Calendar, Cloneable, DateFormat, GregorianCalendar, IllegalArgumentException, Serializable, TimeZone

---

17.4   Dictionary

Synopsis

Class Name:	java.util.Dictionary
Superclass:	java.lang.Object
Immediate Subclasses:	java.util.Hashtable
Interfaces Implemented:	None
Availability:	JDK 1.0 or later

Description

The Dictionary class is an abstract class that associates keys with values. Any non-null object can be used as a key or as a value. Key/value pairs can be stored in a Dictionary, and values can be retrieved or removed using their associated keys.

A subclass of Dictionary should use the equals() method to decide if two keys are equivalent.

Class Summary

```
public abstract class java.util.Dictionary extends java.lang.Object {
    // Instance Methods
    public abstract Enumeration elements();
    public abstract Object get(Object key);
    public abstract boolean isEmpty();
    public abstract Enumeration keys();
    public abstract Object put(Object key, Object value);
    public abstract Object remove(Object key);
    public abstract int size();
}
```

Instance Methods

elements

```
public abstract Enumeration elements()
```

Returns   The values in the dictionary as an Enumeration.

Description   This method returns an Enumeration that iterates through the values in this Dictionary.

get

    public abstract Object get(Object key)

Parameters	key	The key of the value to retrieve.
Returns	The value that corresponds to this key.	
Description	This method returns the value that is associated with the given key.	

isEmpty

    public abstract boolean isEmpty()

Returns	true if there are no values in the Dictionary7thinsp;; false otherwise.
Description	This method returns a boolean value that indicates whether or not the Dictionary is empty.

keys

    public abstract Enumeration keys()

Returns	The keys in the dictionary as an Enumeration.
Description	This method returns an Enumeration that iterates through the keys in this Dictionary.

put

    public abstract Object put(Object key, Object value)

Parameters	key	A key object.
	value	A value object.
Returns	The previous value associated with the given key or null if key has not previously been associated with a value.	
Throws	NullPointerException	
	If either the key or the value is null.	
Description	This method associates the given key with the given value in this Dictionary.	

remove

    public abstract Object remove(Object key)

Parameters	key	The key of the value to remove.
Returns	The value associated with the given key or null if key is not associated with a value.	
Description	This method removes a key/value pair from this Dictionary. If the given key is not in the Dictionary, the method does nothing.	

size

```
public abstract int size()
```

Returns   The number of keys in the `Dictionary`.

Description   This method returns the number of key/value pairs in this `Dictionary`.

Inherited Methods

Method	Inherited From	Method	Inherited From
clone()	Object	equals(Object)	Object
finalize()	Object	getClass()	Object
hashCode()	Object	notify()	Object
notifyAll()	Object	toString()	Object
wait()	Object	wait(long)	Object
wait(long, int)	Object		

See Also

Enumeration, Hashtable, NullPointerException

17.5   EmptyStackException

Synopsis

Class Name: java.util.EmptyStackException

Superclass: java.lang.RuntimeException

Immediate Subclasses: None

Interfaces Implemented: None

Availability: JDK 1.0 or later

Description

An `EmptyStackException` is thrown by methods of the `Stack` class when an operation cannot be completed because the stack is empty.

Class Summary

```
public class java.util.EmptyStackException
            extends java.lang.RuntimeException {
  // Constructors
  public EmptyStackException();
}
```

Constructors

EmptyStackException

```
public EmptyStackException()
```
   Description   This constructor creates an EmptyStackException with no associated detail message.

Inherited Methods

Method	Inherited From	Method	Inherited From
clone()	Object	equals(Object)	Object
fillInStackTrace()	Throwable	finalize()	Object
getClass()	Object	getLocalizedMessage()	Throwable
getMessage()	Throwable	hashCode()	Object
notify()	Object	notifyAll()	Object
printStackTrace()	Throwable	printStack- Trace(PrintStream)	Throwable
printStack- Trace(PrintWriter)	Throwable	toString()	Throwable
wait()	Object	wait(long)	Object
wait(long, int)	Object		

See Also

Exception, RuntimeException, Stack

17.6   Enumeration

Synopsis

Interface Name: java.util.Enumeration
Super-interface: None
Immediate Sub-interfaces:
                        None
Implemented By: java.util.StringTokenizer
Availability: JDK 1.0 or later

Description

An object that implements the Enumeration interface provides a way to access a set of objects sequentially. The Enumeration object hides the actual organization of the set of objects from the code that is using it. An Enumeration can iterate through, or enumerate, its set of objects one at a time. A specific implementation of the interface controls the order in which the objects are presented.

The following is an example of how an Enumeration is used. The example shows a method for printing the values in an Enumeration:

```
void printAll(Enumeration e) {
    while ( e.hasMoreElements() ) {
        System.out.println(e.nextElement());
    }
}
```

Note that an Enumeration can be used only once: it iterates through its collection of objects in one direction and cannot be reset or rewound.

Normally, an Enumeration is not instantiated directly, but instead returned by a method that needs to enumerate a set of values. For example, the elements() method of the Vector class returns an Enumeration of the elements in the Vector. By the same token, the elements() and keys() methods of the Hashtable class return Enumeration objects for the keys and values in the Hashtable.

Interface Declaration

```
public abstract interface java.util.Enumeration {
    // Methods
    public abstract boolean hasMoreElements();
    public abstract Object nextElement() throws NoSuchElementException;
}
```

Methods

hasMoreElements

```
public abstract boolean hasMoreElements()
```

Returns   true if the there are more objects to retrieve; false otherwise.

Description   This method returns true if the nextElement() method of this Enumeration returns an object the next time it is called.

nextElement

```
public abstract Object nextElement()
```

Returns   The next object in this Enumeration.

Throws   NoSuchElementException
                If there are no more objects to return.

Description This method returns the next object in the set of objects encapsulated by this Enumeration.

See Also

Hashtable, StringTokenizer, Vector

17.7   EventListener

Synopsis

Interface Name: java.util.EventListener
Super-interfaces: None
Immediate Sub-interfaces:
                       java.awt.event.ActionListener,
                       java.awt.event.AdjustmentListener,
                       java.awt.event.ComponentListener,
                       java.awt.event.ContainerListener,
                       java.awt.event.FocusListener,
                       java.awt.event.ItemListener,
                       java.awt.event.KeyListener,
                       java.awt.event.MouseListener,
                       java.awt.event.MouseMotionListener,
                       java.awt.event.TextListener,
                       java.awt.event.WindowListener
Implemented by: None
Availability: New as of JDK 1.1

Description

In order for instances of a class to receive events, the class must implement the EventListener interface. It is a semantic interface, meaning that it declares no methods. Classes do not normally implement the EventListener interface directly, but instead implement an interface that extends EventListener.

Prior to Java 1.1, events could only be delivered to AWT components. Java 1.1 introduces a new event model that allows events to be delivered to any object that implements a listener interface and registers to receive events from a particular source.

Interface Declaration

```
public abstract interface java.util.EventListener {
}
```

See Also

ActionListener, AdjustmentListener, ComponentListener, ContainerListener, FocusListener, ItemListener, KeyListener, MouseListener, MouseMotionListener, TextListener, WindowListener

17.8   EventObject

Synopsis

Class Name: java.util.EventObject
Superclass: java.lang.Object
Immediate Subclasses: java.awt.AWTEvent
Interfaces Implemented: java.io.Serializable
Availability: New as of JDK 1.1

Description

The EventObject class is the superclass of all other classes that represent events in the Java 1.1 event model. The class is named EventObject to avoid confusion with java.awt.Event, which was used to represent events in the old Java 1.0 event model.

Class Summary

```
public class java.util.EventObject extends java.lang.Object
            implements java.io.Serializable {
  // Variables
  protected transient Object source;

  // Constructors
  public EventObject(Object source);

  // Instance Methods
  public Object getSource();
  public String toString();
}
```

Variables

source

protected transient Object source

Description   The object that generated this EventObject.

Constructors

EventObject

public EventObject(Object source)

Parameters   source   The object that generated this EventObject.

Description   This constructor creates an EventObject whose source is the given object.

Instance Methods

getSource

public Object getSource()

Returns   The object that generated this EventObject.

Description   This method returns the object that is the source of this Event-Object.

toString

public String toString()

Returns   A string that represents this EventObject.

Overrides   Object.toString()

Description   This method returns a string representation of this Event-Object.

Inherited Methods

Method	Inherited From	Method	Inherited From
clone()	Object	equals()	Object
finalize()	Object	getClass()	Object
hashCode()	Object	notify()	Object
notifyAll()	Object	wait()	Object
wait(long)	Object	wait(long, int)	Object

See Also

AWTEvent, Event, Serializable

17.9   GregorianCalendar

Synopsis

Class Name:	java.util.GregorianCalendar
Superclass:	java.util.Calendar
Immediate Subclasses:	None
Interfaces Implemented:	None
Availability:	New as of JDK 1.1

Description

The GregorianCalendar class is a subclass of the abstract Calendar class. GregorianCalendar provides an implementation of the calendar that much of the world uses. GregorianCalendar has two eras, BC and AD.

GregorianCalendar provides both Gregorian and Julian dates, depending on the date that is represented by the object. The Gregorian calendar was instituted in October 15, 1582, so any dates before this cut-off time are represented as Julian dates. Some countries switched from the Julian and the Gregorian calendar after that date, however. The cutoff date can be changed using the setGregorianChange() method. When using Julian dates, be aware that this class does not account for the fact that the Julian calendar used March 25 as the beginning of the year. You will have to adjust the year on Julian dates that fall between January 1 and March 24.

You can find a fascinating discussion of the history of Western calendars at *http://barroom.visionsystems.com/serendipity/date/jul_greg.html.*

Class Summary

```
public class java.util.GregorianCalendar extends java.util.Calendar {
    // Constants
    public final static int AD;
    public final static int BC;

    // Constructors
    public GregorianCalendar();
    public GregorianCalendar(TimeZone zone);
    public GregorianCalendar(Locale aLocale);
    public GregorianCalendar(TimeZone zone, Locale aLocale);
    public GregorianCalendar(int year, int month, int date);
    public GregorianCalendar(int year, int month, int date,
                             int hour, int minute);
    public GregorianCalendar(int year, int month, int date,
                             int hour, int minute, int second);

    // Instance Methods
```

```
public void add(int field, int amount);
public boolean after(Object when);
public boolean before(Object when);
public Object clone();
public boolean equals(Object obj);
public int getGreatestMinimum(int field);
public final Date getGregorianChange();
public int getLeastMaximum(int field);
public int getMaximum(int field);
public int getMinimum(int field);
public synchronized int hashCode();
public boolean isLeapYear(int year);
public void roll(int field, boolean up);
public void setGregorianChange(Date date);

// Protected Instance Methods
protected void computeFields();
protected void computeTime();
}
```

Constants

AD

```
public final static int AD
```
  Description   A constant value that represents the AD era, which stands for *anno Domini*, Latin for "the year of the Lord". People who do not want to measure years with a Christian connotation call this era CE the Common Era.

BC

```
public final static int BC
```
  Description   A constant value that represents the BC era, which stands for *before Christ*, before the birth of Christ. People who do not want to measure years with a Christian connotation call this era BCE, which stands for Before the Common Era.

Constructors

GregorianCalendar

```
public GregorianCalendar()
```
  Description   This constructor creates a GregorianCalendar that represents the current time using the system's default time zone and locale. The default time zone is that returned by Time-Zone.getDefault(). The default locale is that returned by Locale.getDefault().

`public GregorianCalendar(TimeZone zone)`

Parameters   zone   The `TimeZone` to use.

Description   This constructor creates a `GregorianCalendar` that represents the current time using the supplied time zone and the default locale. The default locale is that returned by `Locale.getDefault()`.

`public GregorianCalendar(Locale aLocale)`

Parameters   aLocale   The `Locale` to use.

Description   This constructor creates a `GregorianCalendar` that represents the current time using the supplied locale and the default time zone. The default time zone is that returned by `TimeZone.getDefault()`.

`public GregorianCalendar(TimeZone zone, Locale aLocale)`

Parameters   zone   The `TimeZone` to use.

               aLocale   The `Locale` to use.

Description   This constructor creates a `GregorianCalendar` that represents the current time using the supplied time zone and locale.

`public GregorianCalendar(int year, int month, int date)`

Parameters   year   The value for the year field.

               month   The value for the month field, where 0 represents the first month.

               date   The value for the day-of-the-month field.

Description   This constructor creates a `GregorianCalendar` that represents the given date in the default time zone and locale. The default time zone is that returned by `TimeZone.getDefault()`. The default locale is that returned by `Locale.getDefault()`.

`public GregorianCalendar(int year, int month, int date,`
`                         int hour, int minute)`

Parameters   year   The value for the year field.

               month   The value for the month field, where 0 represents the first month.

               date   The value for the day-of-the-month field.

               hour   The value for the hour field.

               minute   The value for the minute field.

Description   This constructor creates a `GregorianCalendar` that represents the given date and time in the default time zone and locale. The default time zone is that returned by `TimeZone.getDefault()`. The default locale is that returned by `Locale.getDefault()`.

```
public GregorianCalendar(int year, int month, int date, int hour,
                         int minute, int second)
```

Parameters   year   The value for the year field.

month   The value for the month field, where 0 represents the first month.

date   The value for the day-of-the-month field.

hour   The value for the hour field.

minute   The value for the minute field.

second   The value for the second field.

Description   This constructor creates a GregorianCalendar that represents the given data and time in the default time zone and locale. The default time zone is that returned by Time-Zone.getDefault(). The default locale is that returned by Locale.getDefault().

Instance Methods

add

```
public void add(int field, int amount)
```

Parameters   field   The time field to be modified.

amount   The amount to add to the specified field value. This value can be negative.

Throws   IllegalArgumentException

If field is not a valid time field.

Overrides   Calendar.add()

Description   This method adds the given amount to the specified time field. For example, you can compute a date 90 days beyond the current date of this GregorianCalendar by calling add(Calendar.DATE, 90).

after

```
public boolean after(Object when)
```

Parameters   when   The object to compare to this GregorianCalendar.

Returns   true if this object is after when; false otherwise.

Overrides   Calendar.after()

Description   This method returns true if when is a GregorianCalendar whose value falls before the value of this GregorianCalendar.

before

public boolean before(Object when)

Parameters	when	The object to compare to this GregorianCalendar.
Returns		true if this object is before when; false otherwise.
Overrides		Calendar.before()
Description		This method returns true if when is a GregorianCalendar whose value falls after the value of this GregorianCalendar.

clone

public Object clone()

Returns	A copy of this GregorianCalendar.
Overrides	Calendar.clone()
Description	This method creates a copy of this GregorianCalendar and returns it. In other words, the returned GregorianCalendar has the same time field values and raw time value as this GregorianCalendar.

equals

public boolean equals(Object when)

Parameters	when	The object to be compared with this object.
Returns		true if the objects are equal; false if they are not.
Overrides		Calendar.equals()
Description		This method returns true if when is an instance of GregorianCalendar, and it contains the same value as the object this method is associated with.

getGreatestMinimum

public int getGreatestMinimum(int field)

Parameters	field	A time field constant.
Returns		The highest minimum value for the given time field.
Overrides		Calendar.getGreatestMinimum()
Description		This method returns the highest minimum value for the given time field, if the field has a range of minimum values. If the field has only one minimum value, this method is equivalent to getMinimum(). All of the fields in GregorianCalendar have only one minimum value.

getGregorianChange

public final Date getGregorianChange()

Returns   The date this GregorianCalendar uses as the change date between the Julian and Gregorian calendars.

Description   By default, GregorianCalendar considers midnight local time, October 15, 1582, to be the date when the Gregorian calendar was adopted. This value can be changed using setGregorian-Change().

getLeastMaximum

public int getLeastMaximum(int field)

Parameters   field   A time field constant.

Returns   The lowest maximum value for the given time field.

Overrides   Calendar.getLeastMaximum()

Description   This method returns the lowest maximum value for the given time field, if the field has a range of maximum values. If the field has only one maximum value, this method is equivalent to getMaximum(). For example, for a GregorianCalendar, the lowest maximum value of DATE_OF_MONTH is 28.

getMaximum

public int getMaximum(int field)

Parameters   field   A time field constant.

Returns   The maximum value for the given time field.

Overrides   Calendar.getMaximum()

Description   This method returns the maximum value for the given time field. For example, for a GregorianCalendar, the maximum value of DATE_OF_MONTH is 31.

getMinimum

public int getMinimum(int field)

Parameters   field   A time field constant.

Returns   The minimum value for the given time field.

Overrides   Calendar.getMinimum()

Description   This method returns the minimum value for the given time field. For example, for a GregorianCalendar, the minimum value of DATE_OF_MONTH is 1.

hashCode

`public synchronized int hashCode()`

Returns	A hashcode for this `GregorianCalendar`.
Overrides	`Object.hashCode()`
Description	This method returns a hashcode for this object.

isLeapYear

`public boolean isLeapYear(int year)`

Parameters	year	The year to test.
Returns		true if the given year is a leap year; false otherwise.
Description		This method returns a boolean value that indicates whether or not the specified year is a leap year. Leap years are those years that are divisible by 4, except those that are divisible by 100, unless they are divisible by 400. For example, 1900 is not a leap year because it is divisible by 100 but not by 400. The year 2000 is a leap year.

roll

`public void roll(int field, boolean up)`

Parameters	field	The time field to be adjusted.
	up	A boolean value that indicates if the given field should be incremented.
Throws		IllegalArgumentException
		If field is not a valid time field.
Overrides		Calendar.roll()
Description		This method adds or subtracts one time unit from the given time field. For example, to increase the current date by one day, you can call roll(GregorianCalendar.DATE, true).

The method maintains the field being rolled within its valid range. For example, in a calendar system that uses hours and minutes to measure time, rolling the minutes up from 59 sets that field to 0. By the same token, rolling that field down from 0 sets it to 59.

The roll() method does not adjust the value of any other field than the one specified by its field argument. In particular, for calendar systems that have months with different numbers of days, it may be necessary to adjust the month and also year when the day of the month is rolled up. For example, calling roll(GregorianCalendar.DAY_OF_MONTH, true) on a GregorianCalendar that represents December 31, 1996 changes the date to December 1, 1996. In addition, calling roll() may

make the fields inconsistent. For example, calling
roll(GregorianCalendar.MONTH, true) on a GregorianCalendar that represents January 31, 1997 changes the date to February 31, 1997. It is the responsibility of the caller of roll() to
adjust the other fields.

setGregorianChange

public void setGregorianChange(Date date)

Parameters	date	A Date object that represents the new time value.
Description		This method sets the date that this GregorianCalendar uses as the change date between the Julian and Gregorian calendars. The default is midnight local time, October 15, 1582. This is the date that Pope Gregory instituted the calendar in many Catholic countries in Europe. Most Catholic countries followed within a few years. Protestant England and America did not adopt the new calendar until September 14, 1752.

Protected Instance Methods

computeFields

protected void computeFields()

Overrides	Calendar.computeFields()
Description	This method calculates the time fields of this GregorianCalendar from its raw time value.

computeTime

protected void computeTime()

Overrides	Calendar.computeTime()
Description	This method calculates the raw time value of this Gregorian-Calendar from its time field values.

Inherited Variables

Variable	Inherited From	Variable	Inherited From
areFieldsSet	Calendar	fields	Calendar
isSet	Calendar	isTimeSet	Calendar
time	Calendar		

Inherited Methods

Method	Inherited From	Method	Inherited From
clear()	Calendar	clear(int)	Calendar
complete()	Calendar	finalize()	Object
get(int)	Calendar	getClass()	Object
getFirstDayOfWeek()	Calendar	getMinimumDaysInFirst-Week()	Calendar
getTime()	Calendar	getTimeInMillis()	Calendar
getTimeZone()	Calendar	internalGet(int)	Calendar
isLenient()	Calendar	isSet(int)	Calendar
notify()	Object	notifyAll()	Object
set(int, int)	Calendar	set(int, int, int)	Calendar
set(int, int, int, int, int)	Calendar	set(int, int, int, int, int, int)	Calendar
setFirstDayOfWeek(int)	Calendar	setLenient(boolean)	Calendar
setMinimalDaysInFirst-Week(int)	Calendar	setTime(Date)	Calendar
setTimeInMillis(long)	Calendar	setTimeZone(TimeZone)	Calendar
toString()	Object	wait()	Object
wait(long)	Object	wait(long, int)	Object

See Also

Calendar, Cloneable, Date, IllegalArgumentException, Locale, Serializable, TimeZone

17.10   Hashtable

Synopsis

Class Name:	java.util.Hashtable
Superclass:	java.util.Dictionary
Immediate Subclasses:	java.util.Properties
Interfaces Implemented:	java.lang.Cloneable, java.io.Serializable
Availability:	JDK 1.0 or later

Description

The Hashtable class is a concrete subclass of Dictionary that builds a table of key/value pairs. Any non-null object can be used as a key or as a value. The objects used as keys must implement the equals() and hashCode() methods in a way that computes comparisons and hashcodes from the contents of an object. Once the table is built, a value can be efficiently retrieved by supplying its associated key.

Hashtable is an excellent example of how a well-written class can hide an arcane algorithm. The casual user simply instantiates a Hashtable and uses put() and get() to add and retrieve key and value pairs. However, when performance is an issue, you need to be aware of the considerations discussed in the following paragraphs.

Internally, a Hashtable keeps an array of key/value pairs. When a new key/value pair is added to a Hashtable, it is added to the array at an index that is calculated from the hashcode of the key. If a key/value pair already exists at this index, the new pair is linked to the existing key and value. Thus, a Hashtable has an overall structure of an array of linked lists.

For a given key, the retrieval of the matching value from a Hashtable is quite fast. The Hashtable computes the hashcode of the key and uses it as an index into the array. Then it only needs to search the linked list of key/value pairs at that index to find a match for the given key. If the array is short, but the Hashtable contains many key/value pairs, however, the linked lists will be lengthy, which adversely affects performance.

A Hashtable has a capacity, which is the length of its array, and a load factor, which determines when rehashing is performed. The load factor is a number between 0 and 1. If the number of key/value pairs added to the Hashtable exceeds the capacity multiplied by the load factor, the capacity of the Hashtable is increased and the key/value pairs are rehashed into the new array. Obviously, this is an undesirable performance hit, so if you know approximately how many items you will add to a Hashtable, you should create one with an appropriate initial capacity.

Class Summary

```
public class java.util.Hashtable extends java.util.Dictionary
            implements java.lang.Cloneable, java.io.Serializable {
   // Constructors
   public Hashtable();
   public Hashtable(int initialCapacity);
   public Hashtable(int initialCapacity, float loadFactor);

   // Instance Methods
   public synchronized void clear();
   public synchronized Object clone();
```

```
public synchronized boolean contains(Object value);
public synchronized boolean containsKey(Object key);
public synchronized Enumeration elements();
public synchronized Object get(Object key);
public boolean isEmpty();
public synchronized Enumeration keys();
public synchronized Object put(Object key, Object value);
public synchronized Object remove(Object key);
public int size();
public synchronized String toString();

// Protected Instance Methods
protected void rehash();
}
```

Constructors

Hashtable

public Hashtable()

Description   This constructor creates a Hashtable with a default capacity of
101 and a default load factor of .75.

public Hashtable(int initialCapacity)

Parameters   initialCapacity
The initial capacity.

Throws   IllegalArgumentException
If initialCapacity is less than or equal to zero.

Description   This constructor creates a Hashtable with the given capacity
and a default load factor of .75.

public Hashtable(int initialCapacity, float loadFactor)

Parameters   initialCapacity
The initial capacity.

loadFactor   The load factor.

Throws   IllegalArgumentException
If initialCapacity or loadFactor is less than or
equal to zero.

Description   This constructor creates a Hashtable with the given capacity
and load factor.

Instance Methods

clear

```
public synchronized void clear()
```

Description   This method removes all of the key/value pairs from this Hashtable.

clone

```
public synchronized Object clone()
```

Returns   A copy of this Hashtable.

Overrides   Object.clone()

Description   This method returns a shallow copy of this Hashtable. This means that the internal array of the Hashtable is copied, but the keys and values themselves are not copied.

contains

```
public synchronized boolean contains(Object value)
```

Parameters   value   The value to find.

Returns   true if this Hashtable contains the given value; false otherwise.

Throws   NullPointerException
          If the given value is null.

Description   This method returns true if the given value is contained in this Hashtable object. The entire table is searched, which can be a time-consuming operation.

containsKey

```
public synchronized boolean containsKey(Object key)
```

Parameters   key   The key to find.

Returns   true if this Hashtable contains the given value; false otherwise.

Description   This method returns true if the given key is contained in this Hashtable object. Because the key is hashed to perform the search, this method runs quite fast, especially in comparison to contains().

elements

```
public synchronized Enumeration elements()
```

Returns   The values in this Hashtable as an Enumeration.

Overrides   Dictionary.elements()

Description   This method returns an Enumeration that iterates through the
             values in this Hashtable.

get

```
public synchronized Object get(Object key)
```
Parameters   key   The key of the value to retrieve.
Returns   The value that corresponds to this key or null if the key is not
             associated with any value.
Overrides   Dictionary.get()
Description   This method returns the value that is associated with the given
             key.

isEmpty

```
public boolean isEmpty()
```
Returns   true if there are no values in the Hashtable; false otherwise.
Overrides   Dictionary.isEmpty()
Description   This method returns a boolean value that indicates whether or
             not the Hashtable is empty.

keys

```
public synchronized Enumeration keys()
```
Returns   The keys in the Hashtable as an Enumeration.
Overrides   Dictionary.keys()
Description   This method returns an Enumeration that iterates through the
             keys in this Hashtable.

put

```
public synchronized Object put(Object key, Object value)
```
Parameters   key   A key object.
             value   A value object.
Returns   The previous value associated with the given key or null if key
             has not previously been associated with a value.
Throws   NullPointerException
                            If either the key or the value is null.
Overrides   Dictionary.put()
Description   This method associates the given key with the given value in
             this Hashtable.

remove

```
public synchronized Object remove(Object key)
```

Parameters   key   A key of the value to remove.

Returns   The value associated with the given key, or null if key is not
                associated with a value.

Overrides   `Dictionary.remove()`

Description   This method removes a key/value pair from this Hashtable. If
                the given key is not in the Hashtable, the method does noth-
                ing.

size

```
public int size()
```

Returns   The number of key in the Hashtable.

Overrides   `Dictionary.size()`

Description   This method returns the number of key/value pairs in the
                Hashtable.

toString

```
public String toString()
```

Returns   A string that represents this Hashtable.

Overrides   `Object.toString()`

Description   This method returns a string representation of this Hashtable.
                The string includes every key/value pair that is contained in
                the Hashtable, so the string returned by toString() can be
                quite long.

Protected Instance Methods

rehash

```
protected void rehash()
```

Description   This method increases the capacity of this Hashtable. A larger
                internal array is created and all existing key/value pairs are
                rehashed into the new array.

Inherited Methods

Method	Inherited From	Method	Inherited From
equals(Object)	Object	finalize()	Object
getClass()	Object	hashCode()	Object
notify()	Object	notifyAll()	Object
wait()	Object	wait(long)	Object
wait(long, int)	Object		

See Also

Cloneable, Dictionary, Enumeration, IllegalArgumentException, NullPoint-erException, Properties, Serializable

17.11   ListResourceBundle

Synopsis

Class Name:	java.util.ListResourceBundle
Superclass:	java.util.ResourceBundle
Immediate Subclasses:	None
Interfaces Implemented:	None
Availability:	New as of JDK 1.1

Description

The ListResourceBundle class is an abstract subclass of ResourceBundle that represents a list of resources for a locale. The resources are listed as a set of key/value pairs. Internally, a Hashtable is used for quick lookup of values. To subclass ListResourceBundle, all you need to do is override getContents() to return a two-dimensional array of Objects that contains the key/value pairs.

When ResourceBundle.getBundle() is called, it attempts to find a resource bundle that most closely matches a particular locale. This can be either a ListResourceBundle subclass or a property file, represented by a PropertyResourceBundle. Once the resource bundle has been retrieved, its contents can be used by the application to present locale-specific information.

PropertyResourceBundle inherits a lot of functionality from ResourceBundle; see the class description of ResourceBundle for more information.

Class Summary

```
public abstract class java.util.ListResourceBundle
                    extends java.util.ResourceBundle {
  // Instance Methods
  public Enumeration getKeys();
  public final Object handleGetObject(String key);

  // Protected Instance Methods
  protected abstract Object[][] getContents();
}
```

Instance Methods

getKeys

`public Enumeration getKeys()`

Returns	The keys in the resource bundle as an Enumeration.
Overrides	ResourceBundle.getKeys()
Description	This method returns an Enumeration that iterates through the keys in this ListResourceBundle.

handleGetObject

`public final Object handleGetObject(String key)`

Parameters	key	The key of the resource to retrieve.
Returns	The resource that corresponds to this key.	
Overrides	ResourceBundle.handleGetObject()	
Description	This method returns the resource that corresponds to the given key. This method should not be called directly by your code. Your code should call ResourceBundle.getObject(), which may call the handleGetObject() objects of multiple subclasses of ResourceBundle looking for a particular resource. Calling handleGetObject() directly only finds resources in the object associated with the method.	

Protected Instance Methods

getContents

`protected abstract Object[][] getContents()`

Returns	The key/value pairs that represent the resources as a two-dimensional array.
Description	This method returns a two-dimensional Object array that contains all the key/value pairs for this ListResourceBundle.

Inherited Methods

Method	Inherited From	Method	Inherited From
clone()	Object	equals(Object)	Object
finalize()	Object	getClass()	Object
getObject(String)	ResourceBundle	getString(String)	ResourceBundle
getStringArray(String)	ResourceBundle	hashCode()	Object
notify()	Object	notifyAll()	Object
setParent(ResourceBundle)	ResourceBundle	toString()	Object
wait()	Object	wait(long)	Object
wait(long, int)	Object		

See Also

Enumeration, Hashtable, PropertyResourceBundle, ResourceBundle

---

17.12   Locale

Synopsis

Class Name:	java.util.Locale
Superclass:	java.lang.Object
Immediate Subclasses:	None
Interfaces Implemented:	java.lang.Cloneable, java.io.Serializable
Availability:	New as of JDK 1.1

Description

The Locale class is used for internationalization. Instances of Locale specify language and formatting customs by identifying a language and a country. A Locale object may also specify a platform-specific variant. Other classes throughout the JDK use Locale objects to determine how to represent themselves to the user. The tasks performed by these classes are called locale-sensitive tasks; the tasks should be done in a way that conforms with the conventions of a particular country and language.

There are a number of classes provided with Java that have static methods that create instances of locale-specific subclasses. For example, the NumberFormat class contains static methods named getInstance() that create and return locale-specific instances of subclasses of NumberFormat. A particular NumberFormat instance knows how to format numbers, currency values, and percentages appropriately for a particular locale. Note that it is the responsibiity of a class like NumberFormat to implement the logic needed to translate locale-identifying information into actual subclass instances.

Classes like NumberFormat that can create locale-specific instances are expected to follow certain conventions:

- Methods like getInstance() in NumberFormat are expected to have two variants: one that takes a Locale argument and one that does not. The variant that does not take a locale argument is expected to use the default locale, which is normally determined by calling Locale.getDefault().
- Classes that can create a variety of locale-specific instances are expected to implement a method that has the following signature:

```
public static Locale[] getAvailableLocales()
```

This requirement is not specified through an interface declaration because interfaces cannot declare static methods. The purpose of this method is to facilitate presenting the user with a list or menu of locale choices. The getAvailableLocales() method should return an array of Locale objects that identifies all of the locales for which the class can create locale-specific instances.

Two additional methods are recommended for helping to display the locale choices:

```
public static final String getDisplayName(Locale objectLocale)
public static String getDisplayName(Locale objectLocale,
                                    Locale displayLocale)
```

The first form of getDisplayName() should return a description of objectLocale that is suitable for display in the default locale. The second form should return a description of objectLocale that is suitable for display in the locale specified by displayLocale. Implementations of these methods generally call the getDisplayName() method of the Locale object.

The language, country and variant information that are encapsulated by a Locale object are specified to a constructor as strings. The language for a Locale should be specified as one of the two-letter lowercase language codes defined by ISO-639. Look for a complete list at *http://www.ics.uci.edu/pub/ietf/http/related/iso639.txt*.

The country for a Locale object should be specified as either " " to indicate that no country is specified, or as one of the two-letter uppercase country codes defined by ISO-3166. Check the site, *http://www.chemie.fu-berlin.de/diverse/doc/ISO_3166.html*, for a complete list

Variant codes are platform-specific.

Although the Locale is constructed from these three types of codes, human-readable names can be obtained by calling getDisplayLanguage(), getDisplayCountry(), and getDisplayVariant().

The Locale class defines a number of constant Locale objects that represent some of the major languages and countries of the world.

Class Summary

```
public abstract class java.util.Locale extends java.lang.Object
                      implements java.lang.Cloneable, java.io.Serializable {
// Constants
public final static Locale CANADA;
public final static Locale CANADA_FRENCH;
public final static Locale CHINA;
public final static Locale CHINESE;
public final static Locale ENGLISH;
```

```
public final static Locale FRANCE;
public final static Locale FRENCH;
public final static Locale GERMAN;
public final static Locale GERMANY;
public final static Locale ITALIAN;
public final static Locale ITALY;
public final static Locale JAPAN;
public final static Locale JAPANESE;
public final static Locale KOREA;
public final static Locale KOREAN;
public final static Locale PRC;
public final static Locale SIMPLIFIED_CHINESE;
public final static Locale TAIWAN;
public final static Locale TRADITIONAL_CHINESE;
public final static Locale UK;
public final static Locale US;

// Constructors
public Locale(String language, String country);
public Locale(String language, String country, String variant);

// Class Methods
public static synchronized Locale getDefault();
public static synchronized void setDefault(Locale newLocale);

// Instance Methods
public Object clone();
public boolean equals(Object obj);
public String getCountry();
public final String getDisplayCountry();
public String getDisplayCountry(Locale inLocale);
public final String getDisplayLanguage();
public String getDisplayLanguage(Locale inLocale);
public final String getDisplayName();
public String getDisplayName(Locale inLocale);
public final String getDisplayVariant();
public String getDisplayVariant(Locale inLocale);
public String getISO3Country();
public String getISO3Language();
public String getLanguage();
public String getVariant();
public synchronized int hashCode();
public final String toString();
}
```

Constants

CANADA

```
public final static Locale CANADA
```
    Description   A locale that represents English-speaking Canada.

CANADA_FRENCH

```
public final static Locale CANADA_FRENCH
```
    Description   A locale that represents French-speaking Canada.

CHINA

```
public final static Locale CHINA
```
    Description   A locale that represents China.

CHINESE

```
public final static Locale CHINESE
```
    Description   A locale that represents the Chinese language.

ENGLISH

```
public final static Locale ENGLISH
```
    Description   A locale that represents the English language.

FRANCE

```
public final static Locale FRANCE
```
    Description   A locale that represents France.

FRENCH

```
public final static Locale FRENCH
```
    Description   A locale that represents the French language.

GERMAN

```
public final static Locale GERMAN
```
    Description   A locale that represents the German language.

GERMANY

```
public final static Locale GERMANY
```
    Description   A locale that represents Germany.

ITALIAN

public final static Locale ITALIAN

Description   A locale that represents the Italian language.

ITALY

public final static Locale ITALY

Description   A locale that represents Italy.

JAPAN

public final static Locale JAPAN

Description   A locale that represents Japan.

JAPANESE

public final static Locale JAPANESE

Description   A locale that represents the Japanese language.

KOREA

public final static Locale KOREA

Description   A locale that represents Korea.

KOREAN

public final static Locale KOREAN

Description   A locale that represents the Korean language.

PRC

public final static Locale PRC

Description   A locale that represents the People's Republic of China. It is equivalent to CHINA.

SIMPLIFIED_CHINESE

public final static Locale SIMPLIFIED_CHINESE

Description   A locale that represents the Chinese language as used in mainland China.

TAIWAN

public final static Locale TAIWAN

Description   A locale that represents Taiwan.

TRADITIONAL_CHINESE

    public final static Locale TRADITIONAL_CHINESE
        Description   A locale that represents the Chinese language as used in Tai-
                       wan.

UK

    public final static Locale UK
        Description   A locale that represents the United Kingdom.

US

    public final static Locale US
        Description   A locale that represents the United States.

Constructors

Locale

    public Locale(String language, String country)
        Parameters   language   A two-letter ISO-639 language code.
                      country   A two-letter ISO-3166 country code or "" to omit
                                  the country specification.
        Description   This constructor creates a Locale that represents the given lan-
                      guage and country.

    public Locale(String language, String country, String variant)
        Parameters   language   A two-letter ISO-639 language code.
                      country   A two-letter ISO-3166 country code or "" to omit
                                  the country specification.
                      variant   A vendor-specific variant code.
        Description   This constructor creates a Locale that represents the given lan-
                      guage, country, and variant.

Class Methods

getDefault

    public static synchronized Locale getDefault()
        Returns   The default Locale.
        Description   This method returns the current default Locale. An applica-
                      tion or applet uses this method to find out how to present
                      locale-sensitive information, such as textual strings and num-
                      bers. The method is generally called during application initial-
                      ization to get the default Locale. Once the locale is set, it
                      almost never changes. If you do change the locale, you should
                      probably reload the GUI for your application, so that any
                      locale-sensitive information in the interface is changed.

The initial default Locale is set by the host system.

setDefault

public static synchronized void setDefault(Locale newLocale)

Parameters	newLocale	The new default locale.
Description		This method changes the current default locale to newLocale. Note that calling setDefault() does not change the default locale of the host system.

Instance Methods

clone

public Object clone()

Returns	A copy of this Locale.
Overrides	Object.clone()
Description	This method creates a copy of this Locale and returns it.

equals

public boolean equals(Object obj)

Parameters	obj	The object to be compared with this object.
Returns		true if the objects are equal; false if they are not.
Overrides		Object.equals()
Description		This method returns true if obj is an instance of Locale, and it contains the same value as the object this method is associated with.

getCountry

public String getCountry()

Returns	The country of this Locale.
Description	This method returns a String that represents the country of this Locale. This String is the same String that was passed to the constructor of this Locale object. The String is normally a two-letter ISO-3166 country code.

getDisplayCountry

public final String getDisplayCountry()

Returns	The country of this Locale.
Description	This method returns the country of this Locale as a country name in a form appropriate for this Locale. If the country name cannot be found, this method returns the same value as getCountry().

```
public String getDisplayCountry(Locale inLocale)
```
Parameters   inLocale   The locale to use when finding the country name.

Returns   The country of this Locale, localized to the given locale.

Description   This method returns the country of this Locale as a country name in a form appropriate for inLocale. For example, Locale.ITALY.getDisplayCountry(Locale.GERMAN) returns the German name for Italy, Italien.

getDisplayLanguage

```
public final String getDisplayLanguage()
```
Returns   The language of this Locale.

Description   This method returns the language of this Locale as a language name in a form appropriate for this Locale. If the language name cannot be found, this method returns the same value as getLanguage().

```
public String getDisplayLanguage(Locale inLocale)
```
Parameters   inLocale   The locale to use when finding the language name.

Returns   The language of this Locale, localized to the given locale.

Description   This method returns the language of this Locale as a language name in a form appropriate for inLocale. For example, Locale.ITALY.getDisplayLanguage(Locale.GERMAN) returns the German name for the Italian language, Italienisch.

getDisplayName

```
public final String getDisplayName()
```
Returns   A string that represents this Locale.

Description   This method constructs a string that represents this Locale by calling getDisplayLanguage(), getDisplayCountry(), and getDisplayVariant(). In other words, the method returns a string that contains the country name, language name, and variant in a form appropriate for this Locale. If any of the names cannot be found, the String that was passed to the constructor of this Locale object is used instead. These strings are normally two-letter ISO codes.

```
public String getDisplayName(Locale inLocale)
```
Parameters   inLocale   The locale to use when constructing the string representation.

Returns   A string that represents this Locale.

Description This method constructs a string that represents this Locale by
             calling   getDisplayLanguage(inLocale),   getDisplayCoun-
             try(inLocale), and getDisplayVariant(inLocale). In other
             words, the method returns a string that contains the country
             name, language name, and variant in a form appropriate for
             inLocale. If any of the names cannot be found, the String
             that was passed to the constructor of this Locale object is used
             instead. These strings are normally two-letter ISO codes.

getDisplayVariant

public final String getDisplayVariant()

Returns   The variant of this Locale.

Description This method returns the variant of this Locale as a human-
             readable string in a form appropriate for this Locale. If the
             variant name cannot be found, this method returns the same
             value as getVariant().

public String getDisplayVariant(Locale inLocale)

Parameters   inLocale   The locale to use when finding the variant
                          name.

Returns   The variant of this Locale, localized to the given locale.

Description This method returns the variant of this Locale as a human-
             readable string in a form appropriate for inLocale.

getISO3Country

public String getISO3Country() throws MissingResourceException

Returns   The ISO three-letter country code of this Locale.

Throws   MissingResourceException
                          If the requested code cannot be found.

Description This method returns the country of this Locale as a three-letter
             ISO country code. The country code is obtained from a
             ResourceBundle for this Locale.

getISO3Language

public String getISO3Language() throws MissingResourceException

Returns   The ISO three-letter language code of this Locale.

Throws   MissingResourceException
                          If the requested code cannot be found.

Description This method returns the language of this Locale as a three-
             letter ISO language code. The language code is obtained from
             a ResourceBundle for this Locale.

getLanguage

```
public String getLanguage()
```
Returns   The language of this Locale.

Description   This method returns a String that represents the language of this Locale. This String is the same String that was passed to the constructor of this Locale object. The String is normally a two-letter ISO-639 language code.

getVariant

```
public String getVariant()
```
Returns   The variant of this Locale.

Description   This method returns the variant code of this Locale. If no variant code is specified for this Locale, an empty string is returned.

hashCode

```
public synchronized int hashCode()
```
Returns   A hashcode for this Locale.

Overrides   Object.hashCode()

Description   This method returns a hashcode for this object.

toString

```
public final String toString()
```
Returns   A string representation of this Locale.

Overrides   Object.toString()

Description   This method returns a string representation of this Locale, constructed from the language code, country code, and variant code. The various codes are separated by underscore characters. If a code is missing, it is omitted.

Inherited Methods

Method	Inherited From	Method	Inherited From
finalize()	Object	getClass()	Object
notify()	Object	notifyAll()	Object
wait()	Object	wait(long)	Object
wait(long, int)	Object		

See Also

Cloneable, DateFormat, NumberFormat, ResourceBundle, Serializable

17.13   MissingResourceException

Synopsis

Class Name: java.util.MissingResourceException
Superclass: java.lang.RuntimeException
Immediate Subclasses: None
Interfaces Implemented: None
Availability: New as of JDK 1.1

Description

A MissingResourceException is thrown when a requested resource cannot be found.

Class Summary

```
public class java.util.MissingResourceException
            extends java.lang.RuntimeException {
  // Constructors
  public MissingResourceException(String s, String classname, String key);

  // Instance Methods
  public String getClassName();
  public String getKey();
}
```

Constructors

MissingResourceException

```
public MissingResourceException(String s, String classname,
                                 String key)
```

Parameters   s   The detail message.
              classname   The resource class that generated this exception.
              key   The key that was used to request a resource.
Description   This constructor creates a MissingResourceException with the given information.

Instance Methods

getClassName

```
public String getClassName()
```

Returns   The class name that generated this exception.

Description   This method returns the class name that was used to create this
              exception.

getKey

```
public String getKey()
```

Returns   The key that caused this exception.

Description   This method returns the key that was used to create this excep-
              tion.

Inherited Methods

Method	Inherited From	Method	Inherited From
clone()	Object	equals(Object)	Object
fillInStackTrace()	Throwable	finalize()	Object
getClass()	Object	getLocalizedMessage()	Throwable
getMessage()	Throwable	hashCode()	Object
notify()	Object	notifyAll()	Object
printStackTrace()	Throwable	printStack-Trace(PrintStream)	Throwable
printStack-Trace(PrintWriter)	Throwable	toString()	Throwable
wait()	Object	wait(long)	Object
wait(long, int)	Object		

See Also

Exception, ResourceBundle, RuntimeException

17.14   NoSuchElementException

Synopsis

Class Name: java.util.NoSuchElementException

Superclass: java.lang.RuntimeException

Immediate Subclasses: None
Interfaces Implemented: None
Availability: JDK 1.0 or later

Description

A NoSuchElementException is thrown by Enumeration objects when there are no more elements to be returned.

Class Summary

```
public class java.util.NoSuchElementException
            extends java.lang.RuntimeException {
  // Constructors
  public NoSuchElementException();
  public NoSuchElementException(String s);
}
```

Constructors

NoSuchElementException

```
public NoSuchElementException()
```

Description   This constructor creates a NoSuchElementException with no associated detail message.

```
public NoSuchElementException(String s)
```

Parameters   s   The detail message.

Description   This constructor creates a NoSuchElementException with the specified detail message.

Inherited Methods

Method	Inherited From	Method	Inherited From
clone()	Object	equals(Object)	Object
fillInStackTrace()	Throwable	finalize()	Object
getClass()	Object	getLocalizedMessage()	Throwable
getMessage()	Throwable	hashCode()	Object
notify()	Object	notifyAll()	Object
printStackTrace()	Throwable	printStack-Trace(PrintStream)	Throwable
printStack-Trace(PrintWriter)	Throwable	toString()	Throwable
wait()	Object	wait(long)	Object
wait(long, int)	Object		

See Also

Enumeration, Exception, RuntimeException

17.15   Observable

Synopsis

Class Name: java.util.Observable
Superclass: java.lang.Object
Immediate Subclasses: None
Interfaces Implemented: None
Availability: JDK 1.0 or later

Description

Subclasses of the Observable class are used to implement the model portion of the model-view paradigm. The idea is that an Observable object, the model, represents some data that is being manipulated through a user interface, while Observer objects provide the user with a view of the data. When the Observable object is modified, it tells the Observer objects that the model has been modified by calling notifyObservers(). An Observer object registers with an Observable object to receive notifications when the Observable is modified. The Observer object is then notified of changes via the update() method.

Class Summary

```
public class java.util.Observable extends java.lang.Object {
  // Constructors
  public Observable();

  // Instance Methods
  public synchronized void addObserver(Observer o);
  public synchronized int countObservers();
  public synchronized void deleteObserver(Observer o);
  public synchronized void deleteObservers();
  public synchronized boolean hasChanged();
  public void notifyObservers();
  public void notifyObservers(Object arg);

  // Protected Instance Methods
  protected synchronized void clearChanged();
  protected synchronized void setChanged();
}
```

Constructors

Observable

public Observable()

Description   This constructor creates an Observable object with no registered Observer objects.

InstanceMethods

addObserver

public synchronized void addObserver(Observer o)

Parameters   o   The Observer to be added.

Description   This method registers the given Observer with this Observable object. The given Observer is then notified when notifyObservers() is called.

countObservers

public synchronized int countObservers()

Returns   The number of registered Observer objects for this Observable object.

Description   This method returns the number of Observer objects that are registered with this Observable object.

deleteObserver

public synchronized void deleteObserver(Observer o)

Parameters   o   The Observer to be removed.

Description   This method unregisters the given Observer with this Observable object. The given Observer is no longer notified when notifyObservers() is called.

deleteObservers

public synchronized void deleteObservers()

Description   This method unregisters all of the Observer objects of this Observable object. Thus, no objects are notified if notifyObservers() is called.

hasChanged

public synchronized boolean hasChanged()

Returns   true if this object has been flagged as changed; false otherwise.

Description   This method returns the value of an internal "dirty" flag. The flag can be modified using the `protected` methods `setChanged()` and `clearChanged()`.

notifyObservers

`public void notifyObservers()`

Description   This method calls the `update()` method of all registered `Observer` objects. The value passed as the second argument to each of the `update()` method calls is `null`.

`public void notifyObservers(Object arg)`

Parameters   `arg`   A "hint" object that describes a change.

Description   This method calls the `update()` method of all registered `Observer` objects. The value passed as the second argument to each of the `update()` method calls is the given object `arg`.

This "hint" object can be used to efficiently update the views of a model. For example, an `Observable` object could represent satellite image data. A set of `Observer` objects would provide different graphical views of the data. If the model data changes, the `arg` object describes the part of the data that changed, and the `Observer` views could use this "hint" to update only parts of their displays.

Protected Instance Methods

clearChanged

`protected synchronized void clearChanged()`

Description   This method sets an internal "dirty" flag to `false`. After this method is called, this object's `hasChanged()` method returns `false`.

setChanged

`protected synchronized void setChanged()`

Description   This method sets an internal "dirty" flag to `true`. After this method is called, this object's `hasChanged()` method returns `true`.

Inherited Methods

Method	Inherited From	Method	Inherited From
clone()	Object	equals(Object)	Object
finalize()	Object	getClass()	Object
hashCode()	Object	notify()	Object
notifyAll()	Object	toString()	Object
wait()	Object	wait(long)	Object
wait(long, int)	Object		

See Also

Observer

17.16   Observer

Synopsis

Interface Name:	java.util.Observer
Super-interface:	None
Immediate Sub-interfaces:	
	None
Implemented By:	None
Availability:	JDK 1.0 or later

Description

The Observer interface is used to implement the view portion of the model-view paradigm. The idea is that an Observable object, the model, represents some data that is being manipulated through a user interface, while Observer objects provide the user with a view of the data. When the Observable object is modified, it tells the Observer objects that the model has been modified by calling notifyOb-servers(). An Observer object registers with an Observable object to receive notifications when the Observable is modified. The Observer object is then notified of changes via the update() method.

Interface Summary

```
public abstract interface java.util.Observer {
   // Methods
   public abstract void update(Observable o, Object arg);
}
```

Methods

update

```
void update(Observable o, Object arg)
```

Parameters	o	The object that has been changed.
	arg	A "hint" object that describes the change.
Description		This method is called to indicate that the data in the model implemented by the specified Observable object has been modified. The arg parameter is used to communicate changed information from the model to its view.

This "hint" object can be used to efficiently update the views of a model. For example, an Observable object could represent satellite image data. A set of Observer objects would provide different graphical views of the data. If the model data changed, the arg object would describe the part of the data that changed, and the Observer views could use this "hint" to update only parts of their displays.

See Also

Observable

17.17   Properties

Synopsis

Class Name:	java.util.Properties
Superclass:	java.util.Hashtable
Immediate Subclasses:	None
Interfaces Implemented:	None
Availability:	JDK 1.0 or later

Description

The Properties class is a subclass of Hashtable that deals exclusively with string keys and string values. Furthermore, a Properties object can be written to an OutputStream and read from an InputStream. Note that the load() and save() correctly convert Unicode strings to and from byte streams, using the getLocalizedInputStream() and getLocalizedOutputStream() methods of Runtime.

Class Summary

```
public class java.util.Properties extends java.util.Hashtable {
  // Variables
  protected Properties defaults;

  // Constructors
  public Properties();
  public Properties(Properties defaults);

  // Instance Methods
  public String getProperty(String key);
  public String getProperty(String key, String defaultValue);
  public void list(PrintStream out);
  public void list(PrintWriter out);                    // New in 1.1
  public synchronized void load(InputStream in);
  public Enumeration propertyNames();
  public synchronized void save(OutputStream out, String header);
}
```

Variables

defaults

```
protected Properties defaults
```
> Description   A collection of default property values. If a key/value pair is not found in this Properties object, the defaults object is searched.

Constructors

Properties

```
public Properties()
```
> Description   This constructor creates an empty Properties object.

```
public Properties(Properties defaults)
```
> Parameters   defaults   A set of default key/value pairs.
> Description   This constructor creates an empty Properties object that gets default values for keys that it does not contain from the given Properties object.

Instance Methods

getProperty

```
public String getProperty(String key)
```
> Parameters   key   The key of the value to retrieve.
> Returns   The value of the given property or null if the key is not associated with any value.

Description   This method returns the value that is associated with the given key. If the key is not found, a default value is returned if this object was created with a default `Properties` table that contains a value for the key. If neither a value nor a default value can be found, this method returns `null`.

`public String getProperty(String key, String defaultValue)`

Parameters   `key`   The key of the value to retrieve.

               `defaultValue`

                       The value to return if `key` cannot be found.

Returns   The value of the given property or `defaultValue` if the key is not associated with any value.

Description   This method returns the value that is associated with the given key. If the key is not found, a default value is returned if this object was created with a default `Properties` table that contains a value for the key. If neither a value nor a default value can be found, this method returns `defaultValue`.

list

`public void list(PrintStream out)`

Parameters   `out`   The output stream to use.

Description   This method writes a listing of the contents of this object, in a format suitable for debugging, to the given `PrintStream`. As of JDK 1.1, use `list(PrintWriter)` instead.

`public void list(PrintWriter out)`

Availability   New as of JDK 1.1

Parameters   `out`   The output stream to use.

Description   This method writes a listing of the contents of this object, in a format suitable for debugging, to the given `PrintWriter`.

load

`public synchronized void load(InputStream in) throws IOException`

Parameters   `in`   The input stream to use.

Throws   `IOException`   If any kind of I/O error occurs.

Description   This method reads key/value pairs from the given `InputStream`. Here is the format the method expects:

- Lines that begin with # or ! are comments and are ignored.
- Blank lines are ignored.
- All other lines should specify a key/value pair and be of the form:

```
key = value
```

or

```
key : value
```

or

```
key value
```

All of these forms are equivalent. The method also recognizes the following escape characters and treats them as described:

Character	Treatment
\ *newline*	An escaped newline character is ignored, along with the spaces or tabs that follow it
\n	Expands to a newline character
\r	Expands to a return character
\t	Expands to a tab character
\uxxxx	Expands to the Unicode character code specified by the hexadecimal digits

propertyNames

public Enumeration propertyNames()

Returns   The keys in this Properties object as an Enumeration.

Description   This method returns an Enumeration that iterates through the keys in this Properties object.

save

public synchronized void save(OutputStream out, String header)

Parameters   out   The output stream to use.

                 header   A header string.

Description   This method writes key/value pairs to the given OutputStream. The format of the output is such that it can be read by the load() method.

                 If header is not null, a # followed by header is written to the OutputStream first, thereby making the content of the string a comment that precedes the key/value pairs.

Inherited Methods

Method	Inherited From	Method	Inherited From
clear()	Hashtable	clone()	Hashtable
contains(Object)	Hashtable	containsKey(Object)	Hashtable
elements()	Hashtable	equals(Object)	Object
finalize()	Object	get(Object)	Hashtable

Method	Inherited From	Method	Inherited From
getClass()	Object	hashCode()	Object
isEmpty()	Hashtable	keys()	Hashtable
notify()	Object	notifyAll()	Object
put(Object, Object)	Hashtable	remove(Object)	Hashtable
size()	Hashtable	toString()	Hashtable
wait()	Object	wait(long)	Object
wait(long, int)	Object		

See Also

Enumeration, Hashtable, InputStream, IOException, OutputStream, PrintStream, PrintWriter, Runtime

---

17.18   PropertyResourceBundle

Synopsis

Class Name: java.util.PropertyResourceBundle
Superclass: java.util.ResourceBundle
Immediate Subclasses: None
Interfaces Implemented: None
Availability: New as of JDK 1.1

Description

The PropertyResourceBundle class is a concrete subclass of ResourceBundle that represents a set of resources for a locale. The resources are specified as a set of key/value string pairs in a property file. Internally, a Properties object is used to retrieve the resources from the property file.

When ResourceBundle.getBundle() is called, it attempts to find a resource bundle that most closely matches a particular locale. This can be either a ListResourceBundle subclass or a property file, represented by a PropertyResourceBundle. Once the resource bundle has been retrieved, its contents can be used by the application to present locale-specific information.

PropertyResourceBundle inherits a lot of functionality from ResourceBundle; see the class description of ResourceBundle for more information.

Class Summary

```
public class java.util.PropertyResourceBundle
            extends java.util.ResourceBundle {
  // Constructors
  public PropertyResourceBundle(InputStream stream);

  // Instance Methods
  public Enumeration getKeys();
  public Object handleGetObject(String key);
}
```

Constructors

PropertyResourceBundle

```
public PropertyResourceBundle(InputStream stream)
       throws IOException
```

Parameters	stream	The input stream to use.
Throws	IOException	If any kind of I/O error occurs.
Description		This constructor creates a PropertyResourceBundle that reads properties from the given input stream.

Instance Methods

getKeys

```
public Enumeration getKeys()
```

Returns	The keys in the resource bundle as an Enumeration.
Overrides	ResourceBundle.getKeys()
Description	This method returns an Enumeration that iterates through the keys in this PropertyResourceBundle.

handleGetObject

```
public final Object handleGetObject(String key)
```

Parameters	key	The key of the resource to retrieve.
Returns		The resource that corresponds to this key.
Overrides		ResourceBundle.handleGetObject()
Description		This method returns the resource that corresponds to the given key.

Inherited Methods

Method	Inherited From	Method	Inherited From
clone()	Object	equals(Object)	Object
finalize()	Object	getClass()	Object
getObject(String)	ResourceBundle	getString(String)	ResourceBundle

Method	Inherited From	Method	Inherited From
getStringArray(String)	ResourceBundle	hashCode()	Object
notify()	Object	notifyAll()	Object
setParent(ResourceBundle)	ResourceBundle	toString()	Object
wait()	Object	wait(long)	Object
wait(long, int)	Object		

See Also

Enumeration, IOException, ListResourceBundle, Properties, ResourceBundle

17.19   Random

Synopsis

Class Name: java.util.Random
Superclass: java.lang.Object
Immediate Subclasses: None
Interfaces Implemented: java.io.Serializable
Availability: JDK 1.0 or later

Description

The Random class is a pseudo-random number generator. Pseudo-random numbers are generated by starting with a seed value and then using an algorithm to generate a sequence of numbers that appear to be random. The Random class uses a 48-bit seed and a linear congruential algorithm to modify the seed. As a consequence of this implementation, two Random instances that are constructed with the same seed value generate exactly the same sequence of numbers.

The Random class provides methods that return pseudo-random values for various primitive Java types. The Math.random() method is easier to use if you do not need to fine-tune the generation of random numbers.

Class Summary

```
public class java.util.Random extends java.lang.Object
            implements java.io.Serializable {
    // Constructors
    public Random();
    public Random(long seed);

    // Instance Methods
    public void nextBytes(byte[] bytes);                  // New in 1.1
    public double nextDouble();
```

```
public float nextFloat();
public synchronized double nextGaussian();
public int nextInt();
public long nextLong();
public synchronized void setSeed(long seed);

// Protected Instance Methods
protected synchronized int next(int bits);        // New in 1.1
}
```

Constructors

Random

public Random()

Description   This constructor creates a Random object with the current time
               as its seed value.

public Random(long seed)

Parameters   seed   The seed value to use.
Description   This constructor creates a Random object with the given seed
               value.

Instance Methods

nextBytes

public void nextBytes(byte[] bytes)

Availability   New as of JDK 1.1
Parameters   bytes   The byte array to fill.
Description   This method fills the given array with pseudo-random byte val-
               ues.

nextDouble

public double nextDouble()

Returns   The next pseudo-random double value.
Description   This method returns the next pseudo-random, uniformly dis-
               tributed double value. The value is between 0.0 and 1.0 inclu-
               sive.

nextFloat

public float nextFloat()

Returns   The next pseudo-random float value.
Description   This method returns the next pseudo-random, uniformly dis-
               tributed float value. The value is between 0.0 and 1.0 inclusive.

nextGaussian

public synchronized double nextGaussian()

Returns   The next pseudo-random double value.

Description   This method returns the next pseudo-random, Gaussian distributed double value. The value has a mean of 0.0 and a standard deviation of 1.0 from the random number sequence. The value is between -1.0 and 1.0.

nextInt

public int nextInt()

Returns   The next pseudo-random int value.

Description   This method returns the next pseudo-random, uniformly distributed int value.

nextLong

public long nextLong()

Returns   The next pseudo-random long value.

Description   This method returns the next pseudo-random, uniformly distributed long value.

setSeed

public synchronized void setSeed(long seed)

Parameters   seed   The new seed value.

Description   This method sets this Random object's seed value to the given value.

Protected Instance Methods

next

protected synchronized int next(int bits)

Availability New as of JDK 1.1

Parameters   bits   The number of bits to generate.

Returns   The specified number of pseudo-random bits.

Description   This method generates the given number of bits and returns them as an integer value. A subclass of Random should override this method, as it is used by all of the other random-number generation methods in the class.

Inherited Methods

Method	Inherited From	Method	Inherited From
clone()	Object	equals(Object)	Object
finalize()	Object	getClass()	Object
hashCode()	Object	notify()	Object
notifyAll()	Object	toString()	Object
wait()	Object	wait(long)	Object
wait(long, int)	Object		

See Also

Math, Serializable

17.20   ResourceBundle

Synopsis

Class Name: java.util. ResourceBundle
Superclass: java.lang.Object
Immediate Subclasses: java.util.ListResourceBundle,
                                java.util.PropertyResourceBundle
Interfaces Implemented: None
Availability: New as of JDK 1.1

Description

The ResourceBundle class is an abstract class that represents a set of localized data. An application retrieves a ResourceBundle based on its locale. A Resource-Bundle can contain GUI labels and other locale-specific information that the application needs to run in a specific locale.

Conceptually, a resource bundle is a set of related classes that all inherit from a particular subclass of ResourceBundle. The base resource bundle defines all of the resources for a particular application, while each of the subclasses specifies the appropriate values for a particular locale. Each subclass has the same base name, plus a suffix that identifies its locale.

A static method, getBundle(), is used to locate a resource bundle for a particular locale. This method searches for resources in two forms. First, it looks for a subclass of ResourceBundle or ListResourceBundle with the appropriate name. If one is found, an instance of the class is created and returned. If no appropriate subclass can be found, getBundle() then searches for a property file with the appropriate name. If one is found, a `PropertyResourceBundle` is created from the file and returned.

The `getBundle()` method constructs a name from a specified base resource name and the locale. It then searches for either a class or a property file with this name. If the method fails to find an exact match, it tries to find a close match. The method constructs names by dropping to the next name on the list if the current name cannot be found:

- base + "_" + language + "_" + country + "_" + variant
- base + "_" + language + "_" + country
- base + "_" + language
- base
- base + "_" + default language + "_" + default country + "_" + default variant
- base + "_" + default language + "_" + default country
- base + "_" + default language

For example, if you call `getBundle("Labels", new Locale("it", "IT", "Be"))`, the method looks for a class or property file with one of the following names (assuming the default locale is the United States):

- `Labels_it_IT_Be`
- `Labels_it_IT`
- `Labels_it`
- `Labels`
- `Labels_en_US_Be`
- `Labels_en_US`
- `Labels_en`

A particular `ResourceBundle` object contains a set of key/value pairs that defines the resources for a particular application. The keys are always `String` objects that name the resources, while the values can be any sort of object needed for the application. The `ResourceBundle` class defines convenience methods for retrieving `String` and `String[]` objects. If you need to use other kinds of objects, you can use the `getObject()` method to retrieve them and simply cast the results to the appropriate types.

Class Summary

```
public abstract class java.util.ResourceBundle extends java.lang.Object {
    // Variables
    protected ResourceBundle parent;

    // Class Methods
    public final static ResourceBundle getBundle(String baseName);
    public final static ResourceBundle getBundle(String baseName,
                                      Locale locale);
```

```
    // Instance Methods
    public abstract Enumeration getKeys();
    public final Object getObject(String key)j;
    public final String getString(String key);
    public final String[] getStringArray(String key);

    // Protected Instance Methods
    protected abstract Object handleGetObject(String key);
    protected void setParent(ResourceBundle parent);
}
```

Variables

parent

protected ResourceBundle parent

Description   The parent ResourceBundle of this ResourceBundle. If this
ResourceBundle does not contain a particular resource, its parent is searched. The parent can be set using setParent().

Class Methods

getBundle

public final static ResourceBundle getBundle(String baseName)
                    throws MissingResourceException

Parameters   baseName   The resource name.

Returns   The named ResourceBundle for the default locale.

Throws   MissingResourceException
                        If a matching ResourceBundle can't be located.

Description   This method finds or constructs the appropriate ResourceBundle subclass specified by baseName and localized for the default
locale. See the description of the ResourceBundle class for
more information about how this method works.

public final static ResourceBundle getBundle(String baseName,
                                        Locale locale)

Parameters   baseName   The resource name.
             locale   The Locale to use.

Returns   The named ResourceBundle for the given locale.

Throws   MissingResourceException
                        If a matching ResourceBundle can't be located.

Description   This method finds or constructs the appropriate ResourceBundle subclass specified by baseName and localized for the given
locale. See the description of the ResourceBundle class for
more information about how this method works.

Instance Methods

getKeys

```
public abstract Enumeration getKeys()
```

Returns   The keys in the `ResourceBundle` as an `Enumeration`.

Description   This method returns an `Enumeration` that iterates through the keys in this `ResourceBundle`. A subclass of `ResourceBundle` must provide an implementation for this method.

getObject

```
public final Object getObject(String key)
            throws MissingResourceException
```

Parameters   key   The key of the resource to retrieve.

Returns   The `Object` identified by key.

Throws   `MissingResourceException`
              If the resource cannot be found.

Description   This method returns the named resource as an `Object`. If the named resource is not found in this `ResourceBundle`, the parent `ResourceBundle` is searched.

getString

```
public final String getString(String key)
            throws MissingResourceException
```

Parameters   key   The key of the resource to retrieve.

Returns   The `String` object identified by key.

Throws   `MissingResourceException`
              If the resource cannot be found.

Description   This method returns the named resource as a `String` object. This method is a convenience routine that calls `getObject()` and casts the result to a `String` object.

getStringArray

```
public final String[] getStringArray(String key)
            throws MissingResourceException
```

Parameters   key   The key of the resource to retrieve.

Returns   The `String[]` array identified by key.

Throws   `MissingResourceException`
              If the resource cannot be found.

Description   This method returns the named resource as an array of `String` objects. This method is a convenience routine that calls `getObject()` and casts the result to a `String[]` object.

Protected Instance Methods

handleGetObject

```
protected abstract Object handleGetObject(String key)
                        throws MissingResourceException
```

Parameters	key	The key of the resource to retrieve.
Returns		The resource that corresponds to this key.
Throws	MissingResourceException	
		If the resource cannot be found.
Description		This method returns the resource that corresponds to the given key. This method is called directly by getObject(), so it is called indirectly by getMenu(), getMenuBar(), getString(), and getStringArray().
		A subclass of ResourceBundle must provide an implementation for this method.

setParent

```
protected void setParent(ResourceBundle parent)
```

Parameters	parent	The new parent of this ResourceBundle.
Description		This method sets the parent ResourceBundle of this ResourceBundle. If a requested resource cannot be found in this ResourceBundle, the parent is searched.

Inherited Methods

Method	Inherited From	Method	Inherited From
clone()	Object	equals(Object)	Object
finalize()	Object	getClass()	Object
hashCode()	Object	notify()	Object
notifyAll()	Object	toString()	Object
wait()	Object	wait(long)	Object
wait(long, int)	Object		

See Also

Enumeration, ListResourceBundle, Locale, PropertyResourceBundle, String

17.21   SimpleTimeZone

Synopsis

Class Name: java.util.SimpleTimeZone
Superclass: java.util.TimeZone
Immediate Subclasses: None
Interfaces Implemented: None
Availability: New as of JDK 1.1

Description

The SimpleTimeZone class is a concrete subclass of the abstract TimeZone class. SimpleTimeZone represents a time zone offset for use with GregorianCalendar. SimpleTimeZone does not take into account the historical vicissitudes of daylight savings time, however. Instead, it assumes that the shifts to and from daylight savings time always occur at the same time of the year.

Normally, SimpleTimeZone objects are not created directly, but instead obtained by calling TimeZone.getDefault(). This method creates a subclass of TimeZone that is appropriate for the current locale. You can also call TimeZone.getTimeZone() to obtain a TimeZone object for a specific time zone.

Class Summary

```
public class java.util.SimpleTimeZone extends java.util.TimeZone {
    // Constructors
    public SimpleTimeZone(int rawOffset, String ID);
    public SimpleTimeZone(int rawOffset, String ID, int startMonth,
                    int startDayOfWeekInMonth, int startDayOfWeek,
                    int startTime, int endMonth, int endDayOfWeekInMonth,
                    int endDayOfWeek, int endTime);

    // Instance Methods
    public Object clone();
    public boolean equals(Object obj);
    public int getOffset(int era, int year, int month, int day,
                    int dayOfWeek, int millis);
    public int getRawOffset();
    public synchronized int hashCode();
    public boolean inDaylightTime(Date date);
    public void setEndRule(int month, int dayOfWeekInMonth,
                    int dayOfWeek, int time);
    public void setRawOffset(int offsetMillis);
    public void setStartRule(int month, int dayOfWeekInMonth,
                    int dayOfWeek, int time);
    public void setStartYear(int year);
    public boolean useDaylightTime();
}
```

Constructors

SimpleTimeZone

```
public SimpleTimeZone(int rawOffset, String ID)
```

Parameters	rawOffset	The raw offset of this time zone from GMT, in milliseconds.
	ID	The ID of this time zone.
Description		This constructor creates a SimpleTimeZone that uses the given offset from GMT and has the specified ID. This constructor creates a SimpleTimeZone that does not use daylight savings time.

```
public SimpleTimeZone(int rawOffset, String ID, int startMonth,
                      int startDayOfWeekInMonth, int startDayOfWeek,
                      int startTime, int endMonth,
                      int endDayOfWeekInMonth, int endDayOfWeek,
                      int endTime)
```

Parameters	rawOffset	The raw offset of this time zone from GMT, in milliseconds.
	ID	The ID of this time zone.
	startMonth	The month when daylight savings time begins.
	startDayOfWeekInMonth	The week in the month when daylight savings time begins.
	startDayOfWeek	The day of the week when daylight savings time begins.
	startTime	The time of day when daylight savings time begins, in milliseconds.
	endMonth	The month when daylight savings time ends.
	endDayOfWeekInMonth	The week in the month when daylight savings time ends.
	endDayOfWeek	The day of the week when daylight savings time ends.
	endTime	The time of day when daylight savings time ends, in milliseconds.
Description		This constructor creates a SimpleTimeZone that uses the given offset from GMT, has the specified ID, and uses daylight savings time. Daylight savings time begins and ends at the specified dates and times.

For example, Brazil Eastern Time (BET) is three hours behind GMT. Daylight savings time for BET starts on the first Sunday in

April at 2:00 AM, and ends on the last Sunday in October, also
at 2:00 A.M. To construct a `TimeZone` that represents BET, you
would use the following:

```
new SimpleTimeZone(-3 * 60 * 60 * 1000, "BET",
                    Calendar.APRIL, 1,
                    Calendar.SUNDAY, 2 * 60 * 60 * 1000,
                    Calendar.OCTOBER, -1,
                    Calendar.SUNDAY, 2 * 60 * 60 * 1000)
```

Instance Methods

clone

`public Object clone()`

Returns	A copy of this `SimpleTimeZone`.
Overrides	`TimeZone.clone()`
Description	This method creates a copy of this `SimpleTimeZone` and returns it.

equals

`public boolean equals(Object obj)`

Parameters	`obj` The object to be compared with this object.
Returns	`true` if the objects are equal; `false` if they are not.
Overrides	`Object.equals()`
Description	This method returns `true` if `obj` is an instance of `SimpleTime-Zone`, and it contains the same value as the object this method is associated with.

getOffset

`public int getOffset(int era, int year, int month, int day,`
`            int dayOfWeek, int millis)`

Parameters	`era` The era.
	`year` The year.
	`month` The month.
	`day` The day.
	`dayOfWeek` The day of the week.
	`millis` The time of day in milliseconds.
Returns	An offset from GMT, in milliseconds.
Overrides	`TimeZone.getOffset()`
Description	This method calculates an offset from GMT for the given date for this `SimpleTimeZone`. In other words, the offset takes daylight savings time into account. The return value should be added to GMT to get local time.

getRawOffset

```
public int getRawOffset()
```

Returns   An offset from GMT, in milliseconds.

Overrides   `TimeZone.getRawOffset()`

Description   This method returns the raw offset from GMT for this `Simple-TimeZone`. In other words, the offset does not take daylight savings time into account.

hashCode

```
public synchronized int hashCode()
```

Returns   A hashcode for this SimpleTimeZone.

Overrides   `Object.hashCode()`

Description   This method returns a hashcode for this object.

inDaylightTime

```
public boolean inDaylightTime(Date date)
```

Parameters   date   The date to be tested.

Returns   true if the given date is between the start and end of daylight savings time for this `SimpleTimeZone`; false otherwise.

Overrides   `TimeZone.inDaylightTime()`

Description   This method returns a boolean value that indicates if the given date is in daylight savings time for this `SimpleTimeZone`.

setEndRule

```
public void setEndRule(int month, int dayOfWeekInMonth,
                       int dayOfWeek, int time)
```

Parameters   month   The month when daylight savings time ends.

                DayOfWeekInMonth

                               The week of the month when daylight savings time ends.

                dayOfWeek   The day of the week when daylight savings time ends.

                time   The time of day when daylight savings time ends, in milliseconds.

Description   This method sets the time when daylight savings time ends for this `SimpleTimeZone`. For example, to set the end of daylight savings time to 2 A.M. on the last Sunday in October, you would use the following:

```
setEndRule(Calendar.OCTOBER, -1, Calendar.SUNDAY,
           2 * 60 * 60 * 1000)
```

setRawOffset

```
public void setRawOffset(int offsetMillis)
```

Parameters   offsetMillis

                  The new raw offset from GMT, in milliseconds.

Overrides   `TimeZone.setRawOffset()`

Description   This method is used to set the raw offset value for this Simple-TimeZone.

setStartRule

```
public void setStartRule(int month, int dayOfWeekInMonth,
                         int dayOfWeek, int time)
```

Parameters   month   The month when daylight savings time begins.

              DayOfWeekInMonth

                  The week of the month when daylight savings time begins.

              dayOfWeek   The day of the week when daylight savings time begins.

              time   The time of day when daylight savings time begins, in milliseconds.

Description   This method sets the time when daylight savings time begins for this SimpleTimeZone. For example, to set the beginning of daylight savings time to 2 A.M. on the first Sunday in April, you would use the following:

```
setEndRule(Calendar.APRIL, 1, Calendar.SUNDAY,
           2 * 60 * 60 * 1000)
```

setStartYear

```
public void setStartYear(int year)
```

Parameters   year   The year when daylight savings time begins.

Description   This method sets the year after which the start and end rules for daylight savings time are observed.

useDaylightTime

```
public boolean useDaylightTime()
```

Returns   true if this SimpleTimeZone uses daylight savings time; false otherwise.

Overrides   `TimeZone.useDaylightTime()`

Description   This method returns a boolean value that indicates whether or not this SimpleTimeZone uses daylight savings time.

Inherited Methods

Method	Inherited From	Method	Inherited From
finalize()	Object	getClass()	Object
getID()	TimeZone	notify()	Object
notifyAll()	Object	setID()	TimeZone
toString()	Object	wait()	Object
wait(long)	Object	wait(long, int)	Object

See Also

Calendar, Cloneable, Date, GregorianCalendar, Locale, TimeZone

17.22 Stack

Synopsis

Class Name:	java.util.Stack
Superclass:	java.util.Vector
Immediate Subclasses:	None
Interfaces Implemented:	None
Availability:	JDK 1.0 or later

Description

Stack represents a last-in-first-out (LIFO) object stack. The push() method places an object on the top of the stack, while the pop() method retrieves the top object from the stack. The peek() method returns the top object without removing it from the stack.

Class Summary

```
public class java.util.Stack extends java.util.Vector {
    // Instance Methods
    public boolean empty();
    public synchronized Object peek();
    public synchronized Object pop();
    public Object push(Object item);
    public synchronized int search(Object o);
}
```

Instance Methods

empty

```
public boolean empty()
```

Returns   true if there are no objects on the Stack; false otherwise.

Description   This method returns a boolean value that indicates whether or
                not the Stack is empty.

peek

```
public Object peek()
```

Returns   A reference to the object that is returned by the next call to
                pop().

Throws   EmptyStackException
                        If the stack is empty.

Description   This method returns a reference to the object on the top of this
                Stack without removing it.

pop

```
public Object pop()
```

Returns   The object on top of this Stack.

Throws   EmptyStackException
                        If the stack is empty.

Description   This method returns the object on top of this Stack.

push

```
public Object push(Object item)
```

Parameters   item   The object to be added to the top of the stack.

Returns   The object just pushed.

Description   This method places the object on the top of this Stack.

search

```
public synchronized int search(Object o)
```

Parameters   o   The object to be found.

Returns   The object's distance from the top of the stack or –1 if it cannot
                be found.

Description   This method is used to determine if an object is on this Stack.

Inherited Variables

Method	Inherited From	Method	Inherited From
capacityIncrement	Vector	elementCount	Vector
elementData	Vector		

Inherited Methods

Method	Inherited From	Method	Inherited From
addElement()	Vector	capacity()	Vector
clone()	Vector	contains(Object)	Vector
copyInto(Object[])	Vector	elementAt(int)	Vector
elements()	Vector	ensureCapacity(int)	Vector
equals()	Object	finalize()	Object
firstElement()	Vector	getClass()	Object
hashCode()	Object	indexOf(Object)	Vector
indexOf(Object, int)	Vector	insertElementAt(Object, int)	Vector
isEmpty()	Vector	lastElement()	Vector
lastIndexOf(Object)	Vector	lastIndexOf(Object, int)	Vector
notify()	Object	notifyAll()	Object
removeAllElements()	Vector	removeElement(Object)	Vector
removeElementAt(int)	Vector	setElementAt(Object, int)	Vector
setSize()	Vector	size()	Vector
toString()	Vector	trimToSize()	Vector
wait()	Object	wait(long)	Object
wait(long, int)	Object		

See Also

EmptyStackException, Vector

17.23   StringTokenizer

Synopsis

Class Name: java.util.StringTokenizer

Superclass: java.lang.Object

Immediate Subclasses: None
Interfaces Implemented: `java.util.Enumeration`
Availability: JDK 1.0 or later

Description

The `StringTokenizer` class implements a simple, delimiter-based string tokenizer. In other words, a `StringTokenizer` is used to break a `String` into tokens separated by delimiter characters. By default, the class uses the standard whitespace characters as delimiters, but you can specify any delimiter characters you want, either when the `StringTokenizer` is created or on a token-by-token basis. You can also specify whether the delimiters are returned as tokens or not. A `StringTokenizer` returns the tokens in its `String` in order, either as `String` objects or as `Objects` in an `Enumeration`.

`StringTokenizer` shouldn't be confused with the more complex `java.io.StreamTokenizer`, which parses a stream into tokens that are similar to those used in the Java language.

Class Summary

```
public class java.util.StringTokenizer extends java.lang.Object
            implements java.util.Enumeration {
// Constructors
public StringTokenizer(String str);
public StringTokenizer(String str, String delim);
public StringTokenizer(String str, String delim, boolean returnTokens);

// Instance Methods
public int countTokens();
public boolean hasMoreElements();
public boolean hasMoreTokens();
public Object nextElement();
public String nextToken();
public String nextToken(String delim);
}
```

Constructors

StringTokenizer

public `StringTokenizer(String str)`

   Parameters   str   The `String` to be tokenized.

   Description This constructor creates a `StringTokenizer` that breaks apart the given string using the default delimiter characters. The default delimiters are the standard whitespace characters: space, tab (\t), carriage return (\r), and newline (\n).

```
public StringTokenizer(String str, String delim)
```
    Parameters   str   The String to be tokenized.
                    delim   The delimiter characters.
    Description   This constructor creates a StringTokenizer that breaks apart
                    the given string using the characters in delim as delimiter char-
                    acters.

```
public StringTokenizer(String str, String delim,
                       boolean returnTokens)
```
    Parameters   str   The String to be tokenized.
                    delim   The delimiter characters.
                    returnTokens
                                    A boolean value that indicates whether or not
                                    delimiters should be returned as tokens.
    Description   This constructor creates a StringTokenizer that breaks apart
                    the given string using the characters in delim as delimiter char-
                    acters. If returnTokens is true, the delimiters are returned as
                    tokens; otherwise they are skipped.

Instance Methods

countTokens

```
public int countTokens()
```
    Returns   The number of tokens remaining in the string.
    Description   This method returns the number of tokens that remain in the
                    string, which is the same as the number of times nextToken()
                    can be called before an exception is thrown.

hasMoreElements

```
public boolean hasMoreElements()
```
    Returns   true if there are more tokens to be returned; false otherwise.
    Implements   Enumeration.hasMoreElements()
    Description   This method returns the result of calling hasMoreTokens().

hasMoreTokens

```
public boolean hasMoreTokens()
```
    Returns   true if there are more tokens to be returned; false otherwise.
    Description   This method returns true if this object has more tokens to
                    return.

nextElement

public Object nextElement()

Returns	The next token as an Object.
Throws	NoSuchElementException
	If there are no more tokens in the string.
Implements	Enumeration.nextElement()
Description	This method returns result of calling nextToken().

nextToken

public String nextToken()

Returns	The next token as a String.
Throws	NoSuchElementException
	If there are no more tokens in the string.
Description	This method returns the next token.

public String nextToken(String delim)

Parameters	delim The delimiter characters.
Returns	The next token as a String.
Throws	NoSuchElementException
	If there are no more tokens in the string.
Description	This method sets the delimiter characters to the characters in the given string and then returns the next token. The change in delimiters persists until another call to this method changes them again.

Inherited Methods

Method	Inherited From	Method	Inherited From
clone()	Object	equals(Object)	Object
finalize()	Objxect	getClass()	Object
hashCode()	Object	notify()	Object
notifyAll()	Object	toString()	Object
wait()	Object	wait(long)	Object
wait(long, int)	Object		

See Also

Enumeration, NoSuchElementException, StreamTokenizer, String

17.24   TimeZone

Synopsis

Class Name: `java.util.TimeZone`
Superclass: `java.lang.Object`
Immediate Subclasses: `java.util.SimpleTimeZone`
Interfaces Implemented: `java.io.Serializable, java.lang.Cloneable`
Availability: New as of JDK 1.1

Description

The `TimeZone` class is an abstract class that represents a time zone offset. In addition, the class incorporates knowledge about daylight savings time. Usually, you get a `TimeZone` object by calling `getDefault()`. This method creates a `TimeZone` that is appropriate for the current locale. You can also call `getTimeZone()` to obtain a `TimeZone` object for a specific time zone.

Class Summary

```
public abstract class java.util.TimeZone extends java.lang.Object
                    implements java.io.Serializable, java.lang.Cloneable {
  // Class Methods
  public static synchronized String[] getAvailableIDs();
  public static synchronized String[] getAvailableIDs(int rawOffset);
  public static synchronized TimeZone getDefault();
  public static synchronized TimeZone getTimeZone(String ID);
  public static synchronized void setDefault(TimeZone zone);

  // Instance Methods
  public Object clone();
  public String getID();
  public abstract int getOffset(int era, int year, int month,
                        int day, int dayOfWeek, int milliseconds);
  public abstract int getRawOffset();
  public abstract boolean inDaylightTime(Date date);
  public void setID(String ID);
  public abstract void setRawOffset(int offsetMillis);
  public abstract boolean useDaylightTime();
}
```

Class Methods

getAvailiableIDs

public static synchronized String[] getAvailableIDs()

Returns	An array of strings that contains the predefined time zone IDs.
Description	This method returns a list of the predefined time zone IDs. Time zones are defined for the following ID values, starting from Greenwich, England, and progressing eastward around the world:

GMT	Greenwich Mean Time
ECT	European Central Time
EET	Eastern European Time
ART	(Arabic) Egypt Standard Time
EAT	Eastern African Time
MET	Middle East Time
NET	Near East Time
PLT	Pakistan Lahore Time
IST	India Standard Time
BST	Bangladesh Standard Time
VST	Vietnam Standard Time
CTT	China Taiwan Time
JST	Japan Standard Time
ACT	Australia Central Time
AET	Australia Eastern Time
SST	Solomon Standard Time
NST	New Zealand Standard Time
MIT	Midway Islands Time
HST	Hawaii Standard Time
AST	Alaska Standard Time
PST	Pacific Standard Time
PNT	Phoenix Standard Time
MST	Mountain Standard Time
CST	Central Standard Time
EST	Eastern Standard Time
IET	Indiana Eastern Standard Time
PRT	Puerto Rico and U.S. Virgin Islands Time
CNT	Canada Newfoundland Time
AGT	Argentina Standard Time
BET	Brazil Eastern Time
CAT	Central African Time

```
public static synchronized String[] getAvailableIDs(int rawOffset)
```
Returns   An array of strings that contains the predefined time zone IDs
               with the given raw offset value.
Description   This method returns a list of the predefined time zone IDs that
               have the given raw offset value from GMT. For example, both
               PNT and MST have an offset of GMT-07:00.

getDefault
```
public static synchronized TimeZone getDefault()
```
Returns   A TimeZone that represents the local time zone.
Description   This method returns the default TimeZone object for the local
               system.

getTimeZone
```
public static synchronized TimeZone getTimeZone(String ID)
```
Parameters   ID   The ID of a time zone.
Returns   A TimeZone that represents the time zone with the given ID.
Description   This method returns the TimeZone object that corresponds to
               the time zone with the given ID.

setDefault
```
public static synchronized void setDefault(TimeZone zone)
```
Parameters   zone   The new default time zone.
Description   This method sets the TimeZone that is returned by getDe-
               fault().

Instance Methods
clone
```
public Object clone()
```
Returns   A copy of this TimeZone.
Overrides   Object.clone()
Description   This method creates a copy of this TimeZone and returns it.

getID
```
public String getID()
```
Returns   The ID of this TimeZone.
Description   This method returns the ID string of this TimeZone.

getOffset

```
public abstract int getOffset(int era, int year, int month,
                              int day, int dayOfWeek, int millis)
```

Parameters   era   The era.

                 year   The year.

                 month   The month.

                 day   The day.

                 dayOfWeek   The day of the week.

                 millis   The time of day in milliseconds.

Returns   An offset from GMT, in milliseconds.

Description   This method calculates an offset from GMT for the given date for this TimeZone. In other words, the offset takes daylight savings time into account. The return value should be added to GMT to get local time.

getRawOffset

```
public abstract int getRawOffset()
```

Returns   An offset from GMT, in milliseconds.

Description   This method returns the raw offset from GMT for this TimeZone. In other words, the offset does not take daylight savings time into account.

inDaylightTime

```
public abstract boolean isDaylightTime(Date date)
```

Parameters   date   The date to be tested.

Returns   true if the given date is between the start and end of daylight savings time for this TimeZone; false otherwise.

Description   This method returns a boolean value that indicates if the given date is in daylight savings time for this TimeZone.

setID

```
public void setID(String ID)
```

Parameters   ID   The new time zone ID.

Description   This method sets the ID of this TimeZone.

setRawOffset

```
public abstract void setRawOffset(int offsetMillis)
```

Parameters   offsetMillis

                              The new raw offset from GMT, in milliseconds.

Description   This method is used to set the raw offset value for this Time-
              Zone.

useDaylightTime

    public abstract boolean useDaylightTime()
        Returns   true if this TimeZone uses daylight savings time; false other-
                       wise.
        Description   This method returns a boolean value that indicates whether or
                       not this TimeZone uses daylight savings time.

Inherited Methods

Method	Inherited From	Method	Inherited From
finalize()	Object	getClass()	Object
hashCode()	Object	notify()	Object
notifyAll()	Object	toString()	Object
wait()	Object	wait(long)	Object
wait(long, int)	Object		

See Also

Calendar, Cloneable, GregorianCalendar, Locale, Serializable, SimpleTimeZone

17.25   TooManyListenersException

Synopsis

Class Name: java.util.TooManyListenersException
Superclass: java.lang.Exception
Immediate Subclasses: None
Interfaces Implemented: None
Availability: New as of JDK 1.1

Description

A TooManyListenersException is thrown to indicate that more than one listener is
registered with a *unicast* event source. Normally, an event source multicasts to all
registered listeners. In some special cases, however, an event source is unicast,
meaning it only sends events to a single listener. This exception is thrown if more
than one listener tries to register.

Class Summary

```
public class java.util.TooManyListenersException
            extends java.lang.Exception {
    // Constructors
    public TooManyListenersException();
    public TooManyListenersException(String s);
}
```

Constructors

TooManyListenersException

public TooManyListenersException()

    Description   This constructor creates aTooManyListenersException with no associated detail message

public TooManyListenersException(String s)

    Parameters   s   The detail message.

    Description   This constructor creates a TooManyListenersException with the specified detail message

Inherited Methods

Method	Inherited From	Method	Inherited From
clone()	Object	equals(Object)	Object
fillInStackTrace()	Throwable	finalize()	Object
getClass()	Object	getLocalizedMessage()	Throwable
getMessage()	Throwable	hashCode()	Object
notify()	Object	notifyAll()	Object
printStackTrace()	Throwable	printStack-Trace(PrintStream)	Throwable
printStack-Trace(PrintWriter)	Throwable	toString()	Throwable
wait()	Object	wait(long)	Object
wait(long, int)	Object		

See Also

EventObject, EventListener, Exception

17.26   Vector

Synopsis

Class Name: java.util.Vector
Superclass: java.lang.Object
Immediate Subclasses: java.util.Stack
Interfaces Implemented: java.io.Serializable, java.lang.Cloneable
Availability: JDK 1.0 or later

Description

The Vector class implements a variable-length array that can hold any kind of object. Like an array, the elements in a Vector are accessed with an integer index. However, unlike an array, the size of a Vector can grow and shrink as needed to accommodate a changing number of objects. Vector provides methods to add and remove elements, as well as ways to search for objects in a Vector and iterate through all of the objects.

The initial capacity of a Vector specifies how many objects it can contain before more space must be allocated. The capacity increment specifies how much more space is allocated each time the Vector needs to increase its capacity. You can fine-tune the performance of a Vector by adjusting the initial capacity and capacity increment.

Class Summary

```
public class java.util.Vector extends java.lang.Object
            implements java.io.Serializable, java.lang.Cloneable {
  // Variables
  protected int capacityIncrement;
  protected int elementCount;
  protected Object[] elementData;

  // Constructors
  public Vector();
  public Vector(int initialCapacity);
  public Vector(int initialCapacity, int capacityIncrement);

  // Instance Methods
  public final synchronized void addElement(Object obj);
  public final int capacity();
  public synchronized Object clone();
  public final boolean contains(Object elem);
  public final synchronized void copyInto(Object[] anArray);
  public final synchronized Object elementAt(int index);
  public final synchronized Enumeration elements();
  public final synchronized void ensureCapacity(int minCapacity);
```

```
public final synchronized Object firstElement();
public final int indexOf(Object elem);
public final synchronized int indexOf(Object elem, int index);
public final synchronized void insertElementAt(Object obj, int index);
public final boolean isEmpty();
public final synchronized Object lastElement();
public final int lastIndexOf(Object elem);
public final synchronized int lastIndexOf(Object elem, int index);
public final synchronized void removeAllElements();
public final synchronized boolean removeElement(Object obj);
public final synchronized void removeElementAt(int index);
public final synchronized void setElementAt(Object obj, int index);
public final synchronized void setSize(int newSize);
public final int size();
public final synchronized String toString();
public final synchronized void trimToSize();
}
```

Variables

capacityIncrement

protected int capacityIncrement

Description   The amount by which the internal array grows when more space is needed. If the value is 0, the internal array doubles in size when more space is needed.

elementCount

protected int elementCount

Description   The count of how many objects are contained in this Vector.

elementData

protected Object[] elementData

Description   The array that holds the contents of this Vector.

Constructors

Vector

public Vector()

Description   This constructor creates an empty Vector with the default capacity of 10 and the default capacity increment of 0.

public Vector(int initialCapacity)

Parameters   initialCapacity

The initial capacity of the Vector.

Description   This constructor creates an empty Vector with the given capacity and the default capacity increment of 0.

`public Vector(int initialCapacity, int capacityIncrement)`
Parameters   `initialCapacity`

The initial capacity of the Vector.

`CapacityIncrement`

The amount to increase the capacity when more
space is needed.

Description   This constructor creates an empty Vector with the given capacity and capacity increment.

Instance Methods

addElement

`public final synchronized void addElement(Object obj)`
Parameters   `obj`   The object to be added.
Description   This method adds the given object to this Vector as its last element and increases its size by 1. The capacity of the Vector is
increased if its size becomes greater than its capacity. Any kind
of object can be added to a Vector.

capacity

`public final int capacity()`
Returns   The capacity of this Vector.
Description   This method returns the size of the internal array of this Vec-
tor.

clone

`public synchronized Object clone()`
Returns   A copy of this Vector.
Overrides   `Object.clone()`
Description   This method creates a copy of this Vector and returns it.

contains

`public final boolean contains(Object elem)`
Parameters   `elem`   The object to be found.
Returns   true if the given object is contained in this Vector; false other-
wise.
Description   This method determines whether or not the given object is con-
tained in this Vector.

copyInto

public final synchronized void copyInto(Object[] anArray)

Parameters   anArray   The array to be filled.

Throws   ArrayIndexOutOfBoundsException

If the given array is too small to hold all of the objects in this Vector.

Description   This method copies the object references in this Vector to the given array.

elementAt

public final synchronized Object elementAt(int index)

Parameters   index   The index of the object to be returned.

Returns   The object at the position given by index.

Throws   ArrayIndexOutOfBoundsException

If index is less than zero or greater than the size of this Vector.

Description   This method returns the object at the given index in this Vector.

elements

public final synchronized Enumeration elements()

Returns   The objects in this Vector as an Enumeration.

Description   This method returns an Enumeration that iterates through the objects in this Vector.

ensureCapacity

public final synchronized void ensureCapacity(int minCapacity)

Parameters   minCapacity   The minimum new capacity.

Description   This method expands the internal array, if necessary, to make the capacity of the Vector at least minCapacity.

firstElement

public final synchronized Object firstElement()

Returns   The first object in this Vector.

Throws   NoSuchElementException

If the Vector is empty.

Description   This method returns the object at index 0 in this Vector.

indexOf

public final int indexOf(Object elem)

Parameters	elem	The object to be found.
Returns		The index of the given object or –1 if it cannot be found.
Description		This method returns the index of the first occurrence of the given object in this Vector.

public final int indexOf(Object elem, int index)

Parameters	elem	The object to be found.
	index	The starting index.
Returns		The index of the next occurrence of the given object after the specified index or –1 if it cannot be found.
Description		This method returns the index of the next occurrence of the given object in this Vector after the given index.

insertElementAt

public final synchronized void insertElementAt(Object obj, int index)

Parameters	obj	The object to be inserted.
	index	The index at which to insert the object.
Throws	ArrayIndexOutOfBoundsException	
		If index is less than zero or greater than the size of this Vector.
Description		This method inserts the given object at the given index in this Vector. Each object in the Vector with an index greater than or equal to index is shifted upward in the Vector, so that it has an index of one greater than it did previously.

isEmpty

public final boolean isEmpty()

Returns	true if there are no objects in the Vector; false otherwise.
Description	This method returns a boolean value that indicates whether or not the Vector is empty.

lastElement

public final synchronized Object lastElement()

Returns		The last object in this Vector.
Throws	NoSuchElementException	
		If the Vector is empty.
Description		This method returns the last object in this Vector.

lastIndexOf

```
public final int lastIndexOf(Object elem)
```

Parameters   elem   The object to be found.

Returns   The index of the given object or –1 if it cannot be found.

Description   This method returns the index of the last occurrence of the given object in this Vector.

```
public final synchronized int lastIndexOf(Object elem, int index)
```

Parameters   elem   The object to be found.

               index   The starting index.

Returns   The index of the last occurrence of the given object before the specified index or –1 if it cannot be found.

Description   This method returns the index of the last occurrence of the given object in this Vector before the given index. In other words, the method searches backwards from index for the next occurrence.

removeAllElements

```
public final synchronized void removeAllElements()
```

Description   This method removes all of the objects from this Vector, but does not change its capacity or capacity increment.

removeElement

```
public final synchronized boolean removeElement(Object obj)
```

Parameters   obj   The object to be removed.

Returns   true if the given object is found and removed; false otherwise.

Description   This method searches for the first occurrence of the given object in this Vector and removes it. If the object is found, each object in the Vector with an index greater than or equal to the index of the removed object is shifted downward in the Vector, so that it has an index of one less than it did previously.

removeElementAt

```
public final synchronized void removeElementAt(int index)
```

Parameters   index   The index of the object to be removed.

Throws   ArrayIndexOutOfBoundsException

                            If index is less than zero or greater than the size of this Vector.

Description   This method removes the object at the given index from this Vector. Each object in the Vector with an index greater than or equal to index is shifted downward in the Vector, so that it has an index of one less than it did previously.

setElementAt

```
public final synchronized void setElementAt(Object obj, int index)
```
Parameters	obj	The object to be put in the Vector.
	index	The index at which to put the object.
Throws	ArrayIndexOutOfBoundsException	
		If index is less than zero or greater than the size of this Vector.
Description		This method puts the given object at the given index in this Vector, replacing the object that was previously there.

setSize

```
public final synchronized void setSize(int newSize)
```
Parameters	newSize	The new size.
Description		This method sets the size (not the capacity) of this Vector. If the new size is bigger than the current size, null elements are added to the end of the Vector. If the new size is smaller than the current size, elements are discarded from index newSize to the end of the Vector.

size

```
public final int size()
```
Returns	The size of this Vector.
Description	This method returns the number of objects contained in this Vector.

toString

```
public final synchronized String toString()
```
Returns	A string that represents this Vector.
Overrides	Object.toString()
Description	This method returns a string representation of this Vector. The string includes every object that is contained in the Vector, so the string returned by toString() can be quite long.

trimToSize

```
public final synchronized void trimToSize()
```
Description	This method sets the capacity of this Vector equal to its size. You can use this method to minimize the storage space used by the Vector, but any subsequent calls to addElement() or insertElement() forces the Vector to allocate more space.

Inherited Methods

Method	Inherited From	Method	Inherited From
equals(Object)	Object	finalize()	Object
getClass()	Object	hashCode()	Object
notify()	Object	notifyAll()	Object
wait()	Object	wait(long)	Object
wait(long, int)	Object		

See Also

ArrayIndexOutOfBoundsException, Cloneable, Enumeration, NoSuchElementException, Serializable, Stack

18

The java.util.zip Package

The package `java.util.zip` is new as of Java 1.1. It contains classes that provide support for general-purpose data compression and decompression using the ZLIB compression algorithms. The important classes in `java.util.zip` are those that provide the means to read and write data that is compatible with the popular GZIP and ZIP formats: `GZIPInputStream`, `GZIPOutputStream`, `ZipInputStream`, and `ZipOutputStream`. Figure 18-1 shows the class hierarchy for the `java.util.zip` package.

It is easy to use the GZIP and ZIP classes because they subclass `java.io.FilterInputStream` and `java.io.FilterOutputStream`. For example, to decompress GZIP data, you simply create a `GZIPInputStream` around the input stream that represents the compressed data. As with any `InputStream`, you could be reading from a file, a socket, or some other data source. You can then read decompressed data by calling the `read()` methods of the `GZIPInputStream`. The following code fragment creates a `GZIPInputStream` that reads data from the file *sample.gz*:

```
FileInputStream inFile;
try {
    inFile = new FileInputStream("sample.gz");
} catch (IOException e) {
    System.out.println("Couldn't open file.");
    return;
}
GZIPInputStream in = new GZIPInputStream(inFile);
// Now use in.read() to get decompressed data.
```

Similarly, you can compress data using the GZIP format by creating a `GZIPOutput-Stream` around an output stream and using the `write()` methods of `GZIPOutput-`

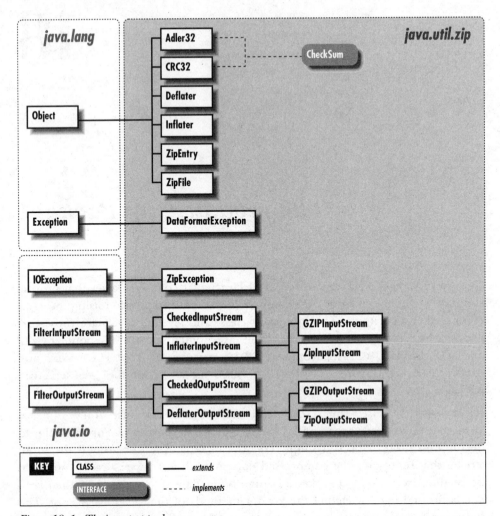

Figure 18–1: The java.text package

Stream. The following code fragment creates a `GZIPOutputStream` that writes data to the file *sample.gz*:

```
FileOutputStream outFile;
try {
    outFile = new FileOutputStream("sample.gz");
} catch (IOException e) {
    System.out.println("Couldn't open file.");
    return;
}
GZIPOutputStream out = new GZIPOutputStream(outFile);
// Now use out.write() to write compressed data.
```

A ZIP file, or archive, is not quite as easy to use because it may contain more than one compressed file. A ZipEntry object represents each compressed file in the archive. When you are reading from a ZipInputStream, you must first call getNextEntry() to access an entry, and then you can read decompressed data from the stream, just like with a GZIPInputStream. When you are writing data to a ZipOutputStream, use putNextEntry() before you start writing each entry in the archive. The ZipFile class is provided as a convenience for reading an archive; it allows nonsequential access to the entries in a ZIP file.

The remainder of the classes in java.util.zip exist to support the GZIP and ZIP classes. The generic Deflater and Inflater classes implement the ZLIB algorithms; they are used by DeflaterOutputStream and InflaterInputStream to decompress and compress data. The Checksum interface and the classes that implement it, Adler32 and CRC32, define algorithms that generate checksums from stream data. These checksums are used by the CheckedInputStream and Checked-OutputStream classes.

18.1 Adler32

Synopsis

Class Name: java.util.zip.Adler32
Superclass: java.lang.Object
Immediate Subclasses: None
Interfaces Implemented: java.util.zip.Checksum
Availability: New as of JDK 1.1

Description

The Adler32 class implements the Checksum interface using the Adler-32 algorithm. This algorithm is significantly faster than CRC-32 and almost as reliable.

Class Summary

```
public class java.util.zip.Adler32 extends java.lang.Object
            implements java.util.zip.Checksum {
  // Constructors
  public Adler32();

  // Instance Methods
  public long getValue();
  public void reset();
  public void update(int b);
  public void update(byte[] b);
  public native void update(byte[] b, int off, int len);
}
```

Constructors

Adler32

public Adler32()

>   Description   This constructor creates an Adler32 object.

Instance Methods

getValue

public long getValue()

>   Returns   The current checksum value.
>
>   Implements   Checksum.getValue()
>
>   Description   This method returns the current value of this checksum.

reset

public void reset()

>   Implements   Checksum.reset()
>
>   Description   This method resets the checksum to its initial value, making it
>   appear as though it has not been updated by any data.

update

public void update(int b)

>   Parameters   b   The value to be added to the data stream for the
>   checksum calculation.
>
>   Implements   Checksum.update(int)
>
>   Description   This method adds the specified value to the data stream and
>   updates the checksum value. The method uses only the lowest
>   eight bits of the given int.

public void update(byte[] b)

>   Parameters   b   An array of bytes to be added to the data stream
>   for the checksum calculation.
>
>   Description   This method adds the bytes from the specified array to the data
>   stream and updates the checksum value.

public native void update(byte[] b, int off, int len)

>   Parameters   b   An array of bytes to be added to the data stream
>   for the checksum calculation.
>
>   off   An offset into the byte array.
>
>   len   The number of bytes to use.
>
>   Implements   Checksum.update(byte[], int, int)
>
>   Description   This method adds len bytes from the specified array, starting at
>   off, to the data stream and updates the checksum value.

Inherited Methods

Method	Inherited From	Method	Inherited From
clone()	Object	equals(Object)	Object
finalize()	Object	getClass()	Object
hashCode()	Object	notify()	Object
notifyAll()	Object	toString()	Object
wait()	Object	wait(long)	Object
wait(long, int)	Object		

See Also

Checksum, CRC32

18.2   CheckedInputStream

Synopsis

Class Name:	java.util.zip.CheckedInputStream
Superclass:	java.io.FilterInputStream
Immediate Subclasses:	None
Interfaces Implemented:	None
Availability:	New as of JDK 1.1

Description

The CheckedInputStream class represents an InputStream with an associated checksum. In other words, a CheckedInputStream wraps a regular input stream and computes a checksum value as data is read from the stream. The checksum can verify the integrity of the data. When you create a CheckedInputStream, you must specify an object that implements the Checksum interface that computes the checksum.

Class Summary

```
public class java.util.zip.CheckedInputStream
        extends java.io.FilterInputStream {
  // Constructors
  public CheckedInputStream(InputStream in, Checksum cksum);

  // Instance Methods
  public Checksum getChecksum();
  public int read();
  public int read(byte[] buf, int off, int len);
```

```
    public long skip(long n);
}
```

Constructors

CheckedInputStream

public CheckedInputStream(InputStream in, Checksum cksum)

Parameters	in	The underlying input stream to use as a data source.
	cksum	The checksum object.
Description		This constructor creates a CheckedInputStream that reads data from the given InputStream and updates the given Checksum.

Instance Methods

getChecksum

public Checksum getChecksum()

Returns	The Checksum associated with this input stream.
Description	This method returns the Checksum object associated with this input stream.

read

public int read() throws IOException

Returns		The next byte from the stream or –1 if the end of the stream has been reached.
Throws	IOException	If any kind of I/O error occurs.
Overrides	FilterInputStream.read()	
Description		This method reads the next byte from the underlying Input-Stream and then updates the checksum. The method blocks until some data is available, the end of the stream is detected, or an exception is thrown.

public int read(byte[] buf, int off, int len) throws IOException

Parameters	buf	An array of bytes to be filled from the stream.
	off	An offset into the byte array.
	len	The number of bytes to read.
Returns		The number of bytes read or –1 if the end of the stream is encountered immediately.
Throws	IOException	If any kind of I/O error occurs.
Overrides	FilterInputStream.read(byte[], int, int)	
Description		This method reads up to len bytes from the underlying Input-Stream and places them into the given array starting at off. The checksum is then updated with the data that has been read. The method blocks until some data is available.

skip

```
public long skip(long n) throws IOException
```

Parameters	n	The number of bytes to skip.
Returns	The actual number of bytes skipped.	
Throws	IOException If any kind of I/O error occurs.	
Overrides	FilterInputStream.skip()	
Description	This method skips over the specified number of bytes in the underlying InputStream. The skipped bytes are not calculated into the checksum.	

Inherited Methods

Method	Inherited From	Method	Inherited From
available()	FilterInputStream	clone()	Object
close()	FilterInputStream	equals(Object)	Object
finalize()	Object	getClass()	Object
hashCode()	Object	mark(int)	FilterInputStream
markSupported()	FilterInputStream	notify()	Object
notifyAll()	Object	read(byte[])	FilterInputStream
reset()	FilterInputStream	toString()	Object
wait()	Object	wait(long)	Object
wait(long, int)	Object		

See Also

Checksum, FilterInputStream, InputStream, IOException

18.3   CheckedOutputStream

Synopsis

Class Name:	java.util.zip.CheckedOutputStream
Superclass:	java.io.FilterOutputStream
Immediate Subclasses:	None
Interfaces Implemented:	None
Availability:	New as of JDK 1.1

Description

The CheckOutputStream class represents an OutputStream with an associated checksum. In other words, a CheckedOutputStream wraps a regular output stream and computes a checksum value as data is written to the stream. The checksum can verify the integrity of the data. When you create a CheckedOutputStream, you must specify an object that implements the Checksum interface that computes the checksum.

Class Summary

```
public class java.util.zip.CheckedOutputStream
            extends java.io.FilterOutputStream {
  // Constructors
  public CheckedOutputStream(OutputStream out, Checksum cksum);

  // Instance Methods
  public Checksum getChecksum();
  public void write(int b);
  public void write(byte[] b, int off, int len);
}
```

Constructors

CheckedOutputStream

public CheckedOutputStream(OutputStream out, Checksum cksum)

Parameters	out	The underlying output stream.
	cksum	The checksum object.
Description		This constructor creates a CheckedOutputStream that writes data to the given OutputStream and updates the given Checksum.

Instance Methods

getChecksum

public Checksum getChecksum()

Returns	The Checksum associated with this output stream.
Description	This method returns the Checksum object associated with this output stream.

write

public void write(int b) throws IOException

Parameters	b	The value to write.
Throws	IOException	If any kind of I/O error occurs.

Overrides	FilterOutputStream.write(int)
Description	This method writes a byte that contains the lowest eight bits of the given integer value to the underlying OutputStream and then updates the checksum.

public void write(byte[] b, int off, int len) throws IOException

Parameters	b	An array of bytes to write to the stream.
	off	An offset into the byte array.
	len	The number of bytes to write.
Throws	IOException	If any kind of I/O error occurs.
Overrides	FilterOutputStream.write(byte[], int, int)	
Description	This method writes len bytes to the underlying OutputStream from the given array, starting at off. The checksum is then updated with the data that has been written.	

Inherited Methods

Method	Inherited From	Method	Inherited From
clone()	Object	close()	FilterOutputStream
equals(Object)	Object	finalize()	Object
flush()	FilterOutputStream	getClass()	Object
hashCode()	Object	notify()	Object
notifyAll()	Object	toString()	Object
wait()	Object	wait(long)	Object
wait(long, int)	Object	write(byte[])	FilterOutputStream

See Also

Checksum, FilterOutputStream, IOException, OutputStream

18.4   Checksum

Synopsis

Interface Name:	java.util.zip.Checksum
Super-interface:	None
Immediate Sub-interfaces:	
	None
Implemented By:	java.util.zip.Adler32, java.util.zip.CRC32
Availability:	New as of JDK 1.1

Description

The Checksum interface defines the methods that are needed to compute a checksum value for a stream of data. The checksum value can be used for error checking purposes. Note, however, that the checksum value must fit into a long value, so this interface is not suitable for cryptographic checksum algorithms.

The Adler32 and CRC32 classes implement the Checksum interface, using the Adler-32 and CRC-32 algorithms, respectively. The CheckedInputStream and CheckedOutputStream classes provide a higher-level mechanism for computing checksums on data streams.

Class Summary

```
public abstract interface java.util.zip.Checksum {
    // Methods
    public abstract long getValue();
    public abstract void reset();
    public abstract void update(int b);
    public abstract void update(byte[] b, int off, int len);
}
```

Methods

getValue

public abstract long getValue()

Returns   The current checksum value.

Description This method returns the current value of this checksum.

reset

public abstract void reset()

Description This method resets the checksum to its initial value, making it appear as though it has not been updated by any data.

update

public abstract void update(int b)

Parameters   b   The value to be added to the data stream for the checksum calculation.

Description This method adds the specified value to the data stream and updates the checksum value. The method uses only the lowest eight bits of the given int.

public abstract void update(byte[] b, int off, int len)

Parameters   b   An array of bytes to be added to the data stream for the checksum calculation.

	off	An offset into the byte array.
	len	The number of bytes to use.

Description   This method adds len bytes from the specified array, starting at off, to the data stream and updates the checksum value.

See Also

Adler32, CheckedInputStream, CheckedOutputStream, CRC32

18.5   CRC32

Synopsis

Class Name:	java.util.zip.CRC32
Superclass:	java.lang.Object
Immediate Subclasses:	None
Interfaces Implemented:	java.util.zip.Checksum
Availability:	New as of JDK 1.1

Description

The CRC32 class implements the Checksum interface using the CRC-32 algorithm. This algorithm is significantly slower than Adler-32 and only slightly more reliable.

Class Summary

```
public class java.util.zip.CRC32 extends java.lang.Object
            implements java.util.zip.Checksum {
  // Constructors
  public CRC32();

  // Instance Methods
  public long getValue();
  public void reset();
  public void update(int b);
  public void update(byte[] b);
  public native void update(byte[] b, int off, int len);
}
```

Constructors

CRC32

public CRC32()

　　Description　　This constructor creates an CRC32 object.

Instance Methods

getValue

public long getValue()

　　Returns　　　　The current checksum value.

　　Implements　　Checksum.getValue()

　　Description　　This method returns the current value of this checksum.

reset

public void reset()

　　Implements　　Checksum.reset()

　　Description　　This method resets the checksum to its initial value, making it appear as though it has not been updated by any data.

update

public void update(int b)

　　Parameters　　b　　　　　　　The value to be added to the data stream for the checksum calculation.

　　Implements　　Checksum.update(int)

　　Description　　This method adds the specified value to the data stream and updates the checksum value. The method uses only the lowest eight bits of the given int.

public void update(byte[] b)

　　Parameters　　b　　　　　　　An array of bytes to be added to the data stream for the checksum calculation.

　　Description　　This method adds the bytes from the specified array to the data stream and updates the checksum value.

public native void update(byte[] b, int off, int len)

　　Parameters　　b　　　　　　　An array of bytes to be added to the data stream for the checksum calculation.

　　　　　　　　　off　　　　　　An offset into the byte array.

　　　　　　　　　len　　　　　　The number of bytes to use.

　　Implements　　Checksum.update(byte[], int, int)

　　Description　　This method adds len bytes from the specified array, starting at off, to the data stream and updates the checksum value.

Inherited Methods

Method	Inherited From	Method	Inherited From
clone()	Object	equals(Object)	Object
finalize()	Object	getClass()	Object
hashCode()	Object	notify()	Object
notifyAll()	Object	toString()	Object
wait()	Object	wait(long)	Object
wait(long, int)	Object		

See Also

Adler32, Checksum

18.6   DataFormatException

Synopsis

Class Name:	java.util.zip.DataFormatException
Superclass:	java.lang.Exception
Immediate Subclasses:	None
Interfaces Implemented:	None
Availability:	New as of JDK 1.1

Description

A DataFormatException is thrown when data is not in the expected format, which can mean that the data is invalid or corrupt. In particular, the inflate() methods of Inflater throw this exception if they encounter data in an unexpected format.

Class Summary

```
public class java.util.zip.DataFormatException
          extends java.lang.Exception {
  // Constructors
  public DataFormatException();
  public DataFormatException(String s);
}
```

Constructors

DataFormatException

protected DataFormatException()

    Description   This constructor creates a DataFormatException with no associ-
ated detail message.

public DataFormatException(String s)

    Parameters   s   The detail message.

    Description   This constructor creates a DataFormatException with the speci-
fied detail message.

Inherited Methods

Method	Inherited From	Method	Inherited From
clone()	Object	equals(Object)	Object
fillInStackTrace()	Throwable	finalize()	Object
getClass()	Object	getLocalizedMessage()	Throwable
getMessage()	Throwable	hashCode()	Object
notify()	Object	notifyAll()	Object
printStackTrace()	Throwable	printStack-Trace(PrintStream)	Throwable
printStack-Trace(PrintWriter)	Throwable	toString()	Throwable
wait()	Object	wait(long)	Object
wait(long, int)	Object		

See Also

Exception, Inflater, Throwable

18.7   Deflater

Synopsis

Class Name:	java.util.zip.Deflater
Superclass:	java.lang.Object
Immediate Subclasses:	None
Interfaces Implemented:	None
Availability:	New as of JDK 1.1

Description

The Deflater class provides support for general-purpose data compression. The class uses the ZLIB compression algorithms described in RFC 1950, RFC 1951, and RFC 1952. These documents can be found at:

- *ftp://ds.internic.net/rfc/rfc1950.txt*
- *ftp://ds.internic.net/rfc/rfc1951.txt*
- *ftp://ds.internic.net/rfc/rfc1952.txt*

The Inflater class uncompresses data that has been compressed using Deflater.

The DeflaterOutputStream uses an internal Deflater to compress data. Typically, you do not need to create a Deflater; instead, you can just use an instance of one of the subclasses of DeflaterOutputStream: GZIPOutputStream or ZipOutputStream.

Class Summary

```
public class java.util.zip.Deflater extends java.lang.Object {
    // Constants
    public static final int BEST_COMPRESSION;
    public static final int BEST_SPEED;
    public static final int DEFAULT_COMPRESSION;
    public static final int DEFAULT_STRATEGY;
    public static final int DEFLATED;
    public static final int FILTERED;
    public static final int HUFFMAN_ONLY;
    public static final int NO_COMPRESSION;

    // Constructors
    public Deflater();
    public Deflater(int level);
    public Deflater(int level, boolean nowrap);

    // Public Instance Methods
    public int deflate(byte[] b);
    public synchronized native int deflate(byte[] b, int off, int len);
    public synchronized native void end();
    public synchronized void finish();
    public synchronized boolean finished();
    public synchronized native int getAdler();
    public synchronized native int getTotalIn();
    public synchronized native int getTotalOut();
    public boolean needsInput();
    public synchronized native void reset();
    public void setDictionary(byte[] b);
    public synchronized native void setDictionary(byte[] b, int off, int len);
    public void setInput(byte[] b);
    public synchronized void setInput(byte[] b, int off, int len);
```

```
public synchronized void setLevel(int level);
public synchronized void setStrategy(int strategy);

// Protected Instance Methods
protected void finalize();
}
```

Constants

BEST_COMPRESSION

```
public static final int BEST_COMPRESSION = 9
```

    Description   A constant that represents a compression level that sacrifices speed for the smallest compressed data size. The compression level for a Deflater object can be set with setLevel(), where the level ranges from 0 to 9.

BEST_SPEED

```
public static final int BEST_SPEED = 1
```

    Description   A constant that represents a compression level that sacrifices compressed data size for speed. The compression level for a Deflater object can be set with setLevel(), where the level ranges from 0 to 9.

DEFAULT_COMPRESSION

```
public static final int DEFAULT_COMPRESSION = -1
```

    Description   A constant that represents the default compression level.

DEFAULT_STRATEGY

```
public static final int DEFAULT_STRATEGY
```

    Description   A constant that represents the default compression strategy.

DEFLATED

```
public static final int DEFLATED
```

    Description   A constant that represents a compression method that uses the deflate algorithm.

FILTERED

```
public static final int FILTERED
```

    Description   A constant that represents a compression strategy that works well for small values with a random distribution.

HUFFMAN_ONLY

public static final int HUFFMAN_ONLY

Description   A constant that represents a compression strategy that uses only Huffman coding.

NO_COMPRESSION

public static final int NO_COMPRESSION = 0

Description   A constant that represents a compression level that does not compress data at all. The compression level for a `Deflater` object can be set with `setLevel()`, where the level ranges from 0 to 9.

Constructors

Deflater

public Deflater()

Description   This constructor creates a `Deflater` that generates compressed data in the ZLIB format using the DEFAULT_COMPRESSION level.

public Deflater(int level)

Parameters   level   The compression level, from 0 (NO_COMPRESSION) to 9 (BEST_COMPRESSION).

Description   This constructor creates a `Deflater` that generates compressed data in the ZLIB format using the given compression level.

public Deflater(int level, boolean nowrap)

Parameters   level   The compression level, from 0 (NO_COMPRESSION) to 9 (BEST_COMPRESSION).

nowrap   A boolean value that specifies whether or not the ZLIB header and checksum data are omitted from the compressed data.

Description   This constructor creates a `Deflater` that generates compressed data using the given compression level. If nowrap is true, the ZLIB header and checksum fields are not used, which means that the compressed data is in the format used by GZIP and PKZIP. If the parameter is false, the data is compressed into ZLIB format.

Public Instance Methods

deflate

```
public int deflate(byte[] b)
```

Parameters	b	A byte array to be filled.
Returns		The number of compressed bytes actually written to the array or 0 if more data may be required.
Description		This method compresses the data passed to setInput() and fills the given array with the compressed data. If this method returns zero, needsInput() should be called to determine whether the Deflater needs more data in its input buffer.

```
public synchronized native int deflate(byte[] b, int off, int len)
```

Parameters	b	A byte array to be filled.
	off	An offset into the byte array.
	len	The number of bytes to fill.
Returns		The number of compressed bytes actually written to the array or 0 if more data may be required.
Description		This method compresses the data passed to setInput() and writes len bytes of the compressed data into the given array, starting at off. If this method returns 0, needsInput() should be called to determine whether the Deflater needs more data in its input buffer.

end

```
public synchronized native void end()
```

Description	This method discards any uncompressed input data and frees up internal buffers.

finish

```
public synchronized void finish()
```

Description	This method tells the Deflater that the compression should end with the data that currently occupies the input buffer.

finished

```
public synchronized boolean finished()
```

Returns	A boolean value that indicates whether or not the end of the compressed data has been reached.
Description	This method returns true if the last of the compressed data has been read using deflate(). Otherwise it returns false.

getAdler

public synchronized native int getAdler()

Returns   The Adler-32 checksum value of the uncompressed data.

Description   This method returns an Adler32 checksum value that is calculated on the uncompressed data passed to setInput().

getTotalIn

public synchronized native int getTotalIn()

Returns   The total number of bytes that have been input so far.

Description   This method returns the number of bytes that have been passed to setInput() since this Deflater was created or since reset() was last called.

getTotalOut

public synchronized native int getTotalOut()

Returns   The total number of bytes that have been output so far.

Description   This method returns the number of bytes that have been read from deflate() since this Deflater was created, or since reset() was last called.

needsInput

public boolean needsInput()

Returns   A boolean value that indicates whether or not the input buffer is empty.

Description   This method returns true if the input buffer is empty. Otherwise it returns false.

reset

public synchronized native void reset()

Description   This method resets the Deflater to the state it was in when it was created, which means that a new set of data can be compressed.

setDictionary

public void setDictionary(byte[] b)

Parameters   b   An array of byte values.

Description   This method sets the preset dictionary for compression using the data in the given array.

```
public synchronized native void setDictionary(byte[] b, int off,
                                               int len)
```

Parameters	b	An array of byte values.
	off	An offset into the byte array.
	len	The number of bytes to use.
Description		This method sets the preset dictionary for compression using len bytes from the given array, starting from off.

setInput

```
public void setInput(byte[] b)
```

Parameters	b	An array of byte values.
Description		This method places the contents of the given array into the input buffer of this Deflater. Use the deflate() method to compress the data and retrieve it in compressed form.

```
public synchronized void setInput(byte[] b, int off, int len)
```

Parameters	b	An array of byte values.
	off	An offset into the byte array.
	len	The number of bytes to use.
Description		This method places len bytes from the given array, starting at off, into the input buffer of this Deflater. Use the deflate() method to compress the data and retrieve it in compressed form.

setLevel

```
public synchronized void setLevel(int level)
```

Parameters	level	The compression level, from 0 (NO_COMPRESSION) to 9 (BEST_COMPRESSION).
Throws	IllegalArgumentException	
		If level is not valid.
Description		This method sets the compression level of this Deflater. A value of 0 corresponds to NO_COMPRESSION. A value of 1 indicates the fastest, least space-efficient compression level (BEST_SPEED). A value of 9 indicates the slowest, most space-efficient compression level (BEST_COMPRESSION).

setStrategy

```
public synchronized void setStrategy(int strategy)
```

Parameters	strategy	The compression strategy.
Throws	IllegalArgumentException	
		If strategy is not valid.

Description   This method sets the compression strategy of this Deflater, which should be one of FILTERED, HUFFMAN_ONLY, or DEFAULT_STRATEGY.

Protected Instance Methods

finalize

protected void finalize()
    Overrides   Object.finalize()
    Description   This method calls end() when this Deflater is garbage collected.

Inherited Methods

Method	Inherited From	Method	Inherited From
clone()	Object	equals(Object)	Object
getClass()	Object	hashCode()	Object
notify()	Object	notifyAll()	Object
toString()	Object	wait()	Object
wait(long)	Object	wait(long, int)	Object

See Also

DeflaterOutputStream, Inflater, GZIPOutputStream, ZipOutputStream

18.8   DeflaterOutputStream

Synopsis

Class Name: java.util.zip.DeflaterOutputStream
Superclass: java.io.FilterOutputStream
Immediate Subclasses: java.util.zip.GZIPOutputStream,
                            java.util.zip.ZipOutputStream
Interfaces Implemented: None
Availability: New as of JDK 1.1

Description

The DeflaterOutputStream class represents an OutputStream with an associated Deflater. In other words, a DeflaterOutputStream wraps a regular output stream, so that data written to the stream is compressed and written to the underlying stream. Two subclasses, GZIPOutputStream and ZipOutputStream, write compressed data in widely-recognized formats.

Class Summary

```
public class java.util.zip.DeflaterOutputStream
          extends java.io.FilterOutputStream {
  // Variables
  protected byte[] buf;
  protected Deflater def;

  // Constructors
  public DeflaterOutputStream(OutputStream out);
  public DeflaterOutputStream(OutputStream out, Deflater def);
  public DeflaterOutputStream(OutputStream out, Deflater def, int size);

  // Public Instance Methods
  public void close();
  public void finish();
  public void write(int b);
  public void write(byte[] b, int off, int len);

  // Protected Instance Methods
  protected void deflate();
}
```

Variables

buf

protected byte[] buf

   Description   A buffer that holds the compressed data that is written to the underlying stream.

def

protected Deflater def

   Description   The Deflater object that is used internally.

Constructors

DeflaterOutputStream

public DeflaterOutputStream(OutputStream out)

Parameters	out	The underlying output stream.
Description		This constructor creates a DeflaterOutputStream that writes data to the given OutputStream. Before being written, the data is compressed by a default Deflater. The DeflaterOutput-Stream uses a compression buffer with the default size of 512 bytes.

public DeflaterOutputStream(OutputStream out, Deflater def)

Parameters	out	The underlying output stream.
	def	The Deflater object.
Description		This constructor creates a DeflaterOutputStream that writes data to the given OutputStream. Before being written, the data is compressed by the given Deflater. The DeflaterOutput-Stream uses a compression buffer with the default size of 512 bytes.

public DeflaterOutputStream(OutputStream out, Deflater def,
                            int size)

Parameters	out	The underlying output stream.
	def	The Deflater object.
	size	The size of the output buffer.
Description		This constructor creates a DeflaterOutputStream that writes data to the given OutputStream. Before being written, the data is compressed by the given Deflater. The DeflaterOutput-Stream uses a compression buffer of the given size.

Public Instance Methods

close

public void close() throws IOException

Throws	IOException If any kind of I/O error occurs.
Overrides	FilterOutputStream.close()
Description	This method closes the stream and releases any system resources that are associated with it.

finish

public void finish() throws IOException

Throws	IOException If any kind of I/O error occurs.

Description   This method finishes writing compressed data to the underlying stream without closing it.

write

```
public void write(int b) throws IOException
```
Parameters   b   The value to write.
Throws   IOException   If any kind of I/O error occurs.
Overrides   FilterOutputStream.write(int)
Description   This method compresses a byte that contains the lowest eight bits of the given integer value and writes it to the underlying OutputStream. The method blocks until the byte is written.

```
public void write(byte[] b, int off, int len) throws IOException
```
Parameters   b   An array of bytes to write to the stream.
              off   An offset into the byte array.
              len   The number of bytes to write.
Throws   IOException   If any kind of I/O error occurs.
Overrides   FilterOutputStream.write(byte[], int, int)
Description   This method takes len bytes from the given buffer, starting at off, and compresses them. The method then writes the compressed data to the underlying OutputStream. The method blocks until all of the bytes have been written.

Protected Instance Methods

deflate

```
protected void deflate() throws IOException
```
Throws   IOException   If any kind of I/O error occurs.
Description   This method asks the internal Deflater to compress the data in the buffer for this DeflaterOutputStream. The method then writes the compressed contents of the buffer to the underlying stream. The method is called by both write() methods.

Inherited Methods

Method	Inherited From	Method	Inherited From
clone()	Object	equals(Object)	Object
finalize()	Object	flush()	FilterOutputStream
getClass()	Object	hashCode()	Object
notify()	Object	notifyAll()	Object
toString()	Object	wait()	Object
wait(long)	Object	wait(long, int)	Object
write(byte[])	FilterOutputStream		

See Also

Deflater, FilterOutputStream, GZIPOutputStream, IOException, OutputStream, ZipOutputStream

18.9   GZIPInputStream

Synopsis

Class Name: java.util.zip.GZIPInputStream
Superclass: java.util.zip.InflaterInputStream
Immediate Subclasses: None
Interfaces Implemented: None
Availability: New as of JDK 1.1

Description

The GZIPInputStream class decompresses data that has been compressed using the GZIP format. To use it, simply construct a GZIPInputStream that wraps regular input stream and use the read() methods to read the compressed data.

Class Summary

```
public class java.util.zip.GZIPInputStream
            extends java.util.zip.InflaterInputStream {
    // Constants
    public static final int GZIP_MAGIC;

    // Variables
    protected CRC32 crc;
    protected boolean eos;

    // Constructors
    public GZIPInputStream(InputStream in);
    public GZIPInputStream(InputStream in, int size);

    // Instance Methods
    public void close();
    public int read(byte[] buf, int off, int len);
}
```

Constants

GZIP_MAGIC

  public static final int GZIP_MAGIC

> Description   A constant that contains the "magic number" that appears in the header of GZIP files.

Variables

crc

  protected CRC32 crc

> Description   A checksum value of the uncompressed data. When an entire file has been read, this checksum is compared to a value stored in the GZIP trailer. If the values do not match, an exception is thrown from read().

eos

  protected boolean eos

> Description   A flag that indicates whether or not the end of the compressed stream has been reached. It is set to true when the compressed data and the GZIP trailer have been read.

Constructors

GZIPInputStream

  public GZIPInputStream(InputStream in) throws IOException

> Parameters   in   The underlying input stream.
>
> Throws   IOException   If an error occurs while reading the GZIP header.
>
> Description   This constructor creates a GZIPInputStream that inflates data from the given InputStream. The GZIPInputStream uses a decompression buffer with the default size of 512 bytes. The GZIP header is read immediately.

  public GZIPInputStream(InputStream in, int size)
      throws IOException

> Parameters   in   The underlying input stream.
>   size   The size of the input buffer.
>
> Throws   IOException   If an error occurs while reading the GZIP header.
>
> Description   This constructor creates a GZIPInputStream that inflates data from the given InputStream. The GZIPInputStream uses a decompression buffer of the given size. The GZIP header is read immediately.

Instance Methods

close

```
public void close() throws IOException
```

Throws   IOException   If any kind of I/O error occurs.

Overrides   FilterInputStream.close()

Description   This method closes this stream and releases any system
                resources that are associated with it.

read

```
public int read(byte[] buf, int off, int len) throws IOException
```

Parameters   buf   An array of bytes to be filled from the stream.

                off   An offset into the byte array.

                len   The number of bytes to read.

Returns   The number of bytes read or -1 if the end of the stream is
                encountered immediately.

Throws   IOException   If any kind of I/O error occurs or the checksum
                              of the uncompressed data does not match that
                              in the GZIP trailer.

Overrides   InflaterInputStream.read(byte[], int, int)

Description   This method reads enough data from the underlying Input-
                Stream to return len bytes of uncompressed data. The uncom-
                pressed data is placed into the given array starting at off. The
                method blocks until some data is available for decompression.

Inherited Methods

Method	Inherited From	Method	Inherited From
available()	FilterInputStream	clone()	Object
equals(Object)	Object	finalize()	Object
getClass()	Object	hashCode()	Object
mark(int)	FilterInputStream	markSupported()	FilterInputStream
notify()	Object	notifyAll()	Object
read()	InflaterInputStream	read(byte[])	FilterInputStream
reset()	FilterInputStream	skip(long)	InflaterInputStream
toString()	Object	wait()	Object
wait(long)	Object	wait(long, int)	Object

See Also

FilterInputStream, Inflater, InflaterInputStream, InputStream, IOException

---

18.10   GZIPOutputStream

Synopsis

Class Name: java.util.zip.GZIPOutputStream
Superclass: java.util.zip.DeflaterOutputStream
Immediate Subclasses: None
Interfaces Implemented: None
Availability: New as of JDK 1.1

Description

The GZIPOutputStream class compresses data using the GZIP format. To use it, simply construct a GZIPOutputStream that wraps a regular output stream and use the write() methods to write compressed data.

Class Summary

```
public class java.util.zip.GZIPOutputStream
            extends java.util.zip.DeflaterOutputStream {
  // Variables
  protected CRC32 crc;

  // Constructors
  public GZIPOutputStream(OutputStream out);
  public GZIPOutputStream(OutputStream out, int size);

  // Instance Methods
  public void close();
  public void finish();
  public synchronized void write(byte[] buf, int off, int len);
}
```

Variables

crc

protected CRC32 crc

Description   A checksum that is updated with the uncompressed stream data. The checksum value is written into the GZIP trailer.

Constructors

GZIPOutputStream

public GZIPOutputStream(OutputStream out) throws IOException

Parameters	out	The underlying output stream.
Throws	IOException	If an error occurs while writing the GZIP header.
Description		This constructor creates a GZIPOutputStream that writes compressed data to the given OutputStream. The GZIPOutput-Stream uses a compression buffer with the default size of 512 bytes.

public GZIPOutputStream(OutputStream out, int size)
        throws IOException

Parameters	out	The underlying output stream.
	size	The size of the output buffer.
Throws	IOException	If an error occurs while writing the GZIP header.
Description		This constructor creates a GZIPOutputStream that writes compressed data to the given OutputStream. The GZIPOutput-Stream uses a compression buffer of the given size.

Instance Methods

close

public void close() throws IOException

Throws	IOException	If any kind of I/O error occurs.
Overrides	DeflaterOutputStream.close()	
Description		This method closes the stream and releases any system resources that are associated with it.

finish

public void finish() throws IOException

Throws	IOException	If any kind of I/O error occurs.
Overrides	DeflaterOutputStream.finish()	
Description		This method finishes writing compressed data to the underlying stream without closing it.

write

public void write(byte[] buf, int off, int len) throws IOException

Parameters	buf	An array of bytes to write to the stream.
	off	An offset into the byte array.
	len	The number of bytes to write.

Throws	IOException If any kind of I/O error occurs.
Overrides	DeflaterOutputStream.write(byte[], int, int)
Description	This method takes len bytes from the given buffer, starting at off, and compresses them. The method then writes the compressed data to the underlying OutputStream. The method blocks until all of the bytes have been written.

Inherited Methods

Method	Inherited From	Method	Inherited From
clone()	Object	equals(Object)	Object
finalize()	Object	flush()	FilterOutputStream
getClass()	Object	hashCode()	Object
notify()	Object	notifyAll()	Object
toString()	Object	wait()	Object
wait(long)	Object	wait(long, int)	Object
write(int)	DeflaterOutputStream	write(byte[])	FilterOutputStream

See Also

Deflater, DeflaterOutputStream, FilterOutputStream, IOException, Output-Stream

18.11   Inflater

Synopsis

Class Name:	java.util.zip.Inflater
Superclass:	java.lang.Object
Immediate Subclasses:	None
Interfaces Implemented:	None
Availability:	New as of JDK 1.1

Description

The Inflater class provides support for general-purpose data decompression. The class uses the ZLIB compression algorithms described in RFC 1950, RFC 1951, and RFC 1952. These documents can be found at:

- *ftp://ds.internic.net/rfc/rfc1950.txt*

- *ftp://ds.internic.net/rfc/rfc1951.txt*
- *ftp://ds.internic.net/rfc/rfc1952.txt*

The Deflater class compresses data that can be uncompressed using Inflater.

The InflaterInputStream uses an internal Inflater to decompress data. Typically, you do not need to create a Inflater; instead, you can just use an instance of one of the subclasses of InflaterInputStream: GZIPInputStream or ZipInput-Stream.

Class Summary

```
public class java.util.zip.Inflater extends java.lang.Object {
    // Constructors
    public Inflater();
    public Inflater(boolean nowrap);

    // Public Instance Methods
    public synchronized native void end();
    public synchronized boolean finished();
    public synchronized native int getAdler();
    public synchronized int getRemaining();
    public synchronized native int getTotalIn();
    public synchronized native int getTotalOut();
    public int inflate(byte[] b);
    public synchronized native int inflate(byte[] b, int off, int len);
    public synchronized boolean needsDictionary();
    public synchronized boolean needsInput();
    public synchronized native void reset();
    public void setDictionary(byte[] b);
    public synchronized native void setDictionary(byte[] b, int off, int len);
    public void setInput(byte[] b);
    public synchronized void setInput(byte[] b, int off, int len);

    // Protected Instance Methods
    protected void finalize();
}
```

Constructors

Inflater

public Inflater()

  Description   This constructor creates an Inflater that decompresses data in
         the ZLIB format.

```
public Inflater(boolean nowrap)
```
Parameters   nowrap   A boolean value that specifies whether or not the ZLIB header and checksum data are expected in the compressed data.

Description   This constructor creates an `Inflater` that decompresses data. If nowrap is true, the ZLIB header and checksum fields are not expected, which means that the compressed data is in the format used by GZIP and PKZIP. If the parameter is false, the data is decompressed in the ZLIB format.

Public Instance Methods

end

```
public synchronized native void end()
```
Description   This method discards any unprocessed input data and frees up internal buffers.

finished

```
public synchronized boolean finished()
```
Returns   A boolean value that indicates whether or not the end of the compressed data has been reached.

Description   This method returns true if the last of the compressed data has been read using `inflate()`. Otherwise it returns false.

getAdler

```
public synchronized native int getAdler()
```
Returns   The Adler32 checksum value of the uncompressed data.

Description   This method returns an Adler32 checksum value that is calculated from the uncompressed data returned by `inflate()`.

getRemaining

```
public synchronized int getRemaining()
```
Returns   The number of bytes remaining in the input buffer.

Description   This method returns the number of bytes that are in the input buffer. It can be called to find out how much data remains after a call to `inflate()`.

getTotalIn

```
public synchronized native int getTotalIn()
```
Returns   The total number of bytes that have been input so far.

Description   This method returns the number of bytes that have been
passed to setInput() since this Inflater was created or since
reset() was last called.

getTotalOut

public synchronized native int getTotalOut()

Returns   The total number of bytes that have been output so far.

Description   This method returns the number of bytes that have been read
from inflate() since this Inflater was created or since
reset() was last called.

inflate

public int inflate(byte[] b) throws DataFormatException

Parameters   b   A byte array to be filled.

Returns   The number of decompressed bytes actually written to the array
or 0 if more data may be required.

Throws   DataFormatException

If the data in the input buffer is not in the correct format.

Description   This method decompresses the data passed to setInput() and
fills the given array with decompressed data. If this method
returns 0, needsInput() and needsDictionary() should be
called in order to determine whether the Inflater needs more
data in its input buffer or whether it needs a preset dictionary.

public synchronized native int inflate(byte[] b, int off, int len)
throws DataFormatException

Parameters   b   A byte array to be filled.

off   An offset into the byte array.

len   The number of bytes to fill.

Returns   The number of decompressed bytes written to the array or 0 if
more data may be required.

Throws   DataFormatException

If the data in the input buffer is not in the correct format.

Description   This method decompresses the data passed to setInput() and
writes len bytes of the decompressed data into the given array,
starting at off. If this method returns 0, needsInput() and
needsDictionary() should be called in order to determine
whether the Inflater needs more data in its input buffer or
whether it needs a preset dictionary.

needsDictionary

`public synchronized boolean needsDictionary()`

Returns   A boolean value that indicates whether or not a preset dictionary is needed.

Description This method returns true if a preset dictionary is needed for decompression. Otherwise it returns false.

needsInput

`public synchronized boolean needsInput()`

Returns   A boolean value that indicates whether or not the input buffer is empty.

Description This method returns true if the input buffer is empty. Otherwise it returns false.

reset

`public synchronized native void reset()`

Description This method resets the Inflater to the state it was in when it was created, which means that a new set of data can be decompressed.

setDictionary

`public void setDictionary(byte[] b)`

Parameters   b   An array of byte values.

Description This method sets the preset dictionary for decompression using the data in the given array.

`public synchronized native void setDictionary(byte[] b, int off,`
                                                        `int len)`

Parameters   b   An array of byte values.

             off   An offset into the byte array.

             len   The number of bytes to use.

Description This method sets the preset dictionary for decompression using len bytes from the given array, starting from off.

setInput

`public void setInput(byte[] b)`

Parameters   b   An array of byte values.

Description This method places the contents of the given array into the input buffer of this Inflater.

```
public synchronized void setInput(byte[] b, int off, int len)
```
Parameters   b   An array of byte values.

off   An offset into the byte array.

len   The number of bytes to use.

Description   This method places len bytes from the given array, starting at off, into the input buffer of this Inflater. Use the inflate() method to decompress the data and retrieve it in decompressed form.

Protected Instance Methods

finalize

```
protected void finalize()
```
Overrides   Object.finalize()

Description   This method calls end() when this Inflater is garbage collected.

Inherited Methods

Method	Inherited From	Method	Inherited From
clone()	Object	equals(Object)	Object
getClass()	Object	hashCode()	Object
notify()	Object	notifyAll()	Object
toString()	Object	wait()	Object
wait(long)	Object	wait(long, int)	Object

See Also

Deflater, GZIPInputStream, InflaterInputStream, ZipInputStream

18.12   InflaterInputStream

Synopsis

Class Name: java.util.zip.InflaterInputStream

Superclass: java.io.FilterInputStream

Immediate Subclasses: java.util.zip.GZIPInputStream,
                        java.util.zip.ZipInputStream

Interfaces Implemented: None

Availability: New as of JDK 1.1

Description

The InflaterInputStream class represents an InputStream with an associated Inflater. In other words, an InflaterInputStream wraps a regular input stream, so that data read from the stream is read from an underlying stream and decompressed. Two subclasses, GZIPInputStream and ZipInputStream, read compressed data in widely recognized formats.

Class Summary

```
public class java.util.zip.InflaterInputStream
            extends java.io.FilterInputStream {
  // Variables
  protected byte[] buf;
  protected Inflater inf;
  protected int len;

  // Constructors
  public InflaterInputStream(InputStream in);
  public InflaterInputStream(InputStream in, Inflater inf);
  public InflaterInputStream(InputStream in, Inflater inf, int size);

  // Public Instance Methods
  public int read();
  public int read(byte[] b, int off, int len);
  public long skip(long n);

  // Protected Instance Methods
  protected void fill();
}
```

Variables

buf

protected byte[] buf

   Description   A buffer that holds the compressed data that is written to the underlying stream.

inf

protected Inflater inf

   Description   The Inflater that is used internally.

len

protected int len

Description   The amount of data that is in the input buffer.

Constructors

InflaterInputStream

public InflaterInputStream(InputStream in)

Parameters	in	The underlying input stream.
Description		This constructor creates an InflaterInputStream that reads data from the given InputStream. Before being read, the data is decompressed by a default Inflater. The InflaterInput-Stream uses a decompression buffer with the default size of 512 bytes.

public InflaterInputStream(InputStream in, Inflater inf)

Parameters	in	The underlying input stream.
	inf	The Inflater object.
Description		This constructor creates an InflaterInputStream that reads data from the given InputStream. Before being read, the data is decompressed by the given Inflater. The InflaterInput-Stream uses a decompression buffer with the default size of 512 bytes.

public InflaterInputStream(InputStream in, Inflater inf, int size)

Parameters	in	The underlying input stream.
	inf	The Inflater object.
	size	The size of the input buffer.
Description		This constructor creates an InflaterInputStream that reads data from the given InputStream. Before being read, the data is decompressed by the given Inflater. The InflaterInput-Stream uses a decompression buffer of the given size.

Instance Methods

read

public int read() throws IOException

Returns		The next uncompressed byte or –1 if the end of the stream is encountered.
Throws	IOException	If any kind of I/O error occurs.
Overrides	FilterInputStream.read()	
Description		This method reads enough data from the underlying Input-Stream to return a byte of uncompressed data. The method blocks until enough data is available for decompression, the end of the stream is detected, or an exception is thrown.

```
public int read(byte[] b, int off, int len) throws IOException
```
Parameters   b   An array of bytes to be filled from the stream.

                   off   An offset into the byte array.

                   len   The number of bytes to read.

Returns   The number of bytes read or –1 if the end of the stream is encountered immediately.

Throws   `IOException` If any kind of I/O error occurs.

Overrides   `FilterInputStream.read(byte[], int, int)`

Description   This method reads enough data from the underlying Input-Stream to return len bytes of uncompressed data. The uncompressed data is placed into the given array starting at off. The method blocks until some data is available for decompression.

skip

```
public long skip(long n) throws IOException
```
Returns   The actual number of bytes skipped.

Throws   `IOException` If any kind of I/O error occurs.

Overrides   `FilterInputStream.skip()`

Description   This method skips over the specified number of uncompressed data bytes by reading data from the underlying InputStream and decompressing it.

Protected Instance Methods

fill

```
protected void fill() throws IOException
```
Throws   `IOException` If any kind of I/O error occurs.

Description   This method fills the input buffer with compressed data from the underlying InputStream.

Inherited Methods

Method	Inherited From	Method	Inherited From
available()	FilterInputStream	clone()	Object
close()	FilterInputStream	equals(Object)	Object
finalize()	Object	getClass()	Object
hashCode()	Object	mark(int)	FilterInputStream
markSupported()	FilterInputStream	notify()	Object
notifyAll()	Object	read()	InflaterInputStream
read(byte[])	FilterInputStream	reset()	FilterInputStream
toString()	Object	wait()	Object
wait(long)	Object	wait(long, int)	Object

See Also

FilterInputStream, GZIPInputStream, Inflater, InputStream, IOException, Zip-InputStream

18.13   ZipEntry

Synopsis

Class Name:	java.util.zip.ZipEntry
Superclass:	java.lang.Object
Immediate Subclasses:	None
Interfaces Implemented:	None
Availability:	New as of JDK 1.1

Description

The ZipEntry class represents a single entry in a ZIP file, which is either a compressed file or an uncompressed file. ZipEntry provides methods that set and retrieve various pieces of information about an entry.

When you are reading a ZIP file, you use ZipInputStream.getNextEntry() to return the next entry in the file. Then you can retrieve information about that particular entry. You can also read the entries in a ZIP file in a nonsequential order using the ZipFile class.

When you are writing a ZIP file, you use ZipOutputStream.putNextEntry() to write an entry, and you must create your own ZipEntry objects. If you are storing compressed (deflated) files, you need only specify a name for the ZipEntry; the other fields are filled in automatically. If, however, you are placing uncompressed entries, you need to specify the size of each entry and provide a CRC-32 checksum value.

Class Summary

```
public class java.util.zip.ZipEntry extends java.lang.Object {
    // Constants
    public static final int DEFLATED;
    public static final int STORED;

    // Constructors
    public ZipEntry(String name);

    // Instance Methods
    public String getComment();
```

```
    public long getCompressedSize();
    public long getCrc();
    public byte[] getExtra();
    public int getMethod();
    public String getName();
    public long getSize();
    public long getTime();
    public boolean isDirectory();
    public void setComment(String comment);
    public void setCrc(long crc);
    public void setExtra(byte[] extra);
    public void setMethod(int method);
    public void setSize(long size);
    public void setTime(long time);
    public String toString();
}
```

Constants

DEFLATED

public static final int DEFLATED

Description   A constant that represents an entry that is stored using the deflate algorithm.

STORED

public static final int STORED

Description   A constant that represents an entry that is stored verbatim; in other words, with no compression applied.

Constructors

ZipEntry

public ZipEntry(String name)

Parameters   name   The name of the entry.

Throws   NullPointerException
                          If name is null.

              IllegalArgumentException
                          If name is longer than 0xFFFF bytes.

Description   This constructor creates a ZipEntry with the given name.

Instance Methods

getComment

`public String getComment()`

Returns	The comment of this entry or null if one has not been specified.
Description	This method returns the comment string for this ZipEntry.

getCompressedSize

`public long getCompressedSize()`

Returns	The compressed size of this entry or –1 is the compressed size is not known.
Description	This method returns the compressed size of this ZipEntry.

getCrc

`public long getCrc()`

Returns	The checksum value for this entry.
Description	This method returns the CRC-32 checksum value for this ZipEntry.

getExtra

`public byte[] getExtra()`

Returns	The extra field data for this entry or null if there is none.
Description	This method returns the bytes in the extra field data for this ZipEntry.

getMethod

`public int getMethod()`

Returns	The compression method of this entry or –1 if it has not been specified.
Description	This method returns the compression method of this ZipEntry. Valid values are DEFLATED and STORED.

getName

`public String getName()`

Returns	The name of this entry.
Description	This method returns the string name of this ZipEntry.

getSize

public long getSize()

Returns   The uncompressed size of this entry or –1 if the uncompressed size is not known.

Description This method returns the uncompressed size of this ZipEntry.

getTime

public long getTime()

Returns   The modification date of this entry.

Description This method returns the modification date of this ZipEntry as the number of milliseconds since midnight, January 1, 1970 GMT.

isDirectory

public boolean isDirectory()

Returns   A boolean value that indicates whether or not this entry is a directory.

Description This method returns true if this ZipEntry represents a directory.

setComment

public void setComment(String comment)

Parameters   comment   The new comment string.

Throws   IllegalArgumentException

             If comment is longer than 0xFFFF bytes.

Description   This method sets the comment string of this ZipEntry.

setCrc

public void setCrc(long crc)

Parameters   crc   The new checksum value.

Description   This method sets the CRC-32 checksum value for this ZipEntry.

setExtra

public void setExtra(byte[] extra)

Parameters   extra   The extra field data.

Throws   IllegalArgumentException

             If extra is longer than 0xFFFF bytes.

Description   This method sets the extra field data for this ZipEntry.

setMethod

`public void setMethod(int method)`

Parameters	method	The new compression method.
Throws	IllegalArgumentException	
		If method is not DEFLATED or STORED.
Description		This method sets the compression method of this ZipEntry. This corresponds to the compression level of Deflater.

setSize

`public void setSize(long size)`

Parameters	size	The new uncompressed entry size.
Throws	IllegalArgumentException	
		If size is less than 0 or greater than 0xFFFFFFFF bytes.
Description		This method sets the uncompressed size of this ZipEntry.

setTime

`public void setTime(long time)`

Parameters	time	The new modification date, expressed as the number of seconds since midnight, January 1, 1970 GMT.
Description		This method sets the modification date of this ZipEntry.

toString

`public String toString()`

Returns	A string representation of this object.
Overrides	Object.toString()
Description	This method returns the name of this ZipEntry.

Inherited Methods

Method	Inherited From	Method	Inherited From
clone()	Object	equals(Object)	Object
finalize()	Object	getClass()	Object
hashCode()	Object	notify()	Object
notifyAll()	Object	wait()	Object
wait(long)	Object	wait(long, int)	Object

See Also

Deflater, IllegalArgumentException, Inflater, NullPointerException, ZipInputStream, ZipOutputStream

18.14   ZipException

Synopsis

Class Name: java.util.zip.ZipException
Superclass: java.io.IOException
Immediate Subclasses: None
Interfaces Implemented: None
Availability: New as of JDK 1.1

Description

A ZipException is thrown when an error occurs when reading or writing a ZIP file. Normally this occurs when data is read that is not in the correct format.

Class Summary

```
public class java.util.ZipException extends java.io.IOException {
  // Constructors
  public ZipException();
  public ZipException(String s);
}
```

Constructors

ZipException

protected ZipException()

Description   This constructor creates a ZipException with no associated
              detail message.

public ZipException(String s)

Parameters   s   The detail message.
Description   This constructor creates a ZipException with the given detail
               message.

Inherited Methods

Method	Inherited From	Method	Inherited From
clone()	Object	equals(Object)	Object
fillInStackTrace()	Throwable	finalize()	Object
getClass()	Object	getLocalizedMessage()	Throwable
getMessage()	Throwable	hashCode()	Object
notify()	Object	notifyAll()	Object
printStackTrace()	Throwable	printStack-Trace(PrintStream)	Throwable
printStack-Trace(PrintWriter)	Throwable	toString()	Throwable
wait()	Object	wait(long)	Object
wait(long, int)	Object		

See Also

Exception, IOException, RuntimeException, Throwable

18.15   ZipFile

Synopsis

Class Name: java.util.zip.ZipFile
Superclass: java.lang.Object
Immediate Subclasses: None
Interfaces Implemented: None
Availability: New as of JDK 1.1

Description

The ZipFile class represents a ZIP file. Unlike with a ZipInputStream, you can read the entries in a ZipFile nonsequentially. Internally, the class uses a RandomAccessFile so that you can read the entries from the file in any order. You can obtain a list of the entries in this ZIP file by calling entries(). Given an entry, you can get an InputStream for that entry using getInputStream().

Class Summary

```
public class java.util.zip.ZipFile extends java.lang.Object {
  // Constructors
  public ZipFile(File file);
  public ZipFile(String name);

  // Instance Methods
  public void close();
  public Enumeration entries();
  public ZipEntry getEntry(String name);
  public InputStream getInputStream(ZipEntry ze);
  public String getName();
}
```

Constructors

ZipFile

`public ZipFile(File file) throws ZipException, IOException`

Parameters	file	The File to read.
Throws	ZipException	
		If the ZIP file cannot be read.
	IOException	If any other kind of I/O error occurs.
Description		This constructor creates a ZipFile for reading from the given File object.

`public ZipFile(String name) throws IOException`

Parameters	name	A string that contains the path name of the file.
Throws	ZipException	
		If the ZIP file cannot be read.
	IOException	If any other kind of I/O error occurs.
Description		This constructor creates a ZipFile for reading from the file specified by the given path.

Instance Methods

close

`public void close() throws IOException`

Throws	IOException	If any kind of I/O error occurs.
Description		This method closes the ZipFile and releases its system resources.

entries

public Enumeration entries()

Returns	An Enumeration of ZipEntry objects.
Description	This method returns an enumeration of ZipEntry objects that represents the contents of this ZipFile.

getEntry

public ZipEntry getEntry(String name)

Parameters	name	The entry name.
Returns		The entry corresponding to the given name or null if there is no such entry.
Description		This method returns the ZipEntry object that corresponds to the given entry name.

getInputStream

public InputStream getInputStream(ZipEntry ze) throws IOException

Parameters	ze	A ZipEntry in this file.
Returns		An InputStream for the given entry.
Throws	ZipException	
		If a ZIP file format error occurs.
	IOException	If any other kind of I/O error occurs.
Description		This method returns an input stream that can read the entry described by the supplied ZipEntry.

getName

public String getName()

Returns	The path of this file.
Description	This method returns the path name of this ZipFile.

Inherited Methods

Method	Inherited From	Method	Inherited From
clone()	Object	equals(Object)	Object
finalize()	Object	getClass()	Object
hashCode()	Object	notify()	Object
notifyAll()	Object	toString()	Object
wait()	Object	wait(long)	Object
wait(long, int)	Object		

See Also

Enumeration, File, InputStream, IOException, RandomAccessFile, String, ZipEntry, ZipException, ZipInputStream

---

18.16   ZipInputStream

Synopsis

Class Name:	java.util.zip.ZipInputStream
Superclass:	java.util.zip.InflaterInputStream
Immediate Subclasses:	None
Interfaces Implemented:	None
Availability:	New as of JDK 1.1

Description

The ZipInputStream class reads files that have been compressed using the ZIP format. To read uncompressed data from a ZIP file, simply construct a ZipInputStream that wraps a regular input stream. The getNextEntry() method returns each entry in the ZIP file in order. Once you have a ZipEntry object, you use the read() method to retrieve uncompressed data from it. If you want to read the entries in a nonsequential order, use a ZipFile instead.

Class Summary

```
public class java.util.zip.ZipInputStream
            extends java.util.zip.InflaterInputStream {
  // Constructors
  public ZipInputStream(InputStream in);

  // Instance Methods
  public void close();
  public void closeEntry();
  public ZipEntry getNextEntry();
  public int read(byte[] b, int off, int len);
  public long skip(long n);
}
```

Constructors

ZipInputStream

public ZipInputStream(InputStream in)

Parameters	in	The underlying input stream.
Description		This constructor creates a ZipInputStream that inflates data from the given InputStream.

Instance Methods

close

public void close() throws IOException

Throws	IOException	If any I/O error occurs.
Overrides	FilterInputStream.close()	
Description		This method closes this stream and releases any system resources that are associated with it.

closeEntry

public void closeEntry() throws IOException

Throws	ZipException
	If a ZIP file format error occurs.
	IOException If any other kind of I/O error occurs.
Description	This method closes the currently open entry in the ZIP file. The stream is then positioned to read the next entry using getNextEntry().

getNextEntry

public ZipEntry getNextEntry() throws IOException

Returns	The ZipEntry for the next entry or null if there are no more entries.
Throws	ZipException
	If a ZIP file format error occurs.
	IOException If any other kind of I/O error occurs.
Description	This method returns a ZipEntry that represents the next entry in the ZIP file and positions the stream to read that entry.

read

public int read(byte[] b, int off, int len) throws IOException

Parameters	b	An array of bytes to be filled from the stream.
	off	An offset into the byte array.

	len	The number of bytes to read.
Returns		The number of bytes read or -1 if the end of the entry is encountered immediately.
Throws	ZipException	
		If a ZIP file format error occurs.
	IOException	If any other kind of I/O error occurs.
Overrides	InflaterInputStream.read(byte[], int, int)	
Description		This method reads enough data from the underlying Input-Stream to return len bytes of uncompressed data. The uncompressed data is placed into the given array starting at off. The method blocks until some data is available for decompression.

skip

```
public long skip(long n) throws IOException
```

Returns	The actual number of bytes skipped.
Throws	ZipException
	If a ZIP file format error occurs.
	IOException If any kind of I/O error occurs.
Overrides	InflaterInputStream.skip()
Description	This method skips over the specified number of uncompressed data bytes by reading data from the underlying InputStream and decompressing it.

Inherited Methods

Method	Inherited From	Method	Inherited From
available()	FilterInputStream	clone()	Object
equals(Object)	Object	finalize()	Object
getClass()	Object	hashCode()	Object
mark(int)	FilterInputStream	markSupported()	FilterInputStream
notify()	Object	notifyAll()	Object
read()	InflaterInputStream	read(byte[])	FilterInputStream
reset()	FilterInputStream	toString()	Object
wait()	Object	wait(long)	Object
wait(long, int)	Object		

See Also

Inflater, InflaterInputStream, InputStream, IOException, ZipEntry, ZipException, ZipFile

18.17   ZipOutputStream

Synopsis

Class Name: java.util.zip.ZipOutputStream
Superclass: java.util.zip.DeflaterOutputStream
Immediate Subclasses: None
Interfaces Implemented: None
Availability: New as of JDK 1.1

Description

The ZipOutputStream class writes compressed files in the ZIP format. To write a ZIP file, construct a ZipOutputStream that wraps a regular output stream. You have to create a ZipEntry for each entry in the file. The putNextEntry() method puts the entry in the file, so that you can then use the write() method to write data for that entry. When you finish writing the data for an entry, call closeEntry() to close that entry and putNextEntry() to start another entry.

The setMethod() method specifies whether the data is compressed or uncompressed by default; setLevel() specifies the level of compression that is used by default. These values can be overridden by the method and level set for a particular entry. If you are storing compressed (deflated) files, you need only specify a name for each ZipEntry; the other fields are filled in automatically. If, however, you are placing uncompressed entries, you need to specify the size of each entry and provide a CRC-32 checksum value.

Class Summary

```
public class java.util.zip.ZipOutputStream
            extends java.util.zip.DeflaterOutputStream {
  // Constants
  public static final int DEFLATED;
  public static final int STORED;

  // Constructors
  public ZipOutputStream(OutputStream out);

  // Instance Methods
  public void close();
  public void closeEntry();
```

```
    public void finish();
    public void putNextEntry(ZipEntry e);
    public void setComment(String comment);
    public void setLevel(int level);
    public void setMethod(int method);
    public synchronized void write(byte[] b, int off, int len);
}
```

Constants

DEFLATED

public static final int DEFLATED

Description   A constant that represents an entry is stored using the deflate algorithm.

STORED

public static final int STORED

Description   A constant that represents a ZIP file entry is stored verbatim; in other words, with no compression applied.

Constructors

ZipOutputStream

public ZipOutputStream(OutputStream out)

Parameters   out   The underlying output stream.

Description   This constructor creates a ZipOutputStream that writes compressed data to the given OutputStream.

Instance Methods

close

public void close() throws IOException

Throws   ZipException

                                If a ZIP file format error occurs.

                IOException   If any other kind of I/O error occurs.

Overrides   DeflaterOutputStream.close()

Description   This method closes the stream and releases any system resources that are associated with it.

closeEntry

public void closeEntry() throws IOException

Throws   ZipException

                                If a ZIP file format error occurs.

| | IOException | If any other kind of I/O error occurs. |
| Description | | This method closes the currently open entry in the ZIP file. A subsequent entry can be started with putNextEntry(). |

finish

```
public void finish() throws IOException
```

Throws	ZipException	
		If a ZIP file format error occurs.
	IOException	If any other kind of I/O error occurs.
Overrides	DeflaterOutputStream.finish()	
Description		This method finishes writing compressed data to the underlying stream without closing it.

putNextEntry

```
public void putNextEntry(ZipEntry e) throws IOException
```

Parameters	e	The new entry.
Throws	ZipException	
		If a ZIP file format error occurs.
	IOException	If any other kind of I/O error occurs.
Description		This method writes the information in the given ZipEntry to the stream and positions the stream for the entry data. The actual entry data can then be written to the stream using write(). The default compression method and level are used if one is not specified for the entry. When all of the entry data has been written, use closeEntry() to finish the entry.

If this method is called when there is already an open entry, that entry is closed and this entry is opened.

setComment

```
public void setComment(String comment)
```

Parameters	comment	The new comment string.
Throws	IllegalArgumentException	
		If comment is longer than 0xFFFF bytes.
Description		This method sets the comment string for this ZIP file.

setLevel

```
public void setLevel(int level)
```

| Parameters | level | A compression level, from 0 (NO_COMPRESSION) to 9 (BEST_COMPRESSION). |

Throws	IllegalArgumentException	
	If level is not valid.	
Description	This method sets the default compression level of subsequent DEFLATED entries. The default value is Deflater.DEFAULT_COMPRESSION.	

setMethod

```
public void setMethod(int method)
```

Parameters	method	A compression method, either DEFLATED or STORED.
Throws	IllegalArgumentException	
	If method is not valid.	
Description	This method sets the default compression method of this ZipOutputStream for entries that do not specify a method.	

write

```
public synchronized void write(byte[] b, int off, int len)
                    throws IOException
```

Parameters	b	An array of bytes to write to the stream.
	off	An offset into the byte array.
	len	The number of bytes to write.
Throws	ZipException	
	If a ZIP file format error occurs.	
	IOException	If any other kind of I/O error occurs.
Overrides	DeflaterOutputStream.write(byte[], int, int)	
Description	This method takes len bytes from the given buffer, starting at off, and compresses them. The method then writes the compressed data to the underlying OutputStream for the current entry. The method blocks until all the bytes have been written.	

Inherited Methods

Method	Inherited From	Method	Inherited From
clone()	Object	equals(Object)	Object
finalize()	Object	flush()	FilterOutputStream
getClass()	Object	hashCode()	Object
notify()	Object	notifyAll()	Object
toString()	Object	wait()	Object
wait(long)	Object	wait(long, int)	Object
write(int)	DeflaterOutputStream	write(byte[])	FilterOutputStream

See Also

Deflater, DeflaterOutputStream, IllegalArgumentException, IOException, OutputStream, ZipEntry, ZipException

III

APPENDIXES

- Appendix A, *The Unicode 2.0 Character Set*
- Appendix B, *The UTF-8 Encoding*

This part provides information about the Unicode 2.0 standard and the UTF-8 encoding used by Java.

A

The Unicode 2.0 Character Set

Characters	Description
\u0000 – \u1FFF	Alphabets
\u0020 – \u007F	Basic Latin
\u0080 – \u00FF	Latin-1 supplement
\u0100 – \u017F	Latin extended-A
\u0180 – \u024F	Latin extended-B
\u0250 – \u02AF	IPA extensions
\u02B0 – \u02FF	Spacing modifier letters
\u0300 – \u036F	Combining diacritical marks
\u0370 – \u03FF	Greek
\u0400 – \u04FF	Cyrillic
\u0530 – \u058F	Armenian
\u0590 – \u05FF	Hebrew
\u0600 – \u06FF	Arabic
\u0900 – \u097F	Devanagari
\u0980 – \u09FF	Bengali
\u0A00 – \u0A7F	Gurmukhi
\u0A80 – \u0AFF	Gujarati
\u0B00 – \u0B7F	Oriya
\u0B80 – \u0BFF	Tamil
\u0C00 – \u0C7F	Telugu
\u0C80 – \u0CFF	Kannada
\u0D00 – \u0D7F	Malayalam
\u0E00 – \u0E7F	Thai
\u0E80 – \u0EFF	Lao
\u0F00 – \u0FBF	Tibetan

Characters	Description
\u10A0 - \u10FF	Georgian
\u1100 - \u11FF	Hangul Jamo
\u1E00 - \u1EFF	Latin extended additional
\u1F00 - \u1FFF	Greek extended
\u2000 - \u2FFF	Symbols and punctuation
\u2000 - \u206F	General punctuation
\u2070 - \u209F	Superscripts and subscripts
\u20A0 - \u20CF	Currency symbols
\u20D0 - \u20FF	Combining diacritical marks for symbols
\u2100 - \u214F	Letterlike symbols
\u2150 - \u218F	Number forms
\u2190 - \u21FF	Arrows
\u2200 - \u22FF	Mathematical operators
\u2300 - \u23FF	Miscellaneous technical
\u2400 - \u243F	Control pictures
\u2440 - \u245F	Optical character recognition
\u2460 - \u24FF	Enclosed alphanumerics
\u2500 - \u257F	Box drawing
\u2580 - \u259F	Block elements
\u25A0 - \u25FF	Geometric shapes
\u2600 - \u26FF	Miscellaneous symbols
\u2700 - \u27BF	Dingbats
\u3000 - \u33FF	CJK auxiliary
\u3000 - \u303F	CJK symbols and punctuation
\u3040 - \u309F	Hiragana
\u30A0 - \u30FF	Katakana
\u3100 - \u312F	Bopomofo
\u3130 - \u318F	Hangul compatibility Jamo
\u3190 - \u319F	Kanbun
\u3200 - \u32FF	Enclosed CJK letters and months
\u3300 - \u33FF	CJK compatibility
\u4E00 - \u9FFF	CJK unified ideographs: Han characters used in China, Japan, Korea, Taiwan, and Vietnam
\uAC00 - \uD7A3	Hangul syllables
\uD800 - \uDFFF	Surrogates
\uD800 - \uDB7F	High surrogates
\uDB80 - \uDBFF	High private use surrogates
\uDC00 - \uDFFF	Low surrogates
\uE000 - \uF8FF	Private use
\uF900 - \uFFFF	Miscellaneous
\uF900 - \uFAFF	CJK compatibility ideographs
\uFB00 - \uFB4F	Alphabetic presentation forms
\uFB50 - \uFDFF	Arabic presentation forms-A

Characters	Description
\uFE20 - \uFE2F	Combing half marks
\uFE30 - \uFE4F	CJK compatibility forms
\uFE50 - \uFE6F	Small form variants
\uFE70 - \uFEFE	Arabic presentation forms-B
\uFEFF	Specials
\uFF00 - \uFFEF	Halfwidth and fullwidth forms
\uFFF0 - \uFFFF	Specials

B

The UTF-8 Encoding

Internally, Java always represents Unicode characters with 16 bits. However, this is an inefficient use of bits when most of the characters being used only need eight bits or less to be represented, which is the case for text written in English and a number of other languages. The UTF-8 encoding provides a more compact way of representing sequences of Unicode when most of the characters are 7-bit ASCII characters. Therefore, UTF-8 is often a more efficient way of storing or transmitting text than using 16 bits for every character.

The UTF-8 encoding is a variable-width encoding of Unicode characters. Seven-bit ASCII characters (\u0000-\u007F) are represented in one byte, so they remain untouched by the encoding (i.e., a string of ASCII characters is a legal UTF-8 string). Characters in the range \u0080-\u07FF are represented in two bytes, and characters in the range \u0800-\uFFFF are represented in three bytes. Java actually uses a slightly modified version of UTF-8, since it encodes \u0000 using two bytes. The advantage of this approach is that a UTF-8 encoded string never contains a null character.

Java provides support for reading characters in the UTF-8 encoding with the read-UTF() methods in RandomAccessFile, DataInputStream, and ObjectInputStream. The writeUTF() methods in RandomAccessFile, DataOutputStream, and ObjectOutputStream handle writing characters in the UTF-8 encoding.

The UTF-8 encoding begins with an unsigned 16-bit quantity that indicates the number of bytes of data that follow. This length value is in the format read by the readUnsignedShort() methods the above input classes and written by the write-UnsignedShort() methods in the above output classes.

The rest of the bytes are variable-length characters. A 1-byte character always has its high-order bit set to 0. A 2-byte character always begins with the high-order bits 110, while a 3-byte character starts with the high-order bits 1110. The second and third bytes of 2- and 3-byte characters always have their high-order bits set to 10, which makes them easy to distinguish from 1-byte characters and the initial bytes of 2- and 3-byte characters. This encoding scheme leaves room for seven bits of data in 1-byte characters, 11 bits of data in 2-byte characters, and 16 bits of data in 3-byte characters.

The table below summarizes the UTF-8 encoding:

Bytes in Character	Minimum Character	Maximum Character	# of Data Bits	Binary Byte Sequence (x = data bit)
1	\u0000	\u007F	7	0xxxxxxx
2	\u0080	\u07FF	11	110xxxxx 10xxxxxx
3	\u0800	\uFFFF	16	1110xxxx 10xxxxxx 10xxxxxx

Index

About the Authors

Mark Grand (*mgrand@mindspring.com*) is a Java consultant, speaker, and instructor. He teaches classes on Java, develops Java-based software, and advises companies on how best to use Java-related technology with databases, networks, and electronic commerce. In addition to writing the *Java Fundamental Classes Reference*, Mark is the author of the *Java Language Reference*. Prior to his involvement with Java, Mark worked for ten years as a designer and implementor of fourth-generation programming languages. His most recent role in this vein was architect of an electronic data interchange product. More information about Mark is available on his Web page at *http://www.mindspring.com/~mgrand/*.

Jonathan Knudsen is a staff writer for O'Reilly & Associates, a position that is the antidote to both the crushing boredom and the kamikaze hours of his previous jobs. In 1993 he graduated cum laude from Princeton University with a degree in mechanical engineering. He is excited about Java, but keeps wondering what the Next Big Thing will be.

Jonathan lives in New Jersey with his wife and technical advisor, Kristen, his daughter, Daphne, and two black and white cats. In his spare time he enjoys playing the piano and bicycling.

Colophon

The blocks image on the cover of *Java Fundamental Classes Reference* is from the CMCD PhotoCD Collection. It was manipulated by Edie Freedman using Adobe Photoshop 3.0 and Adobe Gallery Effects filters. The cover layout was produced with Quark XPress 3.3 using Bitstream Bodoni Bold and URW Bodoni Black fonts.

The inside layout was designed by Nancy Priest. Text was prepared by Erik Ray in SGML DocBook 2.4 DTD. The print version of this book was created by translating the SGML source into a set of gtroff macros using a filter developed at ORA by Norman Walsh. Steve Talbott designed and wrote the underlying macro set on the basis of the GNU troff -gs macros; Lenny Muellner adapted them to SGML and implemented the book design. The GNU groff text formatter version 1.09 was used to generate PostScript output. The heading font is Bodoni BT; the text font is New Baskerville. The illustrations that appear in the book were created in Macromedia Freehand 5.0 by Chris Reilley.

Java Programming *continued*

Java Threads

By Scott Oaks and Henry Wong
1st Edition January 1997
252 pages, ISBN 1-56592-216-6

Java Threads is a comprehensive guide to the intracacies of threaded programming in Java, covering everything from the most basic synchronization techniques to advanced topics like writing your own thread scheduler.

Java Threads uncovers the one tricky but essential aspect of Java programming and provides techniques for avoiding deadlock, lock starvation, and other topics.

Java Network Programming

By Elliotte Rusty Harold
1st Edition February 1997
448 pages, ISBN 1-56592-227-1

Java Network Programming is a complete introduction to developing network programs, both applets and applications, using Java; covering everything from networking fundamentals to remote method invocation (RMI).

It also covers what you can do without explicitly writing network code, how you can accomplish your goals using URLs and the basic capabilites of applets.

Developing Java Beans

By Rob Englander
1st Edition June 1997 (est.)
300 pages (est.), ISBN 1-56592-289-1

With *Developing Java Beans,* you'll learn how to create components that can be manipulated by tools like Borland's Latte or Symantec's Visual Cafe, enabling others to build entire applications by using and reusing these building blocks. Beyond the basics, *Developing Java Beans* teaches you how to create Beans that can be saved and restored properly; how to take advantage of introspection to provide more information about a Bean's capabilities; how to provide property editors and customizers that manipulate a Bean in sophisticated ways; and how to integrate Java Beans into ActiveX projects.

Java in a Nutshell, DELUXE EDITION

By various authors
1st Edition June1997 (est.)
ISBN 1-56592-304-9
includes CD-ROM and books.

Java in a Nutshell, Deluxe Edition, is a Java programmer's dream come true in one small package. The heart of this Deluxe Edition is the Java reference library on CD-ROM, which brings together five indispensable volumes for Java developers and programmers, linking related info across books. It includes: *Exploring Java 2nd Edition, Java Language Reference, 2nd Edition, Java Fundamental Classes Reference, Java AWT Reference*, and *Java in a Nutshell, 2nd Edition*, included both on the CD-ROM and in a companion desktop edition. This deluxe library gives you everything you need to do serious programming with Java 1.1.

Database Programming with JDBC and Java

By George Reese
1st Edition July 1997 (est.)
300 pages (est.), ISBN 1-56592-270-0

Java and databases make a powerful combination. Getting the two sides to work together, however, takes some effort -- largely because Java deals in objects while most databases do not.

This book describes the standard Java interfaces that make portable,object-oriented access to relational databases possible, and offers arobust model for writing applications that are easy to maintain. It introduces the JDBC and RMI packages and uses them to develop three-tier applications (applications divided into a user interface, an object-oriented logic component, and an information store). Covers Java 1.1.

How to stay in touch with O'Reilly

1. Visit Our Award-Winning Web Site

http://www.ora.com/

★"Top 100 Sites on the Web" —*PC Magazine*
★"Top 5% Web sites" —*Point Communications*
★"3-Star site" —*The McKinley Group*

Our web site contains a library of comprehensive product information (including book excerpts and tables of contents), downloadable software, background articles, interviews with technology leaders, links to relevant sites, book cover art, and more. File us in your Bookmarks or Hotlist!

2. Join Our Email Mailing Lists

New Product Releases
To receive automatic email with brief descriptions of all new O'Reilly products as they are released, send email to:
listproc@online.ora.com
Put the following information in the first line of your message (*not* in the Subject field):
subscribe ora-news "Your Name" of "Your Organization" (for example: subscribe ora-news Kris Webber of Fine Enterprises)

O'Reilly Events
If you'd also like us to send information about trade show events, special promotions, and other O'Reilly events, send email to: **listproc@online.ora.com**
Put the following information in the first line of your message (*not* in the Subject field):
subscribe ora-events "Your Name" of "Your Organization"

3. Get Examples from Our Books via FTP

There are two ways to access an archive of example files from our books:

Regular FTP
* ftp to:
  ftp.ora.com
  (login: anonymous
  password: your email address)
* Point your web browser to:
  ftp://ftp.ora.com/

FTPMAIL
* Send an email message to:
  ftpmail@online.ora.com
  (Write "help" in the message body)

4. Visit Our Gopher Site
* Connect your gopher to:
  gopher.ora.com

* Point your web browser to:
  gopher://gopher.ora.com/

* Telnet to:
  gopher.ora.com
  login: gopher

5. Contact Us via Email

order@ora.com
To place a book or software order online. Good for North American and international customers.

subscriptions@ora.com
To place an order for any of our newsletters or periodicals.

books@ora.com
General questions about any of our books.

software@ora.com
For general questions and product information about our software. Check out O'Reilly Software Online at **http://software.ora.com/** for software and technical support information. Registered O'Reilly software users send your questions to: **website-support@ora.com**

cs@ora.com
For answers to problems regarding your order or our products.

booktech@ora.com
For book content technical questions or corrections.

proposals@ora.com
To submit new book or software proposals to our editors and product managers.

international@ora.com
For information about our international distributors or translation queries. For a list of our distributors outside of North America check out:
http://www.ora.com/www/order/country.html

O'Reilly & Associates, Inc.
101 Morris Street, Sebastopol, CA 95472 USA
TEL   707-829-0515 or 800-998-9938
         (6am to 5pm PST)
FAX   707-829-0104

O'REILLY™

Titles from O'Reilly

Please note that upcoming titles are displayed in italic.

WEBPROGRAMMING

Apache: The Definitive Guide
Building Your Own Web Conferences
Building Your Own Website
CGI Programming for the World Wide Web
Designing for the Web
HTML: The Definitive Guide, 2nd Ed.
JavaScript: The Definitive Guide, 2nd Ed.
Learning Perl
Programming Perl, 2nd Ed.
Mastering Regular Expressions
WebMaster in a Nutshell
Web Security & Commerce
Web Client Programming with Perl
World Wide Web Journal

USING THE INTERNET

Smileys
The Future Does Not Compute
The Whole Internet User's Guide & Catalog
The Whole Internet for Win 95
Using Email Effectively
Bandits on the Information Superhighway

JAVA SERIES

Exploring Java
Java AWT Reference
Java Fundamental Classes Reference
Java in a Nutshell
Java Language Reference, 2nd Edition
Java Network Programming
Java Threads
Java Virtual Machine

SOFTWARE

WebSite™ 1.1
WebSite Professional™
Building Your Own Web Conferences
WebBoard™
PolyForm™
Statisphere™

SONGLINE GUIDES

NetActivism   NetResearch
Net Law   NetSuccess
NetLearning   NetTravel
Net Lessons

SYSTEM ADMINISTRATION

Building Internet Firewalls
Computer Crime: A Crimefighter's Handbook
Computer Security Basics
DNS and BIND, 2nd Ed.
Essential System Administration, 2nd Ed.
Getting Connected: The Internet at 56K and Up
Linux Network Administrator's Guide
Managing Internet Information Services
Managing NFS and NIS
Networking Personal Computers with TCP/IP
Practical UNIX & Internet Security, 2nd Ed.
PGP: Pretty Good Privacy
sendmail, 2nd Ed.
sendmail Desktop Reference
System Performance Tuning
TCP/IP Network Administration
termcap & terminfo
Using & Managing UUCP
Volume 8: X Window System Administrator's Guide
Web Security & Commerce

UNIX

Exploring Expect
Learning VBScript
Learning GNU Emacs, 2nd Ed.
Learning the bash Shell
Learning the Korn Shell
Learning the UNIX Operating System
Learning the vi Editor
Linux in a Nutshell
Making TeX Work
Linux Multimedia Guide
Running Linux, 2nd Ed.
SCO UNIX in a Nutshell
sed & awk, 2nd Edition
Tcl/Tk Tools
UNIX in a Nutshell: System V Edition
UNIX Power Tools
Using csh & tsch
When You Can't Find Your UNIX System Administrator
Writing GNU Emacs Extensions

WEB REVIEW STUDIO SERIES

Gif Animation Studio
Shockwave Studio

WINDOWS

Dictionary of PC Hardware and Data Communications Terms
Inside the Windows 95 Registry
Inside the Windows 95 File System
Windows Annoyances
Windows NT File System Internals
Windows NT in a Nutshell

PROGRAMMING

Advanced Oracle PL/SQL Programming
Applying RCS and SCCS
C++: The Core Language
Checking C Programs with lint
DCE Security Programming
Distributing Applications Across DCE & Windows NT
Encyclopedia of Graphics File Formats, 2nd Ed.
Guide to Writing DCE Applications
lex & yacc
Managing Projects with make
Mastering Oracle Power Objects
Oracle Design: The Definitive Guide
Oracle Performance Tuning, 2nd Ed.
Oracle PL/SQL Programming
Porting UNIX Software
POSIX Programmer's Guide
POSIX.4: Programming for the Real World
Power Programming with RPC
Practical C Programming
Practical C++ Programming
Programming Python
Programming with curses
Programming with GNU Software
Pthreads Programming
Software Portability with imake, 2nd Ed.
Understanding DCE
Understanding Japanese Information Processing
UNIX Systems Programming for SVR4

BERKELEY 4.4 SOFTWARE DISTRIBUTION

4.4BSD System Manager's Manual
4.4BSD User's Reference Manual
4.4BSD User's Supplementary Documents
4.4BSD Programmer's Reference Manual
4.4BSD Programmer's Supplementary Documents
X Programming
Vol. 0: X Protocol Reference Manual
Vol. 1: Xlib Programming Manual
Vol. 2: Xlib Reference Manual
Vol. 3M: X Window System User's Guide, Motif Edition
Vol. 4M: X Toolkit Intrinsics Programming Manual, Motif Edition
Vol. 5: X Toolkit Intrinsics Reference Manual
Vol. 6A: Motif Programming Manual
Vol. 6B: Motif Reference Manual
Vol. 6C: Motif Tools
Vol. 8 : X Window System Administrator's Guide
Programmer's Supplement for Release 6
X User Tools
The X Window System in a Nutshell

CAREER & BUSINESS

Building a Successful Software Business
The Computer User's Survival Guide
Love Your Job!
Electronic Publishing on CD-ROM

TRAVEL

Travelers' Tales: Brazil
Travelers' Tales: Food
Travelers' Tales: France
Travelers' Tales: Gutsy Women
Travelers' Tales: India
Travelers' Tales: Mexico
Travelers' Tales: Paris
Travelers' Tales: San Francisco
Travelers' Tales: Spain
Travelers' Tales: Thailand
Travelers' Tales: A Woman's World

O'REILLY™

TO ORDER: **800-998-9938** • **order@ora.com** • **http://www.ora.com/**
OUR PRODUCTS ARE AVAILABLE AT A BOOKSTORE OR SOFTWARE STORE NEAR YOU.
FOR INFORMATION: **800-998-9938** • **707-829-0515** • **info@ora.com**

International Distributors

UK, Europe, Middle East and Northern Africa (except France, Germany, Switzerland, & Austria)

INQUIRIES
International Thomson Publishing
Europe
Berkshire House
168-173 High Holborn
London WC1V 7AA, United Kingdom
Telephone: 44-171-497-1422
Fax: 44-171-497-1426
Email: itpint@itps.co.uk

ORDERS
International Thomson Publishing
Services, Ltd.
Cheriton House, North Way
Andover, Hampshire SP10 5BE,
United Kingdom
Telephone: 44-264-342-832
   (UK orders)
Telephone: 44-264-342-806
   (outside UK)
Fax: 44-264-364418 (UK orders)
Fax: 44-264-342761 (outside UK)
UK & Eire orders: itpuk@itps.co.uk
International orders: itpint@itps.co.uk

France

Editions Eyrolles
61 bd Saint-Germain
75240 Paris Cedex 05
France
Fax: 33-01-44-41-11-44

FRENCH LANGUAGE BOOKS
All countries except Canada
Phone: 33-01-44-41-46-16
Email: geodif@eyrolles.com

ENGLISH LANGUAGE BOOKS
Phone: 33-01-44-41-11-87
Email: distribution@eyrolles.com

Australia

WoodsLane Pty. Ltd.
7/5 Vuko Place, Warriewood NSW 2102
P.O. Box 935, Mona Vale NSW 2103
Australia
Telephone: 61-2-9970-5111
Fax: 61-2-9970-5002
Email: info@woodslane.com.au

Germany, Switzerland, and Austria

INQUIRIES
O'Reilly Verlag
Balthasarstr. 81
D-50670 Köln
Germany
Telephone: 49-221-97-31-60-0
Fax: 49-221-97-31-60-8
Email: anfragen@oreilly.de

ORDERS
International Thomson Publishing
Königswinterer Straße 418
53227 Bonn, Germany
Telephone: 49-228-97024 0
Fax: 49-228-441342
Email: order@oreilly.de

Asia (except Japan & India)

INQUIRIES
International Thomson Publishing Asia
60 Albert Street #15-01
Albert Complex
Singapore 189969
Telephone: 65-336-6411
Fax: 65-336-7411

ORDERS
Telephone: 65-336-6411
Fax: 65-334-1617
thomson@signet.com.sg

New Zealand

WoodsLane New Zealand Ltd.
21 Cooks Street (P.O. Box 575)
Wanganui, New Zealand
Telephone: 64-6-347-6543
Fax: 64-6-345-4840
Email: info@woodslane.com.au

Japan

O'Reilly Japan, Inc.
Kiyoshige Building 2F
12-Banchi, Sanei-cho
Shinjuku-ku
Tokyo 160 Japan
Telephone: 81-3-3356-5227
Fax: 81-3-3356-5261
Email: kenji@ora.com

India

Computer Bookshop (India) PVT. LTD.
190 Dr. D.N. Road, Fort
Bombay 400 001
India
Telephone: 91-22-207-0989
Fax: 91-22-262-3551
Email: cbsbom@giasbm01.vsnl.net.in

The Americas

O'Reilly & Associates, Inc.
101 Morris Street
Sebastopol, CA 95472 U.S.A.
Telephone: 707-829-0515
Telephone: 800-998-9938 (U.S. &
Canada)
Fax: 707-829-0104
Email: order@ora.com

Southern Africa

International Thomson Publishing
Southern Africa
Building 18, Constantia Park
240 Old Pretoria Road
P.O. Box 2459
Halfway House, 1685 South Africa
Telephone: 27-11-805-4819
Fax: 27-11-805-3648

O'REILLY™

TO ORDER: **800-998-9938** • order@ora.com • http://www.ora.com/
OUR PRODUCTS ARE AVAILABLE AT A BOOKSTORE OR SOFTWARE STORE NEAR YOU.
FOR INFORMATION: **800-998-9938** • **707-829-0515** • info@ora.com